BOOKS BY DANNY PEARY

Guide for the Film Fanatic
Close-Ups: The Movie Star Book, editor
Cult Movies
Cult Movies 2
Cult Movies 3
*How to Buy, Trade, and Invest in Baseball
    Cards and Collectibles,* with Bruce
    Chadwick
Cult Baseball Players, editor

Cult MOVIE STARS

DANNY PEARY

A FIRESIDE BOOK PUBLISHED BY SIMON & SCHUSTER

NEW YORK   LONDON   TORONTO   SYDNEY   TOKYO   SINGAPORE

SIMON & SCHUSTER/FIRESIDE

Simon & Schuster Building
Rockefeller Center
1230 Avenue of the Americas
New York, New York 10020

Designed by Hedgerow Design
Manufactured in the United States of America

10 9 8 7 6 5 4 3 2 1
10 9 8 7 6 5 4 3 2 1 PBK

Library of Congress Cataloging-in-Publication Data
Peary, Danny, date.
    Cult movie stars / Danny Peary.
      p.   cm.
    "A Fireside book."
    Includes index.
    1. Motion picture actors and actresses—Biography. I. Title.
PN1998.2.P43   1991
791.43′028′0922—dc20   91-22219 CIP

ISBN 0-671-74924-2
     0-671-69394-8 (pbk)

I DEDICATE THIS BOOK TO:
YOUNG WOMEN WHO DO JOHN WAYNE IMPERSONATIONS

ACKNOWLEDGMENTS

This project was initiated several years ago by the late Tim McGinnis, Laura Yorke, and my agent Chris Tomasino. I am indebted to them. I also would like to acknowledge the people at Fireside/Simon & Schuster who helped me along the way, including my editor Ed Walters, Dan Farley, Wendy Wolf, David Dunton, Bonni Leon, Pat Eisemann, Virginia Clark, Gypsy da Silva, and Jacki Seow. My deepest gratitude to Barbara Young, Tyra Crane, Nora Merhar, Liz Cunningham, Donna Villani, Jeanie Dooha, and Julie Kuehndorf. I acknowledge the various studios and distribution companies whose photos are included in the book. In advance, I thank those readers who will send corrections and suggestions for future printings. And for their endless encouragement, I toast Suzanne and Zoë, Laura and Joe.

CAST OF CHARACTERS

Abbott and Costello
Acquanetta
Brooke Adams
Julie/Julia Adams
John Agar
Jenny Agutter
Priscilla Alden
Kay Aldridge
Karen Allen
Nancy Allen
Kirk Alyn
Luana Anders
Juliet Anderson
Leona Anderson
Ursula Andress
Pier Angeli
Evelyn Ankers
Morris Ankrum
Ann-Margret
Laura Antonelli
Fatty Arbuckle
Jean Arless
Arletty
Robert Armstrong
Rosanna Arquette
John Ashley
Robin Askwith
Lionel Atwill
Stéphane Audran
Mischa Auer
Gene Autry
Frankie Avalon
Lauren Bacall
Barbara Bach
Olga Baclanova/Baclanova
Carroll Baker
Rebecca Balding
Joy Bang
Theda Bara

Adrienne Barbeau
Brigitte Bardot
Lex Barker
Ellen Barkin
Jean-Louis Barrault
Belinda Bauer
Michelle Bauer
Nathalie Baye
Matthew "Stymie" Beard
Louise Beavers
Bonnie Bedelia
Alfonso Bedoya
Jean-Paul Belmondo
Sandahl Bergman
Michael Berryman
Willie Best
Martine Beswick
Turhan Bey
Jane Birkin
Whit Bissell
Karen Black
Linda Blair
Mari Blanchard
Joan Blondell
Eric Blore
Roberts Blossom
Humphrey Bogart
Franklin Bolger
Ray Bolger
Rene Bond
Sandrine Bonnaire
Ernest Borgnine
Carol Borland
Barry Bostwick
David Bowie
William Boyd
Peter Boyle
Sonia Braga
Neville Brand

Marlon Brando
Carolyn Brandt
Bobbie Bresee
Jeff Bridges
Charles Bronson
Louise Brooks
Edward Brophy
Johnny Mack Brown
Ricou Browning
Nigel Bruce
Buckwheat/Billy Thomas
Smiley Burnette
Marilyn Burns
Gary Busey
Susan Cabot
Cherie Caffaro
Rod Cameron
Colleen Camp
Bruce Campbell
Timothy Carey
Anne Carlisle
Richard Carlson
Veronica Carlson
Martine Carol
David Carradine
John Carradine
Keith Carradine
Robert Carradine
Barbara Carrera
Veronica Cartwright
Joanna Cassidy
Kim Cattrall
Marilyn Chambers
Jacky Chan/Jackie Chan/
    Cheng Lung
Lon Chaney
Lon Chaney, Jr.
Geraldine Chaplin
Cyd Charisse

Cheech and Chong
David Chiang
Sonny Chiba
Rae Dawn Chong
Julie Christie
Candy Clark
Susan Clark
Mae Clarke
John Cleese
Montgomery Clift
Colin Clive
Roberta Collins
Jennifer Connelly
Sean Connery
Carol Connors
Eddie Constantine
Elisha Cook, Jr.
Mara Corday
Ray "Crash" Corrigan
Bud Cort
Hazel Court
Desiree Cousteau/
   Clearbranch
Larry "Buster" Crabbe
Barbara Crampton
Joan Crawford
Laird Cregar
Criswell
Peggy Cummins
Tim Curry
Jamie Lee Curtis
Peter Cushing
Zbigniew Cybulski
Arlene Dahl
Joe Dallesandro
Timothy Dalton
Mark Damon
Dorothy Dandridge
Henry Daniell
Sybil Danning
Royal Dano
Ray Danton
Patti D'Arbanville
Marion Davies
Bette Davis
Daniel Day-Lewis
Dead End Kids/East Side
   Kids/Bowery Boys
James Dean
Kristine De Bell

Yvonne De Carlo
Sandra Dee
Eddie Deezen
Albert Dekker
Lisa De Leeuw
Alain Delon
Vanessa Del Rio
William Demarest
Catherine Deneuve
Robert De Niro
Gerard Depardieu
Bo Derek
Bruce Dern
Laura Dern
Patrick Dewaere
Angie Dickinson
Marlene Dietrich
Uschi Digart
Matt Dillon
Divine
Tamara Dobson
Faith Domergue
Troy Donahue
Françoise Dorléac
Diana Dors
Keir Dullea
Margaret Dumont
Deanna Durbin
Dan Duryea
Ann Dusenberry
Robert Duvall
Shelley Duvall
Ann Dvorak
Harry Earles
Clint Eastwood
Shirley Eaton
Nelson Eddy
Julie Ege
Lisa Eichhorn
Anita Ekberg
Bengt Ekerot
Britt Ekland
Jack Elam
Wild Bill/William Elliott
Michael Emil
Marla English
Robert Englund
Dale Evans
Gene Evans
Douglas Fairbanks

Antonio Fargas
Farina
Frances Farmer
Mimsy Farmer
Glenda Farrell
Alice Faye
Stepin Fetchit
W. C. Fields
Carrie Fisher
Cash Flagg
Darlanne Fluegel
Errol Flynn
Peter Fonda
Harrison Ford
Deborah Foreman
Mark Forest
Robert Forster
Jodie Foster
Meg Foster
James Fox
Samantha Fox
Anne Francis
Pamela Franklin
Mark Frechette
Kathleen Freeman
Gert Frobe
Dwight Frye
Annette Funicello
Jean Gabin
Zsa Zsa Gabor
Bruno Ganz
Greta Garbo
Allen Garfield/Goorwitz
Beverly Garland
Judy Garland
Teri Garr
Erica Gavin
Ramon Gay
Judy Geeson
Laura Gemser
Susan George
Giancarlo Giannini
Hoot Gibson
Mel Gibson
Jamie Gillis
Crispin Glover
Jeff Goldblum
Leo Gorcey
Ruth Gordon
Marjoe Gortner

Michael Gough
Gerrit Graham
Gloria Grahame
Shauna Grant
Coleen Gray
Sydney Greenstreet
Pam Grier
Melanie Griffith
Gulpilil/David Gulpilil
Edmund Gwenn
Anne Gwynne
Hugo Haas
Dayle Haddon
Sid Haig
Haji
Jack Haley
Arch Hall, Jr.
Huntz Hall
Jon Hall
Porter Hall
Mark Hamill
George Hamilton
Linda Hamilton
Margaret Hamilton
Gunnar Hansen
Jean Harlow
Jessica Harper
Dolores Hart
Veronica Hart
Raymond Hatton
Rondo Hatton
Rutger Hauer
Wings Hauser
Annette Haven
Linda Hayden
Sterling Hayden
Allison Hayes
George "Gabby" Hayes
Rita Hayworth
Jonathan Haze
John Heard
Tippi Hedren
Brigitte Helm
Percy Helton
Barbara Hershey
Jean Hill
Terence Hill
Candace Hilligoss
Daisy and Violet Hilton
Peter Hinwood

John Holmes
Darla Hood
Dennis Hopper
Edward Everett Horton
Bob Hoskins
John Hoyt
Season Hubley
Rock Hudson
Arthur Hunnicutt
Tab Hunter
John Hurt
Mary Beth Hurt
Rex Ingram
Richard Jaeckel
Sam Jaffe
Brion James
Sidney James
Claudia Jennings
Ron Jeremy
Noble Johnson
Tor Johnson
Buck Jones
Darby Jones
Duane Jones
L. Q. Jones
Marsha Jordan
Jackie Joseph
Brenda Joyce
Valerie Kaprisky
Anna Karina
Boris Karloff
Shintaro Katsu
Stacy Keach
Ruby Keeler
Harvey Keitel
Jim Kelly
Kay Kendall
Suzy Kendall
Edgar Kennedy
George Kennedy
Johnnie/Johnny Keyes
Margot Kidder
Richard Kiel
Udo Kier
Roy Kinnear
Klaus Kinski
Nastassia/Nastassja
  Kinski
Tommy Kirk
Sally Kirkland

Tawny Kitaen
Rudolf Klein-Rogge
Fuzzy Knight
Sylva Koscina
Martin Kosleck
Sho Kosugi
Sylvia Kristel
Machiko Kyo
Veronica Lake
Barbara La Marr
Hedy Lamarr
Christopher Lambert
Dorothy Lamour
Elsa Lanchester
Carole Landis
Laurene Landon
Alan "Rocky" Lane
Diane Lane
Joi Lansing
Al "Lash" La Rue
Tom Laughlin
Carole Laure
Laurel and Hardy
Priscilla Lawson
George Lazenby
Jean-Pierre Léaud
Bernard Lee
Bruce Lee
Christopher Lee
Janet Leigh
Jennifer Jason Leigh
Paul LeMat
Harvey Lembeck
Kay Lenz
Gloria Leonard
Baby LeRoy
John Leslie
Naomi Levine
Fiona Lewis
Jerry Lewis
Elmo Lincoln
Little Nell/Nell Campbell
Desmond Llewellyn
David Lochary
Nancy Loomis
Traci Lords
Peter Lorre
Linda Lovelace
Lynn Lowry
Bela Lugosi

Keye Luke
Lydia Lunch
Dolph Lundgren
Ti Lung
John Lurie
Richard Lynch
Carol Lynley
Sue Lyon
Mercedes McCambridge
Kevin McCarthy
Tim McCoy
Hattie McDaniel
Jeanette MacDonald
Marie McDonald
Malcom McDowell
Spanky McFarland
Vonetta McGee
Tim McIntire
Kyle MacLachlan
Butterfly McQueen
George Macready
Anna Magnani
Marjorie Main
Lorna Maitland
David Manners
Jayne Mansfield
Angela Mao/
   Angela Mao Ying
Jean Marais
Richard "Cheech" Marin
William Marshall
Strother Martin
Lee Marvin
The Marx Brothers
Giulietta Masina
Connie Mason
Edith Massey
Kerwin Mathews
Victor Mature
Carmen Maura
Lois Maxwell
Ken Maynard
Mike Mazurki
Mariangela Melato
Beverly Michaels
Charles Middleton
Toshiro Mifune
Sarah Miles
Sylvia Miles
Dick Miller

Hayley Mills
Yvette Mimieux
Miou-Miou
Carmen Miranda
Helen Mirren
Cameron Mitchell
Sharon Mitchell
Robert Mitchum
Tom Mix
Bridgette Monet
Constance Money
Marilyn Monroe
Maria Montez
Mario Montez
Monty Python
Cleo Moore
Roger Moore
Terry Moore
Mantan Moreland
Michèle Morgan
Cathy Moriarty
Michael Moriarty
Robert Morley
Vic Morrow
Cookie Mueller
Caroline Munro
Audie Murphy
Michael Murphy
George Nader
John/Jack Nance
Charles Napier
Paul Naschy
Francesca "Kitten"
   Natividad
Tom Neal
Franco Nero
Nicholas Brothers
Barbara Nichols
Kelly Nichols
Jack Nicholson
Brigitte Nielsen
Leslie Nielsen
Chuck Norris
Jack Norton
Kim Novak
N!xau
Warren Oates
Dave O'Brien
Richard O'Brien
Glynnis O'Connor

Una O'Connor
Judith O'Dea
Cathy O'Donnell
Bulle Ogier
Miles O'Keeffe
Warner Oland
Gary Oldman
Ron O'Neal
Maureen O'Sullivan
Annette O'Toole
Peter O'Toole
Our Gang/Little Rascals
Maria Ouspenskaya
Betty Page
Jack Palance
Eugene Pallette
Franklin Pangborn
Michael Paré
Reg Park
Kay Parker
Barbara Payton
Mary Vivian Pearce
Anthony Perkins
Millie Perkins
Essy Persson
Mary Philbin
Gérard Philipe
Slim Pickens
Ingrid Pitt
Donald Pleasence
Michael J. Pollard
Eleanor Powell
Paula Prentiss
Elvis Presley
Vincent Price
Jonathan Pryce
Edna Purviance
Randy Quaid
Robert Quarry
Linnea Quigley
Patricia Quinn
Vera Hruba Ralston/Vera
   Hruba
Charlotte Rampling
Basil Rathbone
Aldo Ray
Ronald Reagan
Oliver Reed
Harry Reems
Steve Reeves

Liz Renay
Candice Rialson
Kane Richmond
Molly Ringwald
Tex Ritter
Thelma Ritter
Adam Roarke
Jason Robards/
    Robards, Jr.
Tanya Roberts
Bill "Bojangles" Robinson
German Robles
Jean Rogers
Roy Rogers
Michael Rooker
Richard Roundtree
Mickey Rourke
Candida Royalle
Zelda Rubinstein
Betsy Russell
Craig Russell
Elizabeth Russell
Gail Russell
Jane Russell
Kurt Russell
Theresa Russell
Tina Russell
Margaret Rutherford
Bruno S.
Sabu
Marianne Sägebrecht
Harold Sakata
Santo/Samson
Susan Sarandon
Tura Satana
John Saxon
Maria Schneider
Max Schreck
Arnold Schwarzenegger
Gordon Scott
Hazel Scott
Randolph Scott
Steven Seagal
Jean Seberg
Edie Sedgwick
Seka
Serena
Michel Serrault
Delphine Seyrig
Frank Shannon

Dick Shawn
Wallace Shawn
Moira Shearer
Johnny Sheffield
Barbara Shelley
Fu Sheng/Alexander Fu
    Sheng
Brooke Shields
Henry Silva
Simone Simon
Tod Slaughter
Jack Smith
Rainbeaux Smith/Cheryl
    Smith
William Smith
P. J. Soles
Gale Sondergaard
Renée Soutendijk
Sissy Spacek
Fay Spain
Georgina Spelvin
Bud Spencer
Joe Spinell
Annie Sprinkle
Lionel Stander
Harry Dean Stanton
Charles Starrett
Barbara Steele
Bob Steele
Brinke Stevens
Marc Stevens
Stella Stevens
Catherine Mary Stewart
James Stewart
Sting
Linda Stirling
Dean Stockwell
Mink Stole
Shirley Stoler
Sharon Stone
June Storey
Glenn Strange
Susan Strasberg
Dorothy Stratten
Woody Strode
Grady Sutton
Carl "Alfalfa" Switzer
Shih Szu
Hideko Takamine
Lyle Talbot

Gloria Talbott
Russ Tamblyn
Zoë Tamerlis
Akim Tamiroff
Kinuyo Tanaka
Sharon Tate
Jacques Tati
Shirley Temple
Max Terhune
Terry-Thomas
Ernest Thesiger
Dyanne Thorne
The Three Stooges
Lawrence Tierney
Kenneth Tobey
Thelma Todd
Ugo Tognazzi
Sidney Toler
Angel Tompkins
Rip Torn
Andrea True
Lorenzo Tucker
Sonny Tufts
Lana Turner
Tom Tyler
Susan Tyrrell
Rudolph Valentino
Vampira
Lee Van Cleef
Jean-Claude Van Damme
Mamie Van Doren
Vanity
Edward Van Sloan
Monique Van Vooren
Conrad Veidt
John Vernon
Bruno Vesota
Victoria Vetri
Yvette Vickers
Katherine Victor
Jan-Michael Vincent
Viva
Erich von Stroheim
Max von Sydow
Tomisaburo Wakayama
Anton Walbrook
Christopher Walken
Dee Wallace/Dee Wallace
    Stone
M. Emmet Walsh

David Warner
Fredi Washington
John Wayne
Johnny Weissmuller
Raquel Welch
Tuesday Weld
Peter Weller
Jennifer Welles
Mel Welles
Orson Welles
Oskar Werner
Mae West
Pearl White
Gene Wilder
Dawn Wildsmith

June Wilkinson
Billy Dee Williams
Cindy Williams
Edy Williams
Esther Williams
Fred Williamson
Marlene Willoughby
Dooley Wilson
Marie Windsor
Shelley Winters
Anna May Wong
Natalie Wood
Thomas Wood/William
   Kerwin/Rooney Kerwin
Holly Woodlawn

Bambi Woods
James Woods
Hank Worden
Mary Woronov
Jack Wrangler
Fay Wray
Teresa Wright
Sean Young
Sen Young/
   Victor Sen Young
Wang Yu/
   Jimmy Wang Yu
Pia Zadora
Nick Zedd
George Zucco

INTRODUCTION

Spend just ten minutes in a movie memorabilia store and you'll realize that every actor, actress, and animal who ever appeared on the screen has at least one fanatical fan. In choosing the actors and actresses (no real animals—sorry Rinty—or animated animals, but one masked wrestler) who are included in this volume, I have been more selective, picking only those who have had strong emotional impact on at least a fair-sized number of movie fans. Whether we're talking about great stars like Greta Garbo, James Dean, Rudolph Valentino, or Bette Davis, genre stars like Roy Rogers, Boris Karloff, Pearl White, Johnny Weissmuller, or Barbara Steele, character actors, pinup queens, romantic idols, porno stars, zany comics, midnight-movie favorites, or offbeat performers who defy categorization, they each have sparked an unusual, fiery passion in movie fans. There is a strong bond between these stars and the cults that have formed, a following ranging from enormous to small, from hardcore/fanatical to benign. The admiration and appreciation cultists feel for their favorites is different from that extended to the typical movie star—it borders on guilty pleasure. Cult movie stars have given their fans so much special pleasure and exitement that they are taken to heart, cherished, championed. There is a sense of discovery and a need to spread the word.

This book is, quite simply, a tribute to about 750 cult movie stars (and stars of cult movies) who have made movie-watching so much fun for so many. For each entry, I have provided some biographical information, discussed screen image and special appeal, and listed those films (through the summer of 1991) which showcase the stars in cult-making performances. My intention is to get movie fans to seek out particular stars and discover why others are so devoted to them. Begin with Abbott and Costello, of course, the comedy duo who made me, at age three, a film fanatic. I invite readers to send title suggestions, corrections, missing birth and death dates, and, of course, names of stars that should be included in updated volumes.

ABBOTT AND COSTELLO Bud (1895–1974) and Lou (1906–59) were the most popular comedy team of the forties, and Universal Studios' top attraction. Although not the equals of the Marx Brothers or Laurel and Hardy at their best, their talents have never been fully recognized. Abbott was a peerless straight man, Costello a gifted verbal and physical comedian and a surprisingly sensitive actor, and the team's material was an inspired mix of slapstick, surrealism, and intricate wordplay. Their films often incorporated their classic burlesque and radio routines, like "Who's on First?" in *The Naughty Nineties* and "Slowly I Turned" in *Lost in a Harem*. Typically they played low-rank workers or servicemen. When they (inevitably) get into big trouble, Abbott points his cowardly finger at his partner. He also constantly bosses his pal around, and even slaps him. When the greedy Abbott has good fortune, he immediately dumps Costello. Our sympathy grows for this chubby, bumbling manchild whose one friend treats him cruelly, who is brutalized or aggravated by every stranger who crosses his path, and who won't look into a mirror because he doesn't want to hurt his own feelings. But Costello isn't quite the stupid, innocent, childlike victim he seems. He has a sly, mischievous side: pretending to know nothing of craps, he lets fly with lucky dice and lingo ("Little Joe!") and wipes out Abbott; getting two women for a date, he keeps them both and lets Abbott tag along. The team's popularity has remained constant thanks to television: their delightfully bizarre 1952–53 TV series is rerun and their films are Saturday and Sunday morning staples. Adults should tune in, too.

• **Cult Favorites:** *Buck Privates* (1941, Arthur Lubin), *Abbott and Costello Meet Frankenstein* (1948, Charles T. Barton).

• **Also Recommended:** *Hold That Ghost* (1941, Lubin), *Pardon My Sarong* (1942, Erle C. Kenton), *It Ain't Hay* (1943, Kenton), *Lost in a Harem* (Charles Reisner), *The Naughty Nineties* (1945, Jean Yarborough), *Little Giant* (1946, William A. Seiter), *The Time of Their Lives* (1946, Barton), *The Wistful Widow of Wagon Gap* (1947, Barton).

○

ACQUANETTA (1921–) Alluring, long-haired star of adventure and horror programmers in the forties. Formerly Burno Davenport, she may have been an American Indian but as the "Venezuelan Volcano," she played strange young women in exotic locales, especially jungles. She secured her place in camp lore in her breakthrough films *Captive Wild Women* and its sequel *Jungle Women* as an increasingly violent and sexually aroused woman who was

Acquanetta's image is evident in this publicity shot.

BROOKE ADAMS (1949–) Bright, pretty, hip young leading lady of the late seventies and eighties. She has intentionally avoided Hollywood stardom by choosing unusual roles and turning down major films to perform in small-scale theater productions or teach acting to troubled youngsters. She's best at playing sensitive young women who, for one reason or another, are burdened with great sadness or dissatisfaction. (Her downturned mouth helps give this impression.) While she received her best notices as a migrant worker desired by both Richard Gere and Sam Shepard in *Days of Heaven,* she's better known for taking Dana Wynter's part in the remake of *Invasion of the Body Snatchers.* Science-fiction fans regard her nude scene as one of the sexiest (and one of the creepiest) moments in genre history. Surely her love scene with Christopher Walken in *The Dead Zone* is among the horror genre's most poignant sequences.
- **Cult Favorites:** *Days of Heaven* (1979, Terrence Malick), *Invasion of the Body Snatchers* (1978, Phil Kaufman), *The Dead Zone* (1983, David Cronenberg).
- **Sleepers:** *Shock Waves* (1977, Ken Wiederhorn), *Cuba* (1979, Richard Lester), *Tell Me a Riddle* (1980, Lee Grant), *Utilities* (1983, Harvey Hart).

transformed from an orangutan. She had no dialogue. Her unusual name brought her attention, but excluded her from the big time; no publicist could use the slogan "Gable's back and Acquanetta's got him!"
- **Cult Favorite:** *Captive Wild Woman* (1943, Edward Dmytryk).
- **Other Key Films:** *Jungle Woman* (1944, Reginald LeBorg), *Dead Man's Eyes* (1944, LeBorg), *Tarzan and the Leopard Woman* (1946, Kurt Neumann), *The Lost Continent* (1951, Sam Newfield).

JULIE/JULIA ADAMS (1926–) Although she was a reliable leading lady in numerous fifties and sixties films, including *Bend of the River* with Jimmy Stewart, and television programs, including "The Jimmy Stewart Show," Adams really caught our attention only once: every teenage boy got a cheap thrill watching her swim spreadeagled

Julia Adams is carried away by the Gill Man in Creature from the Black Lagoon.

above the aroused Gill Man in the *Creature from the Black Lagoon.* This was enough to earn her permanent cult status.

- **Cult Favorites:** *Bend of the River* (1952, Anthony Mann), *Creature from the Black Lagoon* (1952, Jack Arnold).
- **Also Recommended:** *Bright Victory* (1951, Mark Robson), *Slaughter on Tenth Avenue* (1957, Arnold Laven).
- **Also of Interest:** *Psychic Killer* (1975, Ray Danton).

○

JOHN AGAR (1921–) Good-looking, clean-cut actor was quite likable in his debut, politely courting real-life wife Shirley Temple in John Ford's western classic *Fort Apache,* and again as a young officer in *She Wore a Yellow Ribbon,* the second entry in Ford's cavalry trilogy. He had good parts in a few other major films, but after a divorce and losing battles to the bottle and blandness he could find steady work only in B films. His cult following is a result of his leading roles in a number of horror and science-fiction films. *Tarantula* and *Revenge of the Creature* were quite fun; the ludicrous titles of some of the others, like *Zontar, the Thing from Venus,* only hint at their low quality. He played one of his few villains—a possessed scientist—in *The Brain from Planet Arous,* a role that required wearing a pair of painful silver

A publicity shot of John Agar with Lori Nelson in Revenge of the Creature.

contact lenses. Agar can supposedly sing, but we never heard him in any of his movies, not even *Curse of the Swamp Creature* or *Women of the Prehistoric Planet.*

• **Cult Favorites:** *Bait* (1954, Hugo Haas), *Tarantula* (1955, Jack Arnold), *The Brain from Planet Arous* (1958, Nathan Juran), *Invisible Invaders* (1959, Edward L. Cahn).

• **Other Key Films:** *Fort Apache* (1948, John Ford), *Adventure in Baltimore* (1949, Richard Wallace), *She Wore a Yellow Ribbon* (1949, Ford), *Sands of Iwo Jima* (1949, Allan Dwan), *Breakthrough* (1950, Lewis Seiter), *Along the Great Divide* (1951, Raoul Walsh), *Revenge of the Creature* (1955, Arnold), *The Mole People* (1956, Virgil Vogel), *Star in the Dust* (1956, Charles Haas), *Daughter of Dr. Jekyll* (1957, Edgar G. Ulmer), *Attack of the*

Puppet People (1958, Bert I. Gordon), *Miracle Mile* (1989, Steve DeJarnatt.)

○

JENNY AGUTTER (1952–) Intelligent, lovely young British actress who became the not-so-innocent crush of many American filmgoers, including adults who still needed someone to replace Hayley Mills. After starring in the ever-popular British drama, *The Railway Children,* she caused an international stir as a uptight teenager in the remarkable erotic odyssey *Walkabout,* trekking across Australia's outback in a very short school uniform and fighting her physical attraction to the young aborigine who leads her (and her young brother) to safety. As an adult, in films like *An American Werewolf in London* and the surprisingly explicit western *China 9, Liberty 37,* she'd play other females experiencing sexual awakenings. Clear-eyed and well

Jenny Agutter in An American Werewolf in London.

spoken (with a great accent), she has always been classy even though her early roles almost always required nudity, including memorable swims in *Walkabout*, *China 9, Liberty 37* and *Logan's Run*.

• **Cult Favorites:** *Walkabout* (1971, Nicolas Roeg), *An American Werewolf in London* (1981, John Landis).

• **Sleepers:** *The Railway Children* (1968, Lionel Jeffries), *China 9, Liberty 37* (1978, Monte Hellman), *Amy* (1981, Vincent McEveety), *Secret Places* (1985, Zelda Barron).

• **Other Key Films:** *Logan's Run* (1976, Michael Anderson), *Equus* (1977, Sidney Lumet), *Sweet William* (1980, Claude Whatham), *Child's Play 2* (1990, John Lafia).

○

PRISCILLA ALDEN Obese actress became a favorite of the horror-movie underground when she played Fat Ethel in the 16mm *Criminally Insane*. She gave an animated performance, alternating stuffing herself with food and annihilating smaller people. Thirteen years later, Alden reprised her role in *Crazy Fat Ethel II*. She had lost neither weight nor presence, and turned in another spectacularly weird performance. Released from prison, Fat Ethel goes on another spree of gluttony and murder, punctuated by flashbacks from the earlier film. Alden also starred in the unpleasant direct-to-video bloodbath *Death Nurse* (no theatrical release). Because Alden's films have been seen by only the most hardcore horror fans, she is somewhat of a legend in the genre.

• **Cult Favorites:** *Criminally Insane* (1974, Nick Phillips), *Crazy Fat Ethel II* (1987, Phillips).

○

KAY ALDRIDGE (1917–) Republic Studios' "Queen of the Serials" in the forties, although she made only three. A former cover girl and a B-film actress, this pretty brunette burst to fame in the extremely popular *Perils of Nyoka*, taking over the role Frances Gifford played so well in *Jungle Girl*. She wasn't as sexy or as athletic as Gifford (although she didn't have to be the latter—David Sharpe did both their stunts), but she was undeniably appealing. Her pretty face had a well-scrubbed, glowing tone, her makeup was perfectly applied, her eyes were clear and determined, her lips ready for hero Clayton Moore, and, like the ideal cliffhanging

Serial Queen Kay Aldridge is in typical jeopardy in the Perils of Nyoka.

heroine, she seemed at once brave (she carried a gun or knife) and, in shorts or short skirts, vulnerable to attack. Aldridge later starred in the action-packed *Daredevils of the West,* opposite Allan "Rocky" Lane, and in *Haunted Harbor,* romancing Kane Richmond. She made 21 features, often playing rich, snobbish young women.

• **Cult Favorite:** *Perils of Nyoka* (1942 serial, William Witney).

• **Also Recommended:** *Daredevils of the West* (1943 serial, John English), *Haunted Harbor* (1944 serial, Spencer Bennet and Wallace Grissell).

○

KAREN ALLEN (1951–) If Myrna Loy was the screen's "perfect wife" for mature men in the mainstream of society, then this appealing, dark-haired actress is the screen's "perfect girlfriend" for young male misfits. Whether in high school in the early sixties, college in the late sixties or early seventies, or at large in the counterculture (and dressed appropriately), the females she plays are spirited, good-natured, sexy *and* sex-minded. Her eyes not only strike you because they are so pretty but because they are so naughty. Her passionate, often unpredictable characters are usually eager to make love—the highlight of *The Wanderers* is when she willingly participates in a strip poker game that she knows the boys have rigged so that she loses. No actress, not even Debra Winger, is better at *acting* (and that includes conversing) during passionate love scenes—note especially *Until September*—but she also proved she can handle action scenes with the best of them in *Raiders of the Lost Ark,* a smash hit destined for cult status. She is feisty and funny, brave and beautiful in this first

Indiana Jones film, the rare woman Harrison Ford's hero could fall for. No wonder fans of the series have been reluctant to accept subsequent heroines.

• **Cult Favorites:** *The Wanderers* (1979, Philip Kaufman), *Shoot the Moon* (1982, Allan Parker).

• **Other Key Films:** *National Lampoon's Animal House* (1978, John Landis), *Small Circle of Friends* (1980, Rob Cohen), *Raiders of the Lost Ark* (1981, Steven Spielberg), *Split Image* (1982, Ted Kotcheff), *Until September* (1984, Richard Marquand), *Starman* (1984, John Carpenter), *The Glass Menagerie* (1987, Paul Newman).

○

NANCY ALLEN (1950–) This cute, curly-haired blonde with a child's voice was cast against type in Brian De Palma's *Carrie,* and as Sissy Spacek's cruel nemesis and John Travolta's domineering girlfriend set the cinema's standard for stuck-up, supersexed, superbitchy high-school girls. Allen later married De Palma, and critics griped when he gave her lead roles in his films, but her offbeat, disarming performances warranted his confidence. She seemed willing to follow any direction: in *Dressed to Kill,* undressing to skimpy underwear to attract Michael Caine, and hurtling over a subway turnstile to escape a pursuer; in *Home Movies,* arguing with a puppet on her hand. De Palma continued to play with her image and cast her as women with dual personalities, one side sweet and sympathetic, the other tough as nails or, in *Home Movies,* quite mad. Since her divorce from De Palma, Allen has continued to play sympathetic leads, but her characters haven't been as interesting and, neither have her films, except for *RoboCop* and

RoboCop II, in which she's Peter Weller's tough, human police partner. Even De Palma didn't take full of advantage of the surprising, natural comic talent she demonstrated in *I Wanna Hold Your Hand,* when she played the last teenager in America to fall hard for the Beatles.

• **Cult Favorites:** *Carrie* (1976, Brian De Palma), *Dressed to Kill* (1980, De Palma), *Blow Out* (1981, De Palma), *Strange Invaders* (1983, Michael Laughlin), *RoboCop* (1987, Paul Verhoeven) *RoboCop II* (1990, Irvin Kershner).

• **Sleeper:** *I Wanna Hold Your Hand* (1978, Robert Zemeckis).

• **Also of Interest:** *Home Movies* (1979, De Palma), *The Philadelphia Experiment* (1984, Stewart Raffill).

○

KIRK ALYN (1910–) He won permanent cult status by playing Superman in two Columbia serials. He didn't have the physical stature for the role—he should have been given lifts and more padding—but that wasn't crucial in those less-than-epic productions. He did, after all, have a pleasant smile and a hank of hair curling down his forehead. While his reputation is based on his "Man of Steel," he also had success as the hero of *Blackhawk* and other action serials at Columbia and Republic. Alyn was cast as Lois Lane's father in the 1978 *Superman* feature, but all that remains of his performance is a shot of the back of his head. (Oddly, for many years he didn't mention *Superman* in his credits, especially when seeking stage roles.)

• **Cult Favorites:** *Superman* (1948 serial, Spencer Bennet and Thomas Carr), *Atom Man vs. Superman* (1950 serial, Bennet).

• **Also of Interest:** *Daughter of Don Q* (1946 serial, Bennet and Fred Bannon), *Radar Patrol vs. Spy King* (1950 serial, Bannon), *Blackhawk* (1952 serial, Bennet).

○

LUANA ANDERS (1940–) Unconventional actress with blond hair, a cleft chin, and sexy demeanor, ideal at playing juvenile delinquents and, when a bit older, uninhibited beats and hippies. As a lead or supporting player, her credits arouse curiosity. Did she seek out chancey, out-of-the-mainstream films, including low-budget horror and fantasy flms, quirky westerns, pictures with drug themes, and early efforts by directors with future fame? Or did the filmmakers go after her? A Roger Corman favorite, her associates also include Dennis Hopper and Jack Nicholson; both acted with her and later directed her. She was the commune dweller who is turned on by Peter Fonda in *Easy Rider,* but cultists best remember her for her erotic and spooky underwater-in-underwear swim in *Dementia 13.* When she comes to the surface, one of the screen's first ax-murderers is waiting for her.

• **Cult Favorites:** *The Pit and the Pendulum* (1961, Roger Corman), *Night Tide* (1963, Curtis Harrington), *Dementia 13* (1963, Francis Ford Coppola), *Easy Rider* (1969, Dennis Hopper), *Greaser's Palace* (1972, Robert Downey), *The Missouri Breaks* (1976, Arthur Penn), *Goin' South* (1978, Jack Nicholson).

• **Sleepers:** *When Legends Die* (1972, Stuart Millar), *Personal Best* (1981, Robert Towne).

• **Also of Interest:** *The Young Racers* (1963, Corman), *That Cold Day in the Park* (1969, Robert Altman), *The Manipulator* (1971, Yabo Yablonsky), *Shampoo* (1975, Hal Ashby).

JULIET ANDERSON Porno star with a string of video hits in the late seventies as "Aunt Peg," a movie producer driven by her libido in the absence of a heart. They were later adapted into feature films. Otherwise, she has mostly played second leads, usually as conniving, bitchy seductresses. She was uninhibited on the screen, but her sex scenes came off as sleazy, without a needed dash of eroticism. What made her different from other blondes of her era was that she was about twice their age and had a truly ugly hairstyle. It's hard to figure out her appeal.

 • **Cult Favorites:** *Pretty Peaches* (1978, Alex DeRenzy), *Aunt Peg* (1980, Arthur Cutter and Wes Brown), *Taboo* (1980, Kirdy Stevens), *Talk Dirty to Me* (1980, Anthony Spinelli).

 • **Other Key Films:** *Randy, the Electric Lady* (1979, Philip Schuman), *A Girl's Best Friend* (1981, Henri Pachard), *Aunt Peg's Fulfillment* (1982, Cutter and Brown), *Aunt Peg Goes Hollywood* (1983, Paul G. Vatelli), *Taboo II* (1983, Stevens).

○

LEONA ANDERSON (1895–1985) Probably the greatest pre-*Psycho* movie shock takes place in *House on Haunted Hill,* when the nervous heroine turns around in the dungeon and screams when she finds, standing inches from her, a cadaverous old lady with electrified white hair; wild, unblinking, sightless eyes; grasping, bony fingers; and a mad, toothy smile with a wide-open mouth and a wiggling lower jaw. Here was the actress who could have played Nosferatu's mother.

 • **Cult Favorite:** *House on Haunted Hill* (1958, William Castle).

○

URSULA ANDRESS (1936–) A statue of a Greek goddess come to life, she would be 45 when cast as Aphrodite in *Clash of the Titans,* yet no younger actress was better suited to the role. After several obscure Italian films, this shapely Swiss beauty made a startling entrance in the first James Bond film, *Dr. No.* In Ian Fleming's book, Honeychile Ryder is nude when Bond first sees her on a beach; in the film, Andress wore a skimpy bikini but no one felt shortchanged. Most aficionados of the series agree that in physical terms alone, there was no better "Bond girl"; certainly she was the best match for the young Sean Connery. Andress immediately became an international sex symbol. She starred in all types of films over the next few years, including the popular comedy *What's New, Pussycat?;* Robert Day's *She,* from H. Ryder Haggard's mythic adventure about an eternally young queen; the satirical science-fiction romance *The Tenth Victim,* in which she played an assassin with a bra that shoots bullets; and *Once Before I Die,* a peculiar war film directed by her then-husband, John Derek. She really couldn't act but faked it by speaking softly, narrowing her eyes, and looking pensive—she had trouble feigning anger because her face was too rigid. But no matter, since all her roles were designed to exploit her anatomy. When her star waned, she accepted roles in Italian exploitation films, like the soft-core comedy *The Sensuous Nurse,* a hit on cable. She has remained a favorite of the pinup crowd.

 • **Cult Favorites:** *Dr. No* (1963, Terence Young), *What's New, Pussycat?* (1965, Clive Donner), *The 10th Victim* (1965, Elio Petri), *The Sensuous Nurse* (1976, Nello Rossati), *Slave of the Cannibal God*

Ursula Andress and Sean Connery in Dr. No.

(1979, Sergio Martini), *Clash of the Titans* (1981, Desmond Davis).

• **Also of Interest:** *Fun in Acapulco* (1963, Richard Thorpe), *4 for Texas* (1963, Robert Aldrich), *Nightmare in the Sun* (1965, Marc Lawrence), *Once Before I Die* (1965, John Derek), *The Blue Max* (1966, John Guillerman), *Casino Royale* (1967, Val Guest, John Huston, Ken Hughes, Joe McGrath, Robert Parrish), *The Southern Star* (1969, Sidney Hayers), *Perfect Friday* (1970, Peter Hall), *Red Sun* (1972, Young).

PIER ANGELI (1932–71) This young Italian actress was brought to America by Fred Zinnemann in 1951 to star in *Teresa* and charmed audiences with her delicate beauty, sensitivity, and accent. She and Paul Newman survived the camp classic *The Silver Chalice* and were reunited for the engaging boxing biography *Somebody Up There Likes Me,* with Angeli as the gentle wife of middleweight champ Rocky Graziano. My strongest, fondest memories of Angeli are of the courtship scenes in that movie and those moments when Graziano's wife, who detests boxing and stays away from the arena and by a radio, suffers each blow that lands on her husband. In real life, Angeli loved James Dean, but her mother forced her to marry singer Vic Damone. After their marriage ended, she returned to Europe and starred in B action and adventure films. Her career wasn't particularly noteworthy—does anyone remember *The Light Touch*, *The Vintage*, *Sombrero*, or *Spy In Your Eye*? Other than Newman, Kirk Douglas in *The Story of Three Loves*, and Danny Kaye in *Merry Andrew*, her leading men were of the Philip Carey–John Erickson–Ty Hardin ilk. But she always played leads—and she had something special. In 1971, she died from an overdose of barbiturates. Actress Marisa Pavan was her less interesting twin.

• **Cult Favorite:** *The Silver Chalice* (1954, Victor Saville).

• **Other Key Films:** *Tomorrow Is Too Late* (1949, Leonide Moguy), *The Story of Three Loves* (1953, Vincente Minnelli), *Somebody Up There Likes Me* (1956, Robert Wise), *Merry Andrew* (1958, Michael Kidd), *S.O.S. Pacific* (1960, Guy Green), *The Angry Silence* (1960, Green), *Sodom and Gomorrah* (1963, Robert Aldrich).

○

EVELYN ANKERS (1918–85) Blond British actress who appeared in a number of Universal films, including the funny Abbott and Costello comedy-spook film *Hold That Ghost*, before making an impression in *The Wolf Man*. She was very appealing as Lon Chaney, Jr.'s imperiled girlfriend in the classy horror film—pretty, smart, and a great screamer. As a result she got leads in

Evelyn Ankers is threatened by Lon Chaney, Jr., in The Wolf Man.

many lesser horror films, several with Chaney, screaming her way to recognition as the studio's "Queen of the Horror Movies." She was always likable and capable but even horror buffs have a hard time placing that pretty face in all those fright films, or even realizing that the same actress is in all of them. In some cases they've forgotten her by the time the movie ends, especially when she costarred with the exotic Acquanetta in *Captive Wild Woman* and *Jungle Woman*. But they do affectionately remember her in the climax of *The Wolf Man*, screaming, being strangled, and fainting, carried through the misty woods by the definitive movie werewolf.

• **Cult Favorites:** *The Wolf Man* (1941, George Waggner), *Captive Wild Woman* (1943, Edward Dmytryk), *Son of Dracula* (1943, Robert Siodmak).

• **Other Key Films:** *Hold That Ghost* (1941, Arthur Lubin), *The Ghost of Frankenstein* (1942, Erle C. Kenton), *Sherlock Holmes and the Voice of Terror* (1942, John Rawlins), *All By Myself* (1943, Felix Feist), *The Mad Ghoul* (1943, James Hogan), *Weird Woman* (1944, Reginald LeBorg), *The Invisible Man's Revenge* (1944, Ford Beebe), *Jungle Woman* (1944, LeBorg), *Pearl of Death* (1944, Roy William Neill), *The Frozen Ghost* (1944, Harold Young), *Tarzan's Magic Fountain* (1949, Lee Sholem).

○

MORRIS ANKRUM (1896–1964) A prolific character actor of A films in the forties, Ankrum became a fixture of B science-fiction films in the fifties. He was ideal at playing low-key, patriotic authority figures, particularly generals, police captains, and scientists. Could he act? I don't know, but he was great at sitting behind a desk, blankly explaining to the hero the grave problem he must resolve, and looking as if he were resigned to the end of the free world.

• **Cult Favorites:** *Rocketship X-M* (1950, Kurt Neumann), *Red Planet Mars* (1952, Harry Horner), *Invaders from Mars* (1953, William Cameron Menzies), *Vera Cruz* (1954, Robert Aldrich), *Earth vs. the Flying Saucers* (1956, Fred F. Sears), *Kronos* (1957, Neumann).

• **Other Key Films:** *Borderland* (1937, Nate Watt), *Flight to Mars* (1951, Lesley Selander), *The Giant Claw* (1957, Sears), *Beginning of the End* (1957, Bert I. Gordon).

○

ANN-MARGRET (1941–) Sexy, voluptuous, soft-voiced, redheaded Ann-Margret Olsson moved from singing and dancing in nightclubs to movie acting in the early sixties. She debuted as Bette Davis's well-bred daughter in *Pocketful of Miracles* but ladylike roles stifled her, and she soon found her niche playing wild, pleasure-seeking flirts and bad girls. She was promoted as a female Elvis Presley, and she wore scandalous shorts when the two were united for *Viva Las Vegas.* "I want you to check my motor," she tells his race-car driver. "It whistles." She was best cast in *Kitten with a Whip,* as an unstable young tease (with frightening friends) who threatens to ruin the life of helpful stranger John Forsythe unless he does her bidding. Although she comes through for him in the end, she is one of the actress's few characters with more than a touch of immorality—there should have been many others. Her acting was wretched in the sixties, but everyone (except the critics) forgave her because she obviously tried hard to compensate for her lack of training, keeping her energy level high and often turning up the sex a notch; while surrounded by other dancers in *Bye Bye Birdie,* she pulls your eyes toward her by squeezing her breasts together with her arms. Both young guys and girls liked her. In 1971's *Carnal Knowledge,* under Mike Nichols's direction, Ann-Margret suddenly turned in a strong performance in a small role, as a woman who, realizing she isn't getting any younger, wants Jack Nicholson to settle down with her. Their bedroom argument is a classic. That one film gave Ann-Margret credibility. It also gave her confidence, as is evident in her later, mature performances.

• **Cult Favorites:** *Viva Las Vegas* (1964, George Sidney), *Kitten with a Whip* (1964, Douglas Heyes), *Carnal Knowledge* (1971, Mike Nichols), *Tommy* (1975, Ken Russell).

Ann-Margret is serenaded by Elvis Presley in Viva Las Vegas.

• **Other Key Films:** *Bye Bye Birdie* (1963, George Sidney), *The Pleasure Seekers* (1964, Jean Negulesco), *Bus Riley's Back in Town* (1965, Harvey Hart), *The Cincinnati Kid* (1965, Norman Jewison), *Twice in a Lifetime* (1985, Bud Yorkin).

• **Also of Interest:** *Magic* (1978, Richard Attenborough), *The Villain* (1979, Hal Needham), *The Return of the Soldier* (1981, Alan Bridges), *52 Pick-Up* (1986, John Frankenheimer), *A New Life* (1988, Alan Alda), *A Tiger's Tail* (1988, Peter Douglas).

○

LAURA ANTONELLI (1942–) Luscious Italian actress with enough talent, beauty, and sensuality to have been at least a minor star without doing nudity, but she became a minor international sex symbol in the seventies by disrobing in each of her pictures. What made her films erotic is that she seemed too classy to strip for the cameras. Her perfect body was actually the source of much of the humor in the foolish *The Naked Cello:* her kneeling

Italian sex symbol Laura Antonelli in Till Marriage Do Us part.

naked form fits snugly into a cello case and it also replaces the instrument in the cellist's mind as he performs. She had her first shot at seducing the American audience as the housekeeper in the Italian import *Malizia,* tantalizing the head of the household and giving his teenage son more than an eyeful. She tried again in the classier, more amusing *Wifemistress,* playing a repressed woman who breaks out of her sexual shackles while exploring the secret life of her philanderer husband, Marcello Mastroianni. Although she worked with famous directors, including Claude Chabrol and Luchino Visconti, and received good notices, for some reason (perhaps she couldn't learn English), she

didn't get offers to appear in American-made films.

• **Key Films:** *Dr. Goldfoot and the Girl Bombs* (1966, Mario Bava), *High Heels* (1972, Claude Chabrol), *Malizia/Malicious* (1973, Salvatore Samperi), *Till Marriage Do Us Part* (1974, Luigi Comenici), *The Innocent* (1976, Luchino Visconti), *Wifemistress* (1977, Marco Vicario), *The Divine Nymph* (1977, Giuseppe Patroni Griffi), *Passion of Love* (1982, Ettore Scola).

○

FATTY ARBUCKLE (1887–1933) The 300-pound Roscoe Arbuckle was one of the first major slapstick comics of the silent era, first with Mack Sennett and then on his own. Wearing makeup that emphasized his baby features, and ill-fitting, childish clothes that emphasized his belly, he looked more like an overgrown Little Rascal than an adult. He was one of the first comics who won over young viewers by coming across as the perfect playmate. Kids liked this fat, unthreatening fellow who was part innocent and part naughty (often dressed in female garb, he would spy on unsuspecting women), and always doing pratfalls. But, as Walter Kerr pointed out, he was "loved not so much for what he did as for what he looked like." His comedy work is actually immature and uninventive, and is interesting largely because of the fledgling comics who worked with him, including Charlie Chaplin, Mabel Normand (his frequent costar), and Buster Keaton. As big as he was, he never tried to hog the screen. Keaton said, "Arbuckle was that rarity, a truly jolly fat man. He had no meanness, malice or jealousy in him." Arbuckle's lasting fame is due to scandal: in 1921, starlet Virginia Rappe went into convulsions at a wild

Fatty Arbuckle (far right) *was first noticed among the skinnier Keystone Cops.*

party and died of a ruptured bladder a few days later. Amid rumors that he had raped and crushed the much smaller actress, Arbuckle was charged with manslaughter. After two hung juries, Arbuckle was acquitted in a third trial. However, his past films were banned, and he was barred by the Hays Office from appearing on screen again. He would continue as a director, under the pseudonym William Goodrich.

• **Sample Films:** *The Knockout* (1914, Mack Sennett), *Fatty and Mabel Adrift* (1916, Arbuckle), *The Rough House* (1916, Arbuckle), *The Butcher Boy* (1917, Arbuckle), *Fatty at Coney Island* (1917, Arbuckle), *The Garage* (1920, Arbuckle).

○

JEAN ARLESS The opening credits of William Castle's horror chiller *Homicidal* say "in-troducing Jean Arless." We don't know if Jean is the stylish, knife-wielding blond murderess (how excited she gets before beheading the invalid, mute housekeeper!) or her brother, Warren, an ugly young man with slick black hair. It turns out that the film ripped off *Psycho* and Arless is both characters. Warren is actually a female who has posed as a male her whole life; now, in order to get an inheritance, she becomes the blond Emily and murders those who know the secret. Got it? At the end of the film, Arless takes bows as both a male and female, and we're not supposed to know if the parts were played by an actor or actress. "Arless" didn't appear in other films, so the mystery was never solved—although anyone can see that the male character looks awfully strange. Who was Arless? According to Castle: Joan Marshall.

• **Cult Favorite:** *Homicidal* (1961, William Castle).

○

ARLETTY (1898–) Born Léonie Bathiat, she starred in several classic French films of the thirties and forties directed by Marcel Carné and written by Jacques Prévert. Her women were realists, passive, stoic, and sphinxlike. They looked as if a deep hurt in the past had permanently shattered their dreams of a happy future. They took love when offered and gave it willingly in return, but realized they'd find no fulfillment or lasting happiness in a world run by immature, insecure, insensitive men. Arletty is most identified as Garance in *Children of Paradise,* the landmark of *le cinéma d'évasion*—the French film industry's brave response to the German occupation. The men who love Garance see her as an angel, a dream, a vision of beauty, Venus. She is the symbol of Paris: beautiful, freedom-loving, full of memories, as tolerant (even as proud) of its gutter dwellers as of its elite, the lover of every man and the betrayer of none. Most important she is a survivor who remains unchanged ("I am free") despite the attempt of a dictatorial man from another class to control her—just as all truly loyal, brave French people refuse to be controlled by a dictator from another country. Garance is the very essence of the unwavering French, so it is ironic and shameful that Arletty would briefly go to prison for having an affair with a German officer during the occupation.

• **Cult Favorites:** *Le Jour Se Lève* (1939, Marcel Carné), *Children of Paradise* (1945, Carné).

• **Also of Interest:** *Désiré* (1938, Sacha Guitry), *Hotel du Nord* (1938, Carné), *Les Visiteurs du Soir* (1942, Carné), *Le Grand Jeu* (1953, Robert Siodmak).

Arletty in Children of Paradise.

○

ROBERT ARMSTRONG (1890–1973) There was nothing remarkable about this character actor—just that he could act tough and talk fast, like a sailor on the make or one of Hart and Kaufman's newspaper men. But he lucked out and was cast as the (human) male lead in *King Kong,* the greatest and most complex of all fantasy films, and got to recite one of the screen's classic lines: "It was beauty killed the beast." He was the wise, ideal choice to play filmmaker-showman Carl Denham, a self-professed he-man who spent his life traveling to the ends of the earth with an all-male crew. Throughout he denies interest in any woman, even Fay Wray's Ann Darrow, but Kong is the physical manifestation of his sexual "beast" side that is attracted to her and wants Bruce Cabot's Jack Driscoll out of the way. The dual personality of Denham and Kong is perhaps the most fascinating in the horror genre. Armstrong would reprise the Denham character in *Son of Kong,* but in that film he is willing to admit his attraction to the female, Helen Mack. Consequently, this film's giant gorilla is tame. Armstrong would appear innocuously in many action-adventure films over the decades, but he did make the spotlight once more in *Mighty Joe Young,* playing a Denham-like white hunter who brings another, friendlier large ape back to civilization. Like Denham, he is tough and money-hungry but, at the expense of his he-man image, ultimately shows he has a heart.
 • **Cult Favorites:** *King Kong* (1933, Merian C. Cooper and Ernest B. Schoedsack), *Mighty Joe Young* (1949, Schoedsack).
 • **Other Key Films:** *A Girl in Every Port* (1928, Howard Hawks), *The Iron Man* (1931, Tod Browning), *The Most Dangerous Game* (1932, Schoedsack and Irving Pichel), *Son of Kong* (1936, Schoedsack).
 • **Also of Interest:** *G-Men* (1935, William Keighley), *Little Big Shot* (1935, Michael Curtiz), *Man of Conquest* (1939, George Nicholls, Jr.), *The Paleface* (1948, Norman Z. McLeod).

○

ROSANNA ARQUETTE (1959–) Not always taken seriously, perhaps because many of her characters talk a spacey blue streak, Arquette is a terrific actress who can skillfully play daffy roles, femme fatales, and real-to-life characters. An atypical leading lady, a flower-child throwback, she comes across as a feisty, flaky free spirit. When this long-haired blonde-brunette smiles broadly she looks like a clown, but there's fire in her blue-green eyes, and when she is free and easy with her shapely body, she is extremely sexy. For those who've seen her topless scene in the European-theatrical and American-video versions of *The Executioner's Song,* her sexiness as Gary Gilmore's obssessed lover obscures the fact that she's giving a *great* dramatic performance. Her varied, memorable roles include her topless hitchhiker in *S.O.B.;* a deaf-mute farm girl in the TV movie *Johnny Belinda;* the slightly snobby and self-centered Jewish high school/college student who's attracted to a wild Italian classmate (Vincent Spano) in *Baby, It's You;* a repressed suburban housewife with kook tendencies in *Desperately Seeking Susan,* her most famous film; Griffin Dunne's zany, soon-dead pick-up date in the surrealistic *After Hours;* and obsessive artist Nick Nolte's fed-up protegé/lover in the best episode of *New York Stories.* Offscreen, the granddaughter of Cliff Arquette, TV's "Charley Weaver," is a political activist.

• **Cult Favorites:** *The Executioner's Song* (1982, Lawrence Schiller), *Baby, It's You* (1983, John Sayles), *Desperately Seeking Susan* (1985, Susan Seidelman), *After Hours* (1985, Martin Scorsese), *Silverado* (1985, Lawrence Kasdan), *New York Stories* (1989, Scorsese episode).

• **Also Recommended:** *S.O.B.* (1981, Blake Edwards), *8 Million Ways to Die* (1986, Hal Ashby), *The Big Blue* (1988, Luc Bresson).

○

JOHN ASHLEY (1934–) If Frankie Avalon had stayed out of movies, this equally handsome, cheery, and innocuous young actor would have been a good choice to star in all those AIP beach movies opposite Annette Funicello. He wasn't particularly tall and he could almost sing. Frankie and Johnny

did make those beach films together, but alas Avalon got Annette while Ashley got sunburned, standing in the background, bare-chested, smiling, and unimportant. Otherwise he was a leading man, in teen-problem and hot-rod pictures, and then horrible low-budget horror films, some of which he produced in the Philippines. I preferred him in action films (and the TV series "Ripcord") because when he'd get a fat lip he'd try to act, and do even better than when he'd comfort young girls by holding their shoulders. He has had a long career without ever playing an interesting character, but he was harmless and had a very young face, which got him the role of Baby Face Nelson in *Young Dillinger*. He produced TV's "The A-Team."

• **Cult Favorites:** *Beach Party* (1963, William Asher), *Beach Blanket Bingo* (1965, Asher), *Brides of Blood* (1968, Eddie Romero and Gerardo de Leon), *Beast of the Yellow Night* (1971, Romero), *Twilight People* (1972, Romero).

John Ashley fights for his life in the horror film shot in the Philippines, Mad Doctor of Blood Island.

• **Other Key Films:** *Dragstrip Girl* (1957, Edward L. Cahn), *Frankenstein's Daughter* (1958, Richard Cunha), *High School Caesar* (1960, O'Dale Ireland), *Muscle Beach Party* (1964, Asher), *Bikini Beach* (1964, Asher), *How to Stuff a Wild Bikini* (1965, Asher), *The Eye Creatures* (1968, Larry Buchanan), *Mad Doctor of Blood Island* (1969, Romero and Gerardo de Leon), *Beast of Blood* (1970, Romero), *Beyond Atlantis* (1973, Romero), *Savage Sisters* (1974, Romero).

○

ROBIN ASKWITH (1950–) Lightweight British actor with a resemblance to Peter Noone, lead singer of Herman's Hermits. He went unnoticed in *If* and *Nicholas and Alexandra*, then achieved culthood as the star in a popular series of silly R-rated Peeping Tom comedies, beginning with *Confessions of a Window Cleaner*. He was fortunate to be paired at times with Linda Hayden, who made the films almost watchable. His dim, young working-class bloke always had jobs where he was put into contact with frustrated (and often naked) females. Invariably, one of them would seduce him about a minute before her husband or father came on the scene. He became adept at slapstick getaways in his underwear. His talent matched the material; his youthful look added to the immature nature of the films.

• **Cult Favorite:** *Confessions of a Window Cleaner* (1974, Val Guest).

• **Other Key Films:** *Confessions of a Pop Performer* (1975), *Confessions of a Driving Instructor* (1976, Norman Cohen), *Confessions from Holiday Camp*.

• **Also of Interest:** *Tower of Evil* (1972, Jim O'Connolly), *Horror Hospital* (1973, Anthony Balch).

○

LIONEL ATWILL (1885–1946) This dark, brooding British actor, with malice in his eyes and a most suspicious mustache, played numerous mad doctors, Nazis, and other fiends, making life miserable for everyone from Fay Wray to Basil Rathbone's Sherlock Holmes to Abbott and Costello. Some of his horror roles were poorly chosen, but the genre was given a dose of respectability by his frequent presence, for he had the talent and voice to have done classic theater. His arrogant generals, Dr. Moriarty, and other sinister characters were highly intelligent and deadly serious, without even the hint of warmth that marked some of Boris Karloff's most wicked characters. Completely unhuggable, he seemed to make the screen grow dark around him. He's surprisingly funny in *To Be or Not to Be* as an actor playing a Nazi—he got to be someone who was supposed to be hammy, which he refused to be in even his most outlandish horror films.

• **Cult Favorites:** *The Mystery of the Wax Museum* (1933, Michael Curtiz), *The Devil Is a Woman* (1935, Josef von Sternberg), *The Hound of the Baskervilles* (1939, Sidney Lanfield), *To Be or Not to Be* (1942, Ernst Lubitsch).

• **Sleepers:** *The Sphinx* (1932, Phil Rosen), *Murders in the Zoo* (1933, A. Edward Sutherland), *The Man Who Reclaimed His Dead* (1934, Edward Ludwig).

• **Other Key Films:** *Doctor X* (1932, Curtiz), *The Vampire Bat* (1933, Frank Strayer), *Nana* (1934, Dorothy Arzner), *Mark of the Vampire* (1935, Tod Browning), *Captain Blood* (1935, Curtiz), *Son of Frankenstein* (1939, Rowland V. Lee), *Man Made Monster* (1941, George Waggner), *The Mad Doctor of Market Street* (1942,

Joseph H. Lewis), *The Ghost of Franken-stein* (1945, Erle C. Kenton), *Sherlock Homes and the Secret Weapon* (1942, Roy William Neill), *Frankenstein Meets the Wolf Man* (1943, Neill), *House of Frankenstein* (1944, Kenton), *House of Dracula* (1945, Kenton).

○

STÉPHANE AUDRAN (1938–) Sleek, smart, and sexy—with a cool demeanor, high cheek-bones, the moves of a dancer, and long legs that some Hollywood studio might have insured for $1 million—Audran has been one of the key leading ladies of the French cinema since the late sixties. She was discovered by her then-husband, director Claude Chabrol, and after some minor parts starred in many of his films, includ-ing several of his classic thrillers. She was marvelous playing aloof or bitchy bourgeois women who get involved in romantic or dangerous intrigue that disrupts their dull lives. But she also was effective as the sweet, sympathetic teacher who is threat-ened by the obsessed village psycho in Chabrol's *Le Boucher*. In Buñuel's hilari-ous *The Discreet Charm of the Bourgeoisie,* she parodied the self-possessed, tight-assed women she played for her husband, keeping a straight face as terrible things happen around her. She became more relaxed in time and if she wasn't required to play someone devoid of feeling, her performances could be almost playful, as in her cameos in Sam Fuller pictures.

• **Cult Favorites:** *Les Biches* (1968, Claude Chabrol), *La Femme Infidèle* (1969, Chabrol), *Le Boucher* (1970, Chabrol), *The Discreet Charm of the Bourgeoisie* (1972, Luis Buñuel), *The Big Red One* (1980, Samuel Fuller).

• **Also Recommended:** *Bluebeard* (1962, Chabrol, *The Champagne Murders* (1967, Chabrol), *Wedding in Blood* (1973, Chabrol), *Violette* (1978, Chabrol), *Coup de Torchon* (1981, Bertrand Tavernier), *Babette's Feast* (1987, Gabriel Axel).

○

MISCHA AUER (1905–67) Born Mischa Oun-skowsky, this tall, thin Russian emigré started out playing swarthy villains but became Hollywood's eccentric-in-waiting. With their wild gestures and ridiculous broken English, his foolish characters in-variably stole scenes and had everyone on- and offscreen laughing. He lost his pants playing cards with Marlene Dietrich in *Destry Rides Again,* brilliantly imperson-ated a gorilla in *My Man Godfrey* (his starving artist–leech was perhaps his best role), danced with "Cuddles" Sakall in *Spring Parade,* and did at least one silly thing per picture to grab your attention, even in noncomedies. He often lent wacky support to Deanna Durbin. One of the great character actors.

• **Cult Favorites:** *My Man Godfrey* (1936, Gregory La Cava), *Destry Rides Again* (1939, George Marshall), *And Then There Were None* (1945, René Clair).

• **Also Recommended:** *The Gay Desperado* (1936, Rouben Mamoulian), *Three Smart Girls* (1936, Henry Koster), *100 Men and a Girl* (1937, Koster), *You Can't Take It with You* (1938, Frank Capra), *Seven Sinners* (1940, Tay Garnett), *Spring Parade* (1940, Koster), *Hold That Ghost* (1941, Arthur Lubin), *Hellzapoppin* (1941, H. C. Potter), *Up in Mabel's Room* (1944, Allan Dwan), *A Royal Scandal* (1945, Ernst Lubitsch), *Brewster's Millions* (1945, Dwan), *Mr. Ar-kadin* (1955, Orson Welles).

○

GENE AUTRY (1907–) Has there ever been a more amiable hero than the Singing Cowboy? We were always surprised that he ever got mad, even when it was at some two-gun hustler or thievin' cattle rustler. Maybe "mad" is too strong a word— "disappointed" is probably more fitting. Autry started out as a radio singer in Tulsa and, inspired by Jimmie Rodgers, became known as "Oklahoma's Yodeling Cowboy." His singing career skyrocketed when he recorded "That Silver-Haired Daddy of Mine," still his best-known song after "Back in the Saddle" and "Rudolph, the Red-Nosed Reindeer." Then he broke into movies and supported singing cowboy Ken Maynard in a couple of pictures at Mascot. When Maynard went elsewhere, Autry was given the lead in the science-fiction– western serial *Phantom Empire,* a predecessor to *Flash Gordon.* Then he made 58 B western–musicals for Republic, becoming the top cowboy star of the era. At first, his westerns were set in the Old West, but later they took place in contemporary times, in almost surreal western towns. Autry went by his own name, though he played a lawman or a radio or rodeo star rather than a movie star. Ann Rutherford, later of the Andy Hardy movies, was his most frequent leading lady at the beginning; in future years it would be June Storey, Faye McKenzie, and Gail Davis (who'd star in the Autry-produced "Annie Oakley" TV series). His horse Champion and sidekicks Smiley Burnette and (later) Pat Buttram shared his popularity. His cowboy was a true-blue hero with an admirable Cowboy Code. A role model for his young fans, he was polite, helpful to anyone in trouble, a pal to kids (with his round, smiling face, he resembled about half of America's fathers), courtly to various school marms (he wasn't too embarrassed to serenade them), unafraid of ornery sidewinders, handy with the six-gun (he merely shot guns out of bad guys' hands), capable at fisticuffs (he'd never hit anyone smaller than himself)—and when the work was done, he'd lead everyone in a cheery campfire song. A lot can be said for adult westerns, but Gene Autry westerns were comforting. An institution.

• **Cult Favorites:** *Phantom Empire* (1935 serial, Otto Brewer and B. Reeves Eason), *Tumbling Tumbleweeds* (1935, Joseph Kane).

• **Also of Interest:** *The Singing Vagabond* (1935, Carl Pierson), *Red River Valley* (1936, Eason), *The Singing Cowboy* (1936, Mack V. Wright), *Ride, Ranger, Ride* (1936, Kane), *Yodelin' Kid from Pine Ridge* (1937, Kane), *Colorado Sunset* (1939, George Sherman), *In Old Monterey* (1939, Kane), *South of the Border* (1939, Sherman), *Back in the Saddle* (1941, Lew Landers), *Last of the Pony Riders* (1953, George Archainbaud).

○

FRANKIE AVALON (1939–) He wasn't the tallest guy around, but since he was cute and sang "Ginger Bread," "Venus," and a bunch of other songs to the top of the charts, he became a teen idol and got to make movies. He made a number of science-fiction and horror films, some comedic, but he had his greatest success in AIP's campy beach party musicals, opposite Annette Funicello. He seemed at ease playing light comedy and standing in the sand with a lot of short actors and actresses smirking and dancing around him. And yes, despite being conceited and smart-alecky, his beach boy always got Annette in the end, after learning she wanted to be romanced instead of bullied or taken for granted. These films taught all young people in the sixties about relationships. In 1987, Avalon was reunited with Annette for *Back to the Beach,* and though the picture lost its charm halfway through, Avalon not only was a good sport about being asked to do self-parody but was also surprisingly funny. When did he improve so much?

• **Cult Favorites:** *Beach Party* (1963, William Asher), *Beach Blanket Bingo* (1965, Asher).

• **Other Key Films:** *Muscle Beach Party* (1964, Asher), *Bikini Beach* (1964, Asher),

Sergeant Deadhead (1965, Norman Taurog), *Back to the Beach* (1987, Lyndall Hobbs).

• **Also of Interest:** *The Alamo* (1960, John Wayne), *Voyage to the Bottom of the Sea* (1961, Irwin Allen).

○

LAUREN BACALL (1924–) Betty Joan Perske was just 19 when Howard Hawks's wife, Slim, saw her beautiful face on the cover of *Harper's Bazaar.* Hawks immediately signed the slender, deep-voiced, erotic-eyed, long-haired brunette and cast her opposite Humphrey Bogart in *To Have and*

Electricity flows between Lauren Bacall and her To Have and Have Not *costar, Humphrey Bogart, as they fall in love on and offscreen.*

Have Not, as "Slim." As on the screen, where Bogart's cynical fishing boat captain falls for Bacall's strong, disarming, loyal nightclub singer, Bogart fell for this woman who was wise beyond her years, wasn't afraid of his tough-guy act, and could match him funny line for funny line. Bacall fell for him, too, which explains the electricity on the screen. She makes the most of her limited screen time: she's incredibly cool just slinking around a room, in control of her sexual impulses but making it obvious what's on her mind; and each time she delivers a line, her manner is so suggestive that she turns it into a *line* ("Anybody got a match?" "You know how to whistle, don't you? You just put your lips together and blow . . ."). She's a dream girl who tells the leading man how much she enjoyed his kiss, who doesn't waste time playing games: "I'm hard to get, all you have to do is ask." Bacall (who was called "The Look") and Bogart were married by the time they made Hawks's *The Big Sleep.* That film was far superior to their first, and Bacall's part was larger, as a playful, spoiled rich girl who attracts detective Philip Marlowe. Yet I don't think their scenes together, though loaded with sexual innuendo, have the same spark. She is perhaps too comfortable with Bogart, and the nervous, erotic edge isn't there. Bacall would make several more sexy appearances in the forties, including *Key Largo* and *Dark Passage* with Bogart, and be a classy, leading lady in the fifties, but nothing she did would equal those two Hawks films, when it was obvious she was having fun on screen. But years later she gave a strong performance in *The Shootist,* as landlady and friend to gunslinger John Wayne, who is dying from cancer.

• **Cult Favorites:** *To Have and Have Not* (1944, Howard Hawks), *The Big Sleep* (1946, Hawks), *Key Largo* (1948, John Huston), *Written on the Wind* (1956, Douglas Sirk).

• **Sleeper:** *The Shootist* (1976, Don Siegel).

• **Other Key Films:** *Confidential Agent* (1945, Herman Shumlin), *Dark Passage* (1947, Delmer Daves), *Young Man with a Horn* (1950, Michael Curtiz), *Bright Leaf* (1950, Curtiz), *How to Marry a Millionaire* (1953, Jean Negulesco), *Designing Woman* (1957, Vincente Minnelli), *Murder on the Orient Express* (1974, Sidney Lumet).

○

BARBARA BACH (1947–) She was from New York but had both a "foreign" look and, having lived 10 years in Italy, a foreign accent that made her suitable as Russian agent Anya Amasova in *The Spy Who Loved Me.* This was the most enjoyable of Roger Moore's James Bond films, and Bach was Moore's best on-screen lover. She was smaller than most Bond girls, but quite sexy and beautiful, with long hair, large lips, and full figure, and seductive, mysterious eyes. The first Bond heroine written with a nod to the women's movement, Anya was Bond's equal in every way: intelligent, witty, a great lover, brave, and capable of both defending herself and killing without guilt (in fact, she threatens to kill Bond as soon as their mission together is complete). Bach again caught one's eye in the prehistoric comedy *Caveman,* playing the coldhearted, stuck-up tribal beauty who is courted by Ringo Starr but spurned when he realizes the Shelley Long character is much sweeter. In real-life, Ringo and Bach got married. Strangely, once the media attention made her familiar, she lost her mysterious quality on screen. It seems that throughout her career, but especially since her marriage, Bach hasn't really pursued good parts. Film offers have usually been limited to exploitation films like *The Unseen,* a perverse psycho picture that for some reason has defenders. She's very popular in Italy, having made several horror and science-fiction pictures there.

• **Cult Favorite:** *The Spy Who Loved Me* (1977, Lewis Gilbert).

• **Sleeper:** *Caveman* (1981, Carl Gottlieb).

• **Also of Interest:** *Black Belly of the Tarantula* (1971, Marcello Danon), *Stateline Motel* (1971, Maurizio Lucidi), *Force Ten from Navarone* (1978, Guy Hamilton), *The Humanoid* (1979, George B. Lewis), *Jaguar Lives* (1979, Ernest Pintoff), *Screamers* (1979, Sergio Martino and Dan T. Miller), *The Great Alligator* (1980, Martino), *The Unseen* (1981, Peter Foleg), *Give My Regards to Broad Street* (1984, Peter Webb).

○

OLGA BACLANOVA/BACLANOVA (1899–1974)
Russian actress ("The People's Artist"), a

Olga Baclanova, after her punishment in Freaks.

blonde with a Mae West build, began cultivating her femme fatale image in silent films. However, she was most impressive in an offbeat role in *Docks of New York,* a tough but sympathetic woman who considered herself "decent" until she married. She kills her unfaithful husband. Originally billed as Baclanova, she is best known as the greedy trapeze artist who marries a midget for his money in *Freaks.* After mistakenly assuming midgets can be treated like children, she is literally cut down to size. No horror movie fan can forget the final morbid shot of Baclanova, with her once proud body transformed into that of a giant feathered hen. It's one of the most gruesome images in film history.

• **Cult Favorite:** *Freaks* (1932, Tod Browning).

• **Other Key Films:** *Street of Sin* (1927, Mauritz Stiller), *The Docks of New York* (1928, Josef von Sternberg), *The Man Who Laughs* (1928, Paul Leni).

○

CARROLL BAKER (1931–) Blond actress came to Hollywood via the Actors Studio, but sex appeal rather than dramatic talent would be the major ingredient in her strange career. She is still most associated with her first starring role, Karl Malden's virginal yet enticing teenage bride in *Baby Doll,* a white-trash comedy adapted from Tennessee Williams. Images of her lying in bed and sucking her thumb, stripping while her horny husband spies through a peephole, and merrily squirming under the foot of seductive neighbor Eli Wallach made her an instant sex symbol and "hot" property. But from the beginning, Baker's career would be plagued by bad role choices. She had neither the acting prowess nor the likability to make hits of her serious films, including *Something Wild*, directed by her then-husband Jack Garfein. When they'd flop, she'd retreat to films that exploited her sex appeal, including *Station Six-Sahara*, in which she is stranded with five men; Joseph E. Levine's steamy *The Carpetbaggers*, playing a Harlow-like movie star in her biggest hit; and Levine's *Harlow*, a flop. Baker could be sensual in love scenes, but outside the bedroom, she didn't have the vulnerability, voice (hers was too raspy) or attitude to be a blond sex goddess on a level with Harlow or Marilyn Monroe. One sensed Harlow and Monroe wanted to be loved by their audiences, but Baker seemed cold, even tough. Baker promoted her image by being the first star to disrobe for *Playboy*, and after being blacklisted in Hollywood (upon winning a $1 million breach-of-contract countersuit against Paramount), by stripping for the cameras in innocuous Italian potboilers like *Orgasmo* and *The Body*. Her career declined dramatically. More than a

Newcomer Carroll Baker shocked viewers as the title character in Baby Doll.

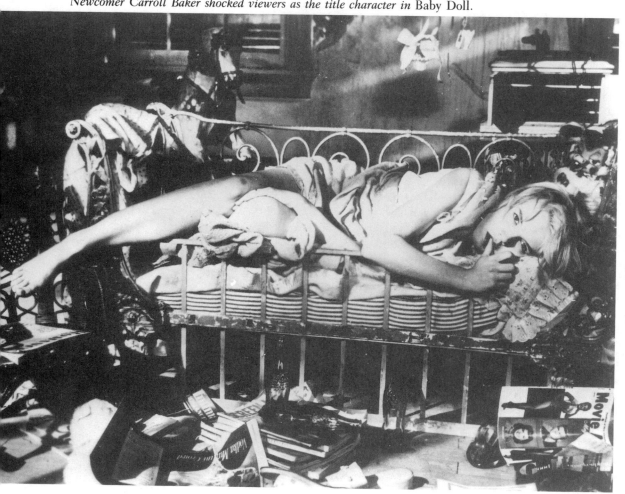

decade later, Baker returned to American films in the absurdist black comedy *Andy Warhol's Bad* as a middle-aged Queens housewife who runs a facial-hair removal business and, to make ends meet, a murder-for-hire operation. No longer having to come across as a sex star, Baker played her part with a straight face but much glee. Again, in *Ironweed*, as Jack Nicholson's deserted wife, she had the comfort of pushing not the earthy but the appealing down-to-earth part of her personality.

• **Cult Favorites:** *Baby Doll* (1956, Elia Kazan), *Giant* (1956, George Stevens), *Andy Warhol's Bad* (1971, Jed Johnson).

• **Sleepers:** *Something Wild* (1961, Jack Garfein), *Bride to the Sun* (1961, Etienne Perier), *Station Six-Sahara* (1964, Seth Holt), *Sylvia* (1965, Gordon Douglas).

• **Other Key Films:** *The Carpetbaggers* (1964, Edward Dmytryk), *Harlow* (1965, Douglas).

• **Also of Interest:** *The Big Country* (1958, William Wyler), *The Miracle* (1959, Irving Rapper), *How the West Was Won* (1962, John Ford, Henry Hathaway, and George Marshall), *Cheyenne Autumn* (1964, Ford), *Orgasmo/Paranoia* (1968, Umberto Lenzi), *Watcher in the Woods* (1980, John Hough), *Native Son* (1986, Jerrold Freedman), *Ironweed* (1987, Hector Babenco).

○

REBECCA BALDING For about fifteen minutes in the early eighties, this pretty young actress was hailed as the horror genre's new "Scream Queen." She did scream but she was no typically stupid, helpless horror heroine; she was smart, her curious eyes sparkled, she was funny, and she fought back. Barbara Steele was also in *The Silent Scream*, but it was Balding who carried the film and lifted it above your run-of-the-mill slasher effort. As another imperiled, college-age female, she also provided energy and humor in *The Boogens*, an okay monster movie that had a title so bad that it conjured up horrific images of characters with terrible colds. Whatever happened to Rebecca Balding?

• **Key Films:** *The Silent Scream* (1980, Denny Harris), *The Boogens* (1982, James L. Conway).

○

JOY BANG (1947–) The name tells all about the type of character she played, always with bubbly good humor. Her cute, upbeat, stoned, sexually uninhibited females graced several pretty good films of and about the seventies. She was available to not only handsome Kris Kristofferson in *Cisco Pike* but even to hapless Woody Allen in *Play It Again, Sam,* at least temporarily—he watches as his date is hijacked by bikers. Her scenes were more like cameos, but she made the most of them. What was exciting was that she gave the impression that she wasn't playing a role—she was playing herself. Watching Joy Bang today, certainly many former male hippies feel nostalgia for that era. Mr. and Mrs. Bang must have been proud of their daughter.

• **Cult Favorites:** *Dealing* (1972, Paul Williams), *Play It Again, Sam* (1972, Herbert Ross), *Cisco Pike* (B. W. L. Norton).

• **Also of Interest:** *Night of the Cobra Woman* (1972, Andrew Meyer).

○

THEDA BARA (1890–1955) The original "vamp" was actually Theodosia Goodman from Cincinnati, the daughter of a Jewish

Theda Bara.

tailor. However, as the first publicity-made movie star she was given a name that was an anagram for Arab Death and placed against an exotic Egyptian background—making her the ideal choice to play Cleopatra. Prevented by her contract to William Fox from going out in public during the day or unveiled at night, she claimed she was a chaste homebody. But Fox made her into the screen's first sex star, the first "other woman"/"femme fatale" to be a main attraction. She first starred for Fox in *A Fool There Was,* based on Kipling's poem "The Vampire," and though she would play an occasional heroine (even Juliet), her fame came from roles as "bloodsucking," emasculating women who take pleasure in ruining weak men's lives. She was a temptress without

soul or conscience who would lure men from good, loyal women; when they were trapped in her web and needed her kisses for survival, she callously moved on to her next conquest. Her most famous line was "Kiss me, my fool!" which she uttered as she happily scattered rose petals over the drained body of a dead lover. Some classic publicity shots showed Bara with the skeletal remains of male victims, among other props of death, while she wears wild jewelry, extreme makeup, and absurd, revealing costumes. Those outrageous stills and footage of her overacting are all that remain from her many films, but it's enough to make her into a camp figure. Ironically, she was an intelligent, outspoken feminist, who complained about her poor treatment at Fox and denounced the ways men exploit women, saying that if women responded by treating men as her vamp did, the men deserved it.

• **Key Films:** *A Fool There Was* (1915, Frank Powell), *The Devil's Daughter* (1915, Powell), *Carmen* (1915, Raoul Walsh), *The Serpent* (1916, Walsh), *The Vixen* (1916, J. Gordon Edwards), *The Tiger Woman* (1917, Edwards), *Camille* (1917, Edwards), *Cleopatra* (1917, Edwards), *Madame Du Barry* (1918, Edwards), *Salome* (1918, Edwards), *The She-Devil* (1919, Edwards).

○

ADRIENNE BARBEAU (1945–) Attractive, buxom brunette spent several years as Bea Arthur's liberated daughter in the TV comedy series "Maude" before enjoying some success as a heroine-in-distress in horror and suspense movies. One of her first significant dramatic roles was as Lauren Hutton's lesbian friend, a murder victim, in the nerve-wracking TV movie, *Someone's Watching Me!* It was directed by John Carpenter, who would marry her and cast her in two features. She was impressive as the smooth-voiced disc jockey who warns her listeners of impending danger in *The Fog,* but, carrying a gun, got lost in the chaos in *Escape for New York.* Barbeau was softer and more appealing in Wes Craven's *The Swamp Thing,* as the creature-hero's love interest, but seemed too classy and mature for the juvenile nonsense; a young California blonde, Heather Locklear, would get the female lead in the sequel. Nevertheless, it remains the film for which she is most remembered, perhaps because of her nude swim. I'd guess she had more fun playing the shrewish wife who gets too close to the monster in the crate in the scariest episode of *Creepshow.* In recent years, Barbeau hasn't made too many films—she looked weary as Rodney Dangerfield's unpleasant wife in *Back to School* and as a feminist anthropologist who has become a tribal leader in the otherwise lively *Cannibal Women in the Avocado Garden of Death.* She has done commendable volunteer work on behalf of teenagers involved in prostitution.

• **Cult Favorites:** *The Fog* (1980, John Carpenter), *Escape from New York* (1981, Carpenter), *Swamp Thing* (1982, Wes Craven).

• **Other Key Films:** *Creepshow* (1982, George Romero), *Open House* (1987, Jay Mundhra).

○

BRIGITTE BARDOT (1934–) I had strange dreams about the cinema's greatest sex symbol long before I was old enough to see any of her films. I studied her photos in magazines, some of which were movie shots of her in towels or with her dresses hiked up as she stood ankle-deep in water. Others were erotic, posed shots—I particularly loved when she ran her hands through her blond hair and pouted seductively. As is true of her film characters, she could "turn on" for photographers, but even when she wasn't aware that anyone was watching her, she was still provocative. This sex kitten even excited female intellectuals; Simone De Beauvoir wrote: "Brigitte Bardot is the most perfect specimen of ambiguous nymphs. Seen from behind, her slender, muscular, dancer's body is almost androgynous. Femininity triumps in her delightful bosom. The long voluptuous tresses of Mélisande flow down to her shoulders, but her hairdo is that of a negligent waif. The line of her lips forms

The slogan was "And God Created Woman, *But the Devil Invented Brigitte Bardot.*"

a childish pout, and at the same time those lips are very kissable. She goes about barefooted, she turns up her nose at the elegant clothes, jewels, girdles, perfumes, makeup, at all artifice. Yet her walk is lascivious and a saint would sell his soul to the devil merely to watch her dance." Moviegoers paid only a small fee to watch her dance, laze on the beach in tiny bikinis, disrobe, and lie naked with various actors. She showed promise early in her career, when she had dark hair, but it was then-husband Roger Vadim's . . . *And God Created Woman* that made her an international sex goddess. Her sexually promiscuous, casually amoral heroine spends time in towels and tight outfits, and standing nude behind a sheet on an outdoor clothesline. She also does one of her sizzling dances. Few later Bardot "sex" films came to America (she also never made a film here), but the famous Vadim film, plus scandals, lovers, suicide attempts, photos, and many imitators kept her sex-symbol status intact. Meanwhile, she occasionally showed talent. She is proudest of her murder suspect in *The Truth*. I prefer her incisive portrait of the fickle wife of screenwriter Michel Piccoli in *Contempt*. When he suggests she ride alone with crass producer Jack Palance, she immediately stops loving him. On- and offscreen Bardot wasn't someone who could be tied to a man.

• **Cult Favorite:** *. . . And God Created Woman* (1956, Roger Vadim).

• **Other Key Films:** *The Girl in the Bikini* (1952, Willy Rozier), *Le Fils de Caroline Chérie* (1954, Jean Devaivre), *Sweet Sixteen* (1955, Marc Allégret), *Doctor at Sea* (1955, Ralph Thomas), *Les Grandes Manoeuvres* (1955, René Clair), *The Light Across the Street* (1955, Georges Lacombe), *Mam'zelle Pigalle* (1955, Michel Boisrond), *Mam'selle Striptease/Please Mr. Balzac* (1956, Allégret, *Une Parisienne* (1959, Boisrond), *The Night Heaven Fell* (1957, Vadim), *Love Is My Profession* (1957, Claude Autant-Lara), *The Female* (1958, Julian Duvivier), *Babette Goes to War* (1959, Christian-Jaque), *The Truth* (1960, Henri-Georges Clouzot), *Only for Love* (1961, Vadim), *A Very Private Affair* (1961, Louis Malle), *Love on a Pillow* (1962, Vadim), *Contempt* (1963, Jean-Luc Godard), *Viva Maria* (1965, Malle), *Spirits of the Dead* (1967, Malle episode), *Les Femmes* (1969, Jean Aurel), *Boulevard du Rhum* (1970, Robert Enrico), *The Legend of Frenchie King* (1971, Christian-Jaque), *If Don Juan Were a Woman* (1973, Vadim).

○

LEX BARKER (1919–73) Tall and handsome, if somewhat stone-faced, this leading man was the tenth screen Tarzan, replacing the irreplaceable Johnny Weissmuller. He was no better than an adequate apeman. The juvenile scripts played up the action rather than exploring the savage aspects of Burroughs' creation, even in *Tarzan's Savage Fury*. As a result, he came across as too calm, civil, and predictable. Barker also was hampered by cheap budgets and producer Sol Lesser's decision to cast a different actress as Jane in each of his films. When Barker pulled out of the Tarzan series, he starred in several westerns, most notably *The Deerslayer*. Never a big star in America, Barker went to Europe in the sixties. He had only a small part in *La Dolce Vita* but became a sensation in adventure films and westerns, particularly in West Germany, where he starred as Shatterhand in films based on Karl May's frontier novels. He was suited for the rugged outdoors and looked fine in buckskin; his reserved style seemed more appropriate for pioneer heroes than the lord of the jungle. His fame in Germany, Italy, and Yugoslavia remains intact long after his death. But in America his heroic image recently was sullied when Cheryl Crane, the daughter of Lana Turner, Barker's third wife, stated he had been a wife beater and child molester.

• **Cult Favorite:** *La Dolce Vita* (1960, Federico Fellini).

• **Key Films:** *Tarzan's Magic Fountain* (1949, Lee Sholem), *Tarzan and the Slave Girl* (1950, Sholem), *Tarzan's Peril* (1951, Byron Haskin), *Tarzan's Savage Fury* (1952, Cyril Endfield), *Tarzan and the She-Devil* (1953, Cyril Endfield), *War Drums* (1957, Reginald LeBorg), *The Deerslayer* (1957, Kurt Neumann), *Treasure of Silver Lake* (1962, Harold Reini), *Apache Gold* (1963, Reini), *Last of the Renegades* (1964), *Shatterhand* (1964), *The Desperado Trail* (1965), *Woman Times Seven* (1967, Vittorio De Sica).

○

ELLEN BARKIN (1954–) Exciting, intelligent, risk-taking, Bronx-born blond actress. An exceptional talent, she is direct, passionate, and energetic. She has a wry wit. She also has a fabulous, usually sweaty body that she drapes in low-cut, form-fitting minidresses. Her unusual face—which Richard Corliss describes as "Diane Sawyer's pressed against a windshield"—is an alluring combination of soft (eyes, skin) and hard features (a sharp nose, an intimidating, down-turned mouth). She can look dangerous, even mean—when she smiles her upper lip rises into a snarl on the right side—but she also can come across as scared, vulnerable, and sympathetic. We remember her being sadistic in *Johnny Handsome* and crazy-vicious in *Made in Heaven;* but we also remember her sizzling sex scenes in *The Big Easy, Siesta,* and *Sea of Love.* And we remember her being hurt just because husband Daniel Stern yells at her for messing up the order of his 45s in *Diner.* The versatility of the actress, the unpredictability of her characters, and her decision to act with her body as well as her head have made her particularly provocative. Her mysterious, extremely lustful woman in the hit *Sea of Love,* who answers cop Al Pacino's ad in the personals, has paved the way for her to become a genuine star, and not only a cult figure.
• **Cult Favorites:** *Diner* (1982, Barry Levinson), *Eddie and the Cruisers* (1983, Martin Davidson), *The Adventures of Buckaroo Bonzai* (1984, W. D. Richter), *Down By Law* (1986, Jim Jarmusch), *Siesta* (1987, Mary Lambert), *Made in Heaven* (1987, Alan Rudolph).
• **Other Key Films:** *Daniel* (1983, Sidney Lumet), *Tender Mercies* (1983, Bruce Be-

resford, *Enormous Changes at the Last Minute* (1983, Ellen Hovde and Muffie Meyer episode), *Desert Bloom* (1983, Eugene Corr), *The Big Easy* (1987, Jim McBride), *Sea of Love* (1989, Harold Becker), *Switch* (1991, Blake Edwards).

○

JEAN-LOUIS BARRAULT (1910–) French actor who will forever be identified with nineteenth-century mime Baptiste Debureau, his role in *Children of Paradise.* Barrault had studied with Etienne Decroux, and his extraordinary mime routines lend magic to a picture already overflowing with romance. A shy, self-pitying dreamer who hasn't the confidence to think he could be a great star or be man enough for the heavenly Garance (Arletty), Baptiste becomes the darling of Paris and eventually makes love to the woman he adores—in a manner that belies his passive demeanor. Baptiste, and Barrault's aging but still lively journalist in *La Nuit de Varennes,* confirm that artists, at least in France, have the passion and talent to be great lovers and romantics.
• **Cult Favorite:** *Children of Paradise* (1945, Marcel Carné).
• **Also Recommended:** *The Lives and Loves of Beethoven* (1936, Abel Gance), *Bizarre, Bizarre* (1937, Carné), *La Ronde* (1950, Max Ophüls), *La Nuit de Varennes* (1983, Ettore Scola).

○

BELINDA BAUER (1956–) Strikingly pretty, sexually exciting Australian brunette was a top model and lived in Hong Kong and India before becoming a movie actress in America. "I think she's a star," director Bill Richert told critic Richard Jameson in

1982. "The definition of a star is somebody I'd have wanted to marry when I was 10½." Though she fits that criterion, Bauer hasn't come close to stardom. A hit movie would have helped but neither of her two films for Richert received adequate distribution. In his legendary political black comedy *Winter Kills,* she played Jeff Bridges's deceitful girlfriend; one of the film's many bizarre scenes has her talking to Bridges while sitting on the toilet. Then in the quirky fable *Success,* she was Bridges's spoiled, infantile wife. Because both films failed, Richert canceled plans to star opposite Bauer and fulfill his childhood dream in *Will You Marry Me?* Bauer later was Fred Ward's lover in another bizarre film, the science-fiction western *Timerider,* adding to her underground reputation. She sold her soul in the TV movie *The Sins of Dorian Grey* and did steamy R-rated scenes in the cable series *The Hitchhiker* without ever making it in the mainstream. Apparently the Hollywood establishment still didn't realize that given the right role, her star could shine.

• **Cult Favorites:** *Winter Kills* (1979, William Richert), *Timerider* (1983, William Dear).

• **Also of Interest:** *Success* (1979, Richert), *Flashdance* (1983, Adrian Lyne), *The Rosary Murders* (1987, Fred Walton).

○

MICHELLE BAUER This one-time *Penthouse* Pet used the name Pia Snow when she began her movie career in porno films, most notably the impressive black comedy *Cafe Flesh,* which has had success on video and as a midnight movie. She gave an adequate performance in the female lead, one of the rare surviving females of a postnuclear future who can have sex without becoming violently ill. Interestingly, she must pretend not to be sexually aroused by her boyfriend, who can't have sex, rather than pretend that her man sexually excites her. Unable to repress her feverish sexual instincts, she abandons him and, in an erotic finale, joins a male and female on stage for a sexual performance for the frustrated onlookers at the Cafe Flesh. As Michelle Bauer, she has often appeared and always sheds her clothes in quickie, outrageous, R-rated, Z-budget exploitation films for Fred Olen Ray and Dave DeCoteau. Many of these go straight to video, where they have a following. Cable viewers were treated to dark-haired bad girl Bauer having a battle of the chain saws with genre queen Linnea Quigley in the obviously stupid but enjoyably laughable *Hollywood Chainsaw Hookers.* She also has used the name Michelle McLennan.

• **Cult Favorites:** *Cafe Flesh* (1982, Rinse Dream), *Hollywood Chainsaw Hookers* (1988, Fred Olen Ray).

• **Other Sample Titles:** *Bad Girls* (1981, Svetlana), *The Tomb* (1986, Ray), *The Phantom Empire* (1987, Ray), *Beverly Hills Vamp* (1988, Ray), *Dr. Alien/I Was a Teenage Sex Mutant* (1988, Dave DeCoteau), *Demon Warp* (1988, Emitt Alston), *Assault of the Party Nerds, Night of the Living Babes, Wild Man.*

○

NATHALIE BAYE (1948–) Attractive French actress with great eyes, a sharp nose, and a face with a lot of character. Even with limited screen time, she was charming as the spirited young director's assistant in Truffaut's *Day for Night*—comrade-in-arms to her troubled boss, stripping by the road for a "quickie" with the young man who changed her flat tire, and uttering the film's most important line: "I'd leave a guy for a film, but I'd never leave a film for a guy!" She gave little indication she could be a leading lady, but Truffaut and Godard recognized her talent and offbeat beauty and cast her in roles that demanded maturity and sex appeal. By and by, Baye proved to be an actress of substance, sensuality, and mystery. She received a lot of attention as the abandoned wife who welcomes the sexual advances of her husband's impostor in *The Return of Martin Guerre* and as a pimp's hardened, self-destructive but loyal girlfriend in *La Balance*. But she was at her most appealing and compelling in *A Week's Vacation* playing her least exotic character, an unmarried teacher who is frustrated by her job and relationships with her boyfriend, parents, children, neighbors, friends, etc. The teacher may be familiar but Baye makes her completely fascinating.

• **Cult Favorites:** *Day for Night* (1973, François Truffaut), *Beau Père* (1981, Bertrand Blier).

• **Sleepers:** *A Week's Vacation* (1980, Bertrand Tavernier), *I Married a Shadow* (1982, Robin Davis), *Honeymoon* (1987, Patrick Jamain).

• **Other Key Films:** *The Last Woman* (1976, Marco Ferreri), *The Man Who Loved Women* (1977, Truffaut), *The Green Room* (1980, Truffaut), *Every Man for Himself* (1980, Jean-Luc Godard), *La Balance* (1982, Bob Swaim), *The Return of Martin Guerre* (1982, Daniel Vigne), *En Toute Innocence* (1989, Alain Jessua), *La Guerre Lasse* (1989, Robert Enrico), *C'est la Vie* (1990, Dian Kurys).

○

MATTHEW "STYMIE" BEARD (1923–81) Bridging the eras of Farina and Buckwheat, Stymie was a funny black boy who ran with "Our

Matthew "Stymie" Beard (second from right) poses with other Our Gang kids. Left to right: Jackie Cooper, Farina, Cubby Chaney, and Bobby "Wheezer" Hutchins.

Gang" in the classic Hal Roach shorts. Whereas the other two boys wore their hair in wild pigtails, so that for a time they could pass as male or female, Stymie was bald, with a mature face that let us know years in advance exactly how he'd look as an adult. He wore a derby hat, and at times covered his dirty, buttoned-at-the-collar shirt with a low-hanging vest or a snazzy zoot suit, looking very much the sharpie. Until Spanky came along, Stymie probably was the little rascal who was closest to a miniature adult. Being independent, he wasn't the leader Spanky would be, but he also was the rare rascal who acted rationally instead of impulsively and was a problem solver—at the time, few black adult on-screen characters showed such restraint or resolve. All the rascals were funny, but Stymie was one of the few who understood comic acting—he was supreme with the double take. He moved his eyes back and forth, pouted, grumbled, and "spoke," writes Donald Bogle, "as if his mouth were full of food." Maybe he wasn't a prime role model for black children, but he wasn't lazy, stupid, or more frightened of their scary world than his white friends.

• **Cult Favorites:** "Our Gang" shorts (1929–1934), *The Return of Frank James* (1940, Fritz Lang).

• **Also of Interest:** *Jezebel* (1938, William Wyler).

○

LOUISE BEAVERS (1902–62) Plump black actress was a former maid who made a career playing maids, housekeepers, and cooks in the movies and on television (starring in "Beulah"). But her characters weren't funny, outspoken, bossy, or suspicious of male strangers as were Hattie McDaniel's

Louise Beavers in Imitation of Life.

"black mamas." They were cheerful, protective, and so loyal that they'd keep working even if their mistresses no longer had the money to pay their salaries. Her most famous role was the Aunt Jemima–like pancake whiz in the original *Imitation of Life,* who felt her place was in the kitchen while her white partner Claudette Colbert handled the business. Beavers could make us laugh, but also in that role, her tears bring on our tears. One of her best moments is in *Made for Each Other* when she consoles and gives sage advice to troubled newlywed Carole Lombard in the park. This scene takes place far away from the kitchen, and the young white girl treats her with respect and love—for once Beavers is not a white person's servant but an equal.

• **Cult Favorites:** *She Done Him Wrong* (1933, Lowell Sherman), *Holiday Inn* (1942, Mark Sandrich).

• **Other Key Films:** *What Price Hollywood?*

(1932, George Cukor), *Bombshell* (1933, Victor Fleming), *Imitation of Life* (1934, John Stahl), *Make Way for Tomorrow* (1937, Leo McCarey), *Made for Each Other* (1939, John Cromwell), *Reap the Wild Wind* (1942, Cecil B. De Mille), *Mr. Blandings Builds His Dream House* (1948, H. C. Potter).

○

BONNIE BEDELIA (1952–) One of Hollywood's most neglected talents. She is best known for her fascinating performance as drag-race champion Shirley "Cha Cha" Muldowney in *Heart Like a Wheel*. She subtly creates a character of depth and determination: not one to lose her cool or have tantrums in the face of (male) adversity, Muldowney's feelings are shown by how she moves her eyes, how she stands (vulnerable or strong), and how her voice quivers. Her confidence peaks when she is behind the wheel and can compete with men on equal terms. I love the way Bedelia smiles as she sits in the driver's seat: she knows that this is where her character, who is unhappy in love, gets the most fulfillment. The wind will blow on her face and lips, the smoke will shoot out from the exhaust, the car will streak toward the finish line—and she never forgets that its engine was built by a man. This is perhaps the only sports film that explores the correlation between sex and competitive sports in regard to the athlete; what is so unusual is that its athlete is female. *Heart Like a Wheel* took a long time to be released and then had poor distribution despite good reviews and Bedelia's Oscar nomination. Afterward, she appeared in several films without fanfare. Until her key role as Harrison Ford's wife in *Presumed Innocent,* playing, ironically, a woman who will no longer tolerate being ignored, her screen time has been only tangential to the story line that brought audiences to the theater. Viewers want to see the teenage romance between Lucy Deakins and Jay Underwood in the lovely fantasy *The Boy Who Could Fly,* not scenes with Deakins's mother; the adult romance between Kevin Kline and Sissy Spacek in *Violets Are Blue,* not scenes with Kline's wife; Bruce Willis fighting terrorists in the surprisingly enjoyable action-thriller *Die Hard,* not scenes with Willis's estranged wife. She has been stuck with routine parts in the films' subplots. Yet, each time, Bedelia—through natural appeal and performances that are clearly conceived and delivered—has made viewers care deeply about what happens to her characters. You may not always recognize Bedelia—though she is very attractive—but sometime during each of her films you'll begin wondering who that uncommonly fine actress is.

• **Cult Favorite:** *Heart Like a Wheel* (1983, Jonathan Kaplan).

• **Sleepers:** *The Big Fix* (1978, Jeremy Paul Kagan), *The Boy Who Could Fly* (1986, Nick Castle), *The Prince of Pennsylvania* (1988, Ron Nyswaner).

• **Also Recommended:** *Lovers and Other Strangers* (1970, Cy Howard), *Die Hard* (1988, John McTiernan).

• **Also of Interest:** *Violets Are Blue* (1986, Jack Fisk), *The Stranger* (1987, Adolfo Aristarain), *Fat Man and Little Boy* (1989, Roland Joffe), *Die Hard 2: Die Harder* (1990, Renny Harlin), *Presumed Innocent* (1990, Alan J. Pakula).

○

ALFONSO BEDOYA (1904–57) Mexican character actor who achieved screen glory in

Alfonso Bedoya's Gold Hat worries Humphrey Bogart's Fred C. Dobbs in The Treasure of the Sierra Madre.

his American debut as the vile, smiling bandito chief who terrorizes the gold diggers and kills Humphrey Bogart in *The Treasure of the Sierra Madre*. When Bogart questions his assertion that he and his men are the mountain police, 'Gold Hat' gives a classic response: "Badges? We ain't got no badges! We don't need no badges. I don't have to show you any stinkin' badges!" One of the most frightening, realistic villains in cinema history—he could have been conceived by Luis Buñuel—Gold Hat has served as a model for numerous bad guys, including other unsavory Mexican highwaymen and the sadistic, bullying punk gang leaders found in the contemporary cinema. Corn chips lovers must know that Gold Hat also was the inspiration for the Frito Bandito.

• **Cult Favorite:** *The Treasure of the Sierra Madre* (1948, John Huston).

• **Also of Interest:** *Angel in Exile* (1948, Allan Dwan), *Border Incident* (1949, Anthony Mann), *California Conquest* (1952, Lew Landers), *The Stranger Wore a Gun* (1953, André de Toth), *Border River* (1954, George Sherman), *The Big Country* (1958, William Wyler).

○

JEAN-PAUL BELMONDO (1933–) He and Alain Delon debuted as teenage gang members in *Sois Belle et Tais-toi*. Before long they were France's top romantic idols. This wasn't surprising in Delon's case because he was strikingly handsome. However Belmondo, with his thick lips and large nose,

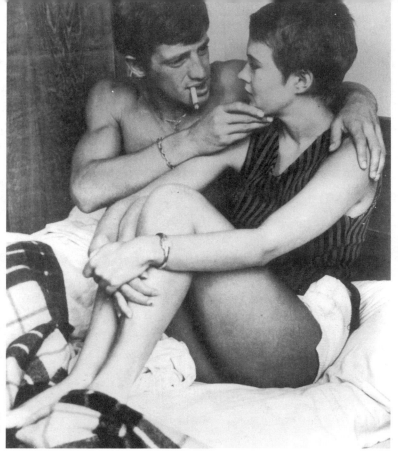

Jean-Paul Belmondo and Jean Seberg in a classic scene from Jean-Luc Godard's Breathless.

was at best "ruggedly handsome." Yet he became a sex symbol overnight by playing a "cool" antihero, destined to be betrayed to the police by his vacuous girlfriend Jean Seberg in *Breathless,* Jean-Luc Godard's ground-breaking New Wave film. Young, alienated viewers not only liked Belmondo's offbeat looks but were excited by his energetic, impulsive, live-dangerously-till-the-end cop killer. Like his idol Humphrey Bogart, the character Michel is a tough guy with wit and the heart of a sentimentalist. That pretty much defines Belmondo's best subsequent characters, as well, particularly his gangsters and tongue-in-cheek adventure heroes. Except for his swindler in *Stavisky,* most of Belmondo's other good roles came early on, including

his swashbuckler in *Cartouche,* priest in *Léon Morin, Prêtre,* imperiled spy in *That Man in Rio,* obsessed thief in *The Thief of Paris,* informer in *Doulos—The Finger Man,* and deserter husband who is on the run with untrustworthy lover Anna Karina in Godard's *Pierrot le Fou,* which ends when he blows himself up. He played opposite Europe's most beautiful actresses, including Claudia Cardinale, Françoise Dorléac, Laura Antonelli, Jacqueline Bisset, Catherine Deneuve, Sophia Loren, Jeanne Moreau, and Gina Lollobrigida. Early in his career, he was regarded as one of the world's great talents, but numerous indifferent performances in uninspired films damaged his acting reputation (especially abroad), though not his star appeal.

Unfortunately, few of his films since the mid-seventies have played in America—it's our loss.

• **Cult Favorites:** *Breathless* (1959, Jean-Luc Godard), *Pierrot le Fou* (1965, Godard).

• **Also Recommended:** *Moderato Cantabile* (1960, Peter Brook), *A Woman Is a Woman* (1960, Godard), *Two Women* (1961, Vittorio de Sica), *Léon Morin, Prêtre* (1961, Jean-Pierre Melville), *Doulos—The Finger Man* (1962, Melville), *Cartouche* (1962, Philippe de Broca), *A Monkey in Winter* (1962, Henri Verneuil), *That Man from Rio* (1963, de Broca), *Sweet and Sour* (1963, Marcel Ophüls), *Banana Peel* (1965, Ophüls), *Is Paris Burning?* (1966, René Clément), *The Thief of Paris* (1967, Louis Malle), *Mississippi Mermaid* (1969, François Truffaut), *Borsalino* (1969, Jacques Deray), *Stavisky* (1974, Alain Resnais).

○

SANDAHL BERGMAN (1951–) Striking blonde of Swedish descent (she grew up in Kansas) is a Sybil Danning with class and, though usually squandered in exploitation films, minor talent. A former dancer, she is not nearly as voluptuous as Danning, but is sexier because there is no trace of vulgarity. She is tall, slim, and athletic; her face has perfect bone structure, her large eyes reveal intelligence but keep emotions hidden (her iciness works both for and against her); and she moves across the screen with amazing grace. She played Cassie in *A Chorus Line* on Broadway, and Bob Fosse used her again in his autobiographical film *All That Jazz*. She is the sexiest of his dancers, the one who rips off her top while gyrating across the floor. Bergman's most popular role is the female warrior who captures the hero's heart and his respect in *Conan the Barbarian*. The scenes in which she and Arnold Schwarzenegger battle their opponents side-by-side with swords are terrifically choreographed, and her fluid dancer's movements are impressive. She was the first screen star since Bruce Lee to turn fighting into a form of sexual expression. Bergman never again got such a good role. In *Red Sonja,* another sword-and-sorcery film from the works of Robert E. Howard, Bergman settled for the villanous second female lead to Brigitte Nielsen. In *Kandyland* she took a smaller part than the unknown Kim Evison but could at least show some emotion as a talented but aging, insecure erotic dancer. After Evison returns to her boyfriend instead of going with her to Las Vegas to build their careers, she takes drugs and commits suicide on the club roof. In *Hell Comes to Frogtown,* she does an erotic dance, kisses wrestler-actor Roddy Piper, and kicks a lot of frog creatures in the crotch.

• **Cult Favorites:** *All That Jazz* (1979, Bob Fosse), *Conan the Barbarian* (1982, John Milius).

• **Also of Interest:** *She* (1983, Avi Nesher), *Red Sonja* (1985, Richard Fleischer), *Kandyland* (1987, Robert Schnitzer), *Programmed to Kill* (1987, Allan Holtzman), *Hell Comes to Frogtown* (1987, R. J. Kizer and Donald G. Jackson).

○

MICHAEL BERRYMAN (1948–) A mental patient in *One Flew Over the Cuckoo's Nest,* he was the most realistic of the deranged desert cannibals who terrorizes a middle-class family in *The Hills Have Eyes*. He was also certainly the scariest-looking,

Michael Berryman is featured on the poster of The Hills Have Eyes.

which is why his image was used in ads for the picture. With his bald, misshapen head, pointy nose, small, oddly placed ears, and askew, menacing eyes sunken beneath a large protruding forehead, he did look like an atomic-test mutant or the product of in breeding. Berryman didn't need any makeup to be "monstrous"—and surely many viewers felt discomfort because he allowed his facial "freakishness" to be used by the filmmakers to scare people, as had been the case with the pitiable Rondo Hatton years earlier. At least those who saw Berryman in *The Hills Have Eyes* weren't shocked when they saw him in later films. They realized he was just another young actor following directions rather than actually being that less-than-human stranger he played so convincingly. Obviously his choice of roles is limited. He was running a plant store when discovered.

• **Cult Favorites:** *One Flew Over the Cuckoo's Nest* (1975, Milos Forman), *The Hills Have Eyes* (1977, Wes Craven).

• **Also of Interest:** *Another Man, Another Chance* (1977, Claude Lelouch), *Deadly Blessing* (1981, Craven), *The Fifth Floor* (1980, Howard Avedis), *The Hills Have Eyes, Part II* (1984, Craven), *Cut and Run* (1985, Ruggero Deodato), *Armed Response* (1986, Fred Olen Ray).

○

WILLIE BEST (1916–62) Like Stepin Fetchit, Willie "Sleep 'n' Eat" Best accepted roles that helped Hollywood perpetuate the myth of the lazy, dim-witted, frightened-by-his-own-shadow black man. His saving grace, like Fetchit's, was that he was almost funny enough to transcend the characters and let you appreciate his genuine comic talent. The character he played for two decades, "Sleep 'n' Eat," would sleep all day if he didn't get hungry. He walked and talked slowly. His eyes bulged with constant fear and/or amazement, and his bottom lip hung low as if he had forgotten to close his mouth. Work was out of the question. Everything terrified him, made him shiver, which is why he was always good for a few laughs when placed in haunted houses. He accepted his stupidity. He accepted being lectured to. He also accepted being the butt of jokes; but of course, he couldn't understand those jokes—no matter, because today they don't seem funny anyway.

Willie Best lends comic support to Bob Hope in Nothing But the Truth.

• **Sample Films:** *The Monster Walks* (1932, Frank Strayer), *The Kentucky Kernels* (1934, George Stevens), *Little Miss Marker* (1943, Alexander Hall), *The Littlest Rebel* (1935, David Butler), *Thank You, Jeeves* (1936, Arthur Collins), *The Ghost Breakers* (1940, George Marshall), *High Sierra* (1941, Raoul Walsh), *Nothing but the Truth* (1941, Elliott Nugent), *Whispering Ghosts* (1942, Alfred L. Werker), *A-Haunting We Will Go* (1942, Werker), *Cabin in the Sky* (1943, Vincente Minnelli), *Hold That Blonde* (1945, Marshall).

○

MARTINE BESWICK (1941–) Curvaceous, raven-haired British beauty who was Hammer Studios' best answer to Barbara Steele. She had a body and a lusty quality that helped her match Steele's sex appeal, but she didn't have Steele's mystery or mystique. She had perfect bone structure—but Steele's "imperfect" face contributed to her aura. Moreover, she didn't have Steele's talent. Beswick first attracted attention as one of the two gypsies who engage in a wild catfight for James Bond's entertainment in *From Russia with Love*. In the opening titles she is billed as Martin. She earned a larger part in a later Bond film, *Thunderball*. A minor role in Hammer's *One Million Years B.C.*, in support of Raquel Welch, led to her first lead, as the queen of a buxom Amazon tribe in *Prehistoric Women*. She got to dance in a skimpy two-piece outfit and be wicked for the first time. She also smoothly segued from being imperious to being a tigress, which pretty much sums up her screen image. Beswick's most interesting role was as Ralph Bates's homicidal female alter ego in *Dr. Jekyll and Sister Hyde*, but also noteworthy is her "Queen of Evil"—

one man's nightmare come to life—in *Seizure*, Oliver Stone's weird debut film. In *The Happy Hooker Goes to Hollywood* she was much less a prude as Xaviera Hollander than either Lynn Redgrave or Joey Heatherton had been in the previous films. Ironically, this was her most ordinary character.

• **Cult Movies:** *From Russia with Love* (1963, Terence Young), *One Million Years B.C.* (1966, Don Chaffey), *Dr. Jekyll and Sister Hyde* (1971, Roy Ward Baker), *Seizure* (1974, Oliver Stone).

• **Also of Interest:** *Thunderball* (1965, Young), *Prehistoric Women* (1966, Michael Carreras), *The Penthouse* (1967, Peter Collinson).

TURHAN BEY (1920–) Undoubtedly the best Czech-Turkish actor to ever appear in Hollywood films. He starred in low-budget juvenile horror and costume-adventure pictures in the forties, mostly for Universal Studios. When he wore a mustache and slicked down his black hair, he looked like an exotic Don Ameche. When he shaved, he looked like Orson Welles's friendly younger brother. He played princes (some evil, some who only seemed evil), phony, turban-clad mystics, and bare-chested slaves, often in support of Maria Montez and Jon Hall. He wore silly outfits, got to shoot wicked George Zucco,

Turhan Bey gazes enigmatically at Lon Chaney, Jr., who hovers over Elyse Knox in The Mummy's Tomb.

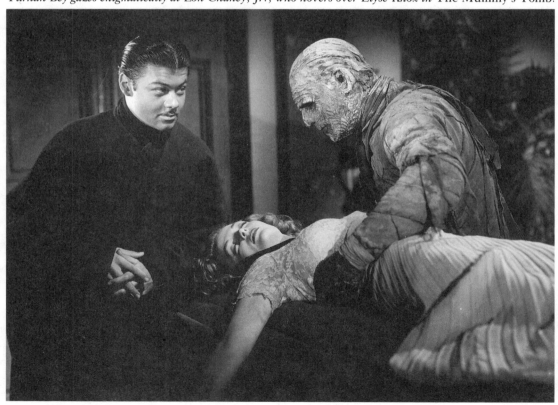

and spent quality time with a mummy, even bringing it to America. The plots were ridiculous, but his characters always seemed to know exactly what was going on, indicating that they had led strange lives. Though not usually a romantic lead (though he had many women fans), he played Aesop in *Night in Paradise* and won the gorgeous Merle Oberon.

• **Cult Favorites:** *Arabian Nights* (1942, John Rawlins), *Ali Baba and the Forty Thieves* (1944, Arthur Lubin).

• **Other Key Films:** *The Mummy's Tomb* (1942, Harold Young), *White Savage* (1943, Lubin), *The Mad Ghoul* (1943, James Hogan), *The Climax* (1944, George Waggner), *Sudan* (1945, Rawlins), *Night in Paradise* (1946, Lubin), *The Spiritualist* (1948, Bernard Vorhaus).

○

JANE BIRKIN (1946–) In *Blow-Up*, this long-legged British brunette and Gillian Hills, playing swinging London teenagers who frolic in photographer David Hemmings's studio, had the distinction of being the first actresses to do full-frontal nudity in a feature film. Soon after, Birkin moved to France where she became a recording sensation (beginning with the lush, erotic "Je t'aime, moi non plus"), a major European movie star, and cover girl and sex symbol almost on par with the early Brigitte Bardot. In fact, there was much publicity surrounding Bardot's love scene with Birkin (Bardot's only female lover in film) in Roger Vadim's *If Don Juan Were a Woman*. Typically, Birkin would play smart, sassy women in stories that centered around sex and allowed her at least one nude scene. In the comical *Catherine & Co.*, a cable favorite in America, she played a prostitute who is also a shrewd businesswoman—she incorporates herself and her friends. Despite all her fame in Europe, Birkin has been disappointed that she hasn't gained fame in America, where she wanted to be seen as a "legit" actress. Her appearances in star-studded Agatha Christie movies didn't exploit her sexuality enough to raise eyebrows in America; she was probably cast only to guarantee that the films attracted European audiences. American critics were impressed by her performance in *Dust*, as an oppressed spinster who kills her cruel father, but the French-Belgian coproduction received little distribution here. There was some controversy surrounding *Kung Fu Master*, directed by Agnes Varda, who once made a documentary about Birkin. Birkin wrote the script and played a 40-year-old who falls passionately in love with her son's 15-year-old friend.

• **Cult Favorite:** *Blow-Up* (1966, Michelangelo Antonioni).

• **Sleepers:** *Romance of a Horsethief* (1971, Abraham Polonsky), *Make Room for Tomorrow* (1982, Peter Kassovitz), *Dust* (1985, Marion Hansel).

• **Also of Interest:** *The Swimming Pool* (1970, Jacques Deray), *If Don Juan Were a Woman* (1973, Roger Vadim), *Love at the Top* (1974, Michel Deville), *Dark Places* (1974, Don Sharp), *Sept Morts sur Ordonnace* (1975, Jacques Rouffio), *Je T'aime, Moi Non Plus* (1975, Serge Gainsbourg), *Death on the Nile* (1978, John Guillerman), *Evil Under the Sun* (1981, Guy Hamilton), *Kung Fu Master* (1989, Agnes Varda), *Daddy Nostalgia* (1991, Bertrand Tavernier).

○

WHIT BISSELL (1919–) In Ray Bradbury's story "The Crowd," the same bystanders turn up at every car accident in the country. In American movies, if there is a major problem, you're likely to find Whit Bissell around. He occasionally caused the problem—for instance, he turned Michael Landon into a monster in *I Was a Teen-age Werewolf*. More often, he just recognized it or was witness to it, while on rare occasions he solved it—he alerted the proper authorities that there was indeed an *Invasion of the Body Snatchers*. This prolific and dependable character actor turned up in key horror and science-fiction films, westerns, dramas, comedies, prison films, soap operas, war movies, low- and high-budget films. There was nothing about him physically that stood out—other than that his hair was always combed—but he made his presence felt, perhaps because his characters spoke their minds. They often told troubled heroes that they were about to go too far. He was particularly good at playing doctors (often working for institutions), scientists, army officers, and trusted family friends. One could usually detect a trace of conceit in his authority figures, so it was fun watching some of them get nervous, become cowardly, or lose control completely. You never left a theater saying that you liked or disliked his characters, but after years of seeing his face and unusual name in the credits, many moviegoers found they'd developed a strange affection for him.

• **Cult Favorites:** *Creature from the Black Lagoon* (1954, Jack Arnold), *Riot in Cell Block 11* (1954, Don Siegel), *Shack Out on 101* (1955, Edward Dein), *Invasion of the Body Snatchers* (1956, Siegel), *The Magnificent Seven* (1960, John Sturges), *The Manchurian Candidate* (1962, John Frankenheimer.

• **Also Recommended:** *Brute Force* (1947, Jules Dassin), *The Caine Mutiny* (1954, Edward Dmytryk), *It Should Happen to You* (1954, George Cukor), *Gunfight at the O.K. Corral* (1957, Sturges), *The Time Machine* (1960, George Pal), *Birdman of Alcatraz* (1962, Frankenheimer), *HUD* (1963, Martin Ritt), *Seven Days in May* (1964, Frankenheimer), *Airport* (1970, George Seaton).

• **Also of Interest:** *I Was a Teenage Frankenstein* (1957, Herbert L. Strock), *Psychic Killer* (1975, Ray Danton).

○

KAREN BLACK (1942–) Today Karen Black has become a camp figure, as a vocal advocate of scientology and the star of second-rate films. Also, she often can be seen on the Late Show as the brave stewardess who flies the jumbo jet to safety in the laughable *Airport 1975*. But from 1970, after she played one of the two New Orleans whores who take acid with Dennis Hopper and Peter Fonda in *Easy Rider*, to 1976, when Alfred Hitchcock gave her the female lead in his last film, *Family Plot*, she was one of the cinema's major leading ladies. She wasn't a classic beauty—she has big lips, an upturned nose, and eyes that seem somewhat crossed—but she was shapely and sexy, did nudity, and walked around in robes and see-through nighties. And she was talented, though it's hard to pinpoint what she did well other than surprise us with offbeat humor and emotional outbursts; perhaps it was that her characters seemed real. She starred in some big-budget studio productions, but was better suited to low-budget, personal films. She received an Oscar nomination for her touching performance as the shallow waitress who can't hold on to Jack Nicholson in *Five Easy Pieces*. In that film, the Nicholson-

Karen Black and Kris Kristofferson in Cisco Pike.

directed *Drive, He Said*, and *Cisco Pike*, opposite Kris Kristofferson, her women were loved by their men, but were neglected just the same. As her characters learned, relationships were tenuous in the seventies. She was also a victim in horror movies, including the weird Canadian devil-worship film, *The Pyx*, and the scary Indian-doll episode of the TV flick, *Trilogy of Terror*. Black had musical talent and when she played Connie White (a combination of Connie Smith and Tammy Wynette) in *Nashville*, Robert Altman let her write and perform her own songs; her singing was fine, but the songs couldn't pass for real country. Altman would use her again in 1982, as the transsexual in

Come Back to the Five and Dime, Jimmy Dean, Jimmy Dean, her only impact role since *Nashville*.

• **Cult Favorites:** *Easy Rider* (1969, Dennis Hopper), *Five Easy Pieces* (1970, Bob Rafelson), *Drive, He Said* (1971, Jack Nicholson), *Cisco Pike* (1972, B. W. L. Norton), *Nashville* (1975, Robert Altman), *Come Back to the Five and Dime, Jimmy Dean, Jimmy Dean* (1982, Altman).

• **Sleepers:** *You're a Big Boy Now* (1967, Francis Ford Coppola), *Born to Win* (1971, Ivan Passer), *The Pyx* (1973, Harvey Hart), *Can She Bake a Cherry Pie?* (1984, Henry Jaglom).

• **Also of Interest:** *Portnoy's Complaint* (1972, Ernest Lehman), *Little Laura and*

Big John (1973, Luke Moberly and Bob Woodburn), *The Great Gatsby* (1974, Jack Clayton), *Airport 1975* (1974, Jack Smight), *The Day of the Locust* (1975, John Schlesinger), *Family Plot* (1976, Alfred Hitchcock), *Burnt Offerings* (1976, Dan Curtis), *Killing Heat* (1984, Michael Raeburn), *Invaders from Mars* (1986, Tobe Hooper).

○

LINDA BLAIR (1959–) As a baby-faced, baby-voiced teenager, she almost won a Best Supporting Actress Oscar as the tormented, possessed girl in *The Exorcist*, until it was revealed that Mercedes McCambridge had dubbed the agonized Devil rantings that appear to come from Blair's lips. Blair repeated her role of Regan in the loony *The Exorcist II: The Heretic*, where her acting was more subdued and she didn't have to wear such gruesome makeup. No one knew what kind of roles Blair would be offered after *The Exorcist*;

alas, one was in *Airport 1975* as the ill but spirited girl who is cheered by nun Helen Reddy's "uplifting" singing on the plane. She made a few such false starts in wholesome pictures, but an indication of things to come was her role in the controversial TV movie *Born Innocent*. Blair played a teenager who is placed in a juvenile detention home, where she is subjected to much trauma, including being raped with a broom handle. The adult Blair ventured into R-rated exploitation films, first horror films and then violent action and prison pictures that have made her a star abroad. She still had that cherubic face and voice—and when she smiled, giggled, or coochy-cooed with a male actor, she seemed 12 years old. But there were other times—when she got serious, clenched her teeth, looked straight ahead with vengeance on her mind, gave advice to her girlfriend, or told some intimidating villain, "Fuck you!"—that she seemed much older, perhaps 15. (In recent years, she has been more "glamorous.") Blair learned

Linda Blair (right) *gets tough in* Chained Heat.

how to play one role in her sleep: an innocent young woman who is thrown into a hellish prison where she is terrified and brutalized by male guards, perverse wardens, and the lesbian bully of her cellblock; initially scared and passive, she finally leads a bloody revolt that leaves all the culprits dead, and wins her freedom. Surprisingly she does nude scenes in these prison fantasies—including one shower scene per film—although she looks uncomfortable and chubby compared to the actresses who play her sexy cellmates. But since she's the star of the film, the other women desire her. Silly scenes include the statuesque Sybil Danning making a play for the short, plump Blair in the shower in *Chained Heat*, and Sylvia Kristel (of *Emmanuelle* fame) lying on top of Blair and licking the captive girl's chin in *Red Heat*. Though she has always been a competent actress, Blair seems completely miscast in these films, but that, I suppose, is what makes them funny rather than repulsive. Anyway, Blair tries and has spirit.

• **Cult Favorites:** *The Exorcist* (1973, William Friedkin), *The Exorcist II: The Heretic* (1977, John Boorman), *Chained Heat* (1983, Paul Nicolas).

• **Also of Interest:** *Hell Night* (1981, Tom Desimone), *Ruckus* (1982, Max Kleven), *Red Heat* (1985, Robert Collector), *Savage Streets* (1985, Danny Steinmann), *Bad Blood* (1988, Chuck Vincent), *Repossessed* (1990, Bob Logan).

○

MARI BLANCHARD (1927–70) Glamorous and sexy, this former bathing-suit model was, according to Ian and Elisabeth Cameron in *Dames*, "the epitome of the fifties B-feature star: hard, very blonde and faintly unreal, like an animated waxwork. She

Mari Blanchard and Forrest Tucker are well matched in this publicity shot from Stagecoach to Fury.

was almost the blonde counterpart of Marie Windsor, though not as human and therefore without the ability to be as blisteringly vicious." She made films set in exotic locales—*Ten Tall Men, The Veils of Bagdad*, and *Son of Sinbad*—and got to wear tantalizing costumes, but she only won supporting roles. She also played saloon girls in westerns. She was quite good in the Dietrich part in *Destry*, though she did seem too much woman for Audie Murphy. Oddly, she made her biggest impression in *She-Devil*, an atrocious B horror film in which Albert Dekker injects her with a fruit fly serum and she becomes less than human. Too bad that she was at her sexiest in her worst film.

• **Key Films:** *Destry* (1954, George Marshall), *She-Devil* (1957, Kurt Neumann), *Twice Told Tales* (1963, Sidney Salkow).

• **Also of Interest:** *Back at the Front* (1952, George Sherman), *Son of Sinbad* (1955, Ted Tetzlaff), *The Return of Jake Slade* (1955, Harold Schuster), *The Cruel Tower* (1956, Lew Landers), *No Place to Land* (1962, Albert Gannaway).

○

JOAN BLONDELL (1909–79) This energetic, round-faced blonde was the least heralded of the great Warners stars of the thirties. She was equally at home in backstage musicals, light comedies, breezy mysteries, and fast-paced action-dramas, as both a romantic lead and supporting player. Some of her women were gold diggers and most were cynical after enduring hard times and bad men. But they were still hard-working, loyal, big-hearted, and good sports about being neglected by the men they loved, often played by her best leading man Jimmy Cagney (who came to Hollywood with her from the Broadway musical *Penny Arcade*). They were friends to other women, patient and resilient, upbeat even when hurt, sexy (she almost falls out of her negligee in *Gold Diggers of 1933*), quick with funny wisecracks, cleverly able to get the men they love out of jams, shrewd enough to see through scams, and perceptive enough to understand (and tolerate) complicated and demanding men. They were great employees (secretaries, dancers), terrific girlfriends, and, as the hero usually realized at the end of the picture, the ideal women to propose to. Blondell's contribution to Warners in the thirties has never been fully recognized. But it's some consolation that her chorine leads the unforgettable tribute to the "Forgotten Man" in *Gold Diggers of 1933*, the classic Busby Berkeley production number that symbolized the studio's Depression-era commitment to social reform. The number also established a bond between women who have to scrape to get by (like Blondell and the other chorines) and the unemployed men (some war vets) who are also caught without jobs or respect. In the forties, Blondell would begin a long second career as a reliable character actress. An actress worthy of a repertory theater retrospective.

• **Cult Favorites:** *The Crowd Roars* (1932, Howard Hawks), *Gold Diggers of 1933* (1933, Mervyn LeRoy), *Footlight Parade* (1933, Lloyd Bacon), *Dames* (1934, Ray Enright), *Nightmare Alley* (1947, Edmund Goulding, *Lizzie* (1957, Hugo Haas), *Will Success Spoil Rock Hunter?* (1957, Frank Tashlin).

• **Sleepers:** *There's Always a Woman* (1938, Alexander Hall), *Angel Baby* (1961, Paul Wendkos and Hubert Cornfield).

• **Other Key Films:** *Sinner's Holiday* (1930, John H. Adolfi), *Public Enemy* (1931, William A. Wellman), *Three On a Match* (1932, LeRoy), *Blondie Johnson* (1933, Enright), *Traveling Saleslady* (1935, Enright), *Broadway Gondolier* (1935, Bacon), *Bullets or Ballots* (1936, William Keighley), *Three Men on a Horse* (1936, LeRoy), *Gold Diggers of 1937* (1936, Bacon), *Topper Returns* (1941, Roy Del Ruth), *A Tree Grows in Brooklyn* (1945, Elia Kazan).

• **Also of Interest:** *Miss Pinkerton* (1932, Bacon), *Colleen* (1936, Alfred E. Green), *Stage Struck* (1936, Busby Berkeley), *Stand-In* (1936, Tay Garnett), *Two Girls on Broadway* (1940, S. Sylvan Simon), *Cry Havoc* (1943, Richard Thorpe), *Waterhole #3* (1967, William Graham), *Support Your Local Gunfighter* (1971, Burt Kennedy).

○

ERIC BLORE (1887–1959) Delightful British-born character actor, with an excited manner, keen (often squinty) eyes, round cheeks, a grin that could expand into a full-faced grimace, and a hairline that receded more with each picture. He appeared in some of the best, most entertaining pictures of the thirties and forties, including five Fred Astaire–Ginger Rogers musicals (he had supported Astaire in the play *Gay Divorce*) as well as two Preston Sturges comedies (plus another which Sturges only wrote). In *I Dream Too Much*, he did a bit with a trained seal, but most often he played hotel managers, dancing school managers, waiters, valets, and butlers—men who don't have lofty positions but who rule their domains. They are energetic, erudite, fussy, interfering, argumentative, critical, and have an air of superiority. They are expert on how one should wear bow ties—Blore often wore them—and just about everything else. His servants, including movie director Joel McCrea's valet in *Sullivan's Travels*, think it ironic that those with money and position know less about being a gentleman than they do—but his fun starts when he's around them. I've long thought that if John Steed, Patrick Macnee's suave, witty spy in television's "The Avengers," had to hire a butler, he'd want Eric Blore.

• **Cult Favorites:** *Flying Down to Rio* (1933, Thornton Freeland), *The Gay Divorcee* (1934, Mark Sandrich), *Top Hat* (1935, Sandrich), *Swing Time* (1936, George Stevens), *Shall We Dance* (1937, Sandrich), *The Lady Eve* (1941, Preston Sturges), *Sullivan's Travels* (1941, Sturges), *The Shanghai Gesture* (1941, Josef von Sternberg).

• **Also Recommended:** *The Good Fairy* (1935, William Wyler), *Diamond Jim* (1935, A. Edward Sutherland), *The Ex-Mrs. Bradford* (1936, Stephen Roberts), *Quality Street* (1937, Stevens), *Breakfast for Two* (1937, Alfred Santell), *Road to Zanzibar* (1941, Victor Schertzinger), *The Moon and Sixpence* (1942, Albert Lewin),

San Diego, I Love You (1944, Reginald LeBorg), *Romance on the High Seas* (1948, Michael Curtiz), *Fancy Pants* (1950, George Marshall).

○

ROBERTS BLOSSOM (1924–) If you need the perfect actor to star in a film about a crazy-eyed, middle-aged backwoodsman who sits all the day on the porch with his hound, drinking moonshine from a jar and shooting strangers, then look no further. Blossom was chillingly authentic as a mama's boy who kills, skins, and mummifies females in the independent horror film *Deranged*, the closest the movies have come to the real-life Ed Gein story. Since then he has had supporting roles in Hollywood films, playing an assortment of cantankerous oddballs who never have a good word or thought for anyone. He's an enjoyable actor to watch, partly because he injects subtle humor into all of his characterizations. He's the sort who'd pick his peculiar name just so there would be typos in film reviews. A poet, writer, and stage actor and director.

• **Cult Favorites:** *Handle with Care/ Citizen's Band* (1977, Jonathan Demme), *Resurrection* (1980, Daniel Petrie), *The Last Temptation of Christ* (1988, Martin Scorsese).

• **Sleepers:** *Deranged* (1974, Jeff Gillen and Alan Ormsby), *Reuben, Reuben* (1983, Robert Ellis Miller).

• **Also of Interest:** *Escape from Alacatraz* (1979, Don Siegel), *Christine* (1983, John Carpenter), *Vision Quest* (1985, Harold Becker), *Candy Mountain* (1987, Robert Frank and Rudy Wurlitzer), *Home Alone* (1990, Chris Columbus).

Humphrey Bogart won an Oscar playing opposite Katharine Hepburn in The African Queen.

○

HUMPHREY BOGART (1899–1957) The Bogart cult began in France with the release of *Breathless*; in it Jean-Paul Belmondo's Bogart-revering tough guy lives dangerously because he knows that he is fated to die soon. In the States, the cult took root at the Brattle Theater in Cambridge, Massachusetts, and spread to revival theaters in other cities and college campuses. Sixties viewers found a new hero. He was the cinema's greatest tough guy, but other than his barbaric Duke Mantee in *The Petrified Forest*, (a Broadway role he reprised in his movie breakthrough), Philip Marlow in *The Big Sleep*, and a few others,

his tough guys always had chinks in their armor. His gangster turns yellow in *The Roaring Twenties*; killer Mad Dog Earle's heart is softened by a dame in *High Sierra*; detective Sam Spade's hand shakes nervously after meeting Sydney Greenstreet in *The Maltese Falcon*; one-time freedom-fighter Rick wallows in self-pity and alcohol after being abandoned by Ingrid Bergman in *Casablanca*; his miner gets gold fever and has hallucinations in *Treasure of the Sierra Madre*; his ex-soldier screenwriter has childish, violent temper tantrums in *In a Lonely Place*; on the stand, his interrogated Captain Queeg reveals he's lost his marbles (rolling little balls in his hand) in *The Caine Mutiny*; his reporter sells out to work for a shady boxing promoter in *The Harder They Fall*. His boat captain gives up liquor in *The African Queen* only when he finds something stronger to lean on—Katharine Hepburn. His flawed tough guys fight losing battles with paranoia, jealousy, greed, cowardice, and insanity. Which isn't to say they aren't also likable men. Most show charm despite their cynicism, humor in a crisis, and some form of integrity. We understand that they talk tough with women while looking for that rare woman who can hand it right back—and soothe their anger: Lauren Bacall in *To Have and Have Not* (it's evident the actors were falling in love) and *The Big Sleep* (by this time they'd married), Ingrid Bergman in *Casablanca*, and Katharine Hepburn in *The African Queen* do this; Gloria Grahame in *In a Lonely Place* fails. We also admire their romantic, sentimental sides and their willingness to make noble sacrifices, like giving up Ingrid Bergman to join the war effort in *Casablanca*. Finally, his appeal is elemental: like only the great stars, he hits a raw nerve.

• **Cult Favorites:** *Marked Woman* (1937, Lloyd Bacon), *Angels with Dirty Faces* (1938, Michael Curtiz), *High Sierra* (1941, Raoul Walsh), *The Maltese Falcon* (1941, John Huston, *Casablanca* (1942, Curtiz), *To Have and Have Not* (1944, Howard Hawks), *The Big Sleep* (1946, Hawks), *The Treasure of the Sierra Madre* (1948, Huston), *Key Largo* (1948, Huston), *In a Lonely Place* (1950, Nicholas Ray), *The African Queen* (1952, Huston), *Beat the Devil* (1954, Huston), *The Caine Mutiny* (1954, Edward Dmytryk).

• **Sleepers:** *Black Legion* (1936, Archie Mayo), *The Harder They Fall* (1956, Mark Robson).

• **Other Key Films:** *The Petrified Forest* (1936, Mayo), *Dead End* (1937, William Wyler), *They Drive By Night* (1940, Walsh), *All Through the Night* (1942, Vincent Sherman), *Action in the North Atlantic* (1943, Bacon), *Sahara* (1943, Zoltan Korda), *Dead Reckoning* (1947, John Cromwell), *Dark Passage* (1947, Delmer Daves), *The Barefoot Contessa* (1954, Joseph L. Mankiewicz).

○

FRANKLIN BOLGER An important member of Russ Meyer's movie repertory company.

Can Franklin Bolger take the stress in Russ Meyer's Cherry, Harry & Raquel?

He was well cast as shrewd, dirty old men and fanatical, self-righteous backwoods preachers in Meyer's early morality plays. Meyer's films were by and large populated by sweaty, overwrought, depraved characters, yet Bolger managed to be more annoying than almost anyone else because he acted as if he were above the other low-lifes around him. It is a pleasure to see his wheelchair-bound pervert run over by a car in *Faster, Pussycat! Kill! Kill!* And no tears are shed when the sliced-up body of his drug dealer is discovered in his hospital bed in *Cherry, Harry, & Raquel.*

• **Cult Favorites:** *Lorna* (1964, Russ Meyer), *Mud Honey* (1965, Meyer), *Faster, Pussycat! Kill! Kill!* (1965, Meyer), *Cherry, Harry, & Raquel* (1970, Meyer).

• **Also of Interest:** *Common Law Cabin* (1967, Meyer).

○

RAY BOLGER (1904–87) With rubbery legs and nimble feet, this ex-vaudevillian and Broadway star danced his way into screen immortality as the Scarecrow in *The Wizard of Oz*, a film that became part of the American psyche. In terms of the story, Bolger's amiable character, Dorothy's first companion in Oz, represents security; he is also the lonely girl's first friend in a picture whose theme is *not* really "There's no place like home" (although this is Dorothy's final line) but "There's nothing more valuable than friends." In terms of cinema history, the brainless strawman, with a chamois-cloth face, is one of the first benevolent "monsters" of fantasy films. Bolger performed some marvelous acrobatic yet relaxed dance numbers in the movies but rarely was placed in the spotlight and allowed to display his versatility. But he did get to sing, act, and be funny

not only in *The Wizard of Oz* but as a student who poses as his own maiden aunt in *Where's Charley?*, the musical version of *Charlie's Aunt*, his successful Broadway show.

• **Cult Favorite:** *The Wizard of Oz* (1939, Victor Fleming).

• **Other Key Films:** *Sunny* (1941, Herbert Wilcox), *The Harvey Girls* (1946, George Sidney), *Where's Charley?* (1952, David Butler). *April in Paris* (1952, Butler), *Babes in Toyland* (1961, Jack Donohue).

• **Also of Interest:** *The Great Ziegfeld* (1936, Robert Z. Leonard), *Rosalie* (1937, Leonard), *Sweethearts* (1937, W. S. Van Dyke), *Four Jacks and a Jill* (1946, Jack Hively, *Look for the Silver Lining* (1949, Butler), *The Daydreamer* (1966, Jules Bass).

○

RENE BOND Young, not-so-cute California brunette who was one of the most prolific and popular of the early porno stars. Some of her films were of the fake "educational" variety. For instance, in the once-controversial *Teenage Fantasies*, her most famous picture, she appears on the screen between seven vignettes, talks to the viewer about her love for oral sex and demonstrates her technique on a different man each time. She would make several other "teenage" sex films, including *Teenage Lovers, Teenage Sex Kitten*, and *Teenage Throat*. Bond was one of the few porno actresses to have any kind of success in legitimate films, including *Invasion of the Bee Girls*, although nudity was usually still required of her. She never improved as an actress.

• **Cult Favorites:** *Teenage Fantasies* (1972, Frank Spokeman), *Invasion of the Bee Girls* (1973, Denis Sanders).

• **Also of Interest:** *Touch Me* (1971, Anthony Spinelli), *Please Don't Eat My Mother* (1972, Carl Munson), *Beach Blanket Bango* (1975, Morris Deal), *Do You Wanna Be Loved?* (1975, B. A. Smith), *Swinger's Massacre* (1975, Ronald V. Garcia).

○

SANDRINE BONNAIRE (1968–) This lovely French actress made a stunning debut in *À Nos Amours* as a 16-year-old who drifts into a series of meaningless, unfulfilling sexual affairs, searching for love that she can't find at home with her squabbling, unhelpful parents. She exhibits a sad lack of self-esteem by picking men who will dump her. Her eyes become progressively more vacant, lonely, and forlorn as the girl's chances for happiness vanish. In *Police*, backing up Sophie Marceau, she is a 19-year-old prostitute who has already lost her ability to feel anything. And in *Vagabond*, she's an ill-fated drifter, young but hard-bitten, having long ago given up thoughts of love, even real human contact, or a real life. In each of these films, she is young but her life has already been irreparably damaged; she searches for something to ease the pain, but when she can't find it, she deadens her emotions.
• **Cult Favorite:** *Vagabond* (1985, Agnes Varda).
• **Other Key Films:** *À Nos Amours* (1984, Maurice Pialat), *Police* (1984, Pialat), *Monsieur Hire* (1989, Patrice Leconte).
• **Also of Interest:** *Tir à Vue* (1984, Marc Angelo), *Le Meilleur de la Vie* (1985, Renaud Victor), *Sous le Soleil de Satan* (1986, Pialat), *La Puritaine* (1986, Jacques Doillon), *Blanc et Marie* (1986, Jacques Renard), *Quelque Jours Avec Toi* (1987, Claude Sautet).

○

ERNEST BORGNINE (1918–) The burly, much-in-demand character actor won a Best Actor Oscar as a kind, lonely butcher in *Marty*. He has played numerous good guys—including the lead on the TV comedy "McHale's Navy"—but is best as a brute, bully, or boss. With his stocky build, unattractive face (with a large gap between his front teeth), broad grin and menacing laugh, he can be a very threatening figure. His prison guard in *From Here to Eternity*, vicious bully in *Bad Day at Black Rock*, and sadistic train conductor in *Emperor of the North* are classic villains. He was a more sympathetic "bad" guy in *The Wild Bunch*, perhaps his most popular role with today's film cultists. He appeared in numerous westerns, as well as other action films, often directed by Robert Aldrich. Horror fans know him best as Bruce Davison's unfriendly boss who gets devoured by rats in *Willard*. He has a tendency to overact, especially when playing self-righteous authority figures, but he's a great deal of fun. Still, everyone wonders why Ethel Merman married him—before divorcing him immediately.
• **Cult Favorites:** *Johnny Guitar* (1953, Nicholas Ray), *Vera Cruz* (1954, Robert Aldrich), *Bad Day at Black Rock* (1955, John Sturges), *The Dirty Dozen* (1967, Aldrich), *The Legend of Lylah Clare* (1968, Aldrich), *The Wild Bunch* (1969, Sam Peckinpah), *Deadly Blessing* (1981, Wes Craven), *Spike of Bensonhurst* (1988, Paul Morrissey).
• **Sleepers:** *The Last Command* (1955, Frank Lloyd), *The Badlanders* (1958, Delmer Daves), *Emperor of the North* (1973, Aldrich), *Shoot* (1976, Harvey Hart), *Escape from New York* (1981, John Carpenter).

• **Other Key Films:** *From Here to Eternity* (1950, Fred Zinnemann), *Run for Cover* (1955, Ray), *Marty* (1955, Delbert Mann), *Jubal* (1956, Daves), *The Catered Affair* (1956, Richard Brooks), *The Vikings* (1958, Richard Fleischer), *The Flight of the Phoenix* (1965, Aldrich), *Ice Station Zebra* (1968, Sturges), *Willard* (1971, Daniel Mann), *The Poseidon Adventure* (1972, Ronald Neame), *Law and Disorder* (1974, Ivan Passer), *Convoy*, (1978, Peckinpah).

○

CAROL BORLAND (1914–) As a teenager, she was so inspired by Bela Lugosi's stage version of *Dracula* that she wrote a sequel to the novel called *Countess Dracula*. Though it couldn't be published because the Bram Stoker estate owned rights to the name, Lugosi took her under his wing and cast her as Lucy in his play. A few years later, she costarred with Lugosi in the movie *Mark of the Vampire*, playing Luna, the vampire girl. Her hair was dark and long, her eyebrows were black and curled at the edges so that they resembled bat wings, her eyes stared straight ahead from her pale face as if she were in a trance; she sleepwalked like an apparition in her flowing white (actually light blue) nightgown. Luna would be the model for Vampira and many later vampire brides, including those in Hammer's Dracula series. Images of Borland's vampire (who turns out to be an actress, not a monster) can be found in almost every horror movie book, often on the cover. Luna's look rather than Borland's haunting performance is the reason for the actress's lasting fame and cult status.

• **Key Film:** *Mark of the Vampire* (1935, Tod Browning).

○

BARRY BOSTWICK (1945–) Stardom was predicted for this tall, handsome actor with musical talents when he appeared in the episode parodying Busby Berkeley musicals in *Movie Movie*. But he simply lacked charisma. If they were recasting television's "The Brady Bunch" today, he could replace Robert Reed. In fact, his lack of star quality is what made him ideal as the superdull Brad (nicknamed "Asshole!") in *The Rocky Horror Picture Show*, his claim to permanent cult fame. His role required him to walk around in his underwear and be seduced by a man and he did it all with good grace . . . and without exciting anyone. He has tried to play action heroes, but hasn't pulled it off. At least his blandness served him well when he portrayed George Washington in a couple of TV movies.

• **Cult Favorite:** *The Rocky Horror Picture Show* (1975, Jim Sharman).

• **Also of Interest:** *Movie Movie* (1978, Stanley Donen), *Red Flag: The Ultimate Game* (1981, Don Taylor), *Megaforce* (1982, Hal Needham).

○

DAVID BOWIE (1947–) British rock superstar who has been surprisingly effective in films, though it's unlikely he's become a bonafide movie star. With his androgynous look and slim, birdlike features, he was perfectly cast as the alien in *The Man Who Fell to Earth*. In that film, he has come to earth to find a way to transport water back to his dying planet, but unlike Atlas, he can't bear the weight of his world because his shoulders are brittle. His mission a failure, stranded on earth, he wallows in self-pity. "Infected" by the earthlings he feels superior to, he loses himself in sex, booze, and television, and acts like the typical depressed, unfulfilled, alcoholic, failed businessman. Bowie also is a tragic figure in *The Hunger*, a vampire who suddenly undergoes centuries of accelerated aging, the sorry fate of all queen-vampire Catherine Deneuve's lovers. When he disappears, the film goes downhill fast. Also in 1983, Bowie played a rigid British officer interned in a Japanese camp who wonders whether to protest the brutal treatment of prisoners; he has tremendous guilt because years ago he was too cowardly to help his younger brother in an analogous situation. Not fully sympathetic in any of these roles, Bowie has been cast as a villain in *Labyrinth*, *Into the Night*, and *The Last Temptation of Christ*, playing Pontius Pilate.

• **Cult Favorites:** *The Man Who Fell to Earth* (1976, Nicolas Roeg), *Just a Gigolo* (1978, David Hemmings), *The Hunger* (1983, Tony Scott), *Merry Christmas, Mr. Lawrence* (1983, Nagisa Oshima), *Absolute Beginners* (1986, Julien Temple), *The Last Temptation of Christ* (1988, Martin Scorsese).

○

WILLIAM BOYD (1895–1972) The first craze in television centered around western hero Hopalong Cassidy, whom Bill Boyd had portrayed 66 times (a record for one actor playing a character) in films from 1935 to 1948 at Paramount. Boyd purchased the rights to Clarence E. Mulford's pulp character and leased the old pictures to television. Cassidy quickly became the medium's first hero, as popular with kids in the late forties and early fifties as Milton Berle was with adults. Boyd became rich, not only from TV but also from radio, where he performed the role anew,

and from merchandising, as youngsters rushed out to buy everything from Hoppy's black outfits and two-gun holsters to Hoppy lunch pails to "Hopalong Cassidy Hair Trainer." Boyd was already gray and 40 when he began playing Cassidy and looked more dignified than other western heroes of his era. For the first film, he used a limp, like Mulford's original character, but eliminated it thereafter. More significantly, Mulford's version was a hardened, heavy-drinking loner who was only one fight away from jail; the movie Cassidy was a noble, law-abiding citizen who didn't drink, smoke, swear, or treat anyone with less than the utmost respect (he rarely even kissed heroines). Though Cassidy was always pleasant in social situations, he was more serious than other

William Boyd as Hopalong Cassidy.

sagebrush heroes, especially the singing cowboys. Usually a rancher, his job was to restore order. He was a calming influence, who rode (on Topper) between a funny, old-timer sidekick (Gabby Hayes or Andy Clyde) and a more impetuous young partner (James Ellison or Russell Hayden). Though there wasn't always enough action in Cassidy films, you could count on a fistfight in a saloon, a gunfight in the hills among giant boulders, and a chase on horseback which ended with Hoppy (actually stuntman Cliff Lyons) jumping on the culprit's back and dragging him to the turf for another fight. Hoppy would unmask the chief villain (a respected citizen), shoot the gun out of someone's hand, and be thanked by a pretty woman for helping her and her pa out of trouble. A former silent movie star, Boyd's career seemed irreparably damaged in 1931 when moviegoers confused him with stage actor William Boyd, who was involved in a scandalous beach party. The Cassidy pictures saved the day.

• **Cult Favorites:** *Hop-A-Long Cassidy* (1935, Howard P. Bretherton), *The Eagle's Brood* (1935, Bretherton), *Bar 20 Rides Again* (1935, Bretherton), *The Texas Trail* (1937, David Selman), *Rustler's Valley* (1937, Nate Watt), *Borderland*, (1937, Watt), *In Old Mexico* (1938, Edward Venturini), *Riders of the Deadline* (1943, Lesley Selander), *False Colors* (1943, George Archainbaud), *Marauders* (1947, Archainbaud), *The Dead Don't Dream* (1948, Archainbaud), and more than fifty other Cassidy pictures.

• **Some Other Key Films:** *The Road to Yesterday* (1925, Cecil B. De Mille), *The Volga Boatman* (1926, De Mille), *King of Kings* (1927, De Mille), *Two Arabian Nights* (1927, Lewis Milestone), *Lady of the Pavements* (1929, D. W. Griffith), *The Painted Desert* (1931, Howard Higgin), *Lucky Devils* (1933, Ralph Ince).

○

PETER BOYLE (1933–90) Balding, heavy-set, forceful character actor who had his greatest successes in the seventies. His characters were stubbornly opinionated, philosophical, often menacing, and usually reactionary. They represented distinctly American types, from bartenders (with gangland connections) to barroom blowhards to gangsters to political advisers to New York cabbies. He is most identified with the title character in *Joe*, a violent, vulgar, unhinged Archie Bunker. The picture presented a false image of the counterculture, but Boyle was frighteningly accurate as an angry working-class jerk whose frustrations about his own life are vented in verbal and then physical attacks on society's dropouts. Hippies and blacks who saw the film recognized this character: he was their worst nightmare. Boyle also made an impression as the cabbie in *Taxi Driver* who holds court with De Niro and the other drivers and spews racist rhetoric. In the acclaimed TV movie *Tail-Gunner Joe*, Boyle was thoroughly convincing as Senator Joe McCarthy, gaining power by capitalizing on the country's paranoia about communist infiltration. Creating right-wing villains must have been an enjoyable challenge for Boyle, who leaned to the left in his own politics. Although most of his characters have been tinged with humor, he really showed comedic flair as the monster in Mel Brooks's *Young Frankenstein*. He is lovable and hilarious, even dignified when he and Gene Wilder, as the doctor, wear top hat and tails and perform "Puttin' on the Ritz."

• **Cult Favorites:** *Medium Cool* (1969, Haskell Wexler), *Joe* (1970, John G. Avildsen), *Young Frankenstein* (1974, Mel Brooks), *Taxi Driver* (1976, Martin Scorsese), *Hammett* (1983, Wim Wenders).

• **Sleepers:** *Steelyard Blues* (1973, Alan Myerson), *The Friends of Eddie Coyle* (1973, Peter Yates).

• **Also of Interest:** *Diary of A Mad Housewife* (1970, Frank Perry), *The Candidate* (1972, Michael Ritchie), *Kid Blue* (1973, James Frawley), *Crazy Joe* (1974, Carlo Lizzani), *Hardcore* (1979, Paul Schrader), *The Dream Team* (1989, Howard Zieff).

○

SONIA BRAGA (1951–) Slim, sultry Brazilian who gained international attention as the star of *Dona Flor and Her Two Husbands*, a comedy (one which, oddly, has more drama than humor) that was an unprecedented smash hit in her native country. All viewers were excited by the steamy sex scenes. Braga turned on men, and women identified with a character who finds sex with her kind second husband to be so dull that she wishes her first, no-good but passionate husband back to life. Later Braga films did well at the box office on the strength of her many nude scenes and the abandon with which she played fairly explicit lovemaking. That she gave good performances and created interesting women seemed incidental assets. In her recent English-language films, her characters are still lusty, but she has toned down the on-screen sex.

• **Cult Favorites:** *Dona Flor and Her Two Husbands* (1977, Bruno Barreto), *Kiss of the Spider Woman* (1985, Hector Babenco).

• **Other Key Films:** *I Love You* (1981, Arnaldo Jabor), *Gabriela* (1983, Barreto), *The Milagro Beanfield War* (1988, Robert Redford).

• **Also of Interest:** *Lady on the Bus* (1978, Neville D'Almelda), *The Man Who Broke 1000 Chains* (1987, Daniel Mann), *Moon Over Parador* (1988, Paul Mazursky).

○

NEVILLE BRAND (1921–) World War II war hero who made a good living as a heavy in Hollywood. He was effective both as gangster leaders (he twice played Al Capone) and mere tough thugs (in *D.O.A.* he kept punching the fatally poisoned Edmond O'Brien in the belly); he also played bad-tempered western outlaws, obnoxious rabble-rousers, convicts, and rotten apples in cavalry and army platoons. He had a gruff, angry voice and unfriendly face, yet did quite well on those rare occasions when he had sympathetic roles, as in *Return from the Sea*, in which he romances Jan Sterling, and the TV western series "Laredo," in which he provided much of the comic relief.

• **Cult Favorites:** *D.O.A.* (1949, Rudolph Maté), *Riot in Cell Block 11* (1954, Don Siegel), *The Ninth Configuration* (1980, William Peter Blatty).

• **Also Recommended:** *Where the Sidewalk Ends* (1950, Otto Preminger), *The Halls of Montezuma* (1950, Lewis Milestone), *Kansas City Confidential* (1952, Phil Karlson), *Stalag 17* (1953, Billy Wilder), *The Tin Star* (1957, Anthony Mann), *The Adventures of Huckleberry Finn* (1960, Michael Curtiz), *The Last Sunset* (1961, Robert Aldrich), *The Scarface Mob* (1962, Karlson), *The Birdman of Alcatraz* (1962, John Frankenheimer).

• **Also of Interest:** *The Charge at Feather River* (1953, Gordon Douglas), *Gun Fury* (1953, Raoul Walsh), *Return from the Sea* (1954, Lesley Selander), *Mohawk* (1956, Kurt Neumann), *Love Me Tender* (1956, Robert D. Webb), *The Lonely Man* (1957, Henry Levin), *That Darn Cat* (1965, Robert Stevenson), *Psychic Killer* (1975, Ray Danton).

○

MARLON BRANDO (1924–) The cinema's most explosive, mesmerizing, controversial, and in the opinion of many, brilliant actor was just 23 when he took Broadway by storm as Stanley Kowalski in *A Streetcar Named Desire*. The charismatic, handsome, solidly built Method actor, with a distinct mumble, terrifying temper, and teary eyes that seemed to search everywhere for his next lines, made an exciting screen debut as an angry G.I. paraplegic in *The Men*. He then reprised his T-shirt–clad brute in Elia Kazan's screen version of *Streetcar*, a devastating performance ("Stella!") that established him as the medium's greatest talent. He solidified his rebel image as a biker in *The Wild One*, and gave his first powerhouse movie performance in a sympathetic role as an ex-boxer who turns against the corrupt longshoreman-union bosses in *On the Waterfront*. In these latter two films he played unfulfilled, inarticulate, seemingly worthless young men who just need someone who cares (Mary Murphy and her sheriff father; Eva Marie Saint and priest Karl Malden) to set them

Marlon Brando is more than attracted to Mary Murphy in The Wild One.

in positive directions. He'd return to this formula when he directed and starred in *One-Eyed Jacks*, in which lovely Pina Pellicer reforms his western outlaw. Since the sixties, he has given his finest performances in roles that allow him to examine what having power does to intelligent men, and what makes some men who could do good commit monstrous acts instead. In *The Godfather*, he showed a man who loves his family and is loyal to friends, yet heads a murderous crime organization. And in the extraordinary *Burn!*, he portrayed a brave, ingenious Englishman who helps black slaves overthrow their Portuguese oppressors, then turns from hero to villain by crushing the rebellion so England can enslave these blacks. Brando's most emotionally devastating performance (and the last time he looked sexy) is in *Last Tango in Paris*. Some viewers think his character, who controls a sexual relationship with young stranger Maria Schneider, is among Brando's most cruel. But Brando feels sympathy for a troubled man in a midlife crisis, broken by his wife's suicide; his excessive sexual demands actually free Schneider from her bourgeois shackles. Alternately ferocious and tender, confident and confused, sympathetic and pathetic, tense and wickedly funny, fatherly and childlike toward Schneider, Brando's performance comes from the gut, the subconscious, the soul. It's Brando at his peerless best.

• **Cult Favorites:** *A Streetcar Named Desire* (1951, Elia Kazan), *The Wild One* (1953, Laslo Benedek), *One-Eyed Jacks* (1961, Marlon Brando), *The Chase* (1966, Arthur Penn), *The Night of the Following Day* (1969, Hubert Cornfield), *Burn!* (1969, Gillo Pontecorvo), *The Godfather* (1972, Francis Ford Coppola), *Last Tango in Paris* (1972, Bernardo Bertolucci), *The Missouri Breaks* (1976, Penn), *Apocalypse Now* (1979, Coppola).

• **Other Key Films:** *The Men* (1950, Fred Zinnemann), *Viva Zapata!* (1952, Kazan), *Julius Caesar* (1953, Joseph L. Mankiewicz), *On the Waterfront* (1954, Kazan), *Guys and Dolls* (1955, Mankiewicz), *The Young Lions* (1958, Edward Dmytryk), *The Fugitive Kind* (1960, Sidney Lumet), *Mutiny on the Bounty* (1962, Lewis Milestone), *The Ugly American* (1963, George H. Englund), *Reflections in a Golden Eye* (1967, John Huston), *The Nightcomers* (1972, Michael Winner), *The Dry White Season* (1989, Euzhan Palcy).

○

CAROLYN BRANDT Buxom brunette was playing a harem girl in something titled *The Magic of Sinbad*, starring Tommy Rettig (of "Lassie" fame) when she caught the eye of young auteur Ray Dennis Steckler. Steckler chased her, married her, and cast her as the female lead in most of his oddball Grade-Z exploitation films, including the first monster musical, *The Incredibly Strange Creatures Who Stopped Living and Became Mixed-Up Zombies*. Steckler under his Cash Flagg alias, often appeared in the films as well (both had bits in Arch Hall's *Eegah!*). In the movies, she wore provocative clothes, she danced, she sang, she was threatened by brutal killers (men carrying axes in *Thrill Killers*), and she got killed off early because Steckler needed her to do the actors' makeup. In later films, she switched from victim to perpetrator. The biggest budget for a Steckler film was barely $38,000. At times, Brandt and Steckler lived in their car.

• **Cult Favorites:** *Eegah!* (1963, Nicholas Merriwether/Arch Hall, Sr.), *The Incredibly Strange Creatures Who Stopped Living*

and Became Mixed-Up Zombies (1963, Ray Dennis Steckler), *Rat Pfink a Boo Boo* (1966, Steckler).
- **Other Key Films:** *Wild Guitar* (1962, Steckler), *The Thrill Killers* (1964, Steckler), *The Lemon Grove Kids Meet the Monsters* (1966, Steckler), *Body Fever* (1969, Steckler), *Blood Shack/The Chopper* (1971, Steckler), *The Hollywood Strangler Meets the Skidrow Slasher* (Steckler).

○

BOBBIE BRESEE Suzanne Sommers pinup type with blond hair and luscious lips has lit up a few cheapie horror films, revealing her breasts to conceal her lack of thespian skills. Not vulnerable enough to be a sympathetic romantic lead, she plays unfeeling seductresses who go after the first males of any age who catch their eyes. She's best known for *Mausoleum*, as a married woman who, when possessed by a demon, seduces several men and then murders them. She turned into another monster in *Evil Spawn* after injecting insect venom into her blood in hopes of becoming younger. At least Bresee doesn't seem to take her films too seriously. A former music teacher and *Playboy* Bunny.
- **Cult Favorite:** *Surf Nazis Must Die* (1987, Peter George).
- **Other Key Films:** *Mausoleum* (1982, Michael Dugan), *Evil Spawn* (1987, Kenneth J. Hall).
- **Also of Interest:** *Star Slammer* (1988, Fred Olen Ray).

○

JEFF BRIDGES (1949–) The blond, boyishly handsome son of Lloyd Bridges and younger brother of Beau Bridges has always infused his characters with his own easygoing, next-door-neighbor personality. Initially he played likable characters with wild streaks that got them into trouble. In *The Last Picture Show*, he stabs friend Timothy Bottoms; in *Bad Company*, he's the leader of a group of young thieves; in *The Last American Hero*, his Junior Johnson mixes moonshine-running and car-racing. His later characters haven't been as reckless or as tough—except for his cold-blooded killer in *Jagged Edge*. One doubts audiences could have accepted him being killed by Glenn Close in that film if he weren't wearing a mask. Audiences like Bridges. He has a friendly smile, an engaging manner, and a protective quality. His characters always seem honest and tender, which is why he was the perfect choice to play the gentle alien in *Spaceman*. His characters don't seem to be driven by money or ambitions, which is why it's easy to root for them. We worry when they get in over their heads and confront imposing villains—as in *Cutter's Way, Winter Kills, Against All Odds*, and *8 Million Ways to Die*; because these guys seem so trusting, we worry about their choices of women. They invariably find themselves helping some sexy woman out of a jam: Rachel Ward, Rosanna Arquette, Kim Basinger, Jane Fonda, Michelle Pfeiffer, etc. He has trimmed off his early baby fat and become quite a sexy leading man. Bridges isn't one of the Hollywood elite, but he's now regarded as one of Hollywood's most dependable leading men, someone (like Joel McCrea used to be) who can give a solid performance and be a suitable screen lover for the sexiest leading ladies. As he did when he made cult films in the seventies and early eighties, Bridges still picks offbeat projects with quirky characters and plot twists. He's still as interesting as he was then, but the films are slicker.

• **Cult Favorites:** *The Last Picture Show* (1971, Peter Bogdanovich), *Fat City* (1971, John Huston), *Rancho Deluxe* (1975, Frank Perry), *Stay Hungry* (1976, Bob Rafelson), *Winter Kills* (1979, William Richert), *Success/The Great American Success Company* (1979, Richert), *Cutter's Way/Cutter and Bone* (1981, Ivan Passer), *Tron* (1982, Steven Lisberger).

• **Sleepers:** *Bad Company* (1972, Robert Benton), *The Last American Hero* (1973, Lamont Johnson), *The Iceman Cometh* (1973, John Frankenheimer), *Hearts of the West* (1975, Howard Zieff), *8 Million Ways to Die* (1986, Hal Ashby), *Tucker: A Man and His Dream* (1988, Francis Ford Coppola).

• **Other Key Films:** *Against All Odds* (1984, Taylor Hackford), *Starman* (1984, John Carpenter), *Jagged Edge* (1985, Richard Marquand), *The Morning After* (1986, Sidney Lumet), *The Fabulous Baker Boys* (1989, Steve Kloves).

• **Also of Interest:** *Lolly Madonna XXX* (1973, Richard C. Sarafian), *Thunderbolt and Lightfoot* (1974, Michael Cimino), *Heaven's Gate* (1980, Cimino), *Nadine* (1987, Benton), *Texasville* (1990, Bogdanovich).

○

CHARLES BRONSON (1921–) In 1957 and 1958, Charles Bronson made two films for director Gene Fowler, Jr., playing a teacher afraid of some violent kids in *Gang War* and a bounty hunter with an inferiority complex because he is short in *Showdown at Boot Hill*. Fowler was shrewd enough to give Bronson (formerly Buchinsky) his first leads, but he obviously didn't understand the actor's appeal. Bronson would eventually become the world's most popular star by playing fearless, ruthless heroes and anti-heroes, in the Old West and in modern-day urban cesspools. Although his acting has never been more than passable, he has tremendous presence. He is unusual-looking, like a cross between an Indian warrior (a role he played several times) and a generic ethnic, working-class type (at one time, he followed his Lithuanian father into the Pennsylvania coal mines). His fascinating face is full of lines and crevices; his eyes are narrow, steely, and untrusting; his voice is deep, dry, without warmth; he is brawny rather than huggable. Although he sometimes flashes a pleasant smile, he looks too cruel to be a sympathetic leading man. His characters have little time for romance; instead they coolly undertake violent missions, often alone, often against the law. They fire guns (appropriately, he got on the right career path by starring in *Machine Gun Kelly*), beat up anyone who angers them (his cops don't bother with due process), and participate in wild car chases that destroy everything in their paths. There are always high body counts in his films. Bronson was already enormously popular when he made *Death Wish*, but his vigilante became his most famous and controversial character—a major hero of reactionary filmgoers. He would wander dark cities and wipe out some more unsavory criminals in several sequels. I much prefer his quiet but lethal gunfighter in Sergio Leone's seminal western *Once Upon a Time in the West*, a mysterious figure whose death signals the end of the mythological West and the true beginning of "civilization" in America. Bronson's contemporary characters conclude that "civilization" doesn't work. Bronson made several films with his late wife, Jill Ireland, including the offbeat, enjoyable western *From Noon Till Three*, in which

Charles Bronson is an assassin in The Mechanic.

he had the rare chance to show he can play comedy—though it was a box-office dud.

- **Cult Favorites:** *The Marrying Kind* (1952, George Cukor), *House of Wax* (1953, André Toth), *Vera Cruz* (1954, Robert Aldrich), *Run of the Arrow* (1957, Samuel Fuller), *Machine Gun Kelly* (1958, Roger Corman), *The Magnificent Seven* (1960, John Sturges), *The Dirty Dozen* (1967, Aldrich), *Once Upon a Time in the West* (1969, Sergio Leone), *Death Wish* (1974, Michael Winner).

- **Sleepers:** *From Noon Till Three* (1976, Frank Gilroy), *Rider on the Rain* (1970, René Clément).

- **Also of Interest:** *Pat and Mike* (1952, Cukor), *Four for Texas* (1953, Aldrich), *Apache* (1954, Aldrich), *Showdown at Boot Hill* (1958, Gene Fowler, Jr.), *Master of the World* (1961, William Witney), *Kid Galahad* (1962, Phil Karlson), *The Great Escape* (1963, Sturges), *This Property is Condemned* (1966, Sydney Pollack), *Lola* (1969, Richard Donner), *The Valachi Papers* (1972, Terence Young), *Chato's Land* (1972, Winner), *The Mechanic* (1972, Winner), *Mr. Majestyk* (1974, Richard Fleischer), *Breakout* (1975, Tom Gries), *Hard Times* (1975, Walter Hill), *Breakheart Pass* (1976, Gries), *Ten to Midnight* (1983, J. Lee Thompson), *The Evil That Men Do* (1984, Thompson).

○

LOUISE BROOKS (1906–85) Lovely, erotic, ex-Follies and Scandals girl had a reputation in the twenties as both a free-spirited party girl and an intellectual. Her short, square black bob resulted in a coiffure craze. Humorist J. P. McEvoy used Brooks as the inspiration for Dixie Dugan, the principal character in his best-selling book *Show Girl*, which later was made into a play with Ruby Keeler in the role first offered to Brooks. When Dixie Dugan became a cartoon character, cartoonist John Strieble used Brooks as a model. Despite her fame, Brooks had trouble getting major roles in American films, not that she particularly cared at the time. But German director G. W. Pabst saw her playing a circus highdiver in Howard Hawks's *A Girl in Every Port* and brought her to Berlin to play the leads in Frank Wedekind's *Pandora's Box* and the equally controversial *Diary of a Lost Girl*, two of the last great silent films. Pabst realized that Brooks had such beauty, vitality, and unique sex appeal (even her women of easy virtue had the glow of innocence) that no viewer would question why every man in his films immediately made advances toward her. Because of the wild life she'd led in Hollywood, Brooks understood the sexual needs and drives of Pabst's fallen heroines. They wanted sex, they needed physical contact. Brooks knew that society would condemn them, and that the men who tried to take advantage of their generosity with their bodies would blame them for their masculine weaknesses. Brooks usually smiled when her characters were being attacked, but she also allowed the pain to slip through when her women were damaged. Not only did Brooks care for her women, but she had the talent to transmit even their deepest thoughts. Even the way she moved (how much energy she had, how erotic she was) expressed feelings. Brooks returned to America after making *Prix de Beauté* for French director René Clair, but was not welcomed back to Hollywood. She drifted into obscurity. Her foreign films were rediscovered in the late fifties, and a 1979 essay about her by Kenneth Tynan in the *New Yorker* secured her cult reputation. Brooks, who was

traced to New York City, went to Rochester as a guest of Eastman House and spent countless hours watching old movies and appreciating them for the first time. She became an astute critic and respected film historian, recounting her unusual career and acquaintances in the candid book *Lulu in Hollywood*.

• **Cult Favorites:** *A Girl in Every Port* (1928, Howard Hawks), *Pandora's Box* (1929, G. W. Pabst), *Diary of a Lost Girl* (1929, Pabst).

• **Other Key Films:** *Love'em and Leave'em* (1926, Frank Tuttle), *Beggars of Life* (1928, William Wellman), *Prix de Beauté* (1930, René Clair).

Louise Brooks.

○

EDWARD BROPHY (1895–1960) Short, short-armed, bald, roly-poly character actor, a Runyonesque Eric Blore. He stood out as the jolly condemned knife-thrower whose hands will be grafted onto pianist Colin Clive in *Mad Love*, as a crooked lawyer who delivers a fabulously flamboyant courtroom spiel in *Beast of the City*, and as a crooked politician in *The Last Hurrah*, but he is better remembered for playing quirky gangsters, foolish cops, and, like Blore, a valet in the "Falcon" series. He dressed impeccably so it was amusing when he'd chirp about dolls and gams, say "ain't," and cheerfully gab about some nasty crime business. He was particularly funny when partnered with Allen Jenkins, who spoke in the same peculiar vernacular. Brophy provided the voice of Timothy Mouse in *Dumbo*.

• **Cult Favorites:** *Freaks* (1932, Tod Browning), *Gold Diggers of 1933* (1933, Mervyn LeRoy), *The Thin Man* (1934, W. S. Van Dyke), *Naughty Marietta* (1935, Van Dyke), *Mad Love* (1935, Karl Freund), *Strike Me Pink* (1936, Norman Taurog).

• **Also Recommended:** *The Champ* (1931, King Vidor), *Flesh* (1932, John Ford), *Beast of the City* (1932, Charles Brabin), *The Whole Town's Talking* (1935, Ford), *China Seas* (1935, Tay Garnett), *The Last Gangster* (1937, Edward Ludwig), *A Silent Case of Murder* (1938, Lloyd Bacon), *You Can't Cheat an Honest Man* (1939, George Marshall), *The Gay Falcon* (1941, Irving Reis), *All Through the Night* (1942, Vincent Sherman), *Air Force* (1943, Howard Hawks), *Cover Girl* (1944, Charles Vidor), *Wonder Man* (1945, H. Bruce Humberstone), *The Falcon in San Francisco*

(1945, Joseph H. Lewis), *The Falcon's Adventure* (1946, William Berke), *The Last Hurrah* (1958, Ford).

○

JOHNNY MACK BROWN (1904–74) Handsome, former Rose Bowl star for the University of Alabama who broke into films at the beginning of the sound era. As a lead or supporting player, he appeared with such actresses as Marion Davies, Mary Pickford, Joan Crawford, and Mae West, and was in successful films from various genres, including *The Secret Six*, a classic gangster film, and King Vidor's big-budget western *Billy the Kid*, playing the title character. It seemed like he would be an all-purpose leading man, but his career faltered in the mid-thirties; Brown turned to quickie westerns, where he'd have success for almost twenty years and win a cult following. Although none of these westerns captured the flavor of the Old West as *Billy the Kid* did, they were generally entertaining, as Brown was one of the most athletic of western stars (until he put on weight late in his career) and had a pleasant, easygoing manner and amiable accent. He usually dressed in black (including gloves) but at times wore light colors or buckskin; he rode a palomino named Rebel; he looked comfortable kissing his leading ladies. Brown starred for several studios, including Universal, paired with comic Fuzzy Knight; but probably his best B westerns were those made for Monogram, costarring Raymond Hatton and featuring efficient, if not original, scripts.

• **Cult Favorites:** about 200 B westerns (1935–1953).

• **Other Key Films:** *Montana Moon* (1930,

Malcolm St. Clair), *Billy the Kid* (1930, King Vidor), *The Secret Six* (1931, George Hill).

• **Also of Interest:** *Slide, Kelly, Slide* (1927, Edward Sedgwick), *The Fair Co-Ed* (1927, Sam Wood), *Our Dancing Daughters* (1928, Harry Beaumont), *Coquette* (1929, Sam Taylor), *Fighting with Kit Carson* (1933 serial, Armand Schaefer and Colbert Clark), *Belle of the Nineties* (1934, Leo McCarey), *Rustlers of Red Dog* (1935 serial, Louis Friedlander), *Wild West Days* (1937 serial, Ford Beebe and Cliff Smith), *Flaming Frontiers* (1938 serial, Ray Taylor and Alan James), *The Oregon Trail* (1939 serial, Beebe), *The Gentleman from Texas* (1946, Lambert Hillyer).

○

RICOU BROWNING (1930–) A handsome Olympic swimmer who donned a scaly rubber suit and hideous mask to play the Gill Man in the underwater scenes in the 3-D *Creature from the Black Lagoon.* Shooting required that the actor playing Gill Man hold his breath for several minutes at a time, which is why Browning, rather than monster-vet Glenn Strange, got the role of the scary yet sympathetic creature, considered by most horror fans to be the best of the many monsters of the fifties. The picture's most famous scene has Julie Adams swimming near the surface while the creature swims below, entranced by the lovely female. Browning reprised his role in *Revenge of the Creature,* also in 3-D. This time he also played the monster in out-of-water scenes, which gave him a little more freedom to act.

• **Cult Favorite:** *Creature from the Black Lagoon* (1954, Jack Arnold).

• **Other Key Film:** *Revenge of the Creature* (1955, Arnold).

○

NIGEL BRUCE (1895–1953) Middle-aged, mustached British character actor who specialized in upper-class gentlemen (usually ex-officers) who love to hear themselves talk, particularly at dinner parties, who quickly jump to wrong conclusions, and who huff and puff if anyone does anything that breaks British social convention. He was most lovable as the bumbling, well-meaning Dr. Watson in Basil Rathbone's "Sherlock Holmes" films, in which he wrongly "solved" a lot of mysteries and was exasperated by a series of defiantly convention-breaking characters who crossed Holmes's path. In truth, Holmes's friendship with Bruce's Watson made about as much sense as Ricky Ricardo's with Fred Mertz in "I Love Lucy"—they didn't seem at all compatible. The scripts always include a line or two where Holmes expresses respect for Watson's noble character, but by and large he merely patronizes him. Watson's major functions in the series were to provide amusement for Holmes and viewers, to represent the staunch, patriotic Britisher (the forties Holmes films were updated to the current war period), and to make viewers see how clever Holmes was. Bruce did his job well.

• **Cult Favorites:** *The Hound of the Baskervilles* (1939, Sidney Lanfield), *The Adventures of Sherlock Holmes* (1939, Alfred L. Werker).

• **Sleeper:** *The Scarlet Claw* (1944, Roy William Neill).

• **Also Recommended:** *Becky Sharp* (1935, Rouben Mamoulian), *She* (1935, Irving Pichel and Lansing C. Holden), *The*

Charge of the Light Brigade (1936, Michael Curtiz), *Rebecca* (1940, Alfred Hitchcock), *Suspicion* (1941, Hitchcock), *Lassie Come Home* (1943, Fred M. Wilcox), *Frenchman's Creek* (1944, Mitchel Leisen), *The Corn Is Green* (1945, Irving Rapper), *Limelight* (1952, Charles Chaplin).

• **Other Key Films:** *Sherlock Holmes and the Voice of Terror* (1942, John Rawlins), *Sherlock Holmes and the Secret Weapon* (1942, Neill), *Sherlock Holmes Faces Death* (1943, Neill), *Sherlock Holmes in Washington* (1943, Neill), *Pearl of Death* (1944, Neill), *Dressed to Kill* (1946, Neill).

○

BUCKWHEAT/BILLIE THOMAS (1931–80) In 1934, 3-year-old Billie Thomas beat out hundreds of black children as the replacement for maturing "Stymie" Beard in Hal Roach's "Our Gang" comedy shorts. His character, Buckwheat, would be the most endearing of the wonderful kids, and with fellow tagalong Porky formed the cutest child tandem in cinema history. Buckwheat was originally supposed to be female, wearing pigtails and little dresses or diapers. "Her" specialties were crying and looking puzzled. Later Buckwheat dressed like a boy, He was a cheery boy, with a round face, frizzy hair, a wide, toothy smile and large, animated eyes that were put to great use when he acted frightened or did double takes. He often wore a straw hat. He got into all kinds of trouble and then he cried, his whines mixed with hiccups. When Spanky would ask, "Where's Buckwheat?" he'd emerge with a jolly, "Here I is." A favorite gesture was his exaggerated I-don't-know-how-that-happened shrug, with shoulders rising almost up to his ears, straight arms spreading slightly at his sides, his head at an angle, and a daffy grin forming. He wasn't as pivotal to the plots as Spanky or Alfalfa, but he was always in on the action, and it's hard to imagine the gang without him. Renewed interest in Buckwheat was sparked when Eddie Murphy played him on "Saturday Night Live."

• **Cult Favorites:** "Our Gang" comedy shorts (1934–44).

○

SMILEY BURNETTE (1911–67) Smiley Burnette was almost out-of-shape enough to be a major-league baseball catcher—in fact he resembled Smoky Burgess, the former catcher. Which is no compliment. If the fat Burgess could play 18 years in the big leagues looking as he did, then Burnette could survive 29 years in the Wild West, particularly in the unreal reel West of Gene Autry pictures. Burnette first worked with Autry on the National Barn Dance radio show: Autry sang, Burnette provided hillbilly humor (often in song). In 1934, they went to Hollywood together to make westerns. And they made more than 60 by 1942, when they split up because Autry enlisted in the air force. By that time Autry was the top-ranked cowboy star and, amazingly, Burnette was also in the top ten, although he was just Autry's comic sidekick. His character was Frog Milhouse, who probably helped inspire Andy Devine's funny, chubby "Jingles" on television's "Wild Bill Hickok." He was flabby, wore a slouch hat that he turned up in front, and wasn't too handy with a gun. He seemed out of place, even though Autry's West was far from rugged. He reminded one of a happy-go-lucky, over-aged farm boy, not someone who would fight outlaws. But though he was clumsy and a bit slow, he wasn't inept and always came through when there was trouble, not just for Autry but for Sunset Carson, Allan "Rocky" Lane, Charles Starrett, and other western leads he supported in his lengthy career. He was Roy Rogers' sidekick in *King of the Cowboys*. Fittingly, he rejoined Autry in the early fifties, and after 6 pictures, both called it quits in film.

• **Cult Favorites:** *The Phantom Empire* (1935 serial, Otto Brower and B. Reeves Eason), *Tumbling Tumbleweeds* (1935, Joseph Kane), *King of the Cowboys* (1943, Kane).

See: Gene Autry's film credits (1934–42).

○

MARILYN BURNS If it were ever determined which female in films suffers the most onscreen torture and torment without actually dying, then surely Marilyn Burns's mistreated young woman in *The Texas Chainsaw Massacre* would rival the heroines of *The Conqueror Worm* and *I Spit on Your Grave* as Queen of Abuse. Abducted by the skin-masked Leatherface and the rest of his sick male cannibal family, she is stuffed into a bag, poked, prodded, bound and gagged, beaten, hit on the head with a hammer, and forced to crash through a second-floor window, cutting her entire body with glass; she then runs on a painfully injured leg with Leatherface and his chain saw at her heels. Her screams are loud, continuous, and thoroughly convincing; the blood that covers her from head to toes and streaks her face seems to be real (and supposedly some of it was). The blond actress wasn't as pretty as some horror movie heroines, but in that film she emerged as one of the genre's great screamers, bedeviled victims, and, ultimately, its most impressive survivor. While viewers were immobilized with fear just watching her be abused, she was able to escape! Interestingly, she doesn't want or get the opportunity to kill those who murdered her companions, like many horror-movie heroines. Escape is victory enough. Burns and Edwin Neal, a real sicko in the film, would reunite for the dismal *Future-Kill*.

• **Cult Favorite:** *The Texas Chainsaw Massacre* (1974, Tobe Hooper).

• **Also of Interest:** *Eaten Alive* (1976, Hooper).

○

GARY BUSEY (1944–) This extremely talented, strapping actor-singer (and imperfect motorcyclist) from Goose Creek, Texas, looks and sounds like an overgrown, big-toothed, big-appetite, common-folks country kid from the Southwest. Indeed, he seemed his most comfortable as a gullible but quick-learning Texas farmboy in *Barbarosa*, well-suited to the land and to blue jeans and suspenders. Busey looks like the quiet type, but instead he's an aggressively funny fast-talker; if he can't get his way with the truth, he'll playfully con you. He wins women by keeping them off-balance. He's polite, but won't be stopped by a closed door or a condescending authority figure. There's a sense of recklessness and danger to him; even his most well-meaning characters make those around him either worry about him or themselves. Busey has gravitated to projects that have myth, legend, or tall-tale aspects: *The Last American Hero*, as the brother of backwoods moonshine-runner and race-car driver Junior Johnson; *Big Wednesday*, about overaged surfers still looking for the perfect wave; *A Star Is Born*, supporting Streisand and Kristofferson in the second remake of the film about a rising star falling for a has-been; *The Buddy Holly Story*, about the long dead but much remembered rockabilly idol; *Carny*, about quirky characters in a traveling carnival; *Barbarosa*, falling in with a mythical outlaw played by Willie Nelson; *Insignificance*, playing a Joe DiMaggio–like ballplayer who's married to a Marilyn Monroe–like actress (Theresa Russell); *Silver Bullet*, about werewolves; and, to a degree, *Lethal Weapon*, as a muscle-toned blond villain who duels with Mel Gibson in a battle of seemingly invincible titans. His best role remains Buddy Holly, a truly exciting, "driven" portrayal—Holly's the only character in the picture who is the least bit unusual. He added another dimension to his performance in that he actually sang rather than lip-synched Holly's familiar songs. He has the raw sound of Holly when he sang live. His moving rendition of "True Love Ways" is actually better than Holly's. In recent years, Busey has recovered from substance abuse, survived a motorcycle crash, and after giving villainy a chilling shot in *Lethal Weapon*, played the hero in some forgettable low-budget action pictures— e.g., *Eye of the Tiger*—that waste his considerable talent.

• **Cult Favorites:** *Big Wednesday* (1978, John Milius), *Straight Time* (1978, Ulu Grosbard), *The Buddy Holly Story* (1978, Steve Rash), *Carny* (1980, Robert Kaylor), *Barbarosa* (1982, Fred Schepisi), *Insignificance* (1985, Nicolas Roeg).

• **Sleeper:** *The Last American Hero/Hard Driver* (1973, Lamont Johnson).

• **Also of Interest:** *Thunderbolt and Lightfoot* (1974, Michael Cimino), *The Gumball Rally* (1976, Chuck Bail), *Foolin' Around* (1980, Richard T. Heffron), *D.C. Cab* (1983, Joel Schumacher), *Silver Bullet*

(1985, Daniel Attias), *Lethal Weapon* (1987, Richard Donner), *Predator 2* (1990, Stephen Hopkins).

○

SUSAN CABOT (1927–86) In her film debut, this dark-haired, dark-eyed starlet gave a weak performance as a sweet native girl who softens tough Jon Hall in *On the Isle of Samoa*. After a few such exotic supporting parts, she redeemed herself as the romantic lead in two solid Audie Murphy westerns, *Gunsmoke* and *Ride Clear of Diablo*. But it would be a few years later

Susan Cabot.

that she found everlasting, though minor, fame, as Roger Corman's female star. In six of his pictures between 1957 and 1959, she alternated between sympathetic young women, bitches (at 30, she was the title character in *Sorority Girl*), bad girls (Charles Bronson's girlfriend in *Machine Gun Kelly*), and finally, a monster. She's best remembered for her final, most enjoyable Corman picture, playing a vain cosmetologist who tries to prolong youth by injecting herself with royal jelly and becomes *The Wasp Woman*. At the time, she was romantically linked to Jordan's King Hussein. Her career ended abruptly, and over the years she became reclusive, suffering several breakdowns. She was bludgeoned to death in 1986, and her dwarf son was charged with the murder.

• **Cult Favorites:** *Machine Gun Kelly* (1958, Roger Corman), *The Wasp Woman* (1959, Corman),

• **Other Key Films:** *Gunsmoke* (1953, Nathan Juran), *Ride Clear of Diablo* (1954, Jesse Hibbs), *Carnival Rock* (1957, Corman), *Sorority Girl* (1957, Corman), *War of the Satellites* (1958, Corman), *Fort Massacre* (1958, Joseph M. Newman).

• **Also of Interest:** *On the Isle of Samoa* (1950, William Berke), *Flame of Araby* (1951, Charles Lamont), *The Viking Women and the Sea Serpent* (1957, Corman), *Surrender—Hell!* (1959, John Barnwell).

○

CHERIE CAFFARO Buxom blonde who enjoyed a dose of fame in the early seventies playing "Ginger" McCallister, an undercover agent who was promoted by herself and her husband, director Don Schain, as "the female James Bond." The low-budget exploitation films were poorly directed, plotted, and acted, but they attracted male viewers because they had violence, sleazy subjects (e.g., white slavers kidnap cheerleaders), and the rare lead actress in action pictures who took off her clothes. Unfortunately, Caffaro wasn't any more enticing naked than with her clothes on. Her hair, face (how did she win a Brigitte Bardot look-alike contest?), and clothes seemed like they belonged to three different women. She was pretty, but seemed cheap, like a combination drag queen and greasy-spoon hash slinger. Perhaps she was appearing in films only until she could get a break as a waitress.

• **Key Films:** *Ginger* (1971, Don Schain), *The Abductors* (1972, Schain), *Girls Are for Loving* (1973, Schain). *Too Hot to Handle* (1976, Schain).

• **Also of Interest:** *A Place Called Today* (1972, Schain), *Savage Sisters* (1974, Eddie Romero).

○

ROD CAMERON (1910–83) As tall and tough as his famous name implied. Handsome, brawny, square-jawed (actually his entire face was kind of square), this 6'4" actor starred in numerous low-budget films that appealed to male viewers because they were long on action and short on romance. A former stunt man, he was most suited for knockdown fistfights, and they were as important to his films as gunplay. He appeared in war, adventure, and detective/secret service pictures (as well a couple of science-fiction films), but he is best known as a western hero. He was no better than an adequate actor and, despite his size, didn't have much dramatic presence (except when pointing a gun), but he could carry a flimsy film on his broad shoulders. Plus he had that he-man name to guarantee him a place in camp annals. There surely would have been even more snickering if he'd used his real name, Rod Cox.

• **Of Interest:** *The Monster and the Girl* (1941, Stuart Heisler), *The Remarkable Andrew* (1942, Heisler), *Fleet's In* (1942, Victor Schertzinger), *Wake Island* (1942, John Farrow), *The Forest Rangers* (1942, George Marshall), *Gung Ho!* (1943, Ray Enright), *G-Men vs. the Black Dragon* (1943 serial, William Witney), *Secret Service in Darkest Africa* (1943 serial, Spencer G. Bennet), *Belle Starr's Daughter* (1948, Lesley Selander), *Stampede* (1949, Selander), *Oh, Susanna* (1951, Joseph Kane), *Ride the Man Down* (1952, Kane), *San Antone* (1953, Kane), *The Electronic Monster* (1958, Montgomery Tully), *The Man Who Died Twice* (1958, Kane), *The Bounty Killer* (1965, Bennet), *Requiem for a Gunfighter* (1965, Bennet), *Evel Knievel* (1972, Marvin Chomsky).

○

COLLEEN CAMP (1953–) Occasionally, this sprite, pretty blonde will show up in a major film, if just for a minute—she was one of the dancers in *Apocalypse Now*—but for the most part she's been a mainstay of low-budget pictures since the mid-seventies, when she was smart, sexy, and stuck-up in *The Swinging Cheerleaders*. Her strangest film was a perverse drama, *Death Game/The Seducers*, in which she and fellow hitchhiker Sondra Locke humiliate, torture, and terrify the middle-class man who gives them a ride. Since then Camp has definitely lightened up. She still plays romantic leads, but is also well cast as teenagers' mothers, as in *Valley Girl*, sexy women who remember what it was like to be sexually confused teenagers. Her offbeat delivery and manner (her characters have quirky minds) make her partic-

ularly adept at comedy. She has been in a number of films with all-star casts, including *Police Academy 2*, *The Gumball Rally*, *Doin' Time*, and Peter Bogdanovich's *They All Laughed*. Bogdanovich is one of the few major directors to have recognized Camp's comedic talent. He also cast her as a daffy murder suspect, opposite Rob Lowe, in his innocuous screwball comedy *Illegally Yours*.

• **Cult Favorites:** *Smile* (1975, Michael Ritchie), *Game of Death* (1979, Robert Clouse), *Apocalypse Now* (1979, Francis Coppola).

• **Sleeper:** *Cloud Dancer* (1980, Barry Brown).

• **Other Key Films:** *Swinging Cheerleaders* (1974, Jack Hill), *Death Game* (1977, Peter Traynor), *They All Laughed* (1981, Peter Bogdanovich), *Valley Girl* (1983, Martha Coolidge).

• **Also of Interest:** *Ebony, Ivory, and Jade* (1976, Cirio H. Santiago), *Deadly Games* (1982, Scott Mansfield), *Rosebud Beach Hotel* (1985, Harry Hurwitz), *Track 29* (1988, Nicholas Roeg).

○

BRUCE CAMPBELL There were so many gory special effects in Sam Raimi's smash, *Evil Dead*, that audiences paid little attention to the young cast, including this dark-haired, good-looking actor. Campbell was thus able to come back as a different character in the comedic sequel, *Evil Dead II*, which he coproduced. About halfway through that film, a definite improvement on the original, you notice that Campbell is turning in a hilarious performance, balancing wild-eyed double takes and straight-faced slapstick, as one god-awful thing after another happens to his semi-possessed character in an isolated house and haunted woods. He played a heel in Raimi's *Crimewave*, but in the low-budget exploitation film, *Maniac Cop*, he capitalized on his image as a hard-luck hero. He played a cop whose wife discovers his infidelity and then is wrongly accused of killing her and everyone else who has been murdered by the title character.

• **Cult Favorite:** *Evil Dead* (1983, Sam Raimi).

• **Sleepers:** *Crimewave* (1986, Raimi), *Evil Dead II* (1987, Raimi).

• **Also of Interest:** *Maniac Cop* (1988, William Lustig), *Moontrap* (1990, Robert Dyke).

○

TIMOTHY CAREY (1925–) The nightmare blind date for your daughter. When I think of Carey, I remember a fifties television anthology series in which his stick-up man shoots a defenseless cop and then sneers sadistically. In movies, this brawny, ugly, mean-looking actor played many other sadistic thugs, ex-cons, and hired guns. They were not just heartless killers—they carried guns, they sneered, they had no manners. He's the cad who shoots the racehorse in *The Killing*. In *One-Eyed Jacks* he bullies a saloon girl and tries to shoot Marlon Brando in the back (also, it is rumored, the actor infuriated Brando by joyfully urinating on the set). He even terrified the Monkees in *Head*. Not worried about his image, he directed, produced, wrote, and starred in (as an egotistical evangelist who sings rock music) *The World's Greatest Sinner*. The ultimate social undesirable.

• **Cult Favorites:** *The Big Carnival/Ace in the Hole* (1951, Billy Wilder), *The Wild*

Timothy Carey enjoys shooting a horse during a race in Stanley Kubrick's The Killing.

One (1954, Laslo Benedek), *East of Eden* (1955, Elia Kazan), *The Killing* (1956, Stanley Kubrick), *Paths of Glory* (1957, Kubrick), *Poor White Trash* (1961, Harold Daniels), *One-Eyed Jacks* (1961, Marlon Brando), *Bikini Beach* (1964, William Asher), *Beach Blanket Bingo* (1965, Asher), *Head* (1968, Bob Rafelson), *What's the Matter with Helen?* (1971, Curtis Harrington), *Minnie and Moskowitz* (1971, John Cassavetes), *The Killing of a Chinese Bookie* (1976, Cassavetes).
• **Other Key Film:** *The World's Greatest Sinner* (1962, Timothy Carey).

○

ANNE CARLISLE Slim young blond actress, painter, aspiring model (I think), filmmaker, and member of New York's avant-garde club scene who was compelling in a dual role in the controversial film *Liquid Sky*, which mixes bizarre science fiction, kinky sex, and social satire. She is Margaret, a drug-dazed, masochistic "hot" New Wave model, who while striving for freedom learns that being fashionable is just as repressive as being traditional; and she is also Jimmy, the gay, heroin-addicted, unsuccessful model who is jealous of her success. I like the way Carlisle slowly reveals Margaret's inner strength beneath her passive-female exterior and the vulnerability (his one redeeming feature) beneath Jimmy's tough-male exterior. This makes me think that if you put Margaret and Jimmy together, you get Anne Carlisle. She also worked on the script. Carlisle had a bit in *Desperately Seeking Susan*.
• **Cult Favorite:** *Liquid Sky* (1983, Slava Tsukerman).
• **Other Key Film:** *Perfect Strangers* (1986, Larry Cohen).

○

RICHARD CARLSON (1912–77) Beginning in the late 1930s, he had steady work, most often as the second male in frivolous films. However, his cult status comes from the leads he had in several science-fiction films of the fifties, particularly three that were released in 3-D: the ground-breaking 3-D film *It Came from Outer Space*, the classic *Creature from the Black Lagoon*, and the lesser-known *The Maze*. Interchangeable with Hugh Marlowe, he was intelligent, bold, intense, earnest, and if unremarkable, then at least reliable. He directed five films. TV fans know him best as FBI agent Herb Philbrick in the fifties series "I Led Three Lives."
• **Cult Favorites:** *It Came from Outer Space* (1953, Jack Arnold), *The Maze* (1953, William Cameron Menzies), *Creature from the Black Lagoon* (1954, Arnold).
• **Sleepers:** *Hold That Ghost* (1941, Arthur Lubin), *Fly by Night* (1942, Robert Siodmak), *The Sound of Fury/Try and Get Me* (1951, Cyril Endfield), *The Last Command* (1955, Frank Lloyd).
• **Also of Interest:** *The Young in Heart* (1938, Richard Wallace), *Too Many Girls* (1941, George Abbott), *The Ghost Breakers* (1940, George Marshall), *Back Street* (1941, Robert Stevenson), *The Little Foxes* (1941, William Wyler), *White Cargo* (1942, Richard Thorpe), *King Solomon's Mines* (1950, Compton Bennett and Andrew Marton), *The Blue Veil* (1951, Curtis Bernhardt), *Retreat, Hell!* (1952, Joseph H. Lewis), *Seminole* (1953, Budd Boetticher), *All I Desire* (1953, Douglas Sirk), *The Magnetic Monster* (1953, Curt Siodmak), *Riders to the Stars* (1954, Richard Carlson), *The Helen Morgan Story* (1957, Michael Curtiz), *The Power* (1968, Byron Haskin).

VERONICA CARLSON (1944–) Blond, statuesque former art student and model whose bikini-clad picture in a British tabloid got her cast as the leading lady in three Hammer Studios horror films. She seemed gentler and more innocent than other Hammer heroines, so it was exciting when directors put her in sexy gowns that revealed her long legs and at least one tender shoulder. When she was bitten on the neck by vampire Christopher Lee in *Dracula Has Risen from the Grave* and raped by mad doctor Peter Cushing in *Frankenstein Must Be Destroyed*, her defilement had that much more power.

• **Key Films:** *Dracula Has Risen from the Grave* (1968, Freddie Francis), *Frankenstein Must Be Destroyed* (1970, Terence Fisher), *The Horror of Frankenstein* (1970, Jimmy Sangster), *The Ghoul* (1975, Francis).

○

MARTINE CAROL (1922–67) France's top female star in the early fifties and, until Bardot replaced her, France's top sex symbol. Playing historical figures known for their physical pursuits, this voluptuous blonde appeared in several costume dramas, some directed by her husband, Christian-Jaque. Viewers came to her films to see her step out of those costumes and into a leisurely bath, bare-breasted. Oddly, her eroticism disappeared when she played the dark-haired beauty every man desires in *Lola Montès*, her most memorable film. She is exciting at rare moments in Max Ophüls cult classic, as when Lola seduces Franz Liszt, but she is unable to project Lola's inner beauty or deep suffering. When she seduces King Louis I (Anton Walbrook) by stripping for him just after they meet, she is more

Martine Carol with Peter Ustinov in Lola Montès.

Maria Montez than *Lola Montès*.

• **Cult Favorite:** *Lola Montès* (1955, Max Ophüls).

• **Other Key Films:** *Carline Chérie* (1951, Richard Pottier), *Les Belles de Nuit* (1952, René Clair), *Adorable Créatures* (1952, Christian-Jaque), *Lucrèce Borgia* (1953, Christian-Jaque), *Madame Du Barry* (1954, Christian-Jaque), *Nana* (1955, Christian-Jaque).

○

DAVID CARRADINE (1936–) The oldest son of John Carradine became an international cult figure portraying a clean-shaven Buddhist monk (a fugitive in the West) with deadly fighting powers and a wealth of wise aphorisms in the TV series "Kung

Fu." Since then he has starred in numerous action films that exploit his martial-arts skills and overall physical prowess (first displayed on Broadway in *The Royal Hunt of the Sun* in the mid-sixties). Most have had low budgets and, to fit his personal philosophy, either a leftist or spiritual slant. He is willing to play bad guys, as he did opposite Chuck Norris in *Lone Wolf McQuade*, but he refuses to let his character lose to the hero in hand-to-hand combat. With his reputation as a free spirit and drug-experimenter, he had trouble at one time getting movie roles until director Paul Bartel and New World's Roger Corman gave him the lead in *Death Race 2000*. As "Frankenstein," one of the drivers in a cross-country run-over-pedestrians-for-points contest, he wore a mask for much of the film. Like most Carradine characters, Frankenstein didn't talk much. He proved that he could play meaty parts in major films when he gave a strong performance as folk singer Woody Guthrie in *Bound for Glory*, yet that fine picture failed at the box office and didn't win him other substantial roles. When you see Carradine in his recent, trivial exploitation films, walking through parts that deserve just that, you wonder if he is disappointed with the course of his career. The only time since *Bound for Glory* that he seemed involved in a role was when he played a Vietnam vet who rebuilds a merry-go-round in Kansas in *Americana*, a film he directed. In it he teamed up with his one-time wife Barbara Hershey, his screen lover in his first starring film, *Boxcar Bertha*.

• **Cult Favorites:** *Boxcar Bertha* (1972, Martin Scorsese), *Mean Streets* (1973, Scorsese), *The Long Goodbye* (1973, Robert Altman), *Death Race 2000* (1975, Paul Bartel), *The Long Riders* (1980, Walter Hill), *Q* (1982, Larry Cohen).

• **Sleeper:** *Bound for Glory* (1976, Hal Ashby).

• **Also of Interest:** *The Good Guys and the Bad Guys* (1969, Burt Kennedy), *Cannonball* (1976, Bartel), *Gray Lady Down* (1978, David Greene), *The Serpent's Egg* (1978, Ingmar Bergman), *Deathsport* (1978, Henry Suto), *Fast Charlie, the Moonbeam Rider* (1979, Steve Carver), *Circle of Iron* (1979, David Carradine), *Americana* (1981, David Carradine), *Lone Wolf McQuade* (1983, Carver), *The Warrior and the Sorceress* (1984, John Broderick).

○

JOHN CARRADINE (1906–88) Gaunt, deep-voiced character actor who appeared in countless films during a 60-year career (which he began as John Peter Richmond). He did his finest work for John Ford, particularly as the vicious guard in *The Prisoner of Shark Island* (his breakthrough film), the gambler in *Stagecoach*, and Preacher Casey in *The Grapes of Wrath*. But he turned in many standout performances at 20th Century-Fox into the early forties, and for smaller studios thereafter. He played all kinds of bizarre characters, some even sympathetic, but he will be remembered because of his villains, a mean lot that included the "scrufty renegade-bastard" Simon Girty in *Daniel Boone*, the one-eyed British officer in *Drums Along the Mohawk*, Robert Ford in both *Jesse James* and *The Return of Jesse James*, Nazi hangman Reinhard Heydrich in *Hitler's Madman* (a shrewd, sinister characterization with a brilliant deathbed scene), the psychotic, wild-eyed artist in *Bluebeard* (his best lead role), and a classy Dracula in many films. He was in *The*

Invisible Man, The Black Cat, and Bride of Frankenstein when he was a bit player, but it wasn't until the forties that his horror roles got notices. He was always hammy, but in the late sixties he began camping it up in one cheapie horror film after another. "Directors never direct me," he boasted. "They just turn me loose." This was often a mistake. He took his Dracula very seriously in the forties—years later he would play him for laughs, as in Billy the Kid vs. Dracula. Kids who know him for his junk horror films should take note of his long and impressive dramatic career. His three talented sons, David, Keith, and Robert, carry on the tradition.

• **Cult Favorites:** The Hound of the Baskervilles (1939, Sidney Lanfield), The Return of Frank James (1940, Fritz Lang), Captive Wild Woman (1943, Edward Dmytryk), Bluebeard (1944, Edgar G. Ulmer), Johnny Guitar (1954, Nicholas Ray), Stranger on Horseback (1955, Jacques Tourneur), The Ten Commandments (1956, Cecil B. De Mille), Tarzan the Magnificent (1960, Robert Day), The Man Who Shot Liberty Valance (1962, John Ford), Billy the Kid vs. Dracula (1966, William Beaudine), Boxcar Bertha (1972, Martin Scorsese), Everything You Always Wanted to Know About Sex But Were Afraid to Ask (1972, Woody Allen), Satan's Cheerleaders (1977, Greydon Clark), The Howling (1981, Joe Dante).

• **Other Key Films:** The Prisoner of Shark Island (1936, Ford), Mary of Scotland (1936, Ford), Winterset (1936, Alfred Santell), Captains Courageous (1937, Victor Fleming), The Hurricane (1937, Ford), Of Human Hearts (1938, Clarence Brown), Four Men and a Prayer (1938, Ford), Submarine Patrol (1938, Ford), Jesse James (1938, Henry King), Stagecoach (1939, Ford), Five Came Back (1939, John Farrow), Drums Along the Mohawk (1939, Ford), The Grapes of Wrath (1940, Ford), Brigham Young—Frontiersman (1940, Henry Hathaway), Blood and Sand (1941, Rouben Mamoulian), Man Hunt (1941, Lang), Swamp Thing (1941, Jean Renoir), Son of Fury (1942, John Cromwell), Reunion in France (1942, Jules Dassin), Hitler's Madman (1943, Douglas Sirk), House of Frankenstein (1945, Erle C. Kenton), House of Dracula (1945, Kenton), Fallen Angel (1945, Otto Preminger), The Last Hurrah (1958, Ford), Cheyenne Autumn (1964, Ford), Peggy Sue Got Married (1986, Francis Coppola).

○

KEITH CARRADINE (1951–) The second son of John Carradine has starred in numerous "off-Hollywood" films (his term), for such cult directors as Walter Hill, Ridley Scott, Louis Malle, and most notably, Robert Altman and his protégé Alan Rudolph. Tall and slender, with intense eyes, the best-looking of the Carradine clan has been considered a romantic lead since his bearded young musician loved and left several women in Nashville. Certainly no Hollywood actor kisses with such passion. His role of a photographer who is sexually comfortable only with the 12-year-old Brooke Shields in Pretty Baby didn't diminish his romantic image. In Choose Me, he sleeps with Genevieve Bujold, Lesley Ann Warren, and Rae Dawn Chong—and each time falls in love; in Nashville, he is after as much sex as he can get. Typically, his impulsive, reckless, moody characters chase women who are off-limits: children; virgins; women who want nothing to do with men (both Bujold and Warren in Choose Me); women who have husbands or

Keith Carradine listens to Shelley Duvall's flirtations in Nashville.

boyfriends (Lili Tomlin in *Nashville*, Monica Vitti in *An Almost Perfect Affair*, Rae Dawn Chong in *Choose Me*, Lori Singer in *Trouble in Mind*, and Linda Fiorentino in *The Moderns* are among those who are tied to other men). He will chase after women even if the men in their lives are violent. In almost all of his films, he enters a dangerous situation and is physically attacked or shot at by jealous men, lawmen, rivals, bullies-punks, or, in *Southern Comfort*, murderous backwoodsmen. His characters are vulnerable, and in several of his early films, they don't survive. Carradine isn't always a likable actor (as in *Welcome to L.A.*), and he has been miscast (as in the still fascinating *The Duellists*), but his impressive, interesting credits and standout performances in such films as *Thieves Like Us* and *Choose Me* should void most criticism. He won a Best Song Oscar for

"I'm Easy," which he wrote and sang in *Nashville*. He won Madonna in her "Material Girl" video.

• **Cult Favorites:** *McCabe and Mrs. Miller* (1971, Robert Altman), *Emperor of the North/Emperor of the North Pole* (1973, Robert Aldrich), *Thieves Like Us* (1974, Altman), *Nashville* (1975, Altman), *Welcome to L.A.* (1977, Alan Rudolph), *The Duellists* (1977, Ridley Scott), *Pretty Baby* (1978, Louis Malle), *The Long Riders* (1980, Walter Hill), *Southern Comfort* (1981, Hill), *Choose Me* (1984, Rudolph), *Trouble in Mind* (1985, Rudolph), *The Moderns* (1988, Rudolph).

• **Also of Interest:** *Lumière* (1976, Jeanne Moreau), *An Almost Perfect Affair* (1979, Michael Ritchie), *Maria's Lovers* (1984, Andrei Konchalovsky), *The Inquiry* (1986, Damiano Damiani), *Cold Feet* (1989, Robert Dornhelm), *The Ballad of the Sad Cafe* (1991, Simon Callow).

ROBERT CARRADINE (1954–) The youngest of the Carradine brothers, the most unpredictable at choosing roles, and by no means the least talented. He has played a series of youthful characters: sex-crazed teens, perpetually stoned teens, psychotic punk teens (he can be very frightening, as in *Jackson County Jail*), nerdy college students (his horse laugh is the funniest thing in *Revenge of the Nerds*), the cigar-chomping young soldier in *The Big Red One*. Most of his characters are merely confused; some are actually off the deep end. An aggressive actor, he has surprising presence. If he hasn't Sean Penn's skill or power, he could certainly do a credible job in all of Penn's roles. He's underappreciated.

• **Cult Favorites:** *Mean Streets* (1973, Martin Scorsese), *Jackson County Jail* (1976, Michael Miller), *The Pom Pom Girls* (1976, Joseph Ruben), *Massacre at Central High* (1976, Renee Daalder), *The Big Red One* (1979, Samuel Fuller), *The Long Riders* (1980, Walter Hill), *Revenge of the Nerds* (1984, Jeff Kanew).

• **Sleeper:** *Heartaches* (1981, Donald Shebib).

• **Also of Interest:** *The Cowboys* (1972, Mark Rydell), *Cannonball* (1976, Paul Bartel), *Coming Home* (1977, Hal Ashby), *Wavelength* (1983, Mike Gray), *Rude Awakening* (1989, Aaron Russo and David Greenwalt).

○

BARBARA CARRERA (1945–) Dark beauty whose exotic looks (her mother was Nicaraguan) were exploited in her early films, as Acquanetta's had been thirty years earlier. She was cast as a woman who evolved from a fetus in a few days' time in scientist Rock Hudson's experiment in *Embryo*, and a woman transformed from a beast in *The Island of Dr. Moreau*. Carrera had natural sex appeal, but it was hard to be attracted to her strange women, considering their peculiar origins. However, as wild and wicked assassin Fatima Blush in the Sean Connery James Bond film *Never Say Never Again*, she was alluring, literally exploding with sexual energy. An ideal foreign villainess in nonserious, high-energy genre films, she'd be a great "spider woman" in Sherlock Holmes pictures.

• **Key Films:** *Embryo* (1976, Ralph Nelson), *The Island of Dr. Moreau* (1977, Don Taylor), *I, the Jury* (1982, Richard T. Heffron), *Never Say Never Again* (1983, Irvin Kershner), *Lone Wolf McQuade* (1983, Steve Carver), *Love at Stake* (1987, John Moffitt).

○

VERONICA CARTWRIGHT (1949–) This curly-haired blonde was the first girl to give the very young Jerry Mathers a kiss in "Leave It to Beaver" (she was Lumpy's sister for one year). She was Rod Taylor's young sister in *The Birds* but had few other occasions in the spotlight, while sister Angela had success in series television. She reemerged in the mid-seventies in a daring adult performance as the addicted porno actress in John Byrum's underrated, X-rated *Inserts*, and has since played a series of quirky supporting characters. A terrific screamer, she is especially adept at women who are on the verge of hysteria, as in the remake of *Invasion of the Body Snatchers*, *Alien*, and *The Right Stuff*. She doesn't mind playing characters who get on your nerves. She also has a vengeful, witch-like expression.

• **Cult Favorites:** *The Birds* (1963, Alfred Hitchcock), *Inserts* (1976, John Byrum), *Invasion of the Body Snatchers* (1978, Philip Kaufman), *Goin' South* (1978, Jack Nicholson), *Alien* (1979, Ridley Scott), *The Right Stuff* (1983, Kaufman).

• **Also of Interest:** *Flight of the Navigator* (1986, Randal Kleiser), *The Witches of Eastwick* (1987, George Miller).

○

JOANNA CASSIDY (1944–) Attractive brunette who was already past her starlet stage when she entered pictures. Soon, we started to notice her and appreciate her special brand of intelligence, wit, and mature sexuality. She was most memorable as the smart, enticingly dressed exotic dancer replicant that Harrison Ford chases and shoots in the back in *Blade Runner*, and as Gene Hackman's journalist girlfriend and Nick Nolte's lover in the excellent leftist Nicaragua-set picture *Under Fire*. She has been cast in other political thrillers—cruel Pierce Brosnan kills her spy after making love to her in *The Fourth Protocol*; she's Bob Hoskins's girlfriend in *Who Framed Roger Rabbit*. But she still doesn't get the star roles she deserves. TV watchers remember her as Dabney Coleman's love interest in "Buffalo Bill." They are married in the original but disappointing comedy *Where the Heart Is*.

• **Cult Favorite:** *Blade Runner* (1982, Ridley Scott).

• **Sleeper:** *Under Fire* (1983, Roger Spottiswoode).

• **Also Recommended:** *Who Framed Roger Rabbit* (1988, Robert Zemeckis), *The Package* (1989, Andrew Davis).

• **Also of Interest:** *Stunts* (1977, Mark L. Lester), *Night Games* (1980, Roger Vadim), *The Fourth Protocol* (1987, John

Mackenzie), *1969* (1988, Ernest Thompson), *Where the Heart Is* (1990, John Boorman).

○

KIM CATTRALL (1956–) She was eerie as the pretty, endlessly energetic, ridiculously upbeat girl who charms depressed Nick Mancuso into joining a cult in the chilling *Ticket to Heaven*. Since then she has played perky heroines in several lousy films. It's not that she's bad, it's just that she seems to be having a much better time acting in the films than we are watching them. Her one unusual, interesting portrayal was as the young but already withering married woman who has an affair with Rob Lowe in *Masquerade*—unfortunately, she was only the second female lead, and the stars, Lowe and Meg Tilly, ruin the film.

• **Cult Favorite:** *Porky's* (1981, Bob Clark).

• **Sleeper:** *Ticket to Heaven* (1981, Ralph L. Thomas).

• **Other Key Films:** *Police Academy* (1984, Hugh Wilson), *Big Trouble in Little China* (1986, John Carpenter), *Mannequin* (1987, Michael Gottlieb).

• **Also of Interest:** *Tribute* (1980, Clark), *Turk 182* (1985, Clark), *City Limits* (1985, Aaron Lipstadt), *Masquerade* (1988, Bob Swaim), *Midnight Crossing* (1988, Roger Holzberg), *Palais Royale* (1988, Martin Lavut), *The Return of the Musketeers* (1989, Richard Lester).

○

MARILYN CHAMBERS (1952–) As Marilyn Briggs she appeared in Sean Cunningham's heavily promoted sexual-awareness "documentary," *Together*—the most famous image in that box-office smash was

Marilyn Chambers in a publicity shot for Behind the Green Door.

her naked dive into a swimming pool. This was in 1971, two years before she would become the Queen of Porno Chic. The fresh-faced, healthy, WASPy, all-American blonde had her face taken off Ivory Snow boxes after she starred in the Mitchell Brothers' notorious *Behind the Green Door*, but audiences raced to the theaters to see the 99⁴⁴/₁₀₀% pure "Ivory Snow Girl" do impure things on the screen. In this groundbreaking porno film, she played a young woman who is kidnapped and taken to a sex club where, before a mixed audience, she is seduced by several women and then willingly performs sexual acts with several men, including black Johnnie Keyes. Photographed in an arty style and emphasizing sensuality rather than raunch, *Green Door* has always been popular with women. Perhaps it visualized their sexual fantasies and/or they identified with Chambers, who seemed to be enjoying herself. Her trapeze act, in which she performs fellatio on one man and simultaneously gives two others hand jobs may have been difficult, but was tame compared to what was done on film by the other two porno superstars of the early seventies, Linda Lovelace in *Deep Throat* and Georgina Spelvin in *The Devil in Miss Jones*. Chambers didn't talk until her follow-up film, *The Resurrection of Eve*, and it turned out she couldn't act. However, she did have a conceited expression—she was either smirking or trying to look wicked—that was kind of sexy. In later Mitchell Brothers films, her sex scenes were extremely masochistic. Because of her fame and natural appeal, David Cronenberg took a chance and cast her as the lead in his R-rated horror film *Rabid*. Her acting had improved and she was acceptable as the heroine who spreads a violence-inducing disease—the part allowed her to strip, seduce people, and writhe on the floor. In 1980 she would return to XXX-rated material with *Insatiable*, for which she gave some nude radio interviews, and engage in kinkier sex than she had done in the pictures that made her famous. That film continues to be popular in the video market with both sexes. Chambers then vowed to give up porno films and has been trying again to make it in R-rated legitimate films, beginning with *Angel of H.E.A.T.* and *Party Incorporated*, with ex-porno director, Chuck Vincent.

• **Cult Favorites:** *Behind the Green Door*, (1972, Jim and Art Mitchell), *Rabid* (1977, David Cronenberg), *Insatiable* (1980, Godfrey Daniels).

• **Other Key Films:** *Together* (1971, Sean

Cunningham), *The Resurrection of Eve* (1973, Mitchell Brothers), *Beyond De Sade* (1973, Mitchell Brothers), *Inside Marilyn Chambers* (1975, Mitchell Brothers), *Never a Tender Moment* (1979, Mitchell Brothers).

○

JACKY CHAN/JACKIE CHAN/CHENG LUNG (1954–)

A challenger for Bruce Lee's empty throne. He too is handsome, incredibly athletic, witty, a fierce fighter, and charismatic, though not on the level of Lee. A former child actor, he was in his early twenties when he got supporting parts in Chinese kung fu films. His first starring roles were in exploitation films that capitalized on Bruce Lee's name (e.g., he would avenge Lee's death) and had Chan utilizing Lee's fighting style. As his fame grew, he became known for his acrobatic, slapstick fighting; his character often devises a special fighting style to defeat a particular villain. He is usually horribly punished before emerging victorious in elaborate half-hour fights with incredible stunts. He does his own stunt work and has almost been killed several times. He actually has a hole in his head! Chan once sought popularity in America (at some point, he had his eyelids enlarged surgically), and Robert Clouse, director of Lee's megahit, *Enter the Dragon*, directed him in *The Big Brawl*, a

Jacky Chan.

lively action-comedy in which he has a blond American girlfriend, Kristine De-Bell. The enjoyable *Jacky Chan's Police Story*, made in Hong Kong, is another good introduction to Chan. Unfortunately, most of his recent self-directed films don't play in the States.

• **Some Key Films:** *Dragon Fist* (1978, Lo Wei), *Eagle's Shadow* (1978, Yuen Woo Ping), *Drunken Master* (1979, Ping), *Fearless Hyena* (1979, Ping), *The Big Brawl* (1980, Robert Clouse), *Project A* (1984, Jacky Chan), *The Protector* (1985, James Glickenhaus), *Jacky Chan's Police Story* (1986, Chan), *Dragons Forever* (1986, Chan), *Armour of God* (1987, Chan), *Project A, Part II* (1987, Chan), *Police Story II* (1988, Chan).

• **Also of Interest:** *New Fist of Fury* (1976, Wei), *Killer Meteor* (1977, Wei), *Magnificent Bodyguard* (1978, Wei), *Spiritual Kung Fu* (1978, Wei), *The Cannonball Run* (1981, Hal Needham), *Winners and Sinners* (1983, Chan), *Painted Faces* (1988, Chan).

○

LON CHANEY (1886–1930) All horror movie fans take pride in "The Man of 1000 Faces," who may have been the silent cinema's greatest dramatic actor yet chose the horror movie in which to exhibit his artistry. Alonso Chaney initially performed pantomime at home, in front of his deaf parents. As he ventured into show business, he began to experiment with makeup, so that when he entered movies, he was able to play several parts in the same film; in one film, one Chaney character kills another Chaney character. Chaney became a major star playing grotesque characters that not only required extensive makeup but called for the actor to distort his body. His menagerie included men who have no arms, have no legs or are crippled; men who have just one eye or are blind or deaf; men whose faces and bodies have been burned or otherwise mutilated or deformed. Some cruel villains, some victims of terrible wrongdoing, these men test the horror axiom: That which looks monstrous acts monstrous. One character who broke the rule is Quasimodo in *The Hunchback of Notre Dame*. The key to Chaney's definitive performance is that his expressions and gestures are subtle, never hammy like the later actors who played the part. Chaney realized that his makeup alone was strong enough to make viewers feel pity. He concentrated on demonstrating that Quasimodo's personality was the opposite of his monstrous exterior, and that this extraordinary figure deserved admiration. Chaney's other unforgettable character was *The Phantom of the Opera*, a victim of torture with a crazed mind and a hideous half-skeletal face that he hides under a mask. Again he absconds with the woman he loves (Mary Philbin) but is too ugly to ever "win." In the earlier film, the hunchback is saddened but resigned to the fact that he'll never have Patsy Ruth Miller; the Phantom goes berserk when he realizes Philbin won't love him. The picture is a first-rate thriller, and Chaney correctly gives a wilder, more audacious portrayal than he did in *Hunchback*. The scene everyone remembers has Philbin unmasking the Phantom as he plays the organ. I love when he points a finger at the horrified woman, directing her to go away—I copy that gesture when I try to send away strange dogs who follow me home. Chaney was excellent in his one sound film, *The Unholy Three*, but died before he could play *Frankenstein* and *Dracula*, making way for the sound horror film's two major stars, Boris Karloff and Bela Lugosi.

• **Cult Favorites:** *The Hunchback of Notre Dame* (1923, Wallace Worsley), *The Phantom of the Opera* (1925, Rupert Julien).

• **Other Key Films:** *Hell Morgan's Girl* (1917, Joseph de Grasse), *The Miracle Man* (1919, George Loane Tucker), *The Penalty* (1920, Worsley), *Shadows* (1922, Tom Forman), *Oliver Twist* (1922, Frank Lloyd), *He Who Gets Slapped* (1924, Victor Seastrom), *The Monster* (1925, Roland West), *The Unholy Three* (1925, Tod Browning), *The Blackbird* (1926, Browning), *Outside the Law* (1926, Browning), *The Road to Mandalay* (1926, Browning), *Mr. Wu* (1927, William Nigh), *The Unknown* (1927, Browning), *London After Midnight* (1927, Browning), *Laugh, Clown, Laugh* (1928, Herbert Brenon), *West of Zanzibar* (1928, Browning), *The Unholy Three* (1930, Jack Conway).

○

LON CHANEY, JR. (1906–73) He began his career using his real name, Creighton, but switched to Lon to cash in on his father's fame. It was a decision he often regretted. It tormented him that he was never considered an artist like his father, taken seriously by critics only once, for his portrayal of the dimwitted Lennie in *Of Mice and Men*; yet all horror fans warmly honor the actor who gave so much to the genre. Though he played Lennie, and assorted monsters (the mummy, Dracula's vampire son, and the Frankenstein monster), starred in Universal's "Inner Sanctum" series, and appeared in numerous westerns, including *High Noon*, he will always be remembered as Lawrence Talbot, wolf man. *The Wolf Man* was a fatalistic film noir merged with a horror film. Those scenes in which Chaney transforms into a werewolf—with the camera trained on his changing face and time-lapse photography employed—are familiar to all horror fans. Talbot was the definitive movie werewolf, a nice guy who suffers because he is cursed to kill everyone who crosses his path, including those he loves (and only those he loves can kill him). As in most of his films, Chaney played a man who could be both gentle and violent, at ease with the world one minute and full of self-pity or rage the next (according to those who knew him, Chaney was exactly the same way). In the original werewolf film, this large, hulking actor was acceptable as a leading man, romancing Evelyn Ankers. He seemed comfortable and gave his most dignified performance. In Chaney's later werewolf films, Talbot's whining about his fate would become annoying. In *The Black Sleep* and *Dracula vs. Frankenstein*, he was anything but dignified. Late in his career he became bloated and his voice became raspy from the throat cancer that eventually killed him in 1973. By that time, he was reduced to cheap horror films and bits in westerns.

• **Cult Favorites:** *The Wolf Man* (1941, George Waggner), *Son of Dracula* (1943, Robert Siodmak), *Cobra Woman* (1944, Siodmak), *Abbot and Costello Meet Frankenstein* (1948, Charles Barton), *Bride of the Gorilla* (1951, Curt Siodmak), *Spider Baby* (1964/1968, Jack Hill).

• **Other Key Films:** *Of Mice and Men* (1939, Lewis Milestone), *One Million B.C.* (1940, Hal Roach and Hal Roach, Jr.), *Man Made Monster* (1941, Waggner), *The Ghost of Frankenstein* (1942, Erle C. Kenton), *The Mummy's Tomb* (1942, Harold Young), *Frankenstein Meets the Wolf Man* (1943, Roy William Neill), *Calling Dr. Death* (1944, Reginald LeBorg,

Late in his career, Lon Chaney, Jr., played in such awful horror films as The Black Sleep, *with Tor Johnson* (left) *and John Carradine* (right).

Weird Woman (1944, LeBorg), *The Mummy's Ghost* (1944, Reginald LeBorg), *Dead Man's Eyes* (1944, LeBorg), *House of Frankenstein* (1945, Kenton), *The Mummy's Curse* (1945, Leslie Goodwins), *House of Dracula* (1945, Kenton), *High Noon* (1952, Fred Zinnemann), *Indian Fighter* (1955, André de Toth), *The Haunted Palace* (1963, Roger Corman).

○

GERALDINE CHAPLIN (1944–) The dark-haired, wispily attractive daughter of Charles Chaplin started out burdened with her father's name but no apparent traces of his film presence or talent; no one thought she'd have success in movies. She has played dramatic leads in Europe, most notably in several Spanish films by Carlos Saura, and the French film *Voyage en Douce*, in which she and traveling companion Dominique Sanda exchange erotic memories and sensual glances. In England and America, she has appeared mostly in ambitious comedies with large ensembles and interweaving stories. She displayed a talent for quirky comedy for Robert Altman, playing a silly British entertainment reporter in *Nashville* and Annie Oakley in *Buffalo Bill and the Indians*, and since then has been a zany presence in some of the

Geraldine Chaplin in Nashville *with Scott Glenn*

unusual films of Altman protégé, Alan Rudolph. In *Welcome to L.A.*, her unhappily married woman is the picture's most interesting character: she's a weirdo with a Camille complex who spends her days in taxis and answers phone calls in the hope that they're wrong numbers. In *Remember My Name*, her ex-con tries to sabotage her ex-husband's life. It was a rare lead in America, and she was impressive. She's to be admired for plugging away until she developed her talents and could carve a comfortable niche for herself. She's had a very respectable career.

• **Cult Favorites:** *The Three Musketeers* (1974, Richard Lester), *Nashville* (1975, Robert Altman), *Buffalo Bill and the Indians* (1976, Altman), *Roseland* (1977, James Ivory), *Welcome to L.A.* (1977, Alan Rudolph, *Remember My Name* (1978, Rudolph), *Voyage en Douce* (1979, Michel Deville), *The Moderns* (1988, Rudolph).

• **Sleeper:** *Cria!* (1976, Carlos Saura).
• **Other Key Films:** *Doctor Zhivago* (1965, David Lean), *Honeycomb* (1969, Saura), *The Hawaiians* (1970, Tom Gries), *Innocent Bystanders* (1972, Peter Collinson), *House Without Boundaries* (1972, Pedro Olea), *The Four Musketeers* (1975, Lester) *Elisa My Love* (1977, Saura), *A Wedding* (1978, Altman), *Bolero* (1981, Claude Lelouch), *Mama Turns 100* (1988, Saura), *White Mischief* (1988, Michael Radford).

○

CYD CHARISSE (1921–) Long-legged, dark-haired, sexy M-G-M dance star, screen partner to Gene Kelly and Fred Astaire, dream dance partner of many male moviegoers, idol of many female fans. I have always found her intimidating: she's all woman without the soft girlish look, fun attitude, or pleasant humor of Ginger Rogers, Debbie Reynolds, Vera-Ellen, Leslie Caron, or Judy Garland. She is elegant and when wrapping a leg around her dance partner and slithering to the floor, she is breathtakingly beautiful. Her dreamlike ballet with Gene Kelly in *Singin' in the Rain* is marvelous. However, I wish she showed some spunk or vulnerability on occasion. In fact, when she wasn't dancing she wasn't very appealing. *The Band Wagon* contains her most memorable staring role (and spectacular choreography) but her character isn't particularly charming—where Ginger Rogers could win us over while thwarting Astaire's romantic advances, Charisse puts us off doing the same. When she stopped dancing and began acting, the excitement disappeared.

- **Cult Favorites:** *Singin' in the Rain* (1951, Gene Kelly and Stanley Donen), *The Band Wagon* (1953, Vincente Minnelli).
- **Other Key Films:** *The Unfinished Dance* (1947, Henry Koster), *Brigadoon* (1954, Minnelli), *It's Always Fair Weather* (1955, Kelly and Donen), *Silk Stockings* (1957, Rouben Mamoulian), *Party Girl* (1958, Nicholas Ray), *Two Weeks in Another Town* (1958, Minnelli), *Un Deux Trois Quatre* (1960, Terence Young).

○

CHEECH AND CHONG Richard "Cheech" Marin, a Mexican-American with sleepy eyes and a droopy mustache, and Tommy Chong, a tall, part-Chinese, part-French, part-Irish Canadian with a thick beard, wire-rim glasses, and a bandanna, were a

Cheech Marin (right) *and Tommy Chong in* Up in Smoke.

popular L.A. comic rock duo before making their first, and by far their best, film, *Up in Smoke*. They still emphasized scatological, sexual, and drug-related humor—but they managed to make it funny, at least in their debut. Cheech and Chong played amiable bozos, harmless affronts to society. They're filthy, lazy, and stoned out of their minds. Chong is oblivious to everything. He's either getting high, passing out, throwing up, talking incoherently, or getting Cheech in trouble. Cheech is more emotional than his partner and just clear-headed enough to worry. Unlike Chong, he is woman-crazy and a nonstop talker. Invariably, his conversation is about sexy females, scoring dope, and his privates. Cheech is the funnier of the two and ideally Chong should be his straight man, but it was decided that they should both be comic figures so there could be humor when only one is on the screen. Their films went downhill after their debut—although they did a guest shot in *After Hours*—and eventually Cheech went off on his own. Chong is the father of actress Rae Dawn Chong.

• **Cult Favorites:** *Up in Smoke* (1978, Lou Adler), *Cheech and Chong's Next Movie* (1980, Thomas Chong), *Cheech and Chong's Nice Dreams* (1981, Chong), *After Hours* (1985, Martin Scorsese).

• **Also of Interest:** *Things Are Tough All Over* (1982, Tom Avildsen), *Still Smokin'* (1983, Chong), *Yellowbeard* (1983, Mel Damski), *The Corsican Brothers* (1984, Chong).

See: Richard "Cheech" Marin.

○

DAVID CHIANG (1947–) One of the most popular of Chinese martial-arts stars preceding Bruce Lee, although he never became known in America. Beginning in the late sixties he was teamed with Ti Lung, another former stuntman, in a series of violent gangster and sword-wielding costume dramas for the Shaw Brothers, tales of betrayal and retribution. Although short and slightly built, Chiang was athletic and handsome, with intense eyes that revealed his characters' determination to carry out vengeance, no matter the risks and who must be killed. Typically, he and Lung would exchange roles from film to film, with one playing the hero and the other playing a misunderstood, mistrusted mystery man who proves himself to be noble when the fighting starts. Or they would be friends or brothers. On occasion, they would avenge each other's deaths, at the cost of their own lives. The fight sequences were quite elaborate, with numerous villains falling to Chiang's death blows. His most memorable role is probably Lei Lei, in *The New One-Armed Swordsman*, in which he singlehandedly invades a fortress and wipes out the army that killed Lung. In 1973, he appeared in his best-distributed picture, a collaboration between the Shaws and Hammer that was the British studio's last Dracula film, *Legend of the Seven Golden Vampires*, using his martial arts skills to help Peter Cushing's Van Helsing on a vampire hunt in China. Chiang, Lung, and their usual director Chang Cheh went off on their own to make socially relevant action films, with Chiang and Lung cast as shrewd conmen. They also joined forces for the popular *Five Masters of Death*. Chiang would often brandish a steel whip.

• **Cult Favorites:** *Vengeance* (1970, Chang Cheh), *The New One-Armed Swordsman* (1970, Cheh), *Legend of the Seven Golden*

Vampires/The Seven Brothers Meet Dracula (1973, Roy Ward Baker), *Five Masters of Death* (1975, Cheh).

• **Other Key Films:** *Dead End* (1968, Cheh), *The Duel* (1969, Cheh) *Have Sword, Will Travel* (1969, Cheh), *The Heroic Ones* (1970, Cheh), *The Boxer from Shantung* (1971, Cheh), *Deadly Duo* (1971, Cheh), *Duel of the Iron Fist* (1971, Cheh), *The Pirate* (1972, Cheh), *Blood Brothers* (1972, Cheh), *The Savage Five* (1979), *Dragon Devil Die* (Pao Hseuh), *The Last Kungfu Secret*, *Six-Direction Boxing*, *A Slice of Death*.

○

SONNY CHIBA (1939–) Solidly built Japanese karate-film star, with thick hair and eyebrows, and dark, sunken eyes. Shinichi Chiba has been criticized by genre fans for having no grace—only brute force—when fighting. He starred in two Yakuza gangster series, "Gambler Cop" and "Lone Wolf Gambler," but is best known for his exceedingly brutal "Streetfighter" series, from which he got his nickname. The original entry, *The Streetfighter*, in which he breaks open a skull with one blow, was the first film to receive an X-rating for violence rather than nudity/sex. Chiba played the vicious fist-for-hire Terry Surugy, who litters the streets with ripped-up bodies. The four authors of *From Bruce Lee to the Ninjas* wrote: "Terry Surugy was an animal, and not a tame one. Surugy's face would contort, incomprehensible cries, grunts, and groans would burble out of his mouth, and then he would tear something off . . . He went for the jugular every time. And if he couldn't get that, he'd shoot for a less polite target." Oddly, his short, pudgy, much older mentor,

Sonny Chiba.

Masafumi Suzuki, is the only man who can beat him in a fight (theirs together are comical scenes). At his most respectable, Chiba top-lined an all-star international cast in the expensive Japanese doomsday film, *Virus*.

• **Cult Favorites:** *The Streetfighter* (1975, S. Ozawa), *Return of the Streetfighter* (1976), *Virus* (1980, Kenji Fukasaki).

• **Some Other Key Films:** *The Bodyguard* (1970), *The Streetfighter's Last Revenge* (1977), *Champion of Death* (1978), *Sister Streetfighter* (1978), *Sonny Chiba's Dragon Princess* (1980), *Legend of the Eight Samurai* (1984, Haruki Kaduwara).

○

RAE DAWN CHONG (1961–) This pretty, sexy, curly-haired Canadian-born actress's mother is half-black and half-Indian, and her father, comic-actor-director-musician Tommy Chong, is part Chinese, part French, and part Irish. Sometimes, she plays a black—as in *The Color Purple* and *Soul Man*—but more often there is no reference to her race. Most of her screen lovers have been white—but one must take into account that few black actors are offered leads. In *Choose Me,* she was well cast as a funny, sexually frustrated flake who sleeps with stranger Keith Carradine although her brutal husband will be coming home soon. I wish she'd play more quirky women. More often she is the loyal, moral friend or lover of the lead male character, providing good companionship, steering him on the right path when he wavers, helping him out when in trouble, and remaining upbeat and strong when he needs just that. She also stimulates him sexually, as her young women are free with their bodies. She was surprisingly well matched with Arnold Schwarzenegger (they're both funny and physical) in the action film *Commando*. She was Mick Jagger's lover in the erotic "Just Another Night" video. She also hosted a controversial "safe sex" video directed at teenagers, chosen because a survey showed an inordinate number of young people knew her and liked her.

• **Cult Favorites:** *Quest for Fire* (1981, Jean-Jacques Annaud), *Choose Me* (1984, Alan Rudolph).

• **Also of Interest:** *Fear City* (1984, Abel Ferrara), *Beat Street* (1984, Stan Latham), *The Color Purple* (1985, Steven Spielberg), *American Flyers* (1985, John Badham), *Commando* (1985, Mark L. Lester),

Soul Man (1986, Steven Miner), *The Principal* (1987, Christopher Cain).

○

JULIE CHRISTIE (1941–) Classy, intelligent, beautiful British actress with long blond hair, blue eyes, and a "look" that females throughout the world, including covergirls and fashion models, have imitated. Her portrayal of an ambitious, amoral model who becomes a bored princess in *Darling*—who can forget her happy disbelief when she won the Best Actress Oscar?—and Lara in *Doctor Zhivago* catapulted the unknown to superstardom. She was adored by the masses, but from the beginning approving film cultists realized that she was different, that she hadn't forgotten her bohemian roots and her preference for art over commercialism. She soon starred in the big-budget romance *Far From the Madding Crowd*, but otherwise chose unusual projects that weren't guaranteed to be box-office successes. Stardom wasn't as important to her as working with directors who were willing to take chances: Truffaut, Lester, Losey, Altman, Roeg. She never sold out. The most romantic of actresses, she also is excitingly lusty—she is truly erotic in such films as *Petulia*, *Don't Look Now* (in which she has a famous nude lovemaking scene with Donald Sutherland), *Shampoo*, and even the deliberately sterile *Demon Seed*, in which she is, literally, raped by a computer. Christie is also funny and, when necessary, appealingly wacky. She always has played women who are passionate, yet, as the men who fall for her discover, unreachable—or at least difficult to hold on to. Her women are defiantly independent and strong, but not as independent and strong as they want to be. In *McCabe*

Julie Christie in Darling.

and Mrs. Miller, her shrewd, ambitious businesswoman-madam must resort to opium when things get really tough and the man she loves (played by her onetime lover Warren Beatty) is in danger. Too often their strength vanishes when excited by handsome suitors. Too often they fall for the wrong men, like the cold Terence Stamp in *Far From the Madding Crowd* and the brutal Richard Chamberlain in *Petulia*. Her kooky Petulia is a symbol of the shaky sixties: miniskirted on wobby legs. Christie stays away from Hollywood, so it's always a treat when one of her films sneaks into the States.

• **Cult Favorites:** *Fahrenheit 451* (1966, François Truffaut), *Petulia* (1968, Richard Lester), *McCabe and Mrs. Miller* (1971, Robert Altman), *Don't Look Now* (1973, Nicolas Roeg), *Nashville* (1975, Altman), *Demon Seed* (1977, Donal Cammell).

• **Other Key Films:** *Billy Liar* (1963, John Schlesinger), *Young Cassidy* (1965, Jack Cardiff), *Darling* (1965, Schlesinger), *Doctor Zhivago* (1965, David Lean), *Far from the Madding Crowd* (1967, Schlesinger), *The Go-Between* (1971, Losey), *Shampoo* (1975, Hal Ashby), *Heaven Can Wait* (1978, Warren Beatty and Buck Henry), *The Return of the Soldier* (1981, Alan Bridges), *Heat and Dust* (1983, James Ivory), *Miss Mary* (1986, Maria Luisa Bemberg), *Fools of Fortune* (1990, Pat O'Connor).

○

CANDY CLARK (1949–) Cute, good-humored, energetic young brunette from Oklahoma (her accent has southern traces) who played several offbeat women in the seventies but, unfortunately, has been relegated to minor roles ever since. Her women are chatty, animated, sexually available, and fun to be with because they want themselves and their men to have good times. She had played the girlfriend of Jeff Bridges's young boxer in *Fat City*, but first attracted attention in *American Graffiti* as the wild blond teenager whom the uncool Charles Martin Smith charms into his car by saying she resembles Connie Stevens. From that Oscar-nominated supporting role, she moved into leads, including the hotel maid who takes care of ailing alien David Bowie (at one point she carries him) and becomes his lover-companion in *The Man Who Fell to Earth*; and Paul LeMat's disenchanted girlfriend in *Handle with Care*. Her choice of men could have been better; she rarely had a relationship that made sense or worked out, which is why her women were frequently exasperated.

• **Cult Favorites:** *American Graffiti* (1973, George Lucas), *The Man Who Fell to Earth* (1976, Nicolas Roeg), *Handle with Care/Citizen's Band* (1977, Jonathan Demme), *Q* (1982, Larry Cohen).

• **Sleeper:** *Fat City* (1972, John Huston).

• **Also of Interest:** *The Big Sleep* (1978, Michael Winner), *More American Graffiti* (1979, B. W. L. Norton), *Blue Thunder* (1983, John Badham), *Cat's Eye* (1985, Lewis Teague).

○

SUSAN CLARK (1940–) This Canadian actress was the female lead in a number of genre films beginning in the late sixties, displaying a winning combination of poise, intelligence, and mature sex appeal. She was particularly classy as mayor Henry Fonda's mistress in *Madigan*. As a con-woman in *Skin Game*, she first revealed her comedic skills; when her movie career sputtered she would use them on the TV series "Webster," costarring her husband Alex Karras. Her women used to be interesting, but that hasn't been the case in recent yeas. She was definitely wasted as the prostitute in the silly *Porky's*. She deservedly won an Emmy as superathlete Babe Didrickson in the TV movie *Babe*; for the role, she even learned to be a hurdler.

• **Cult Favorites:** *Madigan* (1968, Don Siegel), *Coogan's Bluff* (1968, Siegel), *Colossus: The Forbin Project* (1970, Joseph Sargent), *Night Moves* (1975, Arthur Penn), *Porky's* (1981, Bob Clark).

• **Also of Interest:** *Banning* (1967, Ron Winston), *Tell Them Willie Boy Is Here* (1969, Abraham Polonsky), *Valdez Is Coming* (1971, Edwin Sherin), *Skin Game* (1971, Paul Bogart), *Showdown* (1973, George Seaton), *Midnight Man* (1974, Roland Kibbee), *The Apple Dumpling Gang* (1975, Norman Tokar), *The North Avenue Irregulars* (1979, Bruce Bilson), *Murder By Decree* (1979, Clark).

Susan Clark in Coogan's Bluff *with Clint Eastwood.*

MAE CLARKE (1910–66) Spirited blond actress was impressive in several early thirties films, including *The Front Page*, as Molly Malloy; *Frankenstein*, as Colin Clive's endangered fiancée; and *Waterloo Bridge*, as the ballerina who becomes a prostitute but she's best remembered for a smaller role—as the moll who gets a grapefruit pushed into her kisser by gangster James Cagney in *The Public Enemy*. She'd appear with Cagney in other films as well, most notably *Lady Killer*. She was a reliable actress who would have a long career, yet she never fulfilled her early promise.

• **Key Films:** *The Front Page* (1931, Lewis Milestone), *The Public Enemy* (1931, William A. Wellman), *Waterloo Bridge* (1931, James Whale), *Frankenstein* (1931, Whale).

• **Also of Interest:** *Three Wise Girls* (1931, William Beaudine), *Penthouse* (1933, W. S. Van Dyke, *Lady Killer* (1933, Roy Del Ruth), *Nana* (1934, Dorothy Arzner), *The Great Guy* (1936, John G. Blystone).

○

JOHN CLEESE (1939–) The tallest, most aggressive member of Britain's Monty Python comedy troupe and, if not the funniest (which I think he was), he had the easiest time making us laugh. He could do this simply by acting aggravated or pompous, or by complaining or giving orders, or by doing any physical comedy—it is hilarious when his humorless, formidable, uppercrust Englishmen exhibit a silly walk or, in *Monty Python's The Meaning of Life*, strip and wearily demonstrate sex for his students. He was as obstinate and argumentative as the others, but because he was bigger than they, he seemed pettier when he whined or was bossy. He was never one to listen—in *Monty Python and*

the Holy Grail, his Sir Lancelot charges into a castle and wipes out almost everyone at a wedding before realizing he has made a mistake and apologizing: "I just get carried away." Of the Python members, he has had the most solo success. *A Fish Called Wanda*, in which his repressed barrister gets mixed up with some zany criminals, was an enormous hit. His evil western lawman in *Silverado* may be his most unexpected and interesting characterization. He wrote and starred in the cult British TV series "Fawlty Towers."

• **Cult Favorites:** *And Now for Something Completely Different* (1972, Ian McNaughton), *Monty Python and the Holy Grail* (1974, Terry Gilliam and Terry Jones), *Life of Brian* (1979, Jones), *Time Bandits* (1981, Gilliam), *Monty Python's The Meaning of Life* (1983, Jones), *Silverado* (1985, Lawrence Kasdan).

• **Other Key Films:** *The Secret Policemen's Other Ball* (1982, Julien Temple and Roger Graef), *Monty Python Live at the Hollywood Bowl* (1982, Terry Hughes), *Privates on Parade* (1983, Michael Blakemore), *Clockwise* (1987, Christopher Morahan), *A Fish Called Wanda* (1987, Charles Crichton), *Erik the Viking* (1989, Jones).

See: Monty Python.

○

MONTGOMERY CLIFT (1920–66) He broke into movies in 1948, playing a G.I. who cares for a young concentration camp survivor in *The Search* and a nonviolent cowboy who stands up to his tyrant guardian, John Wayne, in *Red River*. He was an immediate sensation. Audiences were taken with this handsome—some say "beautiful"—actor with intense, deeply set eyes, who gave sensitive, deeply introspective performances. His acting was so cerebral that

Six years after A Place in the Sun, *Montgomery Clift was reunited with Elizabeth Taylor in* Raintree County.

another actor would comment: "Monty was the first movie star who seemed obsessed—slightly nuts." Like other actors, he played soldiers, boxers (his soldier in *From Here to Eternity*), and cowboys, only his were nonviolent and vulnerable (but by no means cowardly). He paved the way for Marlon Brando and James Dean with his intellectually conceived characterizations and his ability to make his characters' actions seem natural rather than calculated. However, I do think his performance in *A Place in the Sun* is mannered—rather than intellectual and attractive, his confused young man (in love with rich, beautiful, virginal Elizabeth Taylor but stuck with poor, dumpy, pregnant Shelley Winters) has the expression and stance of someone who is one step away from the psycho ward. Although I admire Clift's work in other films, I always find him an unsettling presence: that his characters seem uncomfortable in their particular lives is probably due to his own discomfort playing such men. They might have had problems similar to his own (they must fight for their individuality and their manhood) but the characters were too unlike him (a cowboy? a career soldier? a lonely hearts columnist?). The exceptions were his priest in *I Confess* and his non-conformist, Jewish soldier in *The Young Lions*, his favorite role. As his biographer Patricia Bosworth points out, he was best at portraying "a man with ethical standards so high he judges himself as harshly as he judges his enemies." Because of his erotically charged scenes with Elizabeth Taylor in *A Place in the Sun*, Clift was regarded as a romantic lead; as he was a homosexual, this must have added to his discomfort. His on-screen lover image would disappear when a car crash in 1955 paralyzed the left side of his face and deformed his lip. But his performances stayed at high caliber because he learned to act more with his eyes, and as Bosworth notes, "he went about perfecting his gift for stillness—his technique for projecting a power deep within himself. In *The Young Lions* . . . some of Monty's best scenes are done entirely in pantomime." After the accident, Clift gave one of his best performances in *Wild River*, as a TVA worker trying to con an old lady into selling her property. That we sense his new insecurity gives added dimension to the role. Clift died of a heart attack at 45.

• **Cult Favorites:** *Red River* (1948, Howard Hawks), *A Place in the Sun* (1951, George Stevens), *Wild River* (1960, Elia Kazan), *The Misfits* (1961, John Huston).

• **Other Key Films:** *The Search* (1948, Fred Zinnemann), *The Heiress* (1949, William Wyler), *I Confess* (1953, Alfred Hitchcock), *From Here to Eternity* (1953, Zinnemann, *Raintree County* (1957, Edward Dmytryk), *The Young Lions* (1958, Dmytryk), *Lonelyhearts* (1958, Vincent J. Donehue), *Suddenly, Last Summer* (1959, Joseph L. Mankiewicz), *Judgment at Nuremberg* (1961, Stanley Kramer) *Freud* (1962, Huston).

○

COLIN CLIVE (1898–1937) This British actor had only a brief career before his untimely death at the age of 39, but he had several memorable roles, especially Dr. Frankenstein in *Frankenstein* and *Bride of Frankenstein*. He was tall and had a slim, angular face that James Whale shot effectively with many wild camera angles during the lightning-creation sequence in *Bride*. His doctor in *Frankenstein* is the model for future cinema scientists who venture into God's dominion. But most horror fans don't realize that his sin was not playing God by creating a monster—the theme of many subsequent horror films—but acting like a god toward that monster. He was erudite and tormented as the doctor in both films, as he would be in many of his roles. In *Mad Love/The Hands of Orlac*, for instance, as a pianist whose severed hands are replaced by those of a dead murderer, he frets that he is responsible for a recent string of strangulations. As *Christopher Strong*, he broods about his fragile marriage to freedom-seeking aviatrix Katharine Hepburn. A fine actor, though perhaps an unappealing romantic lead, he never got his just recognition.

• **Cult Favorites:** *Bride of Frankenstein* (1935, James Whale), *Mad Love/The Hands of Orlac* (1935, Karl Freund).

• **Other Key Films:** *Journey's End* (1930, Whale), *Frankenstein* (1931, Whale), *Christopher Strong* (1933, Dorothy Arzner).

• **Also of Interest:** *The Key* (1934, Michael Curtiz), *One More River* (1934, Whale), *Jane Eyre* (1934, Christy Cabanne), *History Is Made at Night* (1937, Frank Borzage).

ROBERTA COLLINS Vivacious blonde was one of the stars of Roger Corman's formula-setting R-rated women-in-prison films, the enjoyable *The Big Doll House* and the inferior *Women in Cages*. These pictures satisfied anyone wanting to see female breasts, female suffering, female wrestling, female bonding, and female uprisings. She continued to play important roles in future exploitation films at New World. She was my favorite: she was pretty, supersexy, bursting with energy, funny. She didn't even care if she looked bad; she was willing to wrestle another woman in a mud puddle, or draw a mustache on her face and wear baggy men's clothes for a comedy routine in a prison variety show in *Caged Heat*. But she always looked good, whether doing that off-the-wall comedy bit, racing fast cars, or leaping onto a table and firing a machine gun. I'm still waiting for her to be discovered.

• **Cult Favorites:** *The Big Doll House* (1971, Jack Hill), *Women in Cages* (1972, Gerry De Leon), *Unholy Rollers* (1972, Vernon Zimmerman), *Caged Heat* (1974, Jonathan Demme), *Death Race 2000* (1975, Paul Bartel).

• **Sleeper:** *The Arousers* (1972, Curtis Hansen).

Roberta Collins right *and Judy Brown are exciting action heroines in* The Big Doll House.

JENNIFER CONNELLY (1970–) This appealing, dark-haired young beauty was noticed among the stars in *Once Upon a Time in America*, though she had only limited screen time playing Elizabeth McGovern's character as a pre-teen. She was composed and already beautiful and sexy (which is why a young boy—who will grow into Robert De Niro's gangster—spies on her while she undresses). This role won her leads in Dario Argento's disappointing horror film *Creepers*, Jim Henson's fantasy *Labyrinth*, in which she's threatened by evil David Bowie (who thought she looked like the teenage Elizabeth Taylor), and, better, the novel teen comedy *Seven Minutes in Heaven*. Growing into adulthood in the offbeat comedy *Some Girls*, she was the enigmatic girl from a family of eccentrics who suddenly is unresponsive to boyfriend Patrick Dempsey. So far, Connelly's popularity abroad is much greater than in America, but few doubt that as she moves into her twenties, she'll have a shot at stardom.

• **Cult Favorites:** *Once Upon a Time in America* (1984, Sergio Leone), *Creepers* (1985, Dario Argento).

• **Sleeper:** *Some Girls* (1988, Michael Hoffman).

• **Other Key Films:** *Labyrinth* (1986, Jim Henson), *Seven Minutes in Heaven* (1986, Linda Feferman), *The Hot Spot* (1990, Dennis Hopper), *Career Opportunities* (1991, Bryan Gordon), *The Rocketeer* (1991, Joe Johnston).

SEAN CONNERY (1930–) The handsome, dark-haired former lifeguard and bodybuilder (he represented Scotland in a "Mr. Universe" contest) began making films in 1956. In the next six years, he was unable to escape anonymity, though he was the romantic lead in Disney's *Darby O'Gill and the Little People* and a villain who drowns in quicksand in the enjoyable *Tarzan's Greatest Adventure*. Then, with his Scottish burr, he took on Ian Fleming's English spy James Bond in the low-budget *Dr. No*. His dashing, debonaire Agent 007 had a license to kill; knew judo; was a well-educated gentleman; had great taste in clothes, cars, and liquor (he wanted his martinis "shaken, not stirred"); traveled to exotic locations; met only beautiful women (including Ursula Andress's Honeychile Ryder), whom he made love to even if they worked for the other side; could take on villains; didn't panic when the fate of the world rested on his shoulders; and had irresistible charm and a clever sense of humor. The movie was an unexpected smash, initiating a James Bond craze and making Connery an international superstar and sex symbol. He again played Bond in *From Russia with Love*, giving his most realistic portrayal of the spy; in the spectacular (though now dated) *Goldfinger*; and in the lesser *Thunderball*, *You Only Live Twice*, and *Diamonds Are Forever*. Bond fans soon recognized that Connery was a genuine talent, but he quit the series to show the world his versatility. At 53, he'd return to the role in *Never Say Never Again*, confirming that no one could play the part with more gusto and style. Outside of his Bond roles, Connery has invariably given good performances but too often has starred in ponderous, overblown productions, like *Zardoz*, *Highlander*, *Time Bandits*, and *The Name of the Rose*. The exceptions are the fascinating *Marnie*, as a man who is aroused by a frigid thief (Tippi

Hedren); *The Hill*, as a military prisoner who stands up to the sadistic authorities; *A Fine Madness*, as a volatile poet; the glorious *The Man Who Would Be King*, as a British adventurer who poses as a god to dupe natives in a remote area of Afghanistan; *Robin and Marian*, as an aged Robin Hood; *The Untouchables*, as a beat cop (for which he won his only Oscar); and *Indiana Jones and the Last Crusade*, as Indy's father. Connery, now regarded as a living legend, has aged gracefully (there's no need to wear a wig) and is still a commanding presence. On screen, his characters usually give younger men the benefit of their experiences.

• **Cult Favorites:** *Tarzan's Greatest Adven-*

ture (1959, John Guillermin), *The Longest Day* (1962, Ken Annakin, Andrew Marton, and Bernhard Wicki), *Dr. No* (1962, Terence Young), *From Russia with Love* (1964, Young), *Marnie* (1964, Alfred Hitchcock), *Goldfinger* (1964, Guy Hamilton), *Zardoz* (1974, John Boorman), *The Man Who Would Be King* (1975, John Huston), *Time Bandits* (1981, Terry Gilliam).

• **Sleepers:** *The Hill* (1965, Sidney Lumet), *A Fine Madness* (1966, Irvin Kershner), *The Molly Maguires* (1970, Martin Ritt), *Robin and Marian* (1976, Richard Lester), *Cuba* (1979, Lester).

• **Other Key Films:** *Thunderball* (1965, Young), *You Only Live Twice* (1967, Lewis Gilbert), *The Anderson Tapes* (1971, Lu-

Sean Connery as James Bond.

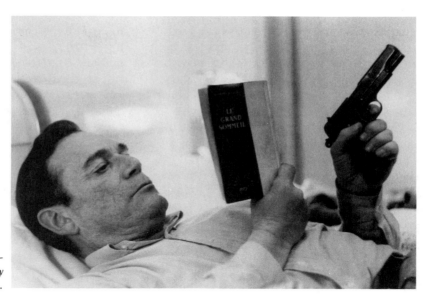

Eddie Constantine is unusual detective Lemmy Caution in Alphaville.

met), *The Great Train Robbery* (1978, Michael Crichton), *Never Say Never Again* (1983, Kershner), *The Untouchables* (1987, Brian De Palma), *Indiana Jones and the Last Crusade* (1989, Steven Spielberg), *The Hunt for Red October* (1990, John McTiernan).

○

CAROL CONNORS Porno actress first noticed as Harry Reems's loopy nurse in *Deep Throat*, but she is better known as the annoying title character in the comedic *The Erotic Adventures of Candy* and *Candy Goes to Hollywood*. In the original, her sweet virgin learns the ins and outs of sex, and in the sequel, her dumb buxom blonde joyously has sex encounters in an attempt to make it in show biz. Candy's one of porno films' too many innocent but uninhibited females who can be talked into bed by anyone. She was more serious but no more impressive as an actress in later films. In *Desire for Men*, which she directed for the Mitchell Brothers, she has

an intense sex scene with one-legged Long Jeanne Silver.

- **Cult Favorites:** *Deep Throat* (1972, Gerard Damiano), *The Erotic Adventures of Candy* (1978, Gail Palmer).
- **Other Key Films:** *Candy Goes to Hollywood* (1979, Palmer), *Sweet Savage* (1979, Anne Perry), *Desire for Men* (1981, Carol Connors).

○

EDDIE CONSTANTINE (1917–) Born in America to Russian parents, he had success singing in France (he was friends with Edith Piaf) before he stuck a gun in his left fist, put on a trench coat, turned up his collar, pulled a hat down over his unanimated, unfriendly face, and became famous there as Peter Cheyney's tough American private eye, Lemmy Caution, in a series of mystery thrillers. He seemed like a cross between Mickey Spillane and Lionel Stander. Jean-Luc Godard cast him against type (though he is billed as himself) in an episode of *Les Sept Péchés Capitaux*, playing a man so lazy that he rejects a beautiful woman's advances because he doesn't want to dress again after making love. "I could do it with Constantine," said Godard, "because he's a solid block, a block of intelligence and precision, but a block just the same." Godard had Constantine play Lemmy Caution in *Alphaville*, a strange concoction of comic books, B detective movies, James Bond, science fiction, and political satire. The picture has the novel twist of having a two-fisted tough guy teaching a sensual female (Anna Karina) the meaning of "love." It is the film for which he is best known in America. However, he had a good bit in the British gangster film *The Long Good Friday*, playing dueling tough guys with Bob Hoskins.

• **Cult Favorite:** *Alphaville* (1965, Jean-Luc Godard).

• **Also of Interest:** *S.O.S. Pacific* (1960, Guy Green), *Lemmy pour les Dames* (1961), *Cleo from 5 to 7* (1962, Agnes Varda), *Hail Mafia* (1965, Raoul Levy), *Attack of the Robots* (1967, Jess Franco), *Malatesta* (1970, Peter Lilienthal), *Beware of a Holy Whore* (1971, Rainer Werner Fassbinder), *Lions Love* (1969, Varda), *It Lives Again* (1978, Larry Cohen), *The Third Generation* (1979, Fassbinder), *The Long Good Friday* (1980, John Mackenzie), *Panic Times* (1980, Udo Lindenberg), *Freak Orlando* (1981, Ulrike Ottinger), *Red Love* (1981, Rosa von Praunheim).

○

ELISHA COOK, JR. (1902–). One of the most familiar character actors, and one whose quirky presence always is welcome. He was short and small and played characters who are well aware they are short and small. Braggarts, they try to bluff strength in order to be part of a man's world, when in fact they are weak and frightened; the nervous edges to their voices and manners reveal their insecurity. In *The Maltese Falcon*, as Wilbur, Sydney Greenstreet's gunsel, Cook formed his image by acting cocky and talking tough (Bogart was *not* intimidated), and wearing a coat that was much too big; in *The Killing*, he was out of his league participating in a racetrack theft, trying to prove himself man enough for greedy wife Marie Windsor; in *Shane*, he tried to impress his rancher friends by foolishly standing up to villainous gunfighter Jack Palance. He was invariably a loser: in *Falcon*, he was the "fall guy" sacrificed to the police; in *The Killing*, he was victim of an ambush; in *Shane*, he was shot down in a mud puddle; and he has memorable death scenes in *The Big Sleep* and *Phantom Lady*. Even when not a victim or in a major role, his characters (the most worrisome of the visitors to the *House on Haunted Hill*, the humorless realtor in *Rosemary's Baby*, the carnival worker in *Carny*, etc.) are odd enough, perverse enough, to be memorable. His characters—whose eyes grow, faces show grave concern, and voices get high and desperate—always make problems seem larger than they are and their own importance in rectifying them far, far greater.

• **Cult Favorites:** *The Maltese Falcon* (1940, John Huston), *Phantom Lady* (1944, Robert Siodmak), *The Big Sleep* (1946, Howard Hawks), *Shane* (1953, George Stevens), *The Killing* (1956, Stanley Kubrick), *House on Haunted Hill* (1958, William Castle), *Platinum High School* (1960, Charles Haas), *One-Eyed Jacks* (1961, Marlon Brando), *Rosemary's Baby* (1968, Roman Polanski), *Blacula* (1972, William Crain), *Electra Glide in Blue*

Trying to act like a big man, Elisha Cook, Jr., points his gun at Humphrey Bogart in The Maltese Falcon, *as Sydney Greenstreet and Mary Astor look on.*

(1973, James William Guerico), *Carny* (1980, Robert Kaylor), *Hammett* (1983, Wim Wenders).

• **Sleepers:** *Stranger on the Third Floor* (1940, Boris Ingster), *I Wake Up Screaming* (1941, H. Bruce Humberstone), *Dark Waters* (1944, André de Toth), *Dillinger* (1944, Max Nosseck), *Plunder Road* (1957, Hubert Cornfield).

• **Also of Interest:** *They Won't Forget* (1937, Mervyn LeRoy), *Don't Bother to Knock* (1952, Roy Ward Baker), *I, the Jury* (1953, Harry Essex), *Chicago Confidential* (1957, Sidney Salkow), *The Haunted Palace* (1963, Roger Corman), *The Outfit* (1974, John Flynn), *Tom Horn* (1980, William Wiard).

○

MARA CORDAY (1932–) A Universal contract player in the fifties, she was given supporting roles in minor westerns (typically playing fiery dancehall girls or Indian squaws) before getting her first lead in *The Man*

from Bitter Ridge. Director Jack Arnold then cast the dark-haired beauty (she'd be a *Playboy* Playmate in 1958) as the heroine in his popular science-fiction film *Tarantula*, which led to her getting parts in two inferior flicks, *The Black Scorpion* and *The Giant Claw*. It is for those three giant-monster films that Corday is remembered with affection. But it's also fun to watch her wield a knife as one of an all-female robbery team in *Girls on the Loose*. Corday didn't have much of a career—her leading men (Lex Barker, Jon Agar, Richard Denning, Rory Calhoun) were unexciting, and her characters were uninteresting—yet she was likable because she never acted too good for her parts. She was content playing a sheepherder or a prim and proper scientist (hair up, makeup in place, and body hidden under white lab coat). She seemed to realize that her talent matched the ordinary quality of her films.

• **Cult Favorite:** *Tarantula* (1955, Jack Arnold).

Mara Corday.

- **Other Key Films:** *The Black Scorpion* (1957, Edward Ludwig), *The Giant Claw* (1957, Fred F. Sears).
- **Also of Interest:** *The Black Castle* (1952, Nathan Juran), *Dawn at Socorro* (1954, George Sherman), *Drums Across the River* (1954, Juran), *Man Without a Star* (1955, King Vidor), *The Man from Bitter Ridge* (1955, Jack Arnold), *Foxfire* (1955, Joseph Pevney), *So This Is Paris* (1955, Richard Quine), *The Day of Fury* (1956, Harmon Jones), *Raw Edge* (1956, John Sherwood), *Girls on the Loose* (1958, Paul Henreid).

○

RAY "CRASH" CORRIGAN (1907–76). Tall, strong former stuntman and action-serial star joined Bob Livingston and Max Ter-
hune as the original likable and formidable leads of Republic's popular, well-made western series "The Three Mesquiteers." Based on the characters of William Colt MacDonald (who borrowed from Dumas), that series would have a number of trios and inspire numerous series with three cowboy heroes, including Monogram's Range Busters, comprised of Corrigan, Terhune, and Dennis Moore. Terhune provided most of the comedy, but Corrigan sometimes wore the silliest tall hat on the range. He made up for it with his stunt work. Beginning in the forties, Corrigan appeared in many low-budget films in and out of the western genre, including bad horror and science-fiction films. He had the sorry distinction of playing the ape in *The Monster and the Ape* (is there really a film with this title?)—which I hope was a better role than the monster—and the large, lumbering alien in *It—The Terror from Beyond Space*, which may have been the inspiration for *Alien*. He'll probably be remembered as much for his exciting nickname as for his often unexciting films.

- **Key Films:** "Three Mesquiteers" westerns (ca. 1935), "Range Busters" westerns (ca. 1940,) *It—The Terror from Beyond Space* (1958, Edward L. Cahn).
- **Also of Interest:** *Undersea Kingdom* (1936 serial, B. Reeves Eason and Joseph Kane), *Darkest Africa* (1936 serial, Eason and Kane), *The Painted Stallion* (1937 serial, William Witney and Ray Taylor).

○

BUD CORT (1950–) As a gentle, passive man-child who is obsessed with flying in *Brewster McCloud* and a gentle, passive man-child who is obsessed with death in *Harold and Maude*, this lanky young actor, who looked liked like he could be Paul

Bud Cort is obsessed with death in Harold and Maude.

McCartney's sweet younger brother, became a certified cult star of the early seventies. Before Robert Altman gave him the lead in *Brewster McCloud*, he had played a small role in Altman's *M*A*S*H*, where he represented all America's rebels who are searching for freedom. In Hal Ashby's *Harold and Maude*, in which he staged fake suicides and had an affair with an elderly woman—Cort and Ruth Gordon are one of the strangest and most delightful pairings in screen history—he represented all of America's young nonconformists who refuse to be crushed by authority figures (mothers, soldiers, priests, police). When you least expect it, he gets a mischievous gleam in his eyes and does or says something outrageous. In both quirky black comedies, he is molded by an older woman: mother-surrogate Sally Kellerman in *Brewster McCloud*, and Gordon in *Harold and Maude*. The first film ends sadly, as he

wasn't taught well; police prevent the young man (who had lost his energy having sex) from flying out of the Astrodome with his harnessed wings. In the second film, it's sad that Maude dies, but she first gives Harold reasons to live—he winds up playing a banjo, happy to be alive, and the movie ends optimistically as nonconformity wins out. No wonder *Harold and Maude* was far more cherished by young fans of the day and became, along with *King of Hearts* and *Night of the Living Dead*, one of *the* "cult" movies of the early seventies— and why it still remains so popular. Cort has made a comeback after a bad car accident. He has tried to get away from his sweet image, playing an occasional villain, doing the voice of a jealous computer in *Electric Dreams,* even playing Freud in *The Secret Diary of Sigmund Freud*.

- **Cult Favorites:** *M*A*S*H* (1970, Robert Altman), *Brewster McCloud* (1970, Alt-

Hazel Court with Robert Urquhart in The Curse of Frankenstein.

man), *Harold and Maude* (1972, Hal Ashby).

• **Sleepers:** *Why Shoot the Teacher?* (1977, Silvio Narizzano), *Love at Stake* (1987, John Moffitt).

• **Also of Interest:** *Love Letters* (1983, Amy Jones), *Electric Dreams* (1984, Steve Barron), *The Secret Diary of Sigmund Freud* (1984, Danford B. Greene), *Out of the Dark* (1988, Michael Schultz).

○

HAZEL COURT (1926–) British actress with the distinction of appearing in both Hammer Studios' early horror films in England and Roger Corman's Edgar Allan Poe horror films in America. Rather than playing sweet vulnerable heroines, she often took the other major female roles, typically regal-looking women who are dominated by the powerful, sadistic men they love. They often try to be as cruel, but a trace of humanity comes through. At some point

her characters usually lose their poise and scream; they rarely survive. She was vital to these films, yet she was rarely remembered by anyone but the filmmakers. For her campiest role, a lead, go back to 1955 when she played a sexy, big-breasted alien who is on the procreation prowl in *Devil Girl from Mars*.

• **Cult Favorite:** *Masque of the Red Death* (1964, Roger Corman).

• **Other Key Films:** *Devil Girl from Mars* (1955, David MacDonald), *The Curse of Frankenstein* (1957, Terence Fisher), *The Man Who Could Cheat Death* (1959, Fisher), *Dr. Blood's Coffin* (1961, Sidney J. Furie), *The Premature Burial* (1962, Corman), *The Raven* (1963, Corman).

• **Also of Interest:** *Ghost Ship* (1952, Vernon Sewell).

○

DESIREE COUSTEAU/CLEARBRANCH Beautiful, cheerful porno superstar of the late

Desiree Cousteau.

seventies–early eighties. She debuted in Alex De Renzy's *Pretty Peaches* as a bubblehead who gets amnesia and is taken sexual advantage of by every man and woman she meets. After winning porno awards for her irritating character, she would continue to play sweet, dizzy young women who are manipulated into having sexual relations and who have the capacity to do and enjoy anything asked of them . . . and more. Mostly she stuck to porno comedies. In *Ecstasy Girls*, she climaxes while standing on her head. She was a hot commodity, due in part to self-promotion, but then disappeared from the business. According to Al Goldstein's *Screw* magazine, rumors spread that the emotional actress wound up in an asylum. She's one of the prisoners in Jonathan Demme's R-rated *Caged Heat*.

• **Cult Favorites:** *Pretty Peaches* (1978, Alex De Renzy), *Randy, the Electric Lady* (1980, Philip Schuman).

• **Other Key Films:** *Easy* (1978, Anthony Spinelli), *The Hot and Saucy Pizza Girls: They Deliver* (1978, Damon Christian), *Ecstasy Girls* (1979, Robert McCallum), 800 *Fantasy Lane* (1979, McCallum), *Ms. Magnificent* (1979, Joe Sherman), *Centerspread Girls* (1982, McCallum), *Inside Desiree Cousteau* (1979, Leon Gucci).

○

LARRY "BUSTER" CRABBE (1907–83) "The King of the Serials." Like a previous Olympic swimming champion, Johnny Weissmuller, Crabbe began his movie career starring in jungle films that allowed him to exhibit both his powerful physique and his swimming talents and overall athleticism. He was Kaspa the Lion Man in *King of the Jungle* and the Lord of the Apes in the cheapie serial *Tarzan the Fearless*, in which he had no dialogue. It would be his first of nine serials. He then replaced Randolph Scott as the star of Paramount's impressive series of B Zane Grey westerns. But his big break came when he got the lead in *Flash Gordon*, dying his hair blond in order to play Alex Raymond's comic-strip space hero. He battled Charles Middleton's Ming the Merciless, romanced and rescued Jean Rogers's Dale Arden, warded off the advances of Priscilla Lawson's Princess Aura, and defied violent death in chapter after chapter. The ambitious, innovative serial was a sensation, and Crabbe became the idol of millions. His voice was high-pitched but he had a muscular chest, handsome features, and strong presence that made him a more than suitable hero. Crabbe never claimed to be a good actor, but he smartly played his character with conviction rather than tongue-in-cheek. He would reprise the role in two successful series. He'd also do a good job as *Buck Rogers*, again venturing into space, but he admitted to not liking "the do-gooder." After the third *Flash Gordon* serial, Crabbe would appear almost exclusively in B west-

Buster Crabbe as Flash Gordon.

winning Crabbe a new generation of fans. No other actor is more associated with the "space adventure," a most enjoyable science-fiction subgenre.

• **Cult Favorites:** *Flash Gordon* (1936 serial, Frederick Stephani), *Flash Gordon's Trip to Mars* (1938 serial, Ford Beebe and Robert F. Hill), *Buck Rogers* (1939 serial, Beebe and Saul Goodking), *Flash Gordon Conquers the Universe* (1940 serial, Beebe and Ray Taylor).

• **Other Key Films:** *King of the Jungle* (1933, H. Bruce Humberstone), *Tarzan the Fearless* (1933 serial, Robert F. Hill), *Red Barry* (1938 serial, Beebe and Alan Jones), *Billy the Kid Wanted* (1941, Sam Newfield).

• **Also of Interest:** *Million Dollar Legs* (1939, Nick Grinde), *Fighting Bill Carson* (1945, Newfield), *Swamp Fire* (1946, William H. Pine), *The Lawless Eighties* (1957, Joseph Kane), *Badman's Country* (1958, Fred F. Sears), *The Bounty Killer* (1965, Spencer G. Bennet).

○

erns, including several as a heroic Billy the Kid (replacing Bob Steele); the name would be changed to Bill Carson after protests by mothers. Fuzzy Al St. John was his comic sidekick. Carson rode a horse named Falcon and dressed in black. Sam Newfield directed the majority of his nearly fifty westerns at PRC studios. Of their quality, film historian William K. Everson jested that Crabbe "only had to saunter into a saloon and Charles King would remark, 'Stranger, I don't like your face,' instantly provoking a vigorous if somewhat unconvincing fight." In the early fifties, the *Flash Gordon* and *Buck Rogers* serials were broadcast on television,

BARBARA CRAMPTON Pretty, uninhibited blonde who starred in Stuart Gordon's outrageous H. P. Lovecraft films, *Re-Animator* and *From Beyond*, both of which are loaded with blood, black humor, and kinky sex. In the wildest scene in *Re-Animator*, her nude body is licked all over by a detached but very much alive head that is held by its owner. In that film she played the dean's daughter; in the follow-up she is a straitlaced scientist who, while engaging in weird experiments involving the dead and another dimension, takes off her glasses, puts on some scanty under-wear, and becomes sexually insatiable. She has enough talent to justify her getting leads in such films, but much of her sex appeal comes from her "natural" manner on-screen.

- **Cult Favorite:** *Re-Animator* (1985, Stuart Gordon).
- **Other Key Film:** *From Beyond* (1986, Gordon).
- **Also of Interest:** *Kidnapped* (1988, Howard Avedis).

○

JOAN CRAWFORD (1906–77) The Texas-born Lucille LeSueur got her screen name from a fan poll organized by M-G-M; she would never underestimate how much stars needed fans and studio publicity machines. Her pivotal early role was in *Dance, Fools, Dance*, which melded her then-popular hedonistic flapper/dancing girl with the noble working girls she'd play in the following years. Watching her as a once-rich girl who becomes a hardworking reporter, one sees her appeal: she's likable and extremely glamorous. Her pulled-back hair emphasizes her sharp nose and beautiful eyes; and she shows an appealing combination of pep, style, sleekness (those shoulders!), and sex (she participates in

Joan Crawford in Paid.

the famous group underwear-swim scene) that can be defined as "star quality." In most of her early films she played sympathetic young women—shopgirls, secretaries—who try to make something of themselves. They reflected her own rise from poverty to shopgirl to dancer to actress. In *Grand Hotel*, she gives a glowing performance as a secretary who wants to be a movie star. These women were glamorous but accessible, strong but vulnerable, resigned to sell their bodies in order to survive but ready to sacrifice their own happiness to maintain the dignity of those they love. In the forties, Crawford revived her career as a successful businesswoman but unsuccessful mother in *Mildred Pierce*, a combination of film noir and the standard "woman's picture"/soap about suffering mothers. She won a Best Actress Oscar for what many consider her quintessential role, but she really isn't very good. She plays every scene in an understated manner. I prefer her in her other melodramas of the forties, when she is more combative or, as in *Harriet Craig*, more selfish and compulsive, manipulating weak men. Also enjoyable is her carnival girl in *Flamingo Road*: she's smart, sincere, and stronger than any man; she alone stands up to corrupt political boss Sydney Greenstreet, slaps him, even points a loaded gun at him. Crawford's overwrought performances in the forties, along with her gun-toting casino owner in the baroque western *Johnny Guitar*, her cripple's sibling rivalry with loony Bette Davis in *What Ever Happened to Baby Jane?*, and star turns in horror films like *Strait-Jacket* (brandishing an axe!) contributed to her camp reputation. This was greatly enhanced by daughter Christina's tell-all tome, *Mommie Dearest*.

• **Cult Favorites:** *Grand Hotel* (1932, Edmund Goulding), *The Women* (1939, George Cukor), *Strange Cargo* (1940, Frank Borzage), *Mildred Pierce* (1945, Michael Curtiz), *Johnny Guitar* (1954, Nicholas Ray), *What Ever Happened to Baby Jane?* (1962, Robert Aldrich), *Strait-Jacket* (1964, William Castle).

• **Also Recommended:** *Our Dancing Daughters* (1928, Harry Beaumont), *Dance, Fools, Dance* (1931, Beaumont), *Paid* (1931, Sam Wood), *Rain* (1932, Lewis Milestone), *Today We Live* (1933, Howard Hawks), *Sadie McKee* (1934, Clarence Brown), *The Bride Wore Red* (1937, Dorothy Arzner), *A Woman's Face* (1941, Cukor), *Humoresque* (1946, Jean Negulesco), *Possessed* (1947, Curtis Bernhardt), *Daisy Kenyon* (1947, Otto Preminger), *Flamingo Road* (1949, Curtiz), *Harriet Craig* (1950, Vincent Sherman), *Female on the Beach* (1955, Joseph Pevney), *Queen Bee* (1955, Ranald MacDougall), *Autumn Leaves* (1955, Aldrich).

○

LAIRD CREGAR (1916–44) He had already made a name for himself as a villain—he was delightful as the Devil in *Heaven Can Wait*—but his final two films, *The Lodger*, in which he played Jack the Ripper, and *Hangover Square*, in which he played a crazed composer, established him as the era's most frightening screen psycho. Once a bouncer, he was a large man, but until his characters had loony spells they didn't seem physically intimidating. What was scary were their creepy eyes and soft, seemingly calm voices that, one can tell, spoke words that belied the vicious thoughts racing through the characters' sick brains. They seemed to have everything under control, yet you sensed that their underwear was soaked with sweat and their fingernails

Laird Cregar with Merle Oberon in The Lodger.

were growing as they contemplated murder. Unhappy to be typecast as insane killers, he went on a crash diet in order to be considered for romantic leads. He died suddenly of a weakened heart at age 28.

• **Key Films:** *The Lodger* (1944, John Brahm), *Hangover Square* (1945, Brahm).

• **Also of Interest:** *Hudson's Bay* (1940, Irving Pichel), *Blood and Sand* (1941, Rouben Mamoulian), *I Wake Up Screaming* (1941, H. Bruce Humberstone), *This Gun for Hire* (1942, Frank Tuttle), *The Black Swan* (1942, Henry King), *Heaven Can Wait* (1943, Ernst Lubitsch), *Holy Matrimony* (1943, John M. Stahl).

○

CRISWELL (1907–82) Among the strange friends of idiosyncratic—and just plain awful—director Edward D. Wood, Jr., was this famous but inaccurate newspaper, radio, and television psychic, who made several appearances with Jack Paar and Johnny Carson. He had incredibly

ridiculous turns as the narrator in Wood's *Plan 9 from Outer Space* and *Night of the Ghouls*, contributing mightily to both the startling wretchedness and camp appeal of those films. In *Plan 9*, regarded by most bad-film freaks as the worst film of all time, he comes on like a street-corner evangelist, telling us the film is based on "sworn testimony" of "miserable souls who survived the ordeal of . . . graverobbers from outer space." Then he challenges us: "Can *you* prove it didn't happen?" After telling us the film story has already happened, he adds: "Future events like these will affect you in the future." At the end, he rises, saying, "God help us in the future." This man belonged in a booby hatch, but Wood stuck him in a coffin, from which he narrated *Night of the Ghouls*. At that film's beginning, he again asked a toughie: "How many of you know the horror, the terror, I will now reveal to you?" Even after seeing the film, that question must go unanswered. But, thanks to Wood's films, Charles Jared Criswell does not go unremembered. I doubt if this forecaster could have predicted that.

• **Cult Movies:** *Plan 9 from Outer Space* (1959, Edward D. Wood, Jr.), *Night of the Ghouls* (1960, Wood).

○

PEGGY CUMMINS (1925–) Blond British leading lady appeared in a number of British and American films in the forties and fifties that made use of her good looks but didn't exploit her sexuality or talent. Only Joseph H. Lewis realized what a sexy actress she could be, and that when she was sexy she was ravishing. He cast her opposite John Dall in *Gun Crazy*, the best of the B couple-on-the-lam pictures. For Cummins and Dall, the firing of guns while committing crimes fuels their sexual flame, as it would do with the couple in *Bonnie and Clyde*. Never has a movie relationship been so intense: Lewis films them throughout in two-shots, constantly grabbing each other, snuggling up, kissing; even when hurt, exhausted, and being chased by police, they stop long enough to hug and kiss. Their exciting initial meeting—Dall beats carnival sharpshooter Cummins in a shooting contest—is dripping with sex. Lewis said: "I told Peggy, 'You're a female dog in heat, and you want

British actress Peggy Cummins was projected to become a Hollywood star, but she was never given the opportunity.

him. But don't let him have it in a hurry. Keep him waiting.' That's exactly how I talked to (her) and I turned (her) loose." The result is that Cummins gave one of the least inhibited performances in film history. Too bad other directors wouldn't exploit Cummins's sexuality; they usually cast her as perky leading ladies in silly comedies, including *Carry On Admiral*. At least she did have a lead in one more memorable film, the top-grade horror thriller *Night of the Demon*. Pretty as she is throughout that film, there are a couple of moments when her sexuality surfaces and catches you completely offguard . . . and you realize this is the same actress who brought electricity to *Gun Crazy*.

• **Cult Favorites:** *Gun Crazy* (1949, Joseph H. Lewis), *Night of the Demon/Curse of the Demon* (1958, Jacques Tourneur).

• **Also of Interest:** *Her Man Gilbey* (1944, Harold French), *The Late George Apley* (1947, Joseph L. Mankiewicz), *Moss Rose* (1947, Gregory Ratoff), *Green Grass of Wyoming* (1948, Louis King), *Escape* (1948, Mankiewicz), *Operation X* (1951, Ratoff), *Both Sides of the Law* (1953, Muriel Box), *The Love Lottery* (1953, Charles Crichton), *Hell Divers* (1958, Cy Endfield), *The Captain's Table* (1960, Jack Lee), *Dentist in the Chair* (1960, Don Chaffey).

○

TIM CURRY (1946–) Multitalented, scenery-chewing British actor-singer is revered by multitudes of *The Rocky Horror Picture Show* fans for his dynamic performance as the flamboyant transvestite monster-creator, Dr. Frank-N-Furter, a role he also played in the original London theater version. Indeed, Tim Curry is the Queen of the cult cinema. Though wearing thick makeup, high heels, and women's underwear, he was anything but an effeminate transsexual as he strutted through the picture, flexing his body into a variety of sexual poses, talking and singing with a booming voice, aggressively seducing both men and women. He comes across as a Mick Jagger who can act. In other films, the curly-haired Curry has continued to play, often with great humor, unlikable characters. Most have been self-serving, arrogant but (you can see in his eyes) cowardly, fussy, gossipy, underhanded, the kind who spit when they talk. He was well cast as the huckster TV evangelist in *Pass the Ammo*, the sleuthing butler in *Clue*, and the evil clown in the TV mini-series of Stephen King's *It!*

• **Cult Favorites:** *The Rocky Horror Picture Show* (1975, Jim Sharman), *The Shout* (1979, Jerzy Skolimowski).

• **Sleeper:** *The Ploughman's Lunch* (1984, Richard Eyre).

• **Also of Interest:** *Annie* (1982, John Huston), *Blue Money* (1984, Colin Bucksey), *Clue* (1985, Jonathan Lynn), *Legend* (1986, Ridley Scott), *Pass the Ammo* (1987, David Beaird), *The Hunt for Red October* (1990, John McTiernan), *Oscar* (1991, John Landis).

○

JAMIE LEE CURTIS (1958–) Talented, poised blond actress, with a shapely figure, a pretty, slender face, and a friendly, toothy grin. She's the daughter of Janet Leigh and Tony Curtis, yet her acting has always been instinctual. She is the most natural of contemporary actresses. Though many of her films have been ludicrous, her women have always been believable. She's an emotional actress who inhabits her characters fully and presents them pre-

Right to Left: *Jamie Lee Curtis, P. J. Soles, and Nancy Loomis became instant cult stars as a result of* Halloween.

cisely. When one of her women is heart-broken, her tears are real. (I remember her being misty-eyed when telling me about the murdered Dorothy Stratten, whom she played in a TV movie.) Directors have wisely included wordless scenes in which Curtis thinks while in close-up; by watching her eyes (which may be teary) and subtle expressions you understand completely what her character is going through. Curtis debuted as the smart, virginal babysitter in *Halloween*, the only girl to survive the wrath of Michael Meyers, and after making several more horror films had trouble shaking her "Scream Queen" tag. She finally did it by being funny and doing a now-famous disrobing scene in *Trading Places*, teaming up with Dan Aykroyd and Eddie Murphy. Recog-

nized as a versatile actress as well as a "sex symbol," she won leads in several sudsy dramas (she obviously cared about such pictures as *Love Letters* and *Grandview, U.S.A.*, but they were unworthy of her performances) and the embarrassing *Perfect*, gyrating ad nauseum as the aerobics instructor who turns on John Travolta. She was sincere and touching as Ray Liotta's girlfriend in *Dominick and Eugene*, one of several noncommercial films she has done because she believed in their themes; the antinuclear *Amazing Grace and Chuck* is another. Curtis recharged her movie career with a funny, sexy, energetic, smart, and extremely composed performance in the hit comedy *A Fish Called Wanda*. She wasted an impressive portrait of a frightened but courageous rookie cop in the infuriating *Blue Steel*. Curtis found popularity with the masses, playing opposite Richard Lewis in the TV sitcom "Anything But Love."

• **Cult Favorites:** *Halloween* (1978, John Carpenter), *The Fog* (1980, Carpenter).

• **Sleepers:** *Road Games* (1981, Richard Franklin), *Trading Places* (1983, John Landis), *Dominick and Eugene* (1988, Robert M. Young).

• **Also of Interest:** *Terror Train* (1980, Roger Spottiswoode), *Love Letters* (1983, Amy Jones), *Grandview, U.S.A.* (1984, Randal Kleiser), *A Fish Called Wanda* (1988, Charles Crichton).

○

PETER CUSHING (1913–) The most important and beloved figure of the British horror-fantasy film. When Hammer Studios de-cided in the late fifties to remake *Frankenstein* and *Dracula* in full color, with explicit violence and sexual content, it hired the 43-year-old British TV star to play the evil monster-maker Baron von Frankenstein in *The Curse of Frankenstein* and vampire-hunter Professor Van Helsing in *The Horror of Dracula*. Christopher Lee, who had been the Frankenstein Monster, played Dracula to great effect with a vivid sexual presence. Lee and Cushing would continue their roles in several *Dracula* sequels; Cushing would go it alone in the Frankenstein sequels. I preferred Cushing's heroic Van Helsing to his Frankenstein, because he seemed miscast as a murderer and rapist. The first two films, both smashes, established Cushing and Lee as the horror cinema's greatest adversaries (although they would be on the same side in a few of their dozen subse-

Peter Cushing in House of Blood.

quent films together). How could Cushing oppose the taller, intimidating Lee? Cushing wasn't big but he could be a formidable figure, as his characters had great intellect and were untiring, driven men; even his heroes were so obsessed with stamping out evil that they had become a bit crazy and dangerously unpredictable (why else would Van Helsing engage in hand-to-hand combat with Dracula?). Cushing could have just as easily played the batlike adversary as the hero. If his head had been shaved and pointed ears attached, Cushing would have certainly looked like a vampire, as his gaunt face, pointed nose, high cheekbones, and penetrating eyes resembled a bat's. His Holmes in *The Hound of the Baskervilles* had so much energy while snooping around the moors that he could barely stand still. In his 19 films for Hammer, Cushing's characters were almost always deadly serious—though Cushing at times had to put tongue firmly in cheek—so he was happy to play funnier characters, like Dr. Who, at Amicus Studios. He was again serious, but having fun, as the cold-blooded Governor Tarkin in *Star Wars*.

• **Cult Favorites:** *The Curse of Frankenstein* (1957, Terence Fisher), *Horror of Dracula* (1958, Fisher), *She* (1965, Robert Day), *Scream and Scream Again* (1970, Gordon Hessler), *The Vampire Lovers* (1970, Roy Ward Baker), *Legend of the Seven Golden Vampires/The Seven Brothers Meet Dracula* (1973, Baker).

• **Other Key Films:** *The Abominable Snowman* (1957, Val Guest), *The Revenge of Frankenstein* (1958, Fisher), *The Hound of the Baskervilles* (1959, Fisher), *The Mummy* (1959, Fisher), *The Brides of Dracula* (1960, Fisher), *The Evil of Frankenstein* (1964, Freddie Francis), *The Gorgon* (1964, Fisher), *Dr. Terror's House of Horrors* (1965, Francis), *The Skull* (1965,

Francis), *Dr. Who and the Daleks* (1965, Gordon Flemyng), *Daleks—Invasion Earth 2150 A.D.* (1966, Flemyng), *Frankenstein Created Woman* (1967, Fisher), *Frankenstein Must Be Destroyed* (1969, Fisher), *Twins of Evil* (1971, John Hough), *Dr. Phibes Rises Again* (1972, Robert Fuest), *Dracula A.D. 1972* (1972, Alan Gibson), *I, Monster* (1972, Stephen Weeks), *The Creeping Flesh* (1973, Francis), *Count Dracula and His Vampire Bride* (1973, Gibson), *Madhouse* (1974, Jim Clark), *Frankenstein and the Monster from Green Hell* (1974, Fisher), *At the Earth's Core* (1976, Kevin Connor), *Shock Waves* (1977, Ken Wiederhorn), *Star Wars* (1977, George Lucas).

○

ZBIGNIEW CYBULSKI (1927–67) The Eastern Bloc didn't turn out many movie idols, but in the late fifties this Polish actor with dark glasses caught the imagination of the era's turbulent youth, not only in his native country but throughout the world. Yes, there are people who would prefer a Zbigniew Cybulski poster to one of James Dean. He became an instant sensation in Andrzej Wajda's internationally acclaimed *Ashes and Diamonds*, as a young resistance fighter who reconsiders assassinating a communist leader after a one-night affair softens his heart. The film's best moment, when the party leader collapses into the young man's arms, was conceived by the actor. He would continue to play young men trying to make sense of their complicated lives in a volatile political climate; they were unsympathetic as often as not. He would later write screenplays and was about to direct his first film at the time of his accidental death boarding a train—a strange death that, like Dean's, contributed to his myth. In 1968, Wajda made *Everything for Sale*, which was inspired by the death of his most famous actor.

• **Key Film:** *Ashes and Diamonds* (1958, Andrzej Wajda).

• **Also of Interest:** *Innocent Sorcerers* (1960, Wajda), *Love at Twenty* (1962, Wajda episode), *How to Be Loved* (1963, Wojciech Has), *The Saragosa Manuscript* (1965, Has).

○

ARLENE DAHL (1924–) Heartstruck boys and men cut out her pictures when they adorned magazines, and girls and women read her beauty books and columns to see if they could ever look like her. They couldn't. The gorgeous, red-haired "Living Dahl" rightly was much more famous for her beauty than for her undistinguished films. She was directed by uninteresting directors (Roy Rowland, Edward Ludwig, etc.) and, with few exceptions, had bland romantic partners like Ricardo Montalban, David Brian, Barry Sullivan, John Payne, Red Skelton, Philip Carey—and Fernando Lamas, whom she married. She generally decorated films rather than acted in them; rarely did she appear in a picture that wasn't principally about the male character. She looked great and was most likable in juvenile costumers, but she was at her best on those few occasions when her women had a hard edge to them: the arsonist in *She Played with Fire*; a klepto-nympho ex-con (Rhonda Fleming's sister!) in *Slightly Scarlet;* and the frigid title character who proves that when pushed around she can be as *Wicked as They Come*.

• **Recommended Films:** A *Southern Yankee* (1948, Edward Sedgwick), *Border Incident* (1949, Roy Rowland), *Ambush* (1949, Sam

Wood), *Slightly Scarlet* (1956, Allan Dwan), *Wicked as They Come* (1957, Ken Hughes), *Journey to the Center of the Earth* (1959, Henry Levin).

• **Also of Interest:** *Three Little Words* (1950, Richard Thorpe), *Inside Straight* (1951, Gerald Mayer), *Sangaree* (1953, Edward Ludwig), *The Diamond Queen* (1953, John Brahm), *Here Come the Girls* (1953, Claude Binyon), *Woman's World* (1954, Jean Negulesco), *She Played with Fire* (1958, Sidney Gilliat).

○

JOE DALLESANDRO (1948–) This muscular, likable, cute though pimply young actor was the male star or an ensemble player in six pictures that represented producer Andy Warhol's venture into the commercial realm. *Flesh* and *Trash* retained elements of the underground cinema, including leading player Dallesandro's Jack Smith–influenced anti-acting style. He was completely natural on screen, casually having sex, shooting up, mumbling his way through hysterical deadpan dialogues with a weird assortment of other lowlifes who inhabit the drug-sex counterculture of New York's Lower East Side. In the first film, he wanders the streets, either hustling gays in order to get money for his disgruntled wife, or meeting and having sex with friends. His passivity in sex (when his wife asks him what he wants her to do next while they are going at it hot and heavy, he suggests his laundry) would be more pronounced in *Trash*, where his heroin addiction keeps him from getting it up, much to the consternation of his nympho girlfriend (played by transvestite Holly Woodlawn). His sex life would never be "normal." In *Heat*, Warhol and Morrissey's variation on *Sunset Boulevard*,

Joe Dallesandro gets ready to shoot up in Andy Warhol's Trash.

he was an unemployed actor who becomes the kept man of aged, has-been actress Sylvia Miles. In the absurd *Andy Warhol's Frankenstein*, he played a stud field worker who has sex with the older, married, rich Monique Van Vooren. His "sex" scene with Van Vooren is hilarious, particularly when she slurps away at his armpit. In *Andy Warhol's Dracula*, his virile Bolshevik gardener in Italy (he didn't bother to hide his New York accent), takes the virginity of his decadent employer's daughters, probably as a political act. Having worked in the fields in two films, Dallesandro's first non-Warhol role was as the title character in *The Gardener*, growing deadly plants. He has since given "professional" performances, albeit in supporting parts, in several commercial pictures.

• **Cult Favorites:** *Lonesome Cowboys* (1967, Andy Warhol), *Flesh* (1968, Paul Morrissey), *Trash* (1970, Morrissey), *Heat/Andy Warhol's Heat* (1972, Morrissey), *Andy Warhol's Frankenstein* (1974, Morrissey), *Andy Warhol's Dracula* (1974, Morrissey).

• **Also of Interest:** *The Gardener/Seeds of Evil* (1974, Jim Kay), *Je t'aime, Moi Non Plus* (1975, Serge Gainsbourg), *The Cotton Club* (1984, Francis Coppola), *Critical Condition* (1987, Michael Apted), *Sunset* (1988, Blake Edwards).

○

TIMOTHY DALTON (1944–) Dark, handsome, theatrically trained Welsh actor who achieved immediate worldwide fame and cult status among hard-core James Bond–movie fans when he was chosen to succeed Roger Moore and be the screen's fourth Agent 007 in *The Living Daylights*. Many moviegoers were surprised that the "new-comer" had been around for almost 20 years. He'd played princes and kings in historical epics in the late sixties and early seventies and been a leading man since

1970, when he was Heathcliff in the confusing but interesting British remake of *Wuthering Heights*. He had survived being Mae West's young lover in the embarrassing "comedy" *Sextette*, and done some credible work, most notably in the atmospheric *The Doctor and the Devils* as a physician who hires a pair of heinous characters to provide bodies for his anatomy experiments. It is hard to find fault with his interpretation of James Bond, whom he has rescued from gimmicks and returned to the acting basics; he's adept in the many action scenes, but unfortunately, when he laughs or jokes, he comes across as humorless. Perhaps Bond should be somber, even brooding, considering his deadly profession—Fleming's original character certainly isn't cheery—but Sean Connery, who played the character with joy, and even the less talented Roger Moore, who played him tongue-in-cheek, had such presences that we believed they were Bond. Dalton was much more comfortable in his second Bond film, *License to Kill*, written specifically for him, than he had been in the inferior *The Living Daylights*, but still, for now, he seems like an imposter.

• **Cult Favorite:** *Sextette* (1978, Ken Hughes and Irving Rapper).

• **Sleeper:** *Agatha* (1979, Michael Apted).

• **Other Key Films:** *The Lion in Winter* (1968, Anthony Harvey), *Wuthering Heights* (1970, Robert Fuest), *The Doctor and the Devils* (1985, Freddie Francis), *The Living Daylights* (1987, John Glen), *License to Kill* (1989, Glen).

○

MARK DAMON (1935–) Handsome, dull actor started out in troubled youth gang and speed-crazy drive-in movies, usually as a wild young man who is tamed by his innocent girlfriend. He was his best opposite Rita Moreno in *This Rebel Breed*. He was the innocuous romantic lead in Roger Corman's impressive *House of Usher*, as Myrna Fahey's fiancé, who isn't so happy when Vincent Price buries her alive. Damon continued to play leads in horror films in the United States and abroad. Most notably he played brothers, opposite sexy Sara Bay's Countess Dracula, in the sleazy Spanish film *The Devil's Wedding Night*. As usual, he just took up space. Eventually, Damon became a producer.

• **Cult Favorites:** *House of Usher/Fall of the House of Usher* (1960, Roger Corman), *The Longest Day* (1962, Ken Annakin, Andrew Marton, and Bernhard Wicki).

• **Sleeper:** *Between Heaven and Hell* (1956, Richard Fleischer).

• **Other Key Films:** *Inside Detroit* (1955, Fred F. Sears), *Young and Dangerous* (1957, William Claxton), *The Party Crashers* (1958, Bernard Girard), *This Rebel Breed/Three Shades of Love* (1960/65, Richard L. Bare), *The Young Racers* (1963, Corman), *Beauty and the Beast* (1963, Edward L. Cahn), *Black Sabbath* (1964, Mario Bava), *Anzio* (1968, Edward Dmytryk), *Little Mother* (1972, Radley Metzger), *The Devil's Wedding Night* (1973, Paul Solvay), *Crypt of the Living Dead/Hannah, Queen of the Vampires* (1973, Ray Danton).

○

DOROTHY DANDRIDGE (1923–65) Playing native girls in low-budget forties movies, this stunningly beautiful black singer-dancer projected an unbridled sexuality that the Hollywood cinema hadn't seen since the pre-Code days. As a jungle queen in *Tarzan's Peril*, for instance, her breasts rise and fall while she lies spread-eagled, tied to stakes. However, in the fifties, when Dandridge went looking for respectability, she suppressed her sexuality in both films and television (as a regular on "Beulah")—but she didn't tone down her hot nightclub act. In *The Harlem Globetrotters* she was a devoted, understanding wife of a young basketball player, and in the odd *Bright Road*, she was a kind, understanding teacher at a black rural elementary school; both unthreatening, pretty but asexual black women, the sort also played by the young Ruby Dee. Dandridge's image changed dramatically when she played the tempestuous femme fatale who leads Harry Belafonte down a destructive path in *Carmen Jones*, Otto Preminger's exceptional all-black musical. In tight, revealing outfits, moving suggestively and flashing hungry eyes, she personified sexuality. Carmen's wanton use of sex and her need for it result in her downfall. Like other Dandridge heroines, she came across as confident and unworried, yet beneath it all was insecurity and vulnerability—the essence of Dandridge herself. Black men were excited by her Carmen Jones; in future films, with the exception of *Porgy and Bess*, white male characters would also drool when looking at her women. In *Island in the Sun*, which caused a stir because of its miscegenation theme, she became the first black actress in a romantic clinch with a white man in a Hollywood film. She would be held by other white men in *The Decks Ran Red*, as the only woman on a ship that already has enough trouble; *Tamango*, as a slave girl whom the ship captain Curt Jurgens lusts after; and *Malaga*, torn between Trevor Howard and Edmund Purdom. Interestingly, her characters never seem surprised that white men desire them. As these films were set up, the fatal "flaw" of her characters was their blackness—they could

Dorothy Dandridge in a publicity pose for Carmen Jones.

never keep the white men who were attracted to them. Dandridge herself suffered because she couldn't overcome Hollywood racism and achieve the success that her talent merited. She was a famous actress, a onetime Best Actress Oscar nominee (for *Carmen Jones* in 1954), a sex goddess, yet she couldn't get any roles in America. Bankrupt because of a business venture that went sour, and getting no script offers, she died of a barbiturate overdose at the age of 41.

• **Cult Favorite:** *Carmen Jones* (1954, Otto Preminger).

• **Other Key Films:** *Island in the Sun* (1957, Robert Rossen), *The Decks Ran Red* (1958, Andrew L. Stone), *Tamango* (1957, John Berry), *Porgy and Bess* (1959, Preminger), *Malaga/Moment of Danger* (1960, Laslo Benedek).

• **Also of Interest:** *Drums of the Congo* (1942, Christy Cabanne), *Tarzan's Peril* (1951, Byron Haskin), *The Harlem Globetrotters* (1951, Phil Brown), *Bright Road* (1953, Gerald Mayer), *Remains to Be Seen* (1953, Don Weis).

○

HENRY DANIELL (1894–1963) This British character actor impeccably played some of the screen's shrewdest and most insidious villains, including Professor Moriarty, Baron de Varville in *Camille*, and various Nazis and traitors. His unfriendly face and snide, conceited voice told moviegoers that he was not to be trusted, yet he usually got away with his treachery until the heroes finally did him in at the film's end. He was particularly well cast as evil advisers in costume dramas, deceiving and manipulating people in positions of power. But he was equally good in the contemporary *The Suspect* as the wife-beating neighbor who tries to blackmail Charles Laughton—a cad only Dan Duryea could have played as well. Daniell got a rare lead (although Boris Karloff was top-billed) and was marvelous in the classy Val Lewton–produced horror film *The Body Snatcher*, playing a doctor who lets henchman Karloff rob graves and commit murder to get the bodies essential for his anatomy classes. Of course, this doctor does dastardly deeds, but he is one of the actor's few characters who has a conscience and suffers guilt.

• **Cult Favorites:** *The Great Dictator* (1940, Charles Chaplin), *The Philadelphia Story*

Henry Daniell (left) *in* The Great Dictator *with Charles Chaplin and Jack Oakie.*

(1941, George Cukor), *The Suspect* (1943, Robert Siodmak), *The Body Snatcher* (1945, Robert Wise).

• **Other Key Films:** *Camille* (1937, Cukor), *Holiday* (1938, Cukor), *The Private Lives of Elizabeth and Essex* (1939, Michael Curtiz), *We Are Not Alone* (1939, Edmund Goulding), *The Sea Hawk* (1940, Curtiz), *Sherlock Holmes and the Voice of Terror* (1942, John Rawlins), *Mission to Moscow* (1943, Curtiz), *Watch on the Rhine* (1943, Herman Shumlin), *Sherlock Holmes and the Woman in Green/The Woman in Green* (1945, Roy William Neill).

• **Also of Interest:** *Nightmare* (1942, Tim Whelan), *Captain Kidd* (1945, Rowland V. Lee), *Song of Love* (1947, Clarence Brown), *The Exile* (1947, Max Ophüls), *Diane* (1955, David Miller), *Witness for the Prosecution* (1958, Billy Wilder), *Voyage to the Bottom of the Sea* (1961, Irwin Allen).

○

SYBIL DANNING Supersexy Austrian-born blonde, with steel blue eyes and a 36-24-36 figure, she's become the goddess of B action-adventure movies, most R-rated for Rotten. In Europe, she began in sex comedies with titles like *Swedish Love Games* and *Loves of a French Pussycat* before breaking into legitimate films as a murder victim in *Bluebeard*, where Richard Burton drops a chandelier on her and her female lover. She appeared in a number of major studio films as part of the decor, then refocused her image, adding strength to the sex appeal as an enticingly dressed superwarrior in the enjoyable *Battle Beyond the Stars* (written by John Sayles). Her character's motto was "live fast, fight well, and have a beautiful ending." Since then she has

Action heroine Sybil Danning.

gained popularity with the pinup crowd by playing other warriors—she is at her best in the Italian-made *The Seven Magnificent Gladiators*—as well as prisoners, prison wardens, killers, a wolfwoman, and a bounty hunter. All are tough characters who are as likely as not to leap into a rough-and-tumble fight; many are villainesses adept at torture; some die gruesomely. Typically, they are sexually insatiable, pursuing men and women; and when dressed at all, it's in an S&M fantasy outfit. She can act if really pressed, but since her films have been bad (some are vile) and she has been cast because of her looks and fame, she has the tendency to give lazy performances. It's no wonder that when her appearance is either clothed or just a cameo, her fans feel gypped.

• **Cult Favorites:** *The Three Musketeers* (1974, Richard Lester), *Battle Beyond the*

Stars (1980, Jimmy T. Murakami), *Chained Heat* (1983, Paul Nicolas), *Reform School Girls* (1986, Tom DeSimone), *Amazon Women on the Moon* (1987, various directors).
- **Sleeper:** *The Man with Bogart's Face* (1980, Robert Day).
- **Other Key Films:** *Bluebeard* (1972, Edward Dmytryk), *The Four Musketeers* (1975, Lester), *Operation Thunderbolt* (1977, Menahem Golan), *Hercules* (1983, Lewis Coates), *The Seven Magnificent Gladiators* (1983, Bruno Mattei), *Howling II: Your Sister Is a Werewolf* (1984, Philippe Mora).
- **Also of Interest:** *Crossed Swords* (1978, Richard Fleischer), *Kill Castro* (1978, Peter Barton), *They're Playing with Fire* (1983, Howard Avidas), *Jungle Warriors* (1983, Ernst von Theumer), *Talking Walls* (1987, Stephen Verona).

○

ROYAL DANO (1922–) Tall, thin, angular character actor with a deep voice, constant frown, and angry manner. Whenever he appears, the audience is jolted. He was equally effective playing bad guys in westerns, Abraham Lincoln on TV's "Omnibus" (a rare nice guy), and crazies, drunks, fanatics and other assorted weirdos. Even when his roles were minor he caught your attention with his special brand of strangeness. Some characters were strange in any event; for instance, his supporting character in the oddball *Johnny Guitar* possesses two unusual traits for western bad guys: he reads and he coughs.
- **Cult Favorites:** *The Red Badge of Courage* (1951, John Huston), *Bend of the River* (1952, Anthony Mann), *Johnny Guitar* (1954, Nicholas Ray), *The Far Country*

(1955, Mann), *Man of the West* (1958, Mann), *7 Faces of Dr. Lao* (1964, George Pal), *Electra Glide in Blue* (1973, James William Guercio), *Big Bad Mama* (1974, Steve Carver), *The Outlaw Josey Wales* (1976, Clint Eastwood), *Handle with Care/ Citizens Band* (1977, Jonathan Demme).
- **Sleepers:** *Hound-Dog Man* (1959, Don Siegel), *Death of a Gunfighter* (1969, "Allen Smithee"), *The Great Northfield, Minnesota Raid* (1972, Philip Kaufman), *Hammett* (1983, Wim Wenders), *Something Wicked This Way Comes* (1983, Jack Clayton).
- **Also of Interest:** *The Trouble with Harry* (1955, Alfred Hitchcock), *Tribute to a Bad Man* (1956, Robert Wise), *Moby Dick* (1956, Huston), *Man in the Shadow* (1957, Jack Arnold), *Saddle the Wind* (1958, Robert Parrish), *Face of Fire* (1959, Albert Band), *The Adventures of Huckleberry Finn* (1960, Michael Curtiz), *Cimarron* (1960, Mann), *King of Kings* (1961, Nicholas Ray), *Welcome to Hard Times* (1967, Burt Kennedy), *Teachers* (1984, Arthur Hiller).

○

RAY DANTON (1931–) This handsome New York actor with thick black hair and a confident attitude broke into films in 1955 as a troublesome Indian in *Chief Crazy Horse*, starring Victor Mature. In the fifties, he had supporting roles in a few big-budget soap operas, including *I'll Cry Tomorrow, Too Much, Too Soon,* and *Ice Palace,* but his first lead was in a low-budget crime drama, *Outside the Law.* He was on the right side of the law in that film, tracking down counterfeiters, but was at his best on the other side, as an insane murderer in *The Night Runner,* a rapist in producer Albert Zugsmith's oddity, *Beat Generation,* and a number of slick, cocky gangsters. He's best remembered for his fancy-dancing, romancing, gun-toting title character in *The Rise and Fall of Legs Diamond*, Budd Boetticher's stylized B gangster film; he later had a bit as Diamond in *Portrait of a Mobster*. Danton played the title character, a real-life gangster-turned-actor, in *The George Raft Story*. He starred in minor action films in America and Europe for the duration of his acting career. He also directed a number of low-budget horror pictures. Married to Julie Adams, with whom he costarred in *Tarawa Beachhead*.

• **Cult Favorites:** *The Rise and Fall of Legs Diamond* (1960, Budd Boetticher), *The Longest Day* (1961, Ken Annakin, Andrew Marton, and Bernhard Wicki).

• **Sleepers:** *The Night Runner* (1957, Abner Biberman), *Six-Pack Annie* (1975, Graydon F. David).

• **Other Key Films:** *I'll Cry Tomorrow* (1955, Daniel Mann), *Beat Generation* (1959, Charles Haas), *The George Raft Story* (1961, Joseph M. Newman).

• **Also of Interest:** *Chief Crazy Horse* (1955, George Sherman), *Outside the Law* (1956, Jack Arnold), *Too Much, Too Soon* (1958, Art Napoleon), *Tarawa Beachhead* (1958, Paul Wendkos), *Yellowstone Kelly* (1959, Gordon Douglas, *Portrait of a Mobster* (1961, Joseph Pevney), *The Chapman Report* (1962, George Cukor), *The Centerfold Girls* (1974, John Peyser).

○

PATTI D'ARBANVILLE (1951–) A green-eyed blonde with a New York accent and often a somewhat hoarse voice, she was a former model (the shortest at Wilhelmina) whom Francesco Scavullo described as a "delec-table beauty with a kittenish quality that's pure enchantment—small, sexy and feminine." Andy Warhol discovered her in a café at age 13, but her mother didn't allow him to use her in a film until she was 17. In Warhol's *Flesh*, Joe Dallesandro finds her in bed with his wife, Geraldine Smith, and joins in. Young Patti would have more lesbian love scenes in photographer David Hamilton's semipornographic *Bilitis*, playing the teenage title character who falls for her adult female guardian. Though many release dates have been given for this French film, she looks a gawky, plump, and flat-chested 15 or 16. After a stint making films in Europe, D'Arbanville returned to Hollywood in 1972. With the exceptions of *The Main Event*, in which she was very funny as Ryan O'Neal's coughing girlfriend, and the Chevy Chase comedy *Modern Problems*, she has remained on the fringes, usually in supporting roles in out-of-the-mainstream films. Typically her characters are extremely sexy, witty, tough, sensitive, wise, and outrageous, as befitting someone who had a *TV Guide* article written about her interestingly placed tattoos. She played Ken Wahl's lover on the TV series "Wiseguy." She had a child by former lover Don Johnson. Cat Stevens wrote many songs about her.

• **Cult Favorites:** *Flesh* (1968, Paul Morrissey), *Rancho Deluxe* (1975, Frank Perry), *Bilitis* (1977, David Hamilton), *Big Wednesday* (1978, John Milius), *Time After Time* (1979, Nicholas Meyer), *The Boys Next Door* (1985, Penelope Spheeris).

• **Other Key Films:** *The Main Event* (1979, Howard Zieff), *Wired* (1989, Larry Peerce).

• **Also of Interest:** *Modern Problems* (1981, Ken Shapiro), *Call Me* (1988, Solace Mitchell).

MARION DAVIES (1897–1961) Newspaper magnate William Randolph Hearst intended to make his blond mistress the cinema's greatest star and formed Cosmopolitan Productions strictly to make pictures with her. Hearst expedited her rise to starring roles and gave her instant fame, but ironically she would have probably become a bigger star if he had then left her alone. She had a knack for comedy, but Hearst thought she was too beautiful to be seen with pie on her face and featured her mostly in lavish, overproduced historical romances. Her early films were so expensive that their distributor, Paramount, lost money, damaging Davies's reputation. Hearst and Davies shifted their affiliation to Goldwyn, which became part of M-G-M. Nurtured by Louis B. Mayer, she had much more success, even making the difficult transition to sound films with relative ease despite a stuttering problem. She'd still make occasional period romances, and her stories still centered around her snaring the man she loved, but she balanced her career with appearances in comedies and musicals and even a Civil War espionage film, *Operator 13*. She played a spy (who poses as a black!), flappers, showgirls, an office girl, poor girls, a trapeze artist, even a basketball player. When Mayer became more supportive of Norma Shearer, Hearst moved Davies to Warner Bros., where she finished her career, playing opposite Dick Powell's French ambassador and not laughing at that casting. It's a shame that so many people who saw the Hearst-Davies relationship as depicted by Orson Welles and Dorothy Comingore in *Citizen Kane* believe Davies was as big a flop as Comingore's character. Davies

Marion Davies.

was a gifted comedienne, and though limited as a dramatic actress, she always exhibited an appealing combination of beauty, intelligence, grit, and spirit, Many of her films were hits, and once the resentment over Hearst's interference died down, she was fairly popular. Catch her on the Late Show: Davies is always fun (and interesting) to watch.

• **Some Key Films:** *When Knighthood Was in Flower* (1933, Robert Vignola), *Zander the Great* (1925, George Hill), *Lights of Broadway* (1925, Monte Bell), *Tillie the Toiler* (1927, Hobart Henley), *Quality Street* (1927, Sidney Franklin), *The Patsy*, (1928, King Vidor), *Show People* (1928, Vidor), *The Floradora Girl* (1930, Harry Beaumont), *It's a Wise Child* (1931, Robert Z. Leonard), *Polly of the Circus* (1932, Alfred Santell), *Blondie of the Follies*

Bette Davis in Hush . . . Hush, Sweet Charlotte.

(1932, Edmund Goulding), *Peg o' My Heart* (1933, Leonard), *Cain and Mabel* (1936, Lloyd Bacon).

○

BETTE DAVIS (1908–89) Just as she was in her personal life, Bette Davis's characters were always at the center of attention, charming or coaxing weak men into doing their bidding and battling those stronger men and women for control of the frame. The cinema still reverberates from her verbal wars on screen and off screen with Warner Bros. over script approval. Fittingly, she fought with Warners to get roles that would feature her in verbal tirades. As she proved with her sluttish Mildred in *Of Human Bondage*, the picture that made her a star, no one threw better low-blow tantrums and was as sarcastic and condescending while screaming than Davis. It's a relief not to be Leslie Howard in *Of Human Bondage*, when Mildred walks back and forth while telling him off, or being in the shoes of Ann Sheridan, Miriam Hopkins, Olivia de Havilland and, of course, Joan Crawford when they competed with her—in and out of character. Davis's high-strung, neurotic women—who try to possess men, control everyone around them, and are resentful of other women—are among the most critical ("What a dump!"), spiteful, and intimidating women in cinema history. That's why they're so much fun. Even when they are mean and horrible, like Regina in *The Little Foxes*, we admire their intelligence, courage, strength, and brutal wit, and the fact that, in their worlds, they have established power. Some of these women are sympathetic, only unleashing venom because of insecurity. For instance, actress Margo Channing in *All About Eve* lashes out at everyone because she worries about advancing age; when she stops comparing herself unfavorably to the ambitious young actress (Anne Baxter), she can see her own value and get on with her life. Channing may be the best role in an incredible career that included hags and queens, tramps and virgins, aristocratic Yankees (she was from Massachusetts) and southern belles, murderers and victims, young dreamers and strict mothers, selfish women and those who'd sacrifice everything for those they love. She had amazing talent and versatility. She also had those remarkable "Bette Davis Eyes" that changed as instantly as she did: flirtatious, angry, thoughtful, sad, perceptive, on and on. Davis was short and not beautiful, but she had the smarts, skills, and eyes to make us believe her characters were.

• **Cult Favorites:** *Marked Woman* (1937, Lloyd Bacon), *Dark Victory* (1939, Edmund Goulding), *The Old Maid* (1939, Goulding), *Now, Voyager* (1942, Irving Rapper), *Beyond the Forest* (1949, King Vidor), *All About Eve* (1950, Joseph L. Mankiewicz), *What Ever Happened to Baby Jane?* (1962, Robert Aldrich).

• **Other Key Films:** *Of Human Bondage* (1934, John Cromwell), *Bordertown* (1935, Archie Mayo), *Dangerous* (1935, Alfred E. Green), *The Petrified Forest* (1936, Mayo), *Jezebel* (1938, William Wyler), *The Private Lives of Elizabeth and Essex* (1939, Michael Curtiz), *The Letter* (1940, William Wyler), *The Great Lie* (1941, Goulding),

The Little Foxes (1941, Wyler), *The Man Who Came to Dinner* (1941, William Keighley), *Old Acquaintance* (1943, Vincent Sherman, *The Corn is Green* (1944, Irving Rapper), *A Stolen Life* (1945, Curtis Bernhardt), *Deception* (1946, Rapper), *Hush . . . Hush, Sweet Charlotte* (1964, Aldrich), *The Nanny* (1965, Seth Holt), *The Anniversary* (1968, Roy Ward Baker).

○

DANIEL DAY-LEWIS (1958–) Handsome, intense, compelling young British actor who has avoided the trappings of stardom just as he has avoided being pigeonholed as an actor. He has intentionally sought diverse parts in small "art" films that don't rely on big-name stars to attract viewers. Typically, he chooses characters who are at odds with the world and/or people around them. He was a streak-haired homosexual street punk in *My Beautiful Laundrette*, a repressed, out-of-synch suitor in *A Room with a View*, a suave, womanizing doctor in occupied Czechoslovakia in *The Unbearable Lightness of Being*, a hopelessly uptight Englishman in America in *Stars and Bars*, and real-life Irish writer-painter, cerebral-palsy victim Christy Brown in *My Left Foot*. He won the Best Actor Oscar for his compassionate, fierce, ask-for-no-sympathy portrayal of the highly sensitive, irascible Brown, a part for which he learned to paint and type with his left foot and spent many hours twisted in a wheelchair. But it's worth noting that he took that role for the challenge, assuming the picture would never be released. Regardless of the fame it brought him, he'll surely continue to make films on the fringes rather than settle into star vehicles.

• **Cult Favorites:** *My Beautiful Laundrette* (1985, Stephen Frears), *The Unbearable Lightness of Being* (1988, Philip Kaufman).

• **Also Recommended:** *The Bounty* (1984, Roger Donaldson), *A Room with a View* (1985, James Ivory), *My Left Foot* (1989, Jim Sheridan).

○

DEAD END KIDS/EAST SIDE KIDS/BOWERY BOYS

They began as a tough, uneducated, unsupervised, and unruly teenage ghetto gang, products and victims of the Depression, in the Broadway social drama *Dead End* and William Wyler's hit Hollywood adaptation, playing it mean and straight. Handsome, bushy-haired Billy Halop was the well-meaning leader, a step up on the evolutionary chart from dangerous, knife-carrying Leo Gorcey (as "Spit"), stupid Huntz Hall (as "Dippy"), Gabe Dell, Bernard Punsley, and the others. The group proved so popular that Warners starred them in several other liberal social dramas, repackaging them as decent but misguided poverty kids who can be reformed by good priests, judges, and adult role models (i.e., the male leads). Their best film was *Angels with Dirty Faces*, in which they idolize gangster James Cagney instead of priest Pat O'Brien, until Cagney pretends to go

The Dead End Kids in Angels with Dirty Faces. *Clockwise from top left: Leo Gorcey, Huntz Hall, Billy Halop, Bernard Punsley, Gabe Dell, and Bobby Jordan.*

"yeller" on his way to execution. Eventually Halop left the group to seek (but not find) solo stardom, and Gorcey and Hall became the central figures in the group, which became the East Side Kids at Universal and the Bowery Boys after a final move to Monogram. Although the pictures continued to be about crime and mysteries (though some had surreal elements), they became increasingly comic, with Gorcey's "Slip" and Hall's "Sach" mixing silly wordplay and wild slapstick. Other regulars included Billy Benedict, Bobby Jordan, Leo's brother, David Gorcey (as Whitey), and Leo's father, Bernard Gorcey, as Louis Dumbrowski, the owner of the gang's headquarters, Louie's Sweet Shop. The programmers were certainly mediocre but were made tolerable by the likable stars. The Bowery Boys continued making pictures into the mid-fifties, when they were approaching middle age. Their movies have long been television staples.

• **Cult Favorites:** *Angels with Dirty Faces* (1937, Michael Curtiz), numerous "Dead End Kids," "East Side Kids," and "Bowery Boys" star vehicles (1940–56).

• **Also Recommended:** *Dead End* (1937, William Wyler), *Crime School* (1938, Lewis Seiler), *They Made Me a Criminal* (1939, Busby Berkeley), *Hell's Kitchen* (1939, Seiler and E. A. Dupont), *Angels Wash Their Faces* (1939, Ray Enright).

See: Leo Gorcey and Huntz Hall.

○

JAMES DEAN (1931–55) Every generation of young people feels that this astonishing young actor is speaking directly to them in *East of Eden*, *Rebel Without a Cause*, and *Giant*, released after his death in a car crash shocked the world. They identify with his sensitive, self-destructive, vulnerable outcasts, who feel everyone misunderstands them. Dean's shy, confused loners can't relate to adults and don't feel they fit in with people their own age—although in *Rebel Without a Cause*, everyone gets to like Jim Stark. There's no one who can explain to Dean's teenagers why they are so unhappy, angry, violent, and restless. Or why their parents and those they love reject their calls for love and understanding. These young men are unable to articulate their own feelings, at least until they find young women (Julie Harris, Natalie Wood, Elizabeth Taylor) who have the patience to listen to them. Appealingly, these females, whose previous men didn't understand their needs, blossom as they get to know Dean. I think female viewers took to Dean for the same reason Wood falls for him in *Rebel*: "A girl wants a man who's gentle and sweet and who doesn't run away." They also want to comfort him, listen to him, and give him the support he needs to get rid of his self-pity—and tame his violent streak. Young males respond to his rebelliousness, his trouble communicating with his father (domineering Raymond Massey in *East of Eden*, weak Jim Backus in *Rebel*), and to his frustration about not knowing how to fit in. I always think of Dean sitting in a chair in *Rebel* and smashing his fists into a policeman's desk, unable to confront his real enemies. Of course, everyone just loved the way Dean looked, mumbled, and moved: the way he shuffles when he walks to show his uncertainty; how he is often in a half-crouch like a boxer who is ready to come out punching; the way he tumbles out of his moving car in *Rebel*, displaying his athleticism; the way he marches off his land in *Giant*; the gentleness with which he responds to people in trouble. Three

James Dean and Elizabeth Taylor in Giant.

bad directors would have ruined it all by telling him to talk clearly, look at the person he is speaking to, sit up straight, correct his posture, and so on. Dean had unusual, highly realistic body movements, often slouching or just slumping to the ground. Kazan smartly went to the ground with him in *East of Eden*; George Stevens even used a ground-level camera in *Giant*. Dean was great as usual in *Giant*—it's a terrific moment when he finds oil on his land—but I never liked him in that film because he gets old. Dean died young. He just wasn't meant to get old, was he?

• **Cult Favorites:** *East of Eden* (1955, Elia Kazan), *Rebel Without a Cause* (1955, Nicholas Ray), *Giant* (1956, George Stevens).

○

KRISTINE DE BELL (1954–) Blond *Playboy* Bunny with brief movie fame as the title character in the amusing adults-only musical, *Alice in Wonderland*. She was comfortable and engaging on the screen, coming across as refreshingly irreverent and uninhibited—on a promotion tour, she temporarily walked off a TV studio set in mid-interview to use the bathroom. She filmed a couple of explicit sex scenes but they were deleted for theatrical release (they have been restored for video). She might have become even more famous if they'd been retained, because the picture could have been the rare successful attempt to incorporate hard-core sex into a legitimate film. Such scenes might have prevented her from making her quick transition into the mainstream cinema, but she hasn't had such a good part again. However, she was likable as Jacky Chan's girlfriend in *The Big Brawl*—her character was perky, like a cheerleader rather than a sexpot.

• **Cult Favorite:** *Alice in Wonderland* (1975, Bud Townsend), *Willie and Phil* (1980, Paul Mazursky).

• **Other Key Films:** *Emmanuelle Around the World* (1977, Joe D'Amato), *Bloodbrothers* (1978, Robert Mulligan), *Meatballs* (1979, Ivan Reitman), *The Big Brawl* (1980, Robert Clouse), *Tag—The Assassination Game* (1982, Nick Castle).

○

YVONNE DE CARLO (1922–) Born in Vancouver, pretty Peggy Middleton became competition to Dorothy Lamour at Paramount. While Lamour had the South Seas to herself—De Carlo wouldn't star in *Flame of the Islands* until 1955—De Carlo heated up the desert and other exotic locales in many campy skimpy-costume pictures. She had leads as Salome and Scheherazade, and in *Slave Girl*, *Casbah*, and *Hotel Sahara*. She also starred in numerous westerns, playing Calamity Jane and Lola Montez (another of her dancers), as well as *Frontier Gal*, *River Lady*, and *The Gal Who Took the West*. She got all dolled up and looked pretty and sexy as saloon girls and riverboat ladies, but this didn't mean she wasn't tough: De Carlo's women, whether temptresses or heroines, never ran away from trouble or backed down from men, which is why she was good in her few melodramas as femmes fatales. In *Criss Cross*, her sneaky female prefers Dan Duryea to Burt Lancaster—that's all you need

to know about her. In the sixties, De Carlo achieved cult status among young TV fans as Lily on the horror-comedy series "The Munsters," which plays everywhere in reruns. She has capitalized on her horror identification by appearing in a number of horror films. Most have been awful (*American Gothic*, *Nocturna*, *Satan's Cheerleaders*, *Cellar Dweller*), but they have won her a new following.

• **Cult Favorites:** *Criss Cross* (1949, Robert Siodmak), *The Ten Commandments* (1956, Cecil B. De Mille), *Satan's Cheerleaders* (1977, Greydon Clark).

• **Sleepers:** *The Captain's Paradise* (1953, Anthony Kimmons), *Silent Scream* (1980, Denny Harris), *The Man with Bogart's Face* (1980, Robert Day), *Liar's Moon* (1981, David Fisher).

• **Other Key Films:** *Salome, Where She Danced* (1945, Charles Lamont), *Frontier Gal* (1945, Lamont), *Song of Scheherazade* (1947, Walter Reisch), *Brute Force* (1947, Jules Dassin), *Slave Girl* (1947, Lamont), *Casbah* (1948, John Berry), *Black Bart* (1948, George Sherman), *River Lady* (1948, Sherman), *Calamity Jane and Sam Bass* (1949, Sherman), *Tomahawk* (1951, Sherman), *Scarlet Angel* (1952, Sidney Salkow), *Border River* (1954, Sherman), *Passion* (1954, Allan Dwan), *Raw Edge* (1956, John Sherwood), *McLintock!* (1963, Andrew V. McLaglen).

○

SANDRA DEE (1942–) In *Grease*, Stockard Channing and her friends sing hopefully, "Look at me, I'm Sandra Dee." Why they and millions of other teenage girls in America in the late fifties and early sixties ever wanted to be Sandra Dee is beyond me. Born Alexandra Zuck, this former child model was one of the least interesting teen idols in cinema history. She may have been perky and could look distressed, but when she was most popular she could barely act. She had a slim figure and was cute at best, looking more like a doll than a girl, with blond hair (usually with bangs flipped perfectly at the edges) and a chubby face. Her colorless lips and fair skin appeared to be covered by Chapstick. Though Tammy and beach bunny Gidget may be endearing to camp-movie lovers, Dee's teenagers are so naive, silly, and obnoxious that it's hard to believe young girls across America could emulate them. Her young heroines have, to varying degrees, trouble communicating with their parents—they feel either overprotected or neglected, as by her actress mother Lana Turner in the Ross Hunter–Douglas Sirk soap opera, *Imitation of Life*, her best film. At the same time, they experience romantic problems. They worry about first love; in some of her dramas, they worry about marriage and about sex. Left to their own devices, they make *mature* decisions. In *A Summer Place*, one of the first films to deal with teenage sex, Dee tells boyfriend Troy Donahue that they must

control their passions because "We've got to be good." Her fans breathed a sigh of relief. She was married for 7 years to her frequent costar, singer Bobby Darin.

• **Cult Favorites:** *Imitation of Life* (1959, Douglas Sirk), *Gidget* (1959, Paul Wendkos), *A Summer Place* (1959, Delmer Daves).

• **Other Key Films:** *The Reluctant Debutante* (1958, Vincente Minnelli), *The Restless Years* (1958, Helmut Kautner), *A Portrait in Black* (1960, Michael Gordon), *Tammy Tell Me True* (1961, Harry Keller), *Come September* (1961, Robert Mulligan), *Tammy and the Doctor* (1963, Harry Keller), *Take Her, She's Mine* (1963, Henry Koster).

• **Also of Interest:** *The Wild and the Innocent* (1959, Jack Sher), *Romanoff and Juliet* (1961, Peter Ustinov), *If a Man Answers* (1962, Henry Levin), *That Funny Feeling* (1965, Richard Thorpe).

○

EDDIE DEEZEN Geeky young actor who looks and acts like he stepped out of the pages of

Sandra Dee is all energy as Gidget.

Mad magazine. He's like a distant cousin of the young, skinny Jerry Lewis. And just as Lewis's otherwise empty-headed character knows everything about comic books in *Artists and Models*, Deezen's funniest nerds are also experts at some facet of our culture: Beatle trivia in *I Wanna Hold Your Hand*, computerese in *WarGames*. It's a shame that Deezen has been exiled to innocuous, big-cast youth comedies and ultracheap Fred Olen Ray horror movies of late, because he is quite hilarious talking up an obnoxious storm about something esoteric and acting like everyone should understand him; his entire face moves with his excited mouth.

• **Sleeper:** *I Wanna Hold Your Hand* (1978, Robert Zemeckis).

• **Other Key Films:** *1941* (1979, Steven Spielberg), *WarGames* (1983, John Badham).

• **Also of Interest:** *Desperate Moves* (1983, Oliver Hellman), *Polish Vampire in Burbank* (1985, Mark Pirro), *The Rosebud Beach Hotel* (1985, Harry Hurwitz), *Beverly Hills Vamp* (1988, Fred Olen Ray).

○

ALBERT DEKKER (1905–68) Hefty actor most memorable in a rare lead, the merciless title character in *Dr. Cyclops*, a jungle-set horror thriller (the first color film to use transparencies, split screen, and double exposures). Completely bald, with a mustache and thick glasses, he was convincing as a madman who shrinks his fellow scientists. He was also frightening as a homicidal mental hospital escapee (and his twin brother) in *Among the Living*, so it's obvious that he could have become a fixture in fright films if he had desired. But Dekker made a slight mark in all genres,

including horror (he was again a mad scientist in 1957's laughable *She-Devil*), usually in supporting roles, almost always as forceful authority figures, many of them villainous.

• **Cult Favorites:** *Dr. Cyclops* (1940, Ernest B. Schoedsack), *Strange Cargo* (1940, Frank Borzage), *The Silver Chalice* (1954, Victor Saville), *East of Eden* (1955, Elia Kazan), *Kiss Me Deadly* (1955, Robert Aldrich), *The Wild Bunch* (1969, Sam Peckinpah).

• **Sleepers:** *The Man in the Iron Mask* (1939, James Whale), *Among the Living* (1941, Stuart Heisler).

• **Other Key Films:** *Wake Island* (1942, John Farrow), *The Killers* (1946, Robert Siodmak), *Gentleman's Agreement* (1947, Kazan), *The Pretender* (1947, W. Lee Wilder), *The Furies* (1950, Anthony Mann), *Wait 'Til the Sun Shines, Nellie* (1952, Henry King), *Suddenly Last Summer* (1959, Joseph L. Mankiewicz).

○

LISA DE LEEUW Red-haired, large-breasted, sexy porno actress. After one look at her cool, hungry eyes under a vixen's sharp eyebrows, directors never thought of casting her as a sweet virgin. She specialized in playing aggressive, sexually experienced temptresses, usually turning in the hottest sex scenes in her films.

• **Cult Favorite:** *Amanda by Night* (1981, Robert McCallum).

• **Other Key Films:** *Downstairs Upstairs* (1980, Lisa Barr), *Plato's, The Movie* (1980, Joe Sherman), *Pink Champagne* (1980, Steven Conrad), *8 to 4* (1981, Louis Lewis), *The Blonde Next Door* (1981, Sherman), *Every Which Way She Can* (1981, Lewis).

○

ALAIN DELON (1935–) In *Borsalino*, a woman tells Delon's character that he never looks satisfied, though he has everything. That almost sums up the career of the actor. He became France's top romantic idol by starring in films for such prestigious directors as Clément, Visconti, Antonioni, and Melville, yet was frustrated in his attempts to export his popularity to America or convince anyone that he was more than a pretty face. He was tall, dark, and exceptionally handsome, and had presence. Yet he was stiff and unexpressive, which made him painful to watch in comedies but, luckily, helped him play cool, emotionless tough guys in numerous gangster and suspense films. He often was cast as a bad guy—he was at his best playing a ruthless killer in Melville's *The Samurai*—usually inhabiting a screen world devoid of good guys. Occasionally, he was teamed with other French idols (Jean Gabin, Yves Montand, Lino Ventura, Jean-Paul Belmondo) in thrillers with male-friendship themes. His screen lovers included Brigitte Bardot, Danielle Darrieux, Claudia Cardinale (they were a gorgeous romantic couple in *The Leopard*, probably Delon's best film), Ann-Margret, Jane Fonda, Catherine Deneuve, his wife Natalie, and his ex-fiancée, Romy Schneider. In France, his fame grew due to his affair with Schneider, a major murder (of his bodyguard) scandal, his acknowledgment that he'd been a homosexual, and bizarre stories about his troubled past. Across the Atlantic, no one cared about his personal life or his American-made movies.

• **Key Films:** *Purple Noon* (1960, René Clément), *Rocco and His Brothers* (1960, Luchino Visconti), *Eclipse* (1962, Michelangelo Antonioni), *The Leopard* (1963, Visconti), *Any Number Can Win/The Big Grab* (1963, Henri Verneuil), *Once a Thief* (1965, Ralph Nelson), *Le Samurai* (1967, Jean-Pierre Melville), *Spirits of the Dead* (1968, Louis Malle episode), *The Sicilian Clan* (1969, Henri Verneuil), *Borsalino* (1970, Jacques Deray), *Le Cercle Rouge* (1970, Melville), *Dirty Money* (1972, Melville), *Mr. Klein* (1976, Joseph Losey).

• **Also of Interest:** *Joy House* (1964, Clément), *Lost Command* (1966, Mark Robson), *Texas Across the River* (1966, Michael Cordon), *Is Paris Burning?* (1967, Clément), *The Last Adventure* (1967, Robert Enrico), *Naked Under Leather/The Girl on the Motorcycle* (1968, Jack Cardiff), *Red Sun* (1972, Terence Young), *The Assassination of Trotsky* (1972, Losey), *Zorro* (1974, Duccio Tessari), *Swann in Love* (1985, Volker Schlöndorff).

○

VANESSA DEL RIO This voluptuous Cuban–New Yorker is the only Latin to become a porno superstar. She appeared in numerous films beginning in the late seventies and has been featured in a successful line of XXX-rated videos. Of course, she is a favorite of the Spanish audience. Whether playing frustrated housewives, housekeepers, cooks, waitresses, or massage parlor attendants, she has excited her fans with charged, lusty performances, giving—as they say of athletes—120 percent in one sex scene after another. Her characters appear to be loving the screen sex, and the kinkier the better. She projects the image of an uninhibited nymphomaniac—unfortunately, at times downright vulgarly. An adequate actress.

• **Cult Favorites:** *Pink Ladies* (1980, Richard Mahler), *Foxtrot* (1982).

• **Other Key Films:** *Odyssey* (1979, Gerard

Alain Delon with Marianne Faithfull in The Girl on a Motorcycle.

Damiano), *Babylon Pink* (1979, Henri Pachard), *Her Name Was Lisa* (1979, Mahler), *Justine* (1980, Robert R. Walters), *Afternoon Delights* (1981, Warren Evans), *The Dancers* (1981, Anthony Spinelli), *Dracula Exotica* (1981, Evans), *A Scent of Heather* (1981, Philip Drexler).

○

WILLIAM DEMAREST (1892–1983) This marvelous character actor is probably best known for his long stint as Uncle Charley on the television comedy series "My Three Sons" (he replaced William Frawley). But it shouldn't be forgotten that he was in about 100 movies, dating back to 1927 with the first sound film, *The Jazz Singer*, starring Al Jolson, as well as *The Jolson Story* and *Jolson Sings Again*, in the late forties. His major contribution came in the

forties when he appeared in several classic comedies written and directed by Preston Sturges, acting cynical, talking fast, saying funny things, being grouchy, doing a slow burn as one character or another irritates him, doing pratfalls. As Andrew Sarris commented, "The Sturges stock company was particularly noted for the contrasting personalities of William Demarest, the rowdy roughneck, and Franklin Pangborn, the prissy prune." Surely Demarest's classic role is as a small-town cop and strict but helpless widower father of two headstrong daughters in Sturges's controversial *The Miracle of Morgan's Creek*. He has some delightful outbursts after finding out his eldest and more high-strung daughter, Betty Hutton (as Trudy Kockenlocker), got knocked up by a soldier (who it turns out also married her before disappearing), during a night of which she has no recollection. Both the scenes in which Demarest intimidates Hutton's meek boyfriend Eddie Bracken and those in which he tries to bring order to his home life are genuinely hilarious. As is usual when he played a father, he gripes constantly, and if not having a tantrum, is on the verge of one—yet he proves to be softhearted.

• **Cult Favorites:** *A Girl in Every Port* (1928, Howard Hawks), *Sullivan's Travels* (1941, Preston Sturges), *The Miracle of Morgan's Creek* (1944, Sturges), *It's a Mad Mad Mad Mad World* (1963, Stanley Kramer).

• **Other Key Films:** *Mr. Smith Goes to Washington* (1939, Frank Capra), *Christmas in July* (1940, Sturges), *The Great McGinty* (1940, Sturges), *The Lady Eve* (1941, Sturges), *Hail the Conquering Hero* (1944, Sturges), *The Jolson Story* (1946, Alfred E. Green).

• **Also Recommended:** *The Jazz Singer* (1927, Alan Crosland), *Easy Living* (1937, Mitchell Leisen), *Big City* (1937, Frank Borzage), *The Devil and Miss Jones* (1941, Sam Wood), *Pardon My Sarong* (1942, Erle C. Kenton), *Night Has a Thousand Eyes* (1948, John Farrow), *Sorrowful Jones* (1949, Sidney Lanfield), *Jolson Sings Again* (1949, Henry Levin), *What Price Glory?* (1952, John Ford), *Viva Las Vegas* (1964, George Sidney).

○

CATHERINE DENEUVE (1943–) This gorgeous, elegant blond French actress, the younger sister of Françoise Dorléac, became her country's greatest female star in the mid-sixties. Her breakthrough film was Jacques Demy's experimental, cynical musical *The Umbrellas of Cherbourg*, in which she played a pregnant 17-year-old shopgirl who must marry when her lover doesn't return from the war. She'd never again play someone so sweet or warm. However, she was again sympathetic in *Repulsion*, which in 1965 many people considered even scarier than *Psycho*. She portrayed a sexually repressed young woman who has brutal-erotic, sexual-attack fantasies and, her mind deteriorating, murders her lascivious landlord and her well-meaning suitor. Whereas viewers of *Psycho* identified with victims, here they bond with an insane murderer. Deneuve would continue to star in erotic films, with male characters still trying to break through her women's sexual defenses and we viewers still trying to understand their complicated minds. Her women became increasingly aloof, icy, and enigmatic. Sex (or the denial of sex) becomes their weapon against men as well as their means to liberation. In Luis Buñuel's *Tristana*, her penniless woman has no choice but to give herself sexually to rich, powerful Fernando Rey, but she comes to realize that by denying herself to him she can offset his control over her and take over. In Buñuel's *Belle de Jour*, her frigid wife of a handsome Parisian doctor has masochistic fantasies and works secretly in a brothel, becoming part of her clients' weird fantasies. Interestingly, as she breaks free of her bourgeois bonds through sex, she begins to reject the depraved, masochistic sex that characterized her early desires—her fantasies become more normal, her self-esteem improves, and she is ready to enter a normal sexual relationship with her husband. With the exception of *Repulsion*, Deneuve's English-language films have been disappointing, especially *The Hunger*, in which she plays a bisexual vampire queen.

• **Cult Favorites:** *The Umbrellas of Cherbourg* (1964, Jacques Demy), *Repulsion*

Catherine Deneuve in Hustle *with Burt Reynolds.*

(1965, Roman Polanski), *Belle de Jour* (1967, Luis Buñuel), *The Hunger* (1983, Tony Scott).

• **Other Key Films:** *Male Hunt* (1965, Edouard Molinaro), *The Young Girls of Rochefort* (1968, Demy), *Mississippi Mermaid* (1969, François Truffaut), *Mayerling* (1969, Terence Young), *Tristana* (1970, Buñuel), *Donkey Skin* (1971, Demy), *Dirty Money* (1972, Jean-Pierre Melville), *A Slightly Pregnant Man* (1973, Demy), *La Grande Bourgeoise* (1974, Mauro Bolognin), *The Last Metro* (1980, Truffaut), *Scene of the Crime* (1987, André Téchiné).

○

ROBERT DE NIRO (1943–) Stunningly talented, one-of-a-kind actor has created some of the cinema's most exciting, powerful portrayals in the last two decades. He first revealed his nobody-will-be-fooled con-man side in Brian De Palma's innovative, low-budget seriocomedy *Greetings*, trying to convince women to pose for "Peeping Tom" films he pretends to be making for the Whitney Museum. He revealed his sweet, inarticulate, mixed-up side in the wonderful baseball movie *Bang the Drum Slowly*, as a dumb catcher whose impending death brings the team together. He also showed his obsessive dedication to his craft, learning to play hardball, just as he'd later learn to box for *Raging Bull* and play the saxophone for *New York, New York*. He punished his body by catching fastballs from the outset just as he would do putting on enormous weight to play an aging Jake LaMotta in *Raging Bull*. Martin Scorsese first began to turn De Niro into a star in his earlier *Mean Streets*, by mixing the pushy con man and the inarticulate, confused, but sweet fuck-up with the third side of what became the De Niro persona: an insensitive, tactless, violent, uncontrollable wild man. (He also was the

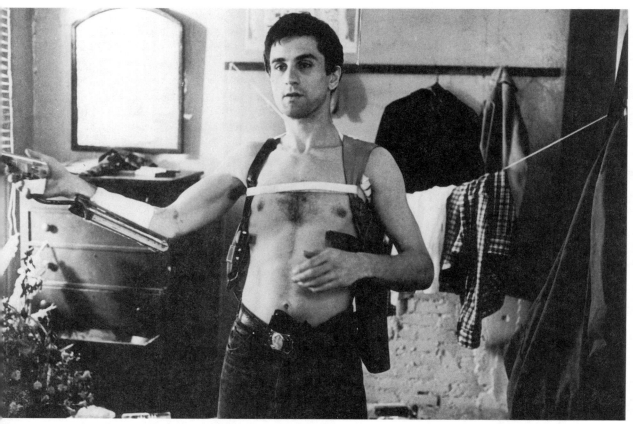

Robert De Niro prepares for battle in Taxi Driver.

first to recognize the grace of De Niro's walking—Coppola would pick up on this for the silent sequences of *The Godfather Part II*.) Since his high-strung Johnny Boy in *Mean Streets*, many of De Niro's characters are like lit fuses. Some—Travis Bickle in *Taxi Driver*, for example—are once well-meaning nobodies who go berserk. Jake LaMotta, a mean somebody, doesn't actually go crazy, but when his temper gets the best of him, he attacks his opponents and his wife. Even Rupert Pupkin, would-be comic in *The King of Comedy*, is dangerous—he kidnaps a talk

show host to gain attention. De Niro's characters talk in a "natural," aggressive, New York street patter, repeating phrases and questions and repeating others' answers as questions. They talk a mad streak but don't really make conversation. We sense they're just biding time, deciding what to destroy next. His characters won't listen and never take advice, though they smile while someone talks to them. When they sense they are being patronized, they do damage. They don't mind causing scenes or being thrown out of places. We want these guys to go away, which is kind of why we enjoy seeing people we dislike get stuck with them. For instance, I like it when his annoying Rupert refuses to leave the hallowed offices of smug TV executives who never let the other hopefuls of the world pass through their doors. However, its hard for us to tolerate pushy Rupert at other times, or De Niro's sax player in *New York, New York*, who's so irritating while courting Liza Minnelli that for the rest of the film we don't realize he's the more sympathetic one in the relationship. Much of the excitement of his early characterizations was that he was young, hyper, and rebellious; it will be interesting to watch his role choices as he gets older, to see if talent wins out.

• **Cult Favorites:** *Greetings* (1968, Brian De Palma), *Bloody Mama* (1969, Roger Corman, *Hi, Mom!* (1970, De Palma), *Bang the Drum Slowly* (1973, John Hancock), *Mean Streets* (1973, Martin Scorsese), *The Godfather Part II* (1974, Francis Ford Coppola), *Taxi Driver* (1976, Scorsese), *New York, New York* (1977, Scorsese), *1900* (1977, Bernardo Bertolucci), *Raging Bull* (1979, Scorsese), *The King of Comedy* (1983, Scorsese), *Once Upon a Time in America* (1984, Sergio Leone), *Brazil* (1985, Terry Gilliam), *Angel Heart* (1987, Alan Parker), *The Untouchables* (1987, De Palma).

• **Other Key Films:** *The Deer Hunter* (1978, Michael Cimino), *GoodFellas* (1990, Scorsese), *Awakenings* (1990, Penny Marshall), *Guilty by Suspicion* (1991, Irwin Winkler).

○

GÉRARD DEPARDIEU (1948–) Forceful, barrel-chested French star, with a handsome face, large nose, strong jaw, narrow eyes, and shaggy blond hair, rated in an *American Film* critics poll as the most significant European actor of the eighties. It's amazing how prolific he is and how many different types of roles he plays (*Time* called him a "One-Man New Wave" when he appeared on its cover) and how he makes viewers believe the role he is playing is the only type he could possibly play. Since many of his characters have been street-punk types, he's often worn black leather jackets—but he's also worn suits, priest's robes, and women's clothes, and been entirely naked. He's played hunks and hunchbacks (in *Jean de Florette*), womanizers and homosexuals, young men without worth and great historical figures (Danton, Rodin). He has played timid men and brutes, sweet men and cads. He's played in the absurd comedies of Bertrand Blier, serious dramas, and everything in between. The one common element is that his characters always seem to view the world differently than anyone else. They're unpredictable and, because of Depardieu's offbeat approach, always interesting. His tremendous talent and appeal aside, Depardieu has been the most daring actor in the cinema.

• **Cult Favorites:** *Going Places* (1973, Bertrand Blier), *1900* (1975, Bernardo Bertolucci), *Maîtresse* (1975, Barbet Schroeder), *Loulou* (1979, Maurice Pialat), *Get Out Your Handkerchiefs* (1977, Blier), *Buffet Froid* (1979, Blier), *Mon Oncle d'Amérique* (1980, Alain Resnais), *The Return of Martin Guerre* (1982, Daniel Vigne), *Moon in the Gutter* (1983, Jean-Jacques Beineix), *Ménage* (1986, Blier).

• **Other Key Films:** *The Last Woman* (1976, Marco Ferrari), *The Last Metro* (1980, François Truffaut), *The Woman Next Door* (1981, Truffaut), *La Chèvre* (1981, Francis Veber), *Danton* (1982, Andrzej Wajda), *Les Compères* (1983, Veber), *La Tartuffe* (1984, Gérard Depardieu),

Gérard Depardieu and Nathalie Baye in The Return of Martin Guerre.

Police (1985, Pialat), *Jean de Florette* (1986, Claude Berri), *Sous le Soleil de Satan* (1987, Pialat), *Camille Claudel* (1988, Bruno Nuytten), *Too Beautiful for You* (1989, Blier), *Cyrano De Bergerac* (1990, Jean-Claude Petit), *Green Card* (1990, Peter Weir).

○

BO DEREK (1957–) Beautiful, shapely blonde became a sensation as the hedonistic young bubblehead who becomes middle-aged Dudley Moore's obsession in Blake Ed-wards's frantic yet sophisticated comedy *'10'*, the title referring to Bo's perfect beauty rating. America's love affair with Bo faded when it realized she came bound to husband John Derek, a onetime actor who had been a sex symbol himself in the fifties. Bo denied they had a Svengali-Trilby rela-tionship, but movie fans sensed she was following Ursula Andress and Linda Evans in the aging Casanova's line of young blondes he conquered and then discarded. John helped promote Bo as a sex symbol and blank-minded love child, even becoming her permanent director. But *Tarzan, the*

Ape Man, *Bolero*, and *Fantasies* were terrible films that teased viewers and left them disappointed. Derek said he wanted the world to see how sexy Bo can be when nude, but his films are anti-erotic. Every time Bo has a love scene, John subverts the passion with disruptive humor, stupid dialogue, or needlessly tricky camerawork. In *Bolero*, there is one unforgettable slow-motion sex scene in which a sheik licks honey off Bo's tummy, and just as we're supposed to be excited, all this disgusting gooey stuff forms on his face and hangs from his nose.

• **Key Films:** *'10'* (1979, Blake Edwards), *Tarzan, the Ape Man* (1981, John Derek), *Bolero* (1984, Derek).

Bo Derek found her physical match, Miles O'Keeffe, in Tarzan, the Ape Man.

• **Also of Interest:** *Orca* (1977, Michael Anderson), *A Change of Seasons* (1980, Richard Lang), *Fantasies* (1984, Derek).

○

BRUCE DERN (1936–) Tall, talented, screen-stealing actor, with a slender, handsome face and crazed blue eyes. He started out as a supporting actor, playing frightening villains (including AIP bikers) who were either psychotic or on the edge. Eventually, he moved into leads, still playing volatile characters who when exasperated seem on the verge of a temper tantrum or a breakdown. At some point, his characters are upset and disappointed—they are never satisfied with their lives, which in some cases seem to be falling apart—and their teary eyes, cracking, high-pitched voices, and sarcastic (quite funny) remarks make it apparent that they are hurt and feel sorry for themselves. Often his characters are overly serious and sensitive about something trivial. Their worlds are limited and they are obsessed with one thing: basketball in *Drive, He Said* (his tongue-in-cheek coach's pep talks are hilarious); his space greenery in *Silent Running*; the army in *Coming Home*; a beauty pageant sponsored by his used-car dealership in *Smile*; his "art" in the sick *Tattoo*; mad experiments in the ludicrous *The Incredible Two-Headed Transplant*; foolish financial schemes in *The King of Marvin Gardens*; capturing getaway driver Ryan O'Neal in *The Driver*; his comeback as a long-distance runner in *On The Edge*, etc. Dern is one ex-supporting actor who continued giving offbeat characterizations after hitting it big. He recently had a great role in *After Dark, My Sweet*, as the seedy, white-haired, pathetic con man Uncle Bud.

Bruce Dern in Silent Running.

• **Cult Favorites:** *Wild River* (1960, Elia Kazan), *Marnie* (1964, Alfred Hitchcock), *St. Valentine's Day Massacre* (1967, Roger Corman) *The Wild Angels* (1966, Corman), *The Trip* (1967, Corman), *Psych-Out* (1968, Richard Rush), *Bloody Mama* (1969, Corman), *Drive, He Said* (1970, Jack Nicholson), *The Incredible Two-Headed Transplant* (1971, Anthony Lanza), *Silent Running* (1971, Douglas Trumbull), *The King of Marvin Gardens* (1972, Nicholson), *Smile* (1975, Michael Ritchie), *The Driver* (1978, Walter Hill).

• **Other Key Films:** *Will Penny* (1968, Tom Gries), *They Shoot Horses, Don't They?* (1969, Sidney Pollack), *Support Your Local Sheriff!* (1969, Burt Kennedy), *The Cowboys* (1972, Mark Rydell), *The Great Gatsby* (1974, Jack Clayton), *Posse* (1975, Kirk Douglas), *Family Plot* (1976, Hitchcock), *Coming Home* (1978, Hal Ashby), *Harry Tracy, Desperado* (1982, William A. Graham), *On the Edge* (1985, Rob Nilsson), *After Dark, My Sweet* (1990, James Foley).

• **Also of Interest:** *Rebel Rousers* (1967, Martin B. Cohen), *The Cycle Savages* (1969, Bill Brame), *The Laughing Policeman* (1974, Stuart Rosenberg), *Black Sunday* (1977, John Frankenheimer), *The Big Town* (1987, John Milius).

○

LAURA DERN (1966–) Slim, extremely appealing blonde, the daughter of Bruce Dern and Diane Ladd has given remarkably intelligent and mature performances as sensitive teenagers in confusing, worrisome romantic or sexual situations. In *Mask*, she is sweet as a blind girl who falls for a boy (Eric Stoltz) with a disfiguring disease, returning the love, tenderness, and respect he gives her. She got her first lead, in the chilling *Smooth Talk*, from an even more depressing story by Joyce Carol Oates. There she was riveting as a tremulous teenage virgin who, excited and bored by the summer heat, chances being a sexual tease and gets more than she bargained for, catching the eye of the older, devil-like Treat Williams. In *Blue Velvet*, director David Lynch plays her blond, virginal teenager against Isabella Rossellini's sexually experienced, sexually perverse dark-haired woman—the two females who attract college student Kyle MacLachlan. Dern represents innocence but, interestingly, she really isn't so innocent: they are attracted to each other by their willingness to commit crimes like theft and breaking and entering. In this film and others, Dern shows that today, "nice girls" aren't necessarily wholesome. In Lynch's violent, batty couple-on-the-run film, *Wild at Heart*, she is openly sexual for a change, but her fantasies (of Oz) are wholesome.

• **Cult Favorites:** *Blue Velvet* (1986, David Lynch), *Wild at Heart* (1990, Lynch).

• **Sleepers:** *Mask* (1985, Peter Bogdanovich), *Smooth Talk* (1985, Joyce Chopra).

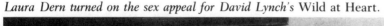
Laura Dern turned on the sex appeal for David Lynch's Wild at Heart.

• **Also of Interest:** *Ladies and Gentlemen, The Fabulous Stains* (1981, Lou Adler), *Haunted Summer* (1988, Ivan Passer).

○

PATRICK DEWAERE (1947–82) A handsome, funny but low-key, rarely smiling French actor, he was discovered while doing improvisational comedy at Paris's popular Café de la Gare with one-time girlfriend Miou-Miou. In movies he played all kinds of parts, from dreamers to outcasts to the temperamental soccer player in *Coup de Tête*. But he typically appeared in unusual films, often dealing with odd sexual themes, strange attractions, or male bonding. He's best known for his work in the bizarre comedies of Bertrand Blier. In *Going Places*, he and Gérard Depardieu race around seducing every pretty woman they meet, wherever they meet them— though the women end up more satisfied than they do. In *Get Out Your Handkerchiefs*, neither macho man can sexually arouse Depardieu's wife, Carole Laure— she rejects them for a boy. In *Beau Père*, his unhappy, weak pianist is seduced by his 14-year-old stepdaughter, who sees only his virtues. While preparing to play boxer Marcel Cerdan, Dewaere committed suicide.

• **Cult Favorites:** *Going Places* (1974, Bertrand Blier), *Get Out Your Handkerchiefs* (1978, Blier), *Beau Père* (1981, Blier).

• **Other Key Films:** *Lily Aime Moi* (1974, Maurice Dugowson), *The Best Way to Walk* (1975, Claude Miller), *Catherine & Co.* (1975, Michael Boisrand), *Le Juge Fayard* (1977, Yves Boisset), *Coup de Tête* (1978, Jean-Jacques Annaud), *Serie Noire* (1979, Alain Corneau), *A Bad Son* (1980, Claude Sautet), *Psy* (1980, Philippe de Broca), *Hotel of the Americas* (1981, André Téchiné), *Plein Sud* (1981, Luc Beraud), *Paradise for All* (1982, Alain Jessua).

○

ANGIE DICKINSON (1931–) Before she became a TV superstar and sex symbol (particularly to men over 40) as the star of "Police Woman" in the mid-seventies, she had a devoted cult following among mostly male movie fans. Beautiful, busty, and with legs that were, according to publicity releases, insured for one million dollars, she made an impression as cynical, savvy, strong but ultimately vulnerable women who believe the world is rotten and run by chauvinistic men, and do whatever has to be done to survive. They "play the game" but are out for themselves. If she was part of the movie's decor, it is because her characters feel part of the decor in their worlds. Her women sell sex, but they also are around when the bullets start flying; Dickinson was always better in films with action and violence than straight comedies or romances. In *Point Blank*, where she is at her most alluring, she accompanies tough Lee Marvin as he goes after gangster leaders. In *The Killers* (made for TV but then deemed too brutal to televise), as gangster kingpin Ronald Reagan's double-dealing mistress, she is slugged and hung out a high window by Marvin and Clu Gulager. Her best role was as Feathers in Howard Hawks's great western, *Rio Bravo*, a wise and witty gambling lady who wins over sheriff John Wayne. As one of Hawks's women who fit into a male world yet retain their femininity, Dickinson both excites Wayne with her aggressive sexuality and saves his life in a gun battle. Although she has a much cheerier ending, Feathers harks back to Dickinson's first important role, in Vietnam-set *China Gate*.

Her provocatively dressed Eurasian, Lucky Legs, left with a baby by her American soldier husband (Gene Barry), joins him in a dangerous mission and gives her life blowing up a Communist supply dump. Dickinson, who was a vicious kidnapper in *Cry Terror*, always played women who are tough and willing to put themselves on the line. She has had fewer movie roles since becoming a major star on "Police Woman," but she has continued to play strong characters. Oddly, whereas she promised sex in her early roles, since she has passed her early forties, she has delivered. In *Dressed to Kill*, she had a celebrated nude shower (plus a sexual encounter with a handsome but syphilitic stranger), and as a gang leader in *Big Bad Mama*, she has a nude lovemaking scene with William Shatner, of all people. She was back robbing banks 13 years later in the sequel; at age 57, she still looked great.

• **Cult Favorites:** *China Gate* (1957, Samuel Fuller), *Rio Bravo* (1959, Howard Hawks), *The Killers* (1964, Don Siegel), *The Chase* (1966, Arthur Penn), *Point Blank* (1967, John Boorman), *Pretty Maids All in a Row* (1971, Roger Vadim), *Big Bad Mama* (1974, Steve Carver), *Dressed to Kill* (1980, Brian De Palma).

• **Also of Interest:** *Man with the Gun* (1955, Richard Wilson), *Cry Terror* (1958, Andrew L. Stone), *Ocean's Eleven* (1960, Lewis Milestone), *The Sins of Rachel Cade* (1961, Gordon Douglas), *Rome Adventure* (1962, Delmer Daves), *The Resurrection of Zachary Wheeler* (1971, Bob Wynn), *Big Bad Mama II* (1987, Jim Wynorski).

○

MARLENE DIETRICH (1901–) One of the cinema's sexiest, most glamorous stars. She was a minor actress in Germany before Josef von Sternberg cast her as songstress-temptress Lola Lola in *The Blue Angel*. This film made her a star in Germany, but it wasn't released in America until after *Morocco* had paved the way. Lola Lola is the role with which Dietrich is most identified. She has a casual, aloof manner toward men, little concern about her image (but has a profound knowledge that she is the only one who can protect herself), an ironic attitude toward the hypocritical world and its strict moral code (men like Emil Jannings's tyrannical professor condemn her but secretly desire her), a willingness to satisfy her own physical needs no matter who gets hurt, and tantalizing beauty. She personified sinful sex. But she's really not the blond devil many critics claim. It's just that her very existence seems to cause men to fall foolishly in love, and she never stops a man from entering a path toward self-destruction. She doesn't plan to humiliate the professor and is loyal until the inevitable moment when she finds herself "Falling in love again, can't help it." Dietrich got rid of her baby fat and went with Sternberg to America, where they made six more classics at Paramount. In these she was erotic and exotic, part of Sternberg's wild decor, under veils and clouds of smoke, singing in costumes that revealed her long legs or in tuxedos and gorilla costumes, alternately acting flirtatious, sluttish, and bored. Her women had a sense of irony, an air of superiority, mystery, and a startling indifference. They lived by their wits and their own code of logic, manipulating weak men, loving strong ones. Her women enjoy sex; they also wisely use it to survive in a man's world. Her Catherine the Great in *The Scarlet Empress* is able to overthrow her demented husband only because she has seduced the powerful men in the Russian

Marlene Dietrich.

court. She gives herself to rich Cary Grant in *Blonde Venus* to get money for her husband's hospital treatment. Her women don't expect men to understand or forgive their sexual trespasses. They don't even attempt to defend their actions—if a man has no faith in her, that's his problem. But if a man will see how brave she is and accept her past (forgiveness isn't important), she will be loyal and loving to him. She will, for instance, follow legionnaire Gary Cooper into the desert (in high heels!) at the end of *Morocco*. Dietrich would have only a few successes after her remarkable collaboration with Sternberg and even that alliance ended in a series of box-office flops. However, the "Marlene" they created will always retain myth status.

• **Cult Favorites:** *The Blue Angel* (1930, Josef von Sternberg), *Morocco* (1930, Sternberg), *Dishonored* (1931, Sternberg), *Shanghai Express* (1932, Sternberg), *Blonde Venus* (1932, Sternberg), *The Scarlet Empress* (1934, Sternberg), *The Devil Is a Woman* (1935, Sternberg), *Destry Rides Again* (1939, George Marshall), *Rancho Notorious* (1952, Fritz Lang), *Touch of Evil* (1958, Orson Welles).

• **Also Recommended:** *Song of Songs* (1933, Rouben Mamoulian), *Desire* (1936, Frank Borzage), *Knight Without Honor* (1937, Jacques Feyder), *Angel* (1937, Ernst Lubitsch), *Seven Sinners* (1940, Tay Garnett), *Manpower* (1940, Raoul Walsh), *The Spoilers* (1942, Ray Enright), *A Foreign Affair* (1948, Billy Wilder), *Stage Fright* (1950, Alfred Hitchcock), *No Highway in* *the Sky* (1951, Henry Koster), *Witness for the Prosecution* (1957, Wilder).

○

USCHI DIGART Huge-breasted, long-haired, usually nude exploitation-film actress. She died a bloody death in the sick, torture-filled *Ilsa: She Wolf of the SS*, but she's more associated with the comic sex films she made with Russ Meyer. Her definitive part is in *Cherry, Harry, & Raquel*, where she neither says a word nor mingles with any of the other actors. Meyer simply shot the superstacked actress romping naked (but for an Indian warbonnet) through the desert, and inserted bits of the silly footage whenever he felt his film needed a dose of sex. Uschi (often written as Ushi) is not to be confused with Haji, who also provided decor for Meyer. Unlike Haji, Digart also made porno films, like *Honey Buns* and *The Maids*.
  • **Cult Favorites:** *Cherry, Harry, & Raquel* (1969, Russ Meyer), *Ilsa: She Wolf of the SS* (1974, Don Edmunds), *Beneath the Valley of the Ultravixens* (1980, Meyer).

○

MATT DILLON (1964–) Handsome, talented young actor with brown hair, thick eyebrows, and deep-set eyes initially was dubbed a "teen idol," a designation he detested. He was promoted as another James Dean, and like Dean played smart but inarticulate, troubled youths. Only his rebel had a cause—he fought for survival. His skinny, mumbling teen who sleeps with Kristy McNichol in *Little Darlings* was his most visible early role, so it took a while for anyone to notice that he was a really thoughtful, dedicated, sensitive ac-

tor. He had been an exciting presence as a doomed, rebellious 14-year-old in his debut, *Over the Edge*, but unfortunately that film wouldn't be released nationally for years. He was terrific in *Tex*, the first, best, but least publicized of his three films based on S. E. Hinton books; he also was good in Coppola's ambitious but muddled *The Outsiders* and *Rumble Fish*, but few critics or moviegoers were taken with anything in those "art films for teenagers." The role that finally won him approval was in *The Flamingo Kid*, where he played a completely likable character for once, even showing he had a flair for comedy in this coming-of-age picture. This time he was a youth with problems, not a problem youth. Since then he has alternated between nasty young hoods and sympathetic characters. But in his best role, in *Drugstore Cowboy*, his nasty young hood becomes sympathetic (though Dillon doesn't play for sympathy) when he decides to stop being an addict and the leader of a young gang that steals drugs from pharmacies. He deserved but failed to get an Oscar nomination; apparently, he still hasn't gotten that much respect.
  • **Cult Favorites:** *Over the Edge* (1979, Jonathan Kaplan), *The Outsiders* (1983, Francis Coppola), *Rumble Fish* (1983, Coppola), *Drugstore Cowboy* (1989, Gus Van Sant, Jr.).
  • **Sleepers:** *My Bodyguard* (1980, Tony Bill), *Liar's Moon* (1981, David Fisher), *Tex* (1982, Tim Hunter).
  • **Also Recommended:** *The Flamingo Kid* (1984, Garry Marshall), *The Big Town* (1987, Ben Bolt).
  • **Also of Interest:** *Little Darlings* (1980, Ronald F. Maxwell), *Native Son* (1986, Jerrold Freedman), *A Kiss Before Dying* (1991, James Dearden).

Divine in Female Trouble.

○

DIVINE (1945–88) The ultimate cult star. John Waters discovered Harris Glenn Milstead (his real name) in Baltimore, standing on street corners with different hair colors each day. This obese, blond, male actor created some of the most dynamic, hilarious females in movie history. Whether as Babs Johnson in *Pink Flamingos*, Dawn Davenport in *Female Trouble*, Francine Fishpaw in *Polyester*, or other females in John Waters's bad-taste celebrations of "crime and beauty," Divine played essentially the same character: a perverted Miss Piggy. Incredibly vain, she laps up compliments and seeks the fame she thinks she deserves, be it making headlines by being electrocuted (for kidnapping and multiple murders) in *Female Trouble*, or being recognized as "the world's filthiest human being" in *Pink Flamingos*. She isn't shy about demonstrating or loudly bragging that she is better than anyone else. Whatever she does or wants is right. For instance, her teenager in *Female Trouble* doesn't understand what is wrong with eating a huge meatball sandwich in class, or why her parents won't buy her cha-cha shoes for Christmas. She considers herself "the new woman"—and if conservative society (or her family) isn't ready for her, then that's their tough luck. She wouldn't think of changing. She believes she is the most beautiful person in the world (even after acid is thrown in her face in *Female Trouble*), and that her tasteless clothes, hideously teased hairdo, and extreme make-up only accentuate her good looks. She doesn't worry that she's flabby. She is supremely confident and in control, but I think she is funniest when she is harried, aggravated, dumped on, or humiliated. She will always exact revenge on those who treat her unfairly—no one wants her mad at them because she becomes increasingly mad and degenerate. She imprisons some of those who anger her, kills others, and, hilariously in *Pink Flamingos*, curses her rivals by licking, spitting, and rubbing herself all over their furniture. This is no ordinary woman—she runs the "Carnival of Perversions" and is raped by a lobster in *Multiple Maniacs*; is raped by herself as a man in *Female Trouble*; has an affair with Tab Hunter in *Polyester*; and has sex with her demented son, walks down the street with a slab of cold, stolen meat against her crotch, and, in her most famous act, actually eats puppy doo doo in *Pink Flamingos*.

It was no ordinary actor who could make us laugh and feel nauseous at the same time. Though usually loud and hammy, he also was adept at deadpan humor and physical comedy, doing an impromptu tumbling act in *Pink Flamingos* that even the great silent comics would have admired. Divine wanted to branch out and made Paul Bartel's *Lust in the Dust*, a disappointing western-comedy with Tab Hunter, and Alan Rudolph's *Trouble in Mind*, a bizarre parallel-world black comedy, playing a male villain. But his last role before his untimely death was in Waters's upbeat *Hairspray*, in a sympathetic part for a change: this time she wanted stardom for her daughter, Rikki Lake.

• **Cult Favorites:** *Mondo Trasho* (1969, John Waters), *Multiple Maniacs* (1970, Waters), *Pink Flamingos* (1972, Waters), *Female Trouble* (1974, Waters), *Polyester* (1981, *Trouble in Mind* (1985, Alan Rudolph), *Hairspray* (1988, Waters).

○

TAMARA DOBSON (1947–) Very tall, very slender, very athletic leading lady of *Cleopatra Jones* and its superior sequel, *Cleopatra Jones and the Casino of Gold*, two of the better-produced, more violent black exploitation films. In both films her cool, confident, and deadly U.S. secret agent got the best of murderous drug lords (Stella Stevens in the sequel). She hadn't the earthiness, talent, or star appeal of Pam Grier, but she was a fairly strong, likable, glamorous (with a close-cropped Afro) heroine. She was fun to watch, whether engaging in good-natured dialogue or winning a brutal karate fight. She and the tiny Tanny, beautiful Chinese martial-arts star, were an exciting duo in the Hong Kong–set *Casino of Gold*. The quick de-

mise of the blaxploitation film curtailed her career, so it was good to see her turn up years later in the all-star-cast women's prison film, *Chained Heat*.

• **Cult Favorites:** *Cleopatra Jones and the Casino of Gold* (1975, Chuck Bail), *Chained Heat* (1983, Paul Nicholas).

• **Other Key Films:** *Cleopatra Jones* (1973, Jack Starrett), *Norman . . . Is That You?* (1976, George Schlatter).

○

FAITH DOMERGUE (1925–) Pretty brunette was promoted by Howard Hughes as a sultry glamour girl, but audiences saw *Vendetta* and didn't buy it. Rather than fade away, though, she gave commendable performances in the campy *Cult of the Cobra Woman*, as a sinister murderess; in good minor westerns, including Don Siegel's *Duel at Silver Creek*, opposite Audie Murphy, and *The Great Sioux Uprising*, opposite Jeff Chandler; and in several enjoyable science-fiction films. All sci-fi fans recall her scientist being carried by a Metaluna mutant in *This Island Earth*, the film for which she is best remembered. Domergue soon retired for about eight years, then beginning in the late sixties, she appeared in several low-budget horror films. Although she was then in her late forties, she was often offered the romantic leads.

• **Cult Favorites:** *This Island Earth*, (1954, Joseph M. Newman), *Cult of the Cobra* (1955, Francis D. Lyon), *Psycho Sisters* (1977, Reginald LeBorg).

• **Also Recommended:** *Duel at Silver Creek*, (1952, Don Siegel), *The Great Sioux Uprising*, (1953, Lloyd Bacon), *It Came from Beneath the Sea* (1955, Robert Gordon).

• **Also of Interest:** *Vendetta* (1950, Mel Ferrer), *Where Danger Lives* (1950, John

Farrow), *This Is My Love* (1954, Stuart Heisler), *The Atomic Man* (1953, Ken Hughes), *Legacy of Blood/Blood Legacy* (1971, Carl Monson), *The House of Seven Corpses* (1973, Paul Harrison).

○

TROY DONAHUE (1936–) It's amazing how many women recall having crushes on this blue-eyed blond hunk when they were in their teens. I think Donahue is best remembered for his starring roles in the Warner Bros. television mystery series "Surfside 6" and "Hawaiian Eye," but he also made his movie mark in some sudsy potboilers of the late fifties and early sixties. He wasn't a good actor—he made Sandra Dee seem like Sarah Bernhardt in those hot clutches and even hotter discussions about going all the way in *A Summer Place*—but he could pout, lose his temper, and express the anguish, confusion, and frustration which was required of all young actors in romance movies of the period. His most dramatic moment came in his one scene in *Imitation of Life*, when he breaks off with Susan Kohner and slaps her after learning she is black. On film, he had quite a group of lovers besides Sandra Dee, including Connie Stevens, Suzanne Pleshette (whom he'd marry), and Joey Heatherton. It's easy to make fun of him— his name always causes chuckles among fans of camp—but he deserves credit for hanging in there and overcoming his pretty-boy image to become an almost passable actor with a long career.
• **Cult Favorites:** *Imitation of Life* (1959, Douglas Sirk), *A Summer Place* (1959, Delmer Daves), *Cockfighter* (1974, Monte Hellman), *Seizure* (1974, Oliver Stone), *Cry-Baby* (1990, John Waters).
• **Other Key Films:** *Parrish* (1961, Daves),

Susan Slade (1961, Daves), *Rome Adventure* (1962, Daves), *Palm Springs Weekend* (1963, Norman Taurog), *A Distant Trumpet* (1964, Raoul Walsh), *Color Me Blood Red* (1965, William Conrad).
• **Also of Interest:** *Monster on the Campus* (1958, Jack Arnold), *The Voice in the Mirror* (1958, Harry Keller), *The Perfect Furlough* (1959, Blake Edwards), *The Crowded Sky* (1960, Joseph Pevney), *The Godfather Part II* (1974, Francis Ford Coppola), *Grandview, U.S.A.* (1984, Randal Kleiser).

○

FRANÇOISE DORLÉAC (1942–67) Beautiful, blond older sister of Catherine Deneuve was killed in a car crash at the height of her career. Just 25, she had already starred in films by some of the most internationally renowned directors of the period, including François Truffaut, Roman Polanski, Jacques Demy, Ken Russell, and Philippe de Broca (she and Jean-Paul Belmondo made a great team in his romantic spy thriller, *That Man from Rio*, her breakthrough film), as well as the French master René Clair. She had already worked in numerous genres, even making a musical, Demy's stylized *The Umbrellas of Cherbourg*, with her sister. She wasn't as cold or mysterious as Deneuve; she was more sensual, more aggressive, more cerebral, warmer, wittier, and wilder. She was arguably sexier than Deneuve in that her women (such as her stewardess in Truffaut's *The Soft Skin*, Donald Pleasence's slutty younger wife in *Cul-de-Sac*, whom we first see on the beach wearing only jeans and lying on top of her young lover) promise more during lovemaking than do her sister's remote women. As Truffaut pointed out, though Dorléac had a fragile,

Françoise Dorléac.

childlike quality, she was from the moment she broke into films an extremely mature actress, both physically ("she had an intelligent, beautiful face and a body that was already built and, like they say in the studios, built well enough to last to the end") and mentally ("she was inflexible, sometimes to the limit of tolerance; she was a moralist whose conversations were rich in aphorisms about life and love"). She was talented and appealing; she had so much energy, so much life, so much promise for the future . . . and suddenly she was dead.

• **Cult Favorites:** *Cul-de-Sac* (1966, Roman Polanski), *The Young Girls of Rochefort* (1967, Jacques Demy).

• **Other Key Films:** *That Man from Rio* (1963, Philippe de Broca), *The Soft Skin* (1964, François Truffaut).

• **Also of Interest:** *Tout l'Or du Monde* (1961, René Clair), *Male Hunt* (1965, Edouard Molinaro), *Genghis Khan* (1965, Henry Levin), *Where the Spies Are* (1965, Val Guest), *Billion Dollar Brain* (1967, Ken Russell).

○

DIANA DORS (1931–) The former Diana Fluck was promoted as the "Blonde Bombshell" in England, that country's answer to Marilyn Monroe, but when Americans got to see her films they couldn't understand why. The young Dors, in her pre–platinum blond days, when she downplayed sex while portraying good-natured teens and young women in lightweight British comedies and thrillers in the late forties, may remind some of the pre-star Monroe. But in the fifties, at the height of their fame, the actresses had little in

England's top sex symbol Diana Dors in As Long As They're Happy.

common, either in role choices (though Dors would have been suitable for Monroe's star-making parts in *The Asphalt Jungle*, *Don't Bother to Knock*, and *Niagara*) or persona (Dors hadn't Monroe's beauty, humor, wild-eyed enthusiasm, vulnerability, or "star quality"). Rather, Dors was a combination of the statuesque Jayne Mansfield—both women dressed to emphasize their breasts—and the femmes fatales played by Lana Turner in the forties and Kim Novak in the fifties. In *The Unholy Wife*, when Dors struts about her humble home in tight purple-and-white outfits more suitable for a pleasure palace, it may remind you of Turner in *The Postman Always Rings Twice*. Like Turner, Dors glows in the dark. Dors was pretty good playing prostitutes, "good-time girls,"

molls, and sinners, but the melodramas themselves were pretty dreary. Unfortunately, because she had to live up to her sex-goddess image, she rarely got to show much dramatic range. However, when she lost her famous figure and became obese—going the Shelley Winters route—she got character parts that let her stretch. Even in shallow films she revealed depth and was fun to watch. One of her most memorable oversexed, aging fat women was in *Deep End*, in which her bathhouse customer has an orgasm while fantasizing about soccer goals.

• **Cult Favorites:** *Baby Love* (1969, Alastair Reid), *Deep End* (1970, Jerzy Skolimowski), *Theatre of Blood* (1973, Douglas Hickox).

• **Also of Interest:** *Dance Hall* (1950,

Charles Crichton), *Lady Godiva Rides Again* (1951, Frank Launder), *The Weak and the Wicked* (1953, J. Lee Thompson), *As Long As They're Happy* (1955, Thompson), *A Kid for Two Farthings* (1955, Carol Reed), *An Alligator Named Daisy* (1955, Thompson), *Yield to the Night/Blonde Sinner* (1956, Thompson), *The Long Haul* (1957, Ken Hughes), *The Unholy Wife* (1957, John Farrow), *Scent of Mystery* (1960, Jack Cardiff), *On the Double* (1961, Melville Shavelson), *King of the Roaring Twenties* (1961, Joseph M. Newman), *Berserk* (1967, Jim O'Connolly), *There's a Girl in My Soup* (1970, Ray Boulting), *Nothing But the Night/The Devil's Undead* (1972, Peter Sasdy), *The Amazing Mr. Blunden* (1972, Lionel Jeffries), *The Infernal Idol/Craze* (1973, Freddie Francis), *Steaming* (1984, Joseph Losey).

○

KEIR DULLEA (1936–) Handsome, youthful-looking actor who has specialized in playing extremely sensitive, emotionally unstable men. He made a strong debut as a troubled juvenile delinquent in *The Hoodlum Priest;* he was a young mental hospital patient in *David and Lisa;* his young, sensitive recruit is at odds with his tough sergeant in *The Thin Red Line;* in *Bunny Lake Is Missing* he kidnaps his young niece because he's jealous that his sister Carol Lynley now plays kid's games with her instead of him. So it was strange seeing him play the completely emotionless space traveler Bowman in *2001: A Space Odyssey,* the role that secured his position as a cult star. Late in the film, he does warm up while battling the rebellious computer "H.A.L." on mankind's behalf; he becomes *very* emotional, to the point where he has trouble controlling himself;

as the only human being in his automative age to regain his human qualities, he is the one who qualifies to meet the aliens. After *2001,* Dullea would play more sensitive and/or unhinged characters, including the title character in the abominable *De Sade.* He also reprised his Bowman character—sort of—in the ill-conceived *2010.*

• **Cult Favorites:** *Bunny Lake Is Missing* (1965, Otto Preminger), *2001: A Space Odyssey* (1969, Stanley Kubrick).

• **Sleeper:** *Black Christmas/Stranger in the House* (1975, Bob Clark).

• **Other Key Films:** *The Hoodlum Priest* (1961, Irvin Kershner), *David and Lisa* (1963, Frank Perry), *The Fox* (1968, Mark Rydell), *The Haunting of Julia* (1976, Richard Loncraine).

• **Also of Interest:** *Mail Order Bride* (1964, Burt Kennedy), *The Thin Red Line* (1964, Andrew Marton), *Madame X* (1966, David Lowell Rich), *Paperback Hero* (1973, Peter Pearson), *Leopard in the Snow* (1978, Gerry O'Hara), *Brainwaves* (1982, Ulli Lommel).

○

MARGARET DUMONT (1889–1965) Stout, dark-haired, middle-aged character actress of the thirties and forties, much loved for being Groucho Marx's comic foil—a stately, smiling, stupefied straightwoman in seven Marx Brothers films. As a number of easily duped, rich, philanthropic widows, she was Groucho's entrance into high society, the political arena, and most grandly, the opera—where he, Harpo, and Chico inflicted their greatest damage. Her stuffy women—Mrs. Potter, Mrs. Rittenhouse, Mrs. Teasdale, Mrs. Claypool, Mrs. Upjohn, Mrs. Dukesbury—are charmed by Groucho's outrageous characters because, unlike every other male in

Margaret Dumont plays straight woman to Chico, Groucho, and Harpo Marx in Animal Crackers.

Dumont's polite, pompous circle, they throw propriety to the wind and make mad, passionate love to them. Her women are so taken by Groucho's brazen advances that they can't tell the difference between his insults and his flirtations. They giggle like schoolgirls as Groucho tries to fit their hefty forms into his arms, and don't listen to the barbs that bombard them. When they finally grasp an insult, Groucho brings back their smiles by making them believe that all he was trying to say was "I love you." *Duck Soup* ends with the Marx Brothers all throwing oranges at Dumont, but for the most part, Groucho had her all to himself. That's why it's a treat to see Dumont's card-game interplay with Chico and Harpo (who virtually molests her and wrestles her to the ground) in *Animal*

Crackers. Also, one shouldn't forget she appeared in films with such comics as W. C. Fields, Laurel and Hardy, Abbott and Costello, Red Skelton, and Jack Benny. She always said that she was able to keep a straight face around Groucho and the others because she never understood the humor directed at her.

• **Cult Favorites:** *Duck Soup* (1933, Leo McCarey), *A Night at the Opera* (1935, Sam Wood), *Never Give a Sucker an Even Break* (1941, Edward Cline), *The Horn Blows at Midnight* (1945, Raoul Walsh).

• **Other Key Films:** *The Cocoanuts* (1929, Joseph Santley and Robert Florey), *Animal Crackers* (1930, Victor Heerman), *A Day at the Races* (1937, Wood), *At the Circus* (1939, Edward Buzzell).

• **Also of Interest:** *The Big Store* (1941,

Charles Riesner), *The Dancing Masters* (1943, Mal St. Clair), *Little Giant* (1946, William A. Seiter).

○

DEANNA DURBIN (1921–) Canadian-born singer-actress was the thirties' first teen star, saving Universal from bankruptcy and prompting M-G-M to develop Judy Garland. Ironically, she debuted singing with Garland in the M-G-M short *Every Sunday,* before that studio cast her aside. Her initial pictures were cheerful and emphasized her youthful energy, wholesome good looks, sweetness, and impressive soprano. She was more of a go-getter than Garland, not as shy, and not as often a victim. But she wasn't flawless—in *Mad About Music* she is inconsiderate to Jackie Cooper! In her early films, she played the matchmaker. In later films, she chased after love, with Robert Stack providing her first screen kiss in *First Love.* She developed into a beautiful romantic lead, mature enough to have a relationship with Joseph Cotten in *Hers to Hold,* in which she was most appealing as a war plant worker. In her early films, her voice was annoyingly shrill and her energy level a bit much, but she later toned down and developed the screen's most relaxed, least-affected delivery. She was no better than adequate in dramatic roles, but her fearless, confident honesty when speaking set her apart. When she suddenly retired, she was the screen's highest-paid female star. Most Durbin films now seem dated, but she remains fresh—she's definitely worth seeking out.

• **Recommended:** *Three Smart Girls* (1937, Henry Koster), *100 Men and a Girl* (1937, Koster), *Mad About Music* (1938, Norman Taurog), *Three Smart Girls Grow Up* (1939, Koster), *First Love* (1939, Koster), *Spring Parade* (1940, Koster), *Nice Girl* (1941, Koster), *The Amazing Mrs. Holliday* (1943, Bruce Manning and, uncredited, Jean Renoir), *Hers to Hold* (1943, Frank Ryan), *Christmas Holiday* (1944, Robert Siodmak), *Lady on a Train* (1945, Charles David).

○

DAN DURYEA (1907–68) I think one of television's funniest moments was on "The Jack Benny Show," when Benny, playing a diner attendant, did one of the longest of his famous exasperated sideways looks at his audience after gangster Dan Duryea, a stranger, walked in and immediately slapped him on the face. That was the moment I started appreciating Duryea, whose obnoxious movie villains weren't the kind kids like. The blond former Broadway actor occasionally played a good guy, but usually portrayed yapping, sneering, clever, amused-with-themselves opportunists, western outlaws, two-bit gangsters, and dapper villains. He was a vicious killer in the exciting western *Winchester '73,* but he's probably better remembered as the scheming, money-hungry scoundrels in *The Woman in the Window* and *Scarlet Street,* Fritz Lang's noir classics. In the first film he blackmails Joan Bennett and Edward G. Robinson; in the second, he and girlfriend Bennett swindle artist Robinson. In both pictures, he outsmarts himself and is killed by the law for crimes he didn't commit. At his best, Duryea was an intriguing combination of James Cagney and Richard Widmark.

• **Cult Favorites:** *The Pride of the Yankees* (1947, Sam Wood), *Scarlet Street* (1945, Fritz Lang), *Winchester '73* (1950, Anthony Mann), *Platinum High School* (1960, Charles Haas).

• **Sleeper:** *Black Angel* (1946, Roy William Neill).

• **Other Key Films:** *The Little Foxes* (1941, William Wyler), *Ball of Fire* (1941, Howard Hawks), *Sahara* (1943, Zoltan Korda), *Ministry of Fear* (1944, Lang), *The Woman in the Window* (1944, Lang), *Along Came Jones* (1945, Stuart Heisler), *Black Bart* (1948, George Sherman), *Another Part of the Forest* (1948, Michael Gordon), *Criss Cross* (1949, Robert Siodmak), *Manhandled* (1949, Lewis R. Foster), *The Underworld Story* (1950, Cy Endfield), *Al Jennings of Oklahoma* (1951, Ray Nazarro), *Thunder Bay* (1953, Mann), *The Burglar* (1956, Paul Wendkos), *Slaughter on Tenth Avenue* (1957, Arnold Laven), *Night Passage* (1957, James Neilson), *Do You Know This Voice?* (1964, Frank Nesbitt), *The Bounty Killer* (1965, Spencer G. Bennet), *The Flight of the Phoenix* (1966, Robert Aldrich).

○

ANN DUSENBERRY (1952–) At first glance, this energetic, blue-eyed blonde looks as though she might be one of the wholesome "Brady Bunch" girls grown up. Yet, while her characters are "good" girls, they exhibit a wicked and enticing sexuality. They are experienced, they are emotional, with backgrounds and lives much different than those possible for the Brady blondes. She held her own with John Heard, Jeff Bridges, and Lisa Eichhorn, who all gave *great* performances, in the offbeat *Cutter's Way*, as the outsider (sister of a murder victim) who joins Heard and Bridges in reckless pursuit of a killer. And she gives a more moving, honest performance than

Heard, Nick Nolte, or a miscast Sissy Spacek in *Heart Beat,* in the small role of Nolte's teenage girlfriend. The changes in her pretty face are wonderful and real when Nolte kisses her then quickly tells her he's dropping her—that's great acting. Underused in Hollywood, she cheerfully starred in *Basic Training,* a stupid sex comedy in which her nude scene is the only highlight. She was more creatively cast in *Lies,* as an unemployed actress who gets involved in a deadly swindle.

• **Cult Favorite:** *Cutter's Way/Cutter and Bone* (1981, Ivan Passer).

• **Sleeper:** *Lies* (1983, Ken and Jim Wheat).

• **Other Key Film:** *Heart Beat* (1980, John Byrum).

• **Also of Interest:** *Basic Training* (1985, Andrew Sugerman).

○

ROBERT DUVALL (1931–) This extremely versatile, dedicated craftsman has been in demand as both a lead and supporting player. Viewers have responded to many of his characters, including his smart lawyer in "The Godfather" movies, Jesse James in *The Great Northfield, Minnesota Raid,* Dr. Watson in *The Seven-Percent Solution,* a marine who is a too-strict father in *The Great Santini,* a Vietnam officer who loves "the smell of napalm in the morning" in *Apocalypse Now,* a tough Mississippi tenant dirt farmer whose life brightens when he raises a boy left to him in *Tomorrow,* and a country singer who is a recovering alcoholic in *Tender Mercies,* the role that won him a Best Actor Oscar. Although some of his characters are gentle, they are moving because we can tell that they also have the capacity for great anger—Duvall can be intimidating. "His range as a performer is extraordinary," writes Horton Foote, who wrote *To Kill a Mockingbird, Tomorrow,* and *Tender Mercies.* "When I go to see him in a role I have no idea how he will play it. [For instance, his Southern characters] were different in speech, mannerisms, and all visual detail . . . He does not choose particular facets of his character to win an audience's sympathy, or aspects that will show off his more appealing qualities as an actor . . . He is after as much truth about the character, good or bad, as he can perceive and his talent can reveal." He has had the talent to create many fascinating, truthful characters.

• **Cult Favorites:** *The Chase* (1966, Arthur Penn), *The Rain People* (1969, Francis Ford Coppola), *M*A*S*H* (1970, Robert Altman), *THX-1138* (1971, George Lucas), *The Godfather* (1972, Coppola), *The Godfather Part II* (1974, Coppola), *The Conversation* (1974, Coppola), *Apocalypse Now* (1979, Coppola), *The Great Santini* (1979, Louis John Carlino).

• **Sleepers:** *The Revolutionary* (1970, Paul Williams), *The Great Northfield, Minnesota Raid* (1972, Philip Kaufman), *Tomorrow* (1972, Joseph Anthony), *The Stone Boy* (1984, Chris Cain).

• **Other Key Films:** *To Kill a Mockingbird* (1962, Robert Mulligan), *Countdown* (1968, Altman), *Bullitt* (1968, Peter Yates), *The Outfit* (1973, John Flynn), *The Killer Elite* (1975, Sam Peckinpah), *The Seven-Percent Solution* (1976, Herbert Ross), *Network* (1976, Sidney Lumet), *True Confessions* (1981, Ulu Grosbard), *Tender Mercies* (1983, Bruce Beresford), *The Natural* (1984, Barry Levinson), *The Lightship* (1985, Jerzy Skolimowski), *Colors* (1988, Dennis Hopper), *The Handmaid's Tale* (1990, Volker Schlöndorff).

SHELLEY DUVALL (1949–) This tall, gangly gawky Texas actress wasn't an actress at all when Robert Altman discovered her at a Houston party and cast her as the weird Astrodome tour guide who seduces virgin Bud Cort in *Brewster McCloud.* She proved to have a marvelous natural talent, with an array of wild-eyed expressions and an offbeat comic delivery. A triple threat who looked funny, acted funny, and dressed funny, she also was so wild-looking, uninhibited, and carelessly vulnerable that somehow she had genuine sex appeal. Altman was impressed and used her in almost all of his films of the period, often as ditsy girls who danced to the beat of a stoned drummer. With her stringbean figure and cartoonish looks, she was the perfect choice to play Olive Oyl in Altman's *Popeye,* and did a wonderful job. But she was more interestingly cast in Altman's dramatic masterpiece *Thieves Like Us,* as the simple, scrawny girl who falls for escaped prisoner Keith Carradine. She got to reveal a sensitive, thoughtful side that hadn't appeared in the Altman comedies. Moreover, her sweet, tender lovemaking scenes with Carradine are quite special. She gave the best, most wondrous performance of her career in Altman's fascinating, cryptic *3 Women,* which won her the Best Actress award at Cannes. She played Millie Lammoreaux, a worker at a center for geriatric invalids, whose kooky new coworker and apartment mate (played by Sissy Spacek) tries to take over her identity—which isn't difficult, since Millie is a nothing. She carries on with a smile, a conceited air, and a motor mouth, refusing to admit that no one pays her the slightest attention. She's a bit like Bob

Uecker. Duvall didn't take on many roles away from Altman, but she did have a hilarious cameo in *Annie Hall,* as Woody Allen's humorless date; after he almost develops lockjaw satisfying her in bed, she comments: "Sex with you is a Kafkaesque experience . . . I mean that as a compliment." Although her acting was first rate, Duvall—best-suited to play surprising characters—was an odd choice as Jack Nicholson's wife in the disappointing *The Shining,* a woman meant to be the only element in the film that is predictable. In the last decade or so, Duvall has been the successful producer of a "Fairy Tales" anthology series and a horror-classics anthology series on cable television. Her

return to movies in a small part in *Roxanne* was most welcome.

• **Cult Favorites:** *Brewster McCloud* (1970, Robert Altman), *McCabe and Mrs. Miller* (1971, Altman), *Thieves Like Us* (1974, Altman), *Nashville* (1975, Altman), *Buffalo Bill and the Indians* (1976, Altman), *Annie Hall* (1977, Woody Allen), *3 Women* (1977, Altman), *The Shining* (1979, Stanley Kubrick), *Time Bandits* (1981, Terry Gilliam).

• **Also of Interest:** *Roxanne* (1987, Fred Schepisi).

○

ANN DVORAK (1912–79) This smart, pretty, exceptionally talented brunette, with hair

Shelley Duvall and former Monty Python member Michael Palin in Terry Gilliam's Time Bandits.

Ann Dvorak and Paul Muni, as brother and sister who have a perverse love for one another, prepare for the final shoot-out in Scarface.

pulled back to emphasize her sharp nose and gorgeous eyes, was a leading lady from the early thirties until her retirement in 1951. Even when her characters lacked class, she gave classy performances; even when her films were nothing special, she was. Even considering that she broke into movies in the pre-Code era, she took some daring parts. For instance, in *Three on a Match,* with Bette Davis and Joan Blondell, she plays a young mother who is turned into a heroin addict (as in most of her films, she suffered because she fell for the wrong man) and then commits suicide. Her most memorable role was in *Scarface,* which the 18-year-old (filming was completed in 1930) stole with an overtly sexual performance as ganglord Paul Muni's fun-seeking sister, the object of his incestuous desires. The censors were so interested in how the gangsters were portrayed that they didn't take a close look at Dvorak's dancing, listen to her double entendres (there is even a reference to an "organ grinder"), or notice the lascivious glances exchanged between the girl and her brother. A typical Dvorak role was that of a woman whose one shot at happiness looks hopeless because the troubled man she loves (a boyfriend or husband) mistreats her. She remains loyal but becomes worn out and depressed trying to cope with his neglect or abuse. She played a role much like this in *The Crowd Roars* opposite James Cagney. Critics have usually assumed the film is Howard Hawks's tribute to race-car drivers, but Hawks's heart is less with driver James Cagney than his loyal girlfriend Dvorak, who turns his life around by giving him support, love, and direction. Dvorak would later star in many films, including a couple of British spy films and westerns with John Wayne and Randolph Scott, playing everything from a knife thrower to a schoolteacher turned spy to a strong-willed saloon singer-dancer in *Abilene Town,* the rare western with feminist themes. But she is still known primarily for the three pictures that she made before she was 21. Obviously a multifilm retrospective is warranted so that more than film connoisseurs can become familiar with her fine work.

• **Cult Favorite:** *Scarface* (1932, Howard Hawks).

• **Sleepers:** *Massacre* (1933, Alan Crosland), *Abilene Town* (1946, Edward L. Marin).

• **Other Key Films:** *Three on a Match* (1932, Mervyn LeRoy), *The Crowd Roars* (1932, Hawks), *Housewife* (1934, Alfred E. Green), *G-Men* (1935, William Keighley), *Blind Alley* (1939, Charles Vidor), *Escape to Danger* (1943, Lance Comfort), *Flame of the Barbary Coast* (1946, Joseph Kane), *The Private Affairs of Bel Ami* (1947, Albert Lewin), *I Was an American Spy* (1951, Lesley Selander).

• **Also of Interest:** *The Strange Love of Mary Louvain* (1932, Michael Curtiz), *Love Is a Racket* (1932, William A. Wellman), *The Way to Love* (1933, Norman Taurog), *College Coach* (1933, Wellman), *Thanks a Million* (1935, Roy Del Ruth), *Bright Lights* (1935, Busby Berkeley), *Dr. Socrates* (1935, William Dieterle), *We Who Are About to Die* (1937, Christy Cabanne), *A Life of Her Own* (1950, George Cukor), *The Return of Jesse James* (1953, Arthur Hilton).

○

HARRY EARLES (1902–85) Born Kurt Schneider, this German midget originally suggested to director Tod Browning that he make *Freaks,* and then starred as Hans, a carnival midget who is duped into marriage by Olga Baclanova's normal-sized, small-hearted trapeze artist so she can collect his inheritance. His face was doll-like and seemed harmless until you looked closely

Harry Earles and Olga Baclanova in Freaks

and saw it was hard and quite eerie. Browning wanted to convey that Hans only looked like a child, and when angered—Browning transformed the freaks from gentle innocents to "monsters" when seeking vengeance—was capable of a revenge so terrible that only an adult could conceive it. In support of Lon Chaney, Earles (disguised in baby garb) was completely unsympathetic in Browning's silent classic *The Unholy Three* and in Jack Conway's sound remake (in which he was unintelligible).

• **Cult Favorite:** *Freaks* (1932, Tod Browning).

• **Other Key Films:** *The Unholy Three* (1925, Browning), *The Unholy Three* (1930, Jack Conway).

○

CLINT EASTWOOD (1930–) A tall, slim, blond, handsome movie bit player and costar of

TV's "Rawhide," he shot to international superstardom as the tight-lipped, vicious bounty hunter in Sergio Leone's spectacular, violent, and witty spaghetti westerns, *A Fistful of Dollars, For a Few Dollars More,* and *The Good, the Bad, and the Ugly.* His casually sadistic Man with No Name, who's much like a mythological superwarrior, is an unusual western "hero": he initiates shoot-outs, often cheats to win, has no sense of remorse, and cares only about making money. In America, Eastwood created the other recurring role that established his screen image: "Dirty Harry" Callahan, a law-and-order policeman whose questionable tactics aim to "re-civilize" America's cities. He is more moral than the Man with No Name be-

cause he kills bad guys to improve society rather than for financial profit. It's rarely recognized that Eastwood often portrays men who vary from the cool/silent/lethal screen persona that made him famous. Aside from their affinity for violence, Eastwood's characters have common traits that are positive. They project traditional American virtues like individuality, bravery, resourcefulness, and, more importantly, dedication, loyalty, and honesty. They are also polite to women and are gentle lovers. Only twice did he portray himself as a cocky ladies' man, and the two men get their comeuppance: as a soldier, his leg is amputated, then he is murdered by the angry females he duped in *The Beguiled;* as a deejay, his crazy spurned

Clint Eastwood played the "Man With No Name" in three Sergio Leone westerns.

lover, Jessica Walter, attacks him with a knife in *Play Misty for Me,* his first directorial effort. Much humor in his films comes from his inability to understand unusual women. His acting has improved considerably from the days when his only facial reaction was his trademark nervously raised upper lip. But he remains our best action hero, playing loners who are superb at what they do: in his westerns, he can outdraw and outshoot anyone; he's a champion bare-knuckles fighter in *Every Which Way But Loose;* a legendary heist man in *Thunderbolt and Lightfoot;* the only pilot who can fly a futuristic plane in *Firefox;* the only prisoner to pull off an *Escape from Alcatraz;* the top police marksman in *Magnum Force;* and so on. As Eastwood has aged, his characters have become gentler and his movies funnier. Such films as *The Outlaw Josey Wales* and *Bronco Billy,* where his characters have diverse friends, indicate that this archconservative has made peace with all Americans.

• **Cult Favorites:** *Tarantula* (1955, Jack Arnold), *A Fistful of Dollars* (1964, Sergio Leone), *For a Few Dollars More* (1966, Leone), *The Good, the Bad, and the Ugly* (1967, Leone), *Coogan's Bluff* (1968, Don Siegel), *The Beguiled* (1971, Siegel), *Play Misty for Me* (1971, Clint Eastwood), *Dirty Harry* (1971, Siegel), *High Plains Drifter* (1973, Eastwood), *The Outlaw Josey Wales* (1976, Eastwood), *Bronco Billy* (1980, Eastwood).

• **Also Recommended:** *Magnum Force* (1973, Ted Post), *Two Mules for Sister Sara* (1970, Siegel), *The Gauntlet* (1977, Eastwood), *Every Which Way But Loose* (1978, James Fargo), *Honky-Tonk Man* (1982, Eastwood), *Sudden Impact* (1983, Eastwood), *Tightrope* (1984, Richard Tuggle), *Pale Rider* (1985, Eastwood).

○

SHIRLEY EATON (1936–) Curvaceous blonde provided spice to a number of British comedies in the fifties, including both Dirk Bogarde's "Doctor Sparrow" and the "Carry On" series. She hardened her image and was even sexier as the duplicitous female lead in the brutal film *The Girl Hunters,* starring author Mickey Spillane himself as detective Mike Hammer. But even that was nothing in comparison to her bikini-clad Jill Masterson, an employee of Gert Frobe's master criminal in the third Sean Connery–James Bond film, *Goldfinger.* It's exciting when Bond seduces her—she's more than willing to cooperate. Too bad she had such little screen time. No Bond fan will forget the tragic moment when Bond discovers his recent lover dead in bed, having suffocated after her entire body had been painted gold. It's Eaton's claim to eternal fame.

• **Cult Favorites:** *Carry on Nurse* (1960, Gerald Thomas), *The Girl Hunters* (1963, Roy Rowland), *Goldfinger* (1964, Guy Hamilton).

• **Also of Interest:** *Doctor at Large* (1957, Ralph Thomas), *Sailor Beware!/Panic in the Parlor* (1957, Gordon Parry), *Your Past Is Showing* (1957, Mario Zampi), *Carry on Sergeant* (1958, Thomas), *The Naked Brigade* (1965, Maury Dexter), *Ten Little Indians* (1966, George Pollock), *The Million Eyes of Su-Muru* (1967, Lindsay Shonteff), *The Blood of Fu Manchu* (1968, Jesus Franco).

○

NELSON EDDY (1901–67) Handsome baritone teamed with Jeanette MacDonald between 1935 and 1942 in eight operettas at M-G-M, forming the most popular singing duo in film history. He had a pleasant smile that made him tolerable, but he was such a wooden actor that he literally came across as MacDonald's straight man, even when they weren't doing comedy! In the period pieces, he'd usually play authority figures—a captain in *Naughty Marietta,* a Royal Mountie (wearing his most memorable costume) in *Rose Marie,* a federal agent in *The Girl of the Golden West,* a soldier in *Rosalie.* He'd stand around stiffly until high-strung and confused MacDonald eventually "came around" and found comfort in his arms. One couldn't really understand why MacDonald's lively women would gravitate toward such dull characters, except when they sang their romantic duets, particularly "Sweetheart" in *Maytime* and their signature tune, "The Indian Love Call," in *Rose Marie.*

• **Cult Favorites:** *Naughty Marietta* (1935, W. S. Van Dyke), *Rose Marie* (1936), Van Dyke).

• **Also Recommended:** *Maytime* (1937, Robert Z. Leonard), *Bitter Sweet* (1940, Van Dyke), *The Phantom of the Opera* (1943, Arthur Lubin).

• **Other Key Films:** *Rosalie* (1937, Van Dyke), *Sweethearts* (1938, Van Dyke), *The Girl of the Golden West* (1938, Leonard), *New Moon* (1940, Leonard), *I Married An Angel* (1942, Van Dyke).

• **Also of Interest:** *Dancing Lady* (1933, Leonard), *The Chocolate Soldier* (1941, Roy Del Ruth), *Northwest Outpost* (1947, Allan Dwan).

○

JULIE EGE (1943–) Shapely, long-haired former Miss Norway was one of villain Blofeld's brainwashed young women in the James Bond film *On Her Majesty's Secret Service.* Before that she'd been in a series of leering British sex comedies. Her later roles would be larger, but she'd still be cast because of her substantial beauty rather than her minor talent. She made her most indelible impression in the last of Hammer Studio's prehistoric adventures, *Creatures the World Forgot,* playing the lead role of a tribal princess in a teensy bikini, sometimes minus the top. She was never shy about revealing her body—with good reason.

• **Cult Favorites:** *On Her Majesty's Secret Service* (1969, Peter Hunt). *Last Days of Man on Earth* (1974, Robert Fuest), *Legend of the Seven Golden Vampires/The Seven Brothers Meet Dracula* (1973, Roy Ward Baker).

• **Other Key Film:** *Creatures the World Forgot* (1971, Don Chaffey).

• **Also of Interest:** *Think Dirty* (1970, Jim Clark), *Rentadick* (1972, Clark), *Craze* (1973, Freddie Francis), *The Mutations* (1974, Jack Cardiff).

○

LISA EICHHORN (1952–) Underappreciated actress whose career inexplicably stalled when she was in her prime. She has given consistently compelling, touching, subtle performances, creating interesting characters. She was sweet as the English shopgirl who falls for American soldier Richard Gere in *Yanks.* In a much different role, she was truly inspiring as the brave Jewish resistance fighter in the TV film *The Wall.* And as Mo, melancholy wife of belligerent handicapped vet John Heard in *Cutter's Way,* she was stunning. Her Mo is still beautiful but has no more beauty in her life. A bottle at her lips, in an open, dirty kimono that reveals a bare breast, she waits for her husband to start living again, realizing he never will. So much is revealed in her voice: it is high and tinny yet full of rage, quivering with sadness, cracking with fear, bristling with sarcasm, gritty with courage. In recent years, Eichhorn has had trouble finding good roles, even humiliating herself (as did other respectable actors) in an exploitation war-prisoner film, *Opposing Force,* and appearing in a TV soap. However, she did star in the obscure *Wildrose,* giving a moving performance as an iron-pit worker who has trouble dealing with the men in the mines and with her uncommitted lover.

• **Cult Favorites:** *Cutter's Way/Cutter and Bone* (1981, Ivan Passer).

• **Sleepers:** *The Europeans* (1979, James Ivory), *Wildrose* (1984, John Hanson).

• **Also of Interest:** *Yanks* (1979, John Schlesinger).

○

ANITA EKBERG (1931–) Tall, voluptuous Swedish blonde was a major sex symbol in the fifties and early sixties, making films in Europe and Hollywood that emphasized her glamour and physical attributes. She appeared in all kinds of films, from Martin and Lewis comedies to Italian gladiator movies to the Hollywood epic *War and Peace* to the kooky low-budget thriller *Screaming Mimi* (as an insane exotic dancer with an enormous dog named

Anita Ekberg had a relatively small part in La Dolce Vita, *but she was highlighted on the poster for the film.*

Devil.) She was a particular favorite of Frank Tashlin and Federico Fellini, two directors who loved actresses who not only had large breasts but also could be photographed as "living caricatures." She's probably best remembered for *La Dolce Vita,* as an international actress who (she confirms to Rome reporters) bathes naked every morning in ice and sleeps "only in two drops of perfume." As they dance, Marcello Mastroianni describes her: "Do you know you are everything, everything . . . You are the first woman on the first day of creation. You are the mother, the sister, the lover, the friend . . . an angel, a devil, the earth, the home . . ." Their long night together ends with her walking into the Trevi Fountain while wearing a black strapless gown. She lifts her arms high and throws her head back and to one side as the water cascades down on her. That striking image of sex, pleasure, and brief freedom was used to promote the film (and would appear on the cover of the published screenplay). No wonder the fully dressed Mastroianni joins her in the water and kisses her—another unforgettably sensual moment. Ekberg stopped making movies when she got heavy, but returned to wear a tight leopardskin outfit for the 1979 TV movie *Gold of the Amazon Women.*

• **Cult Favorites:** *Screaming Mimi* (1958, Gerd Oswald), *La Dolce Vita* (1960, Federico Fellini).

• **Sleeper:** *The Clowns* (1970, Fellini).

• **Also of Interest:** *Artists and Models* (1955, Frank Tashlin), *War and Peace* (1956, King Vidor), *Hollywood or Bust* (1956, Tashlin), *Paris Holiday* (1958, Oswald), *The Mongols* (1960, André de Toth), *Boccaccio '70* (1962, Fellini episode), *Four for Texas* (1963, Robert Aldrich), *The Alphabet Murders* (1966,

Tashlin), *Woman Times Seven* (1967, Vittorio De Sica).

○

BENGT EKEROT Swedish stage actor played one of the cinema's most memorable characters: Death in Ingmar Bergman's *The Seventh Seal.* If he had been an American actor he might have been typecast in the role. He was a striking presence: he wears a black robe, and his pale, hairless, emotionless face looks straight ahead from beneath its hood. His eyes are cold, his nose is sharp, his face mask-like. He's not mean but, of course, he has no heart. Culminating beneath a forbidding sky, his chess game with knight Max von Sydow, which will determine who lives and who dies, is one of the most famous movie confrontations ever.

• **Cult Favorite:** *The Seventh Seal* (1956, Ingmar Bergman).

○

BRITT EKLAND (1942–) Swedish blonde with big, sensuous lips, large eyes, and a striking figure was invariably cast, mostly in British films, to play up her sex appeal. She always delivered on the sex, but she should be given some credit for also trying (at least until recent films) to give decent performances as well and, as often as not, pulling it off. Moreover, she always seemed to be in a good mood. She was energetic, sunny, and funny as Roger Moore's secretary, Mary Goodnight, in *The Man With the Golden Gun,* but ironically, she seemed miscast because she came across as the only actor not sleepwalking through that film and her character grated on one's nerves. Not so in *The Wicker Man,* where she capped a most erotic performance as a redhead with a bizarre nude dance in her room, a prelude to initiating a young boy in sexual practices. She made *After the Fox* and a less amusing comedy, *The Bobo,* with Peter Sellers, her one-time husband. On screen, there was little electricity between them. In recent years, Ekland has made many cheap films, including Fred Olen Ray's sexy, direct-to-video horror movies.

• **Cult Favorites:** *After the Fox* (1966, Vittorio De Sica), *Percy* (1971, Ralph Thomas), *The Wicker Man* (1973, Robin Hardy).

• **Also of Interest:** *The Bobo* (1967, Robert Parrish), *The Double Man* (1967, Franklin Schaffner), *The Night They Raided Minsky's* (1968, William Friedkin), *Stiletto* (1969, Bernard Kowalski), *Get Carter* (1971, Mike Hodges), *Year of the Cannibals* (1971, Liliana Cavani), *Asylum* (1972, Roy Ward Baker), *The Man With the Golden Gun* (1974, Guy Hamilton), *The Monster Club* (1981, Baker).

○

JACK ELAM (1916–) Tall, skinny, mean-looking (he is blind in one eye) character actor who specializes in gunslingers in westerns, henchmen in crime dramas, and drunks in both. His villains are distinguished by their joyous sadism. In some of his later westerns, like *Rio Lobo, Support Your Local Sheriff!,* and *Once Upon a Time in the West* (where he catches a fly in his gun barrel while waiting for his gunfight with Charles Bronson), he showed a real flair for comedy. Elam was always terrific as scummy characters, but I think he was perfectly cast as J. D. Smith in the short-lived TV western series, "The Dakotas"; the tough, dressed-in-black gunslinger turned lawman was even scarier than Elam's villains.

• **Cult Favorites:** *Kansas City Confidential* (1952, Phil Karlson), *Rancho Notorious* (1952, Fritz Lang), *Vera Cruz* (1954, Robert Aldrich), *The Far Country* (1955, Anthony Mann), *Kiss Me Deadly* (1955, Aldrich), *The Man from Laramie* (1955, Mann), *Once Upon a Time in the West* (1969, Sergio Leone), *Rio Lobo* (1970, Howard Hawks), *Pat Garrett and Billy the Kid* (1973, Sam Peckinpah).

• **Also of Interest:** *The Sundowners* (1950, George Templeton), *An American Guerilla in the Philippines* (1950, Lang), *Rawhide* (1951, Henry Hathaway), *Appointment in Honduras* (1953, Jacques Tourneur), *Count the Hours* (1953, Don Siegel), *Cattle Queen of Montana* (1954, Allan Dwan), *Moonfleet* (1955, Lang), *Wichita* (1955, Tourneur), *Jubal* (1956, Delmer Daves), *Pardners* (1956, Norman Taurog). *Gunfight at the O.K. Corral* (1957, John Sturges), *Night Passage* (1957, James Neilson), *Baby Face Nelson* (1957, Siegel), *The Comancheros* (1961, Michael Curtiz), *Support Your Local Sheriff!* (1969, Burt Kennedy), *Dirty Dingus Magee* (1970, Kennedy), *Support Your Local Gunfighter* (1971, Kennedy), *The Villain* (1979, Hal Needham), *Aurora Encounter* (1985, Jim McCullough).

○

WILD BILL/WILLIAM ELLIOTT (1903–65) Formidable cowboy star from the thirties to mid-fifties (as Gordon Elliott, he appeared in nonwesterns beginning in the mid-twenties). He is one of the few to move up from B to big-budget westerns. He played such characters as Wild Bill Hickok; Kit Carson; a Wyatt Earp figure in *In Early*

Arizona; and the title character in the popular "Red Ryder" series, replacing Don "Red" Berry. Except for a few fancy shirts and guns that were placed backward in his holster, Elliott eschewed gimmickry. He is appreciated by genre fans for following the tradition of William S. Hart in playing restrained, realistic characters—flawed heroes or outlaws who reform during the course of the film. His major partners were Tex Ritter at Columbia and Gabby Hayes at Republic; among his female leads were Anne Jeffreys and former skating star Vera Hruba Ralston, wife of Republic's chief, Herbert Yates:

• **Sample Films:** *The Great Adventures of Wild Bill Hickok* (1938 serial, Mack V. Wright and Sam Nelson), *In Early Arizona* (1938, Joseph Levering), *Overland with Kit Carson* (1939 serial, Nelson and Norman Denning), *The Man from Tumbleweed* (1940, Joseph H. Lewis), *The Return of Wild Bill* (1940, Lewis), *In Old Sacramento* (1946, Joseph Kane), *The Plainsman and the Lady* (1946, Kane), *Wyoming* (1947, Kane), *Old Los Angeles* (1948, Kane), *The Last Bandit* (1949, Kane), *The Longhorn* (1952), *Waco* (1952).

○

MICHAEL EMIL He displayed a quirky charm in Nicolas Roeg's *Insignificance*, a fascinating apocalyptic comedy that attacks America for persecuting, victimizing, and exploiting its celebrities, ultimately perverting their knowledge or talent. He played the wild-haired Jewish-German "Scientist" (Albert Einstein) whose life's work (finding the shape of the universe) is threatened by the U.S. government if he dares speak at a 1955 peace conference. There's a wonderful scene in which Theresa Russell's "Actress" (Marilyn Monroe)—who both confuses and flatters him by wanting to sleep with him—teaches him about relativity. Emil is best known for the offbeat pictures of his brother, Henry Jaglom. He invariably plays upbeat, uninhibited, middle-aged motor-mouths who humorously spout weird personal philosophies and debate everything, and explain everything in terms of sex. He can even find a connection between chess and sex or, if in mixed company, chess and masturbation. In his key film, *Sitting Ducks*, he and Zack Norman are a balding odd couple who run off with Mafia money. The gabby Emil, who brags he's the world's best lover, and womanizer Norman, a 60-second man, are a hilarious team—their brief bathtub conversation surpasses Louis Malle's entire dinner with André.

• **Cult Favorites:** *Tracks* (1977, Henry Jaglom), *Sitting Ducks* (1977, Jaglom), *Can She Bake a Cherry Pie?* (1984, Jaglom), *Always* (1985, Jaglom), *Insignificance* (1985, Nicolas Roeg).

• **Other Key Films:** *Someone to Love* (1986, Jaglom), *New Year's Day* (1990, Jaglom)

○

MARLA ENGLISH (1930–) One-time Paramount starlet with a slight resemblance to a young Elizabeth Taylor (only Marla was more of a sex kitten), English was the female lead in a series of ludicrous, very cheap horror films and overheated melodramas in 1956 and 1957, mostly at AIP. Edward L. Cahn made bad movies and she had the misfortune to be in a few of them, not that her acting warranted anything better. As an Indian, she was rescued by John Agar from an anthill in Cahn's *Flesh*

Marla English with Ralph Meeker in Lesley Selander's low-budget Desert Sands.

and the Spur. But she's better remembered playing the title characters in his *The She-Creature* and *Voodoo Woman.* The first film is a Bridey Murphy variation in which her past self, in the form of a prehistoric sea monster, is conjured up while she is under hypnosis. In the follow-up, she is turned into a monster by a mad scientist. Her characters rarely have a good time.

• **Key Films:** *The She-Creature* (1956, Edward L. Cahn), *Voodoo Woman* (1957, Cahn).

• **Also of Interest:** *Flesh and the Spur* (1956, Cahn), *A Strange Adventure* (1956, William Witney).

○

ROBERT ENGLUND (1948–) Meek-looking blond actor seems ideal for sympathetic roles—the kind of guy who can't get a date—but instead he covered himself with cadaverous makeup, put on a hat, a striped shirt, and hands with razor blades for fingers, affected a gruff voice and laugh, and became one of the horror film's most popular villains, Freddy Krueger in the *Nightmare on Elm Street* series. Freddy, who once massacred young children in the Elm Street area and was burned to death by angry parents, refuses to stay dead; he periodically—and gleefully—resumes his killing spree. He keeps turning up in teenagers' nightmares; eventually he appears when they are awake, too, making it impossible for them or the audience to distinguish between dream and reality and to tell if they are really in danger (usually they are). Therein, supposedly, lies the horror, although I find the scare sequences

Robert Englund's Freddy Krueger was as friendly as ever in A Nightmare on Elm Street 3: Dream Warriors.

terribly repetitious. Like Jason in the *Friday the 13th* films, Freddy is, of course, the embodiment of evil and every young person's worst nightmare. I think he's meaner, unfortunately, than he is frightening.

• **Cult Favorite:** *A Nightmare on Elm Street* (1984, Wes Craven), *A Nightmare on Elm Street 2: Freddy's Revenge* (1985, Jack Scholder), *A Nightmare on Elm Street 3: Dream Warriors* (1987, Chuck Russell), *A Nightmare on Elm Street 4: The Dream Master* (1988, Renny Harlin), *A Nightmare on Elm Street 5: The Dream Child* (1989, Stephen Hopkins).

• **Sleeper:** *Don't Cry, It's Only Thunder* (1982, Peter Werner).

• **Other Key Film:** *The Phantom of the Opera* (1989, Dwight H. Little).

○

DALE EVANS (1912–) A former band singer, she became cowboy star Roy Rogers's most popular leading lady in the early forties.

They married in 1947 and, because of public demand, continued to appear together in his films. (They would also costar in the popular early-fifties TV series "The Roy Rogers Show.") Because there wasn't any question that Roy would win Dale at the end of each picture, if they didn't begin the film as a couple, more screen time could be devoted to action and music. In the early films, she often dressed fetchingly, especially if she were a saloon girl. Eventually her dress became more respectable; though her cowgirl outfits weren't any less flashy. "The Queen of the Cowgirls" was a genial partner for "The King of the Cowboys": she was sweet, cute, perky, and noncritical. Roy's characters treated hers as equals.

• **Sample Films:** *In Old Oklahoma/War of the Wildcats* (1943, Albert S. Rogell), *The Cowboy and the Senorita* (1944, Joseph Kane), *The Yellow Rose of Texas* (1944, Kane), *Don't Fence Me In* (1945), *My Pal Trigger* (1946, Frank McDonald), *Helldorado* (1947, William Witney), *Pals of the Golden West* (1951, Witney).

GENE EVANS (1922–) Stocky, rugged-looking character actor, familiar to fans of war films and westerns. In a rare lead role, he gave a tough, convincing portrayal in Samuel Fuller's tense Korean War drama, *The Steel Helmet*, as an American sergeant who is the only member of his platoon to survive an ambush. In Fuller's *Fixed Bayonets*, he was effective as a member of a rearguard platoon whose mission is to hold off Korean troops while the larger U.S. force escapes from the icy mountains. There's a great scene in which all the soldiers put their bare feet together for protection against frostbite and they discover that one foot, which has no claimant, no longer has sensation. When they pull apart, Evans discovers it is his. Fuller would use him again, most notably in *Shock Corridor*, as an atomic scientist who has a breakdown and then, his mind like a child's, ends up in an asylum. He made contributions to a number of popular films over his career without ever getting proper notice.

• **Cult Favorites:** *It Happens Every Spring* (1949, Lloyd Bacon), *The Steel Helmet* (1950, Samuel Fuller), *Ace in the Hole* (1951, Billy Wilder), *Fixed Bayonets* (1951, Fuller), *Park Row* (1952, Fuller), *Shock Corridor* (1963, Fuller), *The Ballad of Cable Hogue* (1970, Sam Peckinpah), *Walking Tall* (1973, Phil Karlson), *Pat Garrett and Billy the Kid* (1973, Peckinpah).

• **Also of Interest:** *I Was an American Spy* (1951, Lesley Selander), *Donovan's Brain* (1953, Felix Feist), *Hell and High Water* (1954, Fuller), *The Giant Behemoth* (1959, Eugene Lourie), *The War Wagon* (1967, Burt Kennedy), *Support Your Local Sheriff!*

(1969, Kennedy), *People Toys/Devil Times Five* (1974, Sean McGregor), *Gentle Savage* (1978, McGregor).

○

DOUGLAS FAIRBANKS (1883–1939) He leapt from high tree limbs, swung perilously across ship decks filled with vicious pirates, vaulted across deep chasms, and gracefully bounded onto tables to engage in deadly swordfights—there was no need for special effects when he was on the screen—and he did these dangerous stunts with the same insouciant grin, good spirits, and relaxed manner he had while romancing his beautiful leading ladies. This dashing, mustached acrobat exemplified the excitement, romance, and youthful exuberance that the early cinema, at its best, represented to entranced viewers.

Douglas Fairbanks in The Thief of Bagdad.

Idolized by young boys, admired by men, adored by females, he was the greatest hero of the silent era, with appeal much broader than Saturday matinee cowboy heroes like Tom Mix. Because he looked like he was having so much fun on the screen, boys wanted to be his Zorro (the inspiration for Batman), Robin Hood, Don Juan, and D'Artagnan, and join in for some swashing and buckling; females wanted to make love to them. His social comedies were extremely popular during their day, but now one can much better see his appeal in his twenties adventure films. Screenwriter Robert Presnell, Jr., wrote of his hero: "There may have been greater athletes, greater romantics, greater performers—but no one has ever looked as marvelous doing what he did." Only Errol Flynn even came close. Fairbanks was a shrewd businessman who formed his own production company and later cofounded United Artists with Charles Chaplin, D. W. Griffith, and Mary Pickford, his wife between 1920 and 1936. He died in his sleep of a heart attack at the age of 56, probably while smiling.

• **Cult Favorites:** *The Mark of Zorro* (1920, Fred Niblo), *The Thief of Bagdad* (1924, Raoul Walsh).

• **Other Key Films:** *The Three Musketeers* (1921, Niblo), *Robin Hood* (1922, Allan Dwan), *The Black Pirate* (1926, Albert Parker).

• **Also Recommended:** *Don Q, Son of Zorro* (1925, Donald Crisp), *The Gaucho* (1927, F. Richard Jones), *The Iron Mask* (1929, Dwan).

• **Also of Interest:** *The Taming of the Shrew* (1929, Sam Taylor), *Mr. Robinson Crusoe* (1932, Edward Sutherland), *The Private Life of Don Juan* (1934, Alexander Korda).

ANTONIO FARGAS (1947–) The son of a West Indian dancer and Puerto Rican father, this slim, humorous black character actor with large lips that he often contorts has been in many low-budget, urban-set exploitation films, too often as a jive-talking pimp or drug connection. In the blaxploitation spoof *I'm Gonna Git You Sucka*, he parodied himself as the winner of the "Pimp of the Year" pageant. Part of the street scene, his characters root themselves to a "safe" spot: a diner counter, a table in a club, a desk in some backroom, where they can count money and wait for the hero to come in. Typically, his cocky characters talk tough but are cowardly. A dull but welcome change of pace was his brothel piano player in *Pretty Baby*. As a youth, he debuted in the Shirley Clarke–Frederick Wiseman "documentary" *The Cool World,* about teenagers in the Harlem slums. He was a regular on TV's "Starsky and Hutch" and had a stint on the soap "All My Children."

• **Cult Favorites:** *Putney Swope* (1969, Robert Downey), *Shaft* (1971, Gordon Parks), *Cisco Pike* (1972, B. W. L. Norton), *Next Stop, Greenwich Village* (1976, Paul Mazursky), *Pretty Baby* (1978, Louis Malle).

• **Also of Interest:** *The Cool World* (1964, Shirley Clarke), *Cleopatra Jones* (1970, Jack Starrett), *Busting* (1974, Peter Hyams), *Car Wash* (1976, Michael Schultz), *Streetwalkin'* (1985, Joan Freeman).

FARINA (1921–80) Allen Hoskins was just 18 months old when Hal Roach picked him to be the playmate to his "lovable little pickaninny" Sunshine Sammy in his popular shorts. He was chosen because his hair was so long that he could pass for male or female. His ability to cry on cue also came in handy. Sammy got older, and Farina—he was named after the breakfast cereal—replaced him. He soon became a fixture in Roach's "Our Gang" series, preceding Stymie and Buckwheat as the resident black boy. He wore suspenders and old, patched gingham clothes (Stymie would wear similar dirty striped shirts) and was known for the half-dozen pigtails that stood on top of his head. While film historian Donald Bogle points out that Farina, like Stymie and Buckwheat, often was presented eating watermelons and fried chicken, spoke in the familiar, unflattering dialect of most pre-fifties black movie characters, and fled "ghosts" as quickly as Willie Best would, he concedes that overall Farina came across in a good light: "With his husky voice and arrogantly pleasant way about him, Farina was noted for his common sense and a certain heroic demeanor. Often he came to the rescue of little white damsels in distress."

• **Cult Favorites:** Many "Our Gang" shorts (1920s).

○

FRANCES FARMER (1913–70) A highly intelligent, headstrong actress of stage (with the leftist Group Theatre) and screen whose career was cut short in the early forties due to a broken marriage with actor Leif Erickson and the combined pressure caused by bouts with alcohol, her mother, Hollywood big shots, the press, and police. As documented in her posthumously published autobiography, *Will There Really Be a Morning?* and Jessica Lange's hit picture,

Frances, she spent several hellish years in mental institutions and was finally forced to have a lobotomy to curb her rebellious nature. The book and film renewed interest in her career, yet a closer look at her pictures has not revealed the special talent that she supposedly had. She was misplaced in *South of Pago-Pago* and *Badlands of Dakota* (an okay western). Her only role of any substance was in *Come and Get It,* and that's only because she played two women, both loved and lost by Edward Arnold. She is pretty, smart, and appealing in that film, but even so, I think she lacked the "spark" to have become a major movie star. Other movie actresses have done more with less.

• **Key Film:** *Come and Get It* (1936, Howard Hawks and William Wyler).
• **Also of Interest:** *Exclusive* (1937, Alexander Hall), *The Toast of New York* (1937, Rowland V. Lee), *Flowing Gold* (1940, Alfred E. Green), *Among the Living* (1941, Stuart Heisler), *Son of Fury* (1942, John Cromwell).

○

MIMSY FARMER (1945–) Pretty, wild blonde starred in several minor troubled-youth drive-in pictures of the late sixties, either playing a "bad girl" (in *Hot Rods to Hell,* she and her two boyfriends harass Dana Andrews and his family) or a good girl who has bad things happen to her as the result of drugs. In *Riot on Sunset Strip,* as policeman Aldo Ray's daughter, she is gang-raped after being slipped LSD; in *More,* she and lover Klaus Grunberg take acid, hoping it will cure them of their heroin addiction. *More* was the first of her several European films. *Code Name: Wild Geese,* directed by Italy's Anthony M. Dawson, is of interest because of her teaming with fellow cult stars Lee Van Cleef, Ernest Borgnine, and Klaus Kinski.

• **Key Films:** *Hot Rods to Hell* (1967, John Brahm), *Devil's Angels* (1967, Daniel Haller), *Riot on Sunset Strip* (1967, Arthur Dreifuss), *The Wild Racers* (1968, Haller), *More* (1969), *Four Flies on Grey Velvet* (1972, Dario Argento).

• **Also of Interest:** *Autopsy* (1978, Armando Crispini), *Code Name: Wild Geese* (1984, Anthony M. Dawson).

○

GLENDA FARRELL (1904–71) Spirited blonde was an unsung talent of many Warner Bros.–First National films of the thirties. She was cast as hard-boiled, wisecracking gold diggers, floozies, chorines, gangsters' molls (as in her debut in *Little Caesar*), and, most notably, reporters. She could be hard as nails, as in *Life Begins,* where she wants no part of her unborn baby, and *I Am a Fugitive from a Chain Gang,* in which she blackmails Paul Muni into marrying her and then betrays him. But more often she was merely cynical ("It's so hard to be good under the capitalistic system"), if not fully sympathetic. Most of her women are likable, funny, resourceful, independent (she is a lawyer in *The Law Is in Her Hands*), and supportive of other women. Joan Blondell, whose image was similar, was her gold-digging partner in several films. Farrell's willingness to play all roles offered, including supporting parts, earned her the part of the indomitable, crime-solving ace reporter Torchy Blane in an eight-picture series beginning with *Smart Blonde.*

• **Cult Favorites:** *I Am a Fugitive from a Chain Gang* (1932, Mervyn LeRoy), *Mystery of the Wax Museum* (1933, Michael Curtiz).

• **Other Key Films:** *Little Caesar* (1931, LeRoy), *Lady for a Day* (1933, Frank Capra), *Gold Diggers of 1935* (1935, Busby Berkeley), *Traveling Saleslady* (1935, Ray Enright), *Gold Diggers of 1937* (1937, Lloyd Bacon), *Smart Blonde* (1937, Frank McDonald), *Fly-Away Baby* (1937, McDonald), *Blondes at Work* (McDonald), *Torchy Gets Her Man* (1938, William Beaudine), *Torchy Blane in Chinatown* (1939, Beaudine), *Torchy Runs for Mayor* (1939, Ray McCarey), *Torchy Plays with Dynamite* (1939, Noel Smith), *Talk of the Town* (1942, George Stevens).

• **Also of Interest:** *Three on a Match* (1932, LeRoy), *Bureau of Missing Persons* (1933, Roy Del Ruth), *Havana Widows* (1933, Enright), *Dark Hazard* (1934, Alfred E. Green), *Hi, Nellie!* (1934, LeRoy), *Kansas City Princess* (1934, William Keighley), *Go into Your Dance* (1935, Archie Mayo), *You Learn and Live* (1937, Arthur Woods), *Hollywood Hotel* (1938, Berkeley), *Stolen Heaven* (1938, Andrew L. Stone), *Girls in the Night* (1953, Jack Arnold), *The Disorderly Orderly* (1964, Frank Tashlin).

○

ALICE FAYE (1912–) Rudy Vallee discovered her in the chorus of *George White's Scandals* and, after signing her to sing with his band, got her the female lead in 20th Century-Fox's film version when Lillian Harvey rejected the part. Fox bleached her already blond hair, penciled in thin eyebrows, and promoted her as a Jean Harlow sex bomb before realizing she could become more popular with a wholesome image that was more in character. Her career was really launched in Shirley Temple films, playing stable, respectable women who would make ideal wives and mothers. Beginning in the late thirties she starred in her own vehicles, mostly frivolous musicals and dramas, and established herself as the first of the Foxy blondes, preceding Betty Grable and Marilyn Monroe. She didn't have their electricity or sex appeal, but she seemed genuine and warmhearted, and audiences rooted for and cried along with her women in *every* film as they had romantic problems with the likes of Tyrone Power and John Payne. Her husky voice could be annoying, but her contralto was soft and pleasant. She benefited from the lavish productions Fox mounted for her.

• **Cult Favorite:** *The Gang's All Here* (1943, Busby Berkeley).

• **Other Key Films:** *Poor Little Rich Girl* (1936, Irving Cummings), *On the Avenue* (1937, Roy Del Ruth), *Wake Up and Live* (1937, Sidney Lanfield), *You Can't Have Everything* (1937, Norman Taurog), *In Old Chicago* (1938, Henry King), *Alexander's Ragtime Band* (1938, King), *Sally, Irene and Mary* (1938, William A. Seiter), *Rose of Washington Square* (1939, Gregory Ratoff), *Lillian Russell* (1940, Cummings), *Tin Pan Alley* (1940, Walter Lang), *Hello, Frisco, Hello* (1943, H. Bruce Humberstone), *Fallen Angel* (1945, Otto Preminger).

• **Also of Interest:** *George White's Scandals* (1934, George White, Thornton Freeland, and Harry Lachman), *Sing, Baby, Sing* (1936, Lanfield), *The Great American Broadcast* (1941, Archie Mayo), *That Night in Rio* (1941, Cummings), *Weekend in Havana* (1941, Lang).

○

STEPIN FETCHIT (1902–85) Born Lincoln Theodore Monroe Andrew Perry (he was named after four presidents), this hilarious ex-vaudeville performer (part of a twosome called Step and Fetch It) became the first black actor to receive feature billing in Hollywood films and be a legitimate drawing card. He'd make $2 million but lived such a flamboyant life that he went bankrupt and fled Hollywood in the late thirties. Tall, thin, and bald (so it seemed like he was scratching directly on his confused brain), he became extremely popular playing dim-witted, lazy, easily frightened, shuffling, stammering plantation hands and small-town handymen. His wide-eyed, open-mouthed expression, his stuttering and idiotic statements were enough to make his audience laugh, but probably his most impressive talent was his much-imitated, slow-motion walk. His movements were as precise and graceful as a ballet dancer's—and much funnier! His career is controversial: his detractors point out that it was he who firmly established the demeaning "coon" stereotype; his fans contend he was so talented that he transcended his material. It's interesting watching him in his four films with Will Rogers: *David Harum, Judge Priest, Steamboat 'Round the Bend,* and *The County Chairman.* Rogers continually insults him for being lazy and slow-thinking and threatens to kick him in the rear to get him to do the work he gave him. Yet the two characters are obviously friends who feel affection for one another and enjoy each other's company; in fact, Rogers is reminded by watching his black friend that small-town life *should* be slow-paced. Also, though Rogers has the upper hand in their characters' relationships in each film, the two actors have equal status in their comedy routines, playing off each other; indeed, Fetchit gets more laughs. It's evident that director John Ford, who used him five times, felt a great deal of warmth for Fetchit and made him part of each film's

Stepin Fetchit with Will Rogers in John Ford's Judge Priest.

ensemble. At the end of *Judge Priest,* he had Fetchit leading a parade through town, high-kicking to "Dixie." Fetchit reprised the role 19 years later, while on the comeback trail, in Ford's even more sentimental remake, *The Sun Shines Bright.*

• **Cult Favorites:** *Judge Priest* (1934, John Ford), *Bend of the River* (1952, Anthony Mann), *The Sun Shines Bright* (1953, Ford).

• **Sleeper:** *Steamboat 'Round the Bend* (1935, Ford).

• **Also of Interest:** *Hearts in Dixie* (1929), *David Harum* (1934, James Cruze), *Stand Up and Cheer* (1934, Hamilton MacFadden), *The County Chairman* (1935, John Blystone), *Dimples* (1936, William Seiter), *On the Avenue* (1937, Roy Del Ruth).

○

W. C. FIELDS (1879–1946) A comic original and genius. The former William Claude Dukenfield, one-time juggler and vaudeville star, was already middle-aged and had his famous bulbous nose when he became a movie star. He would play essentially two characters: an unfriendly, larcenous mountebank and a henpecked husband. Both are cowardly, bumbling, boastful, and freedom-loving, and both cope with an absurd, surreal universe full of dishonest men, grasping women, imbeciles (whom he often employs), and annoying children. The first character type—boat captains, the leader of an itinerant acting troupe, a vagabond medicine man, the owner of traveling carnivals—bluffs, boasts, and

W. C. Fields's misanthropic carnival owner pretends to be "Buffalo Bella" in You Can't Cheat an Honest Man.

bullies his way through a corrupt, hostile world, usually staying one step ahead of an angry sheriff. He's so mean in *You Can't Cheat an Honest Man* that he feeds Charlie McCarthy to the alligators, and in *The Old-Fashioned Way,* he gives Baby LeRoy a stiff kick in the rear. He's so dishonest that he uses ventriloquism to sell a "talking dog" which (he then explains to the sucker who purchased it) is so offended at being sold that it will never speak again. Yet we find him lovable because he's the rare individual who'll wage a war against an oppressive world. In his great unforgettable white-collar comedies, *It's a Gift, The Man on the Flying Trapeze,* and *The Bank Dick,* Fields is trapped in a life of nagging, browbeating wives, mothers-in-law, free-

loaders, bosses, traffic cops, and, as ever, children—even his own. He brags but now no one listens, mumbles and grumbles, putters around (which drives his wives crazy), and is aggravated by everyone who crosses his path. In *It's a Gift,* Baby LeRoy almost kills him with an ice pick, a loud insurance salesman wakes him while looking for Carl LaFong, and blind Mr. Muckle breaks merchandise in his grocery store. Whereas the other Fields spends most of his time drinking, swearing ("Godfrey Daniel!"), smoking cigars, singing off-key, gambling, and talking a blue streak to women, this married Fields must sneak behind his wife's back to enjoy these pleasures. But we mustn't despair: he is just too stubborn to give up his vices, and too much in his own private world to ever conform.

• **Cult Favorites:** *Million Dollar Legs* (1932, Edward Cline), *The Old-Fashioned Way* (1934, William Beaudine), *It's a Gift* (1934, Norman Z. McLeod), *The Man on the Flying Trapeze* (1935, Clyde Bruckman), *You Can't Cheat an Honest Man* (1939, George Marshall), *My Little Chickadee* (1940, Cline), *The Bank Dick* (1940, Cline), *Never Give a Sucker an Even Break* (1941, Cline).

• **Other Key Films:** *Sally of the Sawdust* (1925, D. W. Griffith), *It's the Old Army Game* (1926, Edward Sutherland), *The Golf Specialist* (1930 short, Monte Brice), *If I Had a Million* (1932, James Cruze, H. Bruce Humberstone, Stephen Roberts, William A. Seiter, Ernst Lubitsch, Norman Taurog, Norman Z. McLeod), *The Dentist* (1932 short, Leslie Pearce), *The Fatal Glass of Beer* (1933 short, Bruckman), *The Pharmacist* (1933 short, Arthur Ripley), *The Barber Shop* (1933 short, Ripley), *International House* (1933, Sutherland), *Tillie and Gus* (1933,

McLeod), *Alice in Wonderland* (1933, McLeod), *You're Telling Me* (1934, Erle C. Kenton), *Mrs. Wiggs of the Cabbage Patch* (1934, Taurog), *David Copperfield* (1934, George Cukor), *Mississippi* (1935, Sutherland), *Poppy* (1936, Sutherland), *The Big Broadcast of 1938* (1938, Mitchell Leisen).

○

CARRIE FISHER (1956–) Pretty daughter of Debbie Reynolds and Eddie Fisher had been around before *Star Wars*—her nymphet seduced Warren Beatty in *Shampoo*—but George Lucas's trilogy made her an icon of the era's pop culture. The imperiled heroine, Princess Leia, starts out as a brave, feisty, stubborn (if cold) child-woman, and by *Return of the Jedi* has matured into a sensitive and (in a skimpy outfit) sexy—still brave and feisty—young woman. Actually I think her new wardrobe reflects too drastic a change in her personality from *The Empire Strikes Back,* but it explains why Harrison Ford's Han Solo is willing to give up his solo act. Fisher will never find an equal role. For a time she has had leads and supporting parts in comedies, often trying too hard to be a sex symbol. She is at her best and most amusing as women who have had trouble finding the right men. She wrote the semiautobiographical book *Postcards from the Edge* (which she also adapted for the screen), as well as the novel *Surrender the Pink.*
• **Cult Favorites:** *The Blues Brothers* (1980, John Landis), *Hannah and Her Sisters* (1986, Woody Allen).
• **Other Key Films:** *Star Wars* (1977, George Lucas), *The Empire Strikes Back* (1980, Irvin Kershner), *Return of the Jedi* (1983, Richard Marquand), *When Harry*

Met Sally (1989, Rob Reiner).
• **Also of Interest:** *Shampoo* (1975, Hal Ashby), *Under the Rainbow* (1981, Steve Rash), *Garbo Talks* (1984, Sidney Lumet), *The Man With One Red Shoe* (1985, Stan Dragoti), *Sibling Rivalry* (1990, Carl Reiner).

○

CASH FLAGG The acting pseudonym for Ray Dennis Steckler, auteur director of some of the most idiosyncratic and ridiculous (as well as amusing) mini-budget films in memory. He often lived in his car to cut down expenses. In his most famous film, the first monster musical, *The Incredibly Strange Creatures Who Stopped Living and Became Mixed-Up Zombies,* Cash's character was hypnotized and ordered to commit murders. As a gimmick, actors in Cash Flagg masks raced through the theater trying to scare viewers during the film (and some apparently got punched for their troubles). According to Steckler, Cash Flagg masks were sold in stores. He played a villain named Steak (threatening Arch Hall, Jr.) in *Wild Guitar,* Mad Dog in *Thrill Killers,* a detective in *Body Fever,* and in the California-set "Dead End Kids" take-off, *Lemon Grove Kids Meet the Monsters,* he parodied Huntz Hall, whom he greatly resembled. He was married to his leading lady, Carolyn Brandt. Both had bits in Arch Hall, Sr.'s *Eegah!* In addition to being thrown into a pool by Richard Kiel, he served as cinematographer.
• **Cult Favorites:** *Eegah!* (1962, Nicholas Merriwether/Arch Hall, Sr.), *The Incredibly Strange Creatures Who Stopped Living and Became Mixed-Up Zombies* (1963, Ray Dennis Steckler).
• **Other Key Films:** *Wild Guitar* (1962, Steckler), *Thrill Killers* (1964, Steckler),

Lemon Grove Kids Meet the Monsters (1966, Steckler), *Super Cool/Body Fever* (1969, Steckler), *Revenge of the Stripper* (Steckler).

○

DARLANNE FLUEGEL (1956–) Sexy ex-model with shoulder-length blond hair, a slim figure, sharp features, and forceful gray eyes. She has played beauties with hard edges in a number of violent action films. They risk physical and mental pain by living in a mean world and hanging out with cops and criminals. They think they're tough enough to chance it—but often they're not. In *Once Upon a Time in America,* she is tortured to death by men who want information about her gangster boyfriend, Robert De Niro. In *To Live and Die in L.A.,* she's a junkie informant who resents being controlled by her cop lover, William L. Peterson—she betrays him but his partner takes his place with her. In *Freeway,* in which she has the lead role, she relentlessly tracks down the serial killer who murdered her husband and wrecked her life. In *Running Scared,* she loves cop Billy Crystal; in *Lock Up,* she loves prisoner Sylvester Stallone. In almost every film, including the science-fiction parody *Battle Beyond the Stars,* she falls into the hands of sadistic villains. But she rarely weakens. She has starred on television's "Crime Story" and "Hunter." One of my favorite rising actresses.

• **Cult Favorites:** *Battle Beyond the Stars* (1980, Jimmy T. Murakami), *Once Upon a Time in America* (1984, Sergio Leone), *To Live and Die in L.A.* (1985, William Friedkin).

• **Other Key Films:** *Running Scared* (1986, Peter Hyams), *Freeway* (1988, Francis Della).

• **Also of Interest:** *Eyes of Laura Mars* (1978, Irvin Kershner), *Tough Guys*

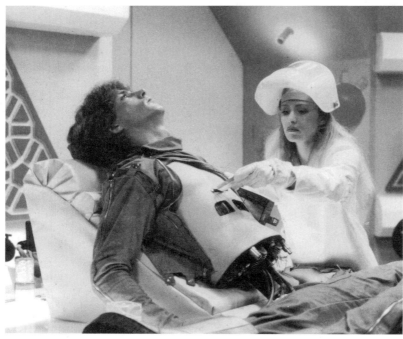

Darlanne Fluegel in Battle Beyond the Stars.

Errol Flynn (far left) *in* Captain Blood.

(1986, Jeff Kanew), *Deadly Stranger* (1988, Max Kleven), *Border Heat* (1988, Tony Gaudloz), *Bulletproof* (1988, Steve Carver), *Lock Up* (1989, John Flynn).

○

ERROL FLYNN (1909–59) Strikingly handsome, mustached, Tasmanian-born actor was the most dashing, romantic action-adventure hero of the sound era, carrying on the Douglas Fairbanks tradition. He was overmatched when opposite Bette Davis, but he was still a great *movie* actor. He certainly thrilled us young boys, who wanted to look like him and clash our swords with Basil Rathbone and Henry Daniell, outbox Ward Bond's John L. Sullivan, and romance Olivia de Havilland, his most frequent and beautiful screen lover. Females were attracted to Flynn, too, including the costars he drove crazy with his pranks. His characters were brash, playful, and egotistical—which is why de Havilland, Alexis Smith in *Gentleman Jim,* and other women they court detest them at first and want them to be humbled—but underneath, these rogues are caring, sincere, and loyal. Their frivolous behavior masks their fear and vulnerability. His brazen Gentleman Jim Corbett mercilessly mocks Sullivan before their championship fight—just as Muhammed Ali would do with Sonny Liston—but in a great scene, he gives Sullivan back his self-respect after taking the title by saying he's lucky he didn't fight him in his prime. Flynn had remarkable eyes, and when his character finally looks directly into the eyes of a woman and speaks from the heart, without bluster or pretense, she inevitably falls for him. Those eyes and that clear delivery also made him, along with John Wayne, the screen's greatest leader. He commands pirates in *Captain Blood* and *The Sea Hawk,* revolutionaries in *The Adventures of Robin Hood,* the 7th Cavalry (as Custer) in *They Died with Their Boots On,* war pilots in *Dawn Patrol,* soldiers in *Objective Burma!,* and so on. When his charismatic men explain their (usually patriotic) motives for attempting brave (though suicidal) acts—with a voice that is true, and eyes shown in close-up—their men will follow them anywhere, sure that their causes are just. Interestingly, coming as they did early in his career, *Captain Blood* and *The Adventures of Robin Hood* established his image as the sensitive champion of the downtrodden underdog, and one of the few freedom-fighter heroes whom conservative Hollywood ever accepted.

• **Cult Favorites:** *The Adventures of Robin Hood* (1938, Michael Curtiz and William Keighley), *Objective, Burma!* (1945, Raoul Walsh), *Cuban Rebel Girls* (1959, Barry Mahon).

• **Other Key Films:** *Captain Blood* (1935, Curtiz), *The Charge of the Light Brigade* (1936, Curtiz), *The Prince and the Pauper* (1937, Keighley), *The Dawn Patrol* (1938,

Edmund Goulding), *Dodge City* (1939, Curtiz), *The Private Lives of Elizabeth and Essex* (1939, Curtiz), *The Sea Hawk* (1940, Curtiz), *Sante Fe Trail* (1940, Curtiz), *Dive Bomber* (1941, Curtiz), *They Died with Their Boots On* (1941, Walsh), *Desperate Journey* (1942, Walsh), *Gentleman Jim* (1942, Walsh), *Edge of Darkness* (1943, Lewis Milestone), *Northern Pursuit* (1943, Walsh), *San Antonio* (1945, David Butler), *The Adventures of Don Juan* (1948, Vincent Sherman), *Against All Flags* (1952, George Sherman), *The Sun Also Rises* (1957, Henry King), *Too Much, Too Soon* (1958, Art Napoleon), *The Roots of Heaven* (1958, John Huston).

○

PETER FONDA (1939–) He had nowhere near the talent of his father Henry Fonda or sister Jane Fonda, but he was popular with young audiences from the early sixties to early seventies because he was good-

Peter Fonda and Luana Anders in Easy Rider.

looking, knew how to ride a motorcycle, made "hip" pictures with drug-related themes, and, to hide his acting limitations, smartly played characters who were tight-lipped, unemotional, and often wore shades. He gave a brain-dead performance as the stoned drug-dealer biker who rides across America in his key film, *Easy Rider,* but viewers just thought the character was supposed to be comatose. Fonda was pivotal to the era. *The Wild Angels,* in which he's the head of an unruly Hell's Angels band, started the outlaw biker film craze; *The Trip,* in which his television-commercial director drops acid, initiated drug films (Fonda would be accused of glamorizing drugs); and *Easy Rider,* which inexplicably made both him and director-costar Dennis Hopper the heroes of the young generation, paved the way for numerous low-budget films with antiestablishment themes. Most of these pictures were downbeat. His biker in *The Wild Angels* concludes: "There's no place else to go"; similarly, at the end of their odyssey to nowhere, and just prior to their murders by southern rednecks, his biker in *Easy Rider* tells Hopper, "We blew it"; in several films he is killed. Fonda eventually realized young viewers identified with his characters and this may have made him uncomfortable, because he gave better performances when he didn't have to represent a particular type. In 1977, he actually played two good parts: a cowboy who comes home after years away and finds his wife (Verna Bloom) has changed, in the interesting feminist western *The Hired Hand,* which he directed; and an ex-convict who is on the lam after he beats up the singer who stole his song in *Outlaw Blues,* an apolitical variation on *The Harder They Come* that is entertaining thanks to his teaming with Susan St. James. He worked well with Warren Oates in *The Hired Hand, 92 in the Shade,* and even the silly *Race with the Devil.* Fonda's last good role was as a cult leader in *Split Image,* his one bad guy.

• **Cult Favorites:** *Lilith* (1964, Robert Rossen), *The Wild Angels* (1966, Roger Corman), *The Trip* (1967, Corman), *Easy Rider* (1969, Dennis Hopper), *The Hired Hand* (1971, Peter Fonda), *Dirty Mary Crazy Larry* (1974, John Hough), *92 in the Shade* (1975, Thomas McGuane).

• **Sleepers:** *Outlaw Blues* (1977, Richard T. Heffron), *Split Image* (1982, Ted Kotcheff).

• **Also of Interest:** *Spirits of the Dead* (1968, Roger Vadim episode), *Two People* (1973, Robert Wise), *Race with the Devil* (1975, Jack Starrett), *Futureworld* (1976, Heffron), *Fighting Mad* (1976, Jonathan Demme), *Wanda Nevada* (1979, Fonda).

○

HARRISON FORD (1942–) He was to kids and adults in the late seventies and eighties what the greatest serial heroes had been to kids in the thirties and forties. He was the ultimate action hero, starring in the wondrous "Star Wars" and "Indiana Jones" trilogies, six of the most popular pictures of all time, and all destined for cult status. There was so much money and technology put into those films that one tended to overlook Ford's contribution to their success. It's hard to picture anyone else as Han Solo, cocky con man and mercenary, who reveals his true good nature when he puts his life on the line for young Luke Skywalker and Princess Leia. And certainly no one else could be the indomitable, whip-carrying adventure seeker Indiana Jones, the most resourceful, dependable, and reckless of heroes. It's always surpris-

Harrison Ford in Blade Runner *with Daryl Hannah.*

ing when one re-watches the "Star Wars" films and *Raiders of the Lost Ark* and sees what terrific, creative performances Ford gave; when they came out, we took him for granted. His action scenes are vigorous, with a lot of physicality and humor, as Ford either loudly complains about his own foolishness for getting into such messes (as Solo often does) or excitedly yells at the female for not automatically doing something exceptionally dangerous to save both of their lives (as Jones often does). Much of the humor in both series centers on how his character reacts to each dangerous situation that arises. Everything makes Solo nervous (though he conquers his fears and carries on); only snakes freak out Jones. Audiences have had mixed reactions to Ford in his other

roles. They liked him best as a tough cop who falls in love with the Amish Kelly McGillis character in *Witness,* and as secretary Melanie Griffith's supportive boyfriend in *Working Girl*—roles in which he showed his soft side. They liked him least as an idealist who, after moving his family to the jungle, becomes crazed, obsessive, and domineering in *The Mosquito Coast,* although that may be his best performance. Initially, most people disliked his portrayal of a noir detective in the futuristic *Blade Runner.* However, he does have strong screen presence—it's just hard getting used to a humorless Harrison Ford character. Nobody was impressed by his American tourist who searches for his kidnapped wife in Roman Polanski's predictable *Frantic.* But *Presumed Innocent,* in which he played a man accused of slaying his former mistress, *was* a major hit, despite his wishy-washy character. Now that Ford is finished with Han Solo and Indiana Jones, it will be interesting to see if he can maintain his box-office clout without playing heroes.

• **Cult Favorites:** *American Graffiti* (1973, George Lucas), *The Conversation* (1974, Francis Ford Coppola), *Apocalypse Now* (1979, Coppola), *Blade Runner* (1982, Ridley Scott), *Witness* (1985, Peter Weir), *The Mosquito Coast* (1986, Weir).

• **Sleeper:** *The Frisco Kid* (1979, Robert Aldrich).

• **Other Key Films:** *Star Wars* (1977, Lucas), *The Empire Strikes Back* (1980, Irvin Kershner), *Raiders of the Lost Ark* (1981, Steven Spielberg), *Return of the Jedi* (1983, Richard Marquand), *Indiana Jones and the Temple of Doom* (1984, Spielberg), *Working Girl* (1988, Mike Nichols), *Indiana Jones and the Last Crusade* (1989, Spielberg), *Presumed Innocent* (1990, Alan J. Pakula).

○

DEBORAH FOREMAN One of the most likable actresses to emerge from the endless stream of teen pics of the eighties. Bright, pretty, dimpled, and spirited, she was so much better than her so-so material in *Valley Girl,* where she was courted by a weird Nicholas Cage, and the cable hit, *My Chauffeur*—a couple of sexy but chaste comedies. While everyone "died" around her, she livened up the *Ten Little Indians*–inspired *April Fool's Day,* playing Muffy St. John. However, she did nothing to liven up *Destroyer.* She hasn't found the vehicle to vault her out of obscurity, but she deserves discovery. Perhaps she'll find fame in television.

• **Key Films:** *Valley Girl* (1983, Martha Coolidge), *My Chauffeur* (1986, David Beaird), *April Fool's Day* (1986, Fred Walton), *3:15—The Moment of Truth* (1986, Larry Gross), *Destroyer* (1988, Robert Kirk), *Waxwork* (1988, Anthony Hickox).

○

MARK FOREST (1933–) Like Steve Reeves and several other well-built American "actors," this ex-gymnast and body builder went to Italy and became a star playing mythical musclemen. Actually, he only played one, Maciste, but for export to America that character was renamed in different films Hercules, Samson, or Goliath. The films were pretty much interchangeable—usually his hero had to perform some impossible task to free an enslaved people and/or to clear his name and save his reputation. There was romance with well-endowed women, hand-to-hand combat with either hordes of bad guys or one equally muscular henchman, horseback riding through a lot of dust, and an action-packed finale that usually included the storming of a fortress, rescuing the leading lady from a forest, or a collapsing building and, of course, dispatching the chief villain, often a supernatural creature. Low-budget pictures—all camp lovers' delights—were horribly directed and dubbed for American release.

• **Sample Films:** *Atlas* (1960, Roger Corman), *Son of Samson* (1960), *Goliath and the Dragon* (1960, Vittorio Cottafavi), *Maciste—The Mighty* (1960, Carlo Campogalliani), *Colossus in the Arena* (1962), *Hercules Against the Sons of the Sun* (1963, Osvaldo Civirani), *Maciste in the Valley of Kings, Hercules Against the Barbarians, Goliath and the Sins of Babylon* (1964, Michele Lupo).

○

ROBERT FORSTER (1941–) A dark, strong-jawed leading man, sort of a handsome Charles Bronson, who also played Indians and ethnics. He gave a strong performance in the ground-breaking leftist film *Medium Cool* as an apolitical, detached Chicago reporter who develops a social conscious-ness while covering news before and dur-ing the 1968 Democratic Convention. It seemed like he had the talent, looks, and charisma to become a big star, but besides the romantic lead in Disney's disappoint-ing *The Black Hole,* the best he's managed is being a capable lead in several minor action films, including two lively cult films written by John Sayles and directed by Lewis Teague: *The Lady in Red* and *Alligator.*
   • **Cult Favorites:** *Reflections in a Golden Eye* (1967, John Huston), *Medium Cool* (1969, Haskell Wexler), *The Lady in Red* (1979, Lewis Teague), *Alligator* (1980, Teague).
   • **Also of Interest:** *The Stalking Moon* (1969, Robert Mulligan), *Justine* (1969, George Cukor), *Cover Me Babe* (1970, Noel Black), *Journey Through Rosebud* (1972, Tom Gries), *Stunts* (1977, Mark L. Lester), *The Black Hole* (1979, Gary Nel-son), *Hollywood Harry* (1985, Robert For-ster).

○

JODIE FOSTER (1963–) Supersmart, supertal-ented blonde actress who began her acting career when only three. Viewers who saw the films she made as a child always sensed they had made a remarkable discovery—a clear-eyed, husky-voiced young star who played parts with the maturity and intelli-gence of adult actresses. But being young and being perceptive, she could get into the heads of troubled children. Producers also saw that she had budded years before she was supposed to and cast her in roles that might have traumatized other girls her age. Her most remembered early role is that of the child prostitute in *Taxi Driver*—the part that attracted John Hinckley—but she played other tough, controversial parts, often girls or teenagers (she's especially good in *Foxes*) without stability or safety in their lives. She also played neglected daughters; a dying girl in *Echoes of Summer;* a girl secretly living alone after her father's death and commit-ting murder in *The Little Girl Who Lives Down the Lane.* She was an adult floozie in the innovative musical *Bugsy Malone.* Adult males other than Hinckley found themselves attracted to Foster. It was by design. Writer Ben Starr, who helped pick Foster early in her career to star in a TV pilot, admitted "she was selected because . . . Jodie delivered her lines not like a precocious 9-year-old but like a sophisti-cated young woman. What Jodie offers is the face of a cute little kid, but it's wrapped in a package that titillates. There is the suggestion of future wickedness: 'Hey Mister, I bet you can't wait till I grow up, can you?'" Foster did grow up, but she hasn't stopped playing females who have troubled lives. In several films, she is the victim of attempted rapes; she *is* raped in *Hotel New Hampshire* and *The Accused;* she commits suicide in *Stealing Home.* She won an Oscar for her stunning perfor-mance in *The Accused,* as a powerless young woman who takes to court her attackers and those who urged them on. This was her first character who isn't well-educated since she played the girl who runs off with Gary Busey and Robbie Robertson in *Carny*—although, again, she

Jodie Foster and Martin Sheen in The Little Girl Lives Down the Lane.

is smart and courageous. This was also her first character since *Carny* who is overtly sexual. One of the reasons she got the part was that she was the only tested actress who had no reservations about doing the harrowing rape scene (she said she had more trouble doing the sexy solo dance scene). She still takes parts other actresses can't handle, such as the young F.B.I. agent who tracks down a serial killer in *The Silence of the Lambs*. No one could have played her any better.

• **Cult Favorites:** *Taxi Driver* (1976, Martin Scorsese), *The Little Girl Who Lives Down the Lane* (1977, Nicholas Gessner), *Carny* (1980, Robert Kaylor), *Foxes* (1980, Adrian Lyne), *Hotel New Hampshire* (1984, Tony Richardson), *Siesta* (1987, Mary Lambert).

• **Sleepers:** *Kansas City Bomber* (1972, Jerrold Freedman), *Freaky Friday* (1977, Gary Nelson), *Stealing Home* (1988, Steven Kampmann).

• **Other Key Films:** *Tom Sawyer* (1973, Don Taylor), *Alice Doesn't Live Here Anymore* (1975, Scorsese), *Candleshoe* (1978, Norman Tokar), *Five Corners* (1988, Tony Bill), *The Silence of the Lambs* (1991, Jonathan Demme) *Little Man Tate* (1991, Jodie Foster).

○

MEG FOSTER (1948–) Talented, slender, attractive actress with unearthly, white-blue eyes. Early in her career she often played hippies, and she has always been good in sympathetic parts—as on the cult TV show "Sunshine"—but most often producers have taken one look at those eyes and cast her as villainesses. In her best film, *Ticket to Heaven,* in which she is a creepy high-ranking member of a cult, her eyes are enough to convince us that she can put anyone under a spell. In *They Live,* her eyes make her scarier than any of the aliens in the film (she turns out to be an alien collaborator). In *Masters of the Universe,* she played Evil-Lyn. In the cruddy underwater science-fiction film *Leviathan,* she pretends to be supportive of the hero (Peter Weller), but we look in her eyes and we know better (she's actually forfeiting his life to protect her business interests), and that film ends with him socking her in the jaw. She was originally cast opposite Tyne Daly on television's "Cagney and Lacey," but the producers opted for Sharon Gless, a less hip actress with normal eyes.

• **Cult Favorites:** *Carny* (1980, Robert Kaylor), *Ticket to Heaven* (1981, Ralph Thomas), *The Emerald Forest* (1985, John Boorman).

• **Also of Interest:** *Thumb Tripping* (1972, Quentin Masters), *Welcome to Arrow Beach* (1974, Laurence Harvey), *A Different Story* (1978, Paul Aaron), *The Osterman Weekend* (1983, Sam Peckinpah), *Masters of the Universe* (1987, Gary Goddard), *The Wind* (1987, Nico Mastorakis), *They Live* (1988, John Carpenter), *Stepfather 2: Make Room for Daddy* (1989, Jeff Burr).

○

JAMES FOX (1939–) This handsome blond British actor's characters typically have serious cracks beneath strong exteriors. In *The Servant,* his upper-class gentleman is so weak that he falls under the clutches of manipulative manservant Dirk Bogarde

and his seductive "sister," Sarah Miles, drowning in decadence. And in *Performance,* his brutal gangster becomes anything but macho after being liberated from his tough pose by decadent musician Mick Jagger and his seductive female companions. He has played mostly supporting parts in his interesting career—which he interrupted in 1973 because of religious callings—including a rich southerner in love with Jane Fonda in *The Chase* (she loves both him and fugitive Robert Redford), and the only British man who treats Indians as equals in *A Passage to India.* His film and character choices have been inspired. Fox wrote the novel *White Mischief.*

• **Cult Favorites:** *The Servant* (1963, Joseph Losey), *The Chase* (1966, Arthur Penn), *Isadora/The Loves of Isadora* (1969, Karel Reisz), *Performance* (1970, Donald Cammell and Nicholas Roeg), *Greystoke: The Legend of Tarzan, Lord of the Jungle* (1984, Hugh Hudson), *Absolute Beginners* (1986, Julien Temple).

• **Other Key Films:** *The Loneliness of the Long-Distance Runner* (1962, Tony Richardson), *Those Magnificent Men in Their Flying Machines* (1965, Ken Annakin), *King Rat* (1965, Bryan Forbes), *Thoroughly Modern Millie* (1967, George Roy Hill), *The Whistle Blower* (1987, Simon Langton), *High Season* (1987, Clare Peploe), *The Mighty Quinn* (1989, Carl Schenkel), *Farewell to the King* (1989, John Milius).

○

SAMANTHA FOX Not to be confused with the English pinup and pop singer, this former dancer from New York was one of the top porno actresses of the late seventies and early eighties. She was slightly plump and not particularly busty, but she was a fair actress, adept at comedy (often working with her boyfriend, porno comic Bobby Astyr), and particularly slutty in seduction scenes. In her first role, in *Bad Penny*, she seduces five men in order to claim an inheritance. She played a number of other amoral seductresses as well as a few sympathetic parts (such as women looking for true love and sexual satisfaction). Fox had, according to the authors of *Adult Movies*, "a way of combining stupidity and evil that is unnerving."

• **Cult Favorites:** *Amanda By Night* (1981, Robert McCallum), *Wanda Whips Wall Street* (1982, Larry Revene), *Roommates* (1982, Chuck Vincent).

• **Other Key Films:** *Bad Penny* (1978, Mark Ubell), *Jack 'n Jill* (1979, Felix Miguel Arroyo), *Babylon Pink* (1979, Henri Pachard), *Mystique* (1979, Robert Norman), *Satan Suite* (1979, Philip Drexler, Jr.), *Her Name Was Lisa* (1979, Richard Mahler), *October Silk* (1980, Pachard), *Pink Ladies* (1980, Mahler), *For the Love of Pleasure* (1980, Edwin S. Brown), *Games Women Play* (1980, Vincent), *Platinum Paradise* (1980, Cecil Howard), *The Tiffany Minx* (1981, Robert Walters), *Outlaw Ladies* (1981, Pachard), *Dracula Exotica* (1981, Warren Evans), *Foxtrot* (1982, Howard), *The Playgirl* (1982, Roberta Findlay), *The Lady Is a Tramp* (1982, Vincent), *In Love* (1983, Vincent).

○

ANNE FRANCIS (1930–) Slim, sexy blonde with a distinguishing beauty mark. She earned her cult status in *Forbidden Planet* as the virginal, sexually repressed Alta, the object of forbidden love by both visiting spaceship captain Leslie Nielsen (her first suitor on this planet without men) and her possessive father, Walter Pidgeon (as Mor-

Anne Francis and Leslie Nielsen in a publicity shot for Forbidden Planet.

bius), who conjures up his Id Monster to destroy his new rival and his male crew. Only Robby the Robot can be trusted around her. Francis usually played tough, experienced young women—she's particularly good as a prostitute undergoing psychoanalysis in *Girl of the Night*—so it's ironic that she is remembered most for the innocent, gentle Alta and as Glenn Ford's nice pregnant wife in *The Blackboard Jungle*. She also starred as one of TV's first female detectives in "Honey West."

• **Cult Favorites:** *Bad Day at Black Rock* (1955, John Sturges), *The Blackboard Jungle* (1955, Richard Brooks), *Forbidden Planet* (1956, Fred McLeod Wilcox).

• **Also of Interest:** *So Young, So Bad* (1950, Bernard Vorhaus), *Dreamboat* (1952, Claude Binyon), *A Lion Is in the Streets* (1953, Raoul Walsh), *Susan Slept Here* (1954, Frank Tashlin), *Battle Cry* (1955, Walsh), *The Rack* (1956, Arnold Laven), *Girl of the Night* (1960, Joseph Cates), *The Satan Bug* (1965, Sturges), *Funny Girl* (1968, Herbert Ross).

○

PAMELA FRANKLIN (1949–) Dark-haired, sweet yet sensual British actress debuted as one of the endangered children in *The Innocents,* and it didn't get any safer for her on the screen as she matured into a lovely leading lady. She took her place as one of the most reliable heroines-in-distress of mostly British-made thrillers and horror films of the seventies. Once in her late teens and early twenties, her roles became more daring, as directors explored her budding sexuality: in the Late Late Show staple *And Soon the Darkness,* she is threatened by a sex maniac while stranded in the French countryside; in *The Legend of Hell House,* she is seduced by a ghost in one of the most erotic scenes in the British horror cinema.

• **Cult Favorites:** *The Innocents* (1961, Jack Clayton), *The Nanny* (1965, Seth Holt), *Night of the Following Day* (1969, Hubert Cornfield), *And Soon the Darkness* (1970, Robert Fuest).

• **Other Key Films:** *The Lion* (1962, Jack Cardiff), *Our Mother's House* (1967, Clayton), *Sinful Davey* (1969, John Huston), *Necromancy/The Witching* (1972, Bert I.

Gordon), *The Legend of Hell House* (1973, John Hough).

• **Also of Interest:** *The Third Secret* (1964, Charles Crichton), *A Tiger Walks* (1964, Norman Tokar), *The Prime of Miss Jean Brodie* (1969, Ronald Neame), *Food of the Gods* (1976, Gordon).

○

MARK FRECHETTE (1947–75) In Michelangelo Antonioni's American-set *Zabriskie Point,* arguably the first Hollywood studio film with a pro-revolutionary theme, this handsome young amateur gave a wretched performance as a committed white revolutionary who might have killed a cop at a protest. While on the run, he meets lovely and equally untalented Daria Halprin in Death Valley, and they make love in the dunes; it is one of the era's most remembered sex scenes because it is alternately erotic and ludicrous. Frechette's movie career came to an abrupt halt. But he made the news when he was arrested for robbing a bank, which he claimed was a political act. He was killed while in prison.

• **Cult Favorite:** *Zabriskie Point* (1970, Michelangelo Antonioni).

○

KATHLEEN FREEMAN (1919–) The ideal movie landlady. She is great at rudely answering the door. The familiar, extremely funny character actress has played several imposing, screaming, distrustful, unattractive landladies; uppity maids; school, hospital, and office authority figures; and a tipsy television "microwave chef" in *Gremlins 2: The New Batch.* She has usually played such characters in absurd comedies, including several Jerry Lewis films. Lewis's characters are invariably scared of her tyrants and battleaxes, and with good reason—in one film Freeman picks up Lewis and carries him in her arms. She surprises viewers into laughter: she looks like she doesn't have a funny bone in her large body, but suddenly she is participating in the wildest, silliest slapstick imaginable.

• **Cult Favorites:** *The Far Country* (1955, Anthony Mann), *The Fly* (1958, Kurt Neumann), *The Nutty Professor* (1963, Jerry Lewis), *Psycho Sisters* (1972, Reginald LeBorg).

• **Also Recommended:** *The Naked City* (1948, Jules Dassin), *House by the River* (1950, Fritz Lang), *The Disorderly Orderly* (1964, Frank Tashlin), *Support Your Local Gunfighter!* (1971, Burt Kennedy), *Your Three Minutes Are Up* (1973, Douglas Schwartz), *In the Mood* (1987, Phillip Alden Robinson).

• **Also of Interest:** *The Midnight Story* (1957, Joseph Pevney), *North to Alaska*

(1960, Henry Hathaway), *The Ladies' Man* (1961, Lewis), *Three on a Couch* (1966, Lewis), *Dragnet* (1987, Tom Mankiewicz), *Gremlins 2: The New Batch* (1990, Joe Dante).

○

GERT FROBE (1912–88) Heavyset yet nimble, red-haired, double-chinned, round-faced German actor who etched his mark in film history as the greatest of all James Bond villains, the title character in *Goldfinger*. Cheerful when he has an advantage, vicious to assure that he gains one, he treats villainy like an art: he kills Shirley Eaton by painting her entire body gold, tries to castrate Sean Connery with a laser beam, schemes to rob Fort Knox, and creatively casts his roster of judo-chopping cohorts with the likes of Honor Blackman's fetching Pussy Galore and Harold Sakata's seeming invincible Oddjob. He was a diabolical supervillain, yet audiences took to him because he was exactly like an arro-

Villain Gert Frobe (right) plays a deadly game of golf with Sean Connery's James Bond in Goldfinger.

gent braggart one might find cheating at cards around a Miami Beach swimming pool or out on the golf links.

• **Cult Favorites:** *Goldfinger* (1964, Guy Hamilton).

• **Also of Interest:** *It Happened in Broad Daylight* (1960), *The Thousand Eyes of Dr. Mabuse* (1960, Fritz Lang), *The Longest Day* (1962, Ken Annakin, Andrew Martin, and Bernhard Wicki), *A High Wind in Jamaica* (1965, Alexander Mackendrick), *Banana Peel* (1965, Marcel Ophüls) *Those Magnificent Men in Their Flying Machines* (1965, Annakin), *Chitty Chitty Bang Bang* (1968, Ken Hughes), *$/Dollars* (1972, Richard Brooks), *Shadowman* (1974, Georges Franju), *The Serpent's Egg* (1978, Ingmar Bergman).

○

DWIGHT FRYE (1899–1943) Small, squirmy, crazed-eyed character actor who brought a welcome touch of hysteria and morbid lunacy to a number of classic Universal horror films. He was ideal as the doctor's grubby heart-procuring assistant in *Frankenstein,* a fiendish hunchback who, to show his superiority over at least one creature on earth, brutally beats the Monster—but the Monster will get revenge. He reappeared as Praetorius's grave-robbing, murderous assistant, Karl, in *Bride of Frankenstein,* and was again done in by Karloff's Monster. One wonders which employment agency kept sponsoring him as a lab assistant. His best role

Dwight Frye is Colin Clive's hunchbacked assistant in Frankenstein.

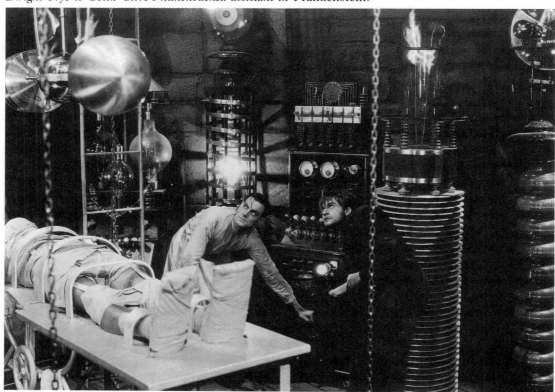

One of the most popular teams of the sixties: Annette Funicello and Frankie Avalon, costars of several AIP "Beach Party" movies.

was Renfield in *Dracula,* where he starts out a respectable, clean-cut young man but after Lugosi becomes his "Master!" turns into a sniveling, spider-eating madman. Beginning in the late thirties, this former concert pianist and musical-comedy stage star was often cast as a Nazi because he was blonde and spoke fluent German.

• **Cult Favorites:** *Dracula* (1931, Tod Browning), *Bride of Frankenstein* (1935, James Whale).

• **Other Key Films:** *Frankenstein* (1931, Whale), *The Vampire Bat* (1933, Frank Strayer), *The Invisible Man* (1933, Whale), *The Crime of Dr. Crespi* (1935, John H. Auer), *The Ghost of Frankenstein* (1942, Erle C. Kenton), *Frankenstein Meets the Wolf Man* (1943, Roy William Neill).

• **Also of Interest:** *The Maltese Falcon* (1931, Roy Del Ruth), *The Cat and the Canary* (1939, Elliott Nugent), *Dead Men Walk* (1943, Sam Newfield).

○

ANNETTE FUNICELLO (1942–) As a teenager, she became the most popular member of television's "The Mickey Mouse Club," not just because she was cute, cheerful, and exuberant but because she was extremely developed for her age—she was the first real crush, and first sex object, of many TV-watching young boys. Annette recorded a number of silly but fun songs, starred in some Disney films, most notably *The Shaggy Dog,* and then found her niche opposite Frankie Avalon (and later Tommy

Kirk and Dwayne Hickman) in a series of campy beach musicals. *Beach Party,* in particular, and its sequels were supposedly about sex, but they were more about courtship. Annette, sexy in a bathing suit but chaste, wanted to be courted with hearts and flowers and not be taken for granted by Avalon; she wanted to be loved rather than mauled. Deprived of affection, the young man eventually came around and treated Annette with sensitivity and respect. Oh, well. She was likable, but her character could also be annoying, and she seemed much stiffer than anyone else in the cast. She was a short brunette, so most of the shapely young actresses who supported her were blonde and shorter. Having kept in the public eye by doing peanut-butter commercials, Annette would reunite with Avalon for *Back to the Beach* in 1987. They still make a nice team.

• **Cult Favorites:** *Beach Party* (1963, William Asher), *Beach Blanket Bingo* (1965, Asher).

• **Other Key Films:** *The Shaggy Dog* (1959), *Muscle Beach Party* (1964, Asher), *Bikini Beach* (1964, Asher), *Pajama Party* (1964, Don Weis), *How to Stuff a Wild Bikini* (1965, Asher), *Thunder Alley* (1967, Richard Rush), *Back to the Beach* (1987, Lyndall Hobbs).

○

JEAN GABIN (1904–76) Except for a brief respite in the early forties (when he made his only two American films and then joined the Free French in North Africa), he has been France's most popular actor, playing leads from the thirties to the seventies. Ruggedly handsome, with a kind but stoic face and eyes that alternately exhibit tenderness and anger, he gained fame playing world-weary, womanizing, tragic anti-heroes—crooks, boulevardiers, army deserters and other fugitives (in trenchcoat and hat). His characters, including his casbah gangster in *Pepe Le Moko,* are often so charming, charismatic, and suave that it's easy to overlook that they aren't such nice guys. They are flawed men who mistakenly fall in love—his sex scenes with Simone Simon in *La Bête Humaine* are particularly intense—and then commit violent acts. They realize that happiness is temporary and that they can neither escape (or return to) their pasts nor avert their sad fates. In the classic fatalistic melodrama *Le Jour se Lève,* his doomed hero barricades himself in his room and waits for the police to make their move. Penelope Houston wrote: "His enemy is not an individual who can be fought, but the remote, inhuman and unshifting form of society itself. [He] is cut off by his own actions; he tries to escape (into his happier past or, more positively, by actual flight), he is pulled back and punished, and he accepts his punishment with fatalistic expectancy. His ambitions have been abandoned before the picture even opens, and his only aim, as we see it, is to survive somehow, through human contacts, against the impersonal forces. Yet it is these contacts, arising more from pity than from love . . . that eventually destroy him." Gabin supposedly stipulated in contracts that some of his characters had to die, so it's a relief that his likable prisoner-of-war officer escapes from the Germans at the end of the antiwar classic *Grand Illusion.* Perhaps Jean Renoir reasoned that if the usually pessimistic and doomed Gabin can survive a film, then perhaps mankind can survive as well. Following the war, Gabin revived his career in films that still required him

Jean Gabin became France's greatest screen lover by starring in Pepe Le Moko, *with Mireille Balin.*

to fall in love, kill and be killed. However, while he continued to be in melodramas, he began playing more bourgeois types, settled men with wives, families, and money. Few of those roles were as interesting as the working-class characters that made him a star, but Gabin always had charisma. Even when costarring with current young French heartthrobs like Jean-Paul Belmondo and Alain Delon, he was never upstaged.

• **Cult Favorites:** *Pépé le Moko* (1937, Julien Duvivier), *Grand Illusion* (1937, Jean Renoir).

• **Other Key Films:** *Maria Chapdelaine* (1934, Duvivier), *Port of Shadows* (1938, Marcel Carné), *La Bête Humaine* (1938, Renoir), *Le Jour se Lève* (1939, Carné),

Touchez pas au Grisbi (1954, Jacques Becker), *French Cancan* (1955, Renoir), *The Magnificent Tramp* (1959, Gilles Grangier), *Any Number Can Win* (1963, Henri Verneuil).

• **Also Recommended:** *La Bandera* (1936, Duvivier), *La Belle Equipe* (1936, Duvivier), *The Lower Depths* (1936, Renoir), *The Walls of Malapaga* (1949, René Clément), *Le Plaisir* (1952, Max Ophüls).

• **Also of Interest:** *Moontide* (1942, Archie Mayo), *The Imposter* (1944, Duvivier), *La Marie du Port* (1950, Carné), *L'Air de Paris* (1954, Carné), *Deadlier Than the Male* (1956, Duvivier), *Les Miserables* (1958, Jean-Paul Le Chanois), *The Possessors* (1958, Denys de la Patelliere), *The Sicilian Clan* (1969, Verneuil).

MANKIND'S FIRST FLIGHT TO VENUS --the Female Planet!

QUEEN OF OUTER SPACE

COLOR BY DELUXE CINEMASCOPE
STARRING
ZSA ZSA GABOR
WITH
ERIC FLEMING · LAURIE MITCHELL · LISA DAVIS

AN ALLIED ARTISTS

From a Story by BEN HECHT · Produced by BEN SCHWALB · Directed by EDWARD BERNDS · Screenplay by CHARLES BEAUMONT

Zsa Zsa Gabor's most famous film, although she didn't even play the title character.

○

ZSA ZSA GABOR (1919–) Former Miss Hungary came to America in the forties and became famous for her glamour, numerous husbands (including George Sanders), and amusing television appearances with Jack Paar—her accent and her familiar "dahling" have long been mimicked. Her film work never seemed relevant, though she had pivotal roles in *Moulin Rouge,* as Jane Avril; in *Death of a Scoundrel,* falling for Sanders; and in *The Girl in the Kremlin,* as Stalin's mistress and her twin. Her roles were usually no more than cameos, as in Orson Welles's *Touch of Evil.* She didn't take her acting seriously; neither did filmmakers, which explains why she was offered and accepted the lead role in the science-fiction camp classic, *Queen of Outer Space.* She didn't want to play the title character, whose face was disfigured, but opted for a Venusian scientist-revolutionary who wears sexy dresses, high heels, and stylish blond hair. It is the movie for which she's best remembered. Despite their promising titles, neither *Picture Mommy Dead* nor *Frankenstein's Great Aunt Tillie* are bad enough to be other must-see Gabor films. But she saved her worst performance for her much-publicized, real-life slapping-a-cop trial, landing in jail for three days.

• **Cult Favorites:** *Lili* (1953, Charles Walters), *Touch of Evil* (1958, Orson Welles), *Queen of Outer Space* (1958, Edward Bernds).

• **Also Recommended:** *Moulin Rouge* (1952, John Huston), *The Story of Three Loves* (1953, Vincente Minnelli), *Death of a Scoundrel* (1956, Charles Martin).

• **Also of Interest:** *Three-Ring Circus* (1954, Joseph Pevney), *The Girl in the Kremlin* (1957, Russell Birdwell), *Picture Mommy Dead* (1966, Bert I. Gordon), *Frankenstein's Great Aunt Tillie* (1985, Myron J. Gold).

○

BRUNO GANZ (1941–) Swiss-born actor spent several years in the Berlin theater before entering films in the mid-seventies. He has since been a compelling, handsome

Bruno Ganz forms an uneasy alliance with Dennis Hopper in Wim Wenders's The American Friend.

lead in "heady" European films that have played America's art-house circuit. His role choices have been interesting and varied: a German journalist covering the war in Lebanon in *Circle of Deceit;* an obsessive chess player in *Black and White Like Day and Night;* a spurned husband in *The Left-Handed Woman;* a brain-damaged biogeneticist who is exploited for political reasons in *Knife in the Head;* a married seaman who abandons his past life and takes refuge *In the White City;* Jonathan Harker (who ends up a vampire) in *Nosferatu, the Vampyre;* a friendly German framemaker who, thinking he's dying, takes money to murder a stranger in *The American Friend;* an angel who wants to be human in *Wings of Desire.* He says that *The American Friend* was his pivotal role because, after fisticuffs with costar Dennis Hopper over differing acting techniques, he realized film acting should be more instinctual than stage acting. If he were an American, he doubtlessly would be one of our most popular stars. Even so, American audiences have responded to his strong performances and found him instantly likable. He was ideal as the angel in *Wings of Desire* because his face has a sweet quality and his eyes, though intense, are extremely gentle. Moreover, you have to like his ill-fated everyman when he sings along to the Kinks in *The American Friend.*

• **Cult Favorites:** *The American Friend* (1977, Wim Wnders), *Nosferatu, the Vampyre* (1977, Werner Herzog), *Wings of Desire* (1988, Wenders).

• **Sleeper:** *In the White City* (1983, Alain Tanner).

• **Other Key Films:** *The Marquise of O* (1976, Eric Rohmer), *The Left-Handed Woman* (1978, Peter Handke), *Knife in the Head* (1978, Reinhard Hauff), *An Italian Woman* (1980, Giuseppe Bertolucci), *Circle of Deceit* (1981, Volker Schlöndorff).

• **Also of Interest:** *Summer Visitors* (1975, Peter Stein), *The Wild Duck* (1976, Hans W. Geissendorfer), *Lumière* (1976, Jeanne Moreau), *Black and White Like Day and Night* (1978, Wolfgang Peterson), *The Boys from Brazil* (1978, Franklin Schaffner), *The Inventor* (1980, Kurt Gloor), *Strapless* (1990, David Hare).

○

GRETA GARBO (1905–90) The greatest romantic actress of both the silent and sound eras, in Sweden and in Hollywood, didn't have to say "I want to be alone"—although her ballerina said something like that in *Grand Hotel*—because it was obvious that no one on screen had any real connection to her, that she was always very much alone. Even screen lovers like John Gilbert and Robert Taylor, who reached her heart, couldn't penetrate her brain, properly read those mysterious eyes, see other than the smile on her extraordinary face, or detect meaning beyond her words. Viewers felt they understood her characters, however, which may explain why they related to or had such sympathy for her troubled women. Life takes a tremendous toll on Garbo's women. They always seem to be under terrible strain, as if they are running out of oxygen—or time. Her women understand the sad realities of the world much more than do the people around her. And only they understand what is expected of women such as themselves in society or the political arena. Her women always go against the grain, do what women aren't supposed to do—including ruling Sweden in my favorite Garbo film, *Queen Christina*—and they accept the conse-

Greta Garbo's first talking picture.

quences: losing the men they love, or, as happens more often, losing their lives. Her women make sacrifices for those brief moments of happiness which come from passionate love affairs. It's significant that she was the only heroine other than Jean Harlow and Marlene Dietrich who played women (as Bosley Crowther wrote) "who had driving, shameless, passionate needs for men." But she pursued men "not merely for sexual satisfaction, but for the deeper fulfillment of the soul." Garbo's women love the finer things in life: flowers, books, art, plays, humor, anything that stimulates the senses. But love is what gives their lives meaning, and they put everything into each kiss, throwing their heads back (her long neck and face form a beautiful profile), obviously memorizing every sensation. When the love ends, their happiness is only as strong as their memories. The Divine Garbo is remembered for her otherworldly beauty, but it should also be recognized that she was an exceptional actress. In almost every role, she skillfully blended humor and intellect with emotion, incorporating her techniques from her silent films into her sound films. Then quite suddenly she quit and became a recluse. It was the saddest of her many fadeouts, but somehow the most appropriate. It certainly has kept her legend intact.

• **Cult Favorites:** *Flesh and the Devil* (1926, Clarence Brown), *Love* (1927, Edmund Goulding), *Grand Hotel* (1932, Edmund Golding), *Queen Christina* (1933, Rouben Mamoulian), *Camille* (1934, George Cukor), *Ninotchka* (1939, Ernst Lubitsch).

• **Other Key Films:** *Gösta Berling's Saga* (1924, Mauritz Stiller), *Joyless Street* (1925, G. W. Pabst), *The Torrent* (1926, Monta Bell), *The Temptress* (1926, Fred Niblo), *The Divine Woman* (1928, Victor Seastrom), *The Kiss* (1929, Jacques Feyder), *Anna Christie* (1930, Brown), *Mata Hari* (1931, George Fitzmaurice), *Anna Karenina* (1934, Brown), *Conquest* (1937, Brown).

○

ALLEN GARFIELD/GOORWITZ (1939–) A plump (though his weight has fluctuated), humorous, distinctly Jewish character actor who has played a number of aggressively garrulous complainers, worriers, and hustlers (the kind who answers his own questions), mostly in offbeat comedies. He is remembered as the protective husband of a country singer (Ronee Blakely) who is on the verge of a breakdown in *Nashville,* and as the screenwriter who is pushed around by director Peter O'Toole in *The Stunt Man,* but he has been equally effective in a wide variety of roles, from newspaper editor to smut peddler. At the beginning of his career, he was usually offered sleazy

parts. His New York hustlers sold porno movies in Brian De Palma's *Greetings* and made porno films in the sequel, *Hi, Mom!;* he had similar, hilarious, seemingly improvised scenes with Robert De Niro's character in the two films. Garfield's one lead came during this period: he was a pot-bellied, balding, sex-crazed private eye in John Avildsen's groundbreaking X-rated comedy *Cry Uncle!,* which attempted to inject sex scenes with full-frontal nudity (even Garfield strips) into a standard commercial story line. Somehow Garfield (who in midcareer used the name Goorwitz) managed to avoid being typecast as a sleazeball and has since appeared in much more respectable roles.

• **Cult Favorites:** *Greetings* (1968, Brian De Palma), *Putney Swope* (1969, Robert Downey), *Hi, Mom!* (1970, De Palma), *Taking Off* (1971, Milos Forman), *Bananas* (1971, Woody Allen), *Cry Uncle!* (1971, John Avildsen), *The Conversation* (1974, Francis Ford Coppola), *Nashville* (1974, Robert Altman), *The Stunt Man* (1980, Richard Rush), *One from the Heart* (1982, Coppola), *The State of Things* (1983, Wim Wenders).

• **Sleepers:** *Continental Divide* (1981, Michael Apted), *Irreconcilable Differences* (1984, Charles Shyer), *Desert Bloom* (1986, Eugene Corr).

• **Other Key Films:** *The Owl and the Pussycat* (1970, Herbert Ross), *The Organization* (1971, Don Medford), *The Candidate* (1972, Michael Ritchie), *Busting* (1974, Peter Hyams), *The Brink's Job* (1978, William Friedkin), *The Cotton Club* (1984, Coppola).

○

BEVERLY GARLAND (1926–) Attractive blonde starred in numerous low-budget westerns,

Beverly Garland, posing with a masterfully designed alien in It Conquered the World.

science-fiction horror films, and crime melodramas in the fifties (often for Roger Corman), earning the title "Queen of the Bs." She claimed that her best film was *Curucu, Beast of the Amazon,* but that "horror" film with a gyp, nonhorror ending may be the dullest picture of her career. Garland's other films weren't gems (though they were almost all better than *Curucu*), but she made them interesting. Her leading ladies were usually women who had been around, and had become wise, cynical, and tough. They were not demure housewives, unless you want to count the understanding one who is married to an alligator man. They were women who stood out. In *Gunslinger,* she is a town marshal who can shoot; in *Swamp Women,* she is an escaped convict who is shot dead. As gutsy as her characters, she did her own stunts: she shattered her nose riding a horse, fell from a tree doing a death scene; singed her hair, eyebrows, and eyelashes while escaping a brush fire; had a boa constrictor wrapped around her; and more. She put a lot into her characters, even in the silliest films, and audiences were appreciative of her conviction as well as her talent. In 1957, Garland had the distinction of becoming television's first police heroine, playing undercover cop Casey Jones in the enjoyable New York–filmed "Decoy." From the fifties through the eighties she would compile an impressive list of television credits (including recurring roles in "My Three Sons" and "Scarecrow and Mrs. King"), at the expense of her movie career. However, she would continue to make an occasional film, most notably *Pretty Poison,* in which one of her nastiest characters is done in by evil daughter Tuesday Weld for being too bossy. Because of her versatility, she is always in demand.

• **Cult Favorites:** *D.O.A.* (1949, Rudolph Maté), *Pretty Poison* (1968, Noel Black).

• **Sleepers:** *Where the Red Fern Grows* (1974, Norman Tokar), *It's My Turn* (1980, Claudia Weill).

• **Other Key Films:** *Swamp Woman* (1955, Roger Corman), *The Gunslinger* (1956, Corman), *It Conquered the World* (1956, Corman), *Curucu, Beast of the Amazon* (1956, Curt Siodmak), *The Joker Is Wild* (1957, Charles Vidor), *Not of This Earth* (1957, Corman), *Chicago Confidential* (1957, Sidney Salkow), *The Alligator People* (1959, Roy Del Ruth).

• **Also of Interest:** *The Miami Story* (1954, Fred F. Sears), *Killer Leopard* (1954, Ford Beebe), *New Orleans Uncensored* (1955, William Castle), *The Steel Jungle* (1956, Walter Doniger), *Naked Paradise/Thunder Over Hawaii* (1957, Corman), *The Saga of Hemp Brown* (1958, Richard Carlson), *Twice Told Tales* (1963, Salkow), *The Mad Room* (1969, Bernard Girard).

○

JUDY GARLAND (1922–69) Beloved singer-actress was 13 when she left vaudeville and signed a contract with M-G-M. The pretty little girl with the highly emotional, adult voice first captured hearts singing "Dear Mr. Gable" to Clark's photo in *Broadway Melody of 1938*. This led to starring roles, including nine films with Mickey Rooney, some Andy Hardys and some let's-put-on-a-show musicals. She played sweet, patient, modest young girls. Rooney respected their musical talents, but didn't think of them as girlfriends until the ends of the films. This would be

a pattern that carried on to her adult films: the male takes her for granted, she puts up with the neglect; just when she gives up and goes away the male realizes how much she means to him. Rarely did her characters have enough nerve to voice disapproval—so it stands out when Dorothy in *The Wizard of Oz* yells at the Cowardly Lion for frightening her dog and stands up to the Wicked Witch; and when she assaults the boy next door for frightening her younger sister in *Meet Me in St. Louis;* and when she tells off and walks out on egotistical, unpatriotic Gene Kelly in *For Me and My Gal.* It's usually only her solo numbers that fully reveal her character's sadness. Garland was wonderful in *Meet Me in St. Louis, Easter Parade,* and many other musicals, but her key films were *The Wizard of Oz* and *A Star Is Born.* Today when we watch *The Wizard of Oz,* a coming-of-age picture for young girls, our feelings waver between delight in her dynamic, touching performance under trying conditions and grief that we are seeing the role that launched her into the world of superstardom she was never able to handle. When she so beautifully sings "Over the Rainbow," we sense that it is Garland, at 16, as much as Dorothy, who hopes there is a faraway land where there is peace and happiness. *A Star Is Born,* Garland's comeback film after a 4-year hiatus, was the only picture that allowed her to showcase both her dramatic and musical ranges. Through Esther Blodgett/Vicki Lester she fully expressed what singing and performing meant to her. And, as Esther—her most mature character—she could present herself to the public—which regarded her as fragile and irresponsible—as a woman sturdy and responsible enough to care for fading, alcoholic actor Norman Maine (James

Judy Garland with Gene Kelly in Summer Stock.

Mason), with problems similar to her own in real life. Sadly, the masterpiece was drastically cut, and it flopped, ending her comeback attempt instead of earning her a deserved Oscar. The worst cut was of the "Lose That Long Face" number for which a crying Esther, in clownface, manages to smile when the music starts. This scene captured the essence of Judy Garland, who spent a lifetime singing away her tears.

• **Cult Favorites:** *The Wizard of Oz* (1939, Victor Fleming), *Meet Me in St. Louis* (1944, Vincente Minnelli), *The Pirate* (1948, Minnelli), *Easter Parade* (1948, Charles Walters), *A Star Is Born* (1954, George Cukor).

• **Other Key Films:** *Broadway Melody of 1938* (1937, Roy Del Ruth), *Babes in Arms* (1939, Busby Berkeley), *Strike Up the Band* (1940, Berkeley), *Little Nelly Kelly* (1940, Norman Taurog), *Ziegfeld Girl* (1940, Robert Z. Leonard), *For Me and My Gal* (1942, Berkeley), *Girl Crazy* (1943, Taurog), *The Clock* (1945, Minnelli), *The Harvey Girls* (1946, George Sidney), *Ziegfeld Follies* (1946, Minnelli), *Summer Stock* (1940, Walters), *Judgment at Nuremberg* (1961, Stanley Kramer).

○

TERI GARR (1952–) A critics' favorite, this zany-funny, sunny-faced blonde also has won over moviegoers, playing recognizable, often neurotic, always sympathetic characters, often in comedies. For a time she was typecast as harried housewives and mothers; for instance, in both *Oh,*

God!, married to John Denver, and *Close Encounters of the Third Kind,* married to Richard Dreyfuss, she played women who refuse to acknowledge that something strange and troublesome is happening to their husbands—in fact, her married women usually considered their husbands to be just one more of the children. Garr would later play single women and either divorced or widowed mothers. Typically, they have had hard luck, and fight to keep their confidence levels up although everything seems to go wrong; they are resilient, laugh at themselves for being losers yet cry with self-pity at the same time; they feel they need a man yet try to assert their independence. In *Tootsie,* her lonely, exasperated single woman contests (in a speech Garr wrote) that "I read *The Second Sex,* I read *The Cinderella Complex,* I'm responsible for my own orgasm!" Garr has played so many similar roles that it's refreshing to watch her in her few offbeat parts, like her buxom nurse, Fraulein Inga, in *Young Frankenstein,* or the wayward wife who dances her way through the stylized musical *One From the Heart,* or the sneaky murderess in the kooky *Out Cold.* She began as a background dancer in the Elvis Presley–Ann-Margret musical *Viva, Las Vegas.* Today, much of her popularity is a result of frequent appearances on "The David Letterman Show," on which, some say, she continues to play the victim.

• **Cult Favorites:** *Head* (1968, Bob Rafelson), *The Conversation* (1974, Francis Ford Coppola), *Young Frankenstein* (1974, Mel Brooks), *Close Encounters of the Third Kind* (1977, Steven Spielberg), *The Black Stallion* (1979, Carroll Ballard), *One From the Heart* (1982, Francis Ford Coppola), *After Hours* (1985, Martin Scorsese).

• **Other Key Films:** *Oh, God!* (1977, Carl Reiner), *Tootsie* (1982, Sydney Pollack), *Mr. Mom* (1982, Stan Dragoti), *Firstborn* (1984, Michael Apted), *Full Moon in Bright Water* (1988, Peter Masterson), *Out Cold* (1989, Malcolm Mowbray), *Waiting for the Light* (1990, Christopher Monger).

○

ERICA GAVIN (1949–) At the age of 19, this enticing, busty actress became a sex symbol by giving a spirited performance as the most sexually aggressive female of them all, the title character of *Russ Meyer's Vixen.* In a little over 70 minutes, her uninhibited, insatiable backwoods sex predator with painted-on eyebrows and jet black hair (plus a fall) commits adultery, incest, and a lesbian act; is raped; shouts countless racist clichés; and dances with a

Erica Gavin as the venomous heroine of Russ Meyer's Vixen.

dead fish, sticking it inside her mouth and under her blouse. The film was a major breakthrough for sex films seeking a mass audience, and paved the way for the hard-core *Deep Throat*. Gavin experienced a bit of the fame that Linda Lovelace would have playing the next pleasure-seeking heroine. However, Gavin, a feminist-in-the-making, later attacked the film as being "a put-down of women. It says that all that women want is sex, that they're never satisfied, and they'll go anywhere to find it. It shows that women have no loyalty, no sensitivity in sexual relationships." Meyer was disenchanted with Gavin as well, especially because she lost 20 pounds and a cup size or two, and refused to again paint on her eyebrows. He gave her a minor part in *Beyond the Valley of the Dolls* only because he knew she could do a lesbian scene. At the end, he kills off her character by shooting her in the mouth. It was nevertheless a major studio film and a major improvement on films Gavin had done after *Vixen*, including *Captain Milk-shake*, *The Godmother*, and *The Rebel Jesus*. (She also had a bit in *The Strawberry Statement*.) Gavin came back strong as the lead in Jonathan Demme's *Caged Heat*, the best of the women-in-prison flicks. As a new prisoner, she has sexual fantasies about men, but as time passes, she realizes women friends are her greatest need. She leads them in a daring escape. She again gave her all and exhibited the natural talent she had shown in *Vixen*. She's surprisingly adept in scenes where there is no dialogue. This time, we look at her intense eyes as much as we do her body and watch them grow tougher as the film progresses. Her performance warranted her receiving more starring roles, but instead she disappeared. Does anyone know what became of her?

• **Cult Favorites:** *Russ Meyer's Vixen/Vixen* (1968, Russ Meyer), *Beyond the Valley of the Dolls* (1970, Meyer), *Caged Heat* (1974, Jonathan Demme).

○

RAMON GAY (1917–60) Anybody who hangs around with an Aztec mummy called Popoca for three films deserves some credit—but not too much. Gay was the unremarkable leading man of a number of popular but boring (especially in dubbed form) and ridiculous Mexican horror films. Too bad he died before *The Wrestling Women vs. the Aztec Mummy* and its sequel, *Doctor of Doom,* the most enjoyable Mexican horror film, were made, because they might have given him lasting fame with camp fanatics north of the border.

• **Cult Favorites:** *The Aztec Mummy* (1957, Rafael Lopez Portillo), *The Robot vs. the Aztec Mummy* (1959, Portillo), *The Curse of the Aztec Mummy* (1959, Portillo).

• **Other Key Films:** *Cry of the Bewitched* (1956, Alfredo Crevena), *The Curse of the Doll People* (1960, Benito Alazraki).

○

JUDY GEESON (1948–) Among the most familiar of Britain's bright-eyed, blond, miniskirted leading ladies in the late sixties, she looked like a young version of Julie Christie, but without the mystique or star quality. She broke into films as the loose, lost working-class high school student who is won over by caring teacher Sidney Poitier in *To Sir with Love*. She continued to play sexy teenagers and young women in comedies (usually with sexual themes), dramas, and thrillers, most notably the disturbing *10 Rillington Place,* about real-life murderer John Christy, and

Doomwatch, an interesting ecological horror film. She was at best only a competent actress, but she was likable and had a "look" that makes some of us nostalgic when we see her on the screen. Americans thought she represented a distinctly British young female type of the era.

• **Sleeper:** *Doomwatch* (1972, Peter Sasdy).

• **Other Key Films:** *To Sir with Love* (1967, James Clavell), *Berserk* (1968, Jim O'Connolly), *Here We Go Round the Mulberry Bush* (1968, Clive Donner), *Three Into Two Won't Go* (1969, Peter Hall), *The Oblong Box* (1969, Gordon Hessler), *Two Gentlemen Sharing* (1969, Ted Kotcheff), *10 Rillington Place* (1971, Richard Fleischer).

• **Also of Interest:** *Hammerhead* (1968, David Miller), *Nightmare Hotel* (1970, Eugenio Martin), *Fear in the Night/Dynasty of Fear* (1972, Jimmy Sangster), *Percy's Progress/It's Not the Size That Counts* (1975, Ralph Thomas), *The Eagle Has Landed* (1977, John Sturges), *Dominique/Dominique Is Dead* (1978, Michael Anderson), *Inseminoid/Horror Planet* (1981, Norman J. Warren).

○

LAURA GEMSER Beautiful, shapely, darkly exotic star of foreign exploitation films, she succeeded Sylvia Kristel as the star of the "Emmanuelle" series. In her first couple of films, the character continued to seek sexual pleasure and adventures. But later story lines introduced melodramatic themes: drug trafficking, white slavery, rape, blackmail, even murder. She'd play a bisexual reporter-photographer investigating sex cults or drug kingpins who have harems, and so on. Most of these badly dubbed Italian productions, with the sim-ulated sex toned down, are cable staples. They apparently are popular, but I find them sleep-inducing.

• **Key Films:** *Emmanuelle in Bangkok* (1977, Joe D'Amato), *Emmanuelle Around the World* (1977, D'Amato), *Emmanuelle in America* (1978, D'Amato), *Emmanuelle, Queen of the Sados* (1982, Ilias Milonakos), *Endgame* (1983, Steven Benson), *Caged Women* (1984, Vincent Dawn), *Women's Prison Massacre* (1985, Gilbert Roussel).

○

SUSAN GEORGE (1950–) A former child actress, this long-haired British blonde began to have success as a teenager, playing sexy, sex-minded nymphettes. With her shapely figure, risqué clothes, energy, pouty, spoiled-girl expression, slutty manner, large eyes batting under her bangs, and sensual lips (over teeth that needed filing and straightening), her young girls tempted men who should have known better than to respond. Her young girls and women had uncontrollable passions and didn't think of the consequences when they went after the wrong men, who include a porno author (Charles Bronson) 22 years her senior in *Lola;* a robber (Peter Fonda) passing through her bored tart's town in *Dirty Mary Crazy Larry;* the handyman who rapes her sexual tease in *Straw Dogs*—her most memorable character (wimpy Dustin Hoffman's wild wife) rivaled Carroll Baker in *Baby Doll* and Sue Lyon in *Lolita;* and a black slave (Ken Norton) in the abominable *Mandingo.* Despite talent, George soon got too old to play the young sexpots she was so good at, and never found a substitute character.

• **Cult Favorites:** *The Sorceress* (1967, Michael Reeves), *Straw Dogs* (1971, Sam

Susan George is Dustin Hoffman's young bride in Straw Dogs.

Peckinpah), *Dirty Mary Crazy Larry* (1974, John Hough), *Enter the Ninja* (1981, Menahem Golan).

• **Other Key Films:** *The Strange Affair* (1968, David Greene), *Lola/Twinky* (1968, Richard Donner), *Fright* (1971, Peter Collinson), *Mandingo* (1975, Richard Fleischer), *A Small Town in Texas* (1976, Jack Starrett), *Venom* (1982, Piers Haggard).

• **Also of Interest:** *All Neat in Black Stockings* (1969, Christopher Morahan), *Eyewitness/Sudden Terror* (1970, Hough), *Die Screaming, Marianne* (1972, Peter Walker), *Sonny and Jed* (1973, Sergio Corbucci), *Out of Season* (1975, Alan Bridges), *The Jigsaw Man* (1984, Freddie Francis).

○

GIANCARLO GIANNINI (1942–) Handsome, romantic, mustached Italian actor, best known for his powerful leads in Lina Wertmuller films, controversial tragicomedies that deal with sex and politics. In her films, his chauvinist heroes suddenly have their lives turned upside down and find themselves either at the mercy of women or acting irrationally because of women. As his relationships with women change (and he is humbled), his politics change as well. In *The Seduction of Mimi,* his union organizer tries to impregnate the fat wife of the fascist who impregnated his own wife. In *Love and Anarchy,* his country bumpkin turned naive anarchist misses his opportunity to assassinate Mussolini when the concerned prostitutes he stays with don't wake him in time. In *Seven Beauties,* his concentration camp inmate, once a slave-driving pimp, stays alive by being a sexual slave to the obese female commandant (Shirley Stoler). At the end of these films, he learns a political lesson. Only in *Swept Away,* in which his communist shiphand becomes sexual master of a rich fascist bitch (frequent costar Mariangela Melato) once they are shipwrecked on a desert island, does his character turn the tables on a woman. That she is excited by her enslavement and debasement is infuriating—if he weren't handsome and a great lover, would she be so tolerant? But much more objectionable is that Wertmuller has him be such an "expert" on women that he expects her to react this way. Giancarlo has skillfully acted for other directors around the world for more than twenty years, but we remember few of those roles.

• **Cult Favorites:** *The Seduction of Mimi* (1972, Lina Wertmuller), *Love and Anarchy* (1973, Wertmuller), *Swept Away/ Swept Away . . . By an Unusual Destiny in the Blue Sea of August* (1974, Wertmuller), *Seven Beauties* (1976, Wertmuller).

• **Other Key Films:** *All Screwed Up* (1976, Wertmuller), *A Night Full of Rain* (1978, Wertmuller), *The Innocent* (1979, Luchino Visconti), *Lili Marlene* (1980, Rainer Werner Fassbinder).

• **Also of Interest:** *Fräulein Doktor* (1969, Albert Lattuada), *The Secret of Santa Vittoria* (1969, Stanley Kramer), *The Pizza Triangle* (1970, Ettore Scola), *Lovers and Liars* (1979, Mario Monicelli), *Where's Picone?* (1984, Nanni Loy), *Saving Grace* (1986, Robert M. Young).

HOOT GIBSON (1892–1962) This former champion rodeo cowboy came to Hollywood and worked as a wrangler, stuntman, double, and supporting player in Harry Carey and Pete Morrison two-reel westerns. In 1917, his apartment-mate John Ford featured Gibson in his first directorial effort, the five-reel *Straight Shooting,* starring Carey. Fittingly, Gibson's last western movie appearance would be a cameo bit in Ford's 1960 western *The Horse Soldiers.* Gibson starred in about 200 silent and 75 sound films during his career. He was at the height of his popularity from the late teens until the early thirties—in the mid-twenties he made almost $15,000 a week—although he continued to have moderate success until the mid-forties. Gibson, who had a dopey look and a mischievous childlike grin, was the first cowboy hero to emphasize comedy, playing a clowning, rope-twirling, light-hearted young westerner, who constantly wanders into trouble, doesn't carry a gun (until he gets really mad at the end and borrows one), and gets knocked about by bullies. His popularity was due to his stunt riding (he didn't need a stand-in) and the fact that he was quite human, far more vulnerable than W. S. Hart, Tom Mix, and his other bigger-than-life cowboy-hero rivals. Eventually, fans tired of having humor at the expense of action, and Gibson retired in 1939, only to return for one more moment in the western sun, costarring with other veterans Ken Maynard and Bob Steele in a popular "Trail-Blazer" series.

• **Sample Films:** *Straight Shooting* (1917, John Ford), *The Black Horse Bandit* (1919, Harry Harvey), *Action* (1921, Ford), *The Bearcat* (1922, Edward Sedgwick), *Ride for*

Your Life (1924, Sedgwick), *The Phantom Bullet* (1926, Clifford S. Smith), *The Flaming Frontier* (1926, Sedgwick), *The Long, Long Trail* (1929, Arthur Rossen), *Powdersmoke Range* (1935, Wallace Fox), *The Last Outlaw* (1936, Christy Cabanne), *Wild Horse Stampede* (1943, Alan James), *The Law Rides Again* (1943, James), *Blazing Guns* (1943, Robert Tansey), *Death Valley Rangers* (1943, Tansey), *Arizona Whirlwind* (1944, Tansey), *Outlaw Trail* (1944, Tansey), *Sonora Stagecoach* (1944, Tansey), *Trigger Law* (1944, Victor Keyes), *The Horse Soldiers* (1960, Ford).

○

MEL GIBSON (1956–) Unfairly handsome, blue-eyed, dark-haired New York–born Australian actor who became an international sensation as the star of George Miller's thrilling "Mad Max" series. In *Mad Max,* Max is a highway policeman in a post-apocalyptic Australia overrun by barbarians. When his wife and baby are killed, he goes "Mad" and hits the road seeking cruel vengeance, completely giving in to his reptilian side. His mission complete, in *The Road Warrior* he wanders

Mel Gibson returned as Mad Max in The Road Warrior.

into the wasteland, avoiding human contact, but then decides (for partly selfish reasons), to help a civilized "tribe" defeat a vicious band of warriors. Having come almost full circle in *Mad Max Beyond Thunderdome*, he is able to interact with other human beings and care about his own survival. The Max character appealed to fans all over the world because of his myth-hero implications. Gibson himself appealed to men because he was terrific in the pictures' amazing action sequences, and was so good-looking that women were drawn to the films despite their violence, car stunts, and movie-western orientation. In other films for Australian and American directors, he plays morally ambivalent, brooding protagonists: rapscallions, criminals, cops who never go by the book. He would never play a straight hero—even his correspondent in Indonesia in *The Year of Living Dangerously* is too ambitious to be fully trusted. His characters exist in crazy worlds or situations, and are themselves borderline crazy, on the edge, even suicidal. Since the death of his L.A. cop's wife in *Lethal Weapon*—the picture that proved he had box-office clout—his character wants risky assignments, has no concern about his safety, and even sticks a loaded gun into his mouth. Just as Max bonded with the tribe, the cop finds comfort in the company of his partner, Danny Glover, and his family, and begins to care about himself. But even Gibson's tamest characters are attracted to danger and are more than willing to risk death. They also feel no guilt about dishing out tremendous punishment, even killing people. We can't always agree with their brutal actions. Gibson has developed into a good dramatic actor (and can be funny), but it's less exciting watching him talk than seeing him fight or run at full speed after a car

(he often runs in his films). This physical actor also has had memorable love scenes with, among others, Diane Keaton in *Mrs. Soffel,* Sigourney Weaver in *The Year of Living Dangerously* (while driving!), and Michelle Pfeiffer in *Tequila Sunrise.* With his recent *Hamlet,* Gibson again made good use of his ability to play a brooding, over-the-edge character. *People*'s first "Sexiest Man Alive" elicits sighs, even when viewers are just seeing previews of his next films.

• **Cult Favorites:** *Mad Max* (1979, George Miller), *The Road Warrior/Mad Max 2* (1981, Miller), *Mad Max Beyond Thunderdome* (1985, Miller and George Ogilvie), *The Year of Living Dangerously* (1983, Peter Weir).

• **Other Key Films:** *Tim* (1979, Michael Pate), *Gallipoli* (1981, Weir), *The Bounty* (1984, Roger Donaldson), *Mrs. Soffel* (1984, Gillian Armstrong), *Lethal Weapon* (1987, Richard Donner), *Tequila Sunrise* (1988, Robert Towne), *Lethal Weapon 2* (1989, Donner), *Hamlet* (1991, Franco Zefferelli).

○

JAMIE GILLIS Handsome and well-built, with dark, curly hair, he is the most recognizable male in porno films other than the late John Holmes. He usually played seducers, bastards, even monsters (as the star of two XXX-rated Dracula films), often appearing as the aggressor in S&M scenes. He starred in many of the better-made porno films from the mid-seventies to the early eighties, getting a reputation for both his sexual proficiency under the hot lights (they called it "professionalism") and his overrated acting talents; in fact, he got to play Lindsay Wagner's boss in the R-rated Sylvester Stallone film *Nighthawks.* This reputation caused two problems: he became overexposed, appearing (it seemed) in almost every major porno film at that time; and when viewers were impatient for sex, he frustrated them with perfectly memorized long bits of dialogue that he delivered slowly and methodically.

• **Cult Favorites:** *The Private Afternoons of Pamela Mann* (1974, Henry Paris/Radley Metzger), *The Opening of Misty Beethoven* (1975, Paris), *Story of Joanna* (1975, Gerard Damiano), *Dracula Sucks* (1979, Phillip Marshak), *Amanda by Night* (1981, Robert McCallum), *Blonde Ambition* (1981, John and Lem Amaro), *Roommates* (1982, Chuck Vincent).

• **Other Key Films:** *Seduction of Lynn Carter* (1975, Wes Brown), *Through the Looking Glass* (1976, Jonas Middleton), *Anna Obsessed* (1978, Martin and Martin), *800 Fantasy Lane* (1979, Svetlana), *Taxi Girls* (1979, Jaccov Jaacovi), *Screwples* (1979, Clair Dia), *Serena* (1979, Fred Lincoln), *Pandora's Mirror* (1981, Warren Evans), *High School Memories* (1981, Anthony Spinelli), *Dracula Exotica* (1981, Evans), *Neon Nights* (1982, Cecil Howard).

○

CRISPIN GLOVER (1964–) Thin young actor, with sharp features, an awkward haircut, a nasal voice, a nervous laugh, a giddy smile, and strange eyes, has specialized in young crazies and eccentrics. One might have predicted an unusual career when he got a meat cleaver stuck in his face in *Friday the 13th—the Final Chapter.* He later made an AFI student film in which he made himself up like Olivia Newton-John and sang one of her songs. It wasn't released. But enough of his films have been released to reveal a most bizarre

Crispin Glover in River's Edge.

talent who has both impressed and annoyed us with his mannered, inspired portrayals. He was quite hilarious as Michael J. Fox's hopelessly nerdy father in *Back to the Future.* His sicko teenager in the disturbing *River's Edge,* who forces his friends to keep secret a classmate's murder, is brilliantly conceived and played, but truly unappealing. Some viewers were turned off by an actor who could get into the brain of such a detestable character. In John Boorman's off-center *Where the Heart Is,* he is no less kooky than anyone else, as a struggling, supposedly gay hairdresser who finally admits—as audiences hiss—that he's straight. Moviegoers are curious about but also fearful of the characters he'll create in the future. He released an album called *The Big Problem*. The son of actor Bruce Glover.

• **Cult Favorites:** *River's Edge* (1986, Tim Hunter), *Wild at Heart* (1990, David Lynch).

• **Other Key Films:** *Back to the Future* (1985, Robert Zemeckis), *Twister* (1988, Michael Almereyda), *Where the Heart Is* (1990, John Boorman).

○

JEFF GOLDBLUM (1952–) Tall, lanky, dark-haired comic actor specializing in characters on their own special wavelengths. He started out in small roles, such as one of the cretins who rape and murder Charles Bronson's wife in *Death Wish,* and the zany stranger on the motorcycle in *Nashville,* one of his many ensemble films. His roles got bigger and he began to specialize in young, eccentric intellectuals—the rock critic in *Between the Lines* and the mud-bath owner in *Invasion of the Body Snatchers.* They talk wildly and amusingly, often telling themselves the punchlines because no one else understands the sad ironies they notice in life. When being funny, he was straight-faced or looked stunned, let his eyes run wild, and talked softly or mumbled (often to himself). His looks seemed too quirky for him to be a lead other than Ichabod Crane (on television), but John Landis gave him a shot at a romantic lead in *Into the Night,* playing an insomniac whose love life perks up when he meets imperiled Michelle Pfeiffer. He then played the title character in *The Fly,* opposite Geena Davis. His brainy scientist was another variation on his typical idiot savant, but for the first time really, Goldblum exhibited sex appeal.

Which means he won't have to return to supporting roles.

• **Cult Favorites:** *Death Wish* (1974, Michael Winner), *Nashville* (1975, Robert Altman), *Annie Hall* (1977, Woody Allen), *Between the Lines* (1977, Joan Micklin Silver), *Remember My Name* (1978, Alan Rudolph), *Invasion of the Body Snatchers* (1978, Philip Kaufman), *The Big Chill* (1983, Lawrence Kasdan), *The Right Stuff* (1983, Kaufman), *The Adventures of Buckaroo Banzai* (1984, W. D. Richter), *Silverado* (1985, Kasdan), *The Fly* (1986, David Cronenberg).

• **Also of Interest:** *Threshold* (1981, Richard Pearce), *Into the Night* (1985, John Landis), *Earth Girls Are Easy* (1989, Julien Temple), *Twisted Obsession* (1990, Fernando Truebo), *The Tall Guy* (1990, Mel Smith).

○

LEO GORCEY (1915–69) The pugnacious, wisecracking, street-smart Dead End Kid, their leader as they became the East Side Kids and then the Bowery Boys. In the beginning, in the play and film of *Dead End,* the gang from the New York slums was comprised of tough juvenile delinquents—victims of society—who got into fights, carried knives, and broke minor laws, and Gorcey's Spit was the most frightening of the bunch. The gang would begin to reform in such films as *Angels with Dirty Faces*—when their gangster idol (James Cagney) proves to be a coward— and *Angels Wash Their Faces,* and by the time the popular group made the East Side Kids programmers at Monogram, Gorcey and the others had evolved into well-intentioned kids who were merely misunderstood. Gorcey (his character's name would eventually become Slip Mahoney), wearing a hat with a brim that was flattened in front, kept increasingly comical Huntz Hall and the others on the right side of the law, although they tried some slightly underhanded money-making schemes. But he still didn't back down when coppers or law-abiding citizens mistakenly accused the gang of some wrong-doing. He would devise the plans that got some friend of the gang or the gang itself out of trouble, and capture the real criminals—earning society's plaudits. As the films became more juvenile and relied more on humor than drama, Gorcey and Hall would do slapstick routines more appropriate for the Three Stooges, with Gorcey taking the Moe role and Huntz taking his slaps and hits on the noggin. As always, Gorcey had trouble with words and phrases: "corpus delicious," "the clam before the storm," "that's a bargain if I ever created one." As he aged, his face

became as flat as his hat brim. At 40, he dropped out of the Bowery Boys after his father, Bernard (also a regular), passed away. The series would continue, but it wouldn't be the same without its leader.

• **Cult Favorites:** *Angels with Dirty Faces* (1938, Michael Curtiz), numerous "Dead End Kids," "East Side Kids," and "Bowery Boys" star vehicles (1940–56).

• **Also Recommended:** *Dead End* (1937, William Wyler), *Mannequin* (1937, Frank Borzage), *Crime School* (1938, Lewis Seiler), *They Made Me a Criminal* (1939, Busby Berkeley), *Hell's Kitchen* (1939, Seiler and E. A. Dupont), *Angels Wash Their Faces* (1939, Ray Enright).

○

RUTH GORDON (1896–1985) Much-missed playwright, screenwriter, and character actress; married writer Garson Kanin (b. 1912) in 1942. She appeared in a few films

Ruth Gordon pinches son George Segal's tush in Where's Poppa?

in the early forties, usually in serious roles, including Mary Todd Lincoln in *Abe Lincoln in Illinois*. When she returned to films in the mid-sixties, she perfected the role of an elderly eccentric, turning in a number of wonderfully zany performances, mostly in black comedies. Her weird old ladies were tough, excitable, fearless, tactless, headstrong, doting, snoopy, independent, full of memories, gossipy, and past the point of listening. Her characters don't follow the rules: as Mia Farrow's strange neighbor (a role that won her a Best Supporting Actress Oscar) in *Rosemary's Baby,* she practices black magic; in *Where's Papa?*, her senile widow embarrasses son George Segal's pretty dinner guest by talking about her son's "pecker" and pulling down his pants and kissing him "on the tush"; as Clint Eastwood's Ma in *Every Which Way But Loose,* she single-handedly routs a motorcycle gang with a rifle; her energetic 80-year-old in *Harold and Maude,* the film for which she's best remembered, has a love affair with a 20-year-old. Memories of her are vivid: the shaky Gordon standing next to the corpse of a girl who fell from a window in *Rosemary's Baby;* the frightened Gordon socking her son in the crotch when he tries to amuse her by wearing a gorilla costume in *Where's Poppa?;* the times in *Harold and Maude* when she, as an Auschwitz survivor who has become a life force for the suicidal boy, lets us glimpse the sadness beneath Maude's smiles. An original.

• **Cult Favorites:** *Inside Daisy Clover* (1965, Robert Mulligan), *Lord Love a Duck* (1966, George Axelrod), *Rosemary's Baby* (1968, Roman Polanski), *Where's Poppa?* (1970, Carl Reiner), *Harold and Maude* (1971, Hal Ashby), *The Big Bus* (1979, James Frawley).

• **Other Key Films:** *Abe Lincoln in Illinois* (1940, John Cromwell), *Dr. Ehrlich's Magic Bullet* (1940, William Dieterle), *Whatever Happened to Aunt Alice?* (1969, Lee H. Katzin), *Every Which Way But Loose* (1978, James Fargo).

• **Sleeper:** *My Bodyguard* (1980, Tony Bill).

• **Also of Interest:** *Two-Faced Women* (1941, George Cukor), *Edge of Darkness* (1943, Lewis Milestone), *The North Star* (1943, Milestone), *Action in the North Atlantic* (1943, Lloyd Bacon), *Boardwalk* (1979, Stephen Verona), *The Trouble with Spies* (1984, Burt Kennedy), *Maxie* (1985, Paul Aaron).

○

MARJOE GORTNER (1941–) His best screen role was as himself, a showy itinerant child evangelist, in the creepy documentary *Marjoe*. The adult Gortner turned to acting and has had some success in minor, action-packed exploitation films, though he hasn't improved since being on the run with Lynda Carter in *Bobbie Jo and the Outlaw*. Tall, with curly hair, a sharp nose, and a too-cheery smile, Gortner isn't very likable, despite his energy and acting competence. He plays an occasional hero but he's better cast as a bad guy (with his background, he's ideal for playing con men). His best performance remains the one that began his acting career, as a violent killer in the superb 1973 TV movie *The Marcus-Nelson Murders*.

• **Key Films:** *Marjoe* (1972, Howard Smith and Sarah Kernochan), *Bobbie Joe and the Outlaw* (1976, Mark L. Lester), *Food of the Gods* (1976, Bert I. Gordon), *Jungle Warriors* (1983, Ernst R. von Theumer), *Mausoleum* (1983, Michael Dugan).

Marjoe Gortner's "magnetic masculinity" (according to Columbia Pictures' publicity department) attracts Candy Clark's young waif in When You Comin' Back, Red Ryder?

• **Also of Interest:** *Sidewinder I,* (1977, Earl Bellamy), *Star Crash* (1979, Lewis Coates), *Hellhole* (1985, Pierre de Moro).

○

MICHAEL GOUGH (1917–) Tall, thin British character actor who has played a number of intense, intellectual, humorless characters, including sinister villains. He has been well cast in prestigious, high-brow films, and has added prestige to juvenile horror movies, moving effortlessly from *Richard III* and *Julius Caesar* to *Konga,* playing everything from royalty to mad doctors. His cult status is the result of his frequent work in horror films. For a time he was more familiar to American horror fans than his occasional costar, Peter Cushing. The two actors have similarities, but Gough can't play heroes as well as

villains. We thought he hit a low point with *Trog,* but then he made the ghastly and grisly *Horror Hospital.*

• **Cult Favorites:** *The Man in the White Suit* (1951, Alexander Mackendrick), *Horror of Dracula* (1958, Terence Fisher), *The Horse's Mouth* (1958, Ronald Neame), *Woman in Love* (1969, Ken Russell).

• **Other Key Films:** *The Small Back Room* (1949, Michael Powell and Emeric Pressburger), *The Sword and the Rose* (1953, Ken Annakin), *Richard III* (1955, Laurence Olivier), *Horrors of the Black Museum* (1959, Arthur Crabtree), *Konga* (1961, John Lamont), *Candidate for Murder* (1962, David Villiers), *Black Zoo* (1963, Robert Gordon), *The Skull* (1965, Freddie Francis), *Berserk* (1967, Jim O'Connolly), *Trog* (1970, Francis).

• **Also of Interest:** *The Phantom of the Opera* (1962, Fisher), *Dr. Terror's House* *of Horrors* (1965, Francis), *They Came from Beyond Space* (1967, Francis), *The Go-Between* (1971, Joseph Losey), *Horror Hospital* (1973, Anthony Balch), *The Boys from Brazil* (1978, Franklin Schaffner), *The Dresser* (1983, Peter Yates), *Out of Africa* (1985, Sydney Pollack), *Caravaggio* (1986, Derek Jarman).

○

GERRIT GRAHAM (1949–) Tall, blond, wild comic actor got his movie break with Brian De Palma, as one of the three leads in his witty, innovative, satirical protest film *Greetings.* He played a young man obsessed with proving Kennedy was shot by more than one assassin; he himself is killed (by a single gunman or a conspiracy?) while on the way to the Statue of Liberty. Later, Graham almost stole De Palma's musical horror film *Phantom of the Paradise,* as a fussy gay pill-popper who is transformed into the frightening rock star Beef, proponent of death—a part that may have inspired Dr. Frank-N-Furter in *The Rocky Horror Picture Show.* Since then he has played many supporting roles, even appearing in dramas (Susan Sarandon's abusive boyfriend in *Pretty Baby,* a victim of the deadly computer in *Demon Seed*), and silly horror/science-fiction and action-oriented exploitation films. He's best when turned loose in irreverent, off-the-wall comedies like *Tunnelvision* and *Used Cars.* But not like *Class Reunion.* His other disasters include *Beware! The Blob, Chopping Mall, The Creature Wasn't Nice/Spaceship,* and *The Annihilators.*
• **Cult Favorites:** *Greetings* (1968, Brian De Palma), *Phantom of the Paradise* (1974, De Palma), *Tunnelvision* (1976, Brad Swirnoff and Neil Israel), *Demon Seed* (1977, Donald Cammell), *Pretty Baby* (1978, Louis Malle), *Used Cars* (1980, Robert Zemeckis).
• **Also of Interest:** *Cannonball* (1976, Paul Bartel), *Bobbie Joe and the Outlaw* (1976, Mark L. Lester), *Home Movies* (1980, De Palma), *Soup for One* (1982, Jonathan Kaufer), *Rat Boy* (1986, Sondra Locke), *The Last Resort* (1986, Zane Busby), *It's Alive III: Island of the Alive* (1987, Larry Cohen), *Child's Play 2* (1990, John Lafia).

○

GLORIA GRAHAME (1925–81) This marvelously offbeat, kittenish actress always came across as if she'd just been punched, with pupils that were above dead center in her eyes and a large, overhanging upper lip that seemed to interfere with her talking. She usually played sensuous, sluttish, flirtatious women—often fallen women—who are unhappy with their lives. They either feel that their men can't satisfy them—like screenwriter Dick Powell in *The Bad and the Beautiful*—or that the men they fancy are too good for them—like James Stewart in *It's a Wonderful Life,* Glenn Ford in *The Big Heat,* and Robert Mitchum in *Macao.* Grateful that these men consider her their friend, she will make sacrifices for them. She is one of many who give Stewart money, she is shot while helping Ford fight her ex-boyfriend, Lee Marvin, she is knifed after freeing Mitchum from the bad guys. She won a Supporting Actress Oscar for her tramp in *The Bad and the Beautiful,* but she steals scenes with equal ease in *The Big Heat,* playing much of the film with blistered-face makeup after Marvin throws hot coffee in her face (she will return the favor!); in *Oklahoma!* as Ado Annie; in *Chilly Scenes of Winter,* as John Heard's loony mother; and *In a Lonely Place,* one of two films she made with one-time husband Nicholas Ray. In this stand-out Ray film, she falls in love with violent neighbor Humphrey Bogart but gradually joins those who think he's a murderer, making him feel persecuted. Halfway through the film, the focus switches from Bogart to Grahame as she becomes the one who is paranoid, fearing he wants to kill her. Now she knows how alone he felt. This fascinating actress played more supporting parts than leads, which explains why she rarely got the man. In her later years, she starred in sleazy, low-budget films.

• **Cult Favorites:** *It's a Wonderful Life* (1946, Frank Capra), *In a Lonely Place* (1950, Nicholas Ray), *The Big Heat* (1953, Fritz Lang), *Head Over Heels/Chilly Scenes of Winter* (1979/82, Joan Micklin Silver).

• **Also Recommended:** *Crossfire* (1947, Edward Dmytryk), *Song of the Thin Man* (1947, Edward Buzzell), *Roughshod* (1947, Mark Robson), *A Woman's Secret* (1949, Ray), *The Greatest Show on Earth* (1952, Cecil B. De Mille), *Macao* (1952, Josef von Sternberg), *Sudden Fear* (1952, David Miller), *The Bad and the Beautiful* (1953, Vincente Minnelli), *Man on a Tightrope*

Gloria Grahame, badly scarred from boyfriend Lee Marvin throwing hot coffee in her face, has just returned the favor in The Big Heat.

(1953, Elia Kazan), *Human Desire* (1954, Lang), *Naked Alibi* (1954, Jerry Hopper), *Oklahoma!* (1955, Fred Zinnemann), *The Man Who Never Was* (1956, Ronald Neame).

• **Also of Interest:** *Not as a Stranger* (1955, Stanley Kramer), *Odds Against Tomorrow* (1959, Robert Wise), *The Todd Killings* (1971, Barry Shear), *Blood and Lace* (1971, Philip Gilbert), *The Loners* (1972, Sutton Roley).

○

SHAUNA GRANT (1963–84) Colleen Applegate, a Catholic girl from Minnesota, went to Hollywood at the age of 18, became a nude model and cover girl, and then a leading lady in the films of porno director Bobby Hollander. She appeared in 30 films in a year and, a genuine phenomenon, jumped to superstar status before her twentieth birthday. She was a nonactress, but she was an extremely pretty blonde who projected exactly what she was, an innocent girl gone bad, a peaches-and-cream kid made up into a glamorous, adult sex bomb. Grant hated having sex on screen and quit at the height of her fame, though her films continued to circulate. Eight months later, broke and a cocaine addict, she agreed to make another film. The day before she was to report to the set, she shot herself in the head. Some in the porno industry capitalized on her death, releasing a compilation film titled *Shauna Grant: Every Man's Fantasy.* Network television made a movie of her short life titled *Shattered Innocence.* She was the subject of a PBS documentary, which regarded her as the prime example of lost, insecure young women who, excited by money and attention, are victimized by the XXX-rated business.

• **Sample Titles:** *Paper Dolls, Summer Camp Girls, Centerfold Celebrities, Flesh and Laces.*

○

COLEEN GRAY (1922–) Beautiful, well-scrubbed brunette played sweet women who gave comfort and remained loyal to the men they loved in such classic crime melodramas as *Kiss of Death,* with Victor Mature; *Nightmare Alley,* with Tyrone Power; and *The Killing,* with Sterling Hayden. Because most of the films she was in were dominated by the male characters, her lovely performances were overlooked. I fell in love with her leading lady of those three titles, plus *Apache Drums, The Copper Sky, Kansas City Confidential* and several other films, as well as the girl whom John Wayne lets get away at the beginning of *Red River*—without realizing they were the same actress. Gray's once-promising career took a downward turn in the fifties, yet she selected roles in what turned out to be impressive B films, including westerns and such crime dramas as *Kansas City Confidential* and *The Killing.* Her choice of horror and science-fiction films was not so wise. However, she managed to upgrade both *The Vampire* and *Leech Woman;* in the latter she had the dubious distinction of playing the title character, a villainess who uses a brain secretion from her victims in an eternal-life serum—with disastrous results.

• **Cult Favorites:** *Kiss of Death* (1947, Henry Hathaway), *Nightmare Alley* (1947, Edmund Goulding), *Kansas City Confidential* (1952, Phil Karlson), *The Killing* (1956, Stanley Kubrick).

• **Sleepers:** *Apache Drums* (1951, Hugo Fregonese), *Copper Sky* (1957, Charles Marquis Warren).

Sydney Greenstreet is an uncouth tycoon in The Hucksters, *starring Clark Gable.*

• **Other Key Films:** *Red River* (1948, Howard Hawks), *The Vampire* (1957, Paul Landres), *The Leech Woman* (1960, Edward Dein).

• **Also of Interest:** *Fury at Furnace Creek* (1948, H. Bruce Humberstone), *Riding High* (1949, Frank Capra), *Father Is a Bachelor* (1950, Norman Foster), *The Sleeping City* (1950, George Sherman), *Lucky Nick Cain* (1951, Joseph M. Newman), *Sabre Jet* (1953, Louis King), *Arrow in the Dust* (1954, Lesley Selander), *Las Vegas Shakedown* (1955, Sidney Salkow), *Tennessee Partner* (1955, Allan Dwan),

Hell's Five Hours (1958, Jack L. Copeland), *Johnny Rocco* (1958, Landres), *The Phantom Planet* (1962, William Marshall), *Town Tamer* (1965, Selander).

○

SYDNEY GREENSTREET (1879–1954) The massive British actor who specialized in Shakespeare during his long stage career was over 60 when he made his screen debut, but had time to establish himself as one of Hollywood's greatest portrayers of villains. His first part, Casper Gutman in

The Maltese Falcon, would serve as the model for most of his future scoundrels. This character is a brilliant conversationalist ("I'm a man who likes talking to a man who likes to talk"), erudite (he reads while the others sleep), witty (his villains always bring smiles to viewers), conceited, corrupt, clever, power-hungry, ruthless, and, of course, fat, although for a 280-pounder, he is quick as a cat. Although he is intelligent and refined, he relishes being involved in criminal activity, enjoys impressing and matching wits with Bogart's lowlife detective Sam Spade, and is greedy enough to conspire with dangerous kooks, like those played by Mary Astor, Elisha Cook, Jr., and Peter Lorre. The much-smaller, worm-playing Lorre would become a frequent movie partner of the rotund (directors used him to balance the frame), civilized Greenstreet. They were an amusingly diabolical odd couple, not trusting each other and getting on each other's nerves, but drawn together by their common greed. Gutman and his later villains work hard to stay composed, yet they become anxious (as does Lorre) and sweat profusely when their prize—or their demise—is in reach. And they ultimately lose, defeated by Bogart in *The Maltese Falcon* or Joan Crawford in *Flamingo Road* (his decadent Sheriff Titus is one of his most memorable miscreants) or their own tragic flaws. Most of Greenstreet's villains would have liked each other's company, but one stands apart: Evan Llewellyn Evans in *The Hucksters,* a vulgar soap tycoon who shocks employee Clark Gable by spitting on a table. Greenstreet never had trouble stealing a scene.

- **Cult Favorites:** *The Maltese Falcon* (1941, John Huston), *They Died with Their Boots On* (1941, Raoul Walsh), *Casablanca* (1942, Michael Curtiz).

- **Other Key Films:** *Across the Pacific* (1942, Huston), *Passage to Marseilles* (1944, Curtiz), *The Mask of Demetrios* (1944, Jean Negulesco), *The Conspirators* (1944, Negulesco), *Three Strangers* (1946, Negulesco), *The Hucksters* (1947, Jack Conway), *Ruthless* (1948, Edgar G. Ulmer), *Flamingo Road* (1949, Curtiz).

- **Also of Interest:** *Background to Danger* (1943, Walsh), *Between Two Worlds* (1944, Edward A. Blatt), *Conflict* (1945, Curtis Bernhardt), *Christmas in Connecticut* (1945, Peter Godfrey), *Devotion* (1946, Bernhardt), *The Verdict* (1946, Don Siegel), *The Woman in White* (1948, Godfrey), *The Velvet Touch* (1948, John Cage), *Malaya* (1949, Richard Thorpe).

○

PAM GRIER (1950–) Black actress with a gorgeous face, untapped talent, and stunning body. She became the Queen of Exploitation Films in the seventies while acting for the likes of Russ Meyer (who gave her a bit in *Beyond the Valley of the Dolls,* her first film), Roger Corman, Jack Hill, and Eddie Romero, who cast her as a Panther Woman in his Philippine-made John Ashley atrocity, *Twilight People.* She was the major figure in Corman's action-packed, R-rated, women-in-prison films, including the groundbreaking *The Big Doll House, The Big Bird Cage,* and *Women in Cages*—as a sadistic lesbian warden. Lots of well-built actresses did nudity in these films, but Grier had no competition. Her fame growing among exploitation fans, she played the title characters in four urban-set blaxploitation films—*Coffy, Foxy Brown, Friday Foster,* and *Sheba Baby*—as two black nurses, a photographer, and a private eye, who, all experts in self-

Pam Grier is Friday Foster.

defense, fearlessly go after drug kingpins and other criminals. These fast-paced low-budget films had enough violence and Grier nudity to be wildly popular. Critics attacked them, yet *Ms.* magazine pointed out that they "have one outstanding redeeming value—they are the only films to show us a woman who is independent, resourceful, self-confident, strong and courageous. Above all, they are the only films to show us a woman who triumphs!" Her characters came across so positively simply because Grier put much of herself into them. While everyone was just paying attention to her body, Grier developed into a terrific actress who could make a weakly written character strong and carry an action picture as well as any of her male counterparts. Those four films secured Grier's position as a cult figure, but they trapped her in the dying black fringe cinema. Grier dropped out of motion pictures for several years, determined to make those in the industry forget her sex-star image and welcome her into the mainstream. She reentered in a role hardly designed to be straight: a drug-crazed, murderous prostitute in *Fort Apache—The Bronx.* Then she was the mysterious, evil "Dust Queen" and a character appropriately billed as "The Most Beautiful Woman on Earth" in the Disney Studio's creepy *Something Wicked This Way Comes.* It was a good start, but since then she has been underutilized in pictures, usually playing the brave friends of her movies' stars. Only on TV, as Philip Michael Thomas's love interest in two episodes of "Miami Vice," could she both turn on the sex appeal and show what a compelling actress she is, completely focused when delivering lines and wonderfully exciting when she's involved in the action.

• **Cult Favorites:** *The Big Doll House* (1971, Jack Hill), *Women in Cages* (1972, Gerry De Leon), *Twilight People* (1972, Eddie Romero), *The Big Bird Cage* (1972, Hill), *Coffy* (1973, Hill), *Foxy Brown* (1974, Hill), *Friday Foster* (1975, Arthur Marks), *Sheba Baby* (1975, William Girdler).

• **Sleepers:** *Something Wicked This Way Comes* (1983, Jack Clayton), *Above the Law* (1988, Andrew Davis).

• **Other Key Films:** *Black Mama, White Mama* (1972, Romero), *Hit Man* (1972, George Armitage), *The Arena* (1973, Steve Carver), *Scream, Blacula, Scream* (1973, Bob Kelljan), *Greased Lightning* (1977, Michael Schultz), *Fort Apache—The Bronx* (1981, Daniel Petrie), *The Class of 1999* (1990, Mark Lester).

○

MELANIE GRIFFITH (1957–) A young-looking, baby-voiced blonde, the daughter of Tippi Hedren put the emphasis on sex for most of her career: as a teenager she did a topless scene in *Night Moves;* grown up, she has played a stripper in *Fear City,* porn actress Holly Body in *Body Double,* and a quirky seductress with handcuffs in *Something Wild.* But with *Body Double* and, more so, *Something Wild, Stormy Monday,* and her breakthrough-into-the-mainstream role as a secretary who won't trade her body for a promotion in *Working Girl,* viewers began to pay attention to her characters and her vast talent. Some viewers find her annoying (they remember her troubles with substance abuse and even criticize her for being a bit plump in *Working Girl*), but most of us find her appealing, and not just on a sexual level. She's perhaps our most vulnerable actress—Mike Nichols says "you can see right into her feelings"—so it has impact when her frightened, powerless women, their baby voices quivering, fight back against the frightening, powerful men and women who want to keep them in their low places. We admire their grit, their willingness to make fools of themselves or put their careers or lives on the line, their refusal to let other people determine their lives (her women think for themselves). And we're happy when nice guys (for instance, Jeff Daniels in *Something Wild,* Harrison Ford in *Working Girl*) join their fights. What's certain is that Griffith really cares about her characters (particularly Lulu in *Something Wild* and Tess in *Working Girl,* women who really make you root for them) because she truly invests herself emotionally in them. When they

get hurt, she takes it personally. Married twice to Don Johnson.
• **Cult Favorites:** *Night Moves* (1975, Arthur Penn), *Smile* (1975, Michael Ritchie), *Body Double* (1984, Brian De Palma), *Something Wild* (1986, Jonathan Demme), *Stormy Monday* (1988, Mike Figgis).
• **Other Key Film:** *Working Girl* (1988, Mike Nichols).
• **Also of Interest:** *The Drowning Pool* (1976, Stuart Rosenberg), *One on One* (1977, Lamont Johnson), *Joyride* (1977, Joseph Ruben), *Fear City* (1985, Abel Ferraro), *Cherry 2000* (1988, Steve DeJarnatt), *The Milagro Beanfield War* (1988, Robert Redford), *Pacific Heights* (1990, John Schlesinger).

○

GULPILIL/DAVID GULPILIL Slender, curly-haired, handsome Australian aborigine was a teenager when he was discovered by Nicolas Roeg while living on a government station in the Outback. In Roeg's compelling *Walkabout,* he played an aborigine who, while making his solo journey of manhood, discovers a white teenage girl (Jenny Agutter) and her young brother lost in the desert. As he walks them back toward civilization, the sexual attraction intensifies between the maturing boy and girl from different cultures; unfortunately, once they reach the outskirts of civilization, he assumes that the confused young girl rejects him. Gulpilil would prove to be a natural actor (he did *act*), open and friendly at times, mysterious at others; so, as it should be, we never fully grasp his character. In future films, his aborigine characters would also be defined by their heritage.

Gulpilil in Walkabout, *filmed in the Australian outback.*

• **Cult Favorites:** *Walkabout* (1971, Nicolas Roeg), *The Last Wave* (1977, Peter Weir).

• **Also Recommended:** *Mad Dog Morgan* (1976, Philippe Mora), *Crocodile Dundee* (1986, Peter Faiman).

○

EDMUND GWENN (1875–1969) Welsh actor was almost 60, and a veteran of the British cinema, before he started to make his mark as a supporting player in American movies. From the mid-thirties to the mid-fifties, he was a popular, familiar figure, playing a series of idiosyncratic characters, including numerous fathers. They were usually curious, ready with sage advice (he had a trusting voice), and gravely worried. When the hero or heroine treated a serious situation with levity, then his serious manner brought them into line; however, in films where the hero or heroine thinks his characters are too frivolous, they can't get his stubborn men to change their attitudes. Among his most memorable characters are Mr. Bennet in *Pride and Prejudice,* Katharine Hepburn's irresponsible father in *Sylvia Scarlett,* a friendly detective who turns out to be an assassin in *Foreign Correspondent,* a vagabond in *Lassie Come Home,* a harmless counterfeiter in *Mister 880,* Captain Wiles (who thinks he shot Harry) in *The Trouble with Harry,* and his elderly but energetic scientist (who worries about giant ants and our future) in *Them!,* the picture that has endeared him to all science-fiction fans. Yet he will always be most identified with his delightful Kris Kringle in *Miracle on 34th Street,* the Christmas classic. I, for one, have always thought of Santa Claus as that altruistic, complex, whimsical *human* being whom Gwenn created.

• **Cult Favorites:** *Sylvia Scarlett* (1936, George Cukor), *Pride and Prejudice* (1940, Robert Z. Leonard), *Miracle on 34th Streeth* (1947, George Seaton), *Them!* (1954, Gordon Douglas).

• **Also Recommended:** *The Skin Game* (1931, Alfred Hitchcock), *Waltzes from Vienna* (1934, Hitchcock), *Anthony Adverse* (1936, Mervyn LeRoy), *A Yank at Oxford* (1938, Jack Conway), *The Earl of Chicago* (1940, Richard Thorpe), *Foreign Correspondent* (1940, Hitchcock), *Cheers for Miss Bishop* (1941, Tay Garnett), *The Devil and Miss Jones* (1941, Sam Wood), *The Meanest Man in the World* (1943, Sidney Lanfield), *Lassie Come Home* (1943, Fred M. Wilcox), *Keys of the Kingdom* (1944, John M. Stahl), *Bewitched* (1945, Arch Oboler), *Life with Father* (1947, Michael Curtiz), *Apartment for Peggy* (1948, Seaton), *The Hills of Home* (1948, Wilcox), *Mister 880* (1950, Edmund Goulding), *The Bigamist* (1953, Ida Lupino), *The Trouble with Harry* (1955, Hitchcock).

• **Also of Interest:** *Between Two Worlds* (1944, Edward A. Blatt), *Dangerous Partners* (1945, Edward L. Cahn), *Undercurrent* (1946, Vincente Minnelli), *Challenge to Lassie* (1949, Thorpe), *A Woman of Distinction* (1950, Edward Buzzell), *For Heaven's Sake* (1950, Seaton), *Mister Scoutmaster* (1953, Henry Levin), *It's a Dog's Life* (1955, Herman Hoffman).

○

ANNE GWYNNE (1918–) Red-haired Texan was a swimsuit model before she signed a contract with Universal in 1939. In the forties, she starred in several programmers and, more significantly, horror films, challenging Evelyn Ankers as the studio's scream queen. Though her career wasn't particularly distinguished overall, she looked lovely and did well as the villainess of the serial *Flash Gordon Conquers the Universe,* a witch married to Lon Chaney, Jr., in the best "Inner Sanctum" film, *Weird Woman,* and Dracula's love interest in *House of Frankenstein.* She also got to star in a haunted house film with musical interludes, *Murder in the Blue Room.* Gwynne should have retired before taking the female lead in the unbearably dull 1957 horror film, *Meteor Monster,* playing a mother whose young boy suddenly becomes a large, hairy, demented killer.

• **Cult Favorites:** *Flash Gordon Conquers the Universe* (1940 serial, Ford Beebe and Ray Taylor), *Weird Woman* (1944, Reginald LeBorg).

• **Other Key Films:** *Black Friday* (1940, Arthur Lubin), *House of Frankenstein* (1944, Erle C. Kenton), *Ride 'Em Cowboy* (1942, Lubin), *The Strange Case of Dr. X* (1942, William Nigh), *Murder in the Blue Room* (1944, Leslie Goodwin), *The Glass*

Alibi (1946, W. Lee Wilder), *The Ghost Goes Wild* (1947, George Blair), *Dick Tracy Meets Gruesome* (1947, John Rawlins).

○

HUGO HAAS (1901–68) Stocky Czech comic star who came to Hollywood and had success as a character actor—since he had an accent, he could play villains—was sort of a poor man's Walter Slezak. His cult is a result of a series of lurid, often campy low-budget melodramas—explorations of human nature—that he always directed, usually produced, sometimes wrote and, with the exception of *Night of the Quarter Moon,* starred in during the fifties and early sixties. He often played civil, mild-mannered (until driven too far), middle-aged men who fall for and are then victimized by young, money-hungry femmes fatales, sleazily played by Beverly Michaels and, later and more often, Cleo Moore. However, he also played a pauper with a dog in *Edge of Hell,* and an aged, philosophical filmmaker who disrupts a neighborhood by making an amateur on-location production in *Paradise Alley,* one of his many offbeat projects.
 • **Cult Favorites:** *Pickup* (1951, Hugo Haas), *Strange Fascination* (1952, Haas), *Bait* (1954, Haas), *Lizzie* (1957, Haas), *Paradise Alley* (1961, Haas).
 • **Other Key Films:** *King Solomon's Mines* (1950, Compton Bennett and Andrew Marton), *Girl on the Bridge* (1951, Haas), *One Girl's Confession* (1953, Haas), *Thy Neighbor's Wife* (1953, Haas), *The Other Woman* (1954, Haas), *Hold Back Tomorrow* (1955, Haas), *Edge of Hell* (1956, Haas), *Born to Be Loved* (1959, Haas).

○

DAYLE HADDON (1949–) Dark-haired Canadian actress with the sensuous features of a cover girl and the distinction of moving from a Walt Disney feature, *The World's Greatest Athlete,* to *Spermula,* a classic tale of female vampires who need sperm (rather than blood) to survive. She would make R-rated sex films in America, Canada, and Europe. While they were ostensibly political thrillers, romances, and murder mysteries, the emphasis was on nudity and sex, with Haddon's special erotic touch. Among her directors was Just Jaeckin, whom she probably reminded of Sylvia Kristel, his star in *Emmanuelle.* In one of her rare appearances in the mainstream, Haddon added healthy doses of sex and sensitivity to the underrated comedy-drama *North Dallas Forty,* helping troubled Nick Nolte realize that there is excitement outside of football. Unfortunately, her fine performance didn't lead to more good roles. She was, for instance, a half-woman, half-robot in *Cyborg.* A cable favorite.
 • **Cult Favorite:** *Cyborg* (1989, Albert Pyun).
 • **Sleeper:** *North Dallas Forty* (1979, Ted Kotcheff).
 • **Other Key Films:** *The World's Greatest Athlete* (1973, Robert Scheerer), *Spermula* (1975, Charles Matton), *Sex With a Smile* (1976, Sergio Martino), *The Cheaters* (1976, Martino), *The Last Romantic Lover* (1978, Just Jaeckin), *The French Woman* (1978, Jaeckin), *Bedroom Eyes* (1986, William Fruet).

○

SID HAIG (1939–) Ugly, ruddy-faced, usually bald, and occasionally bearded—he looks

Sid Haig causes trouble.

like an original member of Frank Zappa's Mothers of Invention—Haig has been a seedy presence in low-budget, sex- and action-packed drive-in movies since the mid-sixties. Director Jack Hill used him often, casting him as sympathetic revolutionaries in his groundbreaking women-in-prison films *The Big Doll House* and *The Big Bird Cage,* both Roger Corman productions. More often Haig played sadistic villains, most memorably in films featuring Pam Grier (his mistress in *The Big Bird Cage*). In the Bond film *Diamonds Are Forever,* he tosses topless Lana Wood out a window. In the demented *Spider Baby,* he has had a lobotomy. In his book *For One Week Only,* Richard Meyers described him as "a hulking man with stringy hair, bulging eyes, rough skin, and a huge smile," yet, speaking for many exploitation film fanatics, admits "it is getting to be a

pleasure to see him in one lightheaded film after another."

• **Cult Favorites:** *Point Blank* (1967, John Boorman), *Spider Baby* (1964/68, Jack Hill), *THX-1138* (1971, George Lucas), *The Big Doll House* (1971, Hill), *The Big Bird Cage* (1972, Hill), *Emperor of the North* (1973, Robert Aldrich), *Coffy* (1973, Hill), *Foxy Brown* (1974, Hill).

• **Other Key Films:** *Pit Stop* (1969, Hill), *Black Mama, White Mama* (1972, Eddie Romero).

• **Also of Interest:** *Blood Bath* (1966, Hill and Stephanie Rothman), *It's a Bikini World* (1967, Rothman), *C.C. and Company* (1970, Seymour Robbie), *Savage Sisters* (1972, Romero), *Busting* (1974, Peter Hyams), *Beyond Atlantis* (1975, Romero), *Galaxy of Terror* (1981, B. D. Clark), *Commando Squad* (1987, Fred Olen Ray).

○

HAJI Dark-haired, buxom beauty usually cast strictly for show in Russ Meyer's dopey T&A potboilers of the seventies. But a decade earlier she had meatier roles in his better films: in her one lead, she was an eye-scratching wildcat surrounded by violent motorcyclists in the gritty *Motor Psycho,* and she was the lover in a horny husband's sexual fantasies in *Good Morning . . . and Goodbye.* Her juiciest part was in *Faster, Pussycat! Kill! Kill!,* where she contributed to the humor and overwrought drama. She used a thick Italian accent to play Rosie, Tura Satana's hot-blooded, bad-tempered lover and knife-wielding accomplice in kidnapping a young girl, plotting to steal money from a dirty old man, and murder. She has the poor luck to be stabbed to death by a character named Vegetable.
• **Cult Favorites:** *Faster, Pussycat! Kill! Kill!* (1966, Russ Meyer), *Beyond the Valley of the Dolls* (1970, Meyer), *Supervixens* (1975, Meyer).
• **Other Key Films:** *Motor Psycho* (1965, Meyer), *Good Morning . . . and Goodbye* (1967, Meyer), *Up!* (1977, Meyer).

○

JACK HALEY (1899–1979) This former vaudevillian and stage actor made his one major mark in film as the Tin Man in *The Wizard of Oz.* Haley should be commended for his amusing, sensitive performance from beneath his coat of armor, because when you put aside the makeup, his character was much less interesting than Ray Bolger's Scarecrow and Bert Lahr's Cowardly Lion, and not so instantly lovable. Still, he captured viewers' hearts while searching for one of his own. Other than

The Wizard of Oz and the Shirley Temple vehicle *Poor Little Rich Girl,* in which Haley and Alice Faye were a vaudeville team, his movie career had few highlights, though he lent able support to the stars in a few diverting musicals.
• **Cult Favorite:** *The Wizard of Oz* (1939, Victor Fleming).
• **Other Key Films:** *Poor Little Rich Girl* (1936, Irving Cummings), *Pigskin Parade* (1936, David Butler), *Rebecca of Sunnybrook Farm* (1938, Allan Dwan), *Alexander's Ragtime Band* (1938, Henry King), *Hold That Co-Ed* (1938, George Marshall), *Moon Over Miami* (1941, Walter Lang), *Navy Blues* (1941, Lloyd Bacon).

○

ARCH HALL, JR. They say that in Hollywood, you gotta know the right people to get breaks. Well, this twerpy, pug-nosed, pompadoured blond actor happened to know his father, who was head honcho of Fairway International Pictures in the early sixties, and at various times and under various names produced, directed, wrote, and acted in shoestring-budget drive-in drivel. His teenage son, who was only slightly better looking than Michael J. Pollard, but without the quirky charm or talent, starred in several of these films. He was quite creepy as the teacher-hating title character of *The Sadist,* going all out in his best performance, but otherwise he was amateurish and obnoxious, whether playing cowboys, rock singers, young hoods, or young gentlemen. It was a double bore to suffer through his romance with a pretty girl who in real life would probably laugh at his advances, and also listen to his band, the Archers, wail one of his rock compositions. I still can't understand why teenager Marilyn Manning (also his girl-

Arch Hall, Jr., with Marilyn Manning in The Sadist.

friend in *The Sadist*) would prefer his dippy Tommy to a gigantic prehistoric caveman in *Eegah!,* his most famous and most enjoyably bad film. He seemed not to actually care about acting and, in fact, he quit to pursue other interests, prompting his father also to call it a career. Apparently, Arch senior used various aliases for reasons other than shame about his son's skills—he actually was proud of the lad.

• **Cult Favorites:** *Eegah!* (1962, Nicholas Merriwether/Arch Hall, Sr.), *The Sadist* (1963, James Landis).

• **Other Key Films:** *The Choppers* (1961, Leigh Jason), *Wild Guitar* (1962, Ray Dennis Steckler), *Deadwood '76* (1965, Landis), *The Nasty Rabbit* (1965, Landis).

HUNTZ HALL (1920–) Like Leo Gorcey, he played a delinquent slum boy in both the Broadway play and movie of *Dead End,* and stayed with Gorcey through two decades, as the tough Dead End Kids mellowed and became the comic East Side Kids and, finally, the Bowery Boys. It was Hall's dumb kicked-in-the-head-by-a-mule expression and ability to do and say funny things that made the transition from drama to comedy possible. Tall and slender, with large eyes and a rubbery face that looked like an extension of his large nose, and always wearing a cap, he was the dumbbell of the group, too stupid to understand orders (by Billy Halop, Gorcey, or the police) or keep his big mouth shut. As Dippy in the Dead End films, his ignorance and stupidity, in conjunction with his energy and aggressiveness, actually made him seem dangerous; but in future years, when he clowned around as Sach (real name, Horace DeBussy Jones), his pea-brain made him sympathetic, as well as driving Gorcey's "Slip" crazy. He was an incorrigible, eternal juvenile. In a fifties film, when Sach says he almost died of manslaughter, Slip chides, "Since when are you a *man?*" He became more and more like Curley of the Three Stooges, with Slip becoming like Moe, loving Sach and needing his companionship but constantly insulting and abusing him. Sach's medical report read: "Everything normal (except patient)."

• **Cult Favorites:** *Angels with Dirty Faces* (1938, Michael Curtiz), numerous "Dead End Kids," "East Side Kids," and "Bowery Boys" star vehicles (1940–56).

• **Also Recommended:** *Dead End* (1937, William Wyler), *Crime School* (1938, Lewis Seiler), *They Made Me a Criminal* (1939, Busby Berkeley), *Hell's Kitchen* (1939, Seiler and E. A. Dupont), *Angels Wash Their Faces* (1939, Ray Enright), *A Walk in the Sun* (1945, Lewis Milestone).

○

JON HALL (1913–79) For those of us who first saw Hall in the fifties as television's stalwart "Ramar of the Jungle," it wasn't surprising to learn that in the thirties and forties he had starred in many juvenile western and adventure films. But it was shocking to learn that this actor, who played a fortyish "Great White Doctor" who lived in the wilds with a male companion, a houseboy, a chimp, and other animals, had been a sex symbol during that period—a hunk who often went bare-chested—and that those movies were full of romance. John Ford put him in a loin-cloth and teamed him with the saronged Dorothy Lamour in his exciting *The Hurricane*—and it's debatable who was better-looking. Hall would be the muscular hero of other tropical-island pictures, often playing handsome young natives, including *Aloma of the South Seas* with Lamour, before starring in a number of colorful, campy "Arabian Nights" films, battling sinister villains to rescue the exotic princesses played by the one and only Maria Montez. Their six escapist, juvenile kitsch classics were all made in Technicolor and overflowed with adventure, palace intrigue, comedy, terrible dialogue, romance, and sex. Although—or perhaps *because*—neither was a very good actor, Hall and Montez were a perfect match, his seriousness keeping us from realizing (at least *all* the time) that she was saying silly things in a very silly way, her enticing costumes diverting our eyes from Hall's horrible wardrobe. We only cared that they seemed to live in a magical screen world which any young viewer would love to visit. Hall and Montez became one of the top romantic teams of the forties and achieved permanent cult status, individually and as a duo.

• **Cult Favorites:** *Arabian Nights* (1942, John Rawlins), *Ali Baba and the Forty Thieves* (1944, Arthur Lubin), *Cobra Woman* (1944, Robert Siodmak).

• **Other Key Films:** *The Hurricane* (1937, John Ford), *South of Pago Pago* (1940, Alfred E. Green), *Kit Carson* (1940, George B. Seitz), *Aloma of the South Seas* (1941, Alfred Santell), *The Tuttles of*

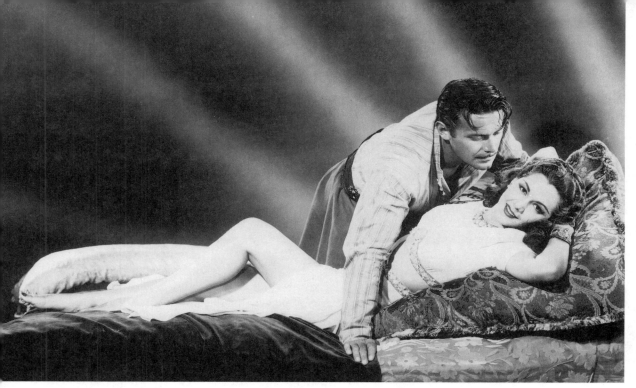

Jon Hall and Maria Montez pose for Ali Baba and the Forty Thieves.

Tahiti (1942, Charles Vidor), *Invisible Agent* (1942, Edwin L. Marin), *White Savage* (1943, Lubin), *The Invisible Man's Revenge* (1944, Ford Beebe), *Gypsy Wildcat* (1944, Roy William Neill), *San Diego, I Love You* (1944, Reginald LeBorg), *Sudan* (1945, Rawlins), *The Prince of Thieves* (1948, Howard Bretherton).

○

PORTER HALL (1888–1953) Familiar character actor, with a shifty mustache and beady eyes surrounded by crooked eyebrows from above and heavy bags from below, who gave amusing performances whether in comedies or dramas. He usually played annoying, grouchy, unhelpful busybodies, snooty little men who are cowards and fools yet exhibit gargantuan self-importance, who never have a good word for anyone and try to crush defenseless heroes and heroines (usually by getting them in trouble with the authorities), and who are almost as suspicious as the hotel clerks played by Franklin Pangborn. He is best remembered as Macy's neurotic psychologist who commits Kris Kringle in *Miracle on 34th Street* and as an unreliable murder witness in *Double Indemnity,* but he was also delightful in other unsympathetic roles.

• **Cult Favorites:** *The Thin Man* (1934, W. S. Van Dyke), *His Girl Friday* (1940, Howard Hawks), *Sullivan's Travels* (1941, Preston Sturges), *The Miracle of Morgan's Creek* (1944, Sturges), *Miracle on 34th Street* (1947, George Seaton), *The Big Carnival/Ace in the Hole* (1951, Billy Wilder).

• **Sleepers:** *Make Way for Tomorrow* (1937, Leo McCarey), *Dark Command*

(1940, Raoul Walsh), *Murder, He Says* (1945, George Marshall).

• **Other Key Films:** *The Petrified Forest* (1935, Archie Mayo), *The Story of Louis Pasteur* (1936, William Dieterle), *Mr. Deeds Goes to Town* (1936, Frank Capra), *Mr. Smith Goes to Washington* (1939, Capra), *Double Indemnity* (1944, Wilder), *Going My Way* (1944, McCarey).

• **Also Recommended:** *Satan Met a Lady* (1936, Dieterle), *The Plainsman* (1936, Cecil B. De Mille), *The General Died at Dawn* (1936, Lewis Milestone), *Wells Fargo* (1937, Frank Lloyd), *Stolen Heaven* (1938, Andrew L. Stone), *Intruder in the Dust* (1949, Clarence Brown).

• **Also of Interest:** *They Shall Have Music* (1939, Mayo), *The Unconquered* (1947, De Mille), *The Beautiful Blonde from Bashful Bend* (1949, Sturges), *Vice Squad* (1953, Arnold Laven).

○

MARK HAMILL (1952–) This boyish, little-known television actor was fortunate to get the key role of Luke Skywalker in *Star Wars,* a character that made him instantly famous and the idol of hundreds of millions worldwide. He would repeat the part in the two sequels, and just as Luke evolved from brave boy to mythic hero, Hamill evolved from an appealing performer to a serious, talented actor who was capable of expressing the often subtle changes taking place in his maturing character. Strongly identified with Luke and the "Star Wars" trilogy, Hamill has had trouble finding other good parts.

• **Cult Favorite:** *The Big Red One* (1980, Sam Fuller).

• **Other Key Films:** *Star Wars* (1977, George Lucas), *The Empire Strikes Back* (1980, Irvin Kershner), *Return of the Jedi* (1983, Richard Marquand).

• **Also Recommended:** *The Night the Lights Went Out in Georgia* (1981, Ronald F. Maxwell).

• **Also of Interest:** *Corvette Summer* (1978, Matthew Robbins).

○

GEORGE HAMILTON (1939–) He was tall, dark, and handsome, but he couldn't act a lick when he broke into films in the late fifties. Like other young leading men of the period, he was called on to project sensitivity and/or rebelliousness in almost all of his roles, but he just came off as slimy, which was no small task for such a well-groomed fellow. He should have been more like Anthony Perkins, but he was drifting toward Laurence Harvey. The most that could be said of his best early performances—courting virginal Dolores Hart in *Where the Boys Are,* promoting evangelist Salome Jens in *Angel Baby*—is that he was inoffensive. His bad-actor reputation intact, he then gave two commendable performances without anyone noticing, bursting out of his stiff-collar acting style to play reckless real-life figures: country-and-western singing legend Hank Williams (who died at 29) in *Your Cheatin' Heart,* and daredevil motorcyclist *Evel Knievel.* Over the years, Hamilton's public image would eclipse his films. He romanced many women, including Lynda Bird Johnson and Elizabeth Taylor; he went skiing a lot; he nurtured the best tan in the world; he seemed like the laziest actor in Hollywood. Anyone making an awful film sought his services, and soon his credits included *Once Is Not Enough, The Happy Hooker Goes to Washington,* and *Sextette.* Hamilton's saving grace is that he started poking fun at himself as well (he turned out to be a funny talk-show guest). And he had an unexpected hit playing, with tongue in cheek, a down-on-his-luck Dracula (who's evicted from his castle) in the wacky vampire parody *Love at First Bite* (for which he was executive producer). No one had any idea that Hamilton could play comedy. The hit film temporarily revived his career and actually won him admiring fans. I preferred his zanier *Zorro, the Gay Blade,* but I was in the minority, as the film flopped and ended his brief period with box-office clout. For years now, he has planned to revive his vampire.

• **Cult Favorites:** *Where the Boys Are* (1960, Henry Levin), *Sextette* (1978, Ken Hughes), *Love at First Bite* (1979, Stan Dragoti).

• **Sleepers:** *Angel Baby* (1961, Paul Wendkos and Hubert Cornfield), *Your Cheatin' Heart* (1964, Gene Nelson), *Zorro, the Gay Blade* (1981, Peter Medak).

• **Other Key Films:** *Crime & Punishment, U.S.A.* (1959, Denis Sanders), *Home from the Hill* (1960, Vincente Minnelli), *All the Fine Young Cannibals* (1960, Michael Anderson), *By Love Possessed* (1961, John Sturges), *Light in the Piazza* (1962, Guy Green), *Two Weeks in Another Town* (1962, Minnelli), *Act One* (1963, Dore Schary), *Viva Maria!* (1965, Louis Malle), *The Power* (1968, Byron Haskin), *The Man Who Loved Cat Dancing* (1973, Richard C. Sarafian), *The Godfather Part III* (1990, Francis Coppola).

○

LINDA HAMILTON (1956–) Before starring in the cult TV series "Beauty and the Beast," this pretty, spunky, extremely appealing young actress, who's sexiest in jeans and sneakers, was the leading lady in several horror and science-fiction films. She'll be remembered as the female star of *The Terminator,* her only good film so far, doing battle with and foiling Arnold Schwarzenegger's robotic assassin from the future. It is an extremely interesting role in fantasy-film annals. Her Sarah Connor evolves from an uninvolved, frightened waitress-servant who is unaware of her strength or potential to a brave, committed "mother" of a revolution against the machines that will govern America in the future. She also represents the Virgin Mary, impregnated by someone who doesn't actually exist in our world (Michael Biehn's emissary from the future can't be termed "mortal"), and will conceive a child, John Connor (note the initials), who will become savior of the people on earth.

• **Cult Favorite:** *The Terminator* (1984, James Cameron).

• **Other Key Films:** *Tag—The Assassination Game* (1982, Nick Castle, *Children of the Corn* (1984, Fritz Kiersch), *Black Moon Rising* (1986, Harley Cokliss), *Terminator 2: Judgment Day* (1991, Cameron).

• **Also of Interest:** *King Kong Lives* (1986, John Guillermin).

○

MARGARET HAMILTON (1902–85) For 40 years, young kids have had nightmares from watching Hamilton in her Halloween garb in *The Wizard of Oz.* She is every child's nightmare school teacher, which is ironic since she was a kindergarten teacher before becoming an actress. Skinny as a rail and hatchet-faced, the shrill-voiced character actress seemed perfectly cast as the Wicked Witch of the West and the mean spinster Miss Gulch. As a hag who truly enjoys being wicked, she was one of the

*Margaret Hamilton, the
Wicked Witch in* The
Wizard of Oz.

scariest villains in movie history (when she points her long-nailed finger and calls Dorothy "my pretty," even adult viewers get chills), so much crueler than one would expect in a kids' film in 1939. Although Hamilton will always be identified with her wicked witch—an unlovable part that won her the eternal love of all movie fans—she stole scenes in films for several decades, usually playing town gossips and hysterics, snoopy neighbors, and housekeepers. She lent her recognizable voice to the animated feature *Journey Back to Oz,* which was made in 1964 but not released until 1974.

• **Cult Favorites:** *The Wizard of Oz* (1939, Victor Fleming), *My Little Chickadee* (1940, Eddie Cline), *Brewster McCloud* (1970, Robert Altman).

• **Also Recommended:** *These Three* (1933, William Wyler), *You Only Live Once* (1937, Fritz Lang), *Nothing Sacred* (1937, William Wellman), *A Slight Case of Murder* (1938, Lloyd Bacon), *The Adventures of Tom Sawyer* (1938, Norman Taurog), *Angels Wash Their Faces* (1939, Ray Enright), *Babes in Arms* (1939, Busby Berkeley), *The Ox-Bow Incident* (1943, William Wellman), *Guest in the House* (1944, John Brahm), *Mad Wednesday/The Sin of Harold Diddlebock* (1947, Preston Sturges), *State of the Union* (1948, Frank Capra), *The Red Pony* (1949, Lewis Milestone), *The Beautiful Blonde from Bashful Bend* (1949, Sturges), *Wabash Avenue* (1950, Henry Koster), *People Will Talk* (1951, Joseph L. Mankiewicz), *13 Ghosts* (1960, William Castle).

○

GUNNAR HANSEN. Stout actor who made one of the most memorable first appearances in movie history: the whirring of his chain saw stops just before he charges through a doorway—and into our sight—wearing a hideous mask made out of a human face and brandishing a huge sledgehammer, which he uses to cream the stunned young male stranger who ventured into his house. His second appearance, a few minutes later, may be even more startling: he grabs the next visitor, hangs the screaming young girl on a meat hook, and resumes chopping up the dead young man with his chain saw. Later on, he will run his chain saw through a paraplegic's stomach, and chase a screaming young woman (Marilyn Burns) through the woods with his buzzing chain saw. Hansen's "Leatherface" (he never removes his mask), speechless son in a cannibal family in Tobe Hooper's shocking, taboo-breaking *The Texas Chainsaw Massacre,* is one of the vilest villains in all horror films. What makes him particularly unnerving is that at the end of the picture he survives! (Unfortunately, when Hooper did the sequel, Leatherface was played by Bill Johnson instead of Hansen.) Hansen, who can't really act, has turned up in a couple of other independent horror films, playing occultists. In the loony *Hollywood Chainsaw Hookers,* his satanist is done in by Linnea Quigley, displaying double chainsaw action. Leatherface would have given her better competition.

• **Cult Favorites:** *The Texas Chainsaw Massacre* (1974, Tobe Hooper), *Hollywood Chainsaw Hookers* (1988, Fred Olen Ray).

• **Other Key Film:** *The Demon Lover* (1976, Donald G. Jackson and Jerry Younkins).

○

JEAN HARLOW (1911–37) The former Harlean Carpenter, from Kansas City, Missouri, was a sexy bit player before shooting to stardom as the female lead in *Hell's Angels,* having replaced Swedish Greta Nissen when Howard Hughes decided it should be a sound picture. She was soon the era's reigning sex goddess, the first movie blonde who wasn't an innocent virgin. She also proved to be a hilarious, wisecracking comedienne. She was quite a package: her voice was husky yet babyish, her delivery was vulgar; she had platinum blonde hair, pastel skin, half-moon brows, a child's pout, and, as her biographer Irving Shulman wrote, "come-on hips, shapely thighs, callipygian rear, marvelous breasts, and a little stomach." Fans were excited that she wore no underwear and fondled herself while speaking to the press. She played cheap, uneducated but strong-willed and savvy women. They wiggle when they walk, strike alluring poses, and wear clinging or revealing outfits. Usually courageous and blessed with hearts of gold, they are never ashamed of themselves—on the contrary, they have strong egos. Society thinks them amoral because they use their bodies to get what they want, yet they have strict moral codes and know the difference between right and wrong. They don't think their sexual conduct is wicked. A "man's woman," she worked well with Clark Gable: they usually played tough characters who reform each other. In *Red Dust,* the unshaven Gable and braless Harlow have immense sexual chemistry, whether he's standing next to her while she takes her famous nude bath in a barrel, or she sits by him as he lies on a bed, reading to him a children's bedtime story while he's putting his hand on her knee. Her comedic talents were best shown in *Dinner at Eight,* as a ditsy (but really smart) sexpot who insists husband Wallace Beery take her to a classy dinner

In the thirties, Jean Harlow and Clark Gable were a sexy team in several films, beginning with Red Dust.

party. Her venomous spat with Beery is a sidesplitter. She's also funny in *Libeled Lady,* holding her own with Spencer Tracy, William Powell, and Myrna Loy. I love the way she huffs and puffs through a room with shoulders and legs working in unison, and how she gives her groom Powell a weak kiss and his best man Tracy a heartfelt smooch. Offscreen, Harlow survived a scandal in 1932 when her new husband, film executive Paul Bern, committed suicide. Five years later, the Blond Bombshell was hospitalized for uremic poisoning and soon after, before completing *Saratoga,* died of cerebral edema. She was just 26 but left behind an impressive body of work and an indelible image. She would be Marilyn Monroe's model, and later, Carroll Baker and Carol Lynley would play Harlow in movies.

• **Cult Favorites:** *The Public Enemy* (1931, William Wellman), *Red Dust* (1932, Victor Fleming), *Dinner at Eight* (1933, George Cukor).

• **Other Key Films:** *Hell's Angels* (1930, Howard Hughes), *The Secret Six* (1931, George Hill), *Platinum Blonde* (1931, Frank Capra), *Beast of the City* (1932, Charles Brabin), *Red-Headed Woman* (1932, Jack Conway), *Hold Your Man*

(1933, Sam Wood), *Bombshell* (1933, Fleming), *The Girl from Missouri* (1934, Conway), *Reckless* (1934, Fleming), *China Seas* (1935, Tay Garnett), *Suzy* (1936, George Fitzmaurice), *Libeled Lady* (1934, Conway), *Saratoga* (1937, Conway).

○

JESSICA HARPER (1949–) Pretty, dark-haired, talented actress-singer, with a minimal acting style (her lips barely open when she speaks; instead she moves her eyes from side to side and does double takes), she has earned the title "The Queen of the Out-of-the-Mainstream Movie." Almost every film she has made has achieved cult status, except the one that was geared for just that, *Shock Treatment,* the horrendous sequel to *The Rocky Horror Picture Show.* It is her bad luck that when she played her one conventional character (Mark Linn-Baker's perky girlfriend) in what was thought to be a surefire popular hit, *My Favorite Year,* it flopped and found only cult success; and that when she made a film for Herbert Ross, a director who had made only commercial films, he decided to become arty with *Pennies from Heaven.* Harper has the face and slim body of a young girl but the delivery and attitude of a woman who has been around. One minute she's demure, the next she's full of energy, even belting

Jessica Harper's Cathy Cake wants to make a porno film for Richard Dreyfuss's Boy Wonder in the underrated Inserts.

out a song. Her ever-changing face can switch quickly from naive to shrewd, from fragile to hard, from sweet to haunting. Filmmakers have exploited her chameleon quality by casting her as women who undergo drastic personality transformations. In *Phantom of the Paradise,* her first lead, she is an angelic singer who loses her soul in a deal with the devil. In *Inserts,* her Cathy Cake is so unpredictable (she impulsively strips to sub for a porno actress) that her demeanor seems to change every time she says something. In *Pennies from Heaven,* she begins as a straitlaced, apathetic midwesterner who is repulsed by the sexual demands of her husband (Steve Martin), then turns into a pathetic creature who tries to satisfy his every whim. In *Stardust Memories,* she is a violinist who just happens to be neurotic. Harper went to Italy to play a typical young-woman-in-peril in Dario Argento's stylized horror film *Suspiria,* but more often she opts for unconventional roles, like a female dictator in the ambitious but poorly made *The Blue Iguana,* a character that she modeled on Edward G. Robinson's gangsters. "You'll notice a lack of willingness on my part to sell myself," she once told me. "I make audiences come to me—if they feel like it—rather than forcing myself on them." She's worth seeking out.

• **Cult Favorites:** *Taking Off* (1971, Milos Forman), *Phantom of the Paradise* (1974, Brian De Palma), *Inserts* (1976, John Byrum), *Suspiria* (1977, Dario Argento), *Stardust Memories* (1980, Woody Allen), *Pennies from Heaven* (1981, Herbert Ross), *My Favorite Year* (1982, Richard Benjamin).

• **Also of Interest:** *Love and Death* (1975, Allen), *The Evictors* (1979, Charles B. Pearce), *Shock Treatment* (1981, Jim Sharman), *The Imagemaker* (1985, Hal Weiner), *The Blue Iguana* (1988, John Lafia).

○

DOLORES HART (1938–) When she was 19, Hal Willis signed her to a seven-year contract and cast her opposite Elvis Presley in *Loving You,* as the pure girl who keeps his small-town country singer from being devoured or corrupted by show biz. One film later, she played opposite Presley in his best film, *King Creole.* Again she was a steadfastly pure girl, this time teaching morality to the troubled youth, at one time speaking to him with a church in the background. She had surprising conviction. Her morality on screen may have been conservative—until she starred in *Where the Boys Are*—yet she seemed sexy rather than wholesome; if the wild Presley settled down with her, he wouldn't be bored. With her well-scrubbed good looks, intelligence, sincerity, natural delivery, genuine talent, and extreme likability, she was quickly recognized as one of the up-and-coming young actresses of the period, was cast as the supportive girlfriend of Montgomery Clift's tormented gossip columnist in *Lonelyhearts,* and had her own love life scrutinized in the fan magazines, which tried to guess when and whom she would marry. When pressed about tying the knot, she was more willing to talk about her religious commitment. Hart would continue to play smart good girls, including her one nun in *Francis of Assisi.* However, she enjoyed playing her "first witchy part" in *Come Fly with Me,* even learning how to smoke for the part. Undoubtedly, Hart's most memorable role is the lead in the fascinating, if campy, *Where the Boys Are,* giving a truly appealing performance as a smart college girl, the loyal friend of three female companions on a trip to Fort Lauderdale, and a strong advocate of premarital sex—although she will decide that in *her* case, she'll be better off if she waits (she even convinces George Hamilton to agree!). It's strange watching her tell her dean she has sexual longings—a scene that contributes to the film's considerable mystique—because at the age of 24, Hart entered a convent in Connecticut. At age 31, Sister Judith, as she was now called, became a full-fledged member of the Benedictine order, pledging to spend the rest of her life in a cloistered monastery, and permanently withdrawing from where the boys are.

- **Cult Favorites:** *King Creole* (1958, Michael Curtiz), *Where the Boys Are* (1960, Henry Levin).
- **Other Key Films:** *Loving You* (1957, Hal Kanter), *Wild Is the Wind* (1957, George Cukor), *Lonelyhearts* (1959, Vincent J. Donahue).
- **Also of Interest:** *Francis of Assisi* (1961, Curtiz), *Sail a Crooked Ship* (1961, Irving S. Brecher), *Lisa* (1962, Philip Dunne), *Come Fly with Me* (1963, Levin).

○

VERONICA HART Sexy former dancer and model who became a porno queen in the early eighties. She did all kinds of kinky things on the screen—after all, she was the title character of *Angel Buns*—yet she still came across as more elegant and classier than most of the other female stars. Perhaps because she can act. She usually played women who were either successful professionally—from high-priced call girls to literary agents to investment brokers—or were trying to sleep their way to success. Another common role was that of women whose disinterested or philandering husbands/boyfriends aren't satisfying them in bed, so they go looking for men and women to put an end to their frustration. Her women both used their bodies for personal gain and needed sex for personal satisfaction. Today, in nonporno adult films and plays, she uses the name Jane Hamilton. In the R-rated comedy *Cleo/Leo* (which anticipated Blake Edwards's mainstream *Switch*), she did a good job as a male chauvinist who is killed and comes back as a woman.

- **Cult Favorites:** *Amanda by Night* (1981, Robert McCallum), *Wanda Whips Wall Street* (1982, Larry Revene), *Roommates* (1982, Chuck Vincent).
- **Other Key Films:** *Pandora's Mirror* (1981, Warren Evans), *Delicious* (1981, Philip Drexler), *Outlaw Ladies* (Henri Pachard), *A Scent of Heather* (1981, Drexler), *Angel Buns* (1981, David Mackenzie), *Neon Nights* (1982, Cecil Howard), *Centerspread Girls* (1982, McCallum), *Foxtrot* (1982, Howard), *The Playgirl* (1982, Roberta Findlay), *In Love* (1983, Vincent), *Cleo/Leo* (1989, Vincent).

○

RAYMOND HATTON (1887–1971) Prolific character actor whose career began in 1911 and ended not long before his death 60 years later. From 1926 to 1929 he made comedies with Wallace Beery, and continued to play quirky characters throughout the sound era. But he is best remembered for his short, sour-looking, often ornery comic sidekicks in B westerns at Republic and Monogram in the thirties and forties. He was in two of the "Three Mesquiteers" groupings, teaming with John Wayne and

Ray "Crash" Corrigan as well as Duncan Renaldo and Bob Livingston, but those films paled in comparison to the exciting "Rough Riders" films he made with Buck Jones and Tim McCoy. Most B-western fans consider them the best of the many trio heroes of the period. Jones's sudden death ended plans for another series with Hatton as his comic partner, so Hatton played that role (as Sandy Hopkins) with Johnny Mack Brown in a number of well-produced minor westerns at Monogram.

• **Cult Favorites:** *Marked Woman* (1937, Michael Curtiz), *Arizona Bound* (1941, Spencer G. Bennet).

• **Also Recommended:** *The Squaw Man* (1931, Cecil B. De Mille), *Polly of the Circus* (1932, Alfred Santell), *Rough Riders' Roundup* (1939, Joseph Kane), *Frontier Pony Express* (1939, Kane), *Texas* (1941, George Marshall), *The Gunman from Bodie* (1941, Bennet), *Forbidden Trails* (1941, Robert North Bradbury), *Below the Border* (1942, Howard Bretherton), *Ghost Town Law* (1942, Bretherton), *Down Texas Way* (1942, Bretherton), *Riders of the West* (1942, Bretherton), *Dawn on the Great Divide* (1942, Bretherton), *Tall in the Saddle* (1944, Edward L. Marin), *The Gentleman from Texas* (1946, Lambert Hillyer) *Black Gold* (1947, Phil Karlson), *Shake, Rattle and Rock* (1956, Edward L. Cahn).

○

RONDO HATTON (1894–1946) He was promoted as the only movie monster who didn't use makeup. His hideous face, misshapen head, and outsized hands were the sad result of acromegaly, a distorting disease of the pituitary gland. He was tastelessly cast as stranglers, back-breakers, and other killers who could barely talk or

Rondo "The Creeper" Hatton poses for evil sculptor Martin Kosleck in House of Horrors.

think. He had no talent whatsoever and no ability to elicit sympathy for his characters (although you couldn't help feeling sorry for the actor himself). He played Moloch the handyman, Mario the Monster Man, and most memorably, "The Creeper" in the Sherlock Holmes film *Pearl of Death*. *The Brute Man*, in which he played a disfigured paranoiac, was such an embarrassment to Universal Studios that they gave it to PRC to release in 1946, the year Hatton died.

• **Key Films:** *The Pearl of Death* (1944, Roy William Neill), *Jungle Captive* (1945, Harold Young), *House of Horrors* (1946, Jean Harbrough), *The Spider Woman Strikes Back* (1946, Arthur Lubin), *The Brute Man* (1946, Yarbrough).

○

RUTGER HAUER (1944–) Charismatic, strikingly handsome Dutch actor with penetrating blue-gray eyes, a sharp nose, and a noble bearing, he came to America after success in Holland with director Paul Verhoeven. He is a dynamic, masculine actor, who puts everything into his rugged, sexually aggressive, arrogant (his arrogance is sexy) outright heroes (which he rarely plays), violent or neurotic antiheroes, and despicable villains, like his political assassin in *Nighthawks*, psycho in *The Hitcher*, and vengeance-bent android (who does one kind final act) in *Blade Runner*. He is completely uninhibited, not worrying if audiences are repulsed by his characters' brutality, amorality, or revolting antics (in *Turkish Delight* his rambunctious, unbridled woman-chaser collects pubic hair, vomits on several people, etc.) or by his own willingness to do semipornographic lovemaking scenes with Monique van de Ven in *Turkish Delight*, Theresa Russell in *Eureka*, Sylvia Kristel in *Mysteries*, and Jennifer Jason Leigh in *Flesh + Blood*. He

Rutger Hauer tells C. Thomas Howell that he was foolish to have given him a lift in The Hitcher.

is confident enough to be shameless, which is why he is so compelling an actor and his characters are so unpredictable.

• **Cult Favorites:** *Soldier of Orange* (1979, Paul Verhoeven), *Spetters* (1980, Verhoeven), *Blade Runner* (1982, Ridley Scott), *Eureka* (1981/1985, Nicolas Roeg), *The Hitcher* (1986, Robert Harmon).

• **Sleeper:** *Turkish Delight* (1975, Verhoeven).

• **Other Key Films:** *Nighthawks* (1981, Bruce Malmuth), *Ladyhawke* (1985, Richard Donner).

• **Also of Interest:** *The Osterman Weekend* (1983, Sam Peckinpah), *A Breed Apart* (1984, Philippe Mora), *Mysteries* (1984, Paul de Lussanet), *Flesh + Blood* (1985, Verhoeven), *Wanted: Dead or Alive* (1987, Gary Sherman), *Blind Fury* (1990, Phillip Noyce).

○

WINGS HAUSER Tall, physical, intense, curly-haired leading man of low-budget exploitation films, specializing in flawed, violent, antisocial characters, particularly villains and vigilantes. He was an acceptable vengeance hero in *Deadly Force*—his ex-cop even beat Dirty Harry to the classic challenge line "Make my day"—but he's easier to dislike than root for. His best role was as a psychotic pimp who stalks hooker Season Hubley in *Vice Squad,* a truly terrifying performance. Also a writer and producer, he has the talent to be in A films, especially as villains, but his name may prevent him from making the move on a permanent basis. He was in major flops by Richard Pryor—such as *Jo Jo Dancer, Your Life Is Calling,* acting decadent; and Norman Mailer—*Tough Guys Don't Dance,* acting psychotic.

• **Cult Favorite:** *Who'll Stop the Rain?* (1978, Karel Reisz).

• **Key Films:** *Vice Squad* (1982, Gary A. Sherman), *Deadly Force* (1983, Paul Aaron), *Mutant* (1983, John "Bud" Cardos), *A Soldier's Story* (1984, Norman Jewison), *Nightmare at Dawn* (1986, Nico Mastorakas).

• **Also of Interest:** *Uncommon Valor* (1983, Ted Kotcheff), *Hostage* (1987, Hanro Mohr), *Tough Guys Don't Dance* (1987, Norman Mailer), *The Wind* (1987, Mastorakas), *Dead Man Walking* (1988, Gregory Brown).

○

ANNETTE HAVEN Slender brunette is regarded as one of porno film's best-looking leading ladies; adult-film reviewer Robert Rimmer rates her: "Sweet face, perfect body, fiery dreamgirl." After debuting in the midseventies, she capped her teeth and went on to star in numerous porn hits; many of the industry's top actors (including John Holmes) and actresses played her sex partners. Her aggressiveness compensated for her inconsistent acting. Often she danced on screen. She turned down R-rated films such as *The Howling* because she objected to their mix of sex and violence.

• **Cult Favorite:** *Barbara Broadcast* (1977, Henry Paris).

• **Other Key Films:** *China Girl* (1974, Paolo Uccello), *Autobiography of a Flea* (1976, Sharon McKnight), *Anna Obsessed* (1977, Martin and Martin), *Soft Places* (1977, Wray Hamilton), *Sex World* (1978, Anthony Spinelli), *V—the Hot One* (Robert McCallum), *High School Memories* (1981, Spinelli).

○

LINDA HAYDEN (1951–) Cute, baby-faced British actress with a naughty demeanor and perverse sex appeal. She made a striking debut at 17 in *Baby Love,* playing an

Linda Hayden in Baby Love.

amoral 15-year-old who seduces a man (who may be her father), his wife, and his son. She angers her movie date by allowing the stranger next to her to put his hand on her bare thigh, and tries to coax young hooligans into molesting her. After this convincing portrayal, she settled into British horror movies, always giving them a sexual charge, and the R-rated *Confessions of a Window Cleaner* sex-comedy series, opposite Robin Askwith. One Hayden-Askwith film was enticingly titled *Let's Get Laid*. Unfortunately, most of her films have been made in England and haven't been well distributed here.

• **Cult Favorite:** *Blood on Satan's Claw* (1971, Piers Haggard).

• **Sleeper:** *Baby Love* (1969, Alastair Reid).

• **Other Key Films:** *Taste the Blood of Dracula* (1970, Peter Sasdy), *Something to Hide* (1972, Reid), *Confessions of a Window Cleaner* (1974, Val Guest), *Madhouse* (1974, Jim Clark).

○

STERLING HAYDEN (1916–86) Tall, tough, deep-voiced leading man of the Robert Ryan school. Hayden moved between routine melodramas, westerns, and some of the most famous classics and cult films of the fifties, sixties, and seventies. He played several memorable heroes and anti-heroes, including the title character of *Johnny Guitar,* Jack D. Ripper in *Dr. Strangelove,* Jim Bowie in *The Last Command,* the drunken writer in *The Long Goodbye,* and a Scandinavian fisherman who uses a harpoon for a weapon in the weird western *Terror in a Texas Town.* He was independent offscreen, and his imposing, self-destructive on-screen characters are also impossible to control, whether they are renegade cops or insane generals who initiate nuclear war. Most of his characters are either leaders (of criminals, of soldiers) or outlaws; they are essentially alone but for the women who put up with

Sterling Hayden is the title character in Johnny Guitar, *with John Carradine.*

them. Almost all die violently or lose those they love.

• **Cult Favorites:** *The Asphalt Jungle* (1950, John Huston), *Johnny Guitar* (1954, Nicholas Ray), *The Killing* (1956, Stanley Kubrick), *Terror in a Texas Town* (1958, Joseph H. Lewis), *Dr. Strangelove* (1964, Kubrick), *The Godfather* (1972, Francis Ford Coppola), *The Long Goodbye* (1973, Robert Altman), *The Last Days of Man on Earth* (1973, Robert Fuest), *1900* (1976, Bernardo Bertolucci), *Winter Kills* (1979, William Richert).

• **Sleepers:** *Suddenly* (1954, Lewis Allen), *The Last Command* (1955, Frank Lloyd), *Loving* (1970, Irvin Kershner).

○

ALLISON HAYES (1930–77) Statuesque star of low-grade late-fifties horror films. She's best known for filling up the screen in the enjoyably bad camp classic, *Attack of the 50 Ft. Woman,* a feminist revenge tale—as well as a lustful teenager's erotic fantasy—that continues to win her fans. She had a great snarl, mean eyes, devilish red lips, a haughty expression, and a body she used as a weapon. She came across like an ex-barfly who hustles old men for drinks. The cheaper she seemed, the more class she gave her pictures. She was best at playing villainesses. She looked the part and seemed to take great pleasure playing

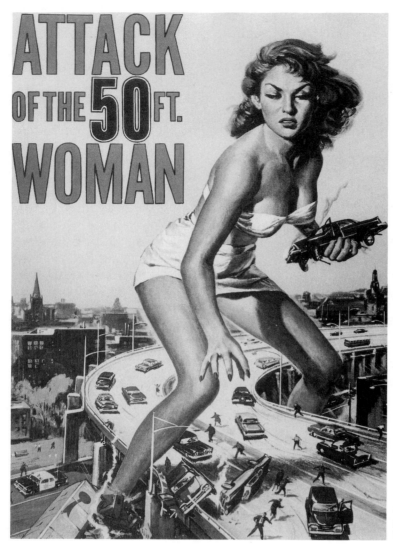

ATTACK OF THE 50 FT. WOMAN

Allison Hayes's biggest part was in Attack of the 50 Ft. Woman.

women who torment men and their lovers.
- **Cult Favorite:** *Attack of the 50 Ft. Woman* (1958, Nathan Juran).
- **Other Key Films:** *The Undead* (1957, Roger Corman), *The Unearthly* (1957, Brooke L. Peters), *The Disembodied* (1957, Walter Grauman), *Zombies of Mora Tau* (1957, Edward L. Cahn), *The Hypnotic Eye* (1960, George Blair), *The Crawling Hand* (1963, Herbert L. Strock).

○

GEORGE "GABBY" HAYES (1885–1969) Beloved, bewhiskered character actor of westerns in the thirties and forties, appearing with such cowboy stars as Ken Maynard, Gary Cooper, Bill Boyd's Hopalong Cassidy, Gene Autry, Roy Rogers, John Wayne, and Wild Bill Elliott. Most often he was the hero's cantankerous sidekick. When the shooting, yodeling, and romancing stopped, he provided the much-needed comedy relief. It seemed that any time a buckboard pulled into town in a quickie western, he was holding the reins, or that anytime the hero and heroine could have used some privacy, he showed up. Although known for low-budget westerns, Hayes appeared in several that were moderately expensive, including Cecil B. De Mille's epic, *The Plainsman*. And sometimes he played it straight and clean-shaven. A significant figure of the movie western.

• **Some Key Films:** *In Old Santa Fe* (1934, David Howard), *The Lost City* (1935 serial, Harry Revier), *The Plainsman* (1936, Cecil B. De Mille), *Hopalong Rides Again* (1938), *Melody Ranch* (1940, Joseph Santley), *Dark Command* (1940, Raoul Walsh), *War of the Wildcats* (1943, Albert S. Rogell), *Tall in the Saddle* (1944, Edwin L. Marin), *My Pal Trigger* (1946, Frank McDonald), *Wyoming* (1947, Joseph Kane), *El Paso* (1949, Lewis R. Foster).

○

RITA HAYWORTH (1918–87) She was, along with Betty Grable, the forties' serviceman's favorite pinup, a ravishing beauty with long, flaming (dyed) red hair, and dancer's legs. Her shapely figure was seen to best advantage in her famous 1941 Bob Landry photograph and in the "Put the Blame on Mame" number in *Gilda* (the film with which she's most identified), when she wore a horse-type harness underneath her black satin Jean-Louis gown. Formerly Margarita Carmen Cansino, who danced professionally with her father (whose relationship with her was far from wholesome), she was a sweet, hardworking, modest young woman whom Hol-

lywood presented as a seductress–love goddess. Her tremendous popularity was, however, indication that viewers detected goodness in the actress-dancer who played the man-killing vamp Doña Sol in *Blood and Sand*, the enticing gypsy in *The Loves of Carmen*, the dancing temptress in *Salome*, the spoiled, pleasure-hungry adultress *Gilda*, and that sinful blonde, *The Lady from Shanghai*. Of course, it helped that she also played likable women in light romances and musicals; she was an enchanting dance partner to Fred Astaire in *You'll Never Get Rich* and *You Were Never Lovelier*, and to Gene Kelly in *Cover Girl*. Following her failed marriage to Orson Welles, she wed Prince Aly Khan, in a fairy-tale love affair that went sour. She then returned to Hollywood and resumed her career. She looked less glamorous, even worn out, but it worked to her advantage because she played a number of fallen women. She was actually sexier then, because she seemed to understand the sexual drives of her women. Her acting was better, even if her pictures weren't. In the eighties, the public was shocked to learn the one-time beauty was being ravaged by Alzheimer's disease. She died in 1987, a sad end to what her biographers insisted was an unhappy life.

• **Cult Favorites:** *Gilda* (1946, Charles Vidor), *The Lady from Shanghai* (1948, Orson Welles).

• **Other Key Films:** *Only Angels Have Wings* (1939, Howard Hawks), *Angels Over Broadway* (1940, Ben Hecht and Lee Garmes), *Blood and Sand* (1940, Rouben Mamoulian), *You'll Never Get Rich* (1941, Sidney Lanfield), *My Gal Sal* (1942, Irving Cummings), *You Were Never Lovelier* (1942, William A. Seiter), *Cover Girl* (1944, Vidor), *The Loves of Carmen* (1948, Vidor), *Affair in Trinidad* (1952, Vincent

In Gilda, *Rita Hayworth heats up the screen while singing "Put the Blame on Mame."*

Sherman), *Salome* (1953, William Dieterle), *Miss Sadie Thompson* (1953, Curtis Bernhardt), *Fire Down Below* (1957, Robert Parrish), *Pal Joey* (1957, George Sidney), *Separate Tables* (1958, Delbert Mann), *They Came to Cordura* (1959, Robert Rossen), *The Story on Page One* (1960, Clifford Odets), *Circus World* (1964, Henry Hathaway).

○

JONATHAN HAZE (1929–) This Pittsburgh-born actor toiled for several years in supporting roles in low-budget science-fiction films and westerns—most directed by Roger Corman and featuring his friend Dick Miller—before securing the only role that would give him fame: Seymour Krelboin, in Corman's black comedy *The Little Shop of Horrors.* His young skid-row plant shop employee, who feeds blood and bodies to a monster plant, courts giddy Audrey (Jackie Joseph), and lives with his hypochondriac mother, is one of the great schlemiels of the screen. He is a Jerry Lewis–like character with a minuscule I.Q., a good heart, a lousy personality, and work habits that drive his boss Gravis Mushnik (Mel Welles) crazy. Haze seems so suited to Seymour that it's a shame that he didn't play any other juvenile numbskulls in his career. In fact, without his silly hat, scarf, and daffy look, it's still hard to recognize him playing it straight in his other films.

• **Cult Favorites:** *East of Eden* (1955, Elia Kazan), *The Little Shop of Horrors* (1960, Roger Corman), *Poor White Trash* (1961, Harold Daniels), *The Terror* (1963, Corman), *X—The Man with the X-Ray Eyes* (1963, Corman), *Heart Like a Wheel* (1982, Jonathan Kaplan).

• **Also of Interest:** *The Monster from the Ocean Floor* (1954, Wyott Ordung), *Five Guns West* (1955, Corman), *Apache Woman* (1955, Corman), *The Day the World Ended* (1956, Corman), *Swamp Women* (1956, Corman), *Gunslinger* (1956, Corman), *The Oklahoma Woman* (1955, Corman), *It Conquered the World* (1956, Corman), *Not of This Earth* (1957, Corman), *Carnival Rock* (1957, Corman), *Viking Women and the Sea Serpent* (1957, Corman), *Stakeout on Dope Street* (1958, Irvin Kershner), *Teenage Caveman* (1958, Corman), *Vice Squad* (1981, Gary Sherman).

○

JOHN HEARD (1946–) It's a shame that this intelligent, talented actor has been wasted in the last few years playing such characters as an FBI agent, a right-wing military officer, a yuppie executive, and a priest. As long as he's going to play irritating individuals, I'd much rather he stay on our side. He thrives as misfits who are at odds with the system, dropouts like Jack Kerouac in *Heart Beat,* survivors of the sixties like his underground newspaper reporter in *Between the Lines,* his angry handicapped Vietnam War vet in *Cutter's Way,* and his romantically obsessed but dead-to-the-rest-of-the-world character in *Chilly Scenes of Winter*—the last three being major cult films of the Woodstock generation. The characters in those films may be off-putting at times, but they are real, holding on to their sixties values, feeling extreme frustration and hostility because things didn't turn out as they had hoped and strived for a decade earlier, and angry because they are being pushed into obsolescence—though they won't go down without a fight. When you watch the bittersweet romantic comedy *Head Over Heels* (which was shortened and re-released three years later as *Chilly Scenes of Winter,* reinstating the title of Ann Beattie's novel on which it was based), you will understand why he lost the woman, Mary Beth Hurt, whom he obsessively tries to win back: he overwhelmed her with his love, his jealousy, his praise. But at the same time, you will come to admire his commitment to her and that he provided her with the love and encouragement she doesn't get in her unfulfilling marriage. In *Cutter's Way,* in which he gave a great performance, you will feel like kicking his cripple down the stairs, because he drinks; he curses, insults, and intentionally embarrasses everyone in sight; makes everyone suffer in his presence (he constantly reminds everyone he is missing an eye, an arm, and a leg); talks nonstop with his raspy voice; has a suicidal bent; and while ignoring his wife, is obsessed with getting back at those fat cats who sent *him* to war to protect *their* concerns. You will think him crazy for going after a rich man he suspects committed a murder that is of no matter to his own life, and for forcing his uninvolved, cowardly friend Jeff Bridges into the pursuit. Yet you will come to admire his romanticism in an age when optimism has been crushed for everyone around him, for his willingness to sacrifice himself for the cause, and for getting Bridges to finally accept moral responsibility.

• **Cult Favorites:** *Between the Lines* (1977, Joan Micklin Silver), *Head Over Heels/Chilly Scenes of Winter* (1979/82, Silver), *Cutter's Way/Cutter and Bone* (1981, Ivan Passer), *Cat People* (1982, Paul Schrader), *After Hours* (1985, Martin Scorsese).

• **Other Key Films:** *On the Yard* (1979, Raphael D. Silver), *Heart Beat* (1980, John Byrum).

• **Also of Interest:** *First Love* (1977, Joan Darling), *Heaven Help Us* (1985, Michael Dinner), *The Trip to Bountiful* (1985, Peter Masterson), *The Milagro Beanfield War* (1988, Robert Redford).

○

TIPPI HEDREN (1935–) Slim, pretty model who briefly became a star when Alfred Hitchcock cast her as his blond heroines in *The Birds* (replacing Vera Miles) and *Marnie* (replacing Grace Kelly). Critics of the day attacked the films and singled out Hedren for abuse, but today both the films and her performances are better appreciated. However, in both cases, it takes a while to warm to Hedren, as she is stiff and remote in the early scenes; but once she becomes softer and more vulnerable, her characters become more sympathetic. While *The Birds* is the better film, *Marnie* is more interesting because it is that rare film which explores the troubled sexual relationship of a married couple. Marnie uses aliases to withdraw from the real world (because of something she doesn't remember from her childhood); she pays back men who molest her with words and lecherous eyes by robbing their safes, committing symbolic rape. Frigid, her excitement comes from riding her male horse.

It's interesting to watch her relationship with new husband Sean Connery, who, also being perverse, falls for her because she is a criminal. We see her change as she gets closer to discovering her own identity by learning about the past; but we almost forget to notice how he changes, too, in order to gain her trust. Still, they don't exactly end up living happily ever after—there isn't even a kiss. Hedren is the mother of Melanie Griffith, who despises Hitchcock for the way he treated Hedren.

• **Cult Favorites:** *The Birds* (1963, Alfred Hitchcock), *Marnie* (1964, Hitchcock).

• **Also of Interest:** *A Countess from Hong Kong* (1967, Charles Chaplin), *The Harrad Experiment* (1973, Ted Post).

○

BRIGITTE HELM (1906–) Blond, blue-eyed German actress was still a teenager when Fritz Lang cast her in *Metropolis*. She was captivating as both the angelic Maria and her evil android double, one trying to protect the workers of the futuristic city and the other trying to destroy them. The robot Maria's tantalizing bare-chested dance at a nightclub remains one of the most erotic scenes in cinema history. Helm would become a major leading lady in Germany in the late twenties and early thirties, playing innocent young women as well as self-destructive vamps. As in *Metropolis*, the duality of her psyche was explored in several of her siren roles, and viewers wondered how women with such beauty could have such empty hearts. For instance in *Alraune*, one of several science-fiction films she made, she played a test-tube creation, a lovely woman without a soul (presumably because she carries the genes of a prostitute mother and criminal father). In fact, Helm did have a soul, and when Hitler came to power, she and her Jewish husband fled to Paris.

• **Cult Favorite:** *Metropolis* (1926, Fritz Lang).

• **Other Key Films:** *Loves of Jeanne Ney* (1927, G. W. Pabst), *At the Edge of the World* (1927, Karl Grune), *Alraune/Unholy Love* (1928, Henrik Galeen), *Crisis* (1928, Pabst), *The Wonderful Lie of Nina Petrovna* (1929, Hans Schwarz), *Alraune* (1930, Richard Oswald), *L'Atlantide* (1932, Pabst), *Gold* (1934, Karl Hartl).

○

PERCY HELTON (1894–1971) Short, round-faced, high-voiced, white-haired, balding character actor, seen in many movies and television shows. One is tempted to say he was a poor man's version of some actor, but he wasn't really like anybody, although he could probably pass as Wallace Shawn's uncle. A court jester in *Diane*, he usually played eccentrics and weasels. He was perfect at projecting cheery innocence, and then turning out to be a rat. For instance, on shows like *The Lone Ranger*, he'd play a respected citizen (a bank owner or town mayor) who expresses great concern about a rash of robberies; at the end, it turned out that he, the least suspected man in town (although we didn't trust his grin, his voice, or his strange breathing pattern), was the mastermind behind the crimes. One of my favorites, he was rarely listed in the opening credits, so his brief appearances were usually wonderful surprises.

• **Cult Favorites:** *Miracle on 34th Street* (1947, George Seaton), *A Star Is Born* (1954, George Cukor), *Kiss Me Deadly* (1955, Robert Aldrich), *Head* (1968, Bob Rafelson).

• **Also of Interest:** *Larceny* (1948, George Sherman), *Criss Cross* (1949, Robert Siodmak), *The Set-Up* (1949, Robert Wise), *My Friend Irma* (1949, George Marshall), *Copper Canyon* (1950, John Farrow), *Cyrano de Bergerac* (1950, Michael Gordon), *Call Me Madam* (1953, Walter Lang), *Scared Stiff* (1953, Marshall), *How to Marry a Millionaire* (1953, Jean Negulesco), *Wicked Woman* (1954, Russell Rouse), *20,000 Leagues Under the Sea* (1954, Richard Fleischer), *Hush . . . Hush, Sweet Charlotte* (1965, Robert Aldrich), *Butch Cassidy and the Sundance Kid* (1969, George Roy Hill).

○

BARBARA HERSHEY (1948–) Those who didn't get a crush on her when she was a teenager on the mid-sixties TV western series "The Monroes," as I did, were hooked by the early seventies, after she'd made a few films, starting with the teenage coming-of-age film *Last Summer,* in which she lay on the beach in a fetching bikini. She was beautiful, with long black hair, exceptional bone structure, exciting eyes, and a large chest. The image she projected on- and offscreen was that of a flighty free spirit, eager to experiment in sex and life. Probably the role that we thought was closest to her real self was the miniskirted hippie who becomes a surrogate mother in *The Baby Maker.* A rebel, she made anti-establishment films. In real life, she married another Hollywood renegade, David Carradine, with whom she had a much-publicized lovemaking scene in *Boxcar Bertha.* They had a child they named Free. She swore the spirit of a seagull entered her and changed her name to Barbara Seagull; when she dropped the Seagull from her billing, it marked the time when

Barbara Hershey and David Carradine in Martin Scorsese's Boxcar Bertha.

she became committed to being accepted in Hollywood and really began to take her work seriously. Her key role in Woody Allen's *Hannah and Her Sisters,* having an affair with her sister Mia Farrow's husband (Michael Caine) while trying to slip out of a destructive relationship with her Svengali-like mentor (Max von Sydow), finally won her the respect of the industry and made her a hot property. To her credit, she continued to search for chancy, adventurous projects. *The Entity,* about a real-life woman who is repeatedly attacked by what she says is an invisible entity, was a silly, mediocre fright film, yet Hershey gave her first great performance (shown in penetrating close-ups), creating a woman who is vulnerable and fearful, yet ultimately strong, confidant, and forceful enough to take responsibility for her own future. She would again play such women in *Shy People,* as a swamp woman; *A World Apart,* as a real-life, politically dedicated writer in South Africa (roles that won her back-to-back Best Actress citations at Cannes); and, to a lesser degree, *The Last Temptation of Christ,* as Mary Magdalene. Past 40, as beautiful as ever (and without the baby fat she had in her early seventies films), with her talent expanding, and unusual, *important* roles being offered, she will likely be one of the most celebrated actresses of the 1990s, popular with cultists as well as the mass audience.

• **Cult Favorites:** *Dealing* (1972, Paul Williams), *Boxcar Bertha* (1972, Martin Scorsese), *The Stunt Man* (1980, Richard Rush), *The Right Stuff* (1983, Philip Kaufman), *The Natural* (1984, Barry Levinson), *A World Apart* (1988, Chris Menges), *The Last Temptation of Christ* (1988, Scorsese).

• **Other Key Films:** *Last Summer* (1969, Frank Perry), *The Baby Maker* (1970, James Bridges), *The Entity* (1983, Sidney J. Furie), *Hannah and Her Sisters* (1986, Woody Allen), *Hoosiers* (1986, David Anspaugh), *Shy People* (1987, Andrei Konchalovsky).

• **Also of Interest:** *The Liberation of L. B. Jones* (1970, William Wyler), *The Pursuit of Happiness* (1971, Robert Mulligan), *Diamonds* (1975, Menahem Golan), *Americana* (1981, David Carradine), *Beaches* (1989, Garry Marshall), *Tune in Tomorrow* (1990, Jon Amiel).

○

JEAN HILL John Waters cast this outrageous, obese personality as insane Mink Stole's 400-pound black maid in *Desperate Living.* She achieved screen glory by sitting on Stole's husband's face and smothering him to death. Later she and Stole must give a policeman their panties and wet soul kisses—and, yes, it's hard to watch her as she arouses the pervert. Hill reminds me of enormous women who try to sit down in a tiny adjoining seat on the bus. In a 1989 issue of *Film Threat,* an entire interview was devoted to Hill's cheerful recollections about being arrested for shoplifting.

• **Cult Favorite:** *Desperate Living* (1977, John Waters).

○

TERENCE HILL (1941–) Handsome, blond, blue-eyed Italian actor of German descent, he began his career using his real name, Mario Giroti, but became an international box-office star as Terence Hill in a string of comedy-laced spaghetti westerns and action films. Often his costar and comic partner was the hefty Bud Spencer; they were equally brutal, but Hill had more finesse. His major role was as a western hero named Trinity, a character he played several times. Like all spaghetti-western heroes, he is lightning quick on the draw and always accurate with his shooting. But he doesn't have the mythical implications of Sergio Leone's better-known characters, and he is lazy, carefree, unbathed, un-shaven, and disheveled, often not bothering to wear a shirt to cover his ripped red underwear. He doesn't worry too much about any grave situation in which he finds himself—he'll be sheepishly smiling, his blue eyes twinkling, before and after killing a few bad guys in a creatively comical manner. Leone, as a producer, would cast Hill as a similar character (but make him part of western movie mythology) in the spoof *My Name Is Nobody,* as a young "unknown" who is capable of filling the void that will exist once Henry Fonda's aged, legendary gunfighter fades into memory. In truth, Hill's characters get on my nerves as much as on those of the characters who meet up with him, including his partner Spencer. Hill, who looks like a cheerful Terence Stamp, is incapable of revealing or even suggesting any subtleties in Trinity or the others. Also, while viewers may laugh while watching Hill, the screenwriters, directors, and Bud Spencer were more responsible for the laughter. Hill just followed direction, adding nothing but his sheepish grin. This is even more evident in the slapstick scenes in his modern-era films.

• **Cult Favorites:** *They Call Me Trinity* (1971, E. B. Clucher/Enzo Barboni), *Trinity Is Still My Name* (1972, Clucher), *My Name Is Nobody* (1974, Tonino Valerii).

• **Other Key Films:** *God Forgives . . . I Don't* (1969, Giuseppe Colizzi), *Ace High* (1969, Colizzi), *Boot Hill* (1969, Colizzi), *Trinity Sees Red* (1972, Mario Camus), *All the Way, Boys* (1973, Colizzi), *Mr. Billion* (1977, Jonathan Kaplan), *Two Supercops/ Crime Busters* (1980, Clucher), *Super Fuzz* (1981, Sergio Corbucci).

○

CANDACE HILLIGOSS Slim, blond, little-known New York stage actress who went to Lawrence, Kansas, to star in Herk Harvey's $30,000, surprisingly effective horror film, *Carnival of Souls,* which has gained increased attention recently after being almost everyone's "private" discovery over the years. The film succeeds more because of Harvey's haunting direction than Hilligoss's performance, but her character is quite interesting. Mary Henry is the lone survivor when a car plunges into a river. Three hours later she emerges from the water and tries to continue her life, only to be pursued by a spooky, cadaverous man (Harvey), lose her hearing on occasion, and find herself at a carnival pavilion watching a dance of ghouls. Mary has always been such a passive, uninvolved (soulless) character—she has no religious convictions, no interest in men, no desire for friendship—that she never was really alive. That's why she can't recognize her own death. Mary is "living" proof that Don Siegel's warning in *Invasion of the Body Snatchers* had merit: we are turning into pod people. Hilligoss went to Stamford, Connecticut, to take a smaller role in Del Tenney's *Curse of the Living Corpse,* Roy Scheider's first film. But she turned down Tenney's *Psychomania* because it required a nude scene, and wouldn't make another film until after *Carnival of Souls* was revived.

• **Cult Favorite:** *Carnival of Souls* (1963, Herk Harvey).
• **Other Key Film:** *Curse of the Living Corpse* (1964, Del Tenney).

○

DAISY AND VIOLET HILTON (1908–69) I tracked down the birth and death dates for each of the sisters before deducing that since they were Siamese twins it was highly likely that those dates would be identical for the two. The twins (I don't remember who was on the right and who was on the left)

were among the less shocking stars of Tod Browning's notorious, long-banned *Freaks.* Browning wanted his carnival sideshow acts to prove that they had real talents and weren't on screen only because of their unusual looks, and the Hilton sisters did him proud as actresses. They even took part in the film's suggestive humor. They each have a man (one husband, one fiancé), and we are made to wonder about their sleeping arrangements. An amusing moment occurs when one of the sisters is kissed on the lips and we see that her twin is enjoying the sensation. The Hilton sisters finally got their own starring vehicle, though it took them 18 years. In the weird exploitation film *Chained for Life,* they play singers in a revue. Violet, as Vivian, goes on trial for killing a gigolo after he dumped sister Dorothy. The picture is dull, but there are a few fascinating moments, including Dorothy fantasizing she is a normal woman (with no attached sister) and dancing with a man (a stand-in doubles for her), Dorothy and Vivian discussing their misery about never being able to be alone with a man, and the twins looking into the possibility of an operation that would separate them.

• **Cult Favorites:** *Freaks* (1932, Tod Browning), *Chained for Life* (1950, Harry L. Fraser).

○

PETER HINWOOD Blond, well-built former photographer and model who found cultdom as Rocky Horror, Dr. Frank-N-Furter's creation and captive lover in *The Rocky Horror Picture Show.* He is treated as a sex object by both the mad doctor and the loopy filmmakers, and undergoes humiliation, torture, and death during one wild night. At least he gets to make love to

Janet, played by Susan Sarandon.

• **Cult Favorite:** *The Rocky Horror Picture Show* (1975, Jim Sharman).

○

JOHN HOLMES (1944–88) A legendary porno actor whose enormous penis, estimated between 11″ and 15″ long when erect, got him starring roles in more than 2,000 loops, stag films, and features in a 20-year career (with a peak $3,000-a-day salary). His lucrative offscreen penis-for-hire business took him all over the world. He would have made even more films, but he dropped out temporarily when his drug addiction kept him from getting an erection. He made money delivering drugs and later was tried for participating in the Laurel Canyon murders. He beat the murder rap but spent time in jail on burglary and contempt-of-court charges. While a cloud still hung over his head, he returned to porno acting. Tall and slim, with light, curly hair, he looked like Ken Osmond (Eddie Haskell on "Leave It to Beaver") with a mustache. He was a terrible, passive actor, but as a lover he was impressive—experienced, dominant, and uninhibited, with the biggest attraction in the business. His most famous character was Long Johnny Wadd, a lusty, always-on-the-make detective he played in several crude porno films like *China Cat, Liquid Lips,* and the best of the lot, *Blonde Fire.* Better were those bigger-budget pictures that costarred some of porno's top leading ladies, including Marilyn Chambers, Seka, Annette Haven, and young Traci Lords. Holmes had the rare distinction of having screen sex with two generations of porno queens, though in later years, some of his appearances were no more than cameos. His last film was *The Rise and Fall of the Roman Empress,* starring the infamous Italian Parliament member, Ilona "Ciccolina" Staller. He claimed to have had sex with 14,000 women (he also made a few gay films), so his AIDS-related death must have terrified many people.

• **Cult Favorites:** *The Erotic Adventures of Candy* (1978, Gail Palmer), *Insatiable* (1980, Godfrey Daniels).

• **Other Key Films:** *Autobiography of a Flea* (1976, Sharon McKnight), *Liquid Lips* (1976, Bob Chinn), *Hard Soap, Hard Soap* (1977, Chinn), *China Cat* (1978, Chinn), *Eruption* (1978, Stanley Kurlan), *Blonde Fire* (1979, Chinn), *Sweet Captive* (1979, Leoni Vallentino), *Prisoner of Paradise* (1980, Palmer and Chin), *Exhausted* (1981, Julia St. Vincent).

○

DARLA HOOD (1931–79) As a 4-year-old, with dark hair, a cherubic, healthy-looking face, rosy cheeks and a cheery smile, she broke the sex barrier by joining Our Gang in 1935. Actually, she remained on the outside of the all-male club (though she was an occasional secretary and telephone operator), too civilized and goody-goody to pal around with Spanky, Alfalfa, Buckwheat, and the rest, but not so snobby that she didn't enjoy their company, particularly the romantic Alfalfa's. Initially, both Spanky and Alfalfa courted her—while they competed, she went off with some other kid—but soon she was exclusively Alfalfa's love interest as Spanky and the others became proud "woman haters." Many shorts were devoted to Alfalfa trying to win Darla by serenading her (off-key), sending her flowers, writing her poetry, acting, or fighting off the bully who was the cowardly boy's romantic rival. Darla usually just allowed Alfalfa to make a fool of himself in order to win her heart; she was also fickle. She did serve another purpose in the shorts: she was a believable witness for the gang members when they were accused of some wrongdoing actually committed by someone else. Darla stayed with the series until she was 14 and then retired. Because of the "Little Rascals" shows on television, she continues to be the first crush of many preschoolers.

• **Cult Favorites:** About 150 "Our Gang" comedies (1935–45).

• **Also of Interest:** *The Bohemian Girl* (1936, James W. Horne and Charles R. Rogers).

○

DENNIS HOPPER (1936–) The one-time bad boy of the American cinema. He was a friend of James Dean and supported him in *Rebel Without a Cause* and, in a bigger part, *Giant*. Offscreen and on the set, Hopper was the moody, sensitive, explosive rebel that Dean projected on screen. He bedded scores of starlets and argued with directors, producers, and studio heads. He had trouble finding pivotal roles outside westerns and the occasional fantasy-horror film; he starred in the interesting experimental fantasy *Night Tide*. So in 1969, he and Peter Fonda joined forces and made their own movie, the breakthrough "youth film" *Easy Rider,* with Hopper directing and both working on the script. Hopper's long-haired, constantly stoned motorcyclist looked like a plump David Crosby (whom he was inspired by), couldn't say anything coherent (he'd end every phrase with "man"), was apolitical, and dealt drugs—yet for some reason he became a hero to many dropouts in the counterculture. His character got on my nerves when the film was first

Dennis Hopper in an uncharacteristic role in The Story of Mankind.

released; today, I can tolerate it because Hopper seemed to be playing him with tongue in cheek (Hopper can be quite funny). Hopper dropped out of films for a while, and became an alcoholic and drug abuser. He came back clean and fulfilled the promise of his youth, turning in several fascinating, high-powered performances in America and abroad, from his seedy criminal in *The American Friend,* who, angry at being slighted by a man (Bruno Ganz), manipulates him into committing murder, to his vile criminal in *Blue Velvet*. His spacy, moody, laughing-as-they-talk characters—emotional, violent, antisocial, ravaged, once-brilliant men—live on the fringes of society. They are outcasts who have gone over the edge due to alcohol, drugs, and/or madness, and are terrifyingly out-of-control. Some are weak and to be pitied, like his alcoholic assistant basketball coach in *Hoosiers*. Some are to be avoided because they are dangerously demented, like his murderous kook in *River's Edge*. Some are detestable, like his soulless sadist in *Blue Velvet*. Many are just plain repulsive—again I think of his characters in *River's Edge* and *Blue Velvet,* as well as his ex-biker in *Out of the Blue*. Hopper does things on screen that other actors would shy away from; then again, it's hard to see anyone else playing his grotesque characters with such conviction. There has been, most definitely, method to his madness.

• **Cult Favorites:** *Rebel Without a Cause* (1955, Nicholas Ray), *Giant* (1956, George Stevens), *Night Tide* (1963, Curtis Harrington), *Cool Hand Luke* (1967, Stuart Rosenberg), *Easy Rider* (1969, Dennis Hopper), *The American Friend* (1977, Wim Wenders), *Apocalypse Now* (1979, Francis Coppola), *Rumble Fish* (1979, Coppola), *Blue Velvet* (1986, David Lynch), *River's Edge* (1986, Tim Hunter).

• **Sleeper:** *Mad Dog Morgan* (1976, Philippe Mora).

• **Other Key Films:** *Queen of Blood/Planet of Blood* (1966, Harrington), *Kid Blue* (1973, James Frawley), *Tracks* (1979, Henry Jaglom), *Out of the Blue* (1980, Hopper), *Hoosiers* (1986, David Anspaugh), *Riders of the Storm* (1988, Maurice Phillips).

○

EDWARD EVERETT HORTON (1886–1970) He starred in low-budget comedies dating back to the silent era, but is best known for his character parts in Lubitsch farces, Astaire-Rogers musicals, and other classy pictures of the thirties and forties, as well as the camp classic musical *The Gang's All Here*. He was funny as nervous, flustered, foppish Milquetoasts, hypochrondriacs, suitors, confidants, and fussbudgets. His face, wrote critic William S. Pechter, was a "marvelous mask of comic incompetence." He always tried to help correct a ridiculous situation, usually involving several people in romantic entanglement ("Oh, dear!" would be his weak comment), and rushed about as if he had just learned his wife had given birth to sextuplets (in *Design for Living,* he realizes his wife Miriam Hopkins loves two other men). He was best cast as the Mad Hatter in *Alice in Wonderland*.

• **Cult Favorites:** *Trouble in Paradise* (1932, Ernst Lubitsch), *The Gay Divorcée* (1934, Mark Sandrich), *The Devil Is a Woman* (1935, Josef von Sternberg), *Top Hat* (1935, Sandrich), *The Gang's All Here* (1943, Busby Berkeley), *The Story of Mankind* (1957, Irwin Allen), *It's a Mad Mad Mad Mad World* (1963, Stanley Kramer), *Cold Turkey* (1971, Norman Lear).

• **Other Key Films:** *Holiday* (1930, Edward H. Griffith), *The Front Page* (1931, Lewis Milestone), *Design for Living* (1933, Lubitsch), *Alice in Wonderland* (1933, Norman Z. McLeod), *The Merry Widow* (1934, Lubitsch), *Lost Horizon* (1937, Frank Capra), *Shall We Dance* (1937, Sandrich), *Bluebeard's Eighth Wife* (1938, Lubitsch), *Holiday* (1938, George Cukor), *Here Comes Mr. Jordan* (1941, Alexander

Hall), *Arsenic and Old Lace* (1944, Capra), *Pocketful of Miracles* (1961, Capra).

○

BOB HOSKINS (1942–) Short, clunky, round-headed English actor, an intriguing combination of Edward Brophy, Edward G. Robinson, Joe E. Ross's Officer Toody on "Car 54, Where Are You?," and a ferocious bulldog. An untrained actor (I believe he was a tailor's assistant), he is a dynamo on camera, full of energy, power, and natural talent, demanding one's attention and getting it. He is always a treat to watch, but I particularly like when he gets anxious, complains, becomes sarcastic, grimaces, literally spits out words, and asks whoever is around him to explain some new, absurd situation that is causing havoc in his life. He often repeats with incredulity the explanation given him. Because of his looks, his amusing cockney delivery, and crude working-class manner, one would think him ideal as a character actor, but he has truly excelled as offbeat leading men, usually jinxed, uneducated characters. He can be sweet, like a cuddly teddy bear, or quite vicious, as he proved as a gangster leader in *The Long Good Friday.* Although he gave a marvelous performance as the ill-fated sheet-music salesman in the splendid British miniseries *Pennies from Heaven,* and was terrific playing a wide variety of characters in a number of movies, it was his riveting British gangster that really got him attention. He would later get raves in *Mona Lisa,* as a former small-time hood who becomes a driver for black call girl Cathy Tyson, and gets caught up in her troubles. Then came his forties private eye, the lead human actor, in the live-action/animation block-buster *Who Framed Roger Rabbit,* the role that brought him at least temporary popular fame. However, I thought that was one of his dreariest parts; I prefer when his characters burst out, whether dramatically or comedically. A great actor, who invariably comes up with a novel approach to his characters.

• **Cult Favorites:** *Inserts* (1976, John Byrum), *Pink Floyd—The Wall/The Wall* (1982, Alan Parker), *Brazil* (1985, Terry Gilliam).

• **Sleepers:** *The Long Good Friday* (1980, John Mackenzie), *Beyond the Limit* (1983, Mackenzie), *Mona Lisa* (1986, Neil Jordan), *The Lonely Passion of Judith Hearne* (1987, Peter Nelson).

• **Also Recommended:** *Who Framed Roger Rabbit* (1988, Robert Zemeckis).

• **Also of Interest:** *The Cotton Club* (1984, Francis Coppola), *Sweet Liberty* (1986, Alan Alda), *Mermaids* (1990, Richard Benjamin).

○

JOHN HOYT (1905–) Stern-looking American character actor with gray (later white) hair; he spent several decades playing unlikable, humorless, imperious authority figures, including Nazis and mad scientists. He was a pleasure to hiss. His most memorable role is as millionaire industrialist Sydney Stanton in George Pal's *When Worlds Collide,* a selfish wretch who finances an enormous space ark so he can be one of the passengers that flees earth before it is destroyed. Stanton is in the tradition of wheelchair-bound egotistical cads in science-fiction films, anticipating Dr. Strangelove. Like Peter Sellers's evil madman, Stanton rises to his feet as the earth's destruction begins; like Strangelove, who had plans of fleeing to a mineshaft, he will not escape death.

- **Cult Favorites:** *The Big Combo* (1955, Joseph H. Lewis), *The Blackboard Jungle* (1955, Richard Brooks), *The Conqueror* (1956, Dick Powell), *Merrill's Marauders* (1962, Sam Fuller), *X—The Man with the X-Ray Eyes* (1963, Roger Corman), *Flesh Gordon* (1972, Howard Ziehm and Michael Benveniste).
- **Other Key Films:** *When Worlds Collide* (1951, Rudolph Maté), *The Lost Continent* (1951, Samuel Newfield), *Attack of the Puppet People* (1958, Bert I. Gordon), *Spartacus* (1960, Stanley Kubrick), *The Time Travelers* (1964, Ib Melchior).
- **Also of Interest:** *My Favorite Brunette* (1947, Elliott Nugent), *Androcles and the Lion* (1952, Chester Erskine), *Casanova's Big Night* (1954, Norman Z. McLeod), *Trial* (1955, Mark Robson), *Death of a Scoundrel* (1956, Charles Martin), *Cleopatra* (1963, Joseph L. Mankiewicz).

○

SEASON HUBLEY (1951–) She made a good first impression in a bad, brutal film, *Lolly Madonna XXX*, playing an innocent (but sexy) girl who is the central figure in a bloody feud between two backwoods families. She made a better second impression a few years later on television, guest-starring in several episodes of "Family," giving a sincere, sensitive performance as a young unwed mother. Then, wearing a wig that probably weighed twenty pounds, she was passable-looking and sympathetic as a young Priscilla Presley in John Carpenter's hit TV movie, *Elvis—the Movie*, opposite a dynamic Kurt Russell. She was married to Russell for a time and had a cameo in his first feature for Carpenter, *Escape to New York*. Back in theatrical movies, she was the best thing in *Hard-core*, playing a sassy young hooker who helps Calvinist George C. Scott track down and rescue (from a pimp) his runaway daughter, only to find herself discarded when he gets his real child back. She was so convincing as an uninhibited prostitute that she was typecast from then on. She was a streetwalker who helps police trap the psychotic pimp Wings Hauser in *Vice Squad*, being terrorized and tortured in the sleazy film, but giving a better performance (as did Hauser) than the script deserved. And she was wasted as still another hooker in *Prettykill*, in love with cop David Birney. She looked bored, perhaps wondering if anyone would remember the varied parts she had skillfully played early in her career.

- **Key Films:** *Lolly Madonna XXX/The Lolly-Madonna War* (1973, Richard C. Sarafian), *Hardcore* (1979, Paul Schrader), *Vice Squad* (1982, Gary A. Sherman).
- **Also of Interest:** *Catch My Soul* (1974, Patrick McGoohan), *Prettykill* (1987, George Kaczender).

○

ROCK HUDSON (1925–85) When Rock Hudson's homosexuality came to light prior to his AIDS-related death in 1985, everyone realized the irony of his being the fifties' most masculine romantic lead, and in that era of rebels like Clift, Brando, Dean, and Newman, a representative of the American ideal. Hudson played well-groomed, polite, nonneurotic, unrebellious men who want to get married and have a stable family life. He was pretty bad in action and adventure films, but was well suited to those contemporary soap-melodramas directed by Douglas Sirk, who believed the perfect-looking, tall-dark-handsome actor

Rock Hudson visits Ozzie, Harriet, David, and Ricky in Here Come the Nelsons.

fit the artificial, dreamlike Hollywood-style America he was trying to create in his films. He also was the first director to realize that Hudson's appeal was based less on strength than on gentleness, sensitivity, and flaws. Hudson gave the best performance of his career as an angry, alcoholic reporter in *The Tarnished Angels,* Sirk's turbulent version of Faulkner's *Pylon.* Beginning with *Pillow Talk* in 1959, Hudson starred in battle-of-the-sexes bedroom farces with Doris Day and others, returning to the cocky playboy he was (before reforming) at the beginning of Sirk's *Magnificent Obsession.* "He had once symbolized simplicity and earthy independence; now he was worldly-wise and manipulative," wrote Michael Stern in *Close-Ups.* "The gentleness that graced his rugged nature in *All That Heaven Allows* turned to quiet cunning and charm." Hudson was amusing in the Day vehicles, but he was genuinely funny parodying his new image in Howard Hawks's *Man's Favorite Sport?,* pretending to be an expert fisherman while being hooked by Paula Prentiss. Two years later, in the science-fiction drama *Seconds,* Hudson starred in his most challenging role, as an old man who gets to start his life over, with a new identity and a young, healthy, handsome body. "There is a profound sadness in Hudson's performance," observed Hudson authority Henry Blinder. "His homosexuality was an open secret in the industry at the time, but it was still extremely difficult for him to perpetrate the lie to his public. During the party scene, in which the drunk [character] makes a desperate plea for the right to his own identity, reality came crashing down on Hudson . . . He lost control and openly wept."

• **Cult Favorites:** *Winchester '73* (1950, Anthony Mann), *Bend of the River* (1952,

Mann), *Magnificent Obsession* (1954, Douglas Sirk), *Giant* (1956, George Stevens), *Written on the Wind* (1956, Sirk), *The Tarnished Angels* (1957, Sirk), *Pillow Talk* (1959, Michael Gordon), *Man's Favorite Sport?* (1964, Howard Hawks), *Seconds* (1966, John Frankenheimer).

• **Sleepers:** *All That Heaven Allows* (1955, Sirk), *Darling Lili* (1970, Blake Edwards).

• **Also of Interest:** *Has Anybody Seen My Gal?* (1952, Sirk), *Scarlet Angel* (1952, Sidney Salkow), *Horizons West* (1952, Budd Boetticher), *The Lawless Breed* (1952, Raoul Walsh), *Seminole* (1953, Boetticher), *Gun Fury* (1953, Walsh), *Battle Hymn* (1956, Sirk), *Something of Value* (1957, Richard Brooks), *A Farewell to Arms* (1957, Charles Vidor), *The Last Sunset* (1961, Robert Aldrich), *Come September* (1961, Robert Mulligan), *Lover, Come Back* (1961, William A. Seiter), *The Spiral Road* (1962, Mulligan), *A Gathering of Eagles* (1963, Delbert Mann), *Blindfold* (1966, Philip Dunne).

○

ARTHUR HUNNICUTT (1911–79) Scene-stealing character actor, with a thick Arkansas accent, usually some whiskers, and an "authentic American face," appeared mostly in westerns in his 35-year career. He often played colorful backwoods or mountain men, characters who grew up with rifles and hunting dogs, have done some trapping, Indian fighting, and gold digging, and have minded their own business. They are independent, opinionated, wise, and chatty, full of advice and tall tales. They drop the first-person pronoun when they begin sentences. Among his most memorable roles are his grizzled fur trapper in *The Big Sky*, cheerful Davy Crockett in *The Last Command,* northern soldier in Audie Murphy's platoon in *The Red Badge of Courage,* and cantankerous old-timer who teams up with John Wayne, Robert Mitchum, and James Caan in *El Dorado.* On television, in a classic "Twilight Zone" episode, his dead hunter refuses to enter "heaven" because it won't allow his dead hunting dog to come in with him; as it turns out, it was hell that he rejected.

• **Cult Favorites:** *The Red Badge of Courage* (1951, John Huston), *El Dorado* (1967, Howard Hawks).

• **Sleepers:** *Stars in My Crown* (1950, Jacques Tourneur), *The Last Command* (1955, Frank Lloyd).

• **Also Recommended:** *Border Incident* (1949, Anthony Mann), *Broken Arrow* (1950, Delmer Daves), *The Big Sky* (1952, Hawks), *The Lusty Men* (1952, Nicholas Ray).

• **Also of Interest:** *Pinky* (1949, Elia Kazan), *Two Flags West* (1950, Robert Wise), *Distant Drums* (1951, Raoul Walsh), *Sugarfoot* (1951, Edwin L. Marin), *Split Second* (1953, Dick Powell), *Devil's Canyon* (1953, Alfred L. Werker), *The Adventures of Bullwhip Griffin* (1967, James Neilson), *Harry and Tonto* (1974, Paul Mazursky).

○

TAB HUNTER (1931–) Tall, blond "pretty boy" who tried to create a rugged movie image by appearing in westerns, war movies, and heated melodramas—and playing a baseball hero in *Damn Yankees.* While critics and other adults weren't impressed, he became an idol of teenagers. (His popularity was also the result of his record "Young Love," which was simultaneously number one for Sonny James). The kids grew up and Hunter faded from sight; his name itself was the principle ingredient in his camp legacy (as with Troy Donahue). He was in the R-rated *The Accusers* in 1973, playing an impotent Romeo who kills women. John Waters brought him back in his disappointing *Polyester,* having him play Todd Tomorrow, the owner of a drive-in that shows art films (including a Marguerite Duras triple feature), and lover of Divine's Francine Fishpaw. It was quite jolting watching Tab and Divine smooch on screen. It was good to see Hunter again, but he reminded us of how bland he had been when he was a star. He never really hurt a film, but he never helped it, either. He and Divine would again join forces and sink together in the dreary western parody, *Lust in the Dust.*

• **Cult Favorites:** *The Loved One* (1965, Tony Richardson), *Polyester* (1981, John Waters).

• **Other Key Films:** *Track of the Cat* (1954, William Wellman), *Battle Cry* (1955, Raoul Walsh), *The Burning Hills* (1956, Stuart Heisler), *Lafayette Escadrille* (1958, Wellman), *Gunman's Walk* (1958, Phil Karlson), *Damn Yankees* (1958, George Abbott and Stanley Donen), *Ride the Wild Surf* (1964, Don Taylor), *War Gods of the Deep* (1965, Jacques Tourneur), *The Arousers* (1973, Curtis Hanson), *Lust in the Dust* (1985, Paul Bartel).

○

JOHN HURT (1940–) Intelligent, slender British actor with a moderately handsome, well-lined face and the precise diction and grand delivery of a serious stage actor; he gravitates toward offbeat lead and supporting roles, alternately dazzling us and hamming it up embarrassingly. Sometimes his intellectual approach to characters is wasted in the films (or on his particular character). He always seems to be deep in thought, often concentrating on sex (his characters' sexual natures are often thematically central to Hurt's films). He specializes in effeminate characters, superior-acting decadent men, sadistic killers, and victims. Almost invariably his characters suffer tragic endings. For instance, he dies in *Alien* when a creature bursts out of his stomach; his Winston Smith in the sadly neglected *1984* is tortured and brainwashed; his deformed *Elephant Man* John Merrick suffers humiliation and finally chokes to death as he sleeps; in *Scandal,* his Stephen Ward descends from being a pal of political giants to a broken, friendless, suicidal man. His unsympathetic characters have similar sorry fates. He made his first major impression on American audiences as Caligula in the PBS miniseries, *I, Claudius,* definitely one of his tour-de-force performances.

• **Cult Favorites:** *The Shout* (1978, Jerzy Skolimowski), *Midnight Express* (1978, Alan Parker), *Alien* (1979, Ridley Scott), *The Hit* (1984, Stephen Frears).

• **Sleeper:** *1984* (1984, Michael Radford).

• **Other Key Films:** *A Man for All Seasons* (1966, Fred Zinnemann), *10 Rillington Place* (1971, Richard Fleischer), *Forbush and the Penguins/Cry of the Penguins* (1971, Roy Boulting and Arne Sucksdorff), *Heaven's Gate* (1980, Michael Cimino), *The Elephant Man* (1980, David Lynch), *White Mischief* (1988, Radford), *Scandal* (1989, Michael Caton-Jones).

○

MARY BETH HURT (1948–) Alternately sunny-faced and down in the dumps, pretty and mousy, this talented blonde with short hair and glasses has gravitated toward the offbeat in both film and character selections. She was most appealing in romantic leads opposite John Heard in *Chilly Scenes of Winter*—you understand why he falls for her immediately—and Robin Williams, as his tender, loving, unfaithful wife in *The World According to Garp*. But being appealing wasn't a concern when she played Randy Quaid's cannibal wife in *Parents,* and Susan Sarandon's snoopy, weird-dressing, plant-castrating neighbor in *Compromising Positions*. And she didn't go for glamour or sympathy as one of the angry, depressed sisters in Woody Allen's ultradramatic, Bergmanesque *Interiors*. In that film, Maureen Stapleton, the new stepmother she has rejected, rescues her from the ocean and gives her mouth-to-mouth resuscitation, giving her life as surely as her first mother did—one of the cinema's most emotional moments. Hurt's

fans most respond to her interesting portrayal in *Chilly Scenes*. She played a smart, funny, adorable but self-deprecating young woman who is torn between a husband who loves her too little and a man who loves her too much. She judges herself in the context of the two men in her life. Only when she is alone at the end, rejecting both, does she establish her own identity.

• **Cult Favorites:** *Interiors* (1978, Woody Allen), *Head Over Heels/Chilly Scenes of Winter* (1979/82, Joan Micklin Silver), *The World According to Garp* (1982, George Roy Hill), *Parents* (1989, Bob Balaban).

• **Also of Interest:** *Compromising Positions* (1985, Frank Perry), *D.A.R.Y.L.* (1985, Simon Wincer).

○

REX INGRAM (1895–1969) Tall, silver-haired, vocally and physically impressive black

Rex Ingram's djinni carries Sabu on his ear in The Thief of Bagdad.

actor, often compared to Paul Robeson because of his intellectual background, athletic build, theatrical experience, booming voice, and the stature of his key roles. Ingram played the wise and kind "De Lawd" in Marc Connelly's heaven-set, all-black dramatic fable, *The Green Pastures,* and the devil who wants the soul of Eddie Anderson's ne'er-do-well in the all-black musical fable *Cabin in the Sky.* He added bravery to intellect in *Sahara,* as a Sudanese soldier who dies fighting Nazis for the sake of white Allied soldiers. In *The Adventures of Huckleberry Finn,* as Jim, and *Moonrise,* as an old black man who takes Dane Clark under his wing, he gives sage advice to much younger white males and leads them to maturation. His most memorable role is the giant, mostly bald, untrustworthy djinni in *The Thief of Bagdad.* His young master, Sabu, tricks him into granting him three wishes. He reluctantly flies the boy to great adventures, which result in both his own freedom (it means something to hear this black man gleefully shout "Freedom!") and that of Sabu's enslaved people. The ridiculous words the djinni recites while in flight sound like poetry coming from Ingram. He would again be the djinni in *A Thousand and One Nights.*

• **Cult Favorites:** *King Kong* (1933, Merian C. Cooper and Ernest B. Schoedsack), *The Thief of Bagdad* (1940, Ludwig Berger, Tim Whelan, and Michael Powell), *Cabin in the Sky* (1943, Vincente Minnelli).

• **Other Key Films:** *The Green Pastures* (1936, William Keighley and Marc Connelly), *The Adventures of Huckleberry Finn* (1939, Richard Thorpe), *Talk of the Town* (1942, George Stevens), *Sahara* (1943, Zoltan Korda), *A Thousand and One Nights* (1945, Alfred E. Green), *Moonrise* (1948, Frank Borzage).

• **Also of Interest:** *Dark Waters* (1944, André de Toth), *Congo Crossing* (1956, Joseph Pevney), *Anna Lucasta* (1958, Arnold Laven), *Watusi* (1959, Kurt Neumann), *Elmer Gantry* (1960, Richard Brooks), *Your Cheatin' Heart* (1964, Gene Nelson), *Hurry Sundown* (1967, Otto Preminger).

○

RICHARD JAECKEL (1926–) Short but formidable blond character actor could usually be found in army or cavalry platoons (as corporals or sergeants), in tough westerns, and in action-packed war movies. He'd often die with blood pouring from his gut, after being shot with a bullet or arrow. In films where he is a troublemaker or bully, his death scenes are most welcome. His best role was probably the creepy assassin in *The Lineup* who writes down his victims' last words. In recent years, he has been turning up as rugged police lieutenants. He still looks best carrying a gun.

• **Cult Favorites:** *The Lineup* (1958, Don Siegel), *Platinum High School* (1960, Charles Haas), *Flaming Star* (1960, Siegel), *The Flight of the Phoenix* (1966, Robert Aldrich), *The Dirty Dozen* (1967, Aldrich), *Ulzana's Raid* (1972, Aldrich), *Pat Garrett and Billy the Kid* (1973, Sam Peckinpah).

• **Other Key Films:** *Guadalcanal Diary* (1943, Lewis Seiler), *Wing and a Prayer* (1944, Henry Hathaway), *Battleground* (1949, William Wellman), *Sands of Iwo Jima* (1948, Allan Dwan), *The Gunfighter* (1950, Henry King), *Attack!* (1956, Aldrich), *3:10 to Yuma* (1957, Delmer Daves), *The Naked and the Dead* (1958,

Raoul Walsh), *Sometimes a Great Notion/ Never Give an Inch* (1971, Paul Newman).

• **Also of Interest:** *Come Back, Little Sheba* (1952, Daniel Mann), *Four for Texas* (1963, Aldrich), *Once Before I Die* (1965, John Derek), *The Dark* (1979, John Cardos), *Starman* (1984, John Carpenter).

○

SAM JAFFE (1891–1984) With his wild hair, eyes, and grin, this marvelous character actor looked like Harpo Marx's sickly twin. He didn't appear in many films in his 40-year acting career, but he created a number of unforgettable roles, including the demented Grand Duke Peter in *The Scarlet Empress*, the ageless High Lama in *Lost Horizon*, the title character in *Gunga Din*, the criminal mastermind ("the Professor") who can't resist sexy young females in *The Asphalt Jungle*, and the scientific genius who befriends alien Michael Rennie in *The Day the Earth Stood Still*. His characters are brainy, often existing on a higher intellectual (or metaphysical) plane; some are also quite batty. You always take notice of them. Television fans best know Jaffe as Dr. Zorba on "Ben Casey." In real life, he was best friends with Edward G. Robinson.

• **Cult Favorites:** *The Scarlet Empress* (1935, Josef von Sternberg), *Gunga Din* (1939, George Stevens), *The Day the Earth Stood Still* (1951, Robert Wise), *Battle Beyond the Stars* (1980, Jimmy T. Murakami).

• **Other Key Films:** *Lost Horizon* (1937, Frank Capra), *Gentleman's Agreement* (1947, Elia Kazan), *The Asphalt Jungle* (1950, John Huston), *Ben-Hur* (1959, William Wyler).

• **Also of Interest:** *13 Rue Madeleine*

(1943, Henry Hathaway), *The Accused* (1948, William Dieterle), *Under the Gun* (1950, Ted Tetzlaff), *I Can Get It for You Wholesale* (1951, Michael Gordon), *The Barbarian and the Geisha* (1958, Huston), *Bedknobs and Broomsticks* (1971, Robert Stevenson).

○

BRION JAMES (1945–) Brawny, unfriendly-looking character actor who is becoming one of the action-film's top villains. Many of his films have been set in the past or future, almost all with unusual geographical locations. He has worn horror makeup, but he's frightening enough without it. He's particularly effective as unremorseful killers and psychotics—he could fill the void left by Joe Spinell. Although best known as the brutal replicant Leon in *Blade Runner,* he's been scarier, if not as interesting, in lesser films. For instance, his murderous albino in *Nightmare at Noon* is particularly despicable. So is his indestructible mass murderer in *The Horror Show.*

• **Cult Favorites:** *Southern Comfort* (1981, Walter Hill), *Blade Runner* (1982, Ridley Scott).

• **Also of Interest:** *Enemy Mine* (1985, Wolfgang Petersen), *Flesh + Blood* (1985, Paul Verhoeven), *Crimewave* (1986, Sam Raimi), *Steel Dawn* (1987, Lance Hool), *Cherry 2000* (1988, Steve DeJarnatt), *Nightmare at Noon* (1988, Nico Mastorakis), *The Horror Show* (1989, James Isaac), *Another 48 HRS.* (1990, Walter Hill).

○

SIDNEY JAMES (1913–76) Short, funny South African–born comedy actor who was one of the most familiar and popular figures in British films and television for thirty years. With his tired, perplexed face, square jaw, tight mouth, baggy eyes, and large, sharp nose, he looked like someone you'd find in a working-class pub at all hours. But he was a nimble comedian who was as quick with a one-liner as with a slapstick turn. He was Alec Guinness's bumbling cockney accomplice in *The Lavender Hill Mob,* but he later abandoned droll humor for the broad, bawdy "Carry On" series of British films, for which he is best known. He always had that dazed look: "Will the craziness never end!" Considering he's the best known of the "Carry On" gang, it's odd that he had just a small part in the series' most familiar entry, *Carry On Nurse,* which was the first to play in America. He was at the center of the absurdity in *Carry on Cleo,* an innovative but neglected parody of ancient times that not only anticipated Monty Python's *Life of Brian* but, until the novelty wears off, is more outrageous and funnier. He was at his best in comedy ensembles.

• **Cult Favorite:** *The Lavender Hill Mob* (1961, Charles Crichton).
• **Sleeper:** *Carry on Cleo* (1965, Gerald Thomas).
• **Other Key Films:** *The Titfield Thunderbolt* (1952, Crichton), *Carry on Henry VIII* (1972, Thomas), *Carry on Camping* (1972, Thomas), and several other "Carry On" films.
• **Also of Interest:** *Joe Macbeth* (1955, Ken Hughes), *What a Carve Up!/No Place Like Homicide!* (1961, Pat Jackson).

○

CLAUDIA JENNINGS (1950–79) Beautiful, charismatic blond actress was killed in a head-on collision less than 10 years after

Claudia Jennings.

she was *Playboy*'s Playmate of the Year and had launched a career in exploitation films that earned her the titles "Queen of the Drive-In Movies" and "Queen of the Bs." She had the most beautiful body in the seventies cinema, and Claudiaphiles didn't deny they went to her films to see her naked or in an unbuttoned blouse, a see-through minidress, or, as in *'Gator Bait,* tight cutoff jeans and an open vest with nothing underneath. Her attitude was "Today, nice girls do take off their clothes," and she gave the men what they wanted. But she had more than a great body. She had strikingly intelligent eyes, a self-assured expression, and infectious vitality. She appealed to female viewers because her women had an exciting blend of courage, confidence, skills (driving fast, shooting straight, loving hard), and strength in the face of adversity; and though they weren't well-educated, they were the sharpest people around. While they fit the mold of Erskine Caldwell's flirtatious, skimpily dressed, sexually promiscuous country-nature girls, they are more cognizant of sexual politics. They know that their bodies are their best weapons in the quest for justice, power, and respect in a world of leering, addle-brained misogynists. Her women are aware of their responsibility to better the socioeconomic standing of their sex. They seek life-styles and occupations that are both challenging and daring: a roller derby star, the driver of a semi, the lawyer for a group of lovers who test the country's marital laws, a racer of superspeed cars, a poacher, a moonshine runner, a bankrobber, etc. We marvel at the way they defy male authorities, and refuse to knuckle under to the powerful people out to destroy them. They are smart, independent, brave women of action—genuine heroines, winners.

• **Cult Favorites:** *The Unholy Rollers* (1972, Vernon Zimmerman), *Truck Stop Women* (1974, Mark Lester), *Group Marriage* (1974, Stephanie Rothman), *The Great Texas Dynamite Chase* (1977, Michael Pressman).

• **Sleeper:** *Moonshine County Express* (1977, Gus Trikonis).

• **Other Key Films:** *'Gator Bait* (1973, Fred and Beverly Sebastian), *Deathsport* (1978, Henry Suso and Allan Arkush).

○

RON JEREMY Porno star of the late seventies and eighties, short and plump but always in demand. He could actually act, was particularly adept at comedy, and, most significantly, had an extremely long penis and the contortionist's ability to perform self-fellatio—a rare talent not lost on those casting kinky films. He's still a prominent figure in the New York sex-entertainment scene.

• **Sample Films:** *Mystique* (1979, Robert Norman), *The Good Girls of Godiva High* (1979, Jim Clark), *Young & Innocent* (1981, J. Angel Martine), *A Girl's Best Friend* (1981, Henri Pachard), *Foxtrot* (1982, Cecil Howard), *Babe* (1982, John Cristorer), *Little Girls Lost* (1983, Ted Roter), *Debbie Does Dallas II* (1983, Clark), *Scoundrels* (1983, Howard), *Eat at the Blue Fox* (1984, Damon Christian).

○

NOBLE JOHNSON (1897–1978) Black actor best known as the imposing and inhospitable native chief in *King Kong*. He would play tribal chiefs and other unfriendly sorts (a zombie in *The Ghost Breakers*) in a number of other fantasy and jungle films in later years. It's often forgotten that he was a pioneer producer of black films in the silent era, as well as one of the first black actors to break into Hollywood pictures (debuting as an Indian in 1914), albeit in bit parts. He played Friday in the 1922 version of *Robinson Crusoe,* and was one of the cannibals who threaten Buster Keaton in *The Navigator.*

• **Cult Favorites:** *The Mummy* (1932, Karl Freund), *King Kong* (1933, Merian C. Cooper and Ernest B. Schoedsack), *She* (1935, Irving Pichel and Lansing C. Holden), *She Wore a Yellow Ribbon* (1949, John Ford).

• **Also of Interest:** *Robinson Crusoe* (1922), *The Ten Commandments* (1923, Cecil B. De Mille), *The Navigator* (1924, Buster Keaton), *The Four Feathers* (1929, Lothar Mendes, Cooper, and Schoedsack), *Moby Dick* (1930, Lloyd Bacon), *East of Borneo* (1931, George Melford), *Murders in the Rue Morgue* (1932, Robert Florey), *The*

Ghost Breakers (1940, George Marshall), *Jungle Book* (1942, Zoltan Korda), *A Game of Death* (1945, Robert Wise).

○

TOR JOHNSON (1903–71) This bald, round-headed, hulking, 300-pound Swede was a wrestler before playing the dim-witted maniac in a number of cheap horror films, and it was obvious he had done his best acting in the arena. He could be a frightening figure (at least he was in one exciting episode of the TV series "Peter Gunn"), but in movies he was laughable, especially in such travesties as *The Black Sleep, The Beast of Yucca Flats,* and Edward D. Wood's camp classics *Plan 9 from Outer Space, Bride of the Monster,* and its sequel, *Night of the Ghouls.* In *Plan 9,* Johnson squeezed into a suit to play a police inspec-

tor (although there is no way he could have passed the exam) who turns into a ghoul (this makes more sense). In the other two films he played the mute brute, Lobo. In *Night of the Ghouls* it looks like he's wearing pajama bottoms and the makeup man cooked an omelette on his face. He could usually be counted on to abduct a female. An ugly fellow, he was appropriately cast as the beast of Yucca Flats rather than of a place with a prettier name. A popular figure with bad-movie freaks.

• **Cult Favorites:** *Bride of the Monster* (1956, Edward D. Wood, Jr.), *Plan 9 from Outer Space* (1959, Wood, Jr.), *Night of the Ghouls* (1960, Wood, Jr.).

• **Other Key Films:** *The Black Sleep* (1956, Reginald LeBorg), *The Unearthly* (1957, Brooke L. Peters), *The Beast of Yucca Flats* (1961, Coleman Francis).

Tor Johnson shocks Mona McKinnon in Plan 9 from Outer Space.

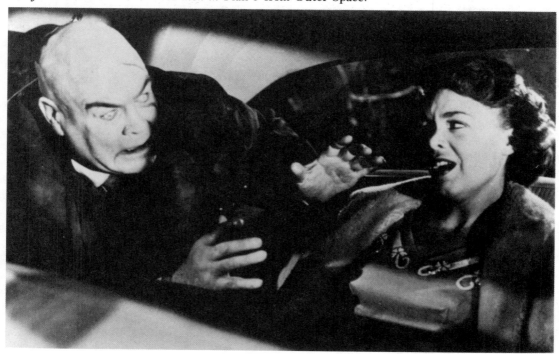

○

BUCK JONES (1889–1942) Former bronc buster became a cowboy idol in the twenties at Fox, playing heroes that, alternately, showed the seriousness of William S. Hart and the flamboyance of Tom Mix, Fox's major star. Although he was adored by kids—5 million joined his Buck Jones Rangers club—his films were aimed at adults, too. Action was usually balanced by plot and characterization, and he often kissed the girl instead of putting on his white Stetson and riding his horse, Silver, into the sunset. He also included comedy bits in his films, often to the chagrin of critics. His characters were usually shy, unassuming men who avoid trouble until circumstances dictate they use their fists and guns; on occasion, he'd be an escaped prisoner out to prove his innocence. Jones was the most successful of the silent cowboy stars at making the transition to sound westerns, the only one to get continuous starring roles with major studios. He would usually produce his own films for Columbia and Universal, and until the advent of the singing cowboy caused a slump in his popularity, he was the top cowboy star in the world. In 1941, he made a dramatic comeback at Monogram, teaming with Tim McCoy and Raymond Hatton for several "Rough Riders" films (beginning with *Arizona Bound*), arguably the best of the many heroic-trio series. The three westerners rode off in different directions at the end of the last "Rough Riders" film, *West of the Law*—plans for a continuation of the series ended when Jones was killed in Boston's Coconut Grove fire, making the farewell scene in *West of the Law* forever poignant.

• **Cult Favorite:** *Arizona Bound* (1941, Spencer G. Bennet).

• **Also Recommended:** *Just Pals* (1920, John Ford), *The Avenger* (1931, Roy William Neill), *The Red Rider* (1934 Serial, Louis Friedlander/Lew Landers), *Rocky Rhodes* (1934, Al Raboch), *The Crimson Trail* (1935, Raboch), *Border Brigands* (1935, Nick Grinde), *Riders of Death Valley* (1941 serial, Ford Beebe and Ray Taylor), *The Gunman from Bodie* (1941, Bennett), *Forbidden Trails* (1941, Robert North Bradbury), *Below the Border* (1942, Howard P. Bretherton), *West of the Law* (1942, Bretherton), *Dawn on the Great Divide* (1942, Bretherton).

○

DARBY JONES (1910–86) Tall, skeletal black who all horror fans remember as the glazed-eyed Carre-Four in the Val Lewton–produced *I Walked with a Zombie*. He has three great scenes in the film: his spooky shadow covers the wall of the room where Nurse Frances Dee sleeps; he leads Dee and her catatonic patient, Christine Gordon, through the jungles to a voodoo ceremony; he follows James Ellison menacingly as he carries Gordon in a poetic silent passage through the jungles, across the beach, and into the ocean. Even more typecast than the typical black actor, Jones's roles were limited to jungle pictures.

• **Cult Favorite:** *I Walked with a Zombie* (1943, Jacques Tourneur).

• **Also of Interest:** *Tarzan the Fearless* (1933 serial, Robert Hill), *Tarzan Escapes* (1936, Richard Thorpe), *Zombies on Broadway* (1945, Gordon Douglas), *Zamba* (1949, William Berke).

○

DUANE JONES (1940–89) Handsome, capable black actor who stood out from amateur

Duane Jones calms Judith O'Dea in Night of the Living Dead.

castmates in George Romero's seminal horror film, *Night of the Living Dead*. He was one of the rare black leads in a horror film outside the *Blacula* series; refreshingly and significantly, no reference is made to his color in the film. The audience sides with him rather than a white bigot when they devise opposite plans to save themselves and everyone else who is trapped in a house surrounded by hungry ghouls. It's usually overlooked that his plan (to hide in the basement), proves wrong, and everyone, including himself, is killed. It would seem that as the star of that commercial blockbuster, Jones would have been offered, at very least, other horror films, yet his small legacy includes only the obscure *Ganja and Hess,* a strange, fascinating black vampire film—Jones develops a bloodlust after being cut by an ancient

dagger—with a compelling sociopolitical subtext.

• **Cult Favorites:** *Night of the Living Dead* (1968, George A. Romero), *Ganja and Hess/Blood Couple* (1973, Bill Gunn).

○

L. Q. JONES (1936–) Familiar villain in fifties and sixties westerns on television and in films, most notably those directed by Sam Peckinpah. When Strother Martin slithered through the Peckinpah dust, Jones was usually there with him, in need of a bath, a shave, a mouthwash to counter the booze, and a long lesson in manners. His characters were leaner and meaner than Martin's, less cowardly, and much scarier. But unlike Martin, he never survived—his death in the windswept mountains in *Ride the High Country* is one of the most memorable in Peckinpah's entire violent work. Jones would team with actor Alvy Moore to produce a number of low-budget horror fantasy films. He also directed the cult classic *A Boy and His Dog*.

• **Cult Favorites:** *Buchanan Rides Alone* (1958, Budd Boetticher), *Flaming Star* (1960, Don Siegel), *Ride the High Country* (1962, Sam Peckinpah), *Hell Is for Heroes* (1962, Siegel), *The Wild Bunch* (1969, Peckinpah), *The Ballad of Cable Hogue* (1970, Peckinpah), *White Line Fever* (1975, Jonathan Kaplan), *Timerider* (1983, William Dear).

• **Sleeper:** *Hound-Dog Man* (1959, Siegel).

• **Also of Interest:** *Love Me Tender* (1956, Robert D. Webb), *Men in War* (1957, Anthony Mann).

○

MARSHA JORDAN The granddaughter of a southern minister and a graduate of a Catholic convent school, she became the "Queen of Soft-Core" in the mid-sixties. Her nude scenes and simulated sex paved the way for the likes of Linda Lovelace, Marilyn Chambers, and others. Her pretty face, sensual mouth, flirtatious eyes, large breasts, and shoulder-length blond hair certainly made her desirable to her male admirers, but she also had a natural, unintimidating, down-home quality that made her extremely popular with women as well. Her popularity, which shouldn't be underestimated, was fueled by her willingness to tour with each film, going to small towns where the people were delighted to meet their first movie star. She refused to do hard-core films in the seven-

ties but tried her hand at R-rated exploitation films, even playing a bit in *Count Yorga, Vampire*.

• **Cult Favorites:** *Head Mistress, Brand of Shame, Lady Godiva Rides, The Daisy Chain, The Golden Box, Diary of a Madam, Marsha, the Erotic Housewife.*

• **Also of Interest:** *Count Yorga, Vampire* (1970, Robert Kelljan).

○

JACKIE JOSEPH L.A. television's first weathergirl, this bubbly, rosy-cheeked actress-singer-dancer gave an endearingly daffy ("I could eat a hearse") comedic performance as Audrey, the monster plant's namesake, in Roger Corman's *The Little Shop of Horrors*. Her Audrey and Jonathan Haze's Seymour Krelboin were one of the oddest romantic duos in film history. On one date, he takes her home to meet his hypochondriac mother and eat cod-liver-oil soup. Audrey, "a dumb brunette" who could compete with any "dumb blonde," was the role of her life and completely obscured her other work in films and on television. She did spend the early seventies in "The Doris Day Show," and has since kept in the public eye working with Day to save homeless animals in Hollywood. Also, she formed L.A.D.I.E.S., a support group for women divorced by celebrities (she had been married to Ken Berry). It was fun to see her and Dick Miller, the plant eater in *Little Shop*, have a joint cameo in *Gremlins*.

• **Cult Favorites:** *The Little Shop of Horrors* (1960, Roger Corman), *Who's Minding the Mint?* (1967, Howard Morris).

• **Also of Interest:** *Gremlins* (1984, Joe Dante), *Gremlins 2: The New Batch* (1990, Dante).

BRENDA JOYCE (1915–) Pretty leading lady of B pictures succeeded Maureen O'Sullivan as Jane in the Tarzan series, costarring with both Johnny Weissmuller and Lex Barker, and was the only other actress to become permanently identified with the role. Tall, blond, and athletic—an All-American girl—she was quite different from her dark-haired, fragile, Ireland-born predecessor. She wasn't as vulnerable, independent-minded, sexy (what boring outfits she wore), romantic, or flirtatious as O'Sullivan had been; in fact, her Jane was a solid, competent wife to Tarzan and mother to Johnny Sheffield's strapping teenage Boy. Still, she was as acceptable as any replacement for the nearly irreplaceable O'Sullivan could have been.

• **Key Films:** *Tarzan and the Amazons* (1945, Kurt Neumann), *Tarzan and the Leopard Woman* (1946, Neumann), *Tarzan and the Huntress* (1947, Neumann), *Tarzan and the Mermaids* (1948, Robert Florey), *Tarzan's Magic Fountain* (1949, Lee Sholem).

• **Also of Interest:** *The Rains Came* (1939, Clarence Brown), *Little Old New York* (1940, Henry King), *Maryland* (1940, Henry King), *Whispering Ghosts* (1942, Alfred L. Werker), *Pillow of Death* (1945, Wallace Fox), *The Spider Woman Strikes Back* (1946, Arthur Lubin), *Little Giant* (1946, William A. Seiter).

○

VALERIE KAPRISKY (1962–) Slender, shapely, and extremely sexy French actress with long brown hair and a young face. She had played the title character in the adaptation of Pierre Louÿs's erotic classic *Aphrodite* when she was offered the Jean Seberg role

Valerie Kaprisky in Breathless.

in the kinetic American remake of Jean-Luc Godard's *Breathless*. She was a French student in Los Angeles who has a fling with cocky punk Richard Gere and contemplates betraying him once she realizes he's wanted for killing a cop. The film was disappointing, with the main selling point being the nude sex scenes between Gere and the then-unknown import; at the time (before Rebecca De Mornay showed up), probably no major American actress would have taken on such an uninhibited part. Kaprisky returned to France and was almost forgotten in America until the successful arrival of *L'Année des Meduses*, a flesh-filled melodrama set on a topless beach on the Riviera. She still looked young enough (she always seems to be pouting) to play a girl in her late teens.

Her shrewd young female learns that men who manipulate women, especially young girls like herself, deserve to be manipulated themselves. By using her body, she usurps the power men have over her, even murdering (in a grisly fashion) a young stud who slept with her mother and then wanted her as well. Where the role in *Breathless* seemed beyond her grasp—Seberg had proved you didn't have to give a shallow performance to play a shallow person—she seemed to understand this young temptress quite well. Because of the nudity, particularly Kaprisky's, the film has become a cable-TV favorite. Her credibility as an actress increased when she gave a strong, multi-layered performance as Kafka's lover, Milena, in *L'Amant.*

• **Key Films:** *Aphrodite* (1982, Robert Fuest), *Breathless* (1983, Jim McBride), *La Femme Publique* (1983, Andrezej Zulawski), *L'Année des Meduses* (1986, Christopher Frank), *L'Amant* (1989, Véra Belmont).

○

ANNA KARINA (1940–) Lovely Danish brunette, a former model, married to French director Jean-Luc Godard in the sixties and the star in some of his most fascinating, influential, and accessible films. Godard often framed her and photographed her as if she were his model. One can tell by the movements of her body, eyes, head, and hair that she understood how the camera can bring out a subject's beauty and at the same time veil her mystery. One recalls Karina's characters being cheery when doing a "mating dance" with an attractive young male in *Vivre Sa Vie,* my favorite Karina film, and an impromptu song and dance with her two male comrades in *Bande à Part.* But for the most part

her enigmatic women are detached, remote, and sad, unable to make romantic connections, illustrating prevailing themes in Godard's films. They are smart women, but either have no idea how to give and receive *true* love or are just reluctant to try it. In *Vivre Sa Vie* and the futuristic *Alphaville,* she plays prostitutes whose mechanical sexual activity pushes them further and further away from true feelings. Men try to reach their hearts: Jean-Paul Belmondo gives up in *Pierrot le Fou,* but in *Alphaville,* tough guy Eddie Constantine (ironically) teaches her sensual female about "love." In Godard's scheme of things, Karina's characters were so anesthetized that it's hard to judge her talent, but in *Bande à Part* she managed to improvise while portraying a play-acting woman who is improvising herself—no easy chore. And she was a captivating presence in *Vivre Sa Vie,* in which her ill-fated prostitute is shot down in the street, and in *Pierrot le Fou,* running off with Belmondo and being as untrustworthy to him as Jean Seberg was in Godard's *Breathless* (a part Karina rejected). In fact, this film hints at what would have happened to Belmondo and Seberg if they had stayed together. Karina also was a sexy, mysterious presence in *Alphaville* and, as a trenchcoat-wearing woman looking for her lover's murderer, in the perplexing *Made in U.S.A.*

• **Cult Favorites:** *Alphaville* (1965, Jean-Luc Godard), *Pierrot le Fou* (1965, Godard), *The Stranger* (1967, Luchino Visconti).

• **Other Key Films:** *A Woman Is a Woman* (1961, Godard), *Vivre Sa Vie/My Life to Live* (1962, Godard), *Le Petit Soldat* (1960/63/65, Godard), *Bande à Part/Band of Outsiders* (1964, Godard), *Made in U.S.A.* (1966, Godard), *La Religieuse* (1966,

Anna Karina and Eddie Constantine in Alphaville.

Jacques Rivette), *Laughter in the Dark* (1969, Tony Richardson), *Justine* (1969, George Cukor), *Michael Kohlhaas—The Rebel* (1969, Volker Schlöndorff), *Rendezvous à Bray* (1971, André Delvaux), *Chinese Roulette* (1976, Rainer Werner Fassbinder), *Bread and Chocolate* (1983, Franco Brusati).

○

BORIS KARLOFF (1887–1969) The gentle, British-born William Henry Pratt didn't star only in horror films—he was a wacko prisoner who kills squealers in *The Criminal Code,* a big-shot gangster who is killed while bowling in *Scarface,* an Oriental sleuth in *Mr. Wong, Detective,* a long-haired Indian in *The Unconquered,* a horror movie icon much like himself in *Targets*—but he contributed even more to the sound horror film than Lon Chaney did to the silent horror film. Every horror fan is familiar with Karloff's face, which looked like it had been chiseled from rock, his eyes menacing from under thick eyebrows, a deep voice that was sinister despite a slight lisp. So dedicated to his craft that at the end of his career he'd climb out of his wheelchair when the cameras rolled. Karloff was a *great* actor, who gave poignant performances even when playing monsters and sinister villains, who was eloquent even as the speechless Monster

Boris Karloff in The Black Room.

in *Frankenstein*—when his cries of "Friend!" are rejected by Elsa Lanchester in *Bride of Frankenstein,* his expression breaks our hearts—and who made us want to understand the motives behind the crimes his characters commit. Only Fu Manchu and a few more of his cruel men elicit no empathy. Hjalmar Poelzig in *The Black Cat* comes close to being purely evil, yet even he has been affected by past suffering. Most of his mad doctors and scientists and even his splendid Val Lewton villains, the Greek general in *Isle of the Dead,* the graverobber-murderer (Mr. Gray) in *The Body Snatcher,* and the ruthless asylum supervisor in *Bedlam,* have become *so* cruel because of circumstances. The inmates who capture and hold him for a mock trial in *Bedlam* even decide to let him go after he pleads his case. While we fear his characters, we have a touch of sadness when, as almost always happens, they are killed. Unfortunately, it seems the man who dignified the horror film and gave us so many great performances and characters died without realizing what a good actor he was and how significant he was to the history of the cinema.

• **Cult Favorites:** *The Criminal Code* (1931, Howard Hawks), *The Mummy* (1932, James Whale), *Scarface* (1932, Hawks), *The Black Cat* (1934, Edgar G. Ulmer), *Bride of Frankenstein* (1935, Whale), *Charlie Chan at the Opera* (1936, H. Bruce Humberstone), *The Devil Commands* (1941, Edward Dmytryk), *The Body Snatcher* (1945, Robert Wise), *Isle of the Dead* (1945, Mark Robson), *Bedlam* (1946, Robson), *The Terror* (1963, Roger Corman), *The Sorcerers* (1967, Michael Reeves), *Targets* (1968, Peter Bogdanovich), *The Crimson Cult* (1970, Vernon Sewell).

• **Other Key Films:** *Frankenstein* (1931,

Whale), *The Mask of Fu Manchu* (1932, Charles Brabin), *The Old Dark House* (1932, Whale), *The Ghoul* (1933, T. Hayes Hunter), *The Lost Patrol* (1934, John Ford), *The Black Room* (1935, Roy William Neill), *The Raven* (1935, Louis Friedlander/Lew Landers), *The Man Who Changed His Mind/The Man Who Lived Again* (1936, Robert Stevenson), *The Walking Dead* (1936, Michael Curtiz), *The Invisible Ray* (1936, Lambert Hillyer), *Night Key* (1937, Lloyd Corrigan), *Mr. Wong, Detective* (1938, William Nigh), *The Son of Frankenstein* (1939, Rowland V. Lee), *The Man They Could Not Hang* (1939, Nick Grinde), *Tower of London* (1939, Lee), *The Man with Nine Lives* (1949, Grinde), *The Climax* (1944, George Waggner), *House of Frankenstein* (1945, Erle C. Kenton), *The Black Castle* (1952, Nathan Juran), *The Raven* (1963, Corman), *A Comedy of Terrors* (1963, Jacques Tourneur), *Black Sabbath* (1963, Mario Bava).

○

SHINTARO KATSU This Japanese actor became a cult hero in his native country playing the plump, wandering, blind swordsman-masseur Zatoichi in 24 films between 1962 and 1973. His fugitive sword-for-hire was one of the most formidable and novel combatants of that kung fu–martial arts era. Usually surrounded by about 30 bad guys, he stands his ground, holds his sword downward in a defensive position, and uses his four heightened senses (we never see his eyes). The enemy attacks en masse, and he wipes them out, with precision and brutality. The Zatoichi films pretty much blend together, except for *Zatoichi and the One-Armed Swordsman*, in which he befriends Chinese superstar Wang Yu's famous character and clears him of a murder charge, and *Zatoichi Meets Yojimbo*, which paired him with the vicious swordfighter whom Toshiro Mifune played in Akira Kurosawa's classic. Zatoichi and Yojimbo originally take opposite sides in a family feud (the comedy part of the movie), but later form an uneasy alliance to search for gold, engaging in some bloody violence along the way. As played by Katsu, who looks like a chubby Japanese version of Donald Pleasence in this film, Zatoichi is supposed to annoy other characters (especially Yojimbo) because of his astute mind and mastery of his four intact senses, but his whimpering and fake modesty get on my nerves, too. However, even Mifune is irritating in this film. Katsu played Zatoichi on Japanese television, and then starred in a "Sword of Justice" series, playing "Razor" Hanzo, a brutal policeman of the 1800s. Filled with sex and sadism, the pictures were quite popular.

• **Cult Favorites:** *Zatoichi/The Life and Opinion of Zatoichi* (1962/68, Kenji Misumi), *Zatoichi and the One-Armed Swordsman* (1970, Kimiyoshi Yasuda), *Zatoichi Meets Yojimbo* (1970, Kihachi Okamoto), *Zatoichi in Desperation* (1973, Shintaro Katsu); 21 other "Zatoichi" films (1963–72); "Sword of Justice" films (beginning in 1972).

○

STACY KEACH (1941–) Extremely talented, versatile, formidable, chance-taking leading man who has specialized in complex, cerebral characters who are either unstable or psychotic. The scar on his handsome face has come to represent the chink in the armor of his characters, once-nice guys who have been traumatized by dangerous professions. We generally meet them when they are already pathetic men attempting to come back to reality or are calm, slow- and low-talking, deadpan villains. Those who aren't suicidal are at least self-destructive; if they don't deliberately rush toward some terrible fall, they make no attempt to avoid their sad fates. Among Keach's best characterizations are his criminal Wyatt Earp in *Doc*, brutal Frank James in the exceptional western *The Long Riders* (brother James played Jesse), his over-the-hill boxer who foolishly tries a comeback in *Fat City*, his kind, popular small-town cop who is actually a psycho in *The Killer Inside Me* (a chilling portrayal), a crazed Vietnam Vet who thinks he's in charge of (rather than a patient at) an asylum in *The Ninth Configuration*, and, in a hilarious comic turn, the no-nonsense cop who is obsessed with arresting Cheech and Chong for dope-running in *Up in Smoke*. In recent years, he gained fame as television's hardboiled "Mike Hammer." He also was a controversial *Hamlet* on the English stage.

• **Cult Favorites:** *Brewster McCloud* (1970, Robert Altman), *Up in Smoke* (1978, Lou Adler), *Slave of the Cannibal God* (1979, Sergio Martino), *The Ninth Configuration* (1980, William Peter Blatty), *Butterfly* (1981, Matt Cimber).

• **Sleepers:** *End of the Road* (1970, Aram Avakian), *Fat City* (1972, John Huston), *Road Games* (1981, Richard Franklin).

• **Also of Interest:** *The Heart Is a Lonely Hunter* (1968, Robert Ellis Miller), *The Traveling Executioner* (1970, Jack Smight), *Doc* (1971, Frank Perry), *The Life and Times of Judge Roy Bean* (1972, Huston), *The New Centurions* (1972, Richard Fleischer), *Luther* (1974, Guy Green), *The Gravy Train* (1974, Jack Starrett), *The Killer Inside Me* (1976, Burt Kennedy),

Cheech & Chong's Nice Dreams (1981, Thomas Chong).

○

RUBY KEELER (1909–) Canadian-born former chorus girl who became a Broadway musical star, then broke into movies in Warners' *42nd Street*, playing a chorus girl who becomes a Broadway musical star when the lead (Bebe Daniels) sprains her ankle and can't perform opening night. Keeler, who had short, dark hair, a sweet smile, and a delivery that was shy but forceful, would have the ingenue part in other classic Warners' working-class, putting-on-a-show musicals, featuring the outlandish yet extraordinary choreography of Busby Berkeley. Tenor Dick Powell, long before his image hardened, was her brash but supportive romantic lead. In addition, she starred in several lesser, escapist, music-filled romances for the studio. Her partners included Powell and, in *Go Into Your Dance*, her husband, Al Jolson. She wasn't much of an actress, her singing was better suited for the shower than the stage, and her tap dancing, though impressive, wasn't at all graceful (okay, she was *clunky* at times). Yet she was just right for corny backstage and campus romances. She was perky, inno- cent, and had rosier cheeks than anyone but Powell.

• **Cult Favorites:** *42nd Street* (1933, Lloyd Bacon), *Gold Diggers of 1933* (1933, Mervyn LeRoy), *Footlight Parade* (1933, Bacon), *Dames* (1934, Ray Enright).

• **Also Recommended:** *Flirtation Walk* (1934, Frank Borzage), *Colleen* (1936, Alfred E. Green).

• **Also of Interest:** *Go Into Your Dance* (1935, Archie Mayo), *Shipmates Forever* (1935, Borzage), *Ready, Willing and Able*

(1936, Enright), *Mother Craig's Chickens* (1938, Rowland V. Lee), *Sweetheart of the Campus* (1941, Edward Dmytryk).

○

HARVEY KEITEL (1941–) Talented, handsome, imposing Brooklyn actor was discovered by Martin Scorsese, who starred him in his first two films, the obscure *Who's That Knocking at My Door?* and his ground-breaking *Mean Streets,* with Robert De Niro in support. In later Scorsese films, he'd have supporting parts. He was well-suited for Scorsese because, like De Niro, he had a natural, improvisatory style—his rat-a-tat-tat street-patter conversations with De Niro in *Mean Streets* and *Taxi Driver* come across as excitingly spontaneous and authentic. Also, he could play characters with volatile "Italian tempers." Though compact, he is muscular, and his eyes and aggressive manner make him extremely menacing. His wife beater who courts Ellen Burstyn in *Alice Doesn't Live Here Anymore* is absolutely terrifying. While most of Keitel's characters are thinkers, they are also tough, physical men who, though they may wear suits, are still products of the rough streets in which they grew up. Even his period-piece characters and those who live far, far away from Brooklyn or Little Italy seem to have a vicious, eye-for-an-eye urban ghetto sensibility. Keitel's most memorable characters include the young small-time hood in *Mean Streets;* the seductive brute in *Alice;* Jodie Foster's evil, long-nailed pimp in *Taxi Driver;* a crude Napoleonic officer who carries on a violent, lengthy, obsessive feud with Keith Carradine in *The Duellists;* an auto worker who gets in over his head taking on his crooked union in the politically astute *Blue Collar,* with Richard

Harvey Keitel and Jodie Foster in Taxi Driver.

Pryor and Yaphet Kotto as his coworker buddies; a collector for his gangster father who'd rather be a concert pianist in *Fingers;* and the cinema's first sympathetic Judas in *The Last Temptation of Christ.* He's had some flops and been badly miscast at times, but overall he's had an impressive, interesting career.

• **Cult Favorites:** *Mean Streets* (1973, Martin Scorsese), *Taxi Driver* (1976, Scorsese), *Buffalo Bill and the Indians* (1976, Robert Altman), *The Duellists* (1977, Ridley Scott), *Welcome to L.A.* (1977, Alan Rudolph), *Fingers* (1978, James Toback), *Blue Collar* (1978, Paul Schrader), *Bad Timing/A Sexual Obsession* (1980, Nicolas Roeg), *The Last Temptation of Christ* (1988, Scorsese).

• **Sleepers:** *Who's That Knocking at My Door?* (1978, Scorsese), *Death Watch* (1980, Bertrand Tavernier), *La Nuit de Varennes* (1982, Ettore Scola).

• **Also Recommended:** *Alice Doesn't Live Here Anymore* (1975, Scorsese), *Mother, Jugs and Speed* (1976, Peter Yates), *Mortal Thoughts* (1991, Alan Rudolph), *Thelma & Louise* (1991, Ridley Scott).

• **Also of Interest:** *That's the Way of the World/Shining Star* (1975, Sig Shore), *Saturn 3* (1980, Stanley Donen), *The Border* (1982, Tony Richardson), *Exposed* (1983, Toback), *Falling in Love Again* (1984, Ulu Grosbard), *Camorra* (1986, Lina Wertmuller), *The January Man* (1989, Pat O'Connor).

○

JIM KELLY (1948–) Tall, handsome former football player and karate champion made a good impression in *Enter the Dragon,* teaming with Bruce Lee and John Saxon to challenge Han in his well-guarded fortress, and dying in the process. Even with Lee in the film, Kelly's martial-arts display was exciting. The only black in the film, he was also the only character with a political consciousness—back in the ghetto in America, he is wanted by police. He was back in the ghetto in his own starring vehicle, *Black Belt Jones,* a dumb but action-filled and amusing black exploitation film in which he and other blacks in a Watts self-defense school take on the mob. Kelly would later team with Fred Williamson and Jim Brown in several all-black films, including a western. Usually the results were disappointing: three athletes who couldn't show emotion just wasn't a winning formula. Kelly also starred in films in Italy and Hong Kong.

• **Cult Favorites:** *Enter the Dragon* (1973, Robert Clouse).

• **Other Key Film:** *Black Belt Jones* (1974, Clouse).

• **Also of Interest:** *Melinda* (1972, Hugh Robertson), *Three the Hard Way* (1974, Gordon Parks, Jr.), *Take a Hard Ride* (1975, Anthony M. Dawson), *Black Samurai* (1977, Al Adamson), *Black Eliminator* (1978, Adamson), *One Down, Two to Go* (1983, Fred Williamson).

○

KAY KENDALL (1926–59) This former British music-hall performer made movies for nine years before becoming an "overnight" sensation in the annoying four-characters-and-two-cars hit comedy *Genevieve.* She played Kenneth More's model girlfriend (he describes her as a "woman in the *broadest* sense"), who accompanies him in a car race to London against John Gregson and his wife Dinah Sheridan, in their car Genevieve. The two women put up with the childish rivalry of their men. Kendall stole the picture, mixing droll wit with silly physical comedy, and drunkenly play-

Kay Kendall.

ing the title song on a trumpet. The attractive actress (whom Sean Young resembles) became a much-loved star in England while playing in bedroom and drawing-room comedies, usually as a brash showgirl or actress who isn't too shy to speak her mind or get down and dirty. Known for her dry wit and impeccable timing, she particularly sparkled in the sophisticated farces she made with husband Rex Harrison. She was soon courted by American directors. Her early death from leukemia saddened a nation.

• **Cult Favorite:** *Genevieve* (1953, Henry Cornelius).

• **Other Key Films:** *Curtain Up* (1953, Ralph Smart), *Doctor in the House* (1955, Ralph Thomas), *Simon and Laura* (1956, Muriel Box), *The Constant Husband* (1957, Sidney Gilliat), *Les Girls* (1957, George Cukor), *The Reluctant Debutante* (1958, Vincente Minnelli), *Once More with Feeling* (1960, Stanley Donen).

○

SUZY KENDALL (1944–) Pretty English blonde always seemed to me like the adult counterpart to Judy Geeson, perhaps because they both were attracted to Sidney Poitier in *To Sir with Love*. Or perhaps it's because, in their respective films, they each seemed to be repressing their sexuality—Geeson because of her youth, and Kendall because of her nervousness. Maybe she was nervous because she realized that she could be a sexual tigress rather than, say, the school teacher she played in more than one film. We sensed it, too. In later films, Kendall would let loose her sex appeal, and with her buxom figure and wide eyes, she made an ideal imperiled heroine in R-rated suspense and horror films, taking leads in both England and Italy. Obscurity beckoned when she made such pictures as *Spasmo, Adventures of a Private Eye,* and (here's a great title)

Diary of a Cloistered Nun. She was once married to Dudley Moore, her costar in the unimaginative comedy *30 Is a Dangerous Age, Cynthia.*

• **Cult Favorite:** *The Bird with the Crystal Plumage* (1970, Dario Argento).

• **Other Key Films:** *Psycho Circus/Circus of Fear* (1967, John Moxey), *To Sir with Love* (1967, James Clavell), *The Penthouse* (1967, Peter Colinson), *Fräulein Doktor* (1969, Alberto Lattuada), *The Gamblers* (1969, Ron Winston), *Darker Than Amber* (1970, Robert Clouse), *In the Devil's Garden/Assault* (1971, Sidney Hayers), *Tales That Witness Madness* (1973, Freddie Francis), *Craze* (1974, Freddie Francis), *Torso* (1974, Sergio Martino).

○

EDGAR KENNEDY (1890–1948) Bald comic character actor, the originator and master of "the slow burn," appeared in more than 500 shorts and features, surely a Hollywood record. He started with Mack Sen-nett, playing a Keystone Kop and backing Chaplin, before spending time in vaudeville. Beginning in the late twenties, he was the foil in Laurel and Hardy shorts, playing traffic cops, a grouchy uncle in *The Perfect Day,* an irate motorist who destroys the boys' car as they destroy his in the classic *Two Tars,* and so on. He'd also direct some of their films as E. Livingston Kennedy. Kennedy also supported the Marx Brothers in *Duck Soup,* as the lemonade salesman whom Harpo harasses—he cuts off Kennedy's pocket to use as a peanut bag, and stomps barefoot in his lemonade. He'd also appear with W. C. Fields, Eddie Cantor, and even Harold Lloyd, playing a bartender in the 1947 sound comedy *Mad Wednesday.* He wasn't only a supporting player, however: he starred in more than 100 two-reel comedies as "The Average Man," trying to cope with marriage, family, work, and life in a difficult, sometimes hostile world.

• **Cult Favorites:** *Two Tars* (1928 short, James Parrott), *Duck Soup* (1933, Leo

Suzy Kendall in The Penthouse.

McCarey), *A Star Is Born* (1937, William Wellman).

• **Also of Interest:** Numerous shorts (1911–47), *Tillie and Gus* (1933, Francis Martin), *Small Town Girl* (1935, Wellman), *San Francisco* (1936, W. S. Van Dyke), *Three Men on a Horse* (1936, Mervyn LeRoy), *Hitler's Madman* (1943, Douglas Sirk), *Crazy House* (1943, Edward Cline), *Anchors Aweigh* (1945, George Sidney), *Mad Wednesday/The Sin of Harold Diddlebock* (1947, Preston Sturges), *Unfaithfully Yours* (1948, Sturges).

○

GEORGE KENNEDY (1925–) Tall and rugged-looking, this likable, familiar character ac-tor began his career playing tough guys. He was one of the thugs who menaced Audrey Hepburn in *Charade*. He continued to play rough characters in all genres, but they gradually became more sympathetic. He was always a dependable, underpriced ac-tor with a forceful presence and honest delivery, who showed equal concern no matter what level of problem his characters faced. He won a Supporting Actor Oscar as one of Paul Newman's fellow prisoners in *Cool Hand Luke*. He really became popular and something of a camp figure as the re-liable jack-of-all-trades mechanic in the "Airport" films, and was in another major disaster film, *Earthquake*. Of late, he has played more authority figures. He has ap-peared in numerous low-budget films, en-

George Kennedy (right) *with Burt Lancaster in* Airport.

hancing his cult reputation without worrying whether the material matches his talents—he even turned up in the Dereks' *Bolero.* In Albert Brooks's *Modern Romance,* he gave a hilarious tongue-in-cheek performance as himself, performing scenes in a wretched science-fiction film. He could laugh at himself, and make us laugh while doing it. Like Leslie Nielsen, he revealed skills as a straight-faced comic after years of dramatic roles; it made sense that they would play detective partners in the madcap *The Naked Gun.*

• **Cult Favorites:** *Lonely Are the Brave* (1962, David Miller), *Strait-Jacket* (1964, William Castle), *The Dirty Dozen* (1967, Robert Aldrich), *Cool Hand Luke* (1967, Stuart Rosenberg), *Modern Romance* (1981, Albert Brooks).

• **Also Recommended:** *Charade* (1963, Stanley Donen), *In Harm's Way* (1965, Otto Preminger), *The Sons of Katie Elder* (1965, Henry Hathaway), *The Flight of the Phoenix* (1966, Aldrich), *Hurry Sundown* (1967, Preminger), *The Boston Strangler* (1968, Richard Fleischer), *The Good Guys and the Bad Guys* (1969, Burt Kennedy), *Airport* (1970, George Seaton), *Fool's Parade* (1971, Andrew V. McLaglen), *Cahill—U.S. Marshall* (1973, McLaglen), *Earthquake* (1974, Mark Robson), *The Naked Gun* (1988, David Zucker), *The Naked Gun 2½: The Smell of Fear* (1991, Zucker).

• **Also of Interest:** *Island of the Blue Dolphin* (1964, James B. Clark), *Hush . . . Hush, Sweet Charlotte* (1965, Aldrich), *Mirage* (1965, Edward Dmytryk), *. . . tick . . . tick . . . tick* (1970, Ralph Nelson), *Airport 1975* (1974, Jack Smight), *Thunderbolt and Lightfoot* (1974, Michael Cimino), *The Eiger Sanction* (1975, Clint Eastwood), *Airport '77* (1977, Jerry Jameson), *Radioactive Dreams* (1986, Albert Pyun).

○

JOHNNIE/JOHNNY KEYES Probably the only black actor to have any fame in the porno industry, although his mark was minor. Talk about dramatic debuts: in the XXX-rated *Behind the Green Door,* this stud walks onto a stage wearing a leotard which has a hole in front through which his long penis sticks, and he has sex with kidnapped blonde Marilyn Chambers in front of an appreciative audience. In Chambers's next film, *The Resurrection of Eve,* Keyes, an ex-boxer, played a fighter who Chambers's jealous husband believes is having sex with his wife.

• **Cult Favorite:** *Behind the Green Door* (1972, Jim and Art Mitchell).

• **Other Key Films:** *The Resurrection of Eve* (1973, Mitchell Brothers), *Inside Marilyn Chambers* (1975, Mitchell Brothers), *Sodom and Gomorrah* (1977, Mitchell Brothers), *Heavenly Desire* (1979, Jaacov Jaacovi), *Proball Cheerleaders* (1979, Jack Mathews).

○

MARGOT KIDDER (1948–) Underrated, appealingly offbeat Canadian-born leading lady, with long, dark hair, a pretty, elfin face, a slim figure, and a voice that is sexiest when hoarse. She was regarded as a rebellious free spirit early in her career, when she was a political activist, drug experimenter, and proponent of the sexual revolution (even admitting she liked doing screen nudity). Even though she was vital to the box-office success of the first two Superman films and *The Amityville Horror,* studios still haven't felt comfortable casting her in major films. So she has created memorable characters in out-of-the-mainstream films: the American exchange

Margot Kidder in Brian De Palma's Sisters.

student whom Dubliner Gene Wilder falls for and is hurt by in *Quackser Fortune Has a Cousin in the Bronx;* separated Siamese twins, one of whom is homicidal, in *Sisters;* a foul-mouthed, drunk sorority slut in *Black Christmas;* the unpredictably exciting woman who attracts friends Ray Sharkey and Michael Ontkean in *Willie and Phil* (a *Jules and Jim* remake); and a loud, flamboyant, blond-wigged, man-chasing kook who rooms with pregnant Annie Potts in *Heartaches,* earning her Canada's most prestigious acting awards. She was a marvelous Lois Lane in *Superman,* injecting the familiar character with a blend of energy, humor, smarts, sex, and flakiness—she comes across as the ideal modern-day working woman. The "date" the starry-eyed Lois and Christopher Reeve's newly arrived Superman have—

she interviews him on her patio (as he uses X-ray vision to see the color of her underwear), he flies her through space (and her thoughts are poetic)—is one of the cinema's most novel and enjoyable love-sex scenes, paving the way for them to sleep together in *Superman II.* She would have eaten George Reeves alive.

• **Cult Favorites:** *Quackser Fortune Has a Cousin in the Bronx* (1970, Waris Hussein), *Sisters* (1973, Brian De Palma), *92 in the Shade* (1975, Thomas McGuane), *Willie and Phil* (1980, Paul Mazursky).

• **Sleepers:** *Black Christmas/Stranger in the House* (1975, Bob Clark), *Heartaches* (1981, Donald Shebib).

• **Also Recommended:** *The Great Waldo Pepper* (1970, George Roy Hill), *Superman* (1978, Richard Donner), *Superman II* (1980, Richard Lester).

• **Also of Interest:** *Gaily, Gaily* (1969, Norman Jewison), *The Gravy Train* (1974, Jack Starrett), *The Reincarnation of Peter Proud* (1975, J. Lee Thompson), *The Amityville Horror* (1979, Stuart Rosenberg), *Some Kind of Hero* (1982, Michael Pressman), *Trenchcoat* (1983, Michael Tuckner), *Little Treasure* (1985, Alan Sharp), *Superman IV: The Quest for Peace* (1987, Sidney J. Furie).

○

RICHARD KIEL (1939–) Gigantic, brutish-looking ex-bouncer who has played mostly pea-brained thugs and, in science-fiction and horror films, unusual, seemingly invincible villains; he has occasionally played heroes. He was a lusty prehistoric caveman in *Eegah!,* kidnapping modern-day teenager Marilyn Manning. The low-budget film, which stars Arch Hall, Jr., is one of the worst sci-fi–horror films ever made, but Kiel didn't seem to care as he (surely improvising) put his massive hands all over his nervous (frightened?) female costar and tested the ratings code. Kiel also made a bad impression as a giant alien, Kolos, who comes to earth and duplicates George Nader (as if one weren't already too many) in *The Human Duplicators.* Kiel's best role came 12 years later, as Jaws in *The Spy Who Loved Me.* After *Goldfinger's* Oddjob, Jaws—who can chew furniture with his steel teeth—is the scariest henchman in the James Bond series, and a worthy foe to Roger Moore's hero. Jaws returned in *Moonraker,* but the mean man fell in love, provided humor, and became a nice guy—they ruined him. Still, Kiel was rewarded not only with a hero's role, but the lead in *The Humanoid.*
• **Cult Favorites:** *Eegah!* (1962, Nicholas Merriwether/Arch Hall, Sr.), *Las Vegas Hillbillys* (1966, Arthur C. Pierce), *The Spy Who Loved Me* (1977, Lewis Gilbert).
• **Also of Interest:** *The Magic Sword* (1962, Bert I. Gordon), *The Human Duplicators* (1965, Hugo Grimaldi), *The Longest Yard* (1974, Robert Aldrich), *Silver Streak* (1976, Arthur Hiller), *The Humanoid* (1979, George B. Lewis), *The Phoenix* (1980, Richard Caan and Sadamasu Arnkawa), *So Fine* (1981, Andrew Bergman), *Pale Rider* (1985, Clint Eastwood).

○

UDO KIER (1944–) This German actor had a sympathetic part in the torture-filled *Mark of the Devil,* the dubbed, gross-out, rated V-for-Violence horror film for which viewers were provided "Vomit Bags." From such dubious beginnings, he was picked by Paul Morrissey to star in both *Andy Warhol's Frankenstein* and the equally bloody but better-made and funnier *Andy Warhol's Dracula.* His thick accent and excitable, exaggerated, naturally humorous delivery definitely appealed to Warhol and Morrissey. His Frankenstein is perpetually aggravated and bad-tempered. While creating his Monster and talking science non-stop to his sex-crazed assistant, Arno Juerging—funny conversations—his neglected wife, Monique Van Vooren, sleeps with stud field worker Joe Dallesandro. His Dracula is the cinema's skinniest, most sickly vampire. Every time he gets excited, he weakens further. His conversations with his assistant, again Juerging, are continuous arguments, with Kier screaming every line and becoming completely drained. They are hilarious scenes. In this film, Kier goes to Italy for some desperately needed virgin blood, and seduces several young sisters. He becomes violently, disgustingly ill after each encounter because they aren't "weergins" after all; it seems they each slept with their father's Bolshevik gardener, played—naturally—by Joe Dallesandro.

• **Cult Favorites:** *Mark of the Devil* (1970, Michael Armstrong), *Andy Warhol's Frankenstein/Flesh for Frankenstein* (1974, Paul Morrissey), *Andy Warhol's Dracula/Blood for Dracula* (1974, Morrissey), *The Story of O* (1975, Just Jaeckin), *Suspiria* (1976, Dario Argento).

• **Also of Interest:** *The Salzburg Connection* (1972, Lee H. Katzin), *Spermula* (1975, Bernard Lenteric), *The Latest Fad* (1975, Robert van Ackeren), *Bolweiser* (1977, Rainer Werner Fassbinder), *The Third Generation* (1979, Fassbinder), *Lili Marlene* (1980, Fassbinder).

○

ROY KINNEAR (1934–89) Large-bellied, round-headed, pink-cheeked British character actor brought good cheer to all his roles, particularly in Richard Lester comedies. His characters don't have a lot to say or, rather, they are too slow to say very much. Anyway, they often make shrewd observations or deliver bad news that no one wants to hear. In several of the Lester films, it seemed as if his parts weren't in the original scripts but were written in just so he could make an appareance, stutter a bit without anyone paying attention, and flash his funny, confused expression with an open mouth and uncertain grin. Such a role was his overworked, underappreciated Musketeers helper—the part he was reprising in the 1989 sequel (the third in the series), when he was thrown from a horse and killed. His most famous Lester part was as Victor Spinetti's sidekick in the Beatles' *Help!*. Apart from his work with Lester, he is best known as the peanut-tycoon father of a spoiled little girl in *Willy Wonka and the Chocolate Factory*. Even in such an unflattering part, he seemed like a nice man.

• **Cult Favorites:** *Help!* (1965, Richard Lester), *A Funny Thing Happened on the Way to the Forum* (1966, Lester), *How I Won the War* (1967, Lester), *The Bed-Sitting Room* (1969, Lester), *Willy Wonka and the Chocolate Factory* (1971, Mel Stuart), *The Three Musketeers* (1974, Lester), *Hammett* (1983, Wim Wenders).

• **Other Key Films:** *The Hill* (1965, Sidney Lumet), *The Deadly Affair* (1967, Lumet), *Juggernaut* (1974, Lester), *The Four Musketeers* (1975, Lester), *The Adventure of Sherlock Holmes' Smarter Brother* (1975, Gene Wilder), *The Last Remake of Beau Geste* (1977, Marty Feldman), *The Return of the Musketeers* (1989, Lester).

○

KLAUS KINSKI (1926–) A blond, blue-eyed, but unattractive German actor who became famous as the "possessed" star of Werner Herzog movies, he has been alternately magnificent and annoyingly hammy as madmen and human monsters—and even the no-longer-human *Nosferatu, the Vampyre*. He played one individual whose madness is benevolent and inspiring: *Fitzcarraldo,* an excited opera lover who drags a ship over a mountain in order to bring Caruso to the Amazon. But most of his characters are frightening figures—crazies, mad scientists, obsessed politicos (radicals, terrorists), and decadent, morality-be-damned rich men, all capable of shocking cruelty. Jack the Ripper and his pointy-eared Nosferatu are some of his gentler villains! His greatest part was as the title character in Herzog's *Aguirre, the Wrath of God,* a crazed, Hitler-like Spanish

Klaus Kinski as a mad conquistador in Werner Herzog's Aguirre, the Wrath of God.

conquistador who takes prisoner the leader of an expedition in the Amazon, and plans on founding and ruling a kingdom in the jungle, and mating with his daughter to create a new, "pure" race. Kinski plays the role with subtle humor, delivering Aguirre's little dialogue in a dry-throated monotone. But seconds after seeing Kinski—sneering and snarling, gnarled like Richard III, standing at an angle as if to signify he is at odds with the world, twisting his head before moving his body—we recognize how contemptuous he is of the world and the people around him (he'd step on them as if they were ants), and that he is tortured by inner demons. This describes many of Kinski's subsequent villains. Kinski likes to work, which explains why he has played in so many

terrible films in his long career, including gory horror movies and a few of the worst spaghetti westerns. The father of Nastassia Kinski.

• **Cult Favorites:** *For a Few Dollars More* (1965, Sergio Leone), *Aguirre, the Wrath of God* (1972, Werner Herzog), *Woyzeck* (1978, Herzog), *Nosferatu, the Vampyre* (1979, Herzog), *Fitzcarraldo* (1982, Herzog), *Android* (1982, Aaron Lipstadt).

• **Also of Interest:** *Dead Eyes of London* (1961, Alfred Vohrer), *The Million Eyes of Su-Muru* (1967, Lindsay Shonteff), *Venus in Furs* (1970, Jess Franco), *Count Dracula* (1970, Franco), *The French Woman* (1978, Just Jaeckin), *Jack the Ripper* (1979, Franco), *Schizoid* (1980, David Paulsen), *Love and Money* (1982, James Toback), *Venom* (1982, Piers Haggard), *The Little*

Drummer Girl (1984, George Roy Hill), *Code Name: Wild Geese* (1984, Anthony Dawson).

○

NASTASSIA/NASTASSJA KINSKI (1960–) The estranged daughter of Klaus Kinski began in films as a sexy nymphet in minor European films, such as the nifty British horror film *To the Devil—A Daughter,* a title which might have reminded her of her own childhood; and the puerile sex comedy *Boarding School,* a dubbed, cable-TV late-night staple. In the Italian *Stay As You Are,* she romances Marcello Mastroianni, who is not only old enough to be her father but, it turns out, may indeed be him. Offscreen, the teenager had an affair with Roman Polanski, who was over forty. He cast her in the title role in *Tess,* his surprisingly sensitive, feminist adaptation of Thomas Hardy's novel. As the young girl who is victimized by various men, Kinski may not have exhibited much passion, but her portrayal has admirable strength and intelligence, and is both interesting and sympathetic. She also impressed everyone with her beauty: gray-green eyes, full lips, and a face always compared to the young Ingrid Bergman's; she is in fact more sexual and mysterious. Kinski became a hot property, reaching the height of her popularity from 1982 to 1985, when her photos adorned magazines—including a *Time* cover—and she starred in what seemed to be every other picture. She gave commendable performances that benefited from her intelligence, subtle humor, and absolute abandon with her athletic body. However, too often her naturalness was undermined by obsessive directors who turned her into a pawn as they defiantly got across their highly personal, annoyingly stylized visions. Among those, Paul Schrader's sex-drowned horror film, *Cat People,* Francis Coppola's musical, *One from the Heart,* James Toback's espionage tale, *Exposed,* Jean-Jacques Beineix's strange murder-love story, *Moon in the Gutter,* and Hugh Hudson's revolting history lesson, *Revolution,* were major disappointments. Like *Revolution, Unfaithfully Yours,* with Dudley Moore, was unwatchable. Despite Kinski's good critical notices in another personal film, *Paris, Texas,* as a woman who left her family and works in a sex-shop booth, and in the underrated *The Hotel New Hampshire,* as Susie the Bear, audiences overdosed on her and studios decided she no longer had box-office clout. She virtually disappeared from films, but many of us eagerly await her comeback.
• **Cult Favorites:** *Cat People* (1982, Paul Schrader), *Paris, Texas* (1984, Wim Wenders).
• **Sleeper:** *The Hotel New Hampshire* (1984, Tony Richardson).
• **Other Key Films:** *Tess* (1979, Roman Polanski), *One from the Heart* (1982, Francis Ford Coppola), *The Moon in the Gutter* (1983, Jean-Jacques Beineix), *Maria's Lovers* (Andrei Konchalovsky).
• **Also of Interest:** *To the Devil—A Daughter* (1976, Peter Sykes), *The Wrong Move* (1978, Wenders), *Boarding School* (1978, André Farwagi), *Stay As You Are* (1978, Alberto Lattuado), *Exposed* (1983, James Toback).

○

TOMMY KIRK (1941–) The kid who killed Old Yeller. Remember? He had dark hair and looked like Tim Considine (his brother in the Hardy Boys adventures on "The Mickey Mouse Club"). I guess he was forgiven for making all of us cry because he went on to be Walt Disney's top juvenile actor in the fifties and early sixties, appearing in adventures and slapstick comedies with science-fiction themes, including the first, *The Shaggy Dog.* He played the boy-turned-pooch—was he doing penance?—and the superintellectual Merlin in two pictures. After leaving Disney, he starred with other former kid actors and children of stars in the camp science-fiction classic *Village of the Giants.* He then costarred with Disney alumna Annette Funicello in the last of her "Beach Party" movies, *Ghost in the Invisible Bikini,* and the last of the entire beach cycle, Stephanie Rothman's feminist *It's a Bikini World,* as a conceited hunk who tries to win Deborah Walley by posing as an intellectual.

• **Cult Favorites:** *Old Yeller* (1957, Robert Stevenson), *Village of the Giants* (1965, Bert I. Gordon).

• **Other Key Films:** *The Shaggy Dog* (1959, Charles Barton), *Swiss Family Robinson* (1960, Ken Annakin), *The Absent-Minded Professor* (1961, Stevenson), *Moon Pilot* (1962, James Neilson), *Son of Flubber* (1963, Stevenson), *Savage Sam* (1963, Norman Tokar), *The Misadventures of Merlin Jones* (1964, Stevenson), *The Monkey's Uncle* (1965, Stevenson), *Ghost in the Invisible Bikini* (1966, Don Weis), *It's a Bikini World* (1967, Stephanie Rothman).

○

SALLY KIRKLAND (1953–) The tall, talented, attractive blonde, daughter of the late *Life* fashion editor Sally Kirkland, was a familiar figure in the New York arts scene in the sixties. She had the distinction of both making films for Andy Warhol at the Factory and being in the New York Shakespeare Festival's production of *A Midsummer Night's Dream,* as well as appearing in plays on and off-Broadway. Extremely pretty, she broke sexual barriers by spending most of her time in Terrence McNally's 1968 play *Sweet Eros* nude and bound to a chair, and, in 1969, doing topless scenes as neurotic psychiatrist Rip Torn's neurotic patient in *Coming Apart.* This film includes a memorable finale in which she discovers Torn's concealed camera and knocks it loose with a gun butt; as the camera swings freely, she is filmed raging through his office. Kirkland wouldn't have a really good film role until 1987, stunning critics with her range as *Anna,* once Czechoslovakia's greatest actress who, at 44 and in America, can do no better than be an understudy in a horrendous off-Broadway production. The emotional scene in which she lies in bed and tells Paulina Porizkova about her hardships in her homeland is beautifully played, one of the reasons she got a Best Actress Oscar nomination. Because of *Anna,* she has received numerous film offers and has played radically different women, including ostentatious, kooky Maureen Linoleum, who wants to marry outlaw Keith Carradine in Thomas McGuane's comedy *Cold Feet,* and an endangered prostitute who mingles with big business in *High Stakes.* However, everything since *Anna* has been a disappointment. Something of an eccentric and a self-promoter, she is an ordained minister of the New Age Church of the Movement of Inner Spiritual Awareness.

• **Cult Favorites:** *Coming Apart* (1969, Milton Moses Ginsberg), *Anna* (1987, Yurek Bogasyevicz).

• **Also of Interest:** *A Star Is Born* (1976, Frank Pierson), *Private Benjamin* (1980, Howard Zieff), *Fatal Games* (1984,

Michael Elliot), *Talking Walls* (1987, Stephen Verona), *Cold Feet* (1989, Robert Dornhelm), *The Best of the Best* (1989, Bob Radler), *High Stakes* (1989, Amos Kolleck).

○

TAWNY KITAEN A sexy beauty with a long mane of red hair, she was Tom Hanks's clever fiancée in the rowdy comedy *Bachelor Party*—one look at her and you can understand his willingness to marry and commit himself sexually to one woman for the rest of his life. Since then Kitaen has been the female lead in low-budget pictures, usually with a strong sexual content (including obligatory showers, sometimes with a male partner). Kitaen was amateurish in her first starring film, *The Perils of Gwendoline,* a far-fetched adaptation of an old erotic French comic strip, made by the director of *Emmanuelle* and *The Story of O*—and relied on nudity to appease audiences. Her next few films—*Instant Justice, Happy Hour, Crystal Heart*—were terrible, but by the time she made the okay horror film *Witchboard,* playing a violent, possessed woman (speaking in a low, male-devil voice), her acting and energy equalled her sex appeal. She has even developed a screen persona, playing women who are obsessed—with finding her father, with administering

Tawny Kitaen in The Perils of Gwendoline.

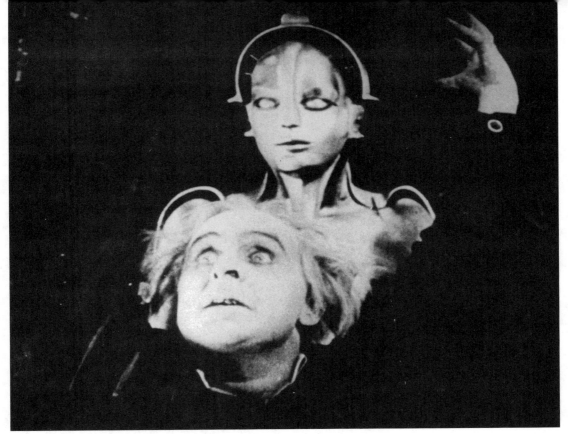

Rudolph Klein-Rogge in Fritz Lang's Metropolis.

revenge, with a Ouija board, with drugs, and so on. She'd still make a great Dallas Cowboys cheerleader or female wrestler, but she is now acceptable as an *actress*. It's time she came back to the mainstream in search of lead roles.

• **Key Films:** *Bachelor Party* (1984, Neil Israel), *The Perils of Gwendoline* (1985, Just Jaeckin), *Witchboard* (1987, Kevin S. Tenney), *White Hot* (1989, Robby Benson).

○

RUDOLPH KLEIN-ROGGE (1888–1955) Beginning in the silent era, under the guidance of Fritz Lang, this unexceptional-looking German actor created some of the most sinister villains in film history. He was the master criminal, *Dr. Mabuse, the Gambler,* who uses mind control to destroy people, using various disguises and forcing some to lose their money to him and others to commit suicide. His pleasure comes from wielding power and manipulating other's lives and determining their fates. A model for other screen villains, he is proof that there is little distinction between genius and madness, that power-lust is the first step toward insanity, and that the criminal mind works similarly to that of great sleuths. Mabuse returned in Lang's talkie, *The Testament of Dr. Mabuse,* using mind control to perpetrate crimes while locked in an insane asylum. An even more famous fiend was his magician Rotwang in

Metropolis, who creates a seductive robot to initiate a worker revolt that will cause their deaths. A mad scientist with an artificial hand, he is a key figure in this German movie tradition. In *Spies,* he played another master criminal who wants to rule the world. Ironically, in *Kriemhild's Revenge,* the second half of Lang's wonderous *Nibelungen Saga,* he played the cinema's only Attila the Hun who respects women, plays with babies, cries, and wants his guests to have a good time. After Lang left Germany, Klein-Rogge married Lang's ex-wife, the writer Thea von Harbou, whom he had supposedly influenced into becoming a Nazi sympathizer.

• **Cult Favorites:** *Dr. Mabuse, the Gambler* (1922, Fritz Lang), *Kriemheld's Revenge* (1924, Lang), *Metropolis* (1926, Lang), *The Testament of Dr. Mabuse* (1933, Lang).

• **Other Key Films:** *Destiny* (1921, Lang), *Spies* (1928, Lang).

○

FUZZY KNIGHT (1901–76) Next to Gabby Hayes and Smiley Burnette, this ex-bandleader and singer was the B western's most likable comic sidekick. Despite his name he was clean-shaven. There was nothing about his appearance that would make one think he was a comic, but he could look dopey, his eyes could seem daffy, and he was adept at stuttering. I never thought he was funny, but he was amiable, sort of like a sagebrush Ray Bolger, and was a good companion for Tex Ritter, Johnny Mack Brown, Brown and Ritter together, Rod Cameron, and Kirby Grant, as they bested killers, rustlers, and mine- and land-jumpers. He also livened up many major-budget pictures.

• **Cult Favorites:** *She Done Him Wrong* (1933, Lowell Sherman), *My Little Chickadee* (1940, Edward Cline).

• **Also of Interest:** *Operator 13* (1934, Richard Boleslawsky), *The Trail of the Lonesome Pine* (1936, Henry Hathaway), *The Plainsman* (1936, Cecil B. De Mille), *Song of the Gringo* (1936, John P. McCarthy), *Spawn of the North* (1938, Hathaway), *The Cowboy and the Lady* (1938, H. C. Potter), *Union Pacific* (1939, De Mille), *Desperate Trails* (1939, Albert Ray), *Oklahoma Frontier* (1939, Ford Beebe), *Johnny Apollo* (1940, Hathaway), *Brigham Young—Frontiersman* (1940, Hathaway), *Law and Order* (1940, Ray Taylor), *The Masked Rider* (1941, Taylor), *Badlands of Dakota* (1941, Alfred E. Green), *Boss of Hangtown Mesa* (1942, Joseph H. Lewis), *Deep in the Heart of Texas* (1942, Elmer Clifton), *The Old Chisolm Trail* (1942, Clifton), *The Silver Bullet* (1942, Lewis), *The Old Texas Trail* (1944, Lewis D. Collins), *Frontier Gal* (1945, Charles Lamont), *Rustler's Roundup* (1946, Wallace C. Fox).

○

SYLVA KOSCINA (1933–) Shapely Yugoslavian-born Italian actress who excited us youngsters as Steve Reeves's bride-to-be in *Hercules* and *Hercules Unchained,* playing the princess who sends Hercules on difficult missions. Reeves's well-built body was not the only one that attracted repeat viewers to the theater. Because of the dubbing, it was impossible to tell that Koscina could act, but in later, adult films, often playing sexy Italians whom the American and British heroes don't know whether to trust, she proved adept at comedy and drama—we already knew she had style. Among her most interesting

parts was a minor role as a circus performer in *Judex*, Georges Franju's bizarre remake of Louis Feuillade's 1917 serial about a caped crusader. Koscina's Daisy, and not Channing Pollock's Judex, does *all* the heroics at the end: she climbs a building, unties Judex's hands, and defeats the archvillain Diane (Francine Bergé) in a fight on the roof. In the seventies, she appeared in bad gore films, *Deadly Sanctuary* (inspired by the writings of the Marquis de Sade), and *Lisa and the Devil* (reedited into *House of Exorcism*), but at least they were made by notables of the genre, Spain's Jess (Jesus) Franco and Italy's Mario Bava.
• **Cult Favorites:** *Hercules* (1959, Pietro Francisci), *Judex* (1963, Georges Franju), *Juliet of the Spirits* (1965, Federico Fellini).
• **Other Key Films:** *Hercules Unchained* (1960, Francisci), *The Little Nuns* (1965, Luciano Sale), *Deadlier Than the Male* (1967, Ralph Thomas), *The Secret War of Harry Frigg* (1968, Jack Smight), *A Lovely Way to Die* (1968, David Lowell Rich), *Hornet's Nest* (1970, Phil Karlson).

○

MARTIN KOSLECK (1907–) Intense, brooding character actor of German-Polish-Russian descent was Hollywood's definitive fascist swine, playing sadistic soldiers (always officers), inquisitors, and doctors-scientists. His specialty was the cruel Nazi: the doctor who drains blood from Russian children in *The North Star* (he even made his superior, Erich von Stroheim, seem sentimental!), the torturing inquisitor Heller in *Underground*, and, several times, Joseph Goebbels, whom he resembled. Of his contemptuous portraits of the Nazi propaganda minister, Kosleck

told John Buras: "I wanted [people] to hate me as I hated the character I was playing." Because he still had family in Germany, he initially used a pseudonym, Nicolai Yoshkin. Although he was mostly in propaganda films from the first time he played Goebbels in *Confessions of a Nazi Spy*, he preferred his villain roles in low-budget horror films, particularly Basil Rathbone's murder partner in *The Mad Doctor*, and the crazed sculptor in *House of Horrors*, who sets the spine-breaking Creeper (acromegalic Rondo Hatton) after art critics.
• **Key Films:** *Confessions of a Nazi Spy* (1939, Anatole Litvak), *Foreign Correspondent* (1940, Alfred Hitchcock), *The Mad Doctor* (1941, Tim Whelan), *Underground* (1941, Vincent Sherman), *All Through the Night* (1942, Sherman), *Berlin Correspondent* (1942, Eugene Forde), *The North Star* (1943, Lewis Milestone), *The Hitler Gang* (1943, John Farrow), *The Mummy's Curse* (1944, Leslie Goodwins), *Strange Holiday* (1942/45, Arch Oboler), *House of Horrors* (1946, Jean Yarbrough), *Hitler* (1962, Stuart Heisler), *The Flesh Eaters* (1964, Jack Curtis).

○

SHO KOSUGI Before there were Mutant Ninja Turtles for the kiddie set, this Japanese martial-arts expert had gained fame as the star of the bloody "Ninja" movie series, playing a stealthy, black-draped killing machine from the mysterious East. He began the first film, *Enter the Ninja*, as a foe of hero Franco Nero's, but would become a hero himself. Except for *Ninja III: The Domination*, which is about a woman possessed by a Ninja warrior, the series is pretty dull and trite, sparked only by Kosugi's bloody fights. Typically, he plays antiterrorists or CIA agents who rescue hostages, stop sabotage, and defeat sadistic villains, who just happen to know kung fu or have mean henchmen who do. Kosugi, who isn't friendly looking, is a dreadful actor, and utterly without humor. His attempts at English are ill-advised, as are his scenes with women. His fight sequences are well-done, if not particularly innovative, and too brutal. They are without the sense of fun of Bruce Lee in combat. Unlike Lee, he uses many weapons along with his martial-arts skills (a favorite trick is to discharge a gun or exotic weapon while flipping through the air). His best film is considered to be *Pray for Death,* in which he dons Ninja garb to avenge his wife and free his kidnapped son. In *Black Eagle,* he defeats an imposing Russian, played by Jean-Claude Van Damme.

• **Cult Favorites:** *Enter the Ninja* (1981, Menaham Golan), *Revenge of the Ninja* (1983, Sam Firstenberg), *Ninja III: The Domination* (1984, Firstenberg), *Pray for Death* (1985, Gordon Hessler).

• **Other Key Films:** *Nine Deaths of the Ninja* (1985, Emmet Alston), *Rage of Honor* (1987, Gordon Hessler), *Black Eagle* (1988, Eric Carson).

○

SYLVIA KRISTEL (1952–) Slender, erotic, multilingual Dutch actress who became an international sex star as the title character in France's soft-core sensation, *Emmanuelle.* As the half-innocent sexual explorer, the sweet-looking Kristel is a turn-on just moving about, seemingly oblivious to the fact that her casual display of her body is exciting anyone on or offscreen. Kristel has wonderful abandon in the way she lifts a leg and allows her robe to open fully, or leans forward so that her blouse shifts and a breast is in view for a second or two. Scantily clad, as she always is, she keeps our eyes alert. Much of Emmanuelle's allure, and Kristel's, is that she isn't shy about her body, or afraid to engage in sexual activity with men or women in semipublic places. She is ready to be seduced. However, when a dirty old man turns her into an exhibitionist who self-consciously displays her body, she is debased in our eyes and loses the appeal that went with her naturally free style. Kristel would play Emmanuelle in inferior sequels that don't even pretend to have themes. She'd also play the leads in other nude-filled exploitation films. Those disguised as "art" films, like *Lady Chatterley's Lover* and *Mata Hari,* were dull because they tried to prove they were legit. Preferable was the sex comedy *Private Lessons,* in which her sneaky-smart French maid seduces a teenager, and *Red Heat,* in which her sadistic lesbian warden forces herself on Linda Blair! She'd also appear in a few mainstream American films, but these had no spark. Despite recent appearances in such travesties as *Dracula's Widow,* her film roles have been sexually exciting on occasion, but for the most part, her appeal vanished with the innocent look that was gone by the end of *Emmanuelle.*

• **Cult Favorites:** *Emmanuelle* (1974, Just Jaeckin).

• **Other Key Films:** *Goodbye, Emmanuelle* (1979, François Letterier), *The Nude Bomb* (1980, Clive Donner), *Private Lessons* (1981, Alan Myerson), *Lady Chatterley's Lover* (1981, Jaeckin), *Mata Hari* (1985, Curtis Harrington).

• **Also of Interest:** *The Fifth Musketeer* (1979, Ken Annakin), *Private School* (1983, Noel Black), *Mysteries* (1984, Paul de Lussanet), *Red Heat* (1985, Robert

Sylvia Kristel being seduced in Emmanuelle.

Collector), *The Big Bet* (1985, Bert I. Gordon), *The Arrogant* (1987, Philippe Blot).

○

MACHIKO KYO (1924–) This pretty former dancer broke into films as a teenager in movies dealing with young people and sex in postwar Japan, and she became the first actress in her country whose sex appeal (specifically, her body), was pivotal to her movies' promotion campaigns. She took an adult role and was striking as the woman in *Rashomon* whose brutal rape and husband's murder is visualized by director Akira Kurosawa in four ways, according to the differing testimony of four witnesses at a trial. This was the first Japanese picture to gain widespread international distribution. Kyo would then star in other films that would be shown in art houses around the world, starring for all the other major Japanese directors, including Ozu, Mizoguchi, Naruse, and Inchikawa. Her fame won her a part in the American film *Teahouse of the August Moon;* she was courted by soldier Glenn Ford in Okinawa. Kyo was versatile, shifting easily between contemporary dramas—usually with sexual themes—and haunting period pieces. She was the clever, brave, energetic female leader of male thieves in *Beauty and the Bandits;* a demonic temptress, who happens to be a ghost, in *Ugetsu*, attracting a married potter into her romantic clutches; and a lovely, smart, and sacrificial married woman whose husband is threatened by a man obsessed with marrying her in *Gate of Hell*. I like her best as the true-life *Princess Yang Kwei Fei*, an eighth-century ex-scullery maid who brought about the downfall of the emperor, her lover. Kwei Fei seems to be Mizoguchi's ideal female, a woman of many attributes who is equally at ease in a palace or mingling with the common people, and who can be both lover and friend to the man in her life.

• **Cult Favorites:** *Rashomon* (1950, Akira Kurosawa), *Ugetsu* (1953, Kenji Mizoguchi).

• **Also Recommended:** *Gate of Hell* (1953, Tienosuke Kinugasa), *Older Brother, Younger Sister* (1953, Mikio Naruse), *The Princess Yang Kwei Fei* (1955, Mizoguchi), *The Teahouse of the August Moon* (1956, Daniel Mann), *Red Light District/Street of Shame* (1956, Mizoguchi), *The Makioka Sisters* (1959, Kojishima), *Odd Obsession/ The Key* (1960, Kon Inchikawa).

• **Other Key Films:** *Clothes of Deception* (1951, Kimisaburo Yoshimura), *The Loyal Forty-Seven Ronin* (1958), *Floating Weeds* (1959, Yasujiro Ozu).

• **Also of Interest:** *A Virgin's Sex Manual* (Hideo Obu), *Bitch* (Keigho Kimura), *Beauty and the Bandits* (Keigo Kimura).

○

VERONICA LAKE (1918–73) A bit player as Constance Keane, she became an overnight sensation in her first role as Veronica Lake, in a small part as a nightclub singer in *I Wanted Wings*. She was only 5′ 2″ and barely topped 90 pounds, but she had a large chest, a sensually husky voice, large eyes, and a lean face with slightly sunken cheeks. (I always found her cute and cuddly; most viewers and critics found her beautiful and cold.) However it was a gimmick that made her a sex siren and glamour queen: long blond tresses covered her right eye in a revolutionary peekaboo style. So many American women copied her look during the war years that the government eventually told her to pull her hair back, in order to cut down on accidents at factories. Ironically, in her first starring role, as The Girl in Preston Sturges's *Sullivan's Travels*, her character spent most of the picture with her hair under a cap and her body under a coat, dressed like a boy hobo. She gave what was probably her best, most endearing performance. She was sweet, tender, playful, sexy in her romantic scenes with Joel McCrea (who was a foot taller); smart, caring, and funny (even doing pratfalls, though she was pregnant at the time). Lake was also charming in her only other top-grade comedy, *I Married a Witch*, although she despised leading man Fredric March (he had to play one romantic scene while she drove a knee into his crotch, out of the frame). Most often she played what she called a "zombie sex siren," an icy, sulky, self-sufficient broad, often a nightclub singer (her songs were dubbed by Martha Mears) who had become desensitized after years of being knocked about. In this vogue, she was at her best in four hard-bitten melodramas with Alan Ladd: *This Gun for Hire* (from Graham Greene), *The Glass Key* (from Dashiell Hammett), *The Blue Dahlia* (from Raymond Chandler), and, a couple of notches below the others, *Saigon*. Also short and blond and deep-voiced, Ladd was a perfect screen partner for Lake. "They created," wrote James Robert Parish, "a new brand of screen lovers—calculating, conscience-less, self-possessed individuals. Their love scenes together were the epitome of re-strained ego-feeding, filled with non-sequitur conversation, wisps of cigarette smoke and bristling icy stares." Her career faltering, Lake left Hollywood in the early fifties and appeared in theaters across the country, often in very minor productions. She faded from sight and was found years later working as a hotel barmaid in New York. She died at 55 of hepatitis, with her last film being the horror abomination *Flesh Feast,* which she coproduced. It was a far cry from her exit in the 1943 war film *So Proudly We Hail*—in that film her nurse puts a live grenade down her blouse, walks into a gathering of enemy soldiers, and blows up.

• **Cult Favorite:** *Sullivan's Travels* (1941, Preston Sturges).

• **Also Recommended:** *This Gun for Hire* (1942, Frank Tuttle), *The Glass Key* (1942, Stuart Heisler), *I Married a Witch* (1942, René Clair), *Star-Spangled Rhythm* (1942, George Marshall), *So Proudly We Hail* (1943, Mitchell Leisen), *The Blue Dahlia* (1946, Marshall), *Ramrod* (1947,

Veronica Lake with Allan Ladd in The Blue Dahlia.

André de Toth), *The Sainted Sisters* (1948, William Russell).

○

BARBARA LA MARR (1896–1926) Oddly, she began in films as a storywriter, but soon developed into a voluptuous actress, the "Too-Beautiful Girl," as she was dubbed by Adela Rogers St. John. She had fair skin, in marked contrast to her dark, wavy hair, which was pulled back and parted in the middle, overdoctored lips, quivering eyebrows (particularly active during panting scenes), and soulful eyes that she used to seduce heroes played by a number of the silent cinema's romantic idols, including Douglas Fairbanks, John Gilbert, and Ramon Navarro. She was a more refined and subtle vamp than Theda Bara had been in the previous decade, but just as deadly. Men on- and offscreen were transfixed by what one writer described as "the primitive fire that lurks beneath the surface." Even at an early age, she attracted men into her spiderweb; by the time she was 17, she was twice widowed. She'd marry at least five times in her brief life, once to a man who already was married and once when it was unclear whether *she* wasn't already married. One ex-husband would go to prison, another would commit suicide. She lived life to the fullest, as if she knew she would die young. She partied all night, took many lovers, indulged heavily in opium, cocaine, and alcohol. After a long illness that took its toll on her beauty and energy, she died of a drug overdose at 29.

• **Key Films:** *The Three Musketeers* (1921, Fred Niblo), *The Prisoner of Zenda* (1922, Rex Ingram), *Trifling Women* (1922, Ingram), *Quincy Adams Sawyer* (1922, Clarence Badger), *Strangers of the Night* (1923, Niblo), *The Eternal City* (1924, George Fitzmaurice), *Thy Name Is Woman* (1924, Niblo), *The Shooting of Dan McGrew* (1924, Badger).

○

HEDY LAMARR (1913–) Despite her long Hollywood career, this dark-haired Austrian beauty is still most identified with an early role she had (as Hedwig Kiesler) in the once-banned Czech film *Ecstasy.* Her most famous sequence—a 10-minute nude swim and naked dash through the woods—is certainly a highlight of the film. However, even more startling in this bold, erotic exploration of a young woman's need for sexual fulfillment are two other scenes. Director Gustav Machaty cuts back and forth between sexual imagery and Lamarr's frustrated young bride (her older husband isn't interested in sex) as she

Hedy Lamarr in the famous nude scene in Ecstasy.

stands alone on a balcony, cigarette smoke escaping her wide-open mouth, as she thinks of the young worker who saw her nude; later Machaty's camera stays on her face throughout her lovemaking with the young man, even while she has an orgasm. More than the nude scene, this is why the film had problems with censors. In Hollywood films, Lamarr was promoted as the most beautiful actress in the world—and she might well have been. But while her characters were lusted after by all men, these women were driven by their hearts or their greed, rarely by their libidos. She was excitingly romantic as Charles Boyer's screen lover in *Algiers* (her first and best Hollywood film), exotic in *White Cargo*, funny and spirited in *H. M. Pulham, Esq.*, sexually aggressive (for once!) in *Samson and Delilah*, and mysterious in *The Strange Woman*, *The Conspirators*, and *A Lady Without a Passport*, among others. She was always luscious—glamorous, sexy, and exciting in love scenes—even if her acting impressed no one. However, few of her characters had anything interesting going on beneath the surface.

• **Cult Favorites:** *Ecstasy* (1933, Gustav Machaty), *Algiers* (1938, John Cromwell), *The Story of Mankind* (1957, Irwin Allen).

• **Other Key Films:** *Lady of the Tropics* (1939, Jack Conway), *Boom Town* (1940, Conway), *Comrade X* (1940, King Vidor), *H. M. Pulham, Esq.* (1941, Vidor), *Tortilla Flat* (1942, Victor Fleming), *White Cargo* (1942, Richard Thorpe), *The Heavenly Body* (1943, Alexander Hall), *The Conspirators* (1944, Jean Negulesco), *Experiment Perilous* (1944, Jacques Tourneur), *Samson and Delilah* (1949, Cecil B. De Mille), *A Lady Without a Passport* (1950, Joseph H. Lewis), *My Favorite Spy* (1951, Norman Z. McLeod), *The Female Animal* (1958, Harry Keller).

Christopher Lambert in Highlander.

○

CHRISTOPHER LAMBERT (1958–) New York–born French star of action and adventure films that have been ambitious but invariably disappointing. He made a great Tarzan in *Greystoke, the Legend of Tarzan, Lord of the Apes,* lithe and graceful instead of musclebound (he resembled but was more agile than Bruce Bennett in *Tarzan the Fearless*), interesting-looking rather than matinee-idol handsome, and the first movie apeman to project the proper combination of intellect and savagery. He was also extremely sexual; his love scenes with Andie MacDowell's Jane are truly erotic. But the film failed because the filmmakers, who wanted to make a highbrow, artistic film from a pulp novel, were less interested in the Tarzan as created by Burroughs than in Tarzan as a unique case study—a man whose primal, bestial instincts cannot be suppressed by human conditioning and control. There would not be a sequel to that *Greystoke,* although the ending hinted at one, but Lambert may have found a recurring role as the *Highlander,* a time-jumping, sword-fighting Scottish vengeance hero. His performances in that film, in Michael Cimino's laughably bad *The Sicilian,* and in Luc Bresson's glitzy but empty thriller *Subway,* indicate he must learn at least one new expression. A major sex symbol in France.

• **Cult Favorites:** *Greystoke, the Legend of Tarzan, Lord of the Apes* (1984, Hugh Hudson), *Subway* (1985, Luc Bresson).

• **Other Key Films:** *Asphalte* (1980, Denis Amar), *Love Songs* (1985, Elle Chouraqui), *Highlander* (1986, Russell Mulcahy), *I Love You* (1986, Marco Ferreri), *Le Complot* (1987, Agnieszka Holland).

○

DOROTHY LAMOUR (1914–) Former Miss New Orleans and vocalist for bandleader Herbie Kaye, whom she married, this beautiful brunette became a star at Paramount long before she revealed any acting talent. As exotic South Seas maidens, with her long hair falling to her shoulders, her curvaceous body clad in a sarong in constant jeopardy of opening up or falling off, her body darkened by makeup, and her lovely—and *different*—face, she made hearts flutter. *The Hurricane,* a well-mounted Sam Goldwyn production directed by John Ford, was certainly the best of her South Seas films, but as a fifties kid growing up on the Early Show and Saturday afternoon movies on TV, I was just as excited by *The Jungle Princess, Her Jungle Love,* and *Aloma of the South Seas.* Partly

No one has ever looked better in a sarong than Dorothy Lamour.

because those pictures were geared for kids, but more specifically because her Ulah, Marama, Tura, Manuela, Dea, Mima, Tanoa, Lona, and Tama were pretty interchangeable. Just as many of us boys had crushes on Maureen O'Sullivan's Jane in the Tarzan jungle films, we were enchanted by this sexy South Seas girl. Lamour might have been one of the beautiful women Gauguin found in Tahiti. She was a fantasy lover (as her last name implies)—docile, kind, innocent and trusting, loyal, nurselike but in need of protection herself, as romantic as the songs she sings, virginal but eager to learn (she gets kissing lessons from Ray Milland in one film)—the reason men (and little boys) want to sail away to the South Seas. When

Paramount put her in contemporary films, she was usually cast as an entertainer (allowing her to sing). These were harder, experienced women who know what to expect from men, and how to use looks and promises to gain an advantage. Never comfortable when things on screen got too serious, she was seen to best advantage as the girl both Bob Hope and Bing Crosby fall in love with in their "Road" comedies. She could relax because the comedy was delivered in such a casual manner, and, as when she costarred in Hope's solo comedies, she seemed to be having fun. For once she wasn't the one acting like a child.

• **Cult Favorite:** *Donovan's Reef* (1963, John Ford).

• **Key Films:** *The Jungle Princess* (1935, William Thiele), *The Hurricane* (1937, Ford), *Her Jungle Love* (1938, George Archainbaud), *Spawn of the North* (1938, Henry Hathaway), *St. Louis Blues* (1939, Raoul Walsh), *Johnny Apollo* (1940, Hathaway), *Typhoon* (1940, Louis King), *Road to Singapore* (1940, Victor Schertzinger), *Road to Zanzibar* (Schertzinger), *Caught in the Draft* (1941, David Butler), *Aloma of the South Seas* (1941, Alfred Santell), *Beyond the Blue Horizon* (1942, Santell), *Road to Morocco* (1942, Butler), *They Got Me Covered* (1943, Butler), *And the Angels Sing* (1944, Claude Binyon), *Road to Utopia* (1945, Hal Walker), *My Favorite Brunette* (1947, Elliott Nugent), *Road to Rio* (1947, Norman Z. McLeod), *Road to Bali* (1952, Walker).

• **Also of Interest:** *The Big Broadcast of 1938* (1938, Mitchell Leisen), *Tropic Holiday* (1938, Theodore Reed), *Chad Hanna* (1940, Henry King), *Star-Spangled Rhythm* (1942, George Marshall), *The Greatest Show on Earth* (1952, Cecil B. De Mille), *Road to Hong Kong* (1962, Norman Panama).

O

ELSA LANCHESTER (1902–86) Delightful, bewitching British actress of stage and screen, who often appeared with her husband of 33 years, Charles Laughton. With curly hair pulled back to accentuate a long, upturned nose and a curved forehead, a large dimple in her chin, enormous eyes, and a slim body, she looked like a caricature. Yet despite her peculiar look, there was something oddly attractive about her. Also she was surprisingly agile—she toured in *Peter Pan,* she did impressive Chaplin-like slapstick in several silent shorts directed by Ivor Montagu. Both her unusual face and her physical dexterity came into play in her great performance as the title character in *The Bride of Frankenstein.* In profile, her stitches are barely noticeable because of her wild hairstyle, inspired by Nefertiti; in a white shroud, on two-and-a-half-foot stilts that make her movements birdlike, she half-wobbles, half-glides across the room; when she hisses and screams, she seems monstrous. Although she played the Bride, Lanchester received top billing in movies only in her obscure silent comedies and in one sound film, *Passport to Adventure,* as a char woman (she played many maids) who scrubs her way to Berlin in hopes of assassinating Hitler. Otherwise she had supporting roles, playing spinsters, eccentrics, and a number of quirky characters with annoying traits (e.g., her kooky painter has a great giggle in *The Big Clock).* Almost all her women are cunning; most have touches of brilliance. Best of all were her films with Laughton. Her women knew how to stand strong during his characters' temper tantrums, how to temper their bombast, make them reveal their soft sides, offer sound advice and care when

Elsa Lanchester and Boris Karloff in The Bride of Frankenstein.

they are too proud to admit they are confused, afraid, or hurt, and put up with or simply ignore their idiosyncracies (as no other woman would). Laughton's men are thrown off guard by her unusual women, and exasperated by their quirks and feisty natures, yet come to appreciate them and love their company. This pattern began in *The Private Life of Henry VIII,* in which Laughton's king decides not to kill Lanchester's Anne of Cleves when she dares beat him at cards. She understands him. He gives up on finding the perfect wife, granting all her demands in exchange for his freedom.

• **Cult Favorites:** *Naughty Marietta* (1935, W. S. Van Dyke), *The Bride of Frankenstein* (1935, James Whale), *The Spiral Staircase* (1946, Robert Siodmak),

Bell, Book, and Candle (1958, Richard Quine), *Willard* (1971, Daniel Mann).

• **Other Key Films:** *The Private Life of Henry VIII* (1933, Alexander Korda), *Rembrandt* (1936, Korda), *Vessel of Wrath/The Beachcomber* (1936, Erich Pommer), *The Big Clock* (1948, John Farrow), *Come to the Stable* (1949, Henry Koster), *The Inspector General* (1949, Koster), *Witness for the Prosecution* (1957, Billy Wilder).

• **Also of Interest:** *The Ghost Goes West* (1936, René Clair), *Ladies in Retirement* (1941, Charles Vidor), *Son of Fury* (1942, John Cromwell), *Lassie, Come Home* (1943, Fred M. Wilcox), *Passport to Adventure* (1944, Ray McCarey), *The Bishop's Wife* (1947, Koster), *Mystery Street* (1950, John Sturges), *Dreamboat* (1952, Claude Binyon), *The Glass Slipper* (1955,

Charles Walters), *Mary Poppins* (1964, Robert Stevenson), *Terror in the Wax Museum* (1973, Georg Fenady).

○

CAROLE LANDIS (1919–48) Vivacious blonde (the "Ping Girl") whose much-publicized legs and figure were shown to great advantage when she wore a cavewoman outfit in her first lead, in *One Million B.C.* She followed that enjoyable, campy adventure film with another odd Hal Roach project, *Turnabout,* an ahead-of-its-time comedy in which Landis and husband, John Hubbard, exchange personalities. Landis would star in several pictures, but more often she had the second female lead, supporting Betty Grable, Joan Blondell, Rita Hayworth, or Sonja Henie. In *I Wake Up Screaming,* the leads figure out who killed her character. *Four Jills in a Jeep,* in which she was billed behind Kay Francis and Martha Raye but ahead of Mitzi Mayfair, was a fictional account of their adventures as entertainers with the USO during World War II. The lighter the film, the better Landis was. However, her enduring fame is less the result of her movies than her offscreen life. She married four times, beginning by eloping at 15. She competed in beauty contests from the time she was 12, and as a teenager worked as a hula dancer in San Francisco. She came to Hollywood in 1937, and Busby Berkeley placed her in the chorus of *Varsity Show* and got her a contract at Warners. Soon Landis's husband, Irving Wheeler, tried to sue Berkeley for $250,000 for stealing his wife's affections. Landis signed a contract at 20th Century-Fox, where, according to Kenneth Anger in *Hollywood Babylon II,* she became known as the "studio hooker" and was "the most constant visitor in attendance in the back room of Darryl F. Zanuck's office." In 1948, her love for Rex Harrison not reciprocated, she intentionally overdosed on barbiturates.

• **Cult Favorites:** *Daredevils of the Red Circle* (1939 serial, William Witney and John English), *One Million B.C.* (1940, Hal Roach, Hal Roach, Jr., and D. W. Griffith), *I Wake Up Screaming* (1941, H. Bruce Humberstone).

• **Also of Interest:** *Turnabout* (1940, Roach), *Topper Returns* (1941, Roy Del Ruth), *Moon Over Miami* (1941, Walter Lang), *My Gal Sal* (1942, Irving Cummings), *Orchestra Wives* (1942, Archie Mayo), *Four Jills in a Jeep* (1944, William Seiter), *Secret Command* (1944, A. Edward Sutherland), *Having a Wonderful Crime* (1945, Sutherland), *It Shouldn't Happen to a Dog* (1946, Herbert I. Leeds).

Carole Landis.

○

LAURENE LANDON Canadian-born, California-raised actress is tall (6' in heels), physical, and sexy, with long and wild blond hair that often hides her face. At times, she resembles Veronica Lake, but is much bigger and much more athletic; though their actual roles are very different, she, like Lake, also plays women with sensitivity and vulnerability beneath hard exteriors. One senses that Landon is much softer than her characters. She was impressive costarring with Vicki Frederick as wrestling tag-team partners, managed by Peter Falk, in the surprisingly enjoyable comedy-drama . . . *All the Marbles.* Neither actress used doubles in the exciting and physically demanding wrestling sequences. I expected Frederick's career to take off, but Landon has actually done better, although she has been stuck in violent exploitation films, some that go directly to video. She has played barbarian women who swing swords, like the title character in *Hundra,* and tough broads who shoot machine guns. Her characters are excitable and usually unhappy, allowing her to use her hurt-puppy look. Most can take care of themselves. Although she doesn't do nudity, she does her own, often dangerous, stunts. Asked by *Prevue* editor Steranko if she wears protective padding, she replied: "Hell, no! Who do you think I am, Arnold Schwarzenegger? I *never* use that stuff—it's for sissy heroes."
- **Sleeper:** . . . *All the Marbles* (1981, Robert Aldrich).
- **Other Key Films:** *I, the Jury* (1982, Richard T. Heffron), *Hundra* (1984, Matt Cimber), *Yellow Hair and the Fortress of Gold* (1985, Cimber), *America 3000* (1986, Dave Engelbach), *Armed Response* (1986, Fred Olen Ray), *It's Alive III: Island of the*

Alive (1987, Larry Cohen), *Maniac Cop* (1988, William Lustig).

○

ALAN "ROCKY" LANE (1904–73) Handsome, marginally talented cowboy star at Republic came to the B studio after being a supporting player and occasional lead at major studios. Among those he supported were Shirley Temple and Laurel and Hardy; one of his leading ladies was Joan Fontaine in her prestar days. At Republic, Lane had some success in serials, particularly opposite genre queens Kay Aldridge in *Daredevils in the West* and Linda Stirling in *The Tiger Woman.* After supporting roles in westerns, he got his own western series, a level below those of Republic's stars, Gene Autry and Roy Rogers. When Autry and Rogers were in the military, Republic got behind Lane and he became a top cowboy star. There was nothing special about his westerns, but he was a likable presence and a sturdy action hero, quick on the trigger and handsome enough to romance the ladies. His wonderhorse was Black Jack, and among his sidekicks were Al St. John and Eddy Waller. Lane is best remembered for the "Red Ryder" series, replacing William Elliott; costar Bobby Blake was Little Beaver. He was still at the peak of his popularity when the television western killed off the B western.
- **Key Films:** *The Law West of Tombstone* (1938, Glenn Tyron), *King of the Royal Mounted* (1940 serial, William Witney and John English), *King of the Mounties* (1942 serial, Witney), *Daredevils of the West* (1943, English), *The Tiger Woman* (1944 serial, Spencer Bennet and Wallace Grissell), *Sheriff of Sundown* (1944, Lesley Selander), *Trail of Kit Carson* (1945, Selander), *Out California Way* (1946, Se-

lander), *Stagecoach to Denver* (1946), *The Wyoming Bandit* (1949), *Night Riders of Montana* (1951, Witney), *Fort Dodge Stampede* (1951, Harry Keller), *Savage Frontier* (1953, Keller), *El Paso Stampede* (1953, Keller).

• **Also of Interest:** *Stowaway* (1936, William A. Seiter), *Charlie Chan at the Olympics* (1937, H. Bruce Humberstone), *The Dancing Masters* (1943, Mal St. Clair), *Bells of Rosarita* (1945, Frank Mc-Donald), *Trail of Robin Hood* (1950, Witney), *Hell Bent for Leather* (1960, George Sherman).

○

DIANE LANE (1965–) She debuted in films when she was just 13—after eight years of theater. She was sweet and pretty and impressive in the charming *A Little Romance* (she has never had as good a screen lover as young Thelo Bernard), and everyone predicted that the young blonde would grow into a beautiful woman and a major actress. She made the cover of *Time,* was referred to as a "budding" Grace Kelly, and was besieged by film offers. But she was reluctant to exploit her obvious sex appeal and opted for roles that called for extreme modesty (except for her unruly teen rock singer in a see-through blouse in *Ladies and Gentlemen: The Fabulous Stains*). She turned down such star-making roles as those in *Pretty Baby, The Blue Lagoon,* and, later, the part Jodie Foster played in *Hotel New Hampshire.* Lane was a seductive mix of naiveté and precociousness as a teenager in Francis Coppola's S. E. Hinton adaptations *The Outsiders* and *Rumble Fish,* a delectable female in these films about troubled male teens, but audiences stayed away. She was miscast as an adult singer, lost among the

Diane Lane in Streets of Fire.

action and confusion in both *Streets of Fire* and *The Cotton Club.* Her unfocused characters became less interesting as the films unravel. No longer refusing to do nudity, Lane was more effective in less "important" films, as a deceitful stripper in *The Big Town* (her third picture with Matt Dillon) and a window dresser with a kinky artistic slant in *Lady Beware.* In the latter film, there are moments when she recalls Natalie Wood, both in voice and expression. When her character overcomes her fears and goes after the killer who is stalking her, she has more screen presence than in her earlier films. It was as if Lane suddenly realized *she* could be a film's main attraction. Her new-found confidence was also apparent when she played a sympathetic prostitute in the TV western miniseries *Lonesome Dove.* Perhaps she can now find the stardom that has eluded her.

• **Cult Favorites:** *Ladies and Gentlemen: The Fabulous Stains* (1981, Lou Adler), *The Outsiders* (1983, Francis Coppola), *Rumble Fish* (1983, Coppola), *Streets of Fire* (1984, Walter Hill).

• **Sleepers:** *A Little Romance* (1979, George Roy Hill), *Cattle Annie and Little Britches* (1980, Lamont Johnson).

• **Other Key Films:** *Touched By Love* (1980, Guy Trikonis), *The Cotton Club* (1984, Coppola), *The Big Town* (1987, Ben Bolt), *Lady Beware* (1987, Karen Arthur), *Vital Signs* (1990, Marisa Silver).

○

JOI LANSING (1936–72) I liked this blond, shapely, round-cheeked starlet who had minor roles on television (she was Lester Flatt's wife on "The Beverly Hillbillies") and in films. She was always spirited and amusing as sexy, flirtatious neighbors, models, and dates of someone else at the dinner table. She was Barbara Nichols's sister—they played the Coogle Sisters!—in *Who Was That Lady?* Underappreciated, she would have to take roles in abysmal films toward the end of her career, but she never lost her pizzazz. She died at an early age without really accumulating decent credits. Nevertheless, many of us remember her fondly.

• **Films of Interest:** *The Brave One* (1957, Irving Rapper), *A Hole in the Head* (1959, Frank Capra), *The Atomic Submarine* (1959, Spencer Bennet), *Who Was That Lady?* (1960, George Sidney), *Marriage on the Rocks* (1965, Jack Donohue), *Hillbillys in a Haunted House* (1967, Jean Yarbrough), *Big Foot* (1971, Robert Slatzer).

○

AL "LASH" LA RUE (1917–) Lash La Rue was a cowboy hero who dressed in black and—this is what made him excitingly different—brandished a 15-foot bullwhip. He was the hero of a number of minor, action-packed B westerns in the late forties. It's probably just as well that they are nearly impossible to see nowadays, because most western-movie historians agree that they were insignificant. I haven't seen any since the fifties, and though I remember liking La Rue, I don't know if it's because of the films themselves or the spin-off Lash La Rue comic books. I did like that whip—though with hindsight, it was a mighty sadistic weapon. In real life, La Rue would become an evangelist and a lawbreaker, winding up in jail on charges of vagrancy, being drunk and disorderly, and possession of marijuana. He had more than 10 wives.

• **Sample Titles:** *Song of Old Wyoming* (1945), *Law of the Lash* (1946), *Border Feud* (1947), *Mark of the Lash* (1948), *The Fighting Vigilantes* (1948), *Son of Billy the Kid* (1949), *Dead Men's Gold* (1949).

○

TOM LAUGHLIN (1938–) Former studio bit player who first hit pay dirt directing and starring as a loner biker in *Born Losers*. As writer-director-(at times using an alias) producer-star-distributor, Laughlin reprised his violent champion of the helpless in *Billy Jack*, which became an enormous hit with the alienated-youth audience of 1971. The title character is a half-Indian, half-white man who returns to his Arizona reservation after being a Green Beret in Vietnam, a war he came to oppose. He now turns his back on an unjust, racist society. A hapkido expert, he uses violent

Tom Laughlin in Billy Jack.

means to protect Indians, wild horses, and the children at an alternative school run by his pacifist girlfriend (played by wife Dolores Taylor). Laughlin proved to be a solid, charismatic action hero—his hapkido is spectacular—and he is believable as he spouts his personal philosophy (except when doing a bad Brando impersonation). However, it took gall for Laughlin to present his violent character as the savior of the pacifist youth culture. (Unfortunately, many otherwise peace-loving young viewers thrilled to his violent acts.) When the kids give him the same "power" salute that they give Christ earlier in the film, it is downright eerie. This was especially disturbing because the picture and Laughlin's ad campaign were designed to make Billy Jack and Tom Laughlin one and the same in the public's eye. Laughlin would play the hero-savior-martyr in two more films. They bought it in the first sequel, but the young audience matured and

wanted no part of *Billy Jack Goes to Washington.* Laughlin went the way of the original Washington Senators.

• **Cult Favorites:** *Gidget* (1959, Paul Wendkos), *Born Losers* (1967, T. C. Frank), *Billy Jack* (1971, Frank), *The Trial of Billy Jack* (1974, Frank Laughlin), *The Master Gunfighter* (1975, Frank Laughlin), *Billy Jack Goes to Washington* (1977, Tom Laughlin).

○

CAROLE LAURE (1951–) Gorgeous French-Canadian actress-singer-dancer starred in several films in Quebec in the early seventies, all written for her by her director and mentor Gilles Carle. Low-budget, personal films, they emphasized Laure's erotic allure when acting freely for the camera. Because she was willing to do nudity and kinky material, she was offered many X-rated roles, including *Emmanuelle* and

Carole Laure tries some kinky role playing with Shannon Tweed in The Surrogate.

The Story of O, but turned them down. Laure got more than she bargained for playing Miss Canada (Miss World) in Dušan Makavejev's loony *Sweet Movie,* with her beauty-contest winner taking part in several nude scenes that border (cross the border, many say), on tastelessness; she is humiliated in a variety of ways, and ultimately drowns in a vat of chocolate. She again did nudity and some unusual sex scenes but still managed to gain international respectability in Bertrand Blier's bizarre Academy Award–winning comedy, *Get Out Your Handkerchiefs.* She was funny and sexy as a woman who is frigid during seduction attempts by her virile husband, Gérard Depardieu, and his helpful friend Patrick Dewaere—but gets turned on by a young boy. In Joyce Buñuel's *Dirty Dishes,* she had a change of pace as a housewife rebelling against her household "duties." Somehow stardom escaped Laure, but she turns up every once in a while, speaking French or English, providing exotic beauty

and an almost lethal dose of eroticism to pictures that deserve less.

- **Cult Favorites:** *Sweet Movie* (1974, Dušan Makavejev), *Get Out Your Handkerchiefs* (1978, Bertrand Blier).
- **Other Key Films:** *La Mort d'un Bucheron* (1973, Gilles Carle), *La Tête de Normande* (1976, Carle), *La Menace* (1977, Alain Corneau), *Dirty Dishes* (1978, Joyce Buñuel), *Asphalte* (1980, Denis Amar), *Heartbreakers* (1984, Bobby Roth), *The Surrogate* (1984, Don Carmody).

○

LAUREL AND HARDY Stan Laurel (1890–1965), a skinny Englishman, and fat Oliver Hardy (1892–1957), who was born in Georgia, started out in solo careers (which is hard to believe), but once linked by producer Hal Roach, went on to become the most beloved comedy team of all time. They were not only able to move from shorts to features (27 of their more than

100 films were full-length), but were also the only silent comics other than Chaplin and Fields to move successfully into sound films. Many of their films were mediocre, but when they were at the top of their form, as they were in shorts and features like *Way Out West* and *The Block-Heads*, the team was indisputably brilliant, worthy of their fans' devotion. There are many reasons for their appeal: their distinctive voices and deliveries, their much-imitated walks, Ollie's tie-fiddling (when bragging, flirting, or acting cowardly) and Stan's head-scratching, mindless smile, and hysterical whimpering (when he has done something even more stupid than usual), their physical grace (even Ollie is light on his feet). Also, their innovative and perfectly timed gags (among the few hilarious *destruction* gags in cinema history), that start small and escalate to catastrophic proportions (cars wrecked, houses destroyed, everyone on a city block engaged in a pie fight), their boundless enthusiasm,

their silly songs and dances, and their characters' unflinching camaraderie. Typically, the aggressive Ollie—who is just as big a dumbbell as Stan—tries to prove he's a big shot. Passive, dimwit Stan, his one-man fan club, tags along, encouraging Ollie's foolish and dangerous ploys and sometimes trying to copy his antics. His presence assures Ollie's downfall and physical punishment: he brags on Ollie's behalf, telling the biggest bullies what Ollie secretly threatened to do to them; every time Stan ducks, Ollie is hit in the kisser; if Stan carries a heavy object, it is bound to wind up on Ollie's foot. Ollie appreciates Stan because he's the only one stupid enough to believe his boasts, and the only one devoted enough to stay with him after he is shown up to be a coward and blowhard. The two are like overgrown children who spend each day wreaking havoc and come home with ripped, muddy clothes, and black eyes. Even when they play married characters, they act like kids

Laurel and Hardy with Jean Harlow in the 1929 short Double Whoopie.

who can't wait to sneak away from their mothers to join the other for another day of destruction.

• **Cult Favorites:** *The Battle of the Century* (1927 short, Clyde Bruckman and Leo McCarey), *Two Tars* (1928 short, James Parrott), *Double Whoopie* (1929 short, Lewis Foster), *Men O'War* (1929 short, Foster), *The Music Box* (1932 short, Parrott), *Sons of the Desert* (1933, William A. Seiter), *March of the Wooden Soldiers/Babes in Toyland* (1934, Gus Meins and Charles Rogers).

• **Other Key Films:** numerous shorts (1917–37), *Pardon Us* (1931, Parrott), *The Devil's Brother/Fra Diavolo* (1933, Hal Roach and Rogers), *The Bohemian Girl* (1936, James Horne), *Our Relations* (1936, Harry Lachman), *Way Out West* (1937, Horne), *Swiss Miss* (1938, John Blystone), *The Flying Deuces* (1939, Edward Sutherland), *A Chump at Oxford* (1940, Alfred Goulding), *Saps at Sea* (1940, Gordon Douglas), *Jitterbugs* (1943, Mal St. Clair), *The Bullfighters* (1945, St. Clair).

○

PRISCILLA LAWSON Dark-haired beauty played Princess Aura, one of the cinema's great villainesses, in the most popular serial, *Flash Gordon*. The daughter of Charles Middleton's Ming the Merciless, ruler of the planet Mongo, Aura hopes to take Buster Crabbe's earth visitor away from his girlfriend, Jean Rogers's Dale Arden. Aura is only as wicked as a spoiled college brat, and when she thinks up some dastardly deed—such as unleashing a large, hungry tiger on her blond romantic rival—it is only because she is jealous and hurt by Flash's lack of interest. Aura never does any permanent damage, and

Priscilla Lawson (left) *looks on jealously as Jean Rogers comforts Buster Crabbe in* Flash Gordon.

usually counters her impulsive bad deeds by helping Flash escape danger (Ming would kill Flash quickly if not for his daughter's interference). At the end, she proves to be a gracious loser and even makes sure Flash and Dale get safely back to earth together. I have no idea who Lawson was (a Universal starlet?), but she was surely one of the few actresses who could make viewers think that just maybe Flash should give up Dale. Her Aura was a much stronger character than Dale, more complex and interesting, and with her bare midriff, high, exotic eyebrows, and willingness to do *anything* for the man she loves, she was just as sexy and even a bit more passionate.

• **Cult Favorite:** *Flash Gordon* (1936 serial, Frederick Stephani).

GEORGE LAZENBY (1939–) This Australian-born model had some success doing European magazine and television ads and was known as the "Big Fry" man when he beat out 400 hopefuls to become Sean Connery's replacement as James Bond in *On Her Majesty's Secret Service*. Lazenby had an obnoxious self-satisfied smile, little talent, and no charisma whatsoever—in fact, he came across as a bland computer-generated Saturday-morning cartoon representation of Connery. But ironically, the film works because of his flawed presence. His Bond is more real than Connery's simply because Lazenby was incapable of playing him as a bigger-than-life hero. His Bond is human, which is appropriate for *this* Bond script. He is neurotic, depressed, vulnerable, and actually scared at times, and capable of being touched by a good woman's (Diana Rigg's Tracy di Vicenzo) love and loyalty, admire her intelligence and bravery, and fall in love with her. He's willing to give up his adventurous life and all the women in the world to marry her. With this film, Lazenby received embarrassing notices, and he lost his chance for stardom. The rest of his movie career has been undistinguished but for a surprisingly effective supporting role in the Singapore-set *Saint Jack,* playing an American senator whose night with a boy prostitute is not as concealed as he thinks.

• **Cult Favorites:** *On Her Majesty's Secret Service* (1969, Peter Hunt), *Kentucky Fried Movie* (1977, John Landis), *Saint Jack* (1979, Peter Bogdanovich).

• **Also of Interest:** *Universal Soldier* (1971, Cy Endfield), *The Man from Hong Kong* (1975, Brian Trenchard-Smith), *Never Too Young to Die* (1986, Gil Bettman).

JEAN-PIERRE LÉAUD (1946–) He made a dramatic debut as a well-meaning young boy, Antoine Doinel, who is both troubled and constantly in trouble in the François Truffaut 1959 masterwork *The 400 Blows*, a reflection on the director's own childhood. The final freeze-frame of the sad Antoine, as he turns toward the camera after his path to happiness is blocked by the ocean, is etched on most film fanatics' brains. Léaud would reprise Antoine four times as a young adult, in Truffaut's episode of *Love at Twenty* and Truffaut's features *Stolen Kisses, Bed and Board,* and *Love on the Run.* Antoine would enter the army, work as a detective, a flower-painter, and other jobs before becoming a writer; marry, have affairs, have a son, divorce, fall in love with his wife's lookalike. Taken as a whole, the five films are the profile of a boy who, with little love in his rough childhood, became an incurable romantic as a man—essentially Truffaut's own story. Antoine, who can fall for a woman who is thoughtful enough to put a plastic wrapper on his book, believes love is at the center of the universe. Like Léaud's character in Truffaut's *Two English Girls,* he is obsessed with love, but finds it easier to express his passions in writing, in telephone messages, and through art than face-to-face. He has better luck with a girl's parents than the girl. Oddly, as his love fades, the young women he admires become interested in him; rarely do they love each other with the same strength at the same time. Léaud is marvelous playing these manic, love-obsessed souls, with his sharp nose and slightly mussed hair, his nervous energy, his deadpan humor, and his fast speech. His hands dart as he

Jean-Pierre Léaud with Kika Markham in François Truffaut's Two English Girls.

improvises, and he continues to give the same furtive look he had as the adolescent in *The 400 Blows* when he stood alone in the street, hungrily gulping down stolen milk. Léaud is regarded as Truffaut's alter ego, but he has appeared in the films of many top European directors, including Bernardo Bertolucci's *Last Tango in Paris,* as Marie Schneider's filmmaker fiancé, and six films by Jean-Luc Godard, his favorite director. His role in Godard's *Masculin-Féminin,* as a young man just out of the army who desires love and tenderness from a young woman who won't commit herself to him, is a harder version of Antoine Doinel.
• **Cult Favorites:** *The 400 Blows* (1959, François Truffaut), *The Testament of Orpheus* (1960, Jean Cocteau), *Masculin-Féminin* (1966, Jean-Luc Godard), *Weekend* (1967, Godard), *Stolen Kisses* (1968, Truffaut), *Pigpen* (1969, Pier Paolo Pasolini), *Two English Girls* (1971, Truffaut), *Last Tango in Paris* (1972, Bernardo

Bertolucci), *Day for Night* (1973, Truffaut).
• **Other Key Films:** *Love at Twenty* (1962, episode by Truffaut), *Made in U.S.A.* (1966, Godard), *La Chinoise* (1967, Godard), *Le Départ* (1967, Jerzy Skolimowski), *Le Gai Savoir* (1968, Godard), *Bed and Board* (1970, Truffaut), *The Lion with Seven Heads* (1970, Glauber Rocha), *Une Aventure de Billy le Kid* (1970, Luc Moullet), *Out One: Specter* (1973, Jacques Rivette), *The Mother and the Whore* (1973, Jean Eustache), *Love on the Run* (1979, Truffaut), *Detective* (1985, Godard), *I Hired a Contract Killer* (1990, Aki Kaurismaki).

○

BERNARD LEE (1908–81) This underappreciated, seasoned British actor gave believable, sturdy performances in numerous melodramas during a 40-year career as a supporting player and occasional lead. He played more than his share of inspectors, military officers, and other no-nonsense authority figures. His most famous part was M, the boss of James Bond. He was a familiar face as Bond's changed from Sean Connery's to George Lazenby's to Roger Moore's, and Lee's death was a blow to the series.

• **Cult Favorites:** *The Third Man* (1949, Carol Reed), *Beat the Devil* (1954, John Huston), *Dr. No* (1962, Terence Young), *From Russia with Love* (1963, Young), *Goldfinger* (1964, Guy Hamilton), *On Her Majesty's Secret Service* (1969, Peter Hunt), *The Spy Who Loved Me* (1977, Lewis Gilbert).

• **Also Recommended:** *The Fallen Idol* (1948, Reed), *Quartet* (1949, Ken Annakin, Arthur Crabtree, Harold French, and Ralph Smart), *Odette* (1951, Herbert Wilcox), *Father Brown/The Detective* (1954, Robert Hamer), *The Purple Rain* (1955, Robert Parrish), *The Spanish Gardener* (1956, Philip Leacock), *The Man Upstairs* (1958, Don Chaffey), *The Angry Silence* (1960, Guy Green), *Whistle Down the Wind* (1961, Bryan Forbes), *Ring of Spies/Ring of Treason* (1963, Robert Tronson), *Thunderball* (1965, Young), *You Only Live Twice* (1967, Gilbert).

• **Other Key Films:** *Pursuit of the Graf Spree* (1957, Michael Powell and Emeric Pressburger), *Across the Bridge* (1957, Ken Annakin), *Kidnapped* (1960, Robert Stevenson), *The Spy Who Came In from the Cold* (1965, Martin Ritt), *Diamonds Are Forever* (1971, Hamilton), *Live and Let Die* (1973, Hamilton), *The Man with the Golden Gun* (1974, Hamilton), *Moonraker* (1979, Gilbert).

○

BRUCE LEE (1941–73) A supreme action hero, the undisputed king of martial-arts films was a living legend and has become,

Bruce Lee shows no mercy toward Bob Wall in Enter the Dragon.

since his sudden, mysterious death in 1973, a mythical figure. In the early seventies, the young Chinese-American who had played Kato on "The Green Hornet" TV series became the cinema's most charismatic, sexual film personality. Like other Chinese kung fu heroes, his characters are disciplined, virtuous, diligent, perceptive, polite, patient, and stoical despite misfortunes; loyal to their families, girlfriends, martial-arts schools and instructors, and country; and capable of acquiring heightened powers, like God-given strengths, when all seems lost. Lee created his own distinctive "street-fighting" style, *jeet kune do,* "the fist-intercepting way," a system whereby, through speed and biomechanics, one upsets an opponent's gravity. Unlike his rivals, Lee used no pulleys, trampolines, or fake props in his action scenes, showing only what was real or at least possible. And, unlike his rivals, he exploited his appeal, stripping off his shirt to reveal rippling muscles, posing for battle with legs spread, knees slightly bent, his hands on his thighs—somehow looking relaxed and tense at the same time. Suddenly his hand thrusts forward; either he delivers his trademark one-inch punch or his fingers penetrate flesh; his feet shoot upward toward an opponent's jaw; and he emits his *kiai* (fighting yell), which in conjunction with his acrobatic body movements makes one think of a wild animal in heat. One minute he is small and cute, offering an ingratiating smile, being polite to a pretty young woman, coming off like the country hicks he played, and the next he is a ferocious killing machine. He is simultaneously graceful, balletic, and deadly in battle, leaping through the air, doing back flips, mowing down hordes of villains with quicker-than-the-eye hands and feet. In his first starring film, *Fists of Fury,* his opponents look like amateurs, so we're thankful for an episode in which he single-handedly fights 15 at once (and wipes them out). In *The Chinese Connection,* in which he does some comedy while employing different disguises, he is at his most violent, annihilating the Japanese responsible for his teacher's death. In *Return of the Dragon,* as a Destry-like yokel who refrains from violence until absolutely necessary, he wins a thrilling life-and-death fight with villain Chuck Norris at the Rome Colosseum. In his most famous film, *Enter the Dragon,* his agent (his one character who isn't champion of the underdog) wins several classic one-on-one battles and another against about half an army. Lee's death from a swelling of the brain happened before *Game of Death* was completed, and another actor sporting a beard and mask filled in for Lee in a number of sequences. But Lee could never be replaced. As a youngster in Hong Kong he had made such films as *Birth of a Man* and *My Son's a Chang* and became known as "The Little Dragon," which explains some of his adult film titles.

• **Cult Favorites:** *Fists of Fury* (1972, Lo Wei), *The Chinese Connection* (1972, Wei), *Enter the Dragon* (1973, Robert Clouse), *Return of the Dragon* (1973, Bruce Lee), *Game of Death* (1974, Clouse).

• **Also of Interest:** *Marlowe* (1969, Paul Bogart).

○

CHRISTOPHER LEE (1922–) This 6′ 4″, gaunt, handsome, deep-voiced British actor is one of the icons of the horror cinema. With an angry expression and imposing presence, he has played many monsters, including the Frankenstein Monster, Dracula, and the Mummy, as well as sadistic villains

Christopher Lee and Britt Ekland in The Wicker Man.

like Rasputin, Hyde, and Fu Manchu. He is best known for his numerous wide-eyed, sexual, and cruel portrayals of Dracula, often playing opposite Peter Cushing's Van Helsing in colorful and bloody Hammer Studios productions. Although he has played a large variety of scoundrels inside and outside the horror genre, he has rarely varied his approach. His vile figures are all intelligent, unsympathetic, aggressive (rather than sly or subtle), unfearing, humorless, and ruthless: they personify evil. His most interesting character, and his favorite, is Lord Summerisle, the leader of a modern-day pagan cult in *The Wicker Man*. He seems like a cheery, sincere, and benevolent, if misguided, man—only at the film's end, when he actually carries through on the horrifying execution-sacrifice of the lead character (Edward Woodward) do we realize that he is perhaps Lee's most frightening monster,

for he is a monster who is plausible, even today.

• **Cult Favorites:** *The Crimson Pirate* (1952, Robert Siodmak), *Horror of Dracula* (1958, Terence Fisher), *Horror Hotel* (1960, John Moxey), *Taste of Fear/Scream of Fear* (1961, Seth Holt), *The Face of Fu Manchu* (1965, Don Sharp, *She* (1965, Robert Day), *The Devil's Bride/The Devil Rides Out* (1968, Fisher), *Scream and Scream Again* (1970, Gordon Hessler), *The Private Life of Sherlock Holmes* (1970, Billy Wilder), *Horror Express* (1972, Eugenio Martin), *The Three Musketeers* (1973, Richard Lester), *The Wicker Man* (1973, Robin Hardy), *Raw Meat* (1973, Gary Sherman).

• **Other Key Films:** *Bitter Victory* (1958, Nicholas Ray), *Corridors of Blood* (1958, Day), *The Hound of the Baskervilles* (1959, Fisher), *The Mummy* (1959, Fisher), *The Two Faces of Dr. Jekyll* (1961, Fisher),

The Gorgon (1964, Fisher), *Dr. Terror's House of Horrors* (1965, Freddie Francis), *The Skull* (1965, Francis), *Dracula—Prince of Darkness* (1966, Fisher), *The Brides of Fu Manchu* (1966, Sharp), *Rasputin—The Mad Monk* (1966, Sharp), *Theatre of Death* (1967, Samuel Gallu), *Dracula Has Risen from the Grave* (1968, Francis), *Vengeance of Fu Manchu* (1968, Jeremy Summers), *The Oblong Box* (1969, Hessler), *Scars of Dracula* (1971, Roy Ward Baker), *Dracula A.D. 1972* (1972, Alan Gibson), *I, Monster* (1972, Stephen Weeks), *The Creeping Flesh* (1973, Francis), *The Man with the Golden Gun* (1974, Guy Hamilton), *The Four Musketeers* (1975, Lester), *To the Devil—A Daughter* (1976, Peter Sykes).

○

JANET LEIGH (1927–) Given an M-G-M contract because of her beauty, she learned on the job and became an interesting, daring, much underrated actress. She was pleasant and perky in fluffy comedies and light dramas, vivacious in the joyful musical *My Sister Eileen,* and scrumptious as an imperiled heroine in costume dramas like *Prince Valiant, Scaramouche,* and *The Black Shield of Falworth*—the young boy's blond fantasy princess. Leigh had an amazing figure, but directors were so afraid of damaging her wholesome image that they wouldn't call attention to it—they merely dressed her in tight but "ladylike" tops and repeatedly shot her from the side. It's a shame, because Leigh was at her best those few times directors made full use of her sex appeal. In his sleaze masterpiece *Touch of Evil,* Orson Welles made her a different kind of helpless, imperiled heroine, showing her in sexy underwear and trapping her in a villain's remote, drug-fiend–infested motel. Before her "prince" (husband Charlton Heston) can rescue her, Welles places her, drugged and naked, under sheets in a room in the villain's decrepit hotel. Leigh's classic role in Alfred Hitchcock's *Psycho* is even more sexually explicit: she walks around her room in the Bates Motel in a black bra, strips while Anthony Perkins's deranged Norman Bates watches through a peephole (a scene that recalls the motel sequence in *Touch of Evil*), and finally disrobes completely (a first for a Hollywood star, though we see her only from behind and above the waist) and takes her ill-fated shower. What is fascinating about Marion Crane is her connection to Norman. We learn about *him* through watching her. Her own sexual repression, her sense that her dead mother is watching her illicit affair with John Gavin, her intense guilt and paranoia after committing a crime, and her imagining conversations—all these things tell us how Norman has become progressively insane in the years since he killed his mother and her lover. Marion comes to her senses and wants to return to a normal life; it is too late for abnormal Norman. Following *Psycho,* Leigh's roles were more mature and sexual (even in *The Vikings*). She was particularly adult and mysterious in *The Manchurian Candidate,* as a woman the paranoid Frank Sinatra meets on a train. Married at one time to frequent costar Tony Curtis (they were a Hollywood glamour couple), she is the mother of Jamie Lee Curtis.

• **Cult Favorites:** *Angels in the Outfield* (1951, Clarence Brown), *The Naked Spur* (1953, Anthony Mann), *Jet Pilot* (1957, Josef von Sternberg), *Touch of Evil* (1958, Orson Welles), *Psycho* (1960, Alfred Hitchcock), *The Manchurian Candidate* (1962, John Frankenheimer), *The Fog* (1979, John Carpenter).

- **Sleeper:** *My Sister Eileen* (1955, Richard Quine).
- **Other Key Films:** *Act of Violence* (1949, Fred Zinnemann), *Holiday Affair* (1949, Don Hartman), *Scaramouche* (1952, George Sidney), *Houdini* (1953, George Marshall), *Prince Valiant* (1954, Henry Hathaway), *Living It Up* (1954, Norman Taurog), *The Black Shield of Falworth* (1954, Rudolph Maté), *Pete Kelly's Blues* (1955, Jack Webb), *Safari* (1956, Terence Young), *The Vikings* (1958, Richard Fleischer), *The Perfect Furlough* (1959, Blake Edwards), *Who Was That Lady?* (1960, Sidney), *Bye Bye Birdie* (1963, Sidney).

○

JENNIFER JASON LEIGH (1963–) For those who believe that the preacher's angelic-looking daughter is as interested in sex as the farmer's daughter. This pretty, sweet-looking blonde has played a number of shy and innocent-looking young women who are curious about sex; once they learn, they display wicked imaginations. Leigh seems too gentle and looks too young and innocent to play the parts she has taken. Her females are either hungry for sex and/or have been psychologically affected by past sexual incidents. She has played a teenager who loses her virginity in *Fast Times at Ridgemont High* (her breakthrough film), a blind, mute teen who had been raped as a girl in *Eyes of a Stranger,* a frigid virgin bride in *Easy Money,* a kinky, unfaithful young bride in *Grandview, U.S.A.,* a virgin princess who is kidnapped and raped by Rutger Hauer and then willingly becomes his sex partner in *Flesh + Blood,* a former mental patient (her finest performance!) who is threatened in a one time brothel she inherits in *Heart of*

Jennifer Jason Leigh as a prostitute in Last Exit to Brooklyn.

Midnight, and hookers in *Last Exit to Brooklyn* (defiantly and self-destructively giving herself to all the men in a bar), *The Men's Club, Miami Blues,* etc. Her characters are vulnerable and almost always victimized, but usually they have surprising resilience, and try to use their bad experiences to make themselves stronger. The daughter of late actor Vic Morrow and screenwriter Barbara Turner, she is an interesting, always watchable, and extremely talented young actress who is known for doing extensive research (into characters, eras, and so on) before playing even the simplest parts, and for her obsessive De Niro–like commitment to her craft. For instance, she lost 18 pounds from her 5′ 3″, 102-pound frame to play an anorexic in the TV movie *The Best Little Girl in the World.*

• **Cult Favorites:** *Fast Times at Ridgemont High* (1982, Amy Heckerling), *The Hitcher* (1986, Robert Harmon), *Miami Blues* (1990, George Armitage).

• **Other Key Films:** *Grandview, U.S.A.* (1984, Randal Kleiser), *Flesh + Blood* (1985, Paul Verhoeven), *Sister, Sister* (1987, Bill Condon), *Heart of Midnight* (1989, Matthew Chapman), *Last Exit to Brooklyn* (1989, Uli Edel).

• **Also of Interest:** *The Young Runaways* (1968, Arthur Dreifuss), *Eyes of a Stranger* (1981, Ken Wiederhorn), *Easy Money* (1983, James Signorelli), *Under Cover* (1987, John Stockwell), *The Big Picture* (1989, Christopher Guest).

○

PAUL LEMAT (1952–) One of the many young actors who got their first break in *American Graffiti*. He played Ron Howard's tough-but-goodhearted, supercool, Beach Boys–hating friend who gets stuck with underaged Mackenzie Phillips in his car for a night of cruising and drag-racing—and ends up having a fun time. A brawny actor with the boyish face of hip movie and music teen idols of the fifties (with a mustache he resembles Vince Edwards), he went on to become a leading man, most notably in Jonathan Demme's Americana treats *Handle with Care* and *Melvin and Howard*. In the latter film LeMat played Melvin Dummar, the gas station attendant who claimed Howard Hughes left him a fortune in return for a small kindness he did for him. LeMat's high-school educated characters run around aggressively but aimlessly, trying to save failing relationships and make enough money to pay their next installments. They are likable, well-meaning men, but they are fuck-ups who get in way over their heads and are lucky

to make it back to an even score. LeMat showed his range with a frightening portrayal of Farrah Fawcett's abusive husband in the acclaimed TV movie *The Burning Bed*.

• **Cult Favorites:** *American Graffiti* (1973, George Lucas), *Handle with Care/Citizen's Band* (1977, Jonathan Demme), *Melvin and Howard* (1980, Demme), *Strange Invaders* (1983, Michael Laughlin).

• **Also of Interest:** *Aloha, Bobby and Rose* (1975, Floyd Mutrux), *More American Graffiti* (1979, W. L. Norton), *P.K. & the Kid* (1982, Lou Lombardo), *The Hanoi Hilton* (1987, Lionel Chetwynd, *Private Investigations* (1987, Nigel Dick).

○

HARVEY LEMBECK (1923–82) Short, hefty, dark-haired character actor who appeared in numerous service dramas and comedies, and became familiar to television viewers as Barbella, the righthand man of scheming Sergeant Bilko on "You'll Never Get Rich"/"The Phil Silvers Show." His cult status comes from his continuing roles in the popular "Beach Party" films of the sixties. Parodying Brando in *The Wild One,* he caused Frankie Avalon and Annette Funicello much grief as Eric Von Zipper, the leather-jacketed leader of an overaged gang that is itself the likely model for the inept gang that hounds Clint Eastwood in *Every Which Way But Loose* and *Any Which Way You Can.* Too feeble a villain to challenge anybody but surfers, Von Zipper is repeatedly bested by Frankie and the beach boys in a slapstick finale. He is always upset when it's proved to all that his bark is much worse than his bite.

• **Cult Favorites:** *Beach Party* (1963, William Asher), *Beach Blanket Bingo* (1965, Asher).

• **Sleepers:** *Between Heaven and Hell* (1956, Richard Fleischer), *A View from the Bridge* (1962, Sidney Lumet).

• **Other Key Films:** *Stalag 17* (1953, Billy Wilder), *Girls in the Night* (1953, Jack Arnold), *The Last Time I Saw Archie* (1961, Jack Webb), *Sail a Crooked Ship* (1961, Irving S. Brecher), *Love with the Proper Stranger* (1963, Robert Mulligan), *Muscle Beach Party* (1964, Asher), *Bikini Beach* (1964, Asher), *Pajama Party* (1964, Don Weis).

○

KAY LENZ (1953–) When Clint Eastwood directed his first film without being in the cast himself, he chose this small (5′ 1″, 105 pounds) but shapely, long-haired brunette to play the title character of *Breezy*. The then-unknown California-born actress gave a winning performance as a free-spirited, free-living teenager who has a May-December relationship with middle-aged, divorced William Holden. While her hippie philosophy was annoyingly simplistic, *Breezy*'s energy and freedom with her body perfectly conveyed why many conservative, middle-aged men across America were shocked by but sexually attracted to females in the youth culture. *Breezy* is one of Lenz's few movie roles that let her show off both her sex appeal and acting talent. Sex alone is dominant in such films as *Stripped to Kill*, with Lenz as an undercover cop who discovers that she becomes aroused while posing (and performing) as a stripper; and *Fast-Walking,* in which she contributes one of the recent cinema's most erotic moments when she visits boyfriend Tim McIntire in prison, and later further excites viewers with a nude lovemaking scene with James Woods. Not a conventional-looking leading lady (the camera must catch her at the right angle for her to be pretty), she proved in numerous films, playing troubled on-their-own women, that she is far sexier than most of today's glamour girls. Equally good in sensitive and highly emotional scenes, her acting has been better showcased on television in such projects as *Rich Man, Poor Man, Lisa, Bright and Dark,* and *Heart and Hiding.* She has won several Emmys, one recently for playing an AIDS victim on *Midnight Caller.* She was also featured in a Rod Stewart video—obviously she is part of many men's fantasies.

• **Cult Favorite:** *White Line Fever* (1975, Jonathan Kaplan).

• **Sleepers:** *Breezy* (1973, Clint Eastwood), *Fast-Walking* (1983, James B. Harris).

• **Other Key Films:** *The Great Scout and Cathouse Thursday* (1976, Don Taylor), *House* (1986, Steve Miner), *Stripped to Kill* (1987, Katt Shea Ruben).

○

GLORIA LEONARD The publisher of the glossy sex magazine *High Society* has always been proud of her life before she sat in a lavish office, when she was in the trenches starring in porno films. She was a bit older and heavier than most porno queens, and gave the impression that she thought herself too smart and classy to consider her porno work as anything more than a lark— sort of like when Beverly Sills would sing with Miss Piggy on "The Muppet Show." Nonetheless, her mature, upscale characters were as raunchy in sex scenes as those played by California bimbos. In her pseudo-documentary *All About Gloria Leonard,* obviously her best showcase, the actress-director presented herself as sexually insatiable, uninhibited, and kinky. For instance, in one scene she is the recipient of double insertion; in another she fellates three men simultaneously.

• **Cult Favorites:** *The Opening of Misty Beethoven* (1976, Henry Paris/Radley Metzger), *All About Gloria Leonard* (1978, Gloria Leonard).

• **Other Key Films:** *Heat Wave* (1973, Cecil Howard), *Maraschino Cherry* (1978, Paris/Metzger), *Bon Appétit* (1980, Chuck Vincent), *Tramp* (1980, Vincent), *October Silk* (1980, Henri Pachard).

○

BABY LEROY (1932–) Blond, cheery toddler who stole scenes from W. C. Fields in four pictures. Fields was supposedly jealous of the boy and, the story goes, once spiked his orange juice, but was smart enough to realize that Baby LeRoy's presence in his pictures—annoying Fields's characters— would allow him to confirm his popular (if fraudulent) image as a child-hater. In one publicity shot, LeRoy is hitting Fields on the head with a hammer. This pretty much sums up their relationship in the films themselves. In *The Old-Fashioned Way,* as they sit together during a boardinghouse meal, LeRoy drops Fields's pocketwatch into the molasses, and hits him in the face with a spoonful of cream. When they're alone, Fields sends the boy flying with a kick to his bottom. In *It's a Gift,* LeRoy's Elwood Dunk pours molasses all over the floor of Fields's store. When Fields tries to sleep on a swing on his porch, the tot, who sits on the porch above, drops a grape into Fields's open mouth and an icepick into the wood next to Fields's head. They were a hilarious duo, with Baby LeRoy Winebrenner being

Baby LeRoy in You Can't Get My Goat!

one of many continuous hilarious aggravations in Fields's hostile world.

• **Cult Favorites:** *The Old-Fashioned Way* (1934, William Beaudine), *It's a Gift* (1934, Norman Z. McLeod).

• **Other Key Films:** *A Bedtime Story* (1933, Norman Taurog), *Torch Singer* (1933, Alexander Hall), *Tillie and Gus* (1933, Francis Martin), *Alice in Wonderland* (1933, McLeod), *Miss Fane's Baby Is Stolen* (1934, Hall), *The Lemon Drop Kid* (1934, Marshall Neilan).

○

JOHN LESLIE Prolific San Francisco porno actor, known in the industry for his good looks, acting ability, and dependability under the hot lights. He has been the ideal leading man in films starring the prettiest porno actresses, from Marilyn Chambers to Annette Haven. According to Robert Rimmer, he "has the knack of combining sex-making with a sense of laughter and a feeling that he likes each and every woman he screws." Typically, his leads are charming, sensitive lovers, confident in bed and great in conversation, too. He has played all kinds of characters—from seducers to sultans, playboys to proles—but no matter who they are, they have *lots* of dialogue. He can't even stop gabbing (in a raunchy manner) while making love in his most famous films, *Talk Dirty to Me* and *Talk Dirty to Me II*. Leslie is also a director of videotape porno movies.

• **Cult Favorites:** *Pretty Peaches* (1978, Alex DeRenzy), *Insatiable* (1980, Godfrey Daniels), *Talk Dirty to Me* (1980, Anthony Spinelli), *Talk Dirty to Me II* (1983, Tim McDonald).

• **Other Key Films:** *A Coming of Angels* (1977, Joel Scott), *The Other Side of Julie* (1978, Anthony Riverton), *V—The Hot One* (1978, Robert McCallum), *Exposed* (1980, Jeffrey Fairbanks), *"F"* (1980, Svetlana), *Wicked Sensations* (1981, Ron Chrones), *Nothing to Hide* (1981, Spinelli), *High School Memories* (1981, Spinelli and Daniels), *Outlaw Ladies* (1981, Henri Pachard), *Urban Cowgirls* (1981, Tsanuski), *The Dancers* (1981, Spinelli), *A Thousand and One Erotic Nights* (1982, Stephen Lucas).

○

NAOMI LEVINE Former painter became Andy Warhol's first Superstar in the early sixties, as the lead in *Tarzan and Jane Regained . . . Sort of* and several other crude, static-camera films. She spent all 50 minutes of *Kiss* smooching with Rufus Collins, Gerald Malanga, and Ed Saunders. The buxom actress also made films with Ken Jacobs, Jack Smith (playing "the Spider" in *Normal Love*), and Jerry Joffen (who didn't title his works), becoming known as the "Queen of the Underground." She also made her own experimental films, including *Mode Yes* and *Jeremelu*, with Smith.

• **Sample Titles:** *Tarzan and Jane Regained . . . Sort of* (1963, Andy Warhol), *Kiss* (1964, Warhol), *Naomi and Rufus Kiss* (1964, Warhol), *Couch* (1964, Warhol), *Normal Love* (Jack Smith), *Christmas on Earth* (Barbara Rubin), *Naomi Is a Vision of Loneliness* (1965, Ken Jacobs).

○

FIONA LEWIS (1946–) Smart, attractive British brunette who has had a disappointing career considering her talent, sex appeal, and unique presence. At one point she even quit acting to become a journalist and screenwriter. She has been cast almost exclusively in outrageous films, full of wild imagery and, in most cases, bloody violence. Her parts have usually been sex-oriented and have contributed to the lunacy of the films. Her characters are sultry, yet aloof and classy—a weird combination. She was Roger Daltry's aristocratic mistress in Ken Russell's absurd *Lisztomania*. In *The Fury,* she was a government agent whose job is to have sex with teenage psychic Andrew Stevens so he will do whatever the government asks of him. He pays her back for her deception by levitating her, spinning her around in midair, and compressing her so that all her blood bursts out of her veins and orifices—one of the most offensive moments in film history, and perhaps the reason Lewis informed director Brian De Palma she

Fiona Lewis with Roger Daltrey in Ken Russell's Lisztomania.

disliked the movie. In *Strange Behavior,* she got good reviews for playing an evil nurse who inserts long hypodermic needles into teenagers' eyeballs, with the soothing comment, "This will . . . cause extreme pain for just a few short months." She had a funny bit as an alien posing as an Avon Lady in *Strange Invaders.*

• **Cult Favorites:** *The Fearless Vampire Killers* (1967, Roman Polanski), *Joanna* (1968, Michael Sarne), *Lisztomania* (1975, Ken Russell), *The Fury* (1978, Brian De Palma), *Strange Behavior* (1981, Michael Laughlin), *Strange Invaders* (1983, Laughlin).

• **Sleeper:** *Villain* (1979, Hal Needham).

• **Other Key Films:** *Where's Jack?* (1969, James Clavell), *Dr. Phibes Rides Again* (1972, Robert Fuest), *Stunts* (1977, Mark L. Lester), *Wanda Nevada* (1979, Peter Fonda), *Innerspace* (1987, Joe Dante).

○

JERRY LEWIS (1926–) The French critics' adoration of Jerry Lewis can likely be traced back to *The Bellboy,* his seventh film after his breakup with Dean Martin and his first as director. After all, it is an homage to *Mr. Hulot's Holiday,* with Lewis's nontalking bellboy following Jacques Tati's lead by causing drastic physical changes to whatever environment he passes through. Also incorporating silent routines into sound comedies, Lewis became the only comedian other than Tati to react comically to the sound track. The French also appreciated Lewis's surreal world, but Lewis later diverged from Tati by having his movie world be orderly except for his own weird, destructive characters. Lewis made some unfunny films; too often his humor was tasteless, and he sunk into pathos or self-pity. But I admire Jerry Lewis for never being afraid to fall on his face, am in awe of his talent (even if it too often went astray), and his energy. I believe that when you look back on such Martin and Lewis films as *Hollywood or Bust* and *Pardners,* they come off quite well; the young, skinny, frantic but controlled Lewis was truly hilarious. Lewis's mass appeal in America is with children; his adult cult audience adored him when

Jerry Lewis (right) *poses with partner Dean Martin and Lizabeth Scott for* Scared Stiff.

they were children and have remained loyal. Lewis played a character who is old enough to be called an adult, but was actually a "kid." He is a nice guy, a nobody (check the movie titles for his lowly positions in life), with a preteen's mental age (though he is a brilliant authority when it comes to comic books). He is too simple, innocent, and trusting to understand the tough, complicated world around him. He is gawky, nasal-voiced, and weak. He is unappreciated (especially by Dean Martin), pushed around, neurotic, and lonely (though he always ends up with a nice, pretty woman), and so awkward that one would think he had suddenly sprouted up a foot at summer camp. *The Nutty Professor,* a Jekyll-and-Hyde comedy in which his "Buddy Love" reminds one of the narcissistic, sanctimonious Lewis of his later telethons, is his best film, not only because it has the funniest scenes and his most ambitious direction, but also because Lewis went out on a limb by playing a character children would despise. In *The King of Comedy,* spoofing Johnny Carson, he chanced playing an arrogant, patronizing character everyone might dislike—yet even adult viewers liked him.

• **Cult Favorites:** *Hollywood or Bust* (1956, Frank Tashlin), *The Bellboy* (1960, Jerry Lewis), *The Nutty Professor* (1963, Lewis), *The King of Comedy* (1983, Martin Scorsese).

• **Also Recommended:** *At War with the Army* (1951, Hal Walker), *Sailor Beware* (1952, Walker), *Jumping Jacks* (1952, Norman Taurog), *The Stooge* (1953, Taurog), *Scared Stiff* (1953, George Marshall), *The Caddy* (1953, Taurog), *Living It up* (1954, Taurog), *You're Never Too Young* (1955, Taurog), *Artists and Models* (1955, Tashlin), *Pardners* (1956, Taurog), *The Delicate Delinquent* (1957, Don McGuire),

The Sad Sack (1957, Marshall), *Rock-a-Bye Baby* (1958, Tashlin), *Don't Give Up the Ship* (1959, Taurog), *The Errand Boy* (1961, Lewis), *It's Only Money* (1962, Tashlin), *Who's Minding the Store?* (1963, Tashlin), *The Patsy* (1964, Lewis), *The Disorderly Orderly* (1964, Tashlin), *The Family Jewels* (1965, Lewis), *The Big Mouth* (1967, Lewis).

○

ELMO LINCOLN (1899–1952) When Winslow Wilson deserted the production to join the army, Elmo Lincoln—formerly Otto Elmo Linkenhelt—replaced him in the title role in the 1918 silent feature *Tarzan of the Apes.* Chosen because he had bared his barrel chest in D. W. Griffith films, Lincoln became the first movie Tarzan. He wore a loincloth and went bare-chested, using a headband to control his long, wild wig. His knife-carrying apeman is a virile presence, strong-looking because of his chest and jaw, and, a stocky 200-pounder, agile if not swift. While he is aggressively masculine, Enid Markey's Jane is shy and feminine. A highlight of the film is a fight with a real lion—quite a thrill for early moviegoers. Lincoln actually had to stab the old, drugged lion to death when it turned on him during filming. On tour to promote the film and his he-man image, Lincoln wrestled a lion cub prior to each screening. Though now dated and stilted, the picture is still watchable, and at times, one can see Lincoln's appeal. Lincoln and Markey appeared in an inferior sequel, and after several more adventure serials, he returned one more time to the role he was most identified with, in a popular serial, *Adventures of Tarzan,* opposite Universal's serial queen, Louise Lorraine. Ironically, censors then had him partially cover his chest. Typecast, Lincoln had trouble finding roles in non-jungle films.

• **Cult Favorites:** *Intolerance* (1916, D. W. Griffith), *Tarzan of the Apes* (1918, Scott Sidney).

• **Other Key Films:** *Romance of Tarzan* (1918, Wilfred Lucas), *Elmo the Mighty* (1919 serial, Robert F. Hill), *Elmo the Fearless* (1920 serial, Hill), *The Flaming Disk* (1920 serial, Hill), *Under the Crimson Skies* (1920, Rex Ingram), *Adventures of Tarzan* (1921 serial, Hill).

• **Also of Interest:** *The Birth of a Nation* (1915, Griffith), *The Greatest Thing in Life* (1918, Griffith), *Tarzan's Magic Fountain* (1949, Lee Sholem).

○

LITTLE NELL/NELL CAMPBELL Laura Campbell was born in Australia to a Sydney newspaper columnist, who wrote regular stories in which he referred to her as "Little Nell," after the Dickens character. The name stuck when she entered show business—at the lowest level. Arriving in England at 18, she worked as a street performer, busking for change. Singing thirties songs and tap dancing in hat and tails, she was discovered by director Jim Sharman, who cast her as Columbia, Dr. Frank-N-Furter's in-house groupie, in the musical *The Rocky Horror Show.* She also played the role in the movie version. Her high-energy performance is one of the delights of the film; her "Time Warp" dance is certainly one of the highlights; her character's death is one of the shocks. She hasn't had much of a film career otherwise, but she did appear in the outrageous British punk musical-satire, *Jubilee,* which depicts Elizabeth I visiting her country in the late twentieth century and not being too thrilled by what she sees. As

Nell Campbell, she is a club performer and club owner in New York.

- **Cult Favorites:** *The Rocky Horror Picture Show* (1975, Jim Sharman), *Jubilee* (1978, Derek Jarman).
- **Also of Interest:** *Shock Treatment* (1981, Sharman).

○

DESMOND LLEWELLYN Tall, thin Welsh actor, a POW from 1940 to 1945, who contributed deadpan comic relief to all the James Bond films since the second entry in the long-running series. His quirky Q provides Agent 007 with gimmicky secret weapons in every film. He calmly (and with hidden pride and joy) demonstrates how deadly they are, and lectures on their proper use with the same precision and degree of concern a British schoolmaster might have explaining to a student how to use a pencil sharpener. He is an eccentric (what weapons he conceives!) but tries to keep this fact hidden beneath a humorless, matter-of-fact approach to his job and an unimpressed attitude toward Bond, when in fact, he'd love to be with him in the field. Indeed, in *License to Kill,* Q bravely works alongside Bond. With the death of Bernard Lee, the original M, and the departure of Lois Maxwell, the original Miss Moneypenny, Llewellyn is the lone link between the new Bond and the exciting past. Consequently, his popularity has increased.

- **Cult Favorites:** *From Russia With Love* (1963, Terence Young), *Goldfinger* (1964, Guy Hamilton), *On Her Majesty's Secret Service* (1969, Peter Hunt), *The Spy Who Loved Me* (1977, Lewis Gilbert).
- **Other Key Films:** *Thunderball* (1965, Young), *You Only Live Twice* (1967, Gilbert), *Diamonds Are Forever* (1971, Hamilton), *Live and Let Die* (1973, Hamilton), *The Man with the Golden Gun* (1974, Hamilton), *Moonraker* (1979, Gilbert), *For Your Eyes Only* (1981, John Glen), *Octopussy* (1983, Glen), *A View to a Kill* (1985, Glen), *The Living Daylights* (1987, Glen), *License to Kill* (1989, Glen).

○

DAVID LOCHARY The male star of John Waters's earlier bad-taste comedies, dating back to his 8mm and 16mm shorts, *Hag in a Black Leather Jacket, Roman Candles,* and *Eat Your Makeup.* Lochary had a mustache and streaked hair and played degenerates with pride and vigor, sharing the screen with Divine, Mary Vivian Pearce, and Mink Stole. In *Mondo Trasho,* he was Dr. Coat Hanger, mad scientific experimenter. In *Multiple Maniacs,* he and girl friend Divine run a "Carnival of Perversions"—she slices him up and eats his heart after discovering he and his secret lover, Pearce, are plotting to kill her. In *Pink Flamingos,* he had his best and most memorable role as Raymond Marble, who along with wife Connie (Mink Stole) claim they each deserve the title of "the filthiest human being on earth" more than Divine's Babs Johnson. The Marbles invest in pornography and sell heroin in elementary schools; they kidnap women, have their butler rape and impregnate them, and then sell their babies; on the side, Raymond flashes women in the park. In *Female Trouble,* Lochary and fellow hairdresser Pearce pay Divine's Dawn Davenport to commit crimes while they photograph her and launch her into show biz. Who knows what demented roles lay in store for Lochary? Unfortunately, he died from complications after an overdose of angel dust. Upset by his long-time friend's death, Waters made his next film, *Desperate Living,* about women so he wouldn't require an important male character.

• **Cult Favorites:** *Mondo Trasho* (1969, John Waters), *Multiple Maniacs* (1970, Waters), *Pink Flamingos* (1972, Waters), *Female Trouble* (1974, Waters).

○

NANCY LOOMIS Pretty, young, brunette turned in three good performances in John Carpenter films, then virtually disappeared. She had the makings of an offbeat leading lady—or quirky friend of the leading lady, as in *Halloween,* where her witty, boy-crazy high-school girl babysits across the street from the house where Jamie Lee Curtis is babysitting. Unfortunately for her, psychotic Michael Myers visits her house first. Loomis was convincing as a teenager, jabbering away about school, boys, prom dates, and sex. She becomes so endearing and so familiar that her long-drawn-out death—after she opens a car door that she remembers, too late, had been locked—is quite tragic.

• **Cult Favorites:** *Assault on Precinct 13* (1976, John Carpenter), *Halloween* (1978, Carpenter), *The Fog* (1980, Carpenter).

○

TRACI LORDS (1968–) Nora Louise Kuzma was a nude model and the *Penthouse* Pet in the famous Vanessa Williams exposé issue

Traci Lords in John Waters's
Cry-Baby.

before she went on to become an enormous, highly marketable porno star, with a line of Traci Lords Company videos flying out of stores. That the pretty, small but shapely blond star looked like an innocent teenager—who did nasty things and posed with a slutty opened-mouth, narrowed-eyes expression only because she was trying to emulate adult porno actresses—contributed to her success. As she would later say, "My films are real popular with dirty old men." As it turned out, Traci Lords was indeed a teenager when she shot all but one (*Traci, Je t'aime*) of her 100 X-rated films and videos, and the porno industry was shaken by scandal. Her underaged video performances were quickly yanked off shelves, and the photographers who had taken her pictures and directors who had filmed her worried that they were about to be arrested for exploiting a minor. Her porno career over, Lords, who is comfortable in front of the cameras, found acting roles in offbeat, mainstream movies. Producer Roger Corman cast her as a sexy nurse, the lead in the R-rated *Not of This Earth*, and John Waters used her in *Cry-Baby,* where she wore tight tops, wiggled, sneered, and was funny. Now, she's pretty much a curio. It will be interesting to see if her talent and her career develop.

• **Key Non-Porno Films:** *Not of This Earth* (1988, Jim Wynorski), *Cry-Baby* (1990, John Waters).

• **Sample Porno Titles:** *Tracy Decks Tokyo, Beverly Hills Copulator, Passion Pit, Sister Dearest, New Wave Hookers, Traci, Je t'aime.*

○

PETER LORRE (1904–64) One of the greats. The Hungarian-born actor was on the Berlin stage when Fritz Lang wrote *M* for him. His shattering portrayal of a child molester and murderer climaxes when the terrified deviant is captured by other criminals and delivers an hysterical plea-for-mercy monologue about the torment he has endured because of his uncontrollable sickness. The role made him a star in his debut, but at the same time typecast him for the rest of his movie career, both in Germany (which he fled upon Hitler's rise) and in France, England, and America. He wanted romantic roles, like Charles Boyer, whom he resembled slightly, but instead played a succession of villains, from comical cads to sadistic fiends with deep psychological problems. He was short and round-headed, with heavy-lidded Ping-Pong eyes, and an oddly accented, distinct, nasal voice that mimics loved. His weight fluctuated and his basically pudgy frame was at times truly fat and at other times quite thin. He wore his hair in many ugly styles, from bald (his unforgettable Dr. Gogol in *Mad Love*) to black with bangs (his foreign terrorist in *The Man Who Knew Too Much*) to blond (his tribute to Truman Capote in *Beat the Devil*). His criminals are intelligent and often cultured, but invariably too oily to touch. The scariest are philosophical "thinking" men, who have a touch of melancholy or have suffered greatly. Almost all his men are eccentric, nervous, excitable, and frustrated in that they *never* get what they want. They often explode in an infantile rage, literally spitting out words and pulling hair. They are pathetic individuals. Yet many are funny, especially Joel Cairo in *The Maltese Falcon*, who gets mad at Bogart for mussing his shirt, and those other cunning, greedy men who teamed up with Sydney Greenstreet's sly schemers in several enjoyable melodramas.

Peter Lorre with Frances Drake in Mad Love.

Although there were exceptions—like his villains in *M, Mad Love,* and *The Lost One*—even his wickedest men were hard to hate. As Charles Bennett, who wrote several Lorre films, attested: "Peter Lorre, the 'heavy,' could kill—calculatedly, malevolently—and still remain amusingly lovable . . . perhaps because he killed with that alluring smile, or perhaps his personal kindness came through."

• **Cult Favorites:** *M* (1931, Fritz Lang), *Mad Love* (1935, Karl Freund), *Strange Cargo* (1940, Frank Borzage), *The Maltese Falcon* (1941, John Huston), *Casablanca* (1942, Michael Curtiz), *Arsenic and Old Lace* (1944, Frank Capra), *The Lost One* (1951, Peter Lorre), *Beat the Devil* (1954, Huston), *The Story of Mankind* (1957, Irwin Allen), *Scent of Mystery* (1959, Jack Cardiff).

• **Other Key Films:** *The Man Who Knew Too Much* (1934, Alfred Hitchcock), *Crime and Punishment* (1935, Josef von Sternberg), *Secret Agent* (1936, Hitchcock), *Thank You, Mr. Moto* (1938, Norman Foster), *Stranger on the Third Floor* (1940, Boris Ingster), *All Through the Night* (1941, Vincent Sherman), *The Face Behind the Mask* (1941, Robert Florey), *The Cross of Lorraine* (1943, Tay Garnett), *The Conspirators* (1944, Jean Negulesco), *Passage to Marseilles* (1944, Curtiz), *The Mask of Dimitrios* (1944, Negulesco), *Three Strangers* (1946, Negulesco), *The Beast with Five Fingers* (1946, Florey), *The Black Angel* (1946, Roy William Neill), *20,000 Leagues Under the Sea* (1954, Richard Fleischer), *The Big Circus* (1959, Joseph Newman), *Voyage to the Bottom of the Sea* (1961, Allen), *Tales of Terror* (1962,

Roger Corman), *The Raven* (1963, Corman), *Comedy of Terrors* (1963, Jacques Tourneur).

○

LINDA LOVELACE (1952–) The most famous porno actress of all time. In 1972, after starring in *Deep Throat,* which middle-class couples made into the top-grossing porno film ever, she became a household word, a national celebrity, an in-demand talk-show guest, and the punchline of countless jokes. The curly-haired brunette wasn't all that pretty or shapely, but mixed audiences appreciated that she seemed to be having fun in the silly XXX-rated comedy playing a young woman in search of

Linda Lovelace is the happy poster girl for the groundbreaking porno film Deep Throat, *but years later she contended she was forced to be in it.*

sexual pleasure. Her sexually frustrated dum-dum learns from Harry Reems's idiotic doctor that she has never had an orgasm because her clitoris is in her throat. She performs fellatio on him, has an orgasm, and a world of pleasure opens up to her. During the course of the film, the uninhibited Lovelace shaved her pubic hair, engaged in anal sex, and made incredibly long penises disappear down her throat without gagging. Because of her fame, old loops circulated through the underground showing her eagerly having sex with men (employing her deep-throat technique), women, and even a dog. As in *Deep Throat,* it looked as if Lovelace was enjoying herself immensely. However, years later, the actress appeared with Women Against Pornography and swore she was beaten and forced into appearing in porno films by her then-husband David Traynor (who would marry Marilyn Chambers). She said the same in her book, *Ordeal*—but the passages were suspiciously titillating. Those who saw her in action doubt her story. But in case she's telling the truth, it's impossible to still enjoy her films.
  • **Cult Favorite:** *Deep Throat* (1972, Gerard Damiano).

○

LYNN LOWRY Pretty, slender, sexy actress with brown hair that was long enough to cover her bare breasts in several films made by cult directors in the seventies. She had the female lead in *Fighting Mad,* opposite Peter Fonda, but more often she was the second or third female lead in violent horror and R-rated sex films. Her roles were almost always sexual in nature. Her women were wide-eyed, innocent, and more than passive—they were primed to be seduced, attacked, or killed. Remarkably, in three films her character is victimized by a form of plague: in *I Drink Your Blood,* she's one of a group of hippies who get rabies by eating infected pies; in *The Crazies,* she switches from being sexually repressed to sexually aggressive because of a deadly violence-inducing plague; in the creepiest scene in *They Came from Within,* her character swallows a large violence-inducing parasite while kissing infected lover Barbara Steele—and then is killed as hordes of crazed people run wild committing murder and mayhem. And in three other films, she is the passive lover of strong lesbians: Steele obviously controls the younger girl in *They Came from Within,* Mary Woronov seduces her in *Sugar Cookies,* Clare Wilbur seduces her in *Score.* Lowry always looked lost, frightened, and vulnerable. Perhaps she disappeared from the screen because such female characters were no longer in vogue.

• **Cult Favorites:** *I Drink Your Blood* (1971, David Durston), *They Came from Within* (1975, David Cronenberg), *Score* (1975, Radley Metzger).

• **Other Key Films:** *The Crazies* (1973, George A. Romero), *Sugar Cookies* (1975, Theodore Gershuny), *Fighting Mad* (1976, Jonathan Demme).

○

BELA LUGOSI (1882–1956) Former matinee idol and leftist organizer of an actors union in his native Hungary, he became a character actor in Hollywood in the early twenties. He was a great success on stage in *Dracula* and played the lead when Tod Browning adapted it as a film in 1931. It was a box-office sensation and Lugosi became a star. The film is dated, but Lugosi's heavily rouged face, with that grimace and those wide, aggressive eyes, is still frightening today. Lugosi was no great actor but he was a great Dracula. Handsome, with the kind of accent that connotes to impressionable Americans good breeding, Lugosi became a sex symbol as a result of the film. His vampire is intelligent, cultivated, yet comfortable walking through cobwebs. His blood lust is scary, and his seductive attacks on women are the acts of a sex fiend. Although he admits at one point that it would be "glorious" to be really dead, this Dracula is not at all sympathetic—it is by choice rather than happenstance that he does evil. Lugosi would play a couple of sympathetic characters in his film career, like Dr. Verdegast in *The Black Cat,* but even those men are capable of cruel acts. Lugosi was at his best when cast opposite the other horror icon Boris Karloff, and he had few other good roles. He would play the werewolf who bites Lon Chaney, Jr., in *The Wolf Man,* the Frankenstein Monster in *Frankenstein Meets the Wolf Man,* and Igor in a couple of Frankenstein movies, but nothing he did compared to his Dracula. Because he was typecast, unable to speak without an accent, and one of the hammiest actors in Hollywood, he had difficulty finding parts even in bad horror films. With the exception of his Dracula reprise in *Abbott and Costello Meet Frankenstein,* he usually ended up playing mad scientists in Grade-Z fare, often exercises in self-parody. In addition, he had marital problems and an addiction to morphine. By the fifties he was appearing in absolute garbage, including Edward D. Wood atrocities that ironically would add millions of bad-movie fans to his cult. He died while filming *Plan 9 from Outer Space* and was buried in his Dracula cape.

• **Cult Favorites:** *White Zombie* (1932,

Bela Lugosi is Dracula.

Victor Halperin), *Island of Lost Souls* (1933, Erle C. Kenton), *The Black Cat* (1934, Edgar G. Ulmer), *Mark of the Vampire* (1935, Tod Browning), *The Raven* (1935, Louis Friedlander/Lew Landers), *Ninotchka* (1939, Ernst Lubitsch), *The Wolf Man* (1941, George Waggner), *The Body Snatcher* (1945, Robert Wise), *Abbott and Costello Meet Frankenstein* (1948, Charles Barton), *Bela Lugosi Meets a Brooklyn Gorilla* (1952, William Beaudine), *Glen or Glenda?/I Changed My Sex* (1953, Edward D. Wood), *Bride of the Monster* (1955, Wood), *Plan 9 from Outer Space* (1959, Wood).

• **Other Key Films:** *Dracula* (1931, Browning), *Murders in the Rue Morgue* (1932, Robert Florey), *The Death Kiss* (1933, Edward L. Marin), *The Return of Chandu* (1934

serial, Ray Taylor), *Murder By Television* (1935, Clifford Sandforth), *The Invisible Ray* (1936, Lambert Hillyer), *Son of Frankenstein* (1939, Rowland V. Lee), *The Phantom Creeps* (1939 serial, Ford Beebe and Saul A. Goodkind), *Human Monster* (1940, Walter Summers), *Black Friday* (1940, Arthur Lubin), *The Devil Bat* (1941, Jean Yarbrough), *The Ghost of Frankenstein* (1942, Kenton), *The Ape Man* (1943, Beaudine), *Frankenstein Meets the Wolf Man* (1943, Roy William Neill), *The Return of the Vampire* (1943, Lew Landers).

○

KEYE LUKE (1904–91) China-born actor had a long Hollywood career, from *The Good Earth* to *Gremlins*, with a lot of entertaining B pictures along the way. He usually played smart, likable, and distinctly Chinese characters, including his most famous role, Charlie Chan's "Number One Son" in all those films in which Warner Oland played the amusing master detective. (Oland had been in Luke's debut film, *The Painted Veil*.) He was a loyal son and proud of his pop, but he occasionally meddled in his father's cases and was impatient with his father's slower, more methodical approach to crime solving. He wanted to impress his dad. He was often humbled by Charlie's weird but sage words of wisdom. Luke would also be a regular in the *Dr. Gillespie* films, playing a doctor, and he would appear in other series featuring Mr. Moto, the Bowery Boys, the Falcon, and Andy Hardy, and play Kato in two "Green Hornet" serials. At times, he would sport a mustache. And, many years later, in David Carradine's television series "Kung Fu," he would give sage advice of his own. He went out in style as Mia Farrow's shrewd, chain-smoking acupuncturist-herbalist in Woody Allen's *Alice*.

• **Cult Favorites:** *Mad Love* (1935, Karl Freund), *Charlie Chan at the Opera* (1936, H. Bruce Humberstone), *Chinatown* (1974, Roman Polanski).

• **Other Key Films:** *The Painted Veil* (1934, Richard Boleslawsky). *Charlie Chan in Paris* (1934), *Oil for the Lamps of China* (1935, Mervyn LeRoy), *Charlie Chan in Shanghai* (1935, James Tinling), *Charlie Chan at the Circus* (1936, Harry Lachman), *Charlie Chan at the Race Track* (1936, Humberstone), *The Good Earth* (1937, Sidney Franklin), *Charlie Chan at the Olympics* (1937, Humberstone), *Charlie Chan on Broadway* (1937, Eugene Forde), *Charlie Chan at Monte Carlo* (1937, Forde), *Mr. Moto's Gamble* (1938, Tinling), *The Green Hornet* (1940 serial, Ford Beebe and Ray Taylor), *The Green Hornet Strikes Again* (1940 serial, Beebe and John Rawlins), *Across the Pacific* (1942, John Huston), *Dr. Gillespie's New Assistant* (1942, Willis Goldbeck), *Dr. Gillespie's Criminal Case* (1943, Goldbeck), *Three Men in White* (1944, Goldbeck), *Secret Agent X-9* (1945 serial, Taylor and Lewis Collins), *Gremlins* (1984, Joe Dante), *The Mighty Quinn* (1989, Carl Schenkel), *The Two Jakes* (1990, Jack Nicholson), *Alice* (1990, Woody Allen).

○

LYDIA LUNCH (1959–) Superstar of New York's taboo-breaking underground cinema, often referred to as the "cinema of transgression." Short, sexy, black-haired, she definitely has a presence, with her thick lipstick, dark eyes, pins in her ears (sometimes), scowl, and insolent and abusive disposition. She has starred in and written 8mm films with bizarre plot lines and shocking imagery, including bondage and hard-core sex. Her most famous and personally revealing short is *The Right Side of the Brain,* playing a young woman with an increasing preoccupation with sex. Cowritten by Lunch, the topics of the 28-minute film, stated one review, include "obsession, domination, debasement, and just plain life." Her narration contains "Lunch lyricism, pro-foundish rhyme and use of clichés." In the picture she dominates one female sexual partner, but places herself in the victim role with male lovers. What made the film thematically controversial as well as supported by some feminists (though despised by others) is that Lunch's subjugation seems to be by choice, and that by demanding satisfaction from the men, she is actually in charge. Lunch insisted that she was a feminist herself because, as she told *Film Threat*'s Christian Gore, "I'm demanding what I want as a *woman.*" So all her sexual experiences are liberating rather than repressive (which, interestingly, is the response Maria Schneider has when agreeing to Marlon Brando's harsh demands in *The Last Tango in Paris*). Lunch appeared in Beth B. and Scott B.'s *Black Box* and *The Offenders* before stepping a bit out of the underground and playing an engagingly quirky lead in their strange 16mm feature, *Vortex,* a mix of film noir, science fiction, and the experimental film. Lunch is a private eye on a murder case involving industrial espionage and computer theft. As in her underground films, she gets involved with a man sexually rather than romantically. She also contributed to the music track. At 17, she was with the "No Wave" band Teenage Jesus and the Jerks, playing guitar and chanting and shrieking in a monotone; later she helped form the blues-oriented Eight-Eyed Spy.

• **Cult Favorites:** *Vortex* (1982, Beth B. and Scott B.), *The Wild World of Lydia*

Lunch (1983, Nick Zedd), *The Right Side of the Brain* (1984, Richard Kern).
- **Other Sample Titles:** *Black Box* (Beth B. and Scott B.), *The Offenders* (Beth B. and Scott B.), *She Had Her Gun All Ready, Beauty Becomes the Beast, Rome '78.*

○

DOLPH LUNDGREN This blond, muscular Swedish karate champion tips the scales at 6'6" and 240–260 pounds. He was an effective villain, Carl Weathers's killer and Sylvester Stallone's unbeatable nemesis, in the otherwise atrocious *Rocky IV*. His mean Russian boxer, a human machine named Drago—a muscular, no-body-fat giant who represents the apex in advanced Soviet training techniques—is a combination of football linebacker Brian Bosworth and Richard Kiel's "Jaws." Lundgren grew his hair and looked more handsome as He-Man in the entertaining juvenile film, *Masters of the Universe,* based on the popular cartoon series. He proved as likable a hero as he was detestable a villain, which makes him a double threat. He became the logical choice to play the violent comic-book sensation, *The Punisher*. Will there be a 900-number telephone poll to determine who'd win a fight between Lundgren and Jean-Claude Van Damme?
- **Key Films:** *Rocky IV* (1985, Sylvester Stallone), *Masters of the Universe* (1987, Gary Goddard), *Red Scorpion* (1989, Joseph Zito), *"I" Come in Peace* (1990, Craig R. Baxley).

○

TI LUNG He came out of a Peking Opera troupe to become a stuntman and then one of Hong Kong's top martial-arts stars. He often teamed with David Chiang in violent costume dramas and gangster pictures. Typically, they start out as enemies, then help each other out of trouble once they realize they have a common enemy. More majestic and handsome than Chiang, he was an equally adept fighter, using fists (he was a student of tae kwon do), swords, and a staff.
- **Cult Favorites:** *Vengeance* (1970, Chang Cheh), *The New One-Armed Swordsman* (1971, Cheh), *Five Masters of Death* (1975, Cheh).
- **Other Key Films:** *Duel of the Iron Fist* (1971, Cheh), *Deadly Duo* (1971, Cheh), *Ten Tigers of Kwantung* (1979, Cheh), *The Hero Defeating Japs* (1983, Cheh).

○

JOHN LURIE (1952–) The leader and saxophone player of the Lounge Lizards, a popular New York–based progressive jazz ensemble, he appeared in the late seventies–early eighties in Super 8 shorts directed by Eric Mitchell, Becky Johnson, Amos Poe, and himself before being the leading man of Jim Jarmusch's critically acclaimed oddball comedies, *Stranger Than Paradise* and *Down by Law*. Tall and gangly, with a handsome but drawn, interesting face, he was perfectly suited to Jarmusch's distinct style, which makes it seem the actors are improvising. But because of the characters' limitations as people—and this contributes to the pieces' humor—they have trouble coming up with anything interesting to say or do. In both films, Lurie's characters attempt to break out of static, dreary existences. In the first film, he flees his New York tenement for Cleveland's snow and then Florida's sunshine, and is disturbed to discover that everywhere he goes seems exactly the same. In *Down By Law*, he breaks out of a New Orleans jail, and after spending time with livelier ex-cellmates Tom Waits and Roberto Begnini, takes a fork in a road to some unknown destination. Lurie's long-confined charac-ters have no idea of the possibilities there are in the world for better, more fruitful lives. Even when they get to their destina-tions, they are still stuck with themselves. A surprisingly effective, engaging actor, who can realistically play boring people and be funny doing it. He had small parts in Jarmusch's *Permanent Vacation* and Wim Wenders's *Paris, Texas*. He has also scored many films.

• **Cult Favorites:** *Stranger Than Paradise* (1984, Jim Jarmusch), *Down By Law* (1986, Jarmusch).

○

RICHARD LYNCH (1936–) Blond actor with a strong, handsome, but fire-scarred face, an effective villain in numerous horror, sword-and-sandal, and action pictures. His loathsome figures are always intent on spreading evil (in *God Told Me To,* he is the anti-Christ), confident they will suc-ceed, and calm in their approach. Their weapon is a hypnotic, seductive power that almost no one can resist. Lynch used that power as a Jim Jones–like cult guru in *Bad Dreams* and as one of the most terrifying vampires of all in the exciting TV movie *Vampire.*

• **Cult Favorites:** *God Told Me To/Demon* (1977, Larry Cohen), *Invasion U.S.A.* (1985, Joseph Zito), *The Ninth Configura-tion* (1980, William Peter Blatty).

• **Other Key Films:** *Deathsport* (1978, Henry Suso and Allan Arkush), *The Sword and the Sorcerer* (1982, Albert Pyun), *Bad Dreams* (1988, Andrew Fleming), *Little Nikita* (1988, Richard Benjamin).

• **Also of Interest:** *Scarecrow* (1973, Jerry

Schatzberg), *The Seven-Ups* (1973, Philip D'Antonio), *The Premonition* (1976, Rob-ert Allen Schnitzer), *Steel* (1980, Steve Carver), *The Formula* (1980, John G. Avildsen), *Cut and Run* (1985, Ruggero Deodato), *The Barbarians* (1987, Deo-dato).

○

CAROL LYNLEY (1942–) This former teen model, with long blond hair and a sweet, pretty face, gained immediate movie popularity—especially with teenage girls —playing anguished adolescents. She al-ways had major parental and romantic problems. In *Blue Denim,* Brandon de Wilde, of all people, gets her pregnant. Her early films were much like Sandra Dee's. But Lynley had better luck in adult parts, even playing the title role in *Harlow,* the competition to Carroll Baker's version released the same year. She had talent but was usually as bland as her material. Her best performance was in her most inter-esting project, Otto Preminger's bizarre mystery *Bunny Lake Is Missing.* She played an unmarried American woman who can't convince the London police that she has a young daughter, and that she has been kidnapped. Since then her career has been undistinguished.

• **Cult Favorites:** *Bunny Lake Is Missing* (1965, Otto Preminger), *The Poseidon Adventure* (1972, Ronald Neame).

• **Sleeper:** *Hound-Dog Man* (1960, Don Siegel).

• **Other Key Films:** *The Light in the Forest* (1958, Herschel Daugherty), *Holiday for Lovers* (1959, Henry Levin), *Blue Denim* (1959, Philip Dunne), *Return to Peyton Place* (1961, José Ferrer), *The Last Sunset* (1961, Robert Aldrich), *The Stripper* (1963, Franklin Schaffner), *Under the*

Yum Yum Tree (1963, David Swift), *The Cardinal* (1963, Preminger), *The Pleasure Seekers* (1964, Jean Negulesco), *Harlow* (1965, Alex Segal), *The Shuttered Room* (1968, David Greene), *The Washington Affair* (1977, Victor Stoloff).

○

SUE LYON (1946–) Amid much publicity stating she was too young even to see the film, an unknown blonde was cast in the title role in *Lolita,* opposite James Mason's Humbert Humbert. As the 12-year-old nymphet, she gave a self-assured, naughty performance. Lolita's smile indicates she understands that her stepfather's intentions are not honorable. Lyon, who looked 17 though she was a couple of years younger, need do nothing provocative as an actress for her character to excite the older man—she simply lies around in a skimpy bikini and wears heart-shaped glasses. (However, her "Yi Yi" bubble-gum theme song is one of the most sexually suggestive pieces of music ever written.) In *The Night of the Iguana,* trying to seduce Richard Burton's much-older ex-clergyman and

Sue Lyon is bored with James Mason's attention in Lolita.

also attracting a much-older female tour-group leader, in *Seven Women*, attracting Margaret Leighton's much-older, sexually repressed missionary (Ann Bancroft's doctor tries to free the young missionary from her boss's control), Lyon would again stimulate "unhealthy" sexual desires. Lyon's career faded after her promising beginning—she would make the news when she married a prisoner—and she has made only a few scattered film appearances since.

• **Cult Favorites:** *Lolita* (1962, Stanley Kubrick), *Seven Women* (1966, John Ford), *Alligator* (1980, Lewis Teague).

• **Other Key Films:** *The Night of the Iguana* (1964, John Huston), *The Flim-Flam Man* (1967, Irvin Kershner), *Tony Rome* (1967, Gordon Douglas), *Evel Knievel* (1972, Marvin Chomsky).

○

MERCEDES MCCAMBRIDGE (1918–) Unconventional, riveting, dark-haired actress. She won a Best Supporting Actress Oscar for her debut role in *All the King's Men*, as a political aide who is expected to temper the too-truthful grass-roots campaign of a dynamic Huey Long–like candidate (Broderick Crawford) but ends up falling in love with him. Her character Sadie Burke is intelligent, forceful, and has difficulty controlling her emotions. Most of the actress's future characters would be more intense, volatile, and neurotic, paranoid about losing what they have, greedy for what others have, and competitive with other women. Often they behave badly because they are dissatisfied with their plain looks. They include shrill shrews, babblers, interfering sisters (as in *Giant*) and mothers, and, in *Touch of Evil*, a butch druggie in a leather jacket. In the leftist-Freudian *Johnny Guitar*, her character's hysteria is the result of sexual repression; when this jealous, vengeful woman hunts down her rival, Joan Crawford, Nicholas Ray presents her like a witch, complete with black dress, scary shadows, and a fire lighting her crazed face. Like Crawford, she is referred to as a woman who wants to be a man, only her "macho" bearing isn't mitigated by motherly instincts. Wearing holsters and guns, McCambridge and Crawford have one of the few western gunfights between women—a classic scene. A radio costar of Orson Welles on "Ford Theater" in the forties, she had her final screen success providing the devil's gravelly voice that comes out of Linda Blair's mouth in *The Exorcist*. She says she drew on the hellish sounds and curses she heard while recovering from alcoholism in state institutions.

• **Cult Favorites:** *Johnny Guitar* (1954, Nicholas Ray), *Giant* (1956, George Stevens), *Touch of Evil* (1958, Orson Welles), *The Exorcist* (1973, William Friedkin).

• **Sleeper:** *Angel Baby* (1960, Paul Wendkos and Hubert Cornfield).

• **Other Key Films:** *All the King's Men* (1949, Robert Rossen), *Suddenly Last Summer* (1959, Joseph L. Mankiewicz).

• **Also of Interest:** *Lightning Strikes Twice* (1951, King Vidor), *A Farewell to Arms* (1957, Charles Vidor), *Cimarron* (1960, Anthony Mann), *Like a Crow on a June Bug/Sixteen* (1972, Lawrence Dobkin).

○

KEVIN MCCARTHY (1914–) One of the cinema's most chilling scenes features Kevin McCarthy at the end of Don Siegel's science-fiction classic *Invasion of the Body*

Kevin McCarthy in Invasion of the Body Snatchers.

Snatchers—the greatest of all paranoia pictures—as his disheveled, semi-hysterical doctor races back and forth on a busy highway, like a lunatic sidewalk preacher, desperately warning all the drivers of their impending doom ("You're next!") unless they listen to him. (In a cameo appearance, this character also sounded the alarm in the remake 22 years later.) Horror-movie fans also get chills from an earlier scene, when McCarthy kisses Dana Wynter, looks down into her cold eyes, and realizes that she has been taken over by her emotionless alien pod replacement. McCarthy's truly excellent performance in this political allegory, as a man who fights to retain his humanity, earned him cult status. Otherwise, McCarthy, the brother of writer Mary McCarthy and good friend of Montgomery Clift, has played forgettable roles—a letdown from the promise of his debut as Biff in *Death of a Salesman* (a role he had earlier on the London stage and Broadway). Broad-shouldered and handsome, his characters look good in suits, drink martinis, seem Ivy League–educated, and probably played a little fraternity football—that is, they're dull.

• **Cult Favorites:** *Invasion of the Body Snatchers* (1956, Don Siegel), *The Misfits* (1961, John Huston), *Buffalo Bill and the Indians* (1976, Robert Altman), *Piranha* (1978, Joe Dante), *The Howling* (1981, Dante).

• **Also of Interest:** *Death of a Salesman* (1951, Laslo Benedek), *An Annapolis Story* (1955, Siegel), *Nightmare* (1956, Maxwell Shane), *A Gathering of Eagles* (1963, Delbert Mann), *The Best Man* (1964, Franklin Schaffner), *A Big Hand for the Little Lady* (1966, Fielder Cook), *Hotel* (1967, Richard Quine), *Hero at Large* (1980, Martin Davidson).

○

TIM MCCOY (1891–1978) Commanding western hero was the only cowboy star on M-G-M's classy roster in the late twenties. For two decades, he made fairly expensive and expansive westerns, some loaded with action, others emphasizing plot. Having worked on ranches in Wyoming and studied the heritage of the West and the Indians, he insisted that his films be authentic—*War Paint* and *End of the Trail* (perhaps his best film) were about the mistreatment of the Native Americans. He also starred in the first all-talking serial, *The Indians Are Coming,* in 1930. Many of his films were "detective" pictures transferred to the West; his most famous character, Lightnin' Bill Carson, often donned disguises. Posture-perfect and sharply featured (he looked best in profile), his husky characters (cowpokes, lawmen, drifters, gamblers, calvary officers) were confident, determined (they could look very intense), and law-abiding. They were tough fighters, quick on the trigger, and did some fine riding on Ace and the white Baron. They were leader types, whose smiles and handshakes meant something. In the early forties, McCoy went out in style, teaming with Buck Jones and Raymond Hatton in the heralded "Rough Riders" series, which ended with Jones's death and McCoy's unsuccessful run for senator of Wyoming. But McCoy went on to win a Bronze Star, achieve the rank of colonel, and become a real-life war hero.
• **Cult Favorites:** *Arizona Bound* (1941, Spencer G. Bennet), *Run of the Arrow* (1957, Samuel Fuller).
• **Some Other Key Films:** *War Paint* (1926, W. S. Van Dyke), *Winners of the Wilderness* (1927, Van Dyke), *California* (1927, Van Dyke), *The Law of the Range* (1928, William Nigh), *The Indians Are Coming* (1930 serial, Henry McRae), *Texas Cyclone* (1932, Ross Lederman), *The Riding Tornado* (1932, Lederman), *End of the Trail* (1932, Lederman), *Fighting Shadows* (1935, David Selman), *Bulldog Courage* (1935, Sam Newfield), *Lightnin' Bill Carson* (1936, Newfield), *Gun Code* (1940, Peter Stewart), *The Gunman from Bodie* (1941, Bennet), *Forbidden Trails* (1941, Robert North Bradbury), *Below the Border* (1942, Howard Bretherton), *Ghost Town Law* (1942, Bretherton), *Down Texas Way* (1942, Bretherton), *West of the Law* (1942, Bretherton).

○

HATTIE MCDANIEL (1895–1952) This much-loved, heavy-set black actress had been a headline singer on the Pantages and Orpheum circuits (billed as "the colored Sophie Tucker") and on the radio, but other than doing a funny, exciting duet with Paul Robeson in *Show Boat,* she rarely was given a singing part in movies. Instead, she became the cinema's definitive maid, a 200-pound black mammy in an apron and white bandana or lace cap. She will always be best remembered as the assertive, protective, haughty, maternal mammy in *Gone With the Wind,* who practically raises Scarlett O'Hara (Vivian Leigh). For her scene-stealing portrayal, she was the first black to win an Oscar. But she played servants in almost all of her 80 films—mostly comedies—working on screen for Mae West, Jean Harlow, Shirley Temple, Barbara Stanwyck, Carole Lombard, and almost every other leading lady. Occasionally she played an unusual character—such as the far-from-perfect cook-maid Katharine Hepburn mistakenly hopes will impress her rich male guest in *Alice Adams*—but most often she was the loyal, temperamental, perceptive (and hilarious) servant who protects her mistress's house as if she were a fierce bulldog guarding a doghouse. She was always a positive influence. In *Mr. Blandings Builds His Dream House,* for instance, she supplies the slogan that saves Cary Grant's advertising job. Once she was hired, she was the boss, and everyone—including her employer—knew it. McDaniel had trouble finding movie roles in the late forties, when the NAACP protested against blacks always playing characters with menial jobs (and producers hesitated to expand the repertoire). However, she starred as the maid "Beulah" on radio and, until her death, on television.

• **Cult Favorites:** *Blonde Venus* (1932, Josef von Sternberg), *I'm No Angel* (1933, Wesley Ruggles).

• **Also Recommended:** *Alice Adams* (1935, George Stevens), *China Seas* (1935, Tay Garnett), *Libeled Lady* (1936, Jack Conway), *Show Boat* (1936, James Whale), *Saratoga* (1937, Conway), *Nothing Sacred* (1937, William A. Wellman), *The Shopworn Angel* (1938, H. C. Potter), *The Shining Hour* (1938, Frank Borzage), *Gone With the Wind* (1939, Victor Fleming), *ZeNobia* (1939, Gordon Douglas), *The Great Lie* (1941, Edmund Goulding), *The Male Animal* (1942, Elliott Nugent), *George Washington Slept Here* (1942, William Keighley), *In This Our Life* (1942, John Huston), *Since You Went Away* (1944, John Crom-

well), *Song of the South* (1946, Wilfred Jackson), *Mr. Blandings Builds His Dream House* (1948, H. C. Potter).

○

JEANETTE MACDONALD (1901–65) Today, this lovely blond singer-actress is best remembered for her eight M-G-M operettas with Nelson Eddy—they were the most popular singing duo in movie history. Other than with connoisseurs, her cult status, I believe, is mostly the result of the camp reputation of those one-time box-office hits. I don't dislike those films as do many critics, because I feel MacDonald shines even in those series entries that are dull and saccharine, and her emotional characters' duets with the stiff, uniformed Eddy pretty much define escapist entertainment. Her films with other costars, however, show how extremely limiting the pairing was to the versatile actress. For instance, in three classic musical comedies with Maurice Chevalier—Ernst Lubitsch's *The Love Parade* and *The Merry Widow,* and the Lubitsch-imitation *Love Me Tonight,* directed by Rouben Mamoulian—she not only displays a great deal of wit (a good sport, she is not adverse to self-mockery) but is daringly brazen. There weren't many racier scenes than when tailor Chevalier measures the bosom of the slip-clad MacDonald (when she abandoned neck-strangling dresses, no actress was sexier). Her characters were ladies but they had wicked gleams in their eyes and, Chevalier knew, would be something special in the bedroom. In *San Francisco,* MacDonald was at her peak—beautiful, energetic, and splendidly singing both opera and rousing songs with the same command and emotion Kate Smith had booming out "God Bless

Jeanette MacDonald and Nelson Eddy in Rose Marie.

America." What star quality! Moreover, she had the talent and sex appeal to be suited for all kinds of pictures, from melodramas to high-class musicals. Unfortunately, she wouldn't play opposite the likes of Spencer Tracy and Clark Gable again—just more Nelson Eddy.

• **Cult Favorites:** *The Love Parade* (1929, Ernst Lubitsch), *Love Me Tonight* (1932, Rouben Mamoulian), *The Merry Widow* (1934, Lubitsch), *Naughty Marietta* (1935, W. S. Van Dyke), *Rose Marie* (1936, Van Dyke).

• **Also Recommended:** *One Hour With You* (1932, Lubitsch and George Cukor), *The Cat and the Fiddle* (1934, William K. Howard), *San Francisco* (1935, Van Dyke), *Maytime* (1937, Robert Z. Leonard), *Bitter Sweet* (1940, Van Dyke).

• **Also of Interest:** *Monte Carlo* (1930, Lubitsch), *Let's Go Native* (1930, Leo McCarey), *The Firefly* (1937, Leonard), *Sweethearts* (1938, Van Dyke), *The Girl of the Golden West* (1938, Leonard), *New Moon* (1940, Frank Borzage), *Bitter Sweet* (1940, Van Dyke), *Smilin' Through* (1941, Borzage), *I Married an Angel* (1942, Van Dyke), *Follow the Boys* (1944, Edward Sutherland).

○

MARIE MCDONALD (1923–65) Buxom blond former model, showgirl, and singer became a Hollywood starlet in the forties and appeared in several light comedies. She was adequate but unimpressive, and her career fizzled. She couldn't live up to audience expectations, and was dubbed "The Body" a decade before producers knew how to really exploit someone with such a nickname or measurements. (In 1958, however, Frank Tashlin, a director known for exploiting America's breast fetish, cast her to good effect opposite Jerry Lewis in *The Geisha Boy*.) While extremely attractive, she was a touch too glamorous and not slutty enough to be a sex bomb in the Jayne Mansfield–Mamie Van Doren mold. But she did make the scandal sheets as often as they did, due to seven marriages, a kidnapping publicity stunt designed to revive her career in the late fifties, arrests on drug and drunk-driving charges, a nervous breakdown, and, finally, her drug-induced suicide.

• **Key Films:** *Lucky Jordan* (1942, Frank Tuttle), *Guest in the House* (1944, John Brahm), *Living in a Big Way* (1947, Gregory LaCava), *Tell It to the Judge* (1949, Norman Foster), *Once a Thief* (1950, W. Lee Wilder), *The Geisha Boy* (1958, Frank Tashlin).

• **Also of Interest:** *It Started with Eve* (1941, Henry Koster), *Pardon My Sarong* (1942, Erle C. Kenton), *Riding High* (1944, Mark Sandrich), *I Love a Soldier* (1944, Sandrich), *Standing Room Only* (1944, Sidney Lansfield), *Getting Gertie's Garter* (1945, Allan Dwan).

○

MALCOLM McDOWELL (1943–) The only actor with an infectious *smirk* and wicked gleam in his eye, this slim, athletic, light-haired, boyish-looking British star came to America to play a time-traveling H. G. Wells in *Time After Time,* opposite Mary Steenburgen (whom he later married). Breaking away from his devilish image, his Wells was one of the sweetest characters in memory: gentle, shy, romantic, considerate, nonaggressive, and, unlike McDowell's other characters, neither insolent nor conceited about being smarter than anyone else in the story. Now, here was a guy you could root for. In films made back home, he'd gained fame as a rebellious student in *if . . . ,* playing a barely likable hero who,

in a surrealistic sequence, shoots the taskmaster teachers of his oppressive school. Then he became even more famous as Alex, a vicious but somehow likable villain in Stanley Kubrick's controversial *A Clockwork Orange.* Kubrick wanted us to condone the savagery committed by McDowell's violent teenager, and forgive him, because in that futuristic world it is the rare exhibition of free expression. Kubrick was clever to cast McDowell, an actor who can do all kinds of terrible things on screen but still come across sympathetically. As Alex, McDowell is disturbingly appealing: he's extremely energetic, handsome, and witty, as dynamic as the young, gangster-playing James Cagney, another actor who seemed to dance when he moved. McDowell's coffee salesman in *O Lucky Man!* gave that loony picture an anchor. He played it well, but we can't really root for someone who wants only to be part of the capitalist system and a business success; moreover, he is a neutral figure used by director Lindsay Anderson to introduce us to a lot of zany characters and let us travel through a bizarre, often surrealistic, ultra-British world. *Time After Time* seemed to open up new avenues for McDowell, but rather than look for more hero roles, he began playing outright villains no one could empathize with in such disasters as the X-rated *Caligula*—one admired his guts for taking the part, but felt embarrassed because his character, like the rest of the film, came across as vulgar rather than artistic. In *Cat People,* he commits grisly murders in his cat guise and, as in *Caligula,* desires sex with his sister (Nastassia Kinski). Much more tasteful was his bit as editor Maxwell Perkins in *Cross Creek,* again with Steenburgen (as writer Marjorie Kinnan Rawlings). McDowell also returned to Lindsay Anderson's cinematic world of satire and surrealism in *Britannia Hospital,* a not very successful throwback to *O Lucky Man!*

• **Cult Favorites:** *if . . .* (1969, Lindsay Anderson), *A Clockwork Orange* (1971, Stanley Kubrick), *O Lucky Man!* (1973, Anderson), *Time After Time* (1979, Nicholas Meyer), *Caligula* (1980, Tinto Brass), *Cat People* (1982, Paul Schrader), *Britannia Hospital* (1982, Anderson).

• **Also of Interest:** *Figures in Landscape* (1970, Joseph Losey), *Royal Flash* (1975, Richard Lester), *Voyage of the Damned* (1976, Stuart Rosenberg), *Aces High* (1977, Jack Gold), *Blue Thunder* (1983, John Badham), *Cross Creek* (1983, Martin Ritt), *Sunset* (1988, Blake Edwards).

○

SPANKY MCFARLAND (1928–) George Emmett McFarland was only three when he joined Hal Roach's "Our Gang" series. He was round rather than chubby then, and a truly adorable toddler. Looking at the pint-sized boy, I think it's amazing he could walk, much less act—but he was a natural comic in front of the camera. We remember Spanky best when a few years older, with a round cap on his head, as the leader of the "rascals"—who included Alfalfa (his best friend), Buckwheat, Porky, and Pete the dog. He was a nice, savvy kid, who ran a racially integrated girl-haters club (although Darla was secretary), and was always coming up with ideas to get the gang out of trouble, make Alfalfa a star, or butter up the principal. He'd always be the first to notice that disaster was about to happen to another gang member. When things went awry, he clinched his fists, pulled up his pants, did open-mouthed double takes, or smacked himself in the forehead. He was a good actor and fine

partner to the more emotional Alfalfa. However, when McFarland got older, bigger, and fatter, he suddenly became terribly awkward. But generation after generation of Little Rascals fans still fondly think of him in his heyday. He was an important figure in our childhoods, perhaps even a role model.

• **Cult Favorites:** Numerous "Our Gang" comedy shorts (1931–1940s, Hal Roach).

• **Also of Interest:** *General Spanky* (1936, Fred Newmeyer and Gordon Douglas), *Peck's Bad Boy with the Circus* (1938, Edward Cline), *The Woman in the Window* (1944, Fritz Lang).

○

VONETTA MCGEE (1950–) A leading lady of the black cinema of the seventies. She was lovely, intelligent, classy, and sexy. She was usually just the love interest of the leading man (such as Fred Williamson or Richard Roundtree), but she held her own on the screen opposite boyfriend Max Julien in *Thomasine & Bushrod,* a bank-robbers-on-the-run comedy-drama, and with Bernie Casey in *Brothers,* a politically conscious film about Angela Davis and George Jackson. She had a chance to break into the mainstream when she became the rare black female lead in a film directed by and starring whites when Clint Eastwood cast her in his mountain-climbing spy film, *The Eiger Sanction.* But the part, like others in the film, turned out to be uninteresting, and she was strangely reserved. When the black cinema of the seventies died, so did her movie career.

• **Cult Favorites:** *Blacula* (1972, William Crain), *Repo Man* (1984, Alex Cox).

• **Sleeper:** *Thomasine & Bushrod* (1974, Gordon Parks, Jr.).

• **Other Key Films:** *Melinda* (1972, Hugh A. Robertson), *Hammer* (1972, Bruce Clark), *Detroit 9000* (1973, Arthur Marks), *Shaft in Africa* (1973, John Guillerman), *The Big Bust Out* (1973, Richard Jackson), *The Eiger Sanction* (1975, Clint Eastwood), *Brothers* (1977, Arthur Barron).

○

TIM McINTIRE (1944–86) This outstanding, underutilized character actor (the son of actor John McIntire) gave forceful, intelligently conceived performances in a number of films most people have missed. He was the voice of the dog Blood in the postapocalyptic black comedy *A Boy and His Dog,* based on Harlan Ellison's novella. The best parts of the film are the wicked, rat-a-tat dialogues between Blood and his human companion, Vic (Don Johnson), consisting of threats to leave each other, insults, apologies, and martyr-like remarks by Blood, an old-timer who still wants to know he has worth. McIntire properly provided the animal with a sharp, "adult," Mr. Belvedere-like delivery, which keeps viewers from being too sympathetic toward this animal with a vicious streak. McIntire gave a super performance as the lead in *American Hot Wax,* playing Alan Freed, the first white deejay to play black R & B music. Through McIntire, we can picture Freed walking through a cluttered, special world every day: spinning platters on his radio show (we see that Freed really loved the music), sizing up aspiring acts whom agents march through his office, amiably chatting with teens on the street, stopping to listen to doo-wop groups who constantly cross his path, watching a recording session. McIntire's Freed is totally believable. You take heed when he tells the policemen who are closing down a show at the Brooklyn Paramount: "You can stop me, but you'll never stop rock 'n' roll." McIntire's other fine performances include his mountain man who moves his family on to a Paiute burial ground in *Sacred Ground,* and his smart, scheming, fearsome prisoner in *Fast-Walking,* starring James Woods. McIntire's sexy scene with visiting girlfriend Kay Lenz is quite memorable. McIntire died of heart failure at 44.

• **Cult Favorites:** *A Boy and His Dog* (1975, L. Q. Jones), *American Hot Wax* (1978, Floyd Mutrux).

• **Other Key Films:** *The Sterile Cuckoo* (1969, Alan J. Pakula), *aloha, bobby and rose* (1975, Mutrux), *The Gumball Rally* (1976, Chuck Bail), *Fast-Walking* (1982, James B. Harris), *Sacred Ground* (1983, Charles B. Pierce).

○

KYLE MACLACHLAN (1959–) This talented young actor made an impressive debut as the star of the big-budget space epic *Dune,* playing Paul Atreides. The film was awful, but he was believable as the "messiah" of the desert guerillas, perhaps because he is a calm actor and everything else about that film was hurried and chaotic. The part was as poorly conceived and inconsistent as in Frank Herbert's novel, but MacLachlan makes you root for him even though you have no idea what he's up to. *Dune* director David Lynch then cast him as the lead in his controversial black comedy *Blue Velvet,* as a college student who returns to his hometown only to discover it is overrun by vicious criminals. He becomes attracted to both a virginal high school girl (Laura Dern) and masochistic nightclub singer (Isabella Rossellini). He represents the normal American boy who, undergoing a rite of passage through his contact with Rossellini and the criminals, discovers he is not only curious about criminality and perversity, but capable of taking part in it. He gave another funny, understated performance as an alien posing as an FBI agent in order to track down an extraterrestrial murderer in *The Hidden,* an inventive science-fiction comedy-thriller that has a big cult following in France and elsewhere in Europe. Since he is classically handsome straight on but has a caricature-like profile that seems to belong to someone else, it makes sense that he should keep playing strange, otherworldly characters. He expanded his cult by playing the quirky FBI agent in Lynch's bizarre TV series "Twin Peaks." Then, with long blond hair, wire rims, and an overly serious attitude about nothing, he gave a right-on performance as a quite familiar sixties type—though specifically he was band member Ray Manzarek—in Oliver Stone's *The Doors.*

• **Cult Favorites:** *Dune* (1984, David Lynch), *Blue Velvet* (1986, Lynch), *The Hidden* (1987, Jack Sholder), *The Doors* (1991, Oliver Stone).

○

BUTTERFLY MCQUEEN (1911–) Born Thelma McQueen in Tampa, she got her nickname after dancing in the "Butterfly Ballet" in a production of *A Midsummer Night's Dream* put on by the Negro Youth Group in New York. After appearing in several George Abbott productions on Broadway, she went to Hollywood and played the part for which she'll always be fondly remembered: Prissy, the flighty, funny, frightened maid, in *Gone With the Wind.* Audiences responded to this diminutive newcomer with a high-pitched, squeaky voice and daffy manner, who seemed on a different wavelength than anyone else in the film. It is still jarring when Vivien Leigh's Scarlett slaps hysterical Prissy to get her to respond to a panic situation, Melanie's impending delivery ("I don't know nothin' 'bout birthin' babies," Prissy protests). Here is an adult slapping a child (which is how Prissy comes across); a tough woman hitting a weak, defenseless woman; and, of course, a person of one color hitting a person of another color in an era when such things didn't happen on the screen. McQueen never established herself in Hollywood but occasionally she turned up as other kooky, sobbing maids. Peter Weir brought her back in a small role in *The Mosquito Coast* and she still had that spark . . . and that voice.

• **Cult Favorites:** *The Women* (1939, George Cukor), *Cabin in the Sky* (1943, Vincente Minnelli), *Mildred Pierce* (1945, Michael Curtiz), *Duel in the Sun* (1946, King Vidor).

• **Other Key Films:** *Gone With the Wind* (1939, Victor Fleming), *Affectionately Yours* (1941, Lloyd Bacon), *I Dood It* (1943, Minnelli), *Flame of the Barbary Coast* (1945, Joseph Kane), *The Mosquito Coast* (1986, Peter Weir).

○

GEORGE MACREADY (1909–73) Former Broadway actor, with gray (later white) hair and a prominent scar on the right side of his face, specialized in villains who were snobbishly cultured, influential, and cruel—often they turned cowardly when cornered. They wore uniforms, business suits, tuxedos. He's probably best remembered as the villain in *Gilda,* plotting a sorry end for his wife, Rita Hayworth, and her new lover, Glenn Ford. He is certainly good in that film, but I don't think he had the presence necessary for such a key role, and it was hard to believe that Ford wouldn't eventually get the better of him (Orson Welles would have been the ideal villain). I think Macready worked best in major films when he had significant, but supporting, roles—as in *The Big Clock,* in which he was the malicious adviser to chief villain Charles Laughton, relentlessly attempting to frame Ray Milland after Laughton commits murder. He was also well cast in *Paths of Glory,* as the gutless, blundering general who, to cover his rear after getting many of his men killed in a suicidal charge, insists on a trial to execute 3 soldiers after mass disobedience to his order. He was perfect in minor films, in which his villains seemed, quite properly, too strong for the heroes and heroines. He was particularly despicable in *My Name Is Julia Ross,* isolating a defenseless young woman (Nina Foch) in an out-of-the-way mansion, trying to brainwash her into believing she is someone else (who has in fact already been murdered), and then plotting her "accidental" death (expecting authorities to believe her to be the first woman). In *Johnny Allegro,* his sportsman stalks victims with a bow and arrow.

• **Cult Favorites:** *My Name Is Julia Ross* (1945, Joseph H. Lewis), *Gilda* (1946, Charles Vidor), *Vera Cruz* (1954, Robert Aldrich), *Paths of Glory* (1957, Stanley Kubrick).

• **Sleeper:** *A Kiss Before Dying* (1956, Gerd Oswald).

• **Other Key Films:** *The Big Clock* (1948, John Farrow), *Black Arrow* (1948, Gordon Douglas), *The Seventh Cross* (1949, Fred Zinnemann), *Alias Nick Beale* (1949, Farrow), *Johnny Allegro* (1949, Ted Tetzlaff), *A Lady Without a Passport* (1950, Lewis),

Detective Story (1951, William Wyler), *Julius Caesar* (1953, Joseph L. Mankiewicz), *The Stranger Wore a Gun* (1953, André de Toth), *Two Weeks in Another Town* (1962, Vincente Minnelli), *Dead Ringer* (1964, Paul Henreid), *Seven Days in May* (1964, John Frankenheimer).

○

ANNA MAGNANI (1909–73) Highly emotional Italian actress, with raven hair, sad, intense eyes, and a few too many pounds. She was successful on the Italian stage but only a minor film star until she starred as a pregnant, ill-fated mother in Roberto Rossellini's *Open City,* the debut of Italian neorealism (a film about the Occupation, it was secretly started before the Nazis had vacated Rome). She had previously been considered a comedian, but her warm, passionate, heart-felt performance—and her tragic, unforgettable death scene—made viewers recognize her versatility. For the next few years, she would play in comedies and tragedies depicting postwar problems in Italy, giving believable performances as earthy, exuberant, temperamental women with hard lives, hungry children, and lazy husbands who need her motivation (i.e., temper tantrums). Among her most successful roles was the forceful leader of disgruntled tenant dwellers in *Angelina*—when angry, Magnani's women weren't the type anyone wanted to argue with. She was wonderful in *L'Amore* as a raped peasant who believes she is carrying the messiah; in the comedy *Bellissima,* as a mother determined to make her young daughter a star; and in Jean Renoir's *The Golden Coach,* as a beloved actress. Renoir (who described her as "an animal") called her the world's greatest actress, and other directors and critics agreed. Tennessee Williams wrote

Anna Magnani and Marlon Brando in The Fugitive Kind.

plays with Magnani in mind, and she played in the American film versions of *The Rose Tattoo* (for which she won a Best Actress Oscar) and *Orpheus Descending* (which was titled *The Fugitive Kind*). She also appeared in the American-made *Wild Is the Wind,* and more than held her own with powerhouse actors Burt Lancaster, Marlon Brando, and Anthony Quinn. American viewers hadn't seen such emotional, sensual acting since the days of Nazimova. American filmmakers, unfortunately, didn't know what to do with her, and she returned to Italy and minor films.

• **Key Films:** *Open City/Roma Città aperta* (1945, Roberto Rossellini), *L'Amore* (1948, Rossellini), *Bellissima* (1951, Luchino Visconti), *The Golden Coach* (1953, Jean Renoir), *The Rose Tattoo* (1955, Daniel Mann), *The Fugitive Kind* (1960, Sidney Lumet).

• **Also of Interest:** *Theresa Venerdi* (1941, Vittorio De Sica), *Angelina* (1946, Luigi Zampa), *Wild Is the Wind* (1957, George Cukor), *The Passionate Thief* (1961, Mario Monicelli), *Mamma Roma* (1962, Pier Paolo Pasolini), *The Secret of Santa Vittoria* (1969, Stanley Kramer).

○

MARJORIE MAIN (1890–1975) Scene-stealing character actress who usually played poor, imposing, cranky, rambunctious, straight-from-the-lip middle-aged women, many with a hick accent. Most of her films focus thematically on the characters' status and wealth (or lack of it). In the thirties, she was typecast as slum mothers in dramas; she became known for her comedic talents in a series of easy-to-take but now dated films she made with Walter Beery in the forties; and then played her most famous comical character, Ma Kettle, the poor but proud, resilient, overwhelming, and mighty quirky backwoods mother of a dozen or so wild children, and wife to Percy Kilbride's Pa who seemed to produce little other than offspring. It was an extremely popular series that kept Universal afloat. She was good at playing battle axes, such as *The Wistful Widow of Wagon Gap*, but she could also be quite spirited and warmhearted, which is why I think she would have been the ideal person to play Minnie Pearl.

• **Cult Favorites:** *Stella Dallas* (1937, King Vidor), *The Women* (1939, George Cukor), *Meet Me in St. Louis* (1944, Vincente Minnelli).

• **Sleepers:** *Murder, He Says* (1945, George Marshall), *The Wistful Widow of Wagon Gap* (1947, Charles Barton), *The Long, Long Trailer* (1954, Minnelli).

• **Other Key Films:** *Dead End* (1937, William Wyler), *Dark Command* (1940, Raoul Walsh), *Wyoming* (1940, Richard Thorpe), *A Woman's Face* (1941, Cukor), *Heaven Can Wait* (1943, Ernst Lubitsch), *Gentle Annie* (1944, Andrew Marton), *The Harvey Girls* (1946, George Sidney), *The Egg and I* (1947, George Erskine), *Ma and Pa Kettle* (1949, Charles Lamont), 8 other

"Kettles" films (1950–57), *Summer Stock* (1950, Charles Walters).

○

LORNA MAITLAND Extremely well-endowed blonde, a former dancer, starred in Russ Meyer's first serious films with actual plots, *Lorna* and *Mud Honey*, black-and-white fake morality plays set in Erskine Caldwell backwoods country. In the latter film, she is Clarabelle, a prostitute who turns tricks for her mother. She gave a better performance as the more interesting *Lorna*, a sexually frustrated young wife who experiences much of what Hedy Lamarr did years earlier in *Ecstasy*. She even imitates Lamarr with a nude walk in the woods and swim. Only she isn't just spotted by a stranger while swimming—she is raped. Meyer has her so turned on by her rapist that she invites him back to her shack for further lovemaking. Like Hedy Lamarr, whose heroine also was subject to a male director's disapproval, Maitland is punished for her infidelity.

• **Cult Favorites:** *Lorna* (1964, Russ Meyer), *Mud Honey/Rope of Flesh* (1965, Meyer).

○

DAVID MANNERS (1901–) Capable, replaceable Canadian-born leading man and second lead from 1930 to 1936. Yes, his characters had good manners and were particularly well-groomed and civil, but they were consistently ineffectual, dwarfed both by stronger older men, played by such figures as Boris Karloff, Bela Lugosi, John Barrymore, and Claude Rains, and by dynamic women, played by Katharine Hepburn, Barbara Stanwyck, and others. Actresses were typically billed above him. His men stood by patiently while attention was focused on the women, who were making important decisions (e.g., should they dump Manners?). Often, his characters were threatened by scary villains. Manners was in a number of fine films, but when he's remembered it's for his appearances in three horror classics: *Dracula,* as Jonathan Harker; *The Mummy,* as the boyfriend of the imperiled Zita Johann; and *The Black Cat,* in which he is repeatedly knocked unconscious while trying to rescue his screaming bride (Jacqueline Wells) from Karloff.

• **Cult Favorites:** *The Mummy* (1932, Karl Freund), *The Black Cat* (1934, Edgar G. Ulmer).

• **Sleepers:** *Journey's End* (1930, James Whale), *The Death Kiss* (1933, Edward L. Marin).

• **Other Key Films:** *Dracula* (1931, Tod Browning), *The Miracle Woman* (1931, Frank Capra), *A Bill of Divorcement* (1932, George Cukor), *The Devil's in Love* (1933, William Dieterle), *The Mystery of Edwin Drood* (1935, Stuart Walker), *A Woman Rebels* (1936, Mark Sandrich).

• **Also of Interest:** *Kismet* (1930, John Francis Dillon), *The Ruling Voice* (1931, Rowland V. Lee), *Crooner* (1932, Lloyd Bacon), *Roman Scandals* (1933, Frank Tuttle), *Jalna* (1935, John Cromwell).

○

JAYNE MANSFIELD (1933–67) The former Vera Jane Palmer had only modest talent, but having an extremely high I.Q. (which one would never guess from watching her interviews), she immodestly parlayed a 40-18½-36 figure into a moderately successful Hollywood career and worldwide fame. Noting her Broadway success as an actress wearing a towel in *Will Success*

Spoil Rock Hunter?, 20th Century-Fox signed her to a seven-year contract. Though 20th promoted her as another Marilyn Monroe (who was threatening not to return to the studio), she smartly copied Mae West instead, both in life (designing her home with West in mind) and on film. But she didn't understand that West's appeal had not so much to do with her body as with her bawdy, unembarrassed attitude toward sex in general. Mansfield was the rare actress whose vulnerability worked against her, weakening characters who should have been strong, defiant, and confident. She played women who had been around—singers, exotic dancers, prostitutes, nymphos, gangster's molls, even gangsters—but they were "innocent" in that they'd never found anyone who could satisfy them (while West had many good lovers). Because they were available to both handsome and goofy-looking men, male viewers found them accessible when they'd have preferred hard-to-get. In her comedies, when she joked about her figure, she joined men in the audience who teased her for having an "abnormal" body, rather than boasting about having "the best body around" as West would have done. She was too willing to mock herself—allowing, for instance, director Frank Tashlin to have her hold milk bottles in front of her bosom in *The Girl Can't Help It,* and to put her in supertight dresses and have her walk across the screen as if she were a caricature of the "fantasy blond bosom-beauty of the fifties," or, worse, one of the former animation director's sexy female *animals* in the Bugs Bunny and Daffy Duck cartoons. Because of putting up with this she was considered a good sport, but since she didn't seem concerned about establishing herself as an *actress,* no one really took her

Jayne Mansfield and milk bottles in The Girl Can't Help It.

more seriously than she did herself on screen. She was touching in *The Wayward Bus* and funny in both her best film, *The Girl Can't Help It,* and Tashlin's film of *Will Success Spoil Rock Hunter?*—though that film further trapped her with an unflattering image and forever typecast her as a dizzy blonde. But Mansfield never really had a chance to challenge herself in films. Early on she seemed desperate for attention; later when she did sleazy films like *Promises! Promises!* and a seamy nightclub act, she seemed bent on salvaging her career. In a freak accident, she was decapitated when the car she was riding in ran into and under a truck (obscured by mist from mosquito spray!) on her way to a TV appearance in New Orleans.

• **Cult Favorites:** *The Girl Can't Help It* (1956, Frank Tashlin), *Will Success Spoil Rock Hunter?* (1957, Tashlin), *Las Vegas Hillbillys* (1966, Arthur C. Pierce).

• **Sleepers:** *The Burglar* (1956, Paul Wendkos), *The Wayward Bus* (1957, Victor Vicas).

• **Other Key Films:** *Illegal* (1955, Lewis Allen), *Hell on Frisco Bay* (1955, Frank Tuttle), *The Female Jungle* (1956, Bruno VeSota), *Kiss Them for Me* (1957, Stanley Donen), *The Sheriff of Fractured Jaw* (1959, Raoul Walsh), *Too Hot to Handle* (1959, Terence Young), *It Takes a Thief* (1960, John Gilling), *The George Raft Story* (1961, Andrew Marton), *It Happened in Athens* (1962, Andrew Marton), *The Fat Spy* (1965, Joseph Cates), *Single Room*

Furnished (1968, Matteo Ottaviano/Matt Cimber).

○

ANGELA MAO/ANGELA MAO YING (1951–) This beautiful Chinese actress was dubbed "Lady Kung Fu" when she starred in a number of martial-arts costume pictures for Golden Harvest in the early seventies. She had been doing fight routines since the age of 5 in the Chinese opera. She was small and looked fragile, but she was thrilling in combat, with lightning-quick hand thrusts, hand and sword slashes, and flying feet, displaying agility and power. As in *Lady Whirlwind,* she would walk into a bar full of mean, lustful men, and walk out later stepping over the bodies of the men who had underestimated her. American viewers know her from *Enter the Dragon,* in which she played Bruce Lee's sister in a flashback. She put on an exciting martial-arts display—without a trace of Lee's narcissism—as her character battled a ruthless gang single-handedly, but, alas, knowing she had no chance, committed suicide. Mao would die in other films as well, but her warriors, revolutionaries, and women on missions of revenge (for a father, a sister, a martial-arts school) would always go down fighting. She was sexy, charismatic, and a dynamic fighter—it's too bad her films weren't shown widely in America.

• **Cult Favorite:** *Enter the Dragon* (1973, Robert Clouse).

• **Other Key Films:** *Angry River* (1970, Huang Feng), *The Invincible Eight* (1970, Lo Wei), *Lady Whirlwind/Deep Thrust* (1970, Wei), *Hap Ki Do* (1971, Feng), *Stoner—The Shame of Ultimate Bliss* (1971, Feng), *Back Alley Princess* (1972), *The Fate of Lee Khan* (1973, King Hu), *Opium*

Trail (1973), *When Taekwondo Strikes* (1973, Feng).

○

JEAN MARAIS (1913–) Tall, curly-haired, blond French romantic idol was viewed as a Greek god come to life. Beginning in the thirties, Jean Cocteau wrote and directed films (and plays) that starred his housemate Marais: *Beauty and the Beast, L'Aigle à Deux Têtes, Les Parents Terribles, Orpheus.* He became France's most popular young actor as the result of *Beauty and the Beast.* In that film, he played three parts, but I don't think he distinguished himself in any of them: the obnoxious, foolish Avenant; the glorious-looking but wimpish, self-pitying, raspy-sounding Beast; and, worst of all, the effeminate, conceited Prince, who looks like he plays the harp, stuffs snuff in his nostrils, and spends much time at the hairdresser's. Marais was better coping with his mother's incestuous love in *Les Parents Terribles* and as the unhappy poet in *Orpheus* who descends to the underworld and learns about death, life, love, his art, and himself. Not a gifted actor, his eyes expressed torment and yearning, but his face expressed nothing. Outside Cocteau's films, the young Marais appeared in other "poetic" and fantasy films, often as a young woman's Prince Charming. In later years, he'd appear in many costume dramas and swashbucklers. He put on weight but his fans pretended not to notice.

• **Cult Favorites:** *Beauty and the Beast* (1946, Jean Cocteau), *Les Parents Terribles* (1948, Cocteau), *Orpheus* (1950, Cocteau), *The Testament of Orpheus* (1960, Cocteau).

• **Other Key Films:** *L'Éternel Retour* (1943, Jean Delannoy), *L'Aigle à Deux Têtes*

Jean Marais with Josette Day in Beauty and the Beast.

(1947, Cocteau), *Le Secret de Mayerling* (1949, Delannoy), *Le Château de Verre* (1950, René Clément), *White Nights* (1957, Luchino Visconti).

○

RICHARD "CHEECH" MARIN (1946–) Popular, talented Mexican-American comedian (and comic rock singer), with a mustache and friendly smile, who has gone solo after splitting with the much taller, bearded Tommy Chong, his partner in Cheech and Chong. When they were on, Cheech and Chong managed to make drug, sex, and scatalogical humor funny rather than tasteless. *Up in Smoke,* their debut film, is about the stoned twosome's efforts to find some quality grass. It's often hilarious, but their later efforts are lazy. Cheech's screen character is a hapless but cheery Chicano who has no money, no meanness whatsoever, and no understanding of the real world (he lives in a foggy world of his own); he is stupid, stoned, dazed (though not brain-dead like Chong). With a consistently funny delivery, he grumbles to himself whenever he is alone; tries dumb come-on lines with every pretty woman he sees; can't say a sentence without including the word "man." He always gets in trouble with policemen, brutish convicts, and stoned or crazy (e.g., Pee-Wee Herman in *Nice Dreams*) people, yet somehow survives while everyone else's life has fallen into disrepair. My favorite Cheech scene has him desperately searching for a bathroom in Tijuana after eating a bad burrito, and finally finding one which he swears was last used by someone who ate the same burritos. He can be very funny. He's often compared to Cantinflas's *Peladito* (Little Tramp) and Tin-Tan.

• **Cult Favorites:** *Up in Smoke* (1978, Lou Adler), *After Hours* (1985, Martin Scorsese).

• **Sleeper:** *Echo Park* (1986, Robert Dornheim).

• **Other Key Films:** *Cheech and Chong's Next Movie* (1980, Thomas Chong), *Nice Dreams* (1981, Chong), *Born in East L.A.* (1987, Richard "Cheech" Marin), *Rude Awakening* (1989, Aaron Russo and David Greenwalt).

• **Also of Interest:** *Things Are Tough All Over* (1982, Tom Avildsen), *Still Smokin'* (1983, Chong), *Yellowbeard* (1983, Mel Damski), *The Corsican Brothers* (1984, Chong).

○

WILLIAM MARSHALL (1924–) Tall, physically imposing, strong-voiced, ex-Shakespearean black actor. He played forceful characters—including a genie in *Sabu and the Magic Ring,* Haitian King Dick in *Lydia Bailey,* Attorney General Edward D. Brooke in *The Boston Strangler*—before he was smartly cast as the lead in the entertaining horror film *Blacula* and its inferior sequel, *Scream, Blacula, Scream!* His vampire was an interesting character, the black equivalent of Christopher Lee's Dracula—refined, frightening (particularly the way he glided through the air during attacks), evil, and sexual. In fact, he was one of the few black villains of the early seventies. Marshall got the chance to play a good guy, an animated exorcist, in *Abby.* He was an intelligent, impressive performer, but his movie career died.

• **Cult Favorite:** *Blacula* (1972, William Crain).

• **Other Key Films:** *Lydia Bailey* (1952, Jean Negulesco), *Demetrius and the Gladiators* (1954, Delmer Daves), *Something of Value* (1957, Richard Brooks), *The Boston Strangler* (1968, Richard Fleischer), *Scream, Blacula, Scream!* (1973, Bob Kelljan), *Abby* (1974, William Girdler), *Twilight's Last Gleaming* (1977, Robert Aldrich).

○

STROTHER MARTIN (1919–80) It's hard to believe that he had been National Diving Champion runner-up, and listened to Beethoven, because he played—always with wit—untidy, unwholesome characters who were strangers to soap and water and were anything but cultured. His first movie role was a nontalking bit in *The Asphalt Jungle* as a suspect in a police lineup who reaches for his marked neck when it's mentioned he tried to hang himself. After that he appeared in a couple of war films, action-packed melodramas, period pieces, and films of almost every genre—he was the slimy Southern prison farm warden in *Cool Hand Luke,* and had his only leads in the horror films *The Brotherhood of Satan* and *Sssssssss*—but he was best known as a bad guy in dusty westerns of the sixties and seventies. His villains are pathetic little men who are slovenly, sniveling, and mean; stupid, insecure, and cowardly, and act tough only when other bad guys are around to back them up. He was most memorable as one of Lee Marvin's henchmen (along with Lee Van Cleef) in *The Man Who Shot Liberty Valance,* and as one of the vulturous scavengers who crawl around with L. Q. Jones in both Sam Peckinpah's *The Wild Bunch* and *The Ballad of Cable Hogue.* In the latter film, his character (his best role) reforms, and works for hero Jason Robards (who also reformed). In Peckinpah, you can't predict who will change for the better if given the opportunity.

• **Cult Favorites:** *Kiss Me Deadly* (1955, Robert Aldrich), *Attack!* (1956, Aldrich), *The Man Who Shot Liberty Valance* (1962, John Ford), *Cool Hand Luke* (1967, Stuart Rosenberg), *The Wild Bunch* (1969, Sam Peckinpah), *The Ballad of Cable Hogue* (1969, Peckinpah), *Slap Shot* (1977, George Roy Hill), *Up in Smoke* (1978, Lou Adler).

• **Sleepers:** *The Deadly Companions* (1961, Peckinpah), *Red Sky at Morning* (1970, James Goldstone), *Pocket Money* (1972, Rosenberg), *The Villain* (1979, Hal Needham).

• **Also of Interest:** *Sanctuary* (1961, Tony Richardson), *McClintock!* (1963, Andrew V. McLaglen), *The Sons of Katie Elder* (1965, Henry Hathaway), *Harper* (1966, Jack Smight), *The Flim Flam Man* (1967, Irvin Kershner), *True Grit* (1969, Hathaway), *Butch Cassidy and the Sundance Kid* (1969, George Roy Hill), *Fool's Parade* (1971, McLaglen), *The Brotherhood of Satan* (1971, Bernard McEveety), *Sssssss* (1973, Bernard L. Kowalski), *Hard Times* (1975, Walter Hill).

○

LEE MARVIN (1924–1987) The tall, deep-voiced, green-eyed New York actor was lean and mean in supporting roles in the early fifties. He played psychotic cowboys and gangsters—throwing hot coffee in girlfriend Gloria Grahame's face (the disfigured woman will later do him in kind)—and such unwashed, lecherous degenerates as Brando's biker foe in *The Wild One* and Slob in *Shack Out on 101*. Other of his villains are also appropriately vicious and

Lee Marvin in The Killers *with Angie Dickinson.*

disgusting, when opposing Rock Hudson in *Gun Fury,* Spencer Tracy in *Bad Day at Black Rock,* and Randolph Scott in *Seven Men from Now.* Later, his bad guys, like Liberty Valance in *The Man Who Shot Liberty Valance,* would become increasingly intelligent and calculating. But Valance and Marvin's assassin in *The Killers* still kill without remorse. Marvin was the good guy in the popular TV series "M Squad" and the host on "The Lawbreakers," and after his Academy Award–winning portrayal of a funny drunk (as well as a vicious gunslinger) in the otherwise unfunny *Cat Ballou,* he became a movie hero. By this time his hair was turning white and he was no longer skinny but still hard as a rock, with a face that looked as if it had been chiseled out of granite. He was ideal to play tough army officers, as in *The Dirty Dozen*. His heroes were just as violent as his villains—in fact, his "hero" in *Point Blank* (his best starring film) is a brutal bad guy cheered on by viewers simply because he spends the rest of the film killing even worse men than himself. At one point, Angie Dickinson hits him repeatedly, trying to get him to show some emotional response. But Marvin's heroes aren't at all emotional; they don't react to physical pain or the deaths of those they should grieve over. They can do kind acts—for instance, he rescues teenage prostitute Sissy Spacek in *Prime Cut*—but the only sign of tenderness is when his soldier spends time with a dying boy rescued too late from a concentration camp in *The Big Red One*. Even then there are no kind words, no tears. Marvin's characters never render or expect any favors or kindness—they just try to survive. A major figure of the American cinema of violence.

• **Cult Favorites:** *The Big Heat* (1953, Fritz Lang), *The Wild One* (1953, Laslo Benedek), *The Caine Mutiny* (1954, Edward Dmytryk), *Bad Day at Black Rock* (1954, John Sturges), *Shack Out on 101* (1955, Edward Dein), *Seven Men from Now* (1956, Budd Boetticher), *Attack!* (1956, Robert Aldrich), *The Man Who Shot Liberty Valance* (1962, John Ford), *Donovan's Reef* (1963, Ford), *The Killers* (1964, Don Siegel), *The Dirty Dozen* (1967, Aldrich), *Point Blank* (1967, John Boorman), *Emperor of the North* (1973, Aldrich), *The Big Red One* (1979, Samuel Fuller).

• **Other Key Films:** *Gun Fury* (1953, Raoul Walsh), *Gorilla at Large* (1954, Harmon Jones), *A Life in the Balance* (1955, Harry Horner), *Violent Saturday* (1955, Richard Fleischer), *Raintree County* (1957, Dmytryk), *The Commancheros* (1961, Michael Curtiz), *Cat Ballou* (1965, Elliot Silverstein), *Ship of Fools* (1965, Stanley Kramer), *The Professionals* (1965, Richard Brooks), *Hell in the Pacific* (1968, John Boorman), *Monte Walsh* (1970, William Fraker), *Prime Cut* (1972, Michael Ritchie), *The Iceman Cometh* (1973, John Frankenheimer).

○

THE MARX BROTHERS Groucho (1890–1990), Chico (1886–1961), Harpo (1888–1964), and even Zeppo (1901–79) had a surge of popularity in the sixties, particularly on college campuses, when young moviegoers were looking for characters who show no respect for authority figures. Thus their one commercial and critical flop, *Duck Soup,* the only time the anarchists run amuck in a political milieu, was elevated to a masterpiece, the equal of *A Night at the Opera.* One of Groucho's most famous remarks is that he wouldn't belong to a club that would have him as a member. The Marx Brothers' hilarious films well illustrate what he meant. Usually by seducing widow Margaret Dumont, Groucho (with a painted-on mustache, cigar, and silly songs and insults at his disposal) is introduced into high society, and brings his loony brothers with him. When the undignified, destructive, propriety-out-the-window group invades the opera, the political arena, a college, a fancy ship, a high-class party, or a hotel and proceeds to insult everyone, chase women (Harpo's specialty), and wreck the "institution," it becomes clear why Groucho (or anyone else) wouldn't want to belong to anything that would invite him or his brothers to join. Of course, the Marx Brothers' odd characters are at odds with everyone else in the films (except for boorish, naive

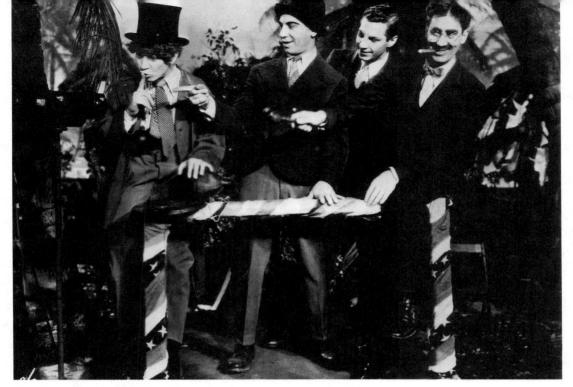

The Marx Brothers in The Cocoanuts.

Dumont, who is flattered by Groucho's attention). But they have an interesting camaraderie. Groucho appreciates Chico and Harpo because they are the only people he can't hustle. He feels kinship with Chico because both are con men and money-grabbers, tell the truth (especially if it means they'll be insulting someone), detest snobbery (while practicing their own reverse snobbery against snobs), and love driving people (including each other) to distraction with intricate, often nonsensical wordplay. Groucho tolerates Harpo only so he can have Chico's company—if he had anything of value, however, he'd worry with kleptomaniac Harpo around. The ever-silent Harpo, grinning under his curly red wig, is a missing link who sleeps with animals, attacks women (beeping the horn he carries), and eats, burns, steals and stores (in his coat) everything in reach. He should be on a leash. Marx Brothers screenwriter Irving Brecher wrote: "Chico's role was always to protect and big-brother the elfin, deliciously manic mute Harpo. And he, grateful for Chico's devotion, did something no other character did—he actually believed Chico was a real Italian."

• **Cult Favorites:** *Duck Soup* (1933, Leo McCarey), *A Night at the Opera* (1935, Sam Wood).

• **Other Key Films:** *The Cocoanuts* (1929, Joseph Santley), *Animal Crackers* (1930, Victor Heerman), *Monkey Business* (1931, Norman Z. McLeod), *Horse Feathers* (1932, McLeod), *A Day at the Races* (1937, Wood).

• **Also of Interest:** *Room Service* (1938, William A. Seiter), *At the Circus* (1939,

Giulietta Masina with Anthony Quinn in La Strada.

Edward Buzzell), *Go West* (1940, Buzzell), *The Big Store* (1941, Charles Reisner), *A Night in Casablanca* (1946, Archie Mayo), *Love Happy* (1949, David Miller).

○

GIULIETTA MASINA (1921–) Independently and in films written for her and directed by her husband, Federico Fellini, this tiny, waif-like Italian actress specialized in tragi-comic portrayals. She has large eyes, a clownish face, and the sweet, sheepish smile of a child who doesn't know if she'll be slapped or praised for a silly act at the dinner table. Because of these clownlike expressions and movements, and the way she conveys sadness through humor, she was often called "Chaplinesque." At her worse, she did too much mugging. She most often played women who are fragile

and without power. She was endearing in two Fellini films, as the lovable but unloved companion-assistant to brutal strongman Anthony Quinn in *La Strada,* and as a street prostitute who wrongly thinks she has found love and happiness in *The Nights of Cabiria.* Her characters deserve love and happiness and remain optimistic, laughing through the tears, but we realize they have nothing to look forward to. Masina also shined in her husband's surrealistic *Juliet of the Spirits,* as a woman who is paranoid about her husband's fidelity, and his more recent, satirical *Ginger and Fred,* in which she and Marcello Mastroianni are reunited on TV years after they were dancers who imitated Rogers and Astaire.

• **Cult Favorites:** *La Strada* (1955, Federico Fellini), *Nights of Cabiria* (1957, Fellini), *Juliet of the Spirits* (1965, Fellini).

• **Other Key Films:** *Without Pity* (1948,

Starring
CONNIE MASON
PLAYBOY'S FAVORITE PLAYMATE
THOMAS WOOD
JEFFREY ALLEN

Box Office Spectaculars, Inc. presents a Friedman-Lewis Production
"TWO THOUSAND MANIACS!"
A TOWN OF MADMEN CRAZED WITH BLOOD LUST!
Produced by DAVID F. FRIEDMAN / Directed by HERSCHELL G. LEWIS

GRUESOME SLAUGHTER
STAINED IN BRUTAL BLOOD COLOR!
with SHELBY LIVINGSTON /
BEN MOORE / YVONNE GILBERT /
JEROME EDEN / LINDA COCHRAN

Connie Mason and Thomas Wood.

Alberto Lattuada), *Variety Lights* (1951, Fellini and Lattuada), *The White Sheik* (1952, Fellini), *Il Bidone* (1955, Fellini), *Ginger and Fred* (1986, Fellini).

• **Also of Interest:** *Europa '51* (1951, Roberto Rossellini), *Landru* (1962, Claude Chabrol).

○

CONNIE MASON Former *Playboy* Playmate gave wretched performances—and kept her clothes on!—in Herschell Gordon Lewis's seminal slice-and-dice sickie *Blood Feast,* as Suzette, and in the equally gruesome but better-made *Two Thousand Maniacs!* Apparently, she got the parts because of her relationship with producer David Friedman. Even Lewis, whose films are filled with bad performances, was aghast: "I've often felt if one took the key out of Connie's back, she'd simply stand in place." Lewis complained that she was never on the set on time, and never knew a line—"Not ever." You can see her look-ing over other actors' shoulders to read cue cards in *Blood Feast,* but that wasn't good enough because Lewis was forced to cut two-thirds of her lines in *Two Thousand Maniacs!* in order to finish the picture on time. Although imperiled by body-part-remover Fuad Ramses (Mal Arnold) in the first film and a whole town of vengeful southern ghosts in the second film, she escaped being chopped up, thanks to two-film hero Tom Wood. Asked by admirer John Waters if audiences thought of her as "the girl you'd love to rip apart," Lewis snapped, "I'm sure the crew would have loved to have ripped her apart."

• **Cult Favorites:** *Blood Feast* (1963, Her-schell Gordon Lewis), *Two Thousand Maniacs!* (1964, Lewis).

○

EDITH MASSEY Late star of John Waters's films, whom he discovered running a Bal-timore bar; she may have been, as Waters contended, the "most lovable" figure in his acting stable. She was certainly the most grotesque: Ugly and aged, she had an obnoxious voice, only about five teeth, and a fat, shapeless body that Waters stuffed into tight, hideous outfits: a bra and girdle in *Pink Flamingos,* a peekaboo leather S & M costume in *Female Trouble,* and so on. Her characters are unbelievably repul-sive: in *Pink Flamingos,* she is a retarded grandmother ("the Egg Lady") who sits in a playpen and constantly fondles, talks about, and eats eggs, and waits for the Egg Man to make his next delivery; in *Female Trouble,* she is Aunt Ida, who tries to convince her straight nephew to turn gay and get a beautician for a boyfriend—and she throws acid in Divine's face; in *Desperate Living,* she is the disagreeable

despot Queen Carlotta, who orders every-one in Mortville to walk and dress back-wards, and injects her daughter Coo-Coo with rabies—and it's no fun watching her have sex with her young, simpering ser-vants; in *Polyester,* she was Divine's friend, Cuddles, and wore outfits meant for some-one 40 years younger, 100 pounds lighter, and had bad taste. Famous from the Wa-ters films, Massey opened a thrift shop in Fell's Point, Baltimore, which became a tourist attraction; she also toured the country heading a punk rock band.

• **Cult Favorites:** *Multiple Maniacs* (1970, John Waters), *Pink Flamingos* (1972, Wa-ters), *Female Trouble* (1974, Waters), *Desperate Living* (1977, Waters), *Polyester* (1981, Waters).

Edith Massey is an evil queen in Desperate Living.

KERWIN MATHEWS (1926–) If Disney had made live-action versions of its animated fairy tales, Mathews would have been ideal as all those dreamy princes. Instead, this dark-haired actor was a dashing leading man in fantasy, horror, and science-fiction films. He was the best movie Sinbad, romancing shrunken princess Kathryn Grant, challenging evil magician Torin Thatcher, and defeating such marvelous Ray Harryhausen creations as a fire-spitting dragon, a giant Cyclops, and a sword-fighting skeleton. He was equally romantic and spirited as the title characters in *Jack the Giant Killer* and *The Three Worlds of Gulliver*, also directed by Nathan Juran and featuring Harryhausen special effects. Mathews is so identified with fantasy films that it's often forgotten that he was also in several exciting contemporary action films, most notably the caper movie *Five Against the House*. Most often he played second male leads.

• **Cult Favorites:** *Five Against the House* (1955, Phil Karlson), *The Seventh Voyage of Sinbad* (1958, Nathan Juran).

• **Other Key Films:** *The Three Worlds of Gulliver* (1960, Juran), *Jack the Giant Killer* (1962, Juran), *Maniac* (1963, Michael Carreras), *The Boy Who Cried Werewolf* (1973, Juran).

• **Also of Interest:** *The Garment Jungle* (1957, Vincent Sherman), *The Last Blitzkrieg* (1958, Arthur Dreifuss), *Man on a String* (1960, André de Toth), *The Warrior Empress* (1960, Pietro Francisci), *The Devil at 4 O'Clock* (1961, Mervyn Leroy), *The Pirates of Blood River* (1962, John Gilling), *The Waltz King* (1963, Steve Previn), *Shadow of Evil* (1964, André Hunebelle), *Battle Beneath the Earth* (1968, Montgomery Tully), *Octaman* (1971, Harry Essex).

VICTOR MATURE (1915–) Tanned and oily hunk, with muscles from his toes to a face that seemed molded by a sculptor whose works had been exiled to the museum's basement. He is often regarded as a joke because of his physique, campy name, limited acting range, and costumes. In historical epics, he seemed uncomfortable in sandals and what looked like diapers or miniskirts; in forties melodramas, he looked like a silly Robert Mitchum in large suits and hats. He always seemed miscast (Mature as songsmith Paul Dresser?), although I can't imagine any sober screenwriter admitting "I've got just the part for Victor Mature!" Yet, while he struggled trying to woo Betty Grable and Rita Hayworth in otherwise pleasant period romances, he wasn't at all an embarrassment as Samson, Crazy Horse, or even a self-loathing, Shakespeare-loving Doc Holliday in *My Darling Clementine*. He was at his best as tough, urban ethnics in crime dramas, giving his finest, most sympathetic performance in the gritty *Kiss of Death*, as an ex-con who reluctantly helps the police capture lunatic criminal Richard Widmark (who pushes a woman in a wheelchair down a flight of stairs). But Mature, who knew his limitations, never craved such praise, and in *After the Fox* and other later films, he was willing to do self-parody. After all those years, who would have thunk that the hunk was adept at comedy?

• **Cult Favorites:** *One Million B.C.* (1940, Hal Roach, Hal Roach, Jr., and, uncredited, D. W. Griffith), *The Shanghai Gesture* (1941, Josef von Sternberg), *My Darling Clementine* (1946, John Ford), *Kiss of Death* (1947, Henry Hathaway), *After the Fox* (1966, Vittorio De Sica), *Head* (1968, Bob Rafelson).

• **Also Recommended:** *I Wake Up Screaming* (1941, H. Bruce Humberstone), *Cry of the City* (1948, Robert Siodmak), *Samson and Delilah* (1949, Cecil B. De Mille), *Easy Living* (1949, Jacques Tourneur), *Androcles and the Lion* (1952, Charles Erskine), *Violent Saturday* (1955, Richard Fleischer).

• **Other Key Films:** *My Gal Sal* (1942, Irving Cummings), *Footlight Serenade* (1942, Gregory Ratoff), *Wabash Avenue* (1950, Henry Koster), *The Robe* (1953, Koster), *Demetrius and the Gladiators* (1954, Delmer Daves).

• **Also of Interest:** *Song of the Islands* (1942, Walter Lang), *Moss Rose* (1947, Ratoff), *Million Dollar Mermaid* (1952, Mervyn LeRoy), *The Egyptian* (1954, Michael Curtiz), *Chief Crazy Horse* (1955, George Sherman), *Safari* (1956, Terence Young), *The Big Circus* (1959, Joseph M. Newman), *Timbuktu* (1959, Tourneur), *Hannibal* (1960, Edgar G. Ulmer), *Every Little Crook and Nanny* (1972, Cy Howard).

○

CARMEN MAURA (1945–) Dark-haired, sharp-nosed, attractive, extremely talented Spanish actress, the granddaughter of Antonio Maura, a famous Spanish politician and historical figure. She became famous herself performing in Madrid's supper

Victor Mature (left) *and wife, Coleen Gray, are forced to be civil to crazy killer Richard Widmark in* Kiss of Death.

clubs, then acted on the stage and really hit it big as a television hostess. She had her first movie successes with Fernando Colomo, but wouldn't be known internationally until she became the star of Pedro Almodóvar's subversive comedies. Sometimes stoic but more often emotional and volatile, she has been particularly impressive as an unhappy married woman dealing with a zany family in his surreal *What Have I Done to Deserve This?*, a transsexual in the weird but more serious *Law of Desire,* and a TV actress whose lover has abandoned her in the megahit, *Women on the Verge of a Nervous Breakdown,* again interacting with a strange array of characters. Her falling out with Almodóvar after that film was only temporary.

• **Cult Favorites:** *Dark Habits* (1984, Pedro Almodóvar), *What Have I Done to Deserve This?* (1984, Almodóvar), *Matador* (1985, Almodóvar), *Law of Desire* (1987, Almodóvar), *Women on the Verge of a Nervous Breakdown* (1988, Almodóvar).

• **Other Key Films:** *Paper Tigers* (1977, Fernando Colomo), *What's a Girl Like You Doing in a Place Like This?* (1978, Colomo), *Black Hand* (1980, Colomo), *The Stylish Man* (1980, Fernando Méndez Leyte), *Pepi, Luci, Bom and a Bunch of Other Girls* (1980, Almodóvar), *Garbage* (1984, Colomo), *Extramuros* (1985, Miguel Picazo), *Be Wanton and Dread No Shame* (1985, Fernando Trueba), *Ay, Carmela* (1990, Carlos Saura).

○

LOIS MAXWELL (1927–) Attractive Canadian-born brunette who made films in the United States, Italy, and England, where, after being a smart, stylish leading lady in minor melodramas, she received the supporting part for which she'll always be identified: Miss Moneypenny in the James Bond films. Already 35 when she first played M's secretary in *Dr. No,* she would always be the one mature female in Bond's world. However, one senses from her flirtatious exchanges with Bond (she has a crush on him) that both of them are thinking that she was once just as ravishing and exciting as the sexy young women he now romances. (Maybe he remembered her eye-catching outfit in *The Big Punch.*) Miss Moneypenny would welcome Bond "home" and comfort him after his arguments with M, in films with Sean Connery, George Lazenby, and Roger Moore. When Timothy Dalton replaced Roger Moore, she was replaced by a younger actress—a mistake.

• **Cult Favorites:** *Lolita* (1962, Stanley Kubrick), *Dr. No* (1962, Terence Young), *The Haunting* (1963, Robert Wise), *From Russia with Love* (1963, Young), *Goldfinger* (1963, Guy Hamilton), *On Her Majesty's Secret Service* (1969, Peter Hunt), *The Spy Who Loved Me* (1977, Lewis Gilbert).

• **Other Key Films:** *Thunderball* (1965, Young), *You Only Live Twice* (1967, Gilbert), *Diamonds Are Forever* (1971, Hamilton), *Live and Let Die* (1973, Hamilton), *The Man with the Golden Gun* (1974, Hamilton), *Moonraker* (1979, Gilbert), *For Your Eyes Only* (1981, John Glen), *Octopussy* (1983, Glen), *A View to a Kill* (1985, Glen).

• **Also of Interest:** *Corridor of Mirrors* (1948, Young), *The Big Punch* (1948, Sherry Shourds), *The Dark Past* (1948, Rudoph Maté), *Satellite in the Sky* (1956, Paul Dickson), *Time Without Pity* (1956, Joseph Losey), *Kill Me Tomorrow* (1957, Terence Fisher).

○

KEN MAYNARD (1895–1973) The handsome, flamboyant former "All-Around Champion Cowboy" was a successful cowboy star for more than twenty years, peaking from 1929 to 1934, when he rivaled Buck Jones as the B western's most popular star. A key attraction in Wild West shows before and at the tail end of his movie career, his appeal, particularly in the silent era, was due to the amazing riding tricks he did with his famous white palomino, Tarzan, "the wonder horse." Viewers thrilled to see Maynard jumping from a balcony into Tarzan's saddle, or the two of them leaping off a cliff into water far below; he also rode two horses simultaneously or switched mounts in midgallop. Stunts were filmed in close-up so it was evident that Maynard wasn't using a double. Often he would complete his stunt with a smile and casual wave, as if he were still playing to a live audience. With the arrival of sound films, Maynard introduced music to the western. There continued to be action in his films, but now even outlaws burst into song. Maynard played four instruments, including the fiddle and banjo, and also sang, paving the way for Gene Autry (whom he introduced in *Old Santa Fe*) and other singing cowboys. Although he was one of the worst actors in cowboy films, he was a dashing hero (until he put on weight). Viewers liked his amiable, white-hatted cowboy who refrained from drinking, was bashful toward women, and always took time to stroke Tarzan. In reality, Maynard was a womanizer and a mean, life-long alcoholic; when drunk, he was known to beat his horse. Because he became too troublesome for producers and was always dissatisfied with salaries, scripts, and co-stars, his departure from the cinema was

hastened. His last hurrah was an inexpensive but entertaining "Trail Blazers" series with Hoot Gibson in 1943–44. Tarzan the horse died in 1940.

• **Some Key Films:** *Fighting Courage* (1925, Clifford S. Elfelt), *The Demon Rider* (1925, Paul Hurst), *Señor Daredevil* (1926, Albert Rogell), *The Overland Stage* (1927, Rogell), *The Red Raiders* (1927, Rogell), *The Wagon Master* (1929, Harry Joe Brown), *Lucky Larkin* (1930, Brown), *Song of the Caballero* (1930, Brown), *Fighting Through* (1930, William Nigh), *Come On, Tarzan* (1932, Alan James), *The Fiddlin' Buckaroo* (1933, Ken Maynard), *In Old Santa Fe* (1934, David Howard), *Mystery Mountain* (1934 serial, B. Reeves Eason and Otto Brower), *Avenging Waters* (1936, Spencer G. Bennet), *Wild Horse Stampede* (1943, James), *The Law Rides Again* (1943, James), *Westward Bound* (1944, Robert Tansey), *Harmony Trail* (1944, Robert Emmett/Tansey).

○

MIKE MAZURKI (1909–90) This 6′6″, muscular actor–pro wrestler of Urkrainian descent, with an unfriendly, deeply lined face, looked like a trimmer, uglier version of ugly heavyweight boxing champion Primo Carnera. He spoke four languages, played the piano, and was an avid reader of Shakespeare and Proust, but he was cast as lugs, thugs, and all kinds of slow-witted barbarians. If a bad guy had Iron Mike as a henchman, you know he meant business; it was even worse when Mazurki was a loose cannon, and didn't have to answer to anyone for his actions. Mazurki was usually way down in the credits, but he did have pivotal parts in *Murder, My Sweet*, as a brute who hires Philip Marlowe (Dick Powell) to find Claire Trevor; in *Dick*

Mike Mazurki (center) *with George Raft and Pat O'Brien in* Some Like It Hot.

Tracy, as a killer stalking the detective's town; in *Seven Women,* as a cruel and lecherous Chinese bandit who holds several females captive; and in his one starring feature, *Challenge to Be Free,* a kiddie film in which he was an Anthony Quinn–type fur trapper. My favorite Mazurki scene is in the offbeat melodrama *Night and the City,* when his vicious henchman grapples to the death with a character played by the much older, long-retired wrestler, Stanislaus Zbyszko, and discovers his confidence was unfounded. Mazurki wisely avoided horror movies.

• **Cult Favorites:** *The Shanghai Gesture* (1941, Josef von Sternberg), *Murder, My Sweet* (1944, Edward Dmytryk), *The Horn Blows at Midnight* (1945, Raoul Walsh), *Nightmare Alley* (1947, Edmund Goulding), *Davy Crockett, King of the Wild Frontier* (1955, Norman Foster), *Some Like It Hot* (1959, Billy Wilder), *Donovan's Reef* (1963, John Ford), *Cheyenne Autumn* (1964, Ford), *Seven Women* (1966, Ford).

• **Sleepers:** *Night and the City* (1950, Jules Dassin), *The Man With Bogart's Face* (1980, Robert Day).

• **Also of Interest:** *Behind the Rising Sun* (1943, Dmytryk), *It Ain't Hay* (1943, Erle C. Kenton), *The Canterville Ghost* (1944, Dassin), *The Spanish Main* (1945, Frank Borzage), *Dakota* (1945, Joseph Kane), *Dick Tracy* (1945, William Berke), *Unconquered* (1947, Cecil B. De Mille), *Rope of Sand* (1949, William Dieterle), *Samson and Delilah* (1949, De Mille), *Dark City* (1950, William Dieterle), *My Favorite Spy* (1951, Norman Z. McLeod), *Comanche* (1956, George Sherman), *The Buccaneer* (1958, Anthony Quinn), *Five Weeks in a Balloon* (1962, Irwin Allen), *Challenge to Be Free* (1976, Tay Garnett).

○

MARIANGELA MELATO (1941–) Slim, attractive, talented Italian actress who usually stars in films with political themes. She played angry revolutionaries in her early films, but is best known as the high-strung leading lady of Lina Wertmuller's controversial comedy-dramas about how love, sex, and social convention undermine politics. Melato usually played opposite Giancarlo Giannini. She is often quite sensual (as is her politically conscious prostitute in *Love and Anarchy*), but in those scenes depicting the Battle of the Sexes, the struggles for power between Melato and men, she proves to be the screen's most forceful arguer, with every shrill complaint or insult topping the previous one, and no space left for retorts. She talks so fast, she sounds like Sid Caesar speeding through "fake Italian." When she is histrionic, she is hilarious. Her constantly complaining, domineering rich bitch in *Swept Away* is, by intention, one of the most annoying screen characters ever. I prefer hearing her insult Giannini's left-wing deckhand to watching her get her comeuppance once she becomes his willing sex slave after they are stranded on a desert island. Her character change has caused much debate among film critics. Melato was in the American fashion-industry comedy, *So Fine,* and was quite funny opposite Ryan O'Neal, adding a bizarre touch to this film about the marketing of pants with see-through backsides.

• **Cult Favorites:** *Love and Anarchy* (1973, Lina Wertmuller), *The Seduction of Mimi* (1974, Wertmuller), *Swept Away* (1975, Wertmuller).

• **Also of Interest:** *Nada/The Nada Gang* (1975, Claude Chabrol), *The Working Class Goes to Heaven* (1975, Elio Petri), *Guernica* (1976, Fernando Arrabal), *The Italian Woman* (1980, Giuseppe Bertolucci), *So Fine* (1981, Andrew Bergman),

Tomorrow We Dance (1982, Maurizio Nichotti), *Summer Night* (1987, Wertmuller).

○

BEVERLY MICHAELS (1927–) Leading lady of tawdry B pictures of the fifties, including the first two directorial efforts of Hugo Haas. She was adept at playing tough, thick-skinned blondes who smoke, drink, and wear tight dresses. They have been around the block and know how to take men for a ride. She was in a couple of women's prison films, but she was usually cast as a gold-digging waitress or femme fatale. Having long ago learned the ways of the world, her women are only out for themselves. In *Blonde Bait,* she was "the kind of mistake a man can make only once"; *Pickup* was "the low-down on a come-on girl."

• **Cult Favorite:** *Pickup* (1951, Hugo Haas).

• **Other Key Films:** *The Girl on the Bridge* (1951, Haas), *Wicked Woman* (1954, Russell Rouse), *Betrayed Women* (1955, Edward L. Cahn), *Blonde Bait* (1956, Elmo Williams).

• **Also of Interest:** *East Side, West Side* (1949, Mervyn LeRoy), *Crashout* (1955, Lewis R. Foster).

○

CHARLES MIDDLETON (1879–1949) This tall, slim actor will always be remembered as the greatest of all serial villains, Ming the Merciless, evil ruler of Mongo, in three Flash Gordon serials. Bald, with a black beard, he repeatedly came up with creative ways to expand his domain—e.g., he spreads a plague dust in *Flash Gordon*

Charles Middleton's Ming the Merciless has only bad intentions for Buster Crabbe and Jean Rogers in Flash Gordon.

Conquers the Universe—and to do away with Buster Crabbe's earth hero. He had terrific presence, the perfect look for a comic strip–level villain, and leered at Jean Rogers' Dale Arden in such a way that we can tell what awful things Ming wants to do to her. A key to Middleton's portrayal is that Ming performs his evil deeds with absolute calmness and faces danger with composure, which is why he always escapes death. Middleton played scoundrels in other serials and in westerns, starring everyone from Bill Boyd to Johnny Mack Brown. His most sympathetic major part in a nonserial was the mist-shrouded ghost of a wrongly executed man in the creepy B chiller *Strangler of the Swamp*.

• **Cult Favorites:** *Duck Soup* (1933, Leo McCarey), *Hop-A-Long Cassidy* (1935, Howard P. Bretherton), *Flash Gordon* (1936 serial, Frederick Stephani), *Flash Gordon's Trip to Mars* (1938, Ford Beebe and Robert Hill), *Daredevils of the Red Circle* (1939 serial, William Witney and John English), *Flash Gordon Conquers the Universe* (1940, Beebe and Ray Taylor), *Perils of Nyoka* (1942 serial, Witney), *Strangler of the Swamp* (1946, Frank Wisbar).

• **Other Key Films:** *Alexander Hamilton* (1931, John Adolfi), *The Miracle Rider* (1935 serial, B. Reeves Eason and Armand Schaefer), *Batman* (1943 serial, Lambert Hillyer), *Jack Armstrong* (1947 serial, Wallace Fox).

○

TOSHIRO MIFUNE (1920–) Vastly talented, charismatic, and imposing (because of his strong voice and physique), the star of most of Akira Kurosawa's classics became the first Japanese actor since Sessue Hayakawa to have international fame. But where Hayakawa became a sex symbol because he was romantic, exotic, and suavely charming (even when playing lecherous villains), Mifune's sex appeal—and appeal to male viewers—was due to his sheer unrefined and uninhibited masculinity. He was attractive even when he was unshaven and unwashed, drunk, wide-eyed, and openly scratching himself all over his sweaty body, as if he were a flea-infested dog. He did indeed have animal magnetism—in fact, he based his wild, growling, scratching, superhyper Samurai recruit in *The Seven Samurai* on a lion. It shouldn't be forgotten that Mifune was terrific in Kurosawa's contemporary social dramas, as detectives or doctors, wearing suits and ties, but he will always be best remembered for his violent and fearless, funny, morally ambivalent samurai heroes for Kurosawa, as well as in Hiroshi Inagaki's classic epic, *The Samurai Trilogy.* Amazingly physical, he was a supreme action hero whose bloody, ritualistic and, ironically, sometimes comical sword-fight sequences in *Yojimbo* and *Sanjuro* are classics, as well-choreographed as the greatest movie dances. His nameless sword-for-hire anticipated Clint Eastwood's "Man With No Name" gunfighter. With intelligence, eyes seemingly in back of his head, and experience evident in every thrust or slice, he has no trouble—and no pity—dispatching twenty opponents at a time (Bruce Lee must have been watching!). It is a testament to his skills as an actor that watching the incredible swordplay does not thrill us any more than watching his face during the battle or just the way he moves, without a trace of panic, across the screen—for no one walks or races with more authority, arrogance, or grace than Mifune's barefoot warriors. For a 20-year period, there was no greater actor—dramatic or action—than Toshiro Mifune. Just look at his credits.

• **Cult Favorites:** *Rashomon* (1951, Akira Kurosawa), *The Life of Oharu* (1952, Kenji Mizoguchi), *The Seven Samurai* (1954, Kurosawa), *The Samurai Trilogy* (1954, Hiroshi Inagaki), *Throne of Blood* (1957, Kurosawa), *Yojimbo* (1961, Kurosawa), *Sanjuro* (1962, Kurosawa), *Zatoichi Meets Yojimbo* (1970, Kihachi Okamoto), *Winter Kills* (1979, William Richert).

• **Sleepers:** *Stray Dog* (1949, Kurosawa), *The Bad Sleep Well* (1960, Kurosawa), *High and Low* (1963, Kurosawa), *Red Beard* (1965, Kurosawa).

• **Other Key Films:** *Drunken Angel* (1949, Kurosawa), *Scandal* (1950, Kurosawa), *The Idiot* (1951, Kurosawa), *Hell in the Pacific* (1968, John Boorman).

• **Also of Interest:** *The Quiet Duel* (1949, Kurosawa), *Record of a Living Being* (1955, Kurosawa), *The Legacy of Five Hundred Thousand* (1964, Toshiro Mifune), *Sword of Doom* (1967, Okamoto), *The Challenge* (1972, John Frankenheimer), *Red Sun* (1972, Terence Young), *Midway* (1976, Jack Smight), *Torasan, Remind Shiretake* (1987, Yoji Yamada).

○

SARAH MILES (1941–) This slim, pretty British actress, with a shy but erotic face, began her career playing young seductresses, first of teacher Laurence Olivier in *Term of Trial,* and then of aristocratic

James Fox in *The Servant,* lying in a chair and wearing only a shirt in a sexual-breakthrough scene in her country's cinema. She would continue to play characters who are defined by their sexuality: David Hemmings's unhappily married mistress, who wears a see-through dress, in *Blow-Up*; Robert Mitchum's sexually frustrated wife who has a passionate love scene in the woods with Christopher Jones in *Ryan's Daughter;* the title character in *Lady Caroline Lamb,* who has an open affair with Lord Bryon. She appeared in progressively more dignified films (she married distinguished screenwriter Robert Bolt) yet her portrayals never lost their sexual edge. We pictured this miniskirted, seemingly uninhibited woman offscreen as leading the decadent life of the perverse, rich character she'd play many years later in *White Mischief.* Males got crushes, had fantasies. In the seventies, she was quoted as saying she would be willing to do a legitimate film with hard-core sex scenes (who knows if she really said it)—and she came mighty close, with a masturbation scene and erotic, nude, simulated sex scenes with Kris Kristofferson (which were highlighted in *Playboy*) in Lewis John Carlino's controversial adaptation of Yukio Mishima's *The Sailor Who Fell from Grace With the Sea.* Only recently, as the spirited mother in *Hope and Glory,* did Miles play a character who was not meant to excite male viewers (but did so anyway). At last she played a woman who was sympathetic and, though she has quirks and faults, quite likable and funny. Her face was still sensual but it was also sweet.

• **Cult Favorites:** *The Servant* (1963, Joseph Losey), *Blow-Up* (1966, Michelangelo Antonioni), *The Sailor Who Fell from Grace With the Sea* (1976, Lewis John Carlino).

• **Other Key Films:** *Term of Trial* (1962, Peter Glenville), *The Ceremony* (1963, Losey), *Ryan's Daughter* (1970, David Lean), *The Hireling* (1973, Alan Bridges), *Hope and Glory* (1987, John Boorman), *White Mischief* (1988, Michael Radford).

• **Also of Interest:** *Those Magnificent Men in Their Flying Machines* (1965, Ken Annakin), *Time Lost and Remembered/I Was Happy There* (1966, Desmond Davis), *Lady Caroline Lamb* (1972, Robert Bolt), *The Man Who Loved Cat Dancing* (1973, Richard C. Sarafian), *The Big Sleep* (1978, Michael Winner), *Priest of Love* (1981, Christopher Miles), *Venom* (1982, Piers Haggard), *Steaming* (1985, Losey).

○

SYLVIA MILES (1932–) Quirky, funny, busty blond New York character actress who has livened up many films as a series of loud, gabby women. Many of her characters aren't able to deal with their increasing years and declining sex appeal. In Andy Warhol's *Heat,* she was a faded actress who is flattered by the attentions of sneaky young actor Joe Dallesandro; in *Midnight Cowboy,* she was a pickup who takes naive hustler Jon Voight back to her fancy apartment—when she acts insulted that he asks her to pay him for sex, he ends up giving *her* money. In *Farewell, My Lovely,* her ill-fated floozie answers Robert Mitchum's questions only when he gives her alcohol; breasts falling out of her garments, she still believes a man might be attracted to her. Miles recently has played down the sex and emphasized the eccentricity: she was the upscale New York real estate agent in *Wall Street* and the matchmaker in *Crossing Delancy.* A much-seen, easy-to-recognize celebrity in New York, she once dumped a plate of food on acerbic

Sylvia Miles accepts money for services rendered from Jon Voight in Midnight Cowboy.

theater and film critic John Simon at a trendy New York restaurant after he gave her a nasty review. She is not one restricted by social proprieties.

• **Cult Favorites:** *Heat* (1972, Paul Morrissey), *92 in the Shade* (1975, Thomas McGuane), *Farewell, My Lovely* (1975, Dick Richards).

• **Also Recommended:** *Midnight Cowboy* (1969, John Schlesinger), *Wall Street* (1987, Oliver Stone), *Crossing Delancey* (1988, Joan Micklin Silver).

• **Also of Interest:** *The Funhouse* (1981, Tobe Hooper), *Evil Under the Sun* (1982, Guy Hamilton), *Spike of Bensonhurst* (1988, Morrissey), *She-Devil* (1989, Susan Seidelman).

○

DICK MILLER (1928–) Popular, very amusing, scene-stealer in low-budget horror films, whose appearances guarantee audience applause. A New York native, he is short (so he couldn't be a romantic lead or a threatening villain, but could play "Shorty" in *Rock All Night*), has wavy hair and long side burns, a sharp nose, and a face as trustful as a used-car dealer's. Beginning in the fifties, he became a mainstay of Roger Corman exploitation films, usually as unlikable sorts. At first he played it straight, but beginning with his vacuum cleaner salesman in *Not of This Earth*, he added large doses of humor. His most memorable lead is the mentally retarded, beatnik artist Walter Paisley, whose sculptures are suspiciously lifelike in *A Bucket of Blood,* but he's better remembered for a supporting part, the flower-eating Vurson Fouch in Corman's other classic black comedy, *The Little Shop of Horrors.* For the last dozen years, as his face has become more recognizable, he has made "cameo" appearances in many films, often playing quirky chatterboxes. One of his best bits was as the funny occult bookshop owner in *The Howling.*

• **Cult Favorites:** *A Bucket of Blood* (1959, Roger Corman), *The Little Shop of Horrors* (1960, Corman), *The Terror* (1963, Corman), *X—The Man with the X-Ray Eyes* (1963, Corman), *The Trip* (1967, Corman), *St. Valentine's Day Massacre* (1967, Corman), *Big Bad Mama* (1974, Steve Carver), *Hollywood Boulevard* (1976, Joe Dante and Alan Arkush), *Piranha* (1978, Dante), *Rock 'n' Roll High School* (1979, Arkush and Dante), *The Lady in Red/ Guns, Sin and Bathtub Gin* (1979, Lewis Teague), *The Howling* (1981, Dante), *Heart Like a Wheel* (1983, Jonathan Kaplan), *After Hours* (1985, Martin Scorsese), *Night of the Creeps* (1987, Fred Dekker).

• **Also of Interest:** *Apache Woman* (1955, Corman), *The Oklahoma Woman* (1955, Corman), *The Gunslinger* (1956, Corman), *It Conquered the World* (1956, Corman), *Not of This Earth* (1956, Corman),

Dick Miller had a rare starring role in Roger Corman's A Bucket of Blood.

Rock All Night (1956, Corman), *The Naked Paradise/Thunder Over Hawaii* (1956, Corman), *Carnival Rock* (1957, Corman), *The Undead* (1957, Corman), *Sorority Girl* (1957, Corman), *War of the Satellites* (1958, Corman), *The Wasp Woman* (1959, Corman), *The Premature Burial* (1962, Corman), *A Time for Killing* (1967, Phil Karlson), *Candy Stripe Nurses* (1974, Allan Holeb), *Dr. Heckyl and Mr. Hype* (1980, Charles B. Griffith), *Gremlins* (1984, Dante), *Explorers* (1985, Dante), *Project X* (1987, Kaplan), *Gremlins 2: The New Batch* (1990, Dante).

○

HAYLEY MILLS (1946–) Blond British actress debuted at the age of 12 in *Tiger Bay,* a thriller starring her father, John Mills. Her intelligent, natural portrayal of a terrified child witness earned her a trip to America to act for Walt Disney, for whom she made such popular family films as *Pollyanna, The Parent Trap,* and *Summer Magic.* I'm surprised when reading contemporary British critics that they weren't all taken by the teenage Mills in the sixties. For instance, David Shipman contended "that she was a joke to many people," and David Thomson wrote that the "Mills family has so crowded us out with insipid, tennis-club talent that it is easy to forget that [John] Mills is a reasonable actor." Here in America everyone adored Hayley Mills. Almost all of us boys (including future critics) had tremendous crushes on her and almost every girl

Hayley Mills with Deborah Kerr in The Chalk Garden.

wanted to be like her. Her appeal with older adults wasn't at all sexual, as would be the case with Jodie Foster—her chastity made both adults and kids secure, and all would have been shocked if she hadn't turned down *Lolita*. I remember turning my head when she kissed Michael Anderson in *In Search of the Castaways;* I drifted away as her roles became more mature. We youngsters did see her as a rebel of sorts—even if only a few of us saw the dramatic British, non-Disney film *Whistle Down the Wind,* in which she and younger kids hide escaped prisoner Alan Bates (whom they believe to be Christ) from their parents and the authorities. In such pictures as *The Parent Trap,* the film for which her loyal fans feel the most nostalgia, her young girls exhibit feelings that the adults around them suppress in themselves, as well as the vibrant energy, wit, imagination and optimistic view of the world that they allowed to slip away years ago. She, in effect, liberates their emotions. These qualities in her characters, along with Mills's mature talent, beauty, and striking, pre-Beatles British accent (her diction, with emphasis on particular words, was unsurpassed), contributed to her immense popularity. Seeing her today, it's hard not to get back those old feelings.

• **Cult Favorite:** *The Parent Trap* (1961, David Swift).

• **Also Recommended:** *Tiger Bay* (1959, J. Lee Thompson), *Pollyana* (1960, Swift), *Whistle Down the Wind* (1961, Bryan Forbes), *The Chalk Garden* (1964, Ronald Neame), *That Darn Cat* (1965, Robert Stevenson), *The Trouble With Angels* (1966, Ida Lupino), *The Family Way* (1966, Roy Boulting), *Cry of the Penguins/ Forbush and the Penguins* (1971, Al Viola and, uncredited, Boulting).

• **Other Key Films:** *In Search of the Castaways* (1962, Stevenson), *Summer Magic* (1963, James Neilson), *The Moon-Spinners* (1964, Neilson), *The Truth About Spring* (1965, Richard Thorpe), *A Matter of Innocence* (1967, Guy Green).

• **Also of Interest:** *Gypsy Girl/Sky West and Crooked* (1966, John Mills), *The Twisted Nerve* (1968, Boulting), *Endless Night* (1972, Sidney Gilliat), *The Kingfisher Caper* (1976, Dick DeVilliers).

○

YVETTE MIMIEUX (1939–) This slim, fragile, long-haired blonde with fairy-tale beauty received much publicity at the beginning of her career (including cover stories when she guested as Richard Chamberlain's ill-fated lover on TV's "Dr. Kildare"). She started out effectively in movies, winning the hearts of us young boys as an innocent (in everything but publicity shots!)—the docile girl of the future in *The Time Machine* and the "Dancing Princess" in *The Wonderful World of the Brothers Grimm;* she excited older males as the virginal college student who makes the usual mistake and pays the price in *Where the Boys Are.* But otherwise, she found herself in turgid soap operas, and lost her chance for stardom. Later she starred in bad, but tougher, action films, no longer as the defenseless innocent. However, she didn't attract much attention until she played an upper-middle-class traveler who is thrown into the *Jackson County Jail,* brutally raped by the guard (in a much-discussed scene), kills him, and goes on the lam with prisoner Tommy Lee Jones. The exploitation film was overrated by those who detected feminist themes, but Mimieux was at her best: strong, mature, and sexy.

• **Cult Favorites:** *Where the Boys Are* (1960, Henry Levin), *Platinum High*

Yvette Mimieux in a publicity shot for Where the Boys Are.

School (1960, Charles Haas), *Jackson County Jail* (1976, Michael Miller).

• **Other Key Films:** *The Time Machine* (1960, George Pal), *The Wonderful World of the Brothers Grimm* (1962, Levin), *Toys in the Attic* (1963, George Roy Hill), *Dark of the Sun* (1968, Jack Cardiff), *Three in the Attic* (1968, Richard Wallace), *The Neptune Factor* (1973, Daniel Petrie), *The Black Hole* (1979, Gary Nelson).

○

MIOU-MIOU (1950–) This beguiling, softspoken French actress—a tiny, fragile, waiflike blonde with a little-girl face and big brown eyes—was born Sylvette Herry, and sewed in an upholstery shop before overcoming her timidity and turning to acting. She was a founder of the Paris café-theater, Café de la Gare, which produced Gérard Depardieu and Patrick Dewaere (with whom she had a child), the costars of her first major film, Bertrand Blier's raucous *Going Places*. When her suburban hairdresser stripped and had sex with them in a car, she jumped to stardom (along with the actors), as a symbol of free-spirited French youth. Years later, Blier would unite her with Depardieu in the even more bizarre comedy *Ménage*, in which his zany crook manipulates her passive suburban housewife and her meek, funny-looking husband (Michel Blanc) into joining his crime spree. Depardieu then seduces each of them—falling for him instead of her. She gave an incisive, mature performance in *Entre Nous* as Isabelle Huppert's long-time friend and confidante—a relationship that worries their insecure husbands (a novel theme!). It was one of her few characters who isn't wildly unpredictable (and anarchic). On her own, she was captivating—erotic and once again, softspoken—reading great literature to various employers in *La Lectrice*.

• **Cult Favorites:** *Going Places/Les Val-*

seuses (1973, Bertrand Blier), *For Jonah Who Will Be 25 in the Year 2000* (1976, Alain Tanner), *Entre Nous* (1983, Diane Kurys), *Ménage* (1986, Blier).

• **Other Key Films:** *Tell Him That I Love Him* (1977, Claude Miller), *My Other Husband* (1981, Georges Lautner), *Blanche et Marie* (1984, Jacques Rénard), *La Lectrice* (1989, Michel Deville), *May Fools* (1990, Louis Malle).

○

CARMEN MIRANDA (1909–55) The "Brazilian Bombshell" debuted in American films in a

Carmen Miranda goes bananas in The Gang's All Here.

close-up that opens *Down Argentine Way*. She is wearing a tall, flashy hat over her dark hair, fancy bracelets, and a colorful outfit that reveals her tummy. Singing the title song, she shimmies back and forth, but her dancing is equally dependent on the constant movements of her fingers, hands, and arms, her expressive eyes, and her animated, brightly made up face. Giving musical and comedic support to the likes of Betty Grable, Alice Faye, and Vivian Blaine, this outrageous entertainer would cheer up 20th Century-Fox color musicals for years, singing some of the silliest songs and wearing a weird selection of fruit hats. In the campy *The Gang's All Here*, she leads Busby Berkeley's most ridiculous musical routine of all, wearing a hat of bananas while scores of beautiful chorus girls make patterns with their bodies and the giant bananas they carry. It's like the worst football halftime routine imaginable, but like all Miranda's kooky numbers, fun to watch. The performer who paved the way for the likes of Charo died of a heart attack when just 46.

• **Cult Favorite:** *The Gang's All Here* (1943, Busby Berkeley).

• **Other Key Films:** *Down Argentine Way* (1940, Irving Cummings), *That Night in Rio* (1941, Cummings), *Week-End in Havana* (1941, Walter Lang), *Springtime in the Rockies* (1942, Cummings), *Greenwich Village* (1944, Lang).

• **Also of Interest:** *Something for the Boys* (Lewis Seiler), *Doll Face* (1945, Seiler), *If I'm Lucky* (1946, Seiler), *Copacabana* (1947, Alfred E. Green), *A Date With Judy* (1948, Richard Thorpe), *Nancy Goes to Rio* (1950, Robert Z. Leonard).

○

HELEN MIRREN (1945–) Lovely, sensuous, strikingly talented blond British actress, with Shakespearean training, who has brought an exciting blend of intelligence, class, and mature, straight-forward sexuality to the cinema. Since playing a sensitive beach girl who poses nude for artist James Mason in Michael Powell's obscure *Age of Consent* in 1969, Mirren has always taken daring parts in nontraditional films. That she would play Malcolm McDowell's amoral wife in the perverse X-rated *Caligula* (which includes a scene where she intensely kisses her young sister-in-law, Teresa Ann Savoy) showed that she isn't concerned about image. She also starred in the scandalous *The Cook, the Thief, His Wife & Her Lover*, as a wife who cheats on her cruel, vulgar husband. She was marvelous in the brutal, fascinating *The Long Good Friday*, as the endangered, confused gangster Bob Hoskins's smart, classy mistress, who tries to keep him calm despite her own escalating fears. She also was memorable in the Ireland-set *Cal*, as a Protestant widow in her thirties who has an affair with a troubled 19-year-old Catholic boy from Belfast. She's too good to be pushed into the background, as she was as Harrison Ford's wife in *The Mosquito Coast*, or saddled with a Russian accent, as has happened on several occasions.

• **Cult Favorites:** *Savage Messiah* (1972, Ken Russell), *O Lucky Man* (1973, Lindsay Anderson), *Caligula* (1980, Tinto Brass), *Excalibur* (1981, John Boorman), *The Cook, the Thief, His Wife & Her Lover* (1989, Peter Greenaway), *The Comfort of Strangers* (1991, Paul Schrader).

• **Sleepers:** *The Long Good Friday* (1980, John MacKenzie), *Cal* (1984, Pat O'Connor), *Pascali's Island* (1988, James Deardon).

• **Also of Interest:** *Age of Consent* (1969, Michael Powell), *The Gospel According to Vic* (1985, Charles Gormley), *White*

Nights (1985, Taylor Hackford), *The Mosquito Coast* (1986, Peter Weir).

○

CAMERON MITCHELL (1918–) Long-active dramatic actor appeared in many mainstream films early in his career, most notably as Happy in *Death of a Salesman* (a role he played on Broadway), the average guy who gold-digging Lauren Bacall falls for who turns out to be a millionaire in *How to Marry a Millionaire,* and drug-addicted boxing champion Barney Ross in *Monkey on My Back.* He also had leads in a number of impressive, offbeat pictures like *Gorilla at Large, Blood and Black Lace, Rebel Rousers,* and the existential western *Ride in the Whirlwind,* which have achieved cult status. But Mitchell's own cult status is due to his appearances since the sixties in bloody, low-grade horror films, made in America and abroad. He has given some of the worst performances on film as mad scientists and demented killers, like the one who commits *The Toolbox Murders.* Forget about pride—at least he continues to work.
• **Cult Favorites:** *They Were Expendable* (1945, John Ford), *House of Bamboo* (1955, Samuel Fuller), *Blood and Black Lace* (1964, Mario Bava), *Ride in the Whirlwind* (1965, Monte Hellman).
• **Sleepers:** *Gorilla at Large* (1954, Harmon Jones), *Face of Fire* (1959, Albert Band), *Silent Scream* (1980, Denny Harris).
• **Also of Interest:** *How to Marry a Millionaire* (1953, Jean Negulesco), *Love Me or Leave Me* (1955, Charles Vidor), *Carousel* (1956, Henry King), *Monkey on My Back* (1957, André de Toth), *No Down Payment* (1957, Martin Ritt), *Erik the Conqueror* (1961, Bava), *Nightmare in Wax* (1966, Bud Townsend), *Rebel Rousers* (1967, Martin B. Cohen), *Buck and the Preacher* (1972, Sidney Poitier), *Haunts* (1976, Herb Freed), *Without Warning* (1980, Greydon Clark).

○

SHARON MITCHELL The popularity of this slim, dark-haired New York porno actress is due, in part, to a funky, androgynous look that sets her apart from the more glamorous, vivacious sex queens. With her slender dancer-contortionist's body, sharp facial features, dark hair that covers her eyebrows, full lips, and a cool expression, she might have been one of Warhol's Superstars—or a male in *Fellini Satyricon.* Often in secondary roles or cameos, she has played seductresses; taken part in lesbian scenes and wild orgies; given, in at least two films, oral sex demonstrations; and, as uninhibited as any porno star, engaged in the kinkiest sex. She was even in the notorious *Sulka's Wedding,* about the sexual exploits of the transsexual Sulka, before and after the operation, and featuring a climactic orgy with some of the strangest couplings in any porno film. She's not for all tastes.
• **Cult Favorites:** *Wanda Whips Wall Street* (1982, Larry Revene), *Sulka's Wedding* (1983, Mike Stryker).
• **Also of Interest:** *Joy* (1975, Harley Mansfield), *Joint Venture* (1978), *Dirty Lilly* (1979, Mark Ubell), *Captain Lust and the Pirate* (1979, Beau Buchanon), *Satisfiers of Alpha Blue* (1981, Gerard Damiano), *Foxtrot* (1982, Cecil Howard), *Touch Me in the Morning* (1982, Louis Lewis), *Brief Affair* (1982, Lewis), *Midnight Heat* (1983, Richard Mahler), *Scoundrels* (1983, Howard), *Widespread Scandals of Lydia* (1983, Henri Pachard).

Robert Mitchum with Jane Greer in Out of the Past.

○

ROBERT MITCHUM (1917–) Tall, muscular, rugged, and handsome, with a deep, confident voice, and a strong jaw that looks like it got its dimple from a bullet that stopped on contact, Mitchum has long been one of the cinema's most masculine heroes. He doesn't look like the type who would put on greasepaint and be an actor, and his seemingly effortless, seemingly lazy style—characterized by a tired delivery and his naturally sleepy eyes (a factor in his sex appeal)—always gave us the impression that he'd rather be doing something else if there was anything interesting he could make a living at. Playing characters who know there is no such thing as happiness or fulfillment, he did his *job*, with the same lack of enjoyment and sense of irony that his Philip Marlowe has while doing his detective work. And he is just as good as Marlowe at what he does. Trying to explain why Mitchum is such a fine movie actor is as frustrating as championing John Wayne. As with Wayne, start talking about his tremendous "presence" and how his tough guys will not back down from trouble (a villain, the law, or a woman). Then mention his humor and surprising sensitivity. And, to illustrate his versatility, recall those characters who get killed, as well as his two terrifying villains: the sexual psychopath who menaces lawyer Gregory Peck and his family in *Cape Fear,* and—in what is probably his best performance—his phony preacher (a "wolf in sheep's clothing"), who murders his wife (Shelley Winters) and relentlessly chases after his small stepchildren in pursuit of some missing money in *The Night of the Hunter*. Concede Mitchum has made many bad films, but point out that he was always better than the material, and mention all his excellent films with interesting characterizations. Indeed, Mitchum was underappreciated until the seventies, when it suddenly became obvious that every movie fanatic was fanatical about at least one Mitchum film and that there were strong underground followings for *The Night of the Hunter;* the B moonshine-running favorite *Thunder Road* (for which he sings the title song); and the definitive noir film *Out of the Past*, in which he is an ill-fated detective. The more you see of Mitchum, the more impressed you become. You understand why John Huston claimed he could have played Shakespeare.

• **Cult Favorites:** *Out of the Past* (1947, Jacques Tourneur), *His Kind of Woman* (1951, John Farrow), *Angel Face* (1952, Otto Preminger), *The Night of the Hunter* (1955, Charles Laughton), *Thunder Road* (1958, Arthur Ripley), *The Longest Day* (1962, Andrew Marton, Ken Annakin, and Bernhard Wicki), *El Dorado* (1967, Howard Hawks), *Farewell, My Lovely* (1975, Dick Richards).

• **Other Key Films:** *The Story of G.I. Joe* (1945, William Wellman), *Pursued* (1947, Raoul Walsh), *Crossfire* (1947, Edward Dmytryk), *Blood on the Moon* (1948, Robert Wise), *The Red Pony* (1949, Lewis Milestone), *The Big Steal* (1949, Don Siegel), *Macao* (1952, Josef von Sternberg), *The Lusty Men* (1952, Nicholas Ray), *River of No Return* (1954, Preminger), *Track of the Cat* (1954, Wellman), *Heaven Knows, Mr. Allison* (1957, John Huston), *The Sundowners* (1960, Fred Zinnemann), *Cape Fear* (1960, J. Lee Thompson), *Two for the See-* saw (1962, Wise), *Secret Ceremony* (1968, Joseph Losey), *The Friends of Eddie Coyle* (1973, Peter Yates), *The Yakuza* (1975, Sydney Pollack).

○

TOM MIX (1880–1940) The most popular cowboy hero of all time. He overtook W. S. Hart as cowboy king around 1920, nine years after his first film and three years after he left Selig for Fox, and began making highly entertaining, action-packed, often comedic westerns that deliberately contrasted with Hart's somber, realistic dramas. The strong, good-looking hero wore frilly shirts and 10-gallon hats, was constantly in fist and gun fights (though rarely was anyone killed), chastely courted schoolmarms and rancher's daughters, and did daredevil stunts on a talented chestnut named Tony (he retired his original mount, Old Blue, in 1915), before riding into the sunset. Of course, he never smoke or drank. His clean-living, all-American cowboy became the idol to millions, his popularity fueled by a studio-fabricated life story that made him out to be a hero of several wars around the world and a gun-firing lawman out west. After leaving films in the thirties, he toured in his own circus, still doing riding stunts. He was killed in a car crash in 1940, four years before 34-year-old Tony was put to sleep.

• **Some Key Films:** *Hearts and Saddles* (1917, Tom Mix and Bob Eddy), *Ace High* (1918, Lynn Reynolds), *Sky High* (1922, Reynolds), *Just Tony* (1922, Reynolds), *Three Jumps Ahead* (1923, John Ford), *The Lone Star Ranger* (1923, Lambert Hillyer), *North of Hudson Bay* (1923, Ford), *The Rainbow Trail* (1925, Reynolds), *The Best Bad Man* (1925, John G. Blystone), *The Great K & A Robbery* (1926, Lewis Seiler),

Tom Mix.

Destry Rides Again (1932, Ben Stoloff), *My Pal, the King* (1932, Kurt Neumann), *Rustler's Roundup* (1933, Henry McRae), *The Miracle Rider* (1935 serial, B. Reeves Eason and Armand Schaefer).

○

BRIDGETTE MONET No relation to Claude. This dark-haired porno actress is beautiful, sexy, and has talent in and out of the sack (although much more in it), but she has a high-pitched baby voice that you may respond to as if she were continually squeaking a balloon. Of course, no one pays money for Monet to talk. Her films are more carefully made than most, with attention paid to light, color, music, and costumes, so that eroticism mixes with raunch. She has usually played smart, upscale women who are searching for sexual fulfillment. She finds it and gives it to others along the way.

● **Cult Favorites:** *I Like to Watch* (1982, Paul G. Vatelli), *Talk Dirty to Me II* (1983, Tim McDonald).
● **Also of Interest:** *Brief Affair* (1982, Louis Lewis), *Sorority Sweethearts* (1983, Vatelli), *Let's Talk Sex* (1983, Vatelli), *Nightlife* (1983, Lewis).

○

CONSTANCE MONEY This shapely blonde is considered one of the most beautiful actresses ever in the porno field. In fact, she became so popular because no one could believe someone with her looks would be doing porno movies unless they really enjoyed the work. The films she made were some of the genre's "classier" efforts, where the directors created an erotic mood through photography, music, and set design. Her most famous role was as a street hustler who is turned into an expensive, refined, famous high-class brothel prostitute in *The Opening of Misty Beethoven.* The premise gave her character a chance to become expert in and demonstrate all kinds of sex. But Money still had another trick up her sleeve: an underwater sex scene (with John Leslie) in *Mary! Mary!*

• **Cult Favorites:** *The Opening of Misty Beethoven* (1975, Henri Paris/Radley Metzger), *Barbara Broadcast* (1977, Paris/Metzger).

• **Also of Interest:** *Anna Obsessed* (1977, Martin & Martin), *Mary! Mary!* (1977, Bernard Morris), *Maraschino Cherry* (1978, Paris/Metzger), *Taste of Money* (1983).

○

MARILYN MONROE (1926–1962) When you look at photos of Marilyn Monroe—and

Marilyn Monroe, glamorous and seemingly happy.

her younger incarnation, Norma Jean Baker—it's impossible not to be awed by her beauty, sex appeal, and magical "star" quality—and to feel sadness for the frightened, lonely, unprotected and doomed actress. In the fifties, women felt jealousy and contempt for the sexy, dizzy, blond child-woman with the hushed baby voice, wide eyes, moist ruby lips in the shape of an "O," an hourglass figure, a much-practiced wiggly walk (it was said that she had "a future that was behind her"), and the annoying habit of chasing men in her films who were much like their own flawed husbands (she rarely was cast opposite a virile young actor). They weren't secure with an actress who was a combination (as Groucho Marx quipped) of vamp Theda Bara, who made victims of her male playthings and who represented dangerous sex; Mae West, who made aggressive female sexuality acceptable and who represented fun sex; and Little Bo Beep, the original blond innocent. But today, women have come to love her as much as men, "canonizing her," writes Molly Haskell, "as a martyr to male chauvinism." She is now seen as a victim in her private life (dating back to an unhappy childhood) in Hollywood, where she "played the sexual game" to reach stardom but still felt trapped, and even in the political arena, as mistress of both John Kennedy and, at the time of her suspicious drug overdose, Robert Kennedy. The constant exploitation took its toll. That she was able to give such wonderful, deeply felt performances is a testament to her talents, for she suffered such anxiety from lack of confidence that she invariably caused turmoil and delays on sets, locking herself in her dressing room, and having breakdowns. It's probably easiest for Monroe fans to watch her in *Gentlemen Prefer Blondes*. In other films,

one senses Monroe's brittle sensitivity, her sad isolation, and her crushed romanticism. In her starlet roles in *The Asphalt Jungle* and *All About Eve,* she played parts that were probably similar to her ugly real-life role at the time. At moments in *Bus Stop* and *The Misfits,* so much of the tender, vulnerable Monroe comes across that it can be painful to watch. But as Lorelei Lee in *Gentlemen Prefer Blondes* and, to some degree, Sugar Kane in *Some Like It Hot* (her best film), she at least seems happy, slipping out of the tough real world and into a fantasy world of songs and dances, tight-fitting costumes, and jewelry. This is what she assumed all movies were like when she was a young girl looking for escape. When the camera focuses on her alone, and she's smiling and singing, she is without question the most glamorous movie star of them all.

• **Cult Favorites:** *All About Eve* (1950, Joseph L. Mankiewicz), *Gentlemen Prefer Blondes* (1953, Howard Hawks), *The Seven Year Itch* (1955, Billy Wilder), *Some Like It Hot* (1959, Wilder), *The Misfits* (1961, John Huston).

• **Other Key Films:** *The Asphalt Jungle* (1950, Huston), *Clash by Night* (1952, Fritz Lang), *Don't Bother to Knock* (1952, Roy Baker), *Monkey Business* (1952, Hawks), *Niagara* (1953, Henry Hathaway), *How to Marry a Millionaire* (1953, Jean Negulesco), *Bus Stop* (1956, Joshua Logan).

• **Also of Interest:** *Love Happy* (1949, David Miller), *River of No Return* (1954, Otto Preminger), *The Prince and the Showgirl* (1957, Laurence Olivier), *Let's Make Love* (1960, George Cukor).

○

MARIA MONTEZ (1920–51) This sultry, curvaceous Dominican beauty didn't have much

Maria Montez in Arabian Nights.

impact when Universal tried to launch her as a Dorothy Lamour clone in a sarong in *South of Tahiti,* but she shot to fame and stardom and the lasting admiration of camp enthusiasts when the studio cast her opposite the dashing Jon Hall in several exotic, outrageous adventure-romances. They were perhaps the best-looking screen couple of them all. The "Queen of Technicolor" played princesses, queens, and dancing girls who all wear colorful, erotic outfits (usually with a bare midriff). They lived in lavish surroundings that were decorated with some of the weirdest props Universal could come up with, and usually stood perilously close to an active volcano.

Physically threatened by evil villains like Kurt Katch, George Zucco, Douglas Drumbille, and Edgar Barrier, and faced with tough decisions such as whether to choose her throne or Hall, she always found happiness thanks to Hall, servant Turhan Bey (in the sixth and final series entry, he replaced Hall as the romantic lead), and Sabu. She was a terrible actress, but she was perfect for these ridiculous escapist films. Playing two parts in *Cobra Woman,* she is doubly bad but truly dazzling to look at. It's hard to believe that as a bit player she and the equally flamboyant Carmen Miranda were contained in one film (*That Night in Rio*)! When Montez's star faded in America, she went to Europe with actor husband Jean-Pierre Aumont and continued her career. She died of a heart attack at the age of 31.

• **Cult Favorites:** *Arabian Nights* (1942, John Rawlins), *Ali Baba and the Forty Thieves* (1944, Arthur Lubin), *Cobra Woman* (1944, Robert Siodmak).

• **Other Key Films:** *White Savage* (1943, Lubin), *Gypsy Wildcat* (1944, Roy William Neill), *Sudan* (1945, Rawlins).

• **Also of Interest:** *South of Tahiti* (1941, George Waggner), *The Mystery of Marie Roget* (1942, Phil Rosen), *Tangier* (1946, Waggner), *The Exile* (1947, Max Ophüls), *Pirates of Monterey* (1947, Alfred E. Werker), *Siren of Atlantis* (1948, Gregg Tallas).

○

MARIO MONTEZ The most flamboyant *performer*—he was one of many to emphasize *non-acting*—of the underground experimental film movement of the early to mid-sixties, starring for such major directors as Jack Smith, Ron Rice, and Bill Vehr (of Charles Ludlam's Theatre of the Ridiculous) and Andy Warhol, when both worked with writer Ronald Tavel (also of the Theatre of the Ridiculous). A transvestite, he was first cast-listed as Dolores Flores in Jack Smith's seminal *Flaming Creatures*, dancing a fandango and participating in a transvestite orgy (he'd be in a similar sequence in Rice's *Chumlum*). From then on he was Mario Montez, playing females in all but one film. His women were throwbacks to former Hollywood vamps, whose flamboyance, seductive quality, and narcissism were more important than their acting. For Warhol-Tavel, he was Jean Harlow in *Harlot*, Hedy Lamarr in *Hedy*, Lana Turner in

More Milk, Yvette; always he was Maria Montez. His most poignant scene is the climax of Warhol's *Screen Test Number Two,* in which he is confronted about his sexuality at a movie audition, and must admit he is a male—but he only does so, he says, because he is a woman.

• **Cult Favorite:** *Flaming Creatures* (1963, Jack Smith).

• **Other Key Films:** *Normal Love* (Smith), *In the Trip of the Lobster* (Smith), *Chumlum* (1964, Ron Rice), *Lupita* (José Rodriguez-Soltero), *Avocada* (1965, Bill Vehr), *Screen Test Number Two* (1965, Andy Warhol), *Harlot* (1965, Warhol), *Hedy* (1966, Warhol), *Brothel* (1966, Vehr), *The Mysterious Spanish Lady* (Vehr), *M.M. for M.M.* (Vehr), *Lil Picards* (Vehr), *Beauty Environment of the Year 2065* (Vehr).

○

MONTY PYTHON Innovative, irreverent, and downright silly British comedy troupe, consisting of Englishmen John Cleese (1939–), Graham Chapman (1941–89), Terry Jones (1942–), Eric Idle (c.1942–), and Michael Palin (1943–), and American Terry Gilliam (1940–), began its celebrated cult comedy series, *Monty Python's Flying Circus,* on the BBC in fall 1969. By 1974, it played in a dozen foreign markets, including America, and had an enormous following. Audiences weren't used to serious-seeming men, educated at Oxford and Cambridge, doing ridiculous things. In 1972, the Pythons made their first joint foray into movies with *And Now for Something Completely Different,* featuring some of their most famous lunatic TV sketches: "The Dead Parrot," "The Ministry of Silly Walks," and "The Lumberjack Song." Eventually there would be two more sketch films, *Monty Python Live at the Hollywood Bowl* and *Monty Python's The Meaning of Life*, with original material that includes Cleese as a teacher matter-of-factly demonstrating sex for his students, and Jones as the world's fattest man, devouring food and vomiting buckets while in a fancy restaurant. The group would also appear in two successful narrative films, the hilarious *Monty Python and the Holy Grail*, a send-up of the Arthur legend, and *Life of Brian*, a controversial takeoff on the Christ story. They would blend slapstick, satire, parody, anarchical humor in the Marx Brothers vein with absurdism, surrealism, and offbeat character comedy in the Alec Guinness tradition (with characters ranging from stiff-upper-lipped British to zany, from royalty to lumpen proletariat). Most unusual is that the Python characters are rarely sympathetic. The actors themselves don't have audience-endearing physical quirks (a big nose, a big belly, a weakling's body, bad eyesight) but are imposing men (even when dressed as women), physically and intellectually, who are always on the attack. Their characters are extremely competitive, even combative, whether being historical figures playing soccer, engaging in one-man wrestling matches (a Chapman routine), participating in bizarre races (for people who think they are chickens, for people with no sense of direction, and so on), or arguing. They argue about everything, including whether an argument that is taking place is indeed an argument ("It is!"/"It isn't!"). The characters are also stubborn, conceited, loud, foul-mannered, and full of complaints. No wonder they constantly get on each other's nerves. The great group never broke up, but Chapman's death in 1989 ended an era. The surviving members, particularly Cleese, and as a director, Gilliam, continue to have much individual success.

- **Cult Favorites:** *Monty Python and the Holy Grail* (1974, Terry Gilliam and Terry Jones), *Life of Brian* (1979, Jones).
- **Also Recommended:** *And Now for Something Completely Different* (1972, Ian McNaughton), *Monty Python Live at the Hollywood Bowl* (1982, Terry Hughes), *Monty Python's The Meaning of Life* (1983, Jones).

○

CLEO MOORE (1930–73) Replacing Beverly Michaels, this attractive, buxom, somewhat chunky blonde was an entertaining female lead in seven of Hugo Haas's low-budget, lurid potboilers. Smoking, standing up to Haas (who usually was her costar), scheming to improve her life, her women were usually cheap and trashy—a hooker, a dancer, a waitress, a prisoner—unfaithful, greedy, vengeful, or suicidal. They were, as one poster contended, "the kind of girl every man wants but shouldn't marry." They dislike men: "They're all alike," she says in *One Girl's Confession*, "they only have faces so you can tell them apart." The older, heavy-set Haas looks at her in low-cut bathing suits and other sexy outfits and wants her badly; being self-destructive, he usually marries her. Then she leads him into misery, often enjoying herself in the process. In the strange *One Girl's Confession*, her waitress almost kills him but they end up best buddies. In Haas's morality plays, she often finds salvation. Moore once ran for governor of Louisiana. Might it have been interesting if she'd won?

- **Cult Favorites:** *Strange Fascination* (1952, Hugo Haas), *Bait* (1954, Haas).

• **Other Key Films:** *Thy Neighbor's Wife* (1953, Haas), *The Other Woman* (1954, Haas), *One Girl's Confession* (1955, Haas), *Hold Back Tomorrow* (1955, Haas), *Women's Prison* (1955, Lewis Seiler), *Over-Exposed* (1956, Seiler), *Hit and Run* (1957, Haas).

• **Also of Interest:** *Congo Bill* (1948 serial, Spencer Bennet and Thomas Carr), *Gambling House* (1950, Ted Tetzlaff), *Dynamite Pass* (1950, Lew Landers), *On Dangerous Ground* (1951, Nicholas Ray).

○

ROGER MOORE (1928–) Tall, blond, extremely handsome British actor vaulted to international stardom when he became the movies' third James Bond, following Sean Connery and George Lazenby (who lasted only one film). I was always partial to Moore because he'd been TV's "Ivanhoe," Bret and Bart's cousin Beau on "Maverick," and "The Saint," and had paid his dues in films since the late forties. But the best that can be said of his Bond is that he held the fort for several years during which the series not only survived but thrived— although it did become too gimmicky and tongue-in-cheek during his reign. He was quite good in the exciting *The Spy Who Loved Me,* opposite Barbara Bach, but in films like *Moonraker* he seemed lackadaisical, walking through his paces for his paycheck and constantly giving way to his stunt double. Being handsome, masculine, and debonair, he looked right making love to glamorous actresses and standing amid lavish sets. But he never brought joy to the role, as did Connery. Outside of Bond, Moore starred in a number of action films, giving adequate but unmemorable performances.

• **Cult Favorite:** *The Spy Who Loved Me* (1977, Lewis Gilbert).

• **Other Key Films:** *Live and Let Die* (1973, Guy Hamilton), *The Man with the Golden Gun* (1974, Hamilton), *Moonraker* (1979, Gilbert), *For Your Eyes Only* (1981, John Glen), *Octopussy* (1983, Glen), *A View to a Kill* (1985).

• **Also of Interest:** *Diane* (1956, David Miller), *The Man Who Haunted Himself* (1970, Basil Deardon), *Gold* (1974, Peter Hunt), *The Wild Geese* (1978, Andrew V. McLaglen), *ffolkes* (1980, McLaglen), *The Naked Face* (1984, Bryan Forbes).

○

TERRY MOORE (1929–) Short, pretty, young-looking former child model and actress had a well-scrubbed face and played wholesome American girls, but she was busty enough and made the scandal sheets often enough to be considered a sexpot. That's why everyone wanted to date Moore, including Howard Hughes, who may have married her. Before settling on the name Terry Moore in the late forties, she went by Judy Ford, Jan Ford, and her real name Helen Koford, which was how she was billed for *Son of Lassie.* After that film, she was cast for a brief time in a series of films about unusual animals: a horse that she insists is a dead uncle who has been reincarnated in *The Return of October;* a giant pet gorilla in the wondrous *Mighty Joe Young,* in which she gives her most charming performance; and a trained squirrel in *The Great Rupert.* From there she moved into more adult films. She gave her finest, most emotional performance as Shirley Booth's curious boarder in *Come Back, Little Sheba* (the animal was missing this time), earning a Best Supporting Actress Oscar nomination.

Few of her later films were as classy. She would end up in a lot of B westerns, but certainly her low point was as a waitress who finds her diner overrun by communists in *Shack Out on 101,* once a dud but today a camp classic. The picture opens with Moore being grabbed on the beach by Lee Marvin's lecherous Slob—a hilarious screen moment. Probably her most unusual adult role was as an innocent woman convicted of murder in *Why Must I Die?,* a poor man's *I Want to Live!*—one of her few films that is about *her* character rather than the lead actor's.

• **Cult Favorites:** *Gaslight* (1944, George Cukor), *Mighty Joe Young* (Ernest B. Schoedsack), *Shack Out on · 101* (1955, Edward Dein), *Platinum High School* (1960, Charles Haas).

• **Sleeper:** *Between Heaven and Hell* (1956, Richard Fleischer).

• **Other Key Films:** *The Return of October* (1948, Joseph H. Lewis), *The Great Rupert* (1950, Irving Pichel), *Gambling House* (1950, Ted Tetzlaff), *Come Back, Little Sheba* (1952, Daniel Mann), *Man on a Tightrope* (1953, Elia Kazan), *Beneath the 12 Mile Reef* (1953, Robert Webb), *King of the Khyber Rifles* (1953, Henry King), *Daddy Long Legs* (1955, Jean Negulesco), *Peyton Place* (1957, Mark Robson), *Why Must I Die?* (1960, Roy Del Ruth).

• **Also of Interest:** *The Sunny Side of the Street* (1951, Richard Quine), *Bernadine* (1957, Henry Levin), *A Private's Affair* (1959, Raoul Walsh), *Town Tamer* (1965, Lesley Selander), *Black Spurs* (1965, R. G. Springsteen), *Waco* (1966, Springsteen).

○

MANTAN MORELAND (1901–73) Short, friendly-looking black actor with a resemblance to Eddie Anderson. He played amusing character parts in Hollywood films, most notably chauffeur Birmingham Brown in the Charlie Chan series, and lead roles in "race" movies, some which featured his name in the title. He was very animated, changing his expression almost every time someone spoke to him or, in the black films, a woman demanded an explanation from him. He was known for his eyes, which would get so wide they would look like they were popping out of his face. He'd often do this when scared, while running in place at full speed.

• **Cult Favorites:** *The Palm Beach Story* (1942, Preston Sturges), *Tarzan's New York Adventure* (1942, Richard Thorpe), *Cabin in the Sky* (1943, Vincente Minnelli), *Spider Baby* (1964/68, Jack Hill), *The Comic* (1970, Carl Reiner), *Watermelon Man* (1970, Melvin Van Peebles).

• **Also of Interest:** *Harlem on the Prairie* (1939), *One Dark Night* (1939), *King of the Zombies* (1941, Jean Yarbrough), *Ellery Queen's Penthouse Mystery* (1941, James Hogan), *The Strange Cargo of Dr. Rx* (1942, William Nigh), *Footlight Serenade* (1942, Gregory Ratoff), *Eyes in the Night* (1942, Fred Zinnemann), *Charlie Chan in the Secret Service* (1944, Phil Rosen), *The Chinese Cat* (1944, Rosen), *The Scarlet Clue* (1945, Rosen), *Mantan Messes Up* (1946), *Mantan Runs for Mayor* (1946), *The Spider* (1946, Robert D. Webb), *The Chinese Ring* (1947, William Beaudine), The Feathered Serpent (1948, Beaudine), *Sky Dragon* (1949, Lesley Selander), *Enter Laughing* (1967, Reiner).

○

MICHÈLE MORGAN (1920–) France's most popular actress for more than three decades.

She was not used to best effect in her few Hollywood pictures—though she is quite appealing sacrificing herself for British flyers in *Joan of Paris* and opposite Bogart in *Passage to Marseilles*—and never achieved more than cult appreciation in America. Her alluring eyes, high cheekbones, but otherwise soft features made her face eerily beautiful—expressing intelligence and class, yet eroticism . . . like Deborah Kerr's. Opposite such French romantic idols as Jean Gabin (most notably in the classic *Port of Shadows*), Jean Marais, and Gérard Philipe, she played sympathetic heroines and femme fatales in melodramas, soap operas, costumers, and other pictures in which characters are driven by their hearts and/or greed and ambitions. In her best pictures, including those made in France, she was usually, according to David Shipman, "a remote, spiritual figure. She is serenely beautiful; her smile is sad without being heartbreaking; her emotions are rarely called into play. She is to a flesh-and-blood woman what a Turner painting of Venice is to Venice itself." Long a rival of Danielle Derrieux, she costarred with her in several films late in their careers. They were both murdered in *Landru.*

• **Key Films:** *Heart of Paris* (1937, Marc Allégret), *Port of Shadows* (1938, Marcel Carné), *Stormy Waters* (1940, Jean Grémillon), *Joan of Paris* (1942, Robert Stevenson), *The Heart of a Nation* (1940/43, Julien Duvivier), *Passage to Marseilles* (1944, Michael Curtiz), *La Symphonie Pastorale* (1946, Jean Delannoy), *The Fallen Idol* (1948, Carol Reed), *Le Château de Verre* (1950, René Clément), *The Proud and the Beautiful* (1953, Yves Allégret), *Napoléon* (1955, Sacha Guitry), *Les Grandes Manoevres* (1955, René Clair), *Marie Antoinette* (1956, Delannoy), *The*

Mirror Has Two Faces (1958, André Cayatte), *Landru/Bluebeard* (1962, Claude Chabrol), *Lost Command* (1966, Mark Robson), *Cat and Mouse* (1975, Claude LeLouch).

○

CATHY MORIARTY (1961–) This beautiful blonde from the Bronx, with a low voice and cool style, was 18 and hadn't ever acted before Martin Scorsese cast her as Vickie LaMotta in *Raging Bull,* opposite Robert De Niro as the forties middleweight boxing champion, Jake LaMotta. It was a difficult part because almost all of Vicki's reactions are dependent on the mood of her loving but brutal and jealous husband; the actress herself had to hold back and respond to each of De Niro's particular deliveries, many of them improvised. It also couldn't have been easy playing a woman who at times is tough enough to argue with her husband and risk abuse, yet at other times backs down because of his physical threats. And think of having to costar with the formidable De Niro in your debut! But she gave an excitingly natural performance, neither moving nor talking like a trained actress. Her second film was *Neighbors,* a black comedy in which she and Dan Aykroyd deliberately bring chaos to the life of staid married suburbanite John Belushi. This time she played an aggressor and was quite funny and sultry as she seduced both Belushi and, to aggravate him, his wife. However, critics attacked the film and everyone in it, and the promising actress dropped out of films for several years before giving another compelling performance in the strange *White of the Eye,* as an Arizona housewife who discovers that husband David Keith is an insane killer.

Cathy Moriarty, starring in Neighbors.

- **Cult Favorite:** *Raging Bull* (1980, Martin Scorsese).
- **Other Key Films:** *Neighbors* (1982, John G. Avildsen), *White of the Eye* (1987, David Cammell), *Soapdish* (1991, Michael Hoffman).

○

MICHAEL MORIARTY (1941–) After his exceptional performance as a Tom Seaver/Don Drysdale-like pitcher who takes care of the dying, simple-minded battery mate Robert De Niro in *Bang the Drum Slowly,* the best of baseball movies, this tall, handsome, blond actor—a cross between Jon Voight and Christopher Walken—seemed destined for superstardom. But his career stalled, probably because he was less in- terested in playing strong, romantic heroes than characters who were sensitive, mistake-prone, brittle at the core, unsure (as is evident in their shaky voices and hesitant deliveries), even cowardly. In *Report to the Commissioner,* he established his screen image: his rookie cop mistakenly kills undercover cop Susan Blakely, and then is trapped in an elevator with an armed criminal; he's pointing his own gun but is too scared to shoot. Once it became clear that he would never be a big star, Moriarty accepted roles in films far beneath his talent, including several low-budget horror films by Larry Cohen. In such movies he has had freedom to do anything he wants with his characters, acting like a baseball hurler trying out new pitches once a game's outcome has been decided. Sometimes he has been excitingly original, if mannered and out of place (and wasted), as in Cohen's *Q*, as an ex-druggie who demands a fortune from the city to reveal the whereabouts of a monster bird's nest. Unfortunately other performances seem to be out of rhythm with the films. He starred in the television series, *Law and Order*. He's also a jazz pianist and composer.

• **Cult Favorites:** *Bang the Drum Slowly* (1973, John Hancock), *The Last Detail* (1973, Hal Ashby), *Who'll Stop the Rain?* (1978, Karel Reisz), *Q* (1982, Larry Cohen).

• **Also of Interest:** *My Old Man's Place/Glory Boy* (1971, Edwin Sherin), *Report to the Commissioner* (1975, Milton Ketselas), *Pale Rider* (1985, Clint Eastwood), *The Stuff* (1985, Cohen), *It's Alive III: Island of the Alive* (1986, Cohen), *The Hanoi Hilton* (1987, Lionel Chetwynd).

○

ROBERT MORLEY (1908–) Plump, rosy-cheeked British character actor has brought charm and whimsy to films since the late thirties (and the theater since the late twenties). He has played a number of historical figures—from Louis XVI to W. S. Gilbert to Oscar Wilde—but more often has appeared in comedic roles, or at least they become funny once he inhabits them. Typically he plays quirky, cultured, bubbling-with-energy Britishers who are vain, critical, upbeat (they have a sick smile while they say unpleasant things), and love to eat and talk. His funniest character was the luckless cutthroat swindler in the unbalanced *Beat the Devil*—he does so well in witty repartee with partners Humphrey Bogart and Peter Lorre that

one doesn't even miss Sydney Greenstreet.

• **Cult Favorites:** *The African Queen* (1951, John Huston), *Beat the Devil* (1954, Huston), *The Loved One* (1965, Tony Richardson), *Theatre of Blood* (1973, Douglas Hickox).

• **Other Key Films:** *Marie Antoinette* (1938, W. S. Van Dyke), *Major Barbara* (1941, Gabriel Pascal), *Young Mr. Pitt* (1942, Carol Reed), *The Small Black Room* (1949, Michael Powell and Emeric Pressburger), *Outcast of the Islands* (1951, Reed), *The Story of Gilbert and Sullivan* (1953, Sidney Gilliat), *The Battle of the Sexes* (1960, Charles Crichton), *Oscar Wilde* (1960, Gregory Ratoff), *Murder at the Gallop* (1963, George Pollock), *Topkapi* (1964, Jules Dassin), *Of Human Bondage* (1964, Ken Hughes), *Those Magnificent Men in Their Flying Machines* (1965, Ken Annakin), *Hot Millions* (1968, Eric Till), *Who Is Killing the Great Chefs of Europe?* (1978, Ted Kotcheff).

○

VIC MORROW (1932–82) New York actor with dirty blond hair, a deep voice, and a handsome but puffy, unfriendly face debuted as the mean teenager who terrorizes teacher Glenn Ford's pregnant wife, Anne Francis, in *The Blackboard Jungle*. He would continue to play smart but poorly educated, slurring tough guys; some soldiers (he starred in the TV series "Combat") but mostly cocky, vicious villains. He looked natural in army fatigues and colored T-shirts, talking tough while a cigarette dangles from his lips. In *Hell's Five Hours*, he threatened to blow up several hostages. In *Portrait of a Mobster*, he was Dutch Schultz. Less extreme was his ruthless Little League coach in the comedy *The Bad News Bears;* his browbeaten pitcher son eventually stages a defiant protest against him on the mound, and audiences cheer Morrow's humiliation. Morrow was playing a bigot in *Twilight Zone—The Movie,* when he and two children were killed by a low-flying helicopter in a war sequence—a sad way to assure his lasting fame. He was the father of actress Jennifer Jason Leigh.

• **Cult Favorites:** *The Blackboard Jungle* (1955, Richard Brooks), *Dirty Mary Crazy Larry* (1974, John Hough), *Message from Space* (1978, Kinji Fukasaku).

• **Other Key Films:** *Tribute to a Bad Man* (1956, Robert Wise), *Men in War* (1957, Anthony Mann), *God's Little Acre* (1958, Mann), *Portrait of a Mobster* (1961, Joseph Pevney), *The Bad News Bears* (1976, Michael Ritchie), *Twilight Zone—The Movie* (1983, John Landis).

• **Also of Interest:** *Hell's Five Hours* (1958, Jack L. Copeland), *Cimarron* (1960, Mann), *Posse from Hell* (1961, Herbert Coleman), *Treasure of Matecumbe* (1976, Vincent McEveety).

○

COOKIE MUELLER (1949–89) One of John Waters's "Dreamland Girls," this heavily made-up blonde was impressive in minor parts in three of his pictures. In *Multiple Maniacs,* she was Divine's teenage daughter, who does a topless dance to "Jailhouse Rock" and talks about mixing sex and revolution. In *Pink Flamingos,* she spies on Divine's Babs Johnson for the Marbles, Babs's opponents in the "world's filthiest human being" contest. She is Divine's only high school friend in *Female Trouble,* which doesn't speak well for either of them. Mueller also had a bit in Eric

Mitchell's intentionally static takeoff on *Sunset Boulevard, Underground U.S.A.;* she also worked with underground filmmaker Amos Poe, modeled, and did some off-Broadway. Waters once claimed, "If she was handled right, she could become the New Wave Charo."

• **Cult Favorites:** *Multiple Maniacs* (1970, John Waters), *Pink Flamingos* (1972, Waters), *Female Trouble* (1974, Waters), *Underground U.S.A.* (1980, Eric Mitchell).

○

CAROLINE MUNRO (1951–) As a teen, she won a "Face of the Year" contest—if there had been a "Body of the Year" contest, she

Caroline Munro in At the Earth's Core.

undoubtedly would have won that too. This tall, shapely, dark-haired British sex siren is the fantasy cinema's most exciting pinup, with her near-nude photos (always her waist and hips are bare) adorning many teenage boys' walls. In the films themselves, she has been used as tantalizing decor. She played slave girls and barbarian maidens in bikini outfits who tag along on the heroes' journeys in such films as *Captain Kronos: Vampire Hunter* (in which she does her one topless scene), *The Golden Voyage of Sinbad,* and *At the Earth's Core.* Cast solely because of her looks in both *The Abominable Dr. Phibes* and *Dr. Phibes Rises Again,* she was Vincent Price's dead but well-preserved wife. In several horror films, her part called for a sexy female to be chased by a murderous madman. In the tasteless *Maniac,* she escapes being killed and scalped. She was a Bond girl in *The Spy Who Loved Me,* the villain's seductive, temptingly clad helicopter pilot. Rarely was she given a chance to act in movies. It was because of her appearance on posters and in commercials (she was the "Navy Rum" girl) that she became the only female signed to a Hammer Studios contract. A suggestive commercial she did for Noxzema was banned in the Bible Belt. Munro was raised in a convent.

• **Cult Favorites:** *The Abominable Dr. Phibes* (1971, Robert Fuest), *Captain Kronos: Vanpire Hunter* (1974, Brian Clemens), *The Golden Voyage of Sinbad* (1974, Gordon Hessler), *The Spy Who Loved Me* (1977, Lewis Gilbert), *Maniac* (1980, William Lustig).

• **Also of Interest:** *A Talent for Loving* (1969, Richard Quine), *Dr. Phibes Rises Again* (1972, Fuest), *Dracula A.D. 1972* (1972, Alan Gibson), *The Devil Within Her* (1975, Peter Sasdy), *At the Earth's Core* (1976, Kevin Connor), *Star Crash* (1979, Lewis Coates), *The Last Horror Film* (1984, David Winters), *Don't Open Until Christmas* (1985, Edmund Purdom), *Slaughter High* (1986, George Dugdale).

○

AUDIE MURPHY (1924–71) He was America's most decorated soldier in World War II, winning the Congressional Medal of Honor after being wounded three times and killing more than 240 Germans. He starred in only a few films about war, including John Huston's poetic adaptation of Stephen Crane's Civil War classic, *The Red Badge of Courage,* and *To Hell and Back,* an exciting adaptation of Murphy's autobiography. Instead, he became a major figure of the dying B western. He may have made *Life*'s cover in 1945, but he looked young and wholesome enough to have been a Norman Rockwell cover boy for *Boy's Life.* As part of the juvenile delinquent movie trend, he played "Kid" outlaws (Billy the Kid, the young Jesse James, *The Cimarron Kid*) until he was almost 30. His later westerners were still at odds with the system. He played gunslingers who may or may not reform (in the unusual *No Name on the Bullet,* he is a hired assassin); decent men who break the law in order to exact revenge; or white men who take the side of mistreated Indians. He was short, soft-spoken, and polite, but because he was quick and accurate with a gun, and had a determined, nononsense, fearless expression, he was quite formidable. Even without formal training, Murphy had poise and confidence, and his westerns were quite agreeable, mixing action, romance, and, in films like *Destry,* comedy. Offscreen, Murphy had a troubled life, partly because he never adapted to civilian ways. Once he was tried for attempted murder. He was killed in a plane crash at the age of 46.

• **Cult Favorites:** *The Red Badge of Courage* (1951, John Huston), *A Time for Dying* (1971, Budd Boetticher).

• **Also Recommended:** *Sierra* (1950, Alfred E. Green), *The Kid from Texas* (1950, Kurt Neumann), *The Cimarron Kid* (1951, Boetticher), *Gunsmoke* (1953, Nathan Juran), *Tumbleweed* (1953, Juran), *Ride Clear at Diablo* (1954, Jesse Hibbs), *Destry* (1954, George Marshall), *To Hell and Back* (1955, Hibbs), *Walk the Proud Land* (1956, Hibbs), *The Guns at Fort Petticoat* (1957, Marshall), *Night Passage* (1957, James Neilson), *The Quiet American* (1958, Joseph L. Mankiewicz), *Ride a Crooked Trail* (1958, Hibbs), *No Name on the Bullet* (1959, Jack Arnold), *Hell Bent for Leather* (1960, George Sherman), *The Unforgiven* (1960, Huston), *Seven Ways from Sundown* (1960, Harry Keller), *Bullet for a Badman* (1964, R. G. Springsteen), *Apache Rifles* (1964, William Witney), *Arizona Raiders* (1965, Witney).

• **Also of Interest:** *Bad Boy* (1949, Neumann), *Kansas Raiders* (1950, Ray Enright), *The Duel at Silver Creek* (1952, Don Siegel), *Column South* (1953, Frederick de Cordova), *Tumbleweed* (1953, Juran), *Drums Across the River* (1954, Juran), *World in My Corner* (1956, Hibbs), *The Gun Runners* (1958, Siegel), *The Wild and the Innocent* (1959, Jack Sher), *Cast a Long Shadow* (1959, Thomas Carr), *Posse from Hell* (1961, Herbert Coleman).

○

MICHAEL MURPHY (1949–) Tall, handsome, amusing actor, a favorite of Robert Altman and other cult directors. He has the looks to be a heroic leading man—his detective in *Brewster McCloud* wears blue contacts that make him look like Steve McQueen— but he typically plays flawed, spineless men. With their ingratiating smiles and cool manners, they pretend to be sincere and sensitive, engage in polite conversation in which they trade quips and feign interest in those they speak with, and constantly try to get these people to do them favors. Well-dressed worms. They will betray their wives (e.g., Jill Clayburgh in *An Unmarried Woman*) or best friends (e.g., Woody Allen in *Manhattan*), yet not understand why they aren't forgiven. To get what they want, they sell out and hurt people, yet think no less of themselves. They are disappointments to others and, when things invariably backfire, losers— like his presidential candidate, Tanner, on cable TV.

• **Cult Favorites:** *Count Yorga, Vampire* (1970, Bob Kelljan), *Brewster McCloud* (1970, Robert Altman), *McCabe and Mrs. Miller* (1971, Altman), *Phase IV* (1974, Saul Bass), *Nashville* (1975, Altman), *Manhattan* (1979, Woody Allen), *Strange Behavior/Dead Kids* (1981, Michael Laughlin), *The Year of Living Dangerously* (1983, Peter Weir), *Salvador* (1986, Oliver Stone).

• **Other Key Films:** *The Front* (1976, Martin Ritt), *An Unmarried Woman* (1978, Paul Mazursky).

• **Also of Interest:** *That Cold Day in the Park* (1969, Altman), *What's Up, Doc?* (1972, Peter Bogdanovich), *The Great Bank Hoax* (1977, Joseph Jacoby), *Cloak & Dagger* (1984, Richard Franklin).

○

GEORGE NADER (1921–) Tall, dark, handsome, and muscular but the type of dull, stiff leading man you're more likely to find in bad summer stock than Hollywood. His otherwise shaky position as a cult movie star was secured when he was top-billed in the junky science-fiction film, *Robot Monster,* where he tries to protect an obnoxious family from the dreaded calcinator death ray being used by an alien in a gorilla costume and diver's mask. My favorite scene: slightly injured, he runs a marathon over hill and dale and then, after this great effort, drops dead. He appeared in many trivial action, adventure, and horror films, but as far as I'm concerned, that was his highlight. His most interesting film, however, was probably *Flood Tide,* in which he played an innocent man accused of murder. Nader was a familiar face on television in the late fifties, appearing in numerous anthology series and starring in "Man and the Challenge" and "The Adventures of Ellery Queen."

• **Cult Favorite:** *Robot Monster* (1953, Phil Tucker).

• **Also of Interest:** *Four Guns to the Border* (1954, Richard Carlson), *Lady Godiva* (1955, Arthur Lubin), *Away All Boats* (1956, Joseph Pevney), *The Unguarded Moment* (1956, Harry Keller), *Four Girls in Town* (1956, Jack Sher), *The Female Animal* (1958, Keller), *The Secret Mark of D'Artagnan* (1962, Siro Marcellini), *The Human Duplicators* (1965, Hugo Grimaldi), *The Million Eyes of Su-Muru* (1967, Lindsay Shonteff), *House of 1,000 Dolls* (1967, Jeremy Summers), *Beyond Atlantis* (1973, Eddie Romero).

○

JOHN/JACK NANCE The star of the midnight movie classic *Eraserhead.* As Henry Spencer, strange inhabitant of a nightmare world or a postapocalyptic age, he dresses like a creep and has electrified hair that makes him look like a fraternity house

reject and the worst blind date imaginable. And he has an unpleasant personality to boot. We start out fearing that his monstrous-looking newborn baby will kill him, but we eventually fear this cad will turn on the crying baby and take over the "monster" role. Our "hero" loses all our sympathy. This one film established him as an icon of the weird cinema. Without his wired hair, he's been hard to immediately recognize in smaller parts in his more recent films and David Lynch's TV series "Twin Peaks."

• **Cult Favorites:** *Eraserhead* (1978, David Lynch), *Hammett* (1982, Wim Wenders), *Dune* (1984, Lynch), *Blue Velvet* (1986, Lynch), *Wild at Heart* (1990, Lynch).

• **Also of Interest:** *Ghoulies* (1985, Luca Bercovici), *Barfly* (1987, Barbet Schroeder).

○

CHARLES NAPIER Rugged blond actor with a square jaw seems to have stepped out of the pages of a comic book—like a Steve Canyon or Dick Tracy. With puffy cheeks, creviced face, and a long, askew smile, he resembles a caricature of a handsome leading man. Russ Meyer, who said Napier had the rare ability to be "smiling on one side of the mouth and sneering on the other," wisely shot him at odd angles. Alternately tough and funny as the corrupt desert sheriff in *Cherry, Harry and Raquel,* his best Meyer film, he's Meyer's only male star to have had any degree of success after moving on. He was amusing as the two-timing, bigamist truck driver in *Handle with Care,* but has since found a home in action pictures, giving sturdy performances as cops, military men, and, in *The Last Embrace,* a government assassin. He dared to double-cross Sylvester

Stallone in *Rambo: First Blood Part II*. He still doesn't look like a hero but occasionally gets to play them in low-budget films.

• **Cult Favorites:** *Cherry, Harry and Raquel* (1969, Russ Meyer), *Beyond the Valley of the Dolls* (1970, Meyer), *Supervixens* (1975, Meyer), *Handle with Care/Citizens Band* (1977, Jonathan Demme), *The Last Embrace* (1979, Demme).

• **Also of Interest:** *Rambo: First Blood Part II* (1985, George P. Cosmatos), *Instant Justice* (1986, Craig T. Rumar), *Night Stalker* (1987, Max Kleven), *Deep Space* (1988, Fred Olen Ray), *The Silence of the Lambs* (1991, Demme).

○

PAUL NASCHY (1936–) A short, stout ex-weightlifter, with dark features, long sideburns, a sharp nose, and an unremarkable, somewhat pudgy face, he became Spain's greatest horror movie star. His films, which he usually wrote (as Jacinto Molina), are distinguished by extreme violence and gore, nudity and sexual content, hand-to-hand fights to the death, torture (characters are often chained to dungeon walls), exotic location shooting, and wild plot intrusions that are alternately ludicrous and imaginative. He played Dracula—his brutal but sympathetic, lovesick vampire commits suicide—and Jack the Ripper, but he is best known for the recurring role of the Lawrence Talbot–influenced werewolf, Waldemar Daninski. The sympathetic Pole, who in most films is attacked by a werewolf and becomes one himself, covets death but keeps being revived, once by doctors who remove silver bullets from his heart in an operation, another time by his girlfriend, who mixes her blood with serum from a rare flower (supposedly ending his curse). But it's a good thing he's around, because he kills bad guys and spends many films chasing after evil vampires, including Elizabeth Bathory. His werewolf walks on two legs, is covered by dark, thick hair—his mask is unconvincing—and has long, pearly white fangs. Oddly, he fights somewhat like a boxer, with his arm shooting out like a jab and his paw almost punching the victim in the neck—only then his claws slash the guy's throat. In America, it's hard to evaluate Naschy's films because they play only in horribly dubbed, badly cut versions.

• **Cult Favorite:** *La Marca del Hombre Lobo/Frankenstein's Bloody Terror* (1968, Enrique L. Eguilez).

• **Other Key Films:** *The Nights of the Werewolf* (1968, René Govar), *La Noche de Walpurgis/The Werewolf vs. the Vampire Woman* (1970, Leon Klimovsky), *Dracula vs. Frankenstein/Assignment Terror* (1970, Tulio Demicheli and Hugo Fregonese), *Fury of the Wolfman* (1970, Jose Maria Zabalza), *Dr. Jekyll and the Wolfman* (1971, Klimovsky), *Dracula's Greatest Love/Vampire Playgirls* (1972, Javier Aguirre), *Horror Rises from the Tomb* (1972, Carlos Aured), *House of the Psychotic Women* (1972, Aured), *Hunchback of the Morgue* (1972, Aguirre), *The Mummy's Revenge* (1973, Aured), *El Retorno de Walpurgis/Curse of the Devil* (1973, Aured), *Night of the Howling Beast/Horror of the Werewolf* (1975, M. I. Bonns), *The People Who Own the Dark* (1975, Klimovsky), *Inquisition* (1976, Paul Naschy), *Human Beasts* (1980, Naschy), *Howl of the Devil* (1987, Naschy).

○

FRANCESCA "KITTEN" NATIVIDAD An erotic dancer and the winner of several nude beauty pageants (what is "Miss Nude

Cosmopolitan"?), she attracted the attention of bosom-mad Russ Meyer. She became his girlfriend and, with good humor, appeared in *Up!* and *Beneath the Valley of the Ultra-vixens,* convincingly playing a cheery nympho. Meyer shot her enormous breasts from a variety of angles. Her sex scenes are hard and kinky, the closest Meyer has come to being pornographic. Later, Kitten would exploit herself in non-Meyer films, including the nude exercise tape, *Eroticism.* In the appropriately titled *Titillation,* she played the only female character whose breasts are so large they need a specially designed bra. In *Takin' It All Off,* she played Betty Boopers.

• **Cult Favorites:** *Up!* (1979, Russ Meyer), *Beneath the Valley of the Ultra-vixens* (1979, Meyer).

• **Also of Interest:** *Titillation* (1982, Damon Christian), *Sizzle* (1982, Chris Tyner), *The Bodacious Ta Ta* (1983), *The Tomb* (1986, Fred Olen Ray), *Takin' It All Off* (1988).

○

TOM NEAL (1914–72) Muscular, often mustached, action-geared actor was an aviator who romances Frances Gifford's Nyoka in the popular serial *Jungle Girl;* eight years later, he played the title character in

Tom Neal (left) *plays a loser in* Detour.

another serial, *Bruce Gentry—Daredevil of the Skies*. Otherwise the lone highlight of his movie career was playing the hard-lucked loser who takes a road to destruction in Edgar G. Ulmer's despairing noir classic, *Detour*. Its legend (and Neal's, too) has grown considerably in recent years as some major critics have called it the best low-budget film ever made. It has also been called the definitive example of fatalistic cinema, yet if you look at it closely you'll see that while Neal's character, Al Roberts, claims that "fate" is responsible for his demise, the foolish fellow clearly initiates his own fall. He steals the clothes and wallet of a dead man and dumps him on the side of the road, thinking he will be wrongly convicted of murdering him; he wears striped pajamas that look like prison garb; he picks up Ann Savage's cold-hearted hitchhiker although he should be keeping a low profile; and he allows himself to be dominated by her and drawn into her schemes. At the end he is arrested for having accidentally killed her when she tried to squeal on him. In his own life, Neal was equally self-destructive. His movie career came to an end when he beat up Franchot Tone for dating his fiancée, actress Barbara Payton. Tone married Payton but soon divorced her for having an affair with Neal; she explained her continuing attraction to Neal in *Confidential*: "He had a chemical buzz that sent red peppers down my thighs." In 1965, in a troubled marriage characterized by infidelity and jealous rage, Neal killed his wife with the automatic Luger he had used in a 1951 play. He was convicted of manslaughter and served six years in prison. Eighteen months after his release, he died of a heart attack. Tom Neal, Jr., starred in the remake of *Detour*.

• **Cult Favorites:** *Jungle Girl* (1941 serial, William Witney and John English), *Detour* (1946, Edgar G. Ulmer).

• **Also of Interest:** *Courageous Dr. Christian* (1940, Bernard Vorhaus), *Ten Gentlemen from West Point* (1942, Henry Hathaway), *Flying Tigers* (1942, David Miller), *First Yank in Tokyo* (1945, Gordon Douglas), *Club Havana* (1945, Ulmer), *Bruce Gentry—Daredevil of the Skies* (1949, serial, Spencer Bennet and Thomas Carr).

○

FRANCO NERO (1942–) Extremely handsome, virile, often mustached Italian leading man. He has played several romantic leads in English-language films, including Lancelot in *Camelot*, the dashing gypsy in *The Virgin and the Gypsy*, and the cinema's greatest lover in the television film *The Legend of Valentino*. However, his cult reputation is based on his male-geared European films. He is the title character, a brutal, quick-on-the-draw drifter-mercenary, in the popular "Django" spaghetti-western series, and has starred in other equally violent Italian westerns, some skillfully directed by Sergio Corbucci. He also had an international hit as the lead in *Enter the Ninja*, testing his martial-arts skills against Sho Kosugi and villain Christopher George in the first of the successful "Ninja" series. In Rainer Werner Fassbinder's final film, *Querelle*, Nero played the character who most diverged from his image: a ship captain who is a latent homosexual. As usual, Nero was better than the material.

• **Cult Favorites:** *Django* (1965, Sergio Corbucci), *The Mercenary* (1968, Corbucci), *Enter the Ninja* (1981, Menahem Golan), *Kamikaze '89* (1982, Wolf

Gremm), *Querelle* (1982, Rainer Werner Fassbinder).

• **Sleeper:** *The Man with Bogart's Face* (1980, Robert Day).

• **Other Key Films:** *Camelot* (1967, Joshua Logan), *A Professional Gun* (1968, Corbucci), *Sardine: Kidnapped* (1968, Gianfranco Mingozzi), *Tristana* (1970, Luis Buñuel), *The Virgin and the Gypsy* (1970, Christopher Miles), *Compañeros* (1971, Corbucci), *Confessions of a Police Captain* (1971, Damiano Damiani), *High Crime* (1973, Enzo G. Castellari), *Django—Il Grande Ritorno* (1977), *The Salamander* (1981, Peter Zinner), *Django 2—The Big Comeback* (1987, Ted Archer/Nello Rossati).

○

NICHOLAS BROTHERS The acrobatic tap duets by Fayard (1917–) and Harold (1924–) Nicholas were as astonishing as the most spectacular dance routines of Fred Astaire and Gene Kelly. However, since they were black entertainers, they were restricted to specialty numbers in Hollywood films and never achieved the great fame they deserved. In fact, few cinema history books even mention them. Although they each made several solo appearances, they were the best dance team in movie history. They began as a child act in vaudeville and, beginning in 1932, became headliners at the Cotton Club. They performed on Broadway in *The Ziegfeld Follies of 1936* and *Babes in Arms,* which was choreographed by George Balanchine. From the start they had amazing speed and precision, and experimented with unusual rhythms and choreography; they would later perfect their high-altitude splits. Their first short film was *Pie Pie Blackbird* in 1932; in 1934, they danced with Eddie Cantor in his *Kid Millions* and

stole the spotlight, as they would always do as adults in their forties films. Their most spectacular number was "Jim Jam Jumpin' Jive" with Cab Calloway and his orchestra in the all-black musical *Stormy Weather.* It's hard not to gasp as they tap up and down a huge staircase, leap over and slide under one another, do splits both six feet off the floor and as they land on the steps and stage. They never stop smiling and they never seem tired. They were equally exuberant and elegant in their mind-boggling performance of "Chattanooga Choo Choo" with Harold's one-time wife Dorothy Dandridge and Glenn Miller in *Sun Valley Serenade,* and "I've Got a Gal in Kalamazoo" with Miller in *Orchestra Wives.* Gene Kelly, who was never afraid of being upstaged, teamed with the Nicholas Brothers for "Be a Clown," a humorous dance-acrobatic routine in *The Pirate.* But where Kelly would go on to make many movie musicals, the equally talented Nicholas Brothers drifted off into relative obscurity. Overdue recognition of the brother team has been sparked by a renewed interest in tap. Harold appeared alone in Gregory Hines's tribute, *Tap,* and acted as well as danced.

• **Cult Favorites:** *Stormy Weather* (1943, Andrew L. Stone), *The Pirate* (1948, Vincente Minnelli).

• **Other Key Films:** *Kid Millions* (1934, Roy Del Ruth), *The Big Broadcast of 1936* (1935, Norman Taurog), *Tin Pan Alley* (1940, Walter Lang), *Down Argentine Way* (1940, Irving Cummings), *Orchestra Wives* (1942, Archie Mayo).

○

BARBARA NICHOLS (1929–76) Likable, pretty but slightly plump New York character actress who specialized in loud, dumb blondes. She played floozies, exotic dancers (she was a former stripper), and gun molls. Some are quite funny and in control of their lives, and others, as in *Sweet Smell of Success,* are pathetic victims. One of my favorite Nichols roles is Lola, a hilarious erotic swimmer (who performs in a tank in a club), in *Where the Boys Are.* A typical Lola line: "I think that's a stinking shame." Nichols appeared in many television shows, most memorably in the "Room for One More" episode (titled "Twenty-Two") of "The Twilight Zone," and as Jack Benny's unimpressive and unimpressed blind date on his comedy show.

• **Cult Favorites:** *Sweet Smell of Success* (1957, Alexander Mackendrick), *Where the Boys Are* (1960, Henry Levin), *The Loved One* (1965, Tony Richardson).

• **Other Key Films:** *Beyond a Reasonable Doubt* (1956, Fritz Lang), *The King and Four Queens* (1956, Raoul Walsh), *The Pajama Game* (1957, George Abbott and Stanley Donen), *Pal Joey* (1957, George Sidney), *Ten North Frederick* (1958, Philip Dunne), *The Naked and the Dead* (1958, Walsh), *Woman Obsessed* (1959, Henry Hathaway), *That Kind of Woman* (1959, Sidney Lumet), *Who Was That Lady?* (1960, Sidney), *The George Raft Story* (1962, Joseph M. Newman), *House of Women* (1962, Walter Doniger), *The Disorderly Orderly* (1964, Frank Tashlin).

○

KELLY NICHOLS Perhaps the best actress ever in the porno field, this pretty brunette, with a slim figure and large, sensual eyes, always managed to make viewers care about her characters, even if they were initially interested only in seeing sex. She starred often for Chuck Vincent in his attempts to make crossover sex films—X-rated but suitable for the mass adult audience. Her sex sequences were erotic rather than raunchy and seemed more part of real, exciting women's lives than scenes staged for the camera. She usually played passionate women who looked for the right permanent partner. She has the talent to get roles in mainstream films and deserved better than to be a victim in *The Toolbox Murders.*

• **Cult Favorite:** *Roommates* (1982, Chuck Vincent).

• **Other Key Films:** *That Lucky Stiff* (1979, Vincent), *Bon Appétit* (1980, Vincent), *In Love* (1983, Vincent), *Puss 'N Boots* (1983, Vincent).

• **Also of Interest:** *Games Women Play* (1980, Vincent), *Society Affair* (1982, Robert MacCallum), *The Mistress* (1983, Jack Remy).

○

JACK NICHOLSON (1937–) B-movie fans discovered him first, in unsavory biker films and Roger Corman's *The Cry Baby Killer* (his first lead), gothic horrors, and *The Little Shop of Horrors,* doing a hilarious bit as a masochistic dental patient. He already had his distinct nasally voice and mad, Cheshire-cat grin. He costarred in and coproduced Monte Hellman's terrific existential westerns, *The Shooting* (playing a sadistic gunman) and *Ride in the Whirlwind,* but distribution was nonexistent. His breakthrough was *Easy Rider,* hitching with Dennis Hopper and Peter Fonda, as a southern ACLU lawyer—talking sensibly one minute about America's hostility toward people who really want freedom, and talking nonsense about Venusians the next. He followed this odd character with another cultural misfit in *Five Easy Pieces:* he was once rich and played classical piano, now he works on an oil rig, is

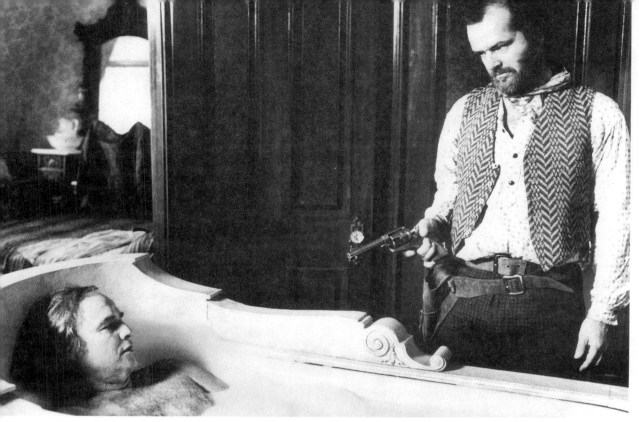

Jack Nicholson (right) *and Marlon Brando in Arthur Penn's quirky, almost forgotten western,* The Missouri Breaks.

attached to ignorant, country-singing waitress Karen Black, and again has wanderlust. Everyone aggravates him, including a complaining female hitchhiker, a stubborn coffee-shop waitress who won't serve him what he wants (Nicholson's first widely seen "blow-up" scene), and the pregnant Black, whom he loves but abandons. In *Carnal Knowledge,* he again takes out his rage on the woman who wants to tie him down, this time Ann-Margret—his second classic "blow-up"—and again ends up alone and pathetic. He smiled in later films and used his sarcasm and condescending tone, but we always waited for his scary explosions. He explodes in *One Flew Over the Cuckoo's Nest,* and again it is his cry for independence, but this time we fully sympathize because he is a mental patient revolting against a Big Nurse who crushes individualism as deliberately as Big Brother. His McMurphy is a nice-guy version of his madman in *The Shining,* even using the same expressions. In future films his outsider either challenges oppressive forces, as does his detective in *Chinatown,* or employs his madman routine to control or terrorize people—he'd play the devil in *The Witches of Eastwick.* This great, thrilling actor always surprises you, whether killing the wife he loves in *Prizzi's Honor* or turning out to be a good, considerate guy and making us cry in *Terms of Endearment.* We constantly wonder what goes on in his head.

• **Cult Favorites:** *The Little Shop of Horrors*

(1960, Roger Corman), *The Terror* (1963, Corman), *The Shooting* (1967, Monte Hellman), *Ride in the Whirlwind* (1967, Hellman), *Hell's Angels on Wheels* (1967, Richard Rush), *The St. Valentine's Day Massacre* (1967, Corman), *Psych-Out* (1968, Rush), *Head* (1968, Bob Rafelson), *Easy Rider* (1969, Dennis Hopper), *Five Easy Pieces* (1970, Rafelson), *Carnal Knowledge* (1971, Mike Nichols), *The King of Marvin Gardens* (1972, Rafelson), *The Last Detail* (1973, Hal Ashby), *Chinatown* (1974, Roman Polanski), *Tommy* (1975, Ken Russell), *The Passenger* (1975, Michelangelo Antonioni), *One Flew Over the Cuckoo's Nest* (1975, Milos Foreman), *The Missouri Breaks* (1976, Arthur Penn), *Goin' South* (1978, Jack Nicholson), *The Shining* (1979, Stanley Kubrick).

• **Other Key Films:** *The Last Tycoon* (1976, Elia Kazan), *The Postman Always Rings Twice* (1981, Rafelson), *Reds* (1981, Warren Beatty), *Terms of Endearment* (1983, James L. Brooks), *Prizzi's Honor* (1985, John Huston), *Heartburn* (1986, Nichols), *Broadcast News* (1987, Brooks), *The Witches of Eastwick* (1987, George Miller), *Batman* (1989, Tim Burton), *The Two Jakes* (1990, Nicholson).

○

BRIGITTE NIELSEN (1963–) A statuesque sex symbol for the pinup set, this Danish actress is often paired with muscular, masculine leading men—Sylvester Stallone, Arnold Schwarzenegger—in sweaty action films. She played the title character in the sword-and-sorcery clinker *Red Sonja*, but even with passable talent, she is most often used for decoration. Not very likable (she'll never be a Will Rogers Foundation spokesperson), she was well cast as a sleek villainess in the otherwise unwatchable

Brigitte Nielsen battles Sandahl Bergman in Red Sonja.

Beverly Hills Cop II. Her well-publicized romance with obnoxious football player Mark Gastineau caused much nausea.

• **Key Films:** *Rocky IV* (1985, Sylvester Stallone), *Red Sonja* (1985, Richard Fleischer), *Cobra* (1986, George Cosmatos), *Beverly Hills Cop II* (1987, Tony Scott), *Domino* (1989, Ivana Massetti).

○

LESLIE NIELSEN (1925–) Nielsen earned his cult stripes as Captain Adams, the dull romantic lead of *Forbidden Planet*. He was stiff from his space shoes to his well-groomed head as he won virgin Anne Francis's kisses and convinced her jealous father, Walter Pidgeon's Dr. Morbius, to reject his Id Monster. For more than 25 years, Nielsen played secondary roles (usually as professionals) in dramatic movies and on television without ever revealing any particular talent or sense of humor. Then he was inspiringly cast as the doctor in the screwy movie spoof *Airplane!*, and displayed a hilarious gift for comedy, including the ability to deliver the most ridiculous lines with a straight face. That film's three writer-directors would cast Nielsen as the intrepid Detective Frank Drebin in their riotous, innovative cult TV series, "Police Squad!," allowing Nielsen to perfect his deadpan style as well as be at the center of their absurd sight gags. The series would last only six weeks in 1982, but in 1988, Drebin would be resurrected in the team's so-stupid-it's-funny film, *The Naked Gun*. He gamely did every absurd bit of action asked of him, including a scene in which the singing, sighing Drebin relieves himself in the men's room, unaware that he's hooked up to a television microphone. Obviously having a good time, the handsome, silver-haired Nielsen energetically carried the film to tremendous commercial success and established himself as one of cinema's funniest actors—which *Forbidden Planet* addicts would have thought an impossibility.

• **Cult Favorites:** *Forbidden Planet* (1956, Fred McLeod Wilcox), *The Poseidon Adventure* (1972, Ronald Neame), *Airplane!* (1980, Jim Abrahams, David Zucker, and Jerry Zucker).

• **Other Key Films:** *Creepshow* (1982, George Romero), *The Naked Gun* (1988, D. Zucker), *The Naked Gun 2½: The Smell of Fear* (1991, D. Zucker).

• **Also of Interest:** *The Resurrection of Zachary Wheeler* (1971, Bob Wynn), *Prom Night* (1980, Paul Lynch), *Nightstick* (1987, Joseph L. Scanlon), *Repossessed* (1990, Bob Logan).

Leslie Nielsen's Lt. Frank Drebin becomes acquainted with the Queen of England in The Naked Gun: From the Files of Police Squad.

○

CHUCK NORRIS (1939–) Blond, often bearded former martial-arts champion started his movie career merely as a combat foe to Bruce Lee, but went on to become one of the world's top action stars. He frequently overstated his importance, claiming he was out to fill a hero void for America's youngsters—but this "role model" has starred in films that contain much bloody violence and many R-rated sex scenes, and which are, in many instances, racist. Hoping to come across as a subtle action hero like Steve McQueen or Gary Cooper, he has told scriptwriters to give him as little dialogue as possible; when he does talk, he is barely audible. In his earliest films, he let his hands and feet do the talking; in later films, his characters use weapons as well as engage in hand-to-hand combat. To be fair, a couple of his martial-arts films—*A Force of One* and *The Octagon*—are relatively exciting, and he is a strong hero despite obvious acting limitations (he is emotionless) and lack of charisma. Moreover, he deserved the good reviews he got as an incorruptible Chicago policeman in *Code of Silence,* a non–martial-arts picture that is definitely his best film to date. However, those films in which he is the standard bearer for America's right, including his blood-thirsty *Missing in Action* films about rescuing MIAs in Vietnam, are truly reprehensible and irresponsible. After seeing those racist films, it's satisfying to watch Bruce Lee brutally kill Norris's villain in the Rome Colosseum in the thrilling fight that climaxes *Return of the Dragon.*

• **Cult Favorites:** *Return of the Dragon* (1973, Bruce Lee), *Force of One* (1979, Paul Aaron), *Good Guys Wear Black* (1979, Ted Post), *The Octagon* (1980, Eric Kar-son), *Game of Death* (1980, Robert Clouse), *Eye for an Eye* (1981, Steve Carver), *Lone Wolf McQuade* (1983, Carver), *Missing in Action* (1984, Joseph Zito), *Missing in Action 2: The Beginning* (1985, Lance Hool), *Invasion U.S.A.* (1985, Zito).

• **Sleepers:** *Silent Rage* (1982, Michael Miller), *Code of Silence* (1985, Andy Davis).

• **Also of Interest:** *Forced Vengeance* (1982, James Fargo), *The Delta Force* (1986, Menahem Golan), *Braddock: Missing in Action III* (1987, Aaron Norris), *Delta Force 2* (1990, A. Norris).

○

JACK NORTON (1889–1958) Middle-aged character actor who appeared in about 100 movies, most of them comedies in which his name was way down in the credits. He played essentially one role: an amiable drunk, a role he perfected in vaudeville. If a film had a saloon, a bar on a train, or a party scene, and a little humor was needed, the call went out for Norton. Well dressed, well groomed, with a neat mustache, he stood on wobbly legs, a highball in his hand, talking nonsense with the likes of Bette Davis, W. C. Fields, or assorted characters in Preston Sturges films. One could tell that he'd remember nothing in the morning—and upset by his loss of memory, he'd head for the nearest bar. In real life, Norton was a teetotaler.

• **Cult Favorites:** *Marked Woman* (1937, Lloyd Bacon), *The Bank Dick* (1940, Eddie Cline), *The Palm Beach Story* (1942, Preston Sturges), *Hail the Conquering Hero* (1944, Sturges).

• **Also of Interest:** *Cockeyed Cavaliers* (1934, Mark Sandrich), *The Farmer's Daughter* (1940, H. C. Potter), *Louisiana*

Kim Novak with Fred MacMurray in Pushover.

Purchase (1941, Irving Cummings), *The Fleet's In* (1942, Victor Schertzinger), *The Spoilers* (1942, Ray Enright), *Wonder Man* (1945, H. Bruce Humberstone), *The Kid from Brooklyn* (1946, Norman Z. McLeod), *Blue Skies* (1946, Stuart Heisler), *The Sin of Harold Diddlebock/Mad Wednesday* (1947/50, Sturges).

○

KIM NOVAK (1933–) This icy blond beauty toured the country as, appropriately, "Miss Deepfreeze," demonstrating refrigerators, before breaking into films. Hoping to find a replacement for troublesome Rita Hay-worth, Columbia's dictatorial Harry Cohn thrust Novak into the limelight too quickly for her to adjust to the demands of being a Hollywood star. Moviegoers were attracted to the mysterious newcomer who sent a mixed message of extreme coolness and thrilling sensuality. But she was stung by critical barbs and constantly worried that her beauty and much-publicized 37-23-37 figure weren't enough to compensate for her lack of acting experience. It surely wasn't reassuring that Cohn boasted he, rather than Novak herself, was responsible for her becoming a star. She was so frightened that each day when filming *Picnic*—the picture that would make her the top box-office star—she went to a church to pray that she would be adequate in the next day's shooting. No wonder she was attracted to *Jeanne Eagles* and the fictional *The Legend of Lylah Clare,* films about other tormented actresses. Novak's vulnerability—the major reason females always liked her—certainly came into play in her role as a southern girl in *Picnic* (although in real life she always seemed even more vulnerable than her women), as did her sexual aggressiveness (her blazing-hot "mating" dance to "Moonglow" with an entranced William Holden is a classic). But it wasn't until *Jeanne Eagles;* the quirky comedy *Bell, Book, and Candle,* in which she played a witch who wants to be human; and her most famous film, *Vertigo,* in which she played both the haunting, suicidal Madeleine and sweet, tarty Judy, that her mysterious, ethereal quality was exploited. Novak never seemed comfortable in Hollywood and in front of the cameras, and she was at her best when her sensual, vulnerable characters were also out of synch with their worlds. Judy, who is made over by an obsessed Jimmy Stewart to look like the dead Madeleine, just as Cohn groomed Novak to be a star, is the Novak character who best represents the actress as her fans conceived her: shaky, passive, unformed, using a false identity (as do all actors), vulnerable, sexy, trying hard to impress, and, in on a plot to deceive Stewart, definitely involved in something that is way over her head. She is, most of all, enigmatic. More than any other star, with the possible exception of Marilyn Monroe, Novak gave viewers the impression that much was going on beneath the surface. We sensed she was deeply unhappy and were glad that she finally fled Hollywood before she became another of its victims.

• **Cult Favorites:** *Five Against the House* (1955, Phil Karlson), *Jeanne Eagles* (1957,

George Sidney), *Vertigo* (1958, Alfred Hitchcock), *Bell, Book, and Candle* (1958, Richard Quine), *Kiss Me, Stupid* (1964, Billy Wilder), *The Legend of Lylah Clare* (1968, Robert Aldrich), *Just a Gigolo* (1979, David Hemmings).

• **Other Key Films:** *Pushover* (1954, Quine), *Phffft!* (1954, Mark Robson), *The Man with the Golden Arm* (1955, Otto Preminger), *The Eddy Duchin Story* (1956, Sidney), *Pal Joey* (1957, Sidney), *Of Human Bondage* (1964, Ken Hughes), *The Amorous Adventures of Moll Flanders* (1965, Terence Young).

• **Also of Interest:** *Middle of the Night* (1959, Delbert Mann), *Strangers When We Meet* (1960, Quine), *The Notorious Landlady* (1962, Quine).

○

N!XAU The bushman's answer to Buster Keaton. He was discovered in the Central Kalahari Reserve in Botswana when South African director Jamie Uys was searching for someone authentic to star in the slapstick-satire *The Gods Must Be Crazy,* as Xi (XiCo), a bushman making his first visit to civilization and encountering a weird assortment of black and white "gods" who, in his eyes, all act crazy. N!xau was well cast, because his nomadic hunter-gatherer band had never left the secluded regions of the Kalahari and he had met only one white person prior to Uys. He agreed to be in the movie and fly off to acting stints over a two-year period simply because he was a nice guy who would never turn down any request. His bemused, unimpressed first view of "civilization" comes across clearly when he plays Xi, and because his reactions seem so honest, viewers must stop and, through his eyes, reflect upon our "superior" way of life. Small and slight, with an Isiah Thomas grin, trusting eyes, and easy manner, he is most endearing. And surprisingly, he is a wonderfully adept comedian, a natural who combines a knowing deadpan style with wild physical comedy. At one point he wears a dress and stands on the hood of a jeep, steering it while it goes backward. It would have been tough for a stuntman, but he handled it with ease. N!xau became a star worldwide, even in Japan, where this sweet fellow who used to think there were only 200 people in the world spoke to 100,000 adoring fans. He returned to his band after the film, and Uys had to search the Kalahari in order to cast him in the less imaginative sequel.

• **Cult Favorite:** *The Gods Must Be Crazy* (1980/84, Jamie Uys).

Warren Oates in Badlands.

• **Other Key Film:** *The Gods Must Be Crazy 2* (1989, Uys).

○

WARREN OATES (1928–82) A dynamic presence in extremely violent pictures. Sam Peckinpah, after using him in his TV westerns, cast him in four of his films. He began in character parts but ultimately moved into leads, most notably in three quirky existential films for Monte Hellman. The short, dark-haired actor could be friendly, ferocious, and funny. In *Two-Lane Blacktop,* he talked a blue streak; in *Cockfighter,* he spoke only once. In *The Shooting,* in which he outsmarts and outfights sadistic Jack Nicholson, he proved

he even was capable of playing a *western hero*, the hardest of tasks for an actor. Oates himself wasn't impressed; as he told F. Albert Bomar and Alan J. Warren: "I feel most uncomfortable in a western role, because my image of the western man is John Wayne, and I'm just a little shit." With scruffy beard, slovenly appearance, and a crazed, puzzled expression, he was ideal playing subhuman villains, as in *Ride the High Country*. But he was a cerebral actor and had much impact when his villains, losers, and heroes were complex figures. There was always something going on behind those bulging eyes and that sheepish grin, something dark that was driving him to be violent (or mean) or tearing him apart. You usually felt his character's pain, and even if you didn't like who he was or what he did, you felt empathy for him. You also marveled at Oates's great performances working for out-of-the-mainstream, often new directors. He really was a *great* actor. His death was a shock—we fans felt robbed.

• **Cult Favorites:** *Ride the High Country* (1962, Sam Peckinpah), *The Shooting* (1967, Monte Hellman), *The Wild Bunch* (1969, Peckinpah), *The Hired Hand* (1971, Peter Fonda), *Badlands* (1973, Terence Malick), *The White Dawn* (1974, Philip Kaufman), *Bring Me the Head of Alfredo Garcia* (1974, Peckinpah), *Cockfighter/Born to Kill* (1974, Hellman), *92 in the Shade* (1975, Thomas McGuane).

• **Sleepers:** *Dillinger* (1973, John Milius), *China 9, Liberty 37* (1978, Hellman).

• **Other Key Films:** *Major Dundee* (1965, Peckinpah), *In the Heat of the Night* (1967, Norman Jewison), *Chandler* (1972, Paul Magwood), *Kid Blue* (1973, James Frawley), *The Thief Who Came to Dinner* (1973, Bud Yorkin), *Race with the Devil* (1975, Jack Starrett), *The Brink's Job* (1978,

William Friedkin), *The Border* (1982, Tony Richardson).

○

DAVE O'BRIEN (1912–69) This tall, neatly attired actor with light, curly hair earned cult status in two different ways. He gave the only sane performance in the camp classic *Reefer Madness,* although his character does go insane from smoking the evil weed and, after attempting rape and killing someone, is sent to a mental hospital for life. Also, from the early forties to the mid-fifties, he was the major star—he'd also devise gags and write scripts—of the extremely popular "Pete Smith Specialties," wacky two-reelers in which his hapless fall guy demonstrates how *not* to fish, play football, cook, do chores, be a landlord, relax, hang telephone wire, etc. Maybe he looked too proper to be a slapstick comedian, but he could do amazing stunts, often hanging upside down. O'Brien was the star of the serial *Captain Midnight,* but otherwise had little opportunity to be an action lead. He later became an Emmy-winning comedy writer.

• **Cult Favorites:** *Reefer Madness* (1936, Louis Gasnier), many "Pete Smith Specialty" shorts (1942–55).

• **Also of Interest:** *The Devil Bat* (1941, Jean Yarbrough), *Spooks Run Wild* (1941, Phil Rosen), *Captain Midnight* (1942 serial, James W. Horne).

○

RICHARD O'BRIEN Bald, sharp-featured, New Zealand–born singer-actor appeared in the British stage production of *Hair,* with Tim Curry, and in *Jesus Christ Superstar,* directed by Jim Sharman. He then wrote the book, lyrics, and music for *The Rocky*

Horror Show, starring Curry and directed by Sharman. The three would again team to make the cult movie *The Rocky Horror Picture Show.* As in the play, O'Brien played Riff-Raff, the hunchback handyman. Actually a cruel secret agent from the planet Transsexual, as is lover-sister Magenta (Patricia Quinn), he undermines their boss, Curry's Dr. Frank-N-Furter. He uses a laser to kill Columbia (Little Nell), Rocky (Peter Hinwood), and Frank. O'Brien and Sharman would reunite for the terrible sequel, *Shock Treatment.*

• **Cult Favorite:** *The Rocky Horror Picture Show* (1975, Jim Sharman).

• **Also of Interest:** *Shock Treatment* (1981, Sharman).

○

GLYNNIS O'CONNOR (1956–) A pretty, much underrated actress who won me over playing sensitive yet feisty teenagers (one's dream high school girlfriend) and young women who have a singular way of looking at the world. Typically they have to make major decisions about men, sex, and the courses their lives should take. Without anyone to give sound advice, they make gutsy choices on their own—in *Jeremy,* her teenager gives up her virginity; in *Melanie,* her young married woman leaves scary husband Don Johnson and runs off with their child—and they turn out to be wise decisions. Her young females, who can be counted on for emotional outbursts, almost always beat the odds. She was marvelous as a smart, emotional farm girl in *Ode to Billy Joe* and as the illiterate mother in the barely released *Melanie,* proving she could create real, deeply layered characters if given the opportunity. But O'Connor lost her baby fat, became an adult, and stopped getting decent movie offers.

• **Key Films:** *Jeremy* (1973, Arthur Barron), *Ode to Billy Joe* (1976, Max Baer).

• **Sleepers:** *The Baby Blue Marine* (1976, John Hancock), *California Dreaming* (1979, Hancock), *Melanie* (1980, Rex Bromfield), *Those Lips, Those Eyes* (1980, Michael Pressman).

• **Also of Interest:** *The White Lions* (1981, Mel Stuart), *Night Crossing* (1981, Delbert Mann).

○

UNA O'CONNOR (1880–1959) Thin, birdlike, middle-aged Irish actress added comic relief to numerous films in the thirties and forties. Her specialty was playing jittery, fussy, gossipy, worrisome barmaids, ladies-in-waiting, and spinsters. In horror films, she'd often get quite hysterical and let out loud, high-pitched shrieks. Her constantly screaming landlady had the misfortune to peek through Claude Rains's door and see him unravel his bandages in *The Invisible Man.* She was sort of an unfrightening version of Margaret Hamilton.

• **Cult Favorites:** *Bride of Frankenstein* (1935, James Whale), *Rose Marie* (1936, W. S. Van Dyke), *The Adventures of Robin Hood* (1938, Michael Curtiz and William Keighley).

• **Other Key Films:** *The Invisible Man* (1933, Whale), *Cavalcade* (1933, Frank Lloyd), *The Informer* (1935, John Ford), *The Plough and the Stars* (1936, Ford), *The Sea Hawk* (1940, Curtiz).

• **Also Recommended:** *David Copperfield* (1935, George Cukor), *How Green Was My Valley* (1941, Ford), *The Strawberry Blonde* (1941, Raoul Walsh), *Holy Matrimony* (1943, John M. Stahl), *The Canterville Ghost* (1944, Jules Dassin), *Cluny Brown* (1946, Ernst Lubitsch), *The Adventures of Don Juan* (1948, Vincent Sherman), *Witness for the Prosecution* (1958, Billy Wilder).

○

JUDITH O'DEA Blond, not particularly pretty or conspicuously talented leading lady of *Night of the Living Dead*. As the only cast member other than Duane Jones with professional experience, she played Barbara, a character partly based on Tippi Hedren's imperiled heroine in Alfred Hitchcock's *The Birds*. She is chased by a zombielike ghoul across a cemetery, locks herself in a car to prevent him from getting at her, takes refuge in a house with other scared humans while cannibalistic ghouls constantly try to break in and eat them, has a nervous breakdown, after which she doesn't speak, and after all that torment, is dragged outside to her death. By that time the film has evolved from being Barbara's nightmare to our own. Her best moment comes when she starts to lose it; she keeps asking an unanswerable question: "What's happening?" The question that remains is: "What happened to Judith O'Dea?"
 • **Cult Favorite:** *Night of the Living Dead* (1968, George A. Romero).

○

CATHY O'DONNELL (1925–70) In the forties and fifties, this pretty brunette played sweet, fragile young women. In her debut, *The Best Years of Our Lives* (she became a favorite of William Wyler) she was the understanding sweetheart of Harold Russell, who returns from World War II as a double amputee. She brings tears to our eyes when she says, "I love you, Homer, and I'm never going to leave you—never!" and kisses him. She is able to soften the world for him, as O'Donnell's women in later films try to do

for the troubled, often violent men in their lives. However, in *They Live by Night*, in which she and Farley Granger are on the run, the world proves too tough for her kind. Director Anthony Mann would reteam them in *Side Street*, where again they were unlucky. A sensitive, likable actress who died too young.
 • **Cult Favorites:** *The Best Years of Our Lives* (1946, William Wyler), *They Live by Night* (1949, Nicholas Ray), *The Man from Laramie* (1955, Anthony Mann).
 • **Also Recommended:** *Side Street* (1949, Mann), *Detective Story* (1951, Wyler), *Ben-Hur* (1959, Wyler).

○

BULLE OGIER (1942–) This blond, pretty, extremely sensual French actress was in demand in the seventies, when she appeared in French, German, and Swiss films. Avoiding straight narratives, she usually played quirky characters in highly unusual projects. In the humorous *La Salamandre,* she works in a sausage factory, finds momentary liberation through loud rock 'n' roll, and has attracted the interest of TV scriptwriters because she may have tried to kill her uncle. In the bizarre *La Vallée,* she's the uptight wife of a French diplomat who changes drastically when she joins an expedition that searches for paradise in remote jungles of New Guinea—some of Barbet Schroeder's film has his cast mingling with Mapuga bushmen. She's best remembered for her dominatrix in Schroeder's *Maîtresse,* who is involved in a power struggle with less-smart, less-successful boyfriend Gérard Depardieu. A real-life dominatrix was Ogier's double for some excruciating torture scenes. She was much hipper than her five bourgeois companions but just as

Bulle Ogier and Gérard Depardieu in Maîtresse.

worthless in Buñuel's surreal comedy *The Discreet Charm of the Bourgeoisie,* and an ill Camille who wants to kill a young girl in order to marry her father (Barbet Schroeder) in the fantasy fairy-tale segments of the delirious but often enchanting *Celine and Julie Go Boating.* She costarred with her late daughter Pascale Ogier in *Le Pont du Nord.*

• **Cult Favorites:** *The Discreet Charm of the Bourgeoisie* (1972, Luis Buñuel), *Celine and Julie Go Boating* (1974, Jacques Rivette), *Maîtresse* (1976, Barbet Schroeder).

• **Sleepers:** *La Salamandre* (1971, Alain Tanner), *La Vallée* (1972, Schroeder).

• **Other Key Films:** *Rendezvous at Bray* (1971, André Delvaux), *Seraile* (1976, Eduardo de Gregorio), *Duelle* (1976, Rivette), *The Third Generation* (1979, Rainer Werner Fassbinder), *Navire Night* (1979, Marguerite Duras), *Le Pont du Nord* (1981, Rivette), *Tricheurs* (1986, Schroeder).

○

MILES O'KEEFFE Muscular, athletic leading man, with long, stringy, light-colored hair that looks unwashed. He made an embarrassing attempt at stardom opposite Bo Derek in *Tarzan, the Ape Man,* a film not even bad-film aficionados like. Director John Derek deserves the blame, but O'Keeffe's fight with a giant water snake ranks with the worst action sequences in cinema history. Tarzan and Jane's romantic scenes lacked any excitement, lending credence to rumors that Bo wasn't enchanted by a sore on the actor's lip. Still, he was able to continue his career, playing bare-chested leads in several sorry sword-and-sorcery adventures. His one okay part was as Sir Arthur's novice knight, Sir Gawain, in *Sword of the Valiant,* in which Sean Connery's brief appearance compensated for the younger actor's wooden performance. O'Keeffe was the title character of *The Drifter,* his one contemporary film. His semi-psycho obsessively courts lovely Kim Delaney and, interestingly, turns out to be her hero.

• **Key Film:** *Tarzan, the Ape Man* (1981, John Derek).

• **Also of Interest:** *Ator: The Fighting Eagle* (1983, David Hills), *The Blade Master* (1984, Hills), *Sword of the Valiant* (1984, Stephen Weeks), *Lone Runner* (1986, Roger Deodato), *Iron Warrior* (1987, Al Bradley), *The Drifter* (1988, Larry Brand).

○

WARNER OLAND (1880–1938) Through typical Hollywood casting, this Swedish character actor regularly played Chinese and Japanese characters. With his menacing eyes, thick mustache, and stocky, barrel-chested figure (not tall, he looked as if he were put together with building blocks), he often played sinister, erudite Oriental villains. He was Wung Fu in the Pearl White silent serial, *The Lightning Raider;* the diabolic title character in *The Mysterious Dr. Fu Manchu* and two sequels; the military tyrant who stops *The Shanghai Express;* the wolfman who fights Henry Hull for an antidote in *The Werewolf of London.* However, his most famous character was a hero, Earl Derr Biggers's sly, indomitable, aphorism-a-minute Chinese sleuth, Charlie Chan, in 16 humor-laced

Warner Oland (left) *and Boris Karloff in* Charlie Chan at the Opera.

B mysteries, beginning in 1931 and continuing until his sudden death in 1938. He was fun to watch as he gathered suspects into a room or confronted villains like Boris Karloff, because he was equally egotistical and capable of devising cruel murder plots. The silent serials' chief villain, he broke into sound films with the first feature, *The Jazz Singer,* playing a Jewish cantor, Al Jolson's father.

• **Cult Favorites:** *Dishonored* (1931, Josef von Sternberg), *Shanghai Express* (1932, Sternberg), *Charlie Chan at the Opera* (1936, H. Bruce Humberstone).

• **Other Key Films:** *Patria* (1917 serial), *The Fatal Ring* (1917 serial), *The Lightning Raider* (1919), *The Third Eye* (1920 serial), *The Jazz Singer* (1927, Alan Crosland), *The Mysterious Dr. Fu Manchu* (1929, Rowland V. Lee), *Charlie Chan Carries On* (1931, Hamilton MacFadden), *Charlie Chan in Egypt* (1935, Louis King), *The Werewolf of London* (1935, Stuart Walker), *Charlie Chan on Broadway* (1937, Eugene Forde), *Charlie Chan at the Olympics* (1937, Humberstone).

• **Also of Interest:** *The Black Camel* (1931, MacFadden), *Daughter of the Dragon* (1931, Lloyd Corrigan), *Charlie Chan's Chance* (1932), *A Passport to Hell* (1932, Frank Lloyd), *Charlie Chan's Greatest Case* (1933, MacFadden), *Charlie Chan's Courage* (1934), *Charlie Chan in London* (1934, Forde), *Bulldog Drummond Strikes Back* (1934, Roy Del Ruth), *The Painted Veil* (1934, Richard Boleslawski), *Charlie Chan in Paris* (1935, Lewis Seiler), *Charlie Chan in Shanghai* (1935, James Tinling), *Charlie Chan's Secret* (1936, Gordon Wiles), *Charlie Chan at the Circus* (1936, Harry Lachman), *Charlie Chan at the Race Track* (1936, Humberstone), *Charlie Chan at Monte Carlo* (1937, Forde).

GARY OLDMAN (1959–) This British actor with a mischievous boy's face, hair combed in both directions, and scary yet sensitive eyes escaped a working-class background to become one of the cinema's most riveting, original actors. Spontaneous and willing to go the limit on screen, he has specialized in playing undisciplined, dangerous characters. He made a tremendous impression in *Sid and Nancy* as punk-music star Sid Vicious, an addict who kills his girlfriend, Nancy Spungen (played by Chloe Webb), and then commits suicide, and also in *Prick Up Your Ears,* as Joe Orton, the playwright who was murdered by his jealous male lover. But his best

Gary Oldman was convincing as Sid Vicious in Sid and Nancy.

performance may have been as a violent New York Irish punk-hood in the little-seen *State of Grace,* a mess but for Old-man. "Acting for me is a passion," he told Graham Fuller, "and I get terribly neu-rotic and anguished about it." All this inner turmoil comes across on screen, and it is, at times, quite thrilling.

• **Cult Movies:** *Sid and Nancy* (1986, Alex Cox), *Prick Up Your Ears* (1987, Stephen Frears), *Track 29* (1988, Nicolas Roeg).

• **Also of Interest:** *We Think the World of You* (1988, Colin Gregg), *Chattahoochee* (1990, Mick Jackson), *State of Grace* (1990, Phil Joanou).

○

RON O'NEAL (1937–) Handsome, "cool"-looking black actor is still remembered for playing Priest, the lead character in *Superfly,* one of the major blaxploitation films of the early seventies. No one had heard of him at the time, and he surprised everyone with an exciting performance that alone made the film an improvement on *Shaft.* Yet, the film was criticized for glorifying his cocaine pusher, who had money, dressed flamboyantly, was a stud in the sack (he had all women swooning), and wouldn't kowtow to honky cops. How-ever, I don't think we're supposed to ad-mire Priest or what he does—I think people mistakenly equate O'Neal having charisma with Priest being presented as a hero. O'Neal played Priest as a reformed dealer-user with a bit of a political con-sciousness in *Superfly T.N.T.*—his acting was solid but his one directional effort here was a disaster. Since then O'Neal has turned up as a supporting player in several action films, playing cops and an occasional bad guy.

• **Cult Favorites:** *Superfly* (1972, Gordon Parks, Jr.), *A Force of One* (1979, Paul Aaron).

• **Other Key Films:** *Superfly T.N.T.* (1973, Ron O'Neal), *The Master Gun-fighter* (1975, Frank Laughlin), *Brothers* (1977, Arthur Barron), *Red Dawn* (1984, John Milius).

○

MAUREEN O'SULLIVAN (1911–) All of us boys who wanted to be Johnny Weissmuller's Tarzan wanted to marry Maureen O'Sul-livan's Jane . . . or Maureen O'Sullivan. It was hard not to fall for this lovely and delicate Irish-born brunette who was cer-tainly a lady (she had fine manners and perfect diction) yet as Jane was willing to forsake civilization to live in the hot jungle with a man in a loincloth, without even being married. Her Jane is Tarzan's play-mate, friend, mother, teacher, intellectual equal, partner, and, most significantly, lover. In the first two entries of their six films together, *Tarzan, the Ape Man* and *Tarzan and His Mate,* there is tremendous eroticism, as the very masculine, muscular hero and very feminine heroine constantly touch, kiss, and make goo-goo eyes at each other. As Jane sheds the pants, shirt, boots, and safari hat she wears in the first film (in which she meets, falls for, and decides to remain with Tarzan), and (for the sequel) slips into a tiny halter top and a loincloth which leaves her midriff bare and thighs and hips exposed—it is one of the sexiest of pre–Hays Code outfits—we realize that she has experienced complete sexual freedom in the year she has spent with him in the jungle. With Tarzan, Lady Jane has reverted to her primitive nature and gone native. Unfortunately, for

Maureen O'Sullivan in
Tarzan and His Mate.

future films, the Hays Office made Jane dress more conservatively, in one-piece outfits, and from then on Jane domesticated the ape-man rather than allowing him to further free her from civilization's bonds. It is the intrusions of the "civilized" world into Tarzan's domain that cause friction in their relationship. Tarzan remains pure but Jane is tempted by what her past world has to offer, and she often falls for the lies of greedy white hunters from back home, always causing Tarzan to be placed in great jeopardy. But Tarzan miraculously escapes, disposes of the hunters, and forgives Jane. He knew no one could replace her. However, O'Sullivan quit the series to try to better her career. Wretched in the first "Tarzan" film, she improved considerably in the early thirties,

but other than the later "Tarzan" films, only was offered ingenue parts in major films. Later she'd play female leads, but usually in films dominated by male characters. Nonetheless, it was good to see her at age 46 play the woman for whom cowboy Randolph Scott falls in *The Tall T.* As in the "Tarzan" films, this sexually repressed woman allows a masculine stranger to love her and set her free from society. In *Hannah and Her Sisters,* she is mother to real-life daughter Mia Farrow, the only actress who seems as fragile as O'Sullivan.

• **Cult Favorites:** *Tarzan, the Ape Man* (1932, W. S. Van Dyke), *Tarzan and His Mate* (1934, Cedric Gibbons and Jack Conway), *The Thin Man* (1934, Van Dyke), *Tarzan's New York Adventure* (1942, Richard Thorpe), *Pride and Preju-*

dice (1940, Robert Z. Leonard), *The Tall T* (1957, Budd Boetticher).

• **Other Key Films:** *Strange Interlude* (1932, Leonard), *The Barretts of Wimpole Street* (1934, Sidney Franklin), *David Copperfield* (1935, George Cukor), *Anna Karenina* (1935, Clarence Brown), *The Devil-Doll* (1936, Tod Browning), *Tarzan Escapes* (1936, Thorpe), *The Big Clock* (1948, John Farrow), *A Day at the Races* (1937, Sam Wood), *Tarzan Finds a Son!* (1939, Thorpe), *Tarzan's Secret Treasure* (1941, Thorpe), *The Big Clock* (1948, Farrow), *Hannah and Her Sisters* (1986, Woody Allen).

○

ANNETTE O'TOOLE (1953–) Young, (usually) red-haired actress has flirted with stardom for years, but hasn't made it big despite undeniable appeal. She's pretty, sexy, energetic, feisty, and good at comedy and drama. So what's gone wrong? Perhaps she looks too much like someone you knew in college rather than the typical Hollywood glamour girl—in fact, she was well cast as stuck-up coeds in *One on One,* opposite Robby Benson, and *Foolin' Around,* opposite Gary Busey. Also, she hasn't had the luck of the Irish: she's either starred in small, neglected films, like the likable *One on One,* or disappointing major releases, like *Cat People* and *Superman III* (perfectly cast as Lana Lang), which her well-received performances couldn't save. It seemed that she had a choice part as Nick Nolte's girlfriend in *48 HRS.,* but her character virtually disappears toward the end. Then it looked like her breakthrough film would be the romantic comedy *Cross My Heart,* where she revealed both her body and quick wit, matching Martin Short every step of the way. As usual critics liked her, but the picture got lukewarm reviews and was soon forgotten. So the wait continues.

• **Cult Favorites:** *Smile* (1975, Michael Ritchie), *Cat People* (1982, Paul Schrader).

• **Other Key Films:** *One on One* (1977, Lamont Johnson), *48 HRS.* (1982, Walter Hill), *Superman III* (1983, Richard Lester), *Cross My Heart* (1987, Armyan Bernstein).

○

PETER O'TOOLE (1932–) Dynamic, lanky British stage actor shot to movie stardom in the sixties in *Lawrence of Arabia,* for which he almost won a Best Actor Oscar; *Lord Jim;* and several historical epics. He could overdo it at times, but he had the talent, diction, and presence—with those steely blue eyes and intense delivery—to hold his own with Katharine Hepburn and keep Richard Burton in line lest he be completely shown up. O'Toole's career faded with ill health and the demise of costume pictures. But he came back strong as a tyrannical movie director in *The Stunt Man* and, fittingly, a one-time movie idol in *My Favorite Year.* O'Toole's philosophic, mesmerizing, scenery-chewing performances are reason enough for studios to resume making historical pieces, but he has revealed a remarkable flair for hip comedy during his comeback, which he certainly didn't have when he made *What's New, Pussycat?* Throughout his career, he has played great, brilliant, flawed men— some are royalty—who tread a fine line between being human beings and being gods, and, if they're not completely evil, struggle to rationalize their godlike actions and attitudes. They include Lawrence, Lord Jim, King Henry II in *Becket* and *The Lion in Winter,* a twisted Nazi general in

Night of the Generals, a British lord who thinks he's Jesus Christ in *The Ruling Class*, Robinson Crusoe in *Man Friday*, Eli Cross in *The Stunt Man*, and the Emperor Tiberius in *Caligula*; although not godlike, his Allan Swann in *My Favorite Year* and Don Quixote in *Man of La Mancha* are also bigger-than-life figures. These aren't men who go to the beach, work in an office, wear a suit and tie, or have families or girlfriends. O'Toole is one of the few male stars who, despite his striking looks and extreme popularity with female viewers, rarely plays romantic parts. But no matter: he's truly a marvelous actor.

• **Cult Favorites:** *Lawrence of Arabia* (1962, David Lean), *What's New, Pussycat?* (1965, Clive Donner), *The Ruling Class* (1972, Peter Medak), *The Stunt Man* (1980, Richard Rush), *My Favorite Year* (1982, Richard Benjamin).

• **Other Key Films:** *Becket* (1964, Peter Glenville), *Lord Jim* (1965, Richard Brooks), *How to Steal a Million* (1966, William Wyler), *The Lion in Winter* (1968, Anthony Harvey), *The Last Emperor* (1987, Bernardo Bertolucci).

○

OUR GANG/LITTLE RASCALS Hal Roach began making comedy shorts about a gang of

Our Gang members (left to right) Alfalfa, Buckwheat, Spanky, and Porky are in perfect harmony, as always.

young poor kids in 1922 and continued turning out little gems until 1944. Of course, his casts changed. His first group included small, freckle-faced Mickey Daniels; hefty Joe Cobb; the black, androgynous Farina; and Pete, a dog with a black circle around his right eye. In the late twenties, a new group formed, featuring Jackie Cooper, "Chubby" Chaney, Bobby "Wheezer" Hutchins, and, replacing Farina, "Stymie" Beard. The group most people remember came next: chubby leader Spanky McFarland, squeaky-voiced, freckle-faced "Alfalfa" Switzer, delightful black Buckwheat, cute tag-along Porky Lee, and pretty Darla Hood (in the steps of Mary Kornman and Jean Darling). Each kid had a distinct personality. All the gangs warred with truant officers, dog catchers, principals and strict teachers, rich kids, and bullies. Poverty was less an issue in the final series, when stories often revolved around Alfalfa's ridiculous but usually successful efforts to win the fickle Darla. The "Our Gang" shorts—Spanky and Buckwheat appeared in the one feature, *General Spanky*—were consistently charming and humorous. And the kids not only were cute but were intuitive actors/comics who created some lovable characters (Farina, "Stymie," Spanky, Alfalfa, Buckwheat, Darla, and even Pete) who aren't just in our memories but are still occasionally found on our television sets.

• **Cult Favorites:** Many "Our Gang" shorts (1922–44, produced by Hal Roach).

• **See:** Matthew "Stymie" Beard, Buckwheat, Darla Hood, Spanky McFarland, Carl "Alfalfa" Switzer.

○

MARIA OUSPENSKAYA (1876–1949) Elderly Russian character actress from the Moscow Art Theater who played in many Hollywood productions from the mid-thirties until her death in 1949. She was equally effective as cruel, autocratic figures (she even played a soldier) and women with great warmth; for instance, she was memorable as both the stern head of Vivien Leigh's dance troupe in *Waterloo Bridge* and Maureen O'Hara's kindly dance mentor in *Dance, Girl, Dance*. She often played snobby, cultured characters, but she also portrayed some truly offbeat women—it's worth seeing *Shanghai Gesture* just for her haircut and outfit. Her wise, sad-eyed gypsy Maleva, who watches over the tormented Lon Chaney, Jr., in *The Wolf Man* and *Frankenstein Meets the Wolf Man,* is one of the horror cinema's most recognizable characters. Who hasn't tried to imitate her thick accent and wearily deliver her familiar refrain: "Even a man who is pure in heart/And says his prayers by night/May become a wolf when the wolfbane blooms/And the autumn [full] moon is bright"?

• **Cult Favorites:** *Waterloo Bridge* (1940, Mervyn LeRoy), *Dance, Girl, Dance* (1940, Dorothy Arzner), *The Wolf Man* (1941, George Waggner), *The Shanghai Gesture* (1941, Josef von Sternberg).

• **Other Key Films:** *Dodsworth* (1936, William Wyler), *Love Affair* (1939, Leo McCarey), *The Rains Came* (1939, Clarence Brown), *Dr. Ehrlich's Magic Bullet* (1940, William Dieterle), *The Mortal Storm* (1940, Frank Borzage), *Kings Row* (1942, Sam Wood), *Frankenstein Meets the Wolf Man* (1943, Roy William Neill).

○

BETTY PAGE Photographer Irving Klaw's fetish pinup queen of post–World War II America also made kinky stag films for him. In some 8mm films, the curvy, animated, dark-haired beauty simply danced with swaying hips, in underwear and high heels, while looking suggestively at the camera. In others she did exotic dances as she stripped. In *Forbidden,* she sat barebreasted in a wading pool, smiling. In some, she and another young woman, both in heels, stockings, and underwear, engaged in cat fights. Her wildest films played out the scenarios hinted at in her famous bondage photos. Typically, she wore black high-heeled shoes and black stockings that ended a few inches beneath her black minidress. Another woman might order her to strip to her black or leopard-skin bra and panties (though this wasn't always the case), tie her spreadeagled to a chair or rack, perhaps gag her, and give her a hard spanking with her hand or paddle. She was skilled at exhibiting terror. Indeed, she was very conscious of the camera, flirting with it, and making an attempt to act. Interest in Page has increased in the last couple of years, with long profiles in both *Rolling Stone* and *Film Threat,* and the emergence of a fanzine titled *Betty Pages.* Her films remain underground favorites, and she is now regarded as an icon of the fifties.

• **Sample Films:** *Betty Page's Dance in High Heels* (Irving Klaw), *Betty's Clown Dance* (Klaw), *Betty's Black Chemise Dance* (Klaw), *Betty Page in Bondage* (Klaw), *Forbidden* (Klaw).

○

JACK PALANCE (1919–) I've always liked this tall, dark, physically imposing former coalminer, boxer, and World War II bomber pilot as good guys—tough American soldiers in *Halls of Montezuma* and *Attack!* (determined to exact revenge from cowardly commander Eddie Albert), the pressured actor in *The Big Knife,* the sympathetic, punch-drunk, sold-out boxer in *Requiem for a Heavyweight* (an extraordinary live performance on television), Lee Marvin's gentle saddle partner in *Monte Walsh,* even the set-designer-turned-artist who paints and then proposes to Marianne Sägebrecht in the more recent *Bagdad Cafe,* and a few others. But if he wasn't born looking like a villain, then plastic surgery (he suffered facial burns after his bomber crashed), which tightened his skin and gave him a distorted, slightly crazed look, did the trick. Apart from these goodguy roles, he became the master of the Method Madman, slow-talking, gleeful or pained, cerebral sadists. His fierce, bullying hired gun in *Shane,* who takes pleasure in gunning down weakling Elisha Cook, Jr., in a mud puddle, is one of the most loathsome of screen villains, and is Palance's signature role—this is the villain I most remember from my childhood. But he was also scary as other remorseless killers, assassins, and mobsters in such films as *Panic in the Streets* (when he was billed as Walter Jack Palance), *Sudden Fear, Second Chance,* and *I Died a Thousand Times.* If those films had been made today, viewers would guess his hyper, smiling bad guys were delirious from drugs. Moreover, he also has played such villainous icons as Jack the Ripper, Dracula, Mr. Hyde, Fidel Castro, and Attila the Hun. Occasionally he has gone overboard on his bad guys (as with Castro), and he has seemed to laugh all the way through some of his recent, low-budget atrocities. But more often he has been on target, making us respond with immediate distaste. Offscreen Palance is funny and poetic.

• **Cult Favorites:** *Shane* (1952, George Stevens), *The Silver Chalice* (1954, Victor

Jack Palance in one of his nastiest roles.

Saville), *Attack!* (1956, Robert Aldrich), *The Mercenary* (1970, Sergio Corbucci), *The Sensuous Nurse* (1978, Nello Rossati), *Cocaine Cowboys* (1979, Ulli Lommel), *Alone in the Dark* (1982, Jack Sholder), *Bagdad Cafe* (1988, Percy Adlon).

• **Other Key Films:** *Panic in the Streets* (1950, Elia Kazan), *Second Chance* (1953, Rudolph Maté), *Arrowhead* (1953, Charles Marquis Warren), *Man in the Attic* (1954, Hugo Fregonese), *Sign of the Pagan* (1955, Douglas Sirk), *The Big Knife* (1955, Aldrich), *I Died a Thousand Times* (1955, Stuart Heisler), *The Lonely Man* (1957, Henry Levin), *The Mongols* (1960, André de Toth), *Barabbas* (1962, Richard Fleischer), *Contempt* (1964, Jean-Luc Godard),

The Professionals (1966, Richard Brooks), *Torture Garden* (1968, Freddie Francis), *Che!* (1969, Fleischer), *Monte Walsh* (1970, William Fraker), *Chato's Land* (1972, Michael Winner), *Batman* (1989, Tim Burton), *City Slickers* (1991, Ron Underwood).

○

EUGENE PALLETTE (1889–1954) This short, increasingly heavy, squawky-voiced character actor's lengthy career dates back to early silent films, including *Birth of a Nation*. In 1929, he played Sargeant Heath, a flustered homicide detective, in the first Philo Vance mystery, *The Canary Murder Case*. He would continue to arrest the wrong suspects in Vance films of the thirties. He became a familiar figure in the sound era, particularly in classic screwball comedies, stealing scenes as loudly grumbling, harried, excitable characters who can never get a straight answer from anyone and whose opinions are usually wrong or ignored. Usually rich, successful men in business, they see themselves as masters of their households, but their wives and flighty daughters pretend to listen to them only when they feel sorry for them. Pallette wasn't limited to comedies, though his delightful roles in such adventures as *The Adventures of Robin Hood,* as a fat Friar Tuck, and *The Mark of Zorro* were full of humor.
• **Cult Favorites:** *The Love Parade* (1929, Ernst Lubitsch), *Shanghai Express* (1932, Josef von Sternberg), *My Man Godfrey* (1936, Gregory La Cava), *The Adventures of Robin Hood* (1938, Michael Curtiz and William Keighley), *The Gang's All Here* (1943, Busby Berkeley).
• **Also Recommended:** *The Three Musketeers* (1921, Fred Niblo), *The Virginian*

(1929, Victor Fleming), *The Kennel Murder Case* (1933, Michael Curtiz), *Bordertown* (1935, Archie Mayo), *Steamboat 'Round the Bend* (1935, John Ford), *The Ghost Goes West* (1936, René Clair), *100 Men and a Girl* (1937, Henry Koster), *Mr. Smith Goes to Washington* (1939, Frank Capra), *The Mark of Zorro* (1940, Rouben Mamoulian), *The Lady Eve* (1941, Preston Sturges), *The Male Animal* (1942, Elliott Nugent), *Heaven Can Wait* (1943, Lubitsch).
• **Other Key Films:** *Lights of New York* (1928, Bryan Foy), *The Canary Murder Case* (1929, Malcolm St. Clair), *Topper* (1937, Norman Z. McLeod), *Young Tom Edison* (1940, Norman Taurog), *The Bride Came C.O.D.* (1941, Keighley), *Swamp Water* (1941, Jean Renoir and, uncredited, Irving Pichel), *Lady in a Jam* (1942, La Cava), *The Big Street* (1942, Irving Reis), *It Ain't Hay* (1943, Erle C. Kenton).

○

FRANKLIN PANGBORN (1893–1958) Comical character actor with a thin, unimpressive mustache and one of the cinema's great names played what Andrew Sarris called "prissy prunes." In comedies, he was often a helpful salesclerk/manager who becomes increasingly flustered by the zany star's appearance in his store, or, more often, a hotel clerk whose smile turns into a sick grin when he realizes that the people checking in will be nothing but trouble. Pangborn also was hilarious as the scavenger-hunt tabulator in *My Man Godfrey.* Another memorable Pangborn character is his bank examiner in *The Bank Dick;* to prevent him from examining the books, W. C. Fields takes him to a hotel bar, has the bartender slip him a Mickey, takes the sick man upstairs to a room,

Franklin Pangborn (second from right) *stands with fellow character actors Robert Warwick, William Demarest, and Porter Hall in* Sullivan's Travels, *starring Joel McCrea* (seated).

accidentally drops him out the second floor window, catches him on the bounce, takes him back upstairs to the room, and makes him excruciatingly ill by discussing weird combinations of greasy food. A funny, "prissy-prunish" Douglas Dumbrille.

• **Cult Favorites:** *My Man Godfrey* (1936, Gregory La Cava), *A Star Is Born* (1937, William Wellman), *The Bank Dick* (1940, Eddie Cline), *Never Give a Sucker an Even Break* (1941, Cline), *Sullivan's Travels* (1942, Preston Sturges), *Now, Voyager* (1942, Irving Rapper), *The Palm Beach Story* (1942, Sturges), *The Horn Blows at Midnight* (1945, Raoul Walsh).

• **Also Recommended:** *International House* (1933, A. Edward Sutherland), *Design for Living* (1933, Ernst Lubitsch), *Easy Living* (1937, Mitchell Leisen), *Stage Door* (1937, La Cava), *Bluebeard's Eighth Wife* (1938, Lubitsch), *Vivacious Lady* (1938, George Stevens), *Carefree* (1938, Mark Sandrich), *The Fifth Avenue Girl* (1939, La Cava), *Christmas in July* (1940, Sturges), *George Washington Slept Here* (1942, William Keighley), *Holy Matrimony* (1943, John M. Stahl), *Crazy House* (1943, Cline), *Hail the Conquering Hero* (1944, Sturges), *The Great Moment* (1944, Sturges), *The Sin of Harold Diddlebock/Mad Wednesday* (1947, Sturges), *Romance on the High Seas* (1948, Michael Curtiz).

MICHAEL PARÉ Tall, handsome, and virile Brooklyn-born leading man seemed to be streaking for stardom with lead roles in *Eddie and the Cruisers,* as a Jim Morrison–inspired, supposedly dead rock legend, and Walter Hill's stylized *Streets of Fire,* as a gun-for-hire tracking down his ex-girlfriend, singer Diane Lane. Both films would become cult items—*Eddie and the Cruisers* reached its fans playing on cable—but were disappointing at the box office. *The Philadelphia Experiment,* a gimmicky science-fiction film with his forties soldier transported to the eighties, excited no one. Since then he has taken leads in bad, violent, low-budget exploitation films, as well as the poorly received *Eddie and the Cruisers II.* Paré has charisma and seems more appealing than most hunks (maybe because he doesn't remove his shirt as often), but it has become increasingly obvious that his range is limited. To become a star, he might follow the route of the comparably talented Ken Wahl, and do a TV series.

• **Cult Favorites:** *Eddie and the Cruisers* (1983, Martin Davidson), *Streets of Fire* (1984, Walter Hill).

• **Other Key Films:** *The Philadelphia Experiment* (1984, Stewart Raffill), *World Gone Wild* (1988, Lee H. Katzkin).

• **Also of Interest:** *Instant Justice* (1986, Craig T. Rumor), *Space Rage* (1988, Conrad E. Palmisano), *The Woman's Club* (1988, Sandra Weintraub), *Eddie and the Cruisers II: Eddie Lives!* (1989, Jean-Claude Lord).

○

REG PARK This American muscleman replaced Steve Reeves as Hercules in Italian epics. With his impressive physique, heavy black beard, and deep (dubbed) voice, he almost passed for Reeves, but because he didn't have Reeves's charisma—or beautiful Sylva Koscina—and the films veered away from mythology (the Spanish are his enemy in *Hercules and the Captive Women*), he didn't seem like the genuine article. Seeing his films today, particularly Mario Bava's stylized *Hercules in the Haunted World,* with Christopher Lee as the evil villain, one recognizes them as being better than Reeves's *Hercules Unchained,* and far superior to those later "Hercules" films starring Kirk Morris, Mark Forest, Dan Vadis, Alan Steel, Rock Stevens, and Gordon Scott. Always playing second fiddle, Park would replace Scott in the Italian "Samson" films (the character was actually Maciste, son of Hercules).

• **Key Films:** *Hercules in the Haunted World* (1961, Mario Bava), *Hercules and the Captive Women* (1963, Vittorio Cottafavi), *Hercules, Prisoner of Evil* (1964/67, Anthony Dawson).

• **Also of Interest:** *Samson in King Solomon's Mines* (1964, Piero Regnoli), *The Challenge of the Giants* (1965).

○

KAY PARKER This attractive, buxom British brunette was an American porno star in the late seventies and early eighties, before getting into the distribution end of the business. No starlet, she became porno's top portrayer of mature women (in their late thirties and forties), including mothers and stepmothers of college-age children. Her films typically included her seducing and having sex with a young actress or actor. If her character had a son, it was likely that they would end up having sex. That was the subject matter of

Taboo, which despite its groundbreaking theme was far less shocking than the majority of porno films. Because Parker was a decent actress and played love scenes for eroticism rather than raunch, she made her films come across as more tasteful than they actually were.

• **Cult Favorites:** *Taboo* (1980, Kirdy Stevens), *Taboo II* (1983, Stevens).

• **Other Key Films:** *Seven into Snowy* (1977, Antonio Sheppard), *Untamed* (1977, Ramsey Carson), *V—the Hot One* (1978, Robert McCallum), *Sex World* (1978, Anthony Spinelli), *The Health Spa* (1978, Clair Dia), *Chorus Call* (1978, Sheppard), *Kate and the Indians* (1979, Allen Swift), *Fast Cars, Fast Women* (1979, Scott McHaley), *Downstairs/Upstairs* (1980, Lisa Barr), *Vista Valley P.T.A.* (1980, Spinelli), *Satisfactions* (1983, McCallum), *Intimate Lessons* (1983, Philip Marshall).

○

BARBARA PAYTON (1927–67) Well-built, leggy, moderately talented blonde had a chance for stardom in the early fifties when she played the female leads opposite James Cagney in *Kiss Tomorrow Goodbye* and

Barbara Payton with Barton MacLaine (far left) *and Ward Bond in* Kiss Tomorrow Goodbye.

Gregory Peck in *Only the Valiant,* but her career took a backseat to her nightclub-hopping, romances, and alcoholism. Married twice by the time she was 17, a mother at 20, separated at 21, she was romantically linked in Hollywood to Howard Hughes, Guy Madison, most of her leading men, many of the filmmakers she worked with, and, most notably, actors Tom Neal and Franchot Tone. Neal made headlines when he brutally beat up Tone in Payton's yard, sending him to the hospital with a concussion and in need of plastic surgery. Payton would marry Tone, but less than two months later return to Neal and their tempestuous relationship. Moreover, gossip columnists claimed that her peculiar friendship with Ava Gardner was one of the reasons Frank Sinatra divorced Gardner. She was also friends with Lana Turner. Because of the scandals, she no longer was offered good parts, settling for the laughable *Bride of the Gorilla, Run for the Hills* with Sonny Tufts, and low-budget films and theater with Neal. She also went to England, capitalizing on her image in *Bad Blonde/The Woman Is Trouble.* Her relationship with Neal was over by 1955, as was her film career. The rest of her life was tragic, with arrests for drunkenness, passing bad checks, and prostitution. It was long rumored that she even made stag films, but no evidence has turned up. Interestingly, she titled her 1963 memoir *I Am Not Ashamed.* She died of heart and liver failure when just 40.

• **Cult Favorite:** *Bride of the Gorilla* (1951, Curt Siodmak).

• **Also of Interest:** *Trapped* (1949, Richard Fleischer), *Dallas* (1950, Stuart Heisler), *Kiss Tomorrow Goodbye* (1950, Gordon Douglas), *Only the Valiant* (1951, Douglas), *Four-Sided Triangle* (1953, Terence Fisher), *Run for the Hills* (1953), *Bad Blonde/The Woman Is Trouble* (1953), *The Great Jesse James Raid* (1953, Reginald LeBorg), *Murder Is My Beat* (1955, Edgar G. Ulmer).

○

MARY VIVIAN PEARCE (1947–) An important member of John Waters's stock company, going all the way back to his 8mm films *Hag in a Black Leather Jacket* and *Roman Candles.* Blond Bonnie from Baltimore, Waters's friend before he became a filmmaker, was the star of his first feature, *Mondo Trasho,* made up as a cheap Jean Harlow. Early in the film, she has her toes sucked by a stranger in a park, after which she is run over by a car driven by Divine, who then pushes her unconscious body around in a wheelchair. The funniest moment has Pearce clicking her heels and turning up in a Baltimore street, where she is mercilessly insulted by two women who try to guess exactly what kind of lowlife she is. In *Multiple Maniacs,* she is a talkative dumbbell who is obsessed with performing "acts" with Divine's boyfriend (David Lochary); Divine gets revenge on them both. In *Female Trouble,* she and Lochary are hairdressers who sponsor Divine's criminality in order to make her a star. Perhaps her best role was in *Desperate Living,* as the seemingly retarded Princess Coo-coo, who wears a fairy-tale outfit better suited for a 10-year-old. Her mother, Queen Carlotta (Edith Massey), injects her with rabies because she's having an affair with the janitor at the nudist colony. She's a mean nun in *Polyester.*

• **Cult Favorites:** *Mondo Trasho* (1969, John Waters), *Multiple Maniacs* (1970, Waters), *Pink Flamingos* (1972, Waters),

Female Trouble (1974, Waters), *Desperate Living* (1977, Waters), *Polyester* (1981, Waters), *Hairspray* (1988, Waters), *Cry-Baby* (1990, Waters).

○

ANTHONY PERKINS (1932–) Tall, lanky, and boyish-looking, this talented New York–born actor began his movie career playing sensitive, shy, awkward, and, often, emotionally troubled adolescents and young men. The parts didn't change much as he got older. His ballplayer Jimmy Piersall in *Fear Strikes Out,* who has a nervous breakdown and is institutionalized because of pressure from his father, anticipated the insane Norman Bates in *Psycho,* whose dead mother still controls his life. Perkins's characters are often dwarfed by dominating or strong-willed parental figures. In three films, he has relationships with stepmothers: Melina Mercouri in *Phaedra,* Sophia Loren in *Desire Under the Elms,* and Marlene Jobert in *Ten Days Wonder,* later in his career. And in *Goodbye Again,* he has a relationship with another older woman, Ingrid Bergman. He always had trouble finding the ideal match: in *Pretty Poison,* fresh out of an institution where he's been since a child, he immediately falls for an evil, excitement-seeking teenager (Tuesday Weld, his best screen partner), who implicates him for her crimes and gets him sent to another institution. Of course, Norman Bates is Perkins's key role, the one with which he is identified and the one that serves as a model for his other crazies. The actor's astonishing, beautifully conceived performance in *Psycho,* exhibiting Norman's gentleness, feeble wit, and pain—along with his deep-rooted madness—is the rea-

son viewers have always been able to sympathize with the crazed young man despite his heinous crimes and perversity. He is something of a folk hero. Playing a not completely cured Norman 23 years later, Perkins gave another remarkable performance in the underrated *Psycho II,* allowing his still sympathetic character to evolve from worried to neurotic to paranoid to insane—the path Norman probably took prior to meeting Janet Leigh in the first film. His performances in *Psycho III* and other psychotic Norman-based roles—such as the knife-carrying preacher who is after prostitute Kathleen Turner in *Crimes of Passion*—have been too hammy. I think the loony he plays in *Winter Kills,* who barely reacts when being shot, pretty much explains other Perkins characters: they have been so hurt emotionally in their pasts that physical pain no longer bothers them.

• **Cult Favorites:** *Psycho* (1960, Alfred Hitchcock), *The Trial* (1963, Orson Welles), *Pretty Poison* (1968, Noel Black), *Catch-22* (1970, Mike Nichols), *Winter Kills* (1979, William Richert), *Crimes of Passion* (1984, Ken Russell).

• **Other Key Films:** *The Actress* (1953, George Cukor), *Friendly Persuasion* (1956, William Wyler), *Fear Strikes Out* (1957, Robert Mulligan), *The Tin Star* (1957, Anthony Mann), *On the Beach* (1959, Stanley Kramer), *The Champagne Murders* (1968, Claude Chabrol), *Lovin' Molly* (1974, Sidney Lumet), *Psycho II* (1983, Richard Franklin).

• **Also of Interest:** *The Matchmaker* (1958, Joseph M. Newman), *Green Mansions* (1959, Mel Ferrer), *Goodbye Again* (1961, Anatole Litvak), *Phaedra* (1962, Jules Dassin), *Five Miles to Midnight* (1963, Litvak), *Is Paris Burning?* (1966, René

Clément), *Play It As It Lays* (1972, Frank Perry), *Ten Days Wonder* (1972, Chabrol).

○

MILLIE PERKINS (1938–) After being discovered in a much-publicized talent hunt and then promoted heavily, this cute, dark-haired, large-eyed unknown was a major disappointment as the teenage heroine of *The Diary of Anne Frank.* Critics claimed she hadn't the emotional depth to play the courageous, ill-fated Anne; audiences were more sympathetic, but were so worried that the young, sweet, fragile-looking actress would shame herself playing such a cherished character that they couldn't involve themselves in the story. Her bubble burst, Perkins has played only occasional roles since. She was likable as Elvis's ditched childhood sweetheart in *Wild in the Country,* but her most intriguing parts were in Monte Hellman's obscure existential westerns *Ride in the Whirlwind,* as a timid farm girl who is dominated by her father, and *The Shooting,* as a mysterious woman who hires Warren Oates to escort her through the desert, but has other plans. In both films, her characters have a hard, unglamorous quality that separates them from her ingenue roles. Her strangest part came a decade later: she was a homicidal maniac and did nude lovemaking scenes in *Witch Who Came from the Sea.*

• **Cult Favorites:** *Ride in the Whirlwind* (1965, Monte Hellman), *The Shooting* (1967, Hellman), *Wild in the Streets* (1968, Barry Shear).

• **Sleepers:** *Wild in the Country* (1961, Philip Dunne), *Cockfighter/Born to Kill* (1974, Hellman).

• **Also of Interest:** *Ensign Pulver* (1964, Joshua Logan), *Lady Cocoa* (1975, Matt Cimber), *Witch Who Came from the Sea* (1976, Cimber), *Table for Five* (1983, Robert Lieberman), *Wall Street* (1987, Oliver Stone), *Slamdance* (1987, Wayne Wang).

○

ESSY PERSSON (1941–) Sensual, dark-haired Swedish actress starred in *I, a Woman,* Mac Ahlberg's erotically photographed, pre-porno sex film about a sexually frustrated woman who becomes increasingly promiscuous. Highlighted by her character's memorable shower, masturbation, and exhibitionism, it was a major financial success and spawned two sequels. Since it was a Danish film, she was dubbed, which made it really peculiar when it was subtitled for American distribution so that it could pose as an "art film." The picture was monotonous, yet Persson's performance was intense. Radley Metzger, who imported *I, a Woman,* cast her as one of the leads in his arty sex film, *Thérèse and Isabelle,* from Violette Leduc's memoir, with Anna Gael as her lover. "She was an extraordinary talent . . . [who] thought of herself as a girl who got famous showing her tits, and doing fuck films," Metzger told Richard Corliss. "And now she had a real part." Unfortunately, while Persson and the film eventually got good reviews, it wasn't until after the daily press ripped her apart for looking too old for the role. Devastated, she retired from films.

• **Cult Favorites:** *I, a Woman* (1965, Mac Ahlberg), *Thérèse and Isabelle* (1968, Radley Metzger).

• **Other Key Films:** *I, a Woman—II* (1968), *Mission Stardust* (1968, Primo Zeglio), *I, a Woman—III* (1969), *Cry of the Banshee* (1970, Gordon Hessler).

○

MARY PHILBIN (1903–) One of the most memorable screams in screen history is, ironically, in a silent film, when Mary Philbin's abducted singer Christine Daaé reacts to her unmasking of the hideous skeletal face of Lon Chaney's *Phantom of the Opera.* That part, and particularly that scene, were enough to fix Philbin in the minds of all horror and most learned movie fans. Discovered by Erich von Stroheim, the pretty, moderately talented actress played sympathetic leads for about 10 years, including in the talkie *The Last Performance.* She was an appealing heroine in the splendid adventure *The Man Who Laughs,* wearing one of her long, curly blond wigs, as the blind girl who falls in love with disfigured hero Conrad Veidt. Most of her other parts are forgotten, but not the actress. When Brian De Palma made his rock musical, *Phantom of the Paradise,* he named one of his male characters Philbin.

• **Cult Favorite:** *Phantom of the Opera* (1925, Rupert Julien and, uncredited, Edward Sedgwick and Lon Chaney).

• **Other Key Films:** *The Merry-Go-Round* (1923, Julien and, uncredited, Erich von Stroheim), *Temple of Venus* (1923, Henry Otto), *Drums of Love* (1928, D. W. Griffith), *Love Me and the World Is Mine* (1928, E. A. Dupont), *The Man Who Laughs* (1928, Paul Leni), *The Last Performance/Erik, the Great Illusionist* (1929, Paul Fejos).

○

GÉRARD PHILIPE (1922–59) Handsome, dark-haired, delicate-featured young actor was France's great romantic idol of the postwar years, carrying the torch of Jean Gabin and Jean Marais. His movie fame was complemented by great success in the theater, where he devotedly worked for far less money. Philipe shot to stardom in 1946 in *Devil in the Flesh,* with a moving performance as a sensitive student who has an affair with a married woman, played by France's leading actress at the time, Micheline Presle. He would continue to excite French moviegoers with his passionate, introspective portrayals of young men—like his two Stendhal heroes, Fabrizio del Dongo in *La Chartreuse de Parme,* and Julien Sorel in *The Red and the Black*—who ambitiously seek happiness through sex, love, and power. In films that have rarely been shown in America, he played anguished young men, soldiers, dreamers/ romantics/lovers, artists (Modigliani in *Montparnasse 19*), and murderers. To fulfill their ambitions, as well as their own need for physical love, they seduce beautiful, emotional, sometimes older women. (His leading ladies included stars with alliterated names—Danielle Darrieux, Anouk Aimee, and Michèle Morgan.) While few of his films were highly praised, he was always captivating. Through it all, writes David Shipman, "there was something about Gérard Philipe's screen presence that suggested he was not quite of this world." His untimely death at age 36 (attributed to a heart attack and cancer) was a shock to the French people and added to his legend. Two years later he and Raimu became the only actors to be honored by French commemorative stamps.

• **Cult Favorites:** *Devil in the Flesh* (1946, Claude Autant-Lara), *La Ronde* (1950, Max Ophüls).

• **Other Key Films:** *Le Pays Sans Étoiles* (1945, Georges Lacombe), *The Idiot* (1945, Georges Lampin), *La Chartreuse de Parme*

(1947, Christian-Jaque), *Une Si Jolie Petit Plage/Riptide* (1948, Yves Allégret), *Beauty and the Devil* (1949, René Clair), *Souvenirs Perdus* (1950, Christian-Jaque), *Fanfan the Tulip* (1951, Christian-Jaque), *The Seven Deadly Sins* (1951, Lacombe), *Les Orgueilleux/The Proud and the Beautiful* (1953, Allégret), *Royal Affairs in Versailles* (1954, Sacha Guitry), *Monsieur Ripois/Knave of Hearts* (1954, René Clément), *The Red and the Black* (1954, Autant-Lara), *The Grand Maneuver* (1955, Clair), *Pot-Bouille* (1957, Julien Duvivier), *Montparnasse 19* (1957, Jacques Becker), *Le Jouer* (1958, Autant-Lara), *Les Liaisons Dangereuses* (1959, Roger Vadim).

• **Also of Interest:** *Tous les Chemins Mènent à Rome* (1948, Jean Boyer), *Juliette ou la Clé des Songes* (1951, Marcel Carné), *Villa Borghese* (1953, Gianni Franciolini), *La Meilleure Part* (1955, Allégret), *Bold Adventure* (1956, Gérard Philipe and Joris Ivens), *Republic of Sin* (1960, Luis Buñuel).

○

SLIM PICKENS (1919–83) A strapping former rodeo clown with a thick, country-boy accent, he played character parts in numerous westerns from the fifties until the eighties. He was the mean guard who bullied Marlon Brando in *One-Eyed Jacks,* but mostly he played likable characters who spout terms like "Oh, shoot!" "Dad-burned," and "What in tarnation . . .?" His chatter and accent added authenticity to the films. He also injected humor, though his westerners weren't buffoons. Oddly, his most memorable role—a near buffoon—wasn't in a western: in Stanley Kubrick's doomsday black comedy, *Dr. Strangelove,* he is the superpatriotic bomber captain, who—in one of the mem-

Slim Pickens in Dr. Strangelove.

orable moments of the cinema—rides the nuclear bomb like a bronco, whooping it up, as it falls on Russia.

• **Cult Favorites:** *One-Eyed Jacks* (1961, Marlon Brando), *Dr. Strangelove or: How I Learned to Stop Worrying and Love the Bomb* (1964, Stanley Kubrick), *Major Dundee* (1965, Sam Peckinpah), *The Ballad of Cable Hogue* (1970, Peckinpah), *The Getaway* (1972, Peckinpah), *Pat Garrett and Billy the Kid* (1973, Peckinpah), *Blazing Saddles* (1974, Mel Brooks), *White Line Fever* (1975, Jonathan Kaplan), *Rancho Deluxe* (1975, Frank Perry), *The Howling* (1981, Joe Dante).

• **Sleepers:** *The Last Command* (1955,

Frank Lloyd), *Will Penny* (1968, Tom Gries), *Pony Express Rider* (1976, Hal Harrison, Jr.).

• **Also of Interest:** *The Great Locomotive Chase* (1956, Frank D. Lyon), *The Sheepman* (1958, George Marshall), *Savage Sam* (1963, Norman Tokar), *In Harm's Way* (1965, Otto Preminger), *The Flim Flam Man* (1967, Irvin Kershner), *The Cowboys* (1972, Mark Rydell), *Hawmps!* (1976, Joe Camp), *Honeysuckle Rose* (1980, Jerry Schatzberg).

○

INGRID PITT (1944–) Voluptuous, sensuous femme fatale of Hammer horror films in England. She was born in Poland and relocated in East Berlin after the war; she began her movie career in Spain, making a film about bullfighting, and spaghetti westerns. In the sixties, she had minute parts in such films as *Chimes at Midnight, Doctor Zhivago,* and *A Funny Thing Happened on the Way to the Forum,* before getting a decent role in the American-made *Where Eagles Dare.* She went to England but couldn't find work before Hammer Studios took an interest. She achieved permanent cult status with *The Vampire Lovers,* starring as a lesbian vampire in the erotic adaptation of Sheridan Le Fanu's novella, *Carmilla.* Hammer's films had been becoming increasingly sexy, but no one was

Ingrid Pitt seduces Madeleine Smith in The Vampire Lovers.

prepared for all the nudity and sexual activity, or Pitt's unabashedly physical performance. Hell-bent for physical pleasure, Pitt's Carmilla rarely displays the remorse of Le Fanu's vampire, but there's an effective scene in which she cries upon seeing a funeral procession, realizing all but she will die. She's wrong—Peter Cushing cuts off her head. Pitt's other famous role is the evil Elizabeth Bathory, who retains her beauty by bathing in the blood of murdered virgins in *Lady Dracula,* another film full of sex and nudity. This time, her villainess is walled up for life.

• **Cult Favorites:** *The Vampire Lovers* (1970, Roy Ward Baker), *Lady Dracula* (1971, Peter Sasdy), *The Wicker Man* (1973, Robin Hardy).

• **Also of Interest:** *The Omegans* (1969, W. Lee Wilder), *The House That Dripped Blood* (1971, Peter Duffell), *Transmutations* (1985, George Pavlou).

○

DONALD PLEASENCE (1919–) Coming from the theater in the mid-fifties, this intense, mannered, short British character actor, with beady, pale blue eyes and a bald, round head, has specialized in villains (various Nazis; James Bond villain Blofeld; and men with twitches, beards, and scars), and as-

Donald Pleasence in Halloween.

sorted obsessive oddballs. His few leads include the title character, a mild-mannered wife-murderer, in *Dr. Crippen,* and Françoise Dorléac's weak, masochistic, older husband in Roman Polanski's absurdist black comedy *Cul-de-Sac.* Because of the latter role, Pleasence's presence in films over the next few years hinted (often for no good reason) that they were arty or classy. So people even paid attention to the cannibal horror film *Raw Meat,* with Pleasence as a detective, and were justly rewarded. However, in time, Pleasence seemed to accept any role offered, and his art status diminished. He was well cast as the obsessively loony, doomsayer psychiatrist who tracks escaped psycho Michael Myers in *Halloween,* which gave him a career boost, but too many of his later films, including the sequels, have been exercises in self-parody.

• **Cult Favorites:** *Fantastic Voyage* (1966, Richard Fleischer), *Cul-de-Sac* (1968, Roman Polanski), *THX-1138* (1971, George Lucas), *Raw Meat* (1973, Gary Sherman), *Halloween* (1978, John Carpenter), *Escape from New York* (1981, Carpenter), *Alone in the Dark* (1982, Jack Sholder).

• **Sleepers:** *The Guest/Caretaker* (1964, Clive Donner), *Will Penny* (1968, Tom Gries), *Outback* (1971, Ted Kotcheff), *Wedding in White* (1972, William Fruet), *The Monster Club* (1981, Roy Ward Baker).

• **Also of Interest:** *The Beachcomber* (1955, Muriel Box), *1984* (1956, Michael Anderson), *Sons and Lovers* (1960, Jack Cardiff), *The Great Escape* (1963, John Sturges), *Dr. Crippen* (1964, Robert Lynn), *You Only Live Twice* (1967, Lewis Gilbert), *Soldier Blue* (1970, Ralph Nelson), *From Beyond the Grave* (1973, Kevin Connor), *The Black Windmill* (1974, Don Siegel), *Hearts of the West* (1975, Howard Zieff),

Escape to Witch Mountain (1975, John Hough), *The Devil Within Her* (1975, Peter Sasdy), *The Last Tycoon* (1976, Elia Kazan), *Dracula* (1979, John Badham), *The Devonsville Terror* (1983, Ulli Lommel), *Black Arrow* (1984, Hough), *Creepers* (1985, Dario Argento), *Ground Zero* (1987, Michael Pattinson), *Halloween 4: The Return of Michael Myers* (1988, Dwight H. Little).

○

MICHAEL J. POLLARD (1939–) Likable, funny character actor with a smiley, off-kilter face that would make him perfect as either Leo Gorcey's brother or Santa's largest elf. Instead he has given charming portrayals of easygoing, quirky characters, many of whom live in small towns and/or work at small-scale operations (local cab companies, theaters, newspapers). Though unimportant figures, they are observant, philosophical, and wise, and if you are a stranger to their worlds, they're the guys you'd probably strike up a conversation with. Not all of his characters have been genial and gentle: he was a scummy Billy the Kid in *Dirty Little Billy,* a motorcycle gang member in *The Wild Angels,* a moronic killer in the moronic *American Gothic,* and, in his most famous role, C. W. Moss, the youngest member of the gang in *Bonnie and Clyde.*

• **Cult Favorites:** *The Wild Angels* (1966, Roger Corman), *Bonnie and Clyde* (1967, Arthur Penn), *Between the Lines* (1977, Joan Micklin Silver), *Melvin and Howard* (1979, Jonathan Demme).

• **Sleeper:** *Enter Laughing* (1967, Carl Reiner).

• **Other Key Films:** *Summer Magic* (1963, James Neilson), *Hannibal Brooks* (1969, Michael Winner), *Little Fauss and Big*

Halsy (1970, Sidney J. Furie), *Dirty Little Billy* (1972, Stan Dragoti).

• **Also of Interest:** *Hemingway's Adventures of a Young Man* (1962, Martin Ritt), *The Stripper* (1963, Franklin Schaffner), *The Russians Are Coming! The Russians Are Coming!* (1966, Norman Jewison), *The Legend of Frenchie King* (1971, Christian-Jaque), *Roxanne* (1987, Fred Schepisi), *Riders of the Storm* (1988, Maurice Phillips), *Dick Tracy* (1990, Warren Beatty).

○

ELEANOR POWELL (1912–82) Standing still, she looked like an awkward "Amateur Hour" contestant, but she was a thrilling dancer, the greatest of all female tappers. Though she had a pleasant personality, she wasn't much of an actress, so most of her M-G-M films were essentially musical revues. The slim plots were corny and campy, with forced comedy and fluffy romance, but when Powell danced in the spotlight—Roger Edens arranged her spectacular production numbers—it was all worth it. In *Born to Dance,* she tapped on a battleship full of sequined cannons. She was an exuberant performer, with a wide smile, colorful costumes (even a hula outfit with a bare midriff), a flexible body, long, long legs, amazingly quick feet, and great endurance. Her "Begin the Beguine" number with Fred Astaire in *Broadway Melody of 1940* is awesome; supposedly, the feet of both dancers were bleeding by the time they finished rehearsing and filming the grueling dance.

• **Cult Favorites:** *Born to Dance* (1936, Roy Del Ruth), *Broadway Melody of 1940* (1940, Norman Taurog).

• **Other Key Films:** *Broadway Melody of 1936* (1935, Del Ruth), *Broadway Melody of 1938* (1937, Del Ruth), *Rosalie* (1937,

W. S. Van Dyke), *Honolulu* (1939, Edward Buzzell), *Lady Be Good* (1941, Norman Z. McLeod), *Ship Ahoy* (1942, Buzzell), *I Dood It* (1943, Vincente Minnelli), *Sensations of 1945* (1944, Andrew L. Stone).

• **Also of Interest:** *George White's 1935 Scandals* (1935, George White and Thornton Freeland), *Thousands Cheer* (1945, George Sidney), *Duchess of Idaho* (1950, Robert Z. Leonard).

○

PAULA PRENTISS (1939–) Tall, talented, Texas-born brunette made her film debut in *Where the Boys Are,* as a witty, husband-chasing college student. She lassoed Jim Hutton, who would be her frequent and best screen partner. Trading quips with various leading men in her comedies, she'd play other funny, intelligent, aggressive females whose idea of happiness is to be married and have kids. They are threats to the freedom of wary males, but win them just the same, throwing them off-guard with their openness and delighting them with their personalities. Strong women, they aren't intimidated by soldiers, sailors, cops, or gangsters. But her funniest, pushiest character snares timid Rock Hudson, posing as a sportsman, in the screwball comedy *Man's Favorite Sport?* In the early seventies, Prentiss became more sexual on screen, even doing nudity; in *The Parallax View,* the usually funny actress became dead serious, a murder victim in a political conspiracy. She is remembered for her convincing performance in the otherwise disappointing satire *The Stepford Wives,* as a feminist who, as Katherine Ross discovers one day, is replaced by a look-alike android designed for male pleasure. In real life, Prentiss is married to Richard Benjamin, who was her costar in the short-lived TV comedy series "He & She," one of the only showcases for her sophisticated comedy talents.

• **Cult Favorites:** *Where the Boys Are* (1960, Henry Levin), *Man's Favorite Sport?* (1964, Howard Hawks), *What's New, Pussycat?* (1965, Clive Donner), *Catch-22* (1970, Mike Nichols), *The Parallax View* (1974, Alan J. Pakula), *The Stepford Wives* (1975, Bryan Forbes).

• **Other Key Films:** *The Honeymoon Machine* (1961, Richard Thorpe), *The Horizontal Lieutenant* (1962, Thorpe), *Follow the Boys* (1963, Thorpe), *The World of Henry Orient* (1964, George Roy Hill), *In Harm's Way* (1965, Otto Preminger), *Born to Win* (1971, Ivan Passer), *The Black Marble* (1980, Harold Becker).

○

ELVIS PRESLEY (1935–77) The "king of rock 'n' roll" began making films in 1955, and much of his popularity carried over. In the sixties, when his recording career slumped, his movies continued to pack them in (doing extremely well at drive-

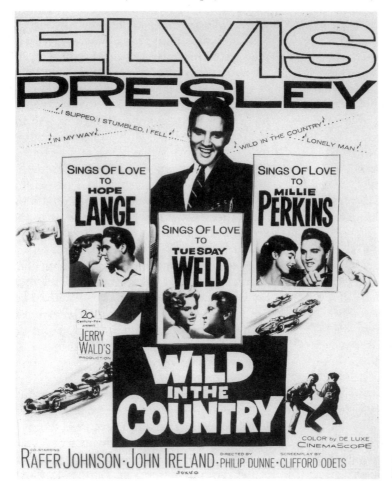

One of Elvis's best films, scripted by Clifford Odets.

ins), and he was one of the decade's highest-priced movie stars. Variations on juvenile-delinquent pictures, his earliest films were his best, as he did a good job playing restless, brooding young men who get angry and impatient with the unfair rules of the world, allow themselves to be corrupted, dump the people who have been kind to them, and are, finally, reformed by the loving, patient young women who detect their inner decency: Judy Tyler in *Jailhouse Rock,* Dolores Hart in both *Loving You* and his best film, *King Creole,* and so on. In the sixties, he'd play brash, women-chasing young men of action who, again, are tamed by the love of good women. His later films, mostly comedies, were assembly-line jobs with fistfights, car races, bad songs, and pretty actresses—fun to watch, up to a point. By that time, Presley showed more confidence in his acting—he was even okay doing comedy—but his characters were no longer interesting.

• **Cult Favorites:** *Jailhouse Rock* (1957, Richard Thorpe), *King Creole* (1958, Michael Curtiz), *Flaming Star* (1960, Don Siegel), *Viva Las Vegas* (1964, George Sidney).

• **Also Recommended:** *Love Me Tender* (1955, Robert D. Webb), *Loving You* (1957, Hal Kanter), *G.I. Blues* (1960, Norman Taurog), *Wild in the Country* (1961, Philip Dunne), *Kid Galahad* (1962, Phil Karlson), *Frankie and Johnny* (1966, Frederick de Cordova), *The Chautauqua/ The Trouble with Girls* (1969, Peter Tewksbury), *Elvis—That's the Way It Is* (1970, Denis Sanders).

○

VINCENT PRICE (1911–) This tall, mustached, cultured former stage actor played varied roles for the first twenty years of his movie career; then, in the late fifties, he began devoting himself almost exclusively to horror films, and became one of the genre's icons. He played sadistic, egocentric villains: brooding aristocrats with deep, dark secrets, or obsessive scientists and artists who once were decent but have forgotten the nobility of their work and seek revenge on those who ruined their lives. Price is well remembered for Roger Corman's gloomy, psychological Edgar Allan Poe films, in which the crumbling mansions represent the minds of his characters. Price may have given his best performance in a non-Corman Poe film, Michael Reeves's shocking *The Conqueror Worm,* playing monstrous, real-life seventeenth-century witchhunter Matthew Hopkins. He conveys the scorn that someone of Hopkins's breeding and intelligence would have for a world which allows him—even financially enables him—to commit what he knows are terrible acts. His angel of death is a menacing figure—shrewd, arrogant, brutal—and Price properly plays him with a great deal of restraint, keeping him *real.* Elsewhere Price has usually overacted, but his hamminess has pretty much suited his mad characters, like the vengeful actor in *Theatre of Blood* and the titular murderer in *The Abominable Dr. Phibes.* So forget the criticism, and watch *The Tingler, House of Wax, House on Haunted Hill,* the Poe films, and *Theatre of Blood.* He has appeared in an amazing number of truly enjoyable movies.

• **Cult Favorites:** *Laura* (1944, Otto Preminger), *The Baron of Arizona* (1950, Samuel Fuller), *His Kind of Woman* (1951, John Farrow), *House of Wax* (1953, André de Toth), *The Ten Commandments* (1956, Cecil B. De Mille), *The Story of Mankind* (1957, Irwin Allen), *The Fly* (1958, Kurt

Vincent Price loses control when he realizes what Peter Lorre has in store for him and Joyce Jameson in The Comedy of Terrors.

Neumann), *House on Haunted Hill* (1959, William Castle), *The Tingler* (1959, Castle), *House of Usher* (1960, Roger Corman), *The Pit and the Pendulum* (1961, Corman), *Confessions of an Opium Eater* (1962, Albert Zugsmith), *Beach Party* (1963, William Asher), *The Masque of the Red Death* (1964, Corman), *The Tomb of Ligeia* (1965, Corman), *The Conqueror Worm/The Witchfinder General* (1968, Michael Reeves), *Scream and Scream Again* (1970, Gordon Hessler), *The Abominable Dr. Phibes* (1971, Robert Fuest), *Theatre of Blood* (1973, Douglas Hickox).

• **Other Key Films:** *The Private Lives of Elizabeth and Essex* (1939, Michael Curtiz), *Tower of London* (1939, Rowland V. Lee), *The Invisible Man Returns* (1940, Joe May), *The House of Seven Gables* (1940, May), *The Song of Bernadette* (1943, Henry King), *Keys of the Kingdom* (1944, John M. Stahl), *Leave Her to Heaven* (1945, Stahl), *Dragonwyck* (1946, Joseh L. Mankiewicz), *Champagne for Caesar* (1950, Richard Whorf), *The Mad Magician* (1954, John Brahm), *While the City Sleeps* (1956, Fritz Lang), *The Bat* (1959, Crane Wilbur), *Master of the World* (1961, William Witney), *The Last Man on Earth* (1961, Sidney Salkow), *Tower of London* (1963, Corman), *Tales of Terror* (1963, Corman), *The Raven* (1963, Corman), *Diary of a Madman* (1963, Reginald LeBorg), *Comedy of Terrors* (1963, Jacques Tourneur), *The Haunted Palace* (1964, Corman), *The Oblong Box* (1969, Hessler), *Dr. Phibes Rises Again* (1972, Fuest), *Madhouse* (1974, Jim Clark).

JONATHAN PRYCE (1947–) Versatile, vastly talented, creepy-eyed British stage and screen actor has given intriguing portrayals in a number of unusual, out-of-the-mainstream films. In period pieces, he was menacing as Ray Bradbury's demonic Mr. Black, who runs a frightening traveling carnival in *Something Wicked This Way Comes,* and was vile as a procurer of bodies in *The Doctor and the Devils.* In modern-era films, he draws sympathy as a junkie musician in Hazel O'Connor's punk-rock band in *Breaking Glass,* and makes your skin crawl as an opportunist reporter in *The Ploughman's Lunch.* Pryce's grandest role was the lead in Terry Gilliam's ambitious, controversial near-masterpiece, *Brazil.* His Walter Mittyish low-level bureaucrat for an oppressive state ends up as the tortured prisoner of the state, but his lovely dreams survive the pain and brainwashing. Pryce caused much controversy by playing a Eurasian pimp in *Miss Saigon,* when the play moved from London to Broadway in 1991.
- **Cult Favorites:** *Breaking Glass* (1980, Brian Gibson), *Brazil* (1985, Terry Gilliam), *The Adventures of Baron Munchausen* (1989, Gilliam).
- **Sleepers:** *Something Wicked This Way Comes* (1983, Jack Clayton), *The Ploughman's Lunch* (1983, Richard Eyre).
- **Other Key Films:** *The Doctor and the Devils* (1985, Freddie Francis), *Consuming Passions* (1988, Giles Foster).

○

EDNA PURVIANCE (1894–1958) A pretty blonde from Paradise Valley, Nevada, with large, beautiful eyes and a sensitive mouth, she played opposite Charlie Chaplin in all his films (except the two that had no females) from 1915 to 1923, beginning with *A Night Out.* As noted in *The Films of Charles Chaplin,* "Whether she played a waif, a woman of wealth, a country girl, or a most alluring Carmen, she was the perfect leading lady for Chaplin, often providing a center of tranquillity in a world of comic madness." She was a charming presence and, more than being the prettiest part of the decor—the reason Chaplin originally hired her—she unexpectedly proved adept at light comedy. When some of her women look at Chaplin's tramp with love and admiration, we believe it—not surprising since the two had an offscreen attraction. In 1923, Purviance played the lead in *A Woman of Paris,* a serious feature with comic moments that Chaplin directed but wasn't in. Purviance's country girl flees to Paris when the young man she loves doesn't keep a rendezvous; she becomes mistress of Adolphe Menjou—then the country boy shows up. Because the response to the picture was unfavorable and because Chaplin and Purviance had a permanent falling out (she wouldn't make another film for him, though he continued to pay her salary), Chaplin kept it out of circulation for 50 years, a shame since it broke ground by simply portraying—without accusing—a single woman for whom sex is an integral part of life. Also, she was the rare Chaplin female lead whom he didn't idealize.
- **Cult Favorite:** *A Woman of Paris* (1923, Charles Chaplin).
- **Other Key Films:** *The Kid* (1921, Chaplin), 33 shorts with Charles Chaplin (1915–23, Chaplin).

○

RANDY QUAID (1953–) Tall, large-bodied, curly-haired Texan has only recently emerged from years in supporting parts—and from the shadow of handsome younger brother Dennis. A former stand-up comic who was briefly a regular on "Saturday Night Live," he has a flair for creating strange comic characters, including Chevy Chase's awful relative in *National Lampoon's Vacation* and *National Lampoon's Christmas Vacation*. But even his dramatic characters have been off-the-wall types who make us smile, beginning with the simple, sweet-faced, kleptomaniac soldier whom MPs Jack Nicholson and Otis Young escort to the brig in *The Last Detail*. Because he is big and can yell, his characters can be intimidating, as is his outlaw in *The Long Riders,* and the creepy, too orderly father in *Parents*. The roles that have best shown his versatility and dramatic power have been in television movies, especially as Lyndon Johnson.

• **Cult Favorites:** *The Last Picture Show* (1971, Peter Bogdanovich), *The Last Detail* (1973, Hal Ashby), *Midnight Express* (1978, Alan Parker), *Foxes* (1980, Adrian Lyne), *The Long Riders* (1980, Walter Hill), *Parents* (1989, Bob Balaban).

• **Sleepers:** *The Apprenticeship of Duddy Kravitz* (1974, Ted Kotcheff), *Bound for Glory* (1976, Ashby), *National Lampoon's Vacation* (1983, Harold Ramis).

• **Also of Interest:** *Breakout* (1975, Tom Gries), *Fool for Love* (1985, Robert Altman), *National Lampoon's Christmas Vacation* (1989, Jeremiah S. Chechik), *Out Cold* (1989, Malcolm Mowbray), *Texasville* (1990, Bogdanovich).

○

ROBERT QUARRY (1928–) An actor since he was a child—his credits include *Shadow of a Doubt* and *A Kiss Before Dying*—he was 42 when he lucked into the lead in *Count Yorga, Vampire,* a low-budget picture that was originally intended to be primarily a sex film but instead became a lurid horror film that made a lot of money and Quarry temporarily famous. He was effectively evil as the vampire who stalks Los Angeles, killing boys and making their pretty girl-friends his vampire brides. He almost seemed too professional for the sloppy production. Quarry played Yorga once more, and then in *The Deathmaster,* which he produced, he was a vampire who becomes a Manson-like guru. He would take supporting roles in two Vincent Price films made in England and in the exploitation film *Sugar Hill* before disappearing. Recently he returned in minor roles in cheap Fred Olen Ray action films.

• **Cult Favorite:** *Count Yorga, Vampire* (1970, Bob Kelljan).

• **Other Key Films:** *Return of Count Yorga* (1971, Kelljan), *Dr. Phibes Rises Again* (1972, Robert Fuest), *The Deathmaster* (1972, Ray Danton), *Madhouse* (1973, Jim Clark).

• **Also of Interest:** *Sugar Hill* (1974, Paul Maslansky), *Cyclone* (1986, Fred Olen Ray), *Commando Squad* (1987, Ray), *The Phantom Empire* (1987, Ray).

○

LINNEA QUIGLEY This tiny, cute, shapely blonde from Iowa had bounced around unnoticed for about five years in minor parts in Grade-Z horror films and a couple of Cheech & Chong comedies when she gained instant notoriety with her role in *Return of the Living Dead.* She was a wild-haired punker named Trash who strips naked and dances under the moon in a cemetery before being devoured by ghouls. Horror fans took notice, adolescents fell in love, and soon she was starring in her own horror films. She has been

The Queen of the Zs, Linnea Quigley, does her signature moon dance with special implements in The Hollywood Chainsaw Hookers.

billed as the "Queen of the Bs," but her campy, quickly made films have rarely been expensive enough to qualify as Bs. They are rated R, which has helped Linnea become the horror film's current sex queen. Made with the video market in mind, most have outlandish titles—we have been promised *Space Sluts in the Slammer*—and feature Quigley nude. In *Treasure of the Moon Goddess,* she plays a rock singer (Quigley used to play guitar for the L.A. band The Skirts) who is taken for a tribal queen. In other films, she has done variations of her nude "moon dance." She dances topless while holding two chain saws in *The Hollywood Chainsaw Hookers,* before she does in the villain. She was gruesomely victimized in her early small roles, but her later heroines emerge victorious. Her acting range is limited, but she is one of the fun celebrities of today's offbeat cinema.

• **Cult Favorites:** *Return of the Living Dead* (1985, Dan O'Bannon), *Sorority Babes in the Slime Bowl-O-Rama* (1987, David DeCoteau), *Treasure of the Moon Goddess* (1988, Joseph Louis Agraz), *Night of the Demons/Halloween Party* (1988, Kevin S.

Tenney), *The Hollywood Chainsaw Hookers* (1988, Fred Olen Ray).

• **Other Key Films:** *The Young Warriors* (1983, Lawrence D. Foldes), *Savage Streets* (1984, Danny Steinman), *Silent Night, Deadly Night* (1984, Charles E. Seller), *Creepozoids* (1987, DeCoteau), *Nightmare Sisters* (1988, DeCoteau).

• **Also of Interest:** *Stone Cold Dead* (1980, George Menduluk), *American Gigolo* (1980, Paul Schrader), *Don't Go Near the Park* (1981), *Graduation Day* (1981, Herb Freed), *The Black Room* (1981, Elly Kenner and Norman Thaddeus Vane), *Cheech & Chong's Nice Dreams* (1981, Thomas Chong), *Still Smoking* (1983, Chong), *A Nightmare on Elm Street 4: The Dream Master* (1988, Renny Harlin).

○

PATRICIA QUINN (1944–) Belfast-born actress played the wild-haired, heavily made-up Magenta (A Domestic) in *The Rocky Horror Picture Show,* having originated the role in the London stage production. At the beginning, Magenta wears a maid's outfit and follows the orders of Dr. Frank-N-Furter (Tim Curry), even pulling a switch that turns the visitors into stone. But at the end, she and her lover/brother Riff-Raff (Richard O'Brien) turn up in space outfits and threaten Frank with an antimatter laser blast, leading to his death. Quinn has appeared in theater, television, and film in London, but nothing else has brought her attention in America, including the disappointing sequel, *Shock Treatment.* It's hard to even pick her out in such films as *Up the Chastity Belt, Up the Front,* and *Rentadick.*

• **Cult Favorite:** *The Rocky Horror Picture Show* (1975, Jim Sharman).

• **Also of Interest:** *Shock Treatment* (1981, Sharman).

○

VERA HRUBA RALSTON/VERA HRUBA (1919–) At 17, representing Czechoslovakia, Vera Hruba finished seventeenth in the women's figure-skating competition at the 1936 Winter Olympics. She was an attractive blonde, with exotic eyes, and a few years later, she followed the Olympic winner, Norway's Sonja Henie, to Hollywood. Her publicity would eventually claim she finished second in the Olympics and was born in 1921 or later. At first she appeared in films that featured her athleticism, *Ice-Capades* and *Ice-Capades Revue,* but graduated to leads in B movies as Vera Hruba Ralston and then (to stop hearing the "Hubba-Hubba"/"Hruba-Hruba" jokes), just Vera Ralston. She wouldn't get far in melodramas (she might have been a good "foreign" villainess during the war years, but didn't get such parts), but she carved out a niche for herself in the higher-budgeted westerns that were made by Republic, starring William "Wild Bill" Elliott and John Wayne. It was difficult to find an excuse for having a well-dressed female with a Czech accent in a film about the Old West, especially when the actress neither had much range nor looked at home on the range (she often played French chanteuses). That she was the mistress and eventual bride (1952) of studio head Herbert Yates wasn't considered an acceptable reason, at least not by the stockholders who sued Yates for using their money to finance what they claimed were 18 Ralston flops in a row. Word got out that after two pictures with Ralston, John Wayne refused to be in any more, because he thought them damaging to his career; some exhibitors refused to book Ralston films or to put her name on the marquee. Ralston would eventually be

Vera Hruba Ralston and John Wayne in Dakota.

called the "Queen of the Clinkers," but it's likely only a couple of her films lost money (a reason the suit was dropped). In spite of it all, she injected those westerns with both exoticism and class. And she was particularly good at one thing: she was extremely alluring when she looked, wide-eyed, up at the heroes with whom she was falling in love, such as John Wayne in *The Fighting Kentuckian*. She was more romantically aggressive than her American-born competition. Never as bad as camp enthusiasts claim, she improved over the years, and was quite good as a native girl in *Fair Wind to Java*.
• **Key Films:** *The Lady and the Monster* (1944, George Sherman), *Storm over Lis-*

bon (1944, Sherman), *Lake Placid Serenade* (1944, Steve Sekely), *Dakota* (1945, Joseph Kane), *The Plainsman and the Lady* (1946, Kane), *Wyoming* (1947, Kane), *I, Jane Doe* (1948, John H. Auer), *Angel on the Amazon* (1948, Auer), *The Fighting Kentuckian* (1949, George Waggner), *The Wild Blue Yonder* (1951, Allan Dwan), *Hoodlum Empire* (1952, Kane), *Fair Wind to Java* (1953, Kane), *Jubilee Trail* (1954, Kane), *The Man Who Died Twice* (1958, Kane).

○

CHARLOTTE RAMPLING (1945–) Very slim, mysterious, naughty-looking, long-haired brunette of the smart-cool Lauren Bacall school. This English-born actress never reached the stardom many critics predicted for her—though she was enticing in her best shot, deceiving her lover, lawyer Paul Newman, in *The Verdict*—but she has made good impressions in a number of films, playing intelligent, classy women who can't—or make no attempt to—deny their sexual urges. They either throw themselves at men (as her slutty married woman does to Robert Mitchum's Philip Marlowe in *Farewell, My Lovely*), or excite males in the audience by wearing see-through clothes (as in *Zardoz* and *Foxtrot*) or nothing at all. Her most controversial role was in an ugly film, *The Night Porter*, as a masochistic Jewish concentration-camp survivor who willingly resumes a perverse sexual relationship with the German (Dirk Bogarde) who abused her as a teenager in the camp. Her bare-chested dance remains her most famous movie scene, but is by no means the most erotic.

• **Cult Favorites:** *Zardoz* (1974, John Boorman), *The Night Porter* (1974, Liliana Cavani), *Farewell, My Lovely* (1975, Dick Richards), *Stardust Memories* (1980, Woody Allen), *Angel Heart* (1987, Alan Parker).

• **Other Key Films:** *Georgy Girl* (1966, Silvio Narizzano), *The Damned* (1969, Luchino Visconti), *Henry VIII and His Six Wives* (1973, Waris Hussein), *The Purple Taxi* (1977, Yves Boisset), *The Verdict* (1982, Sidney Lumet).

• **Also of Interest:** *Rotten to the Core* (1965, John Boulting), *Asylum* (1972, Roy Ward

Charlotte Rampling and Sean Connery in Zardoz.

Baker), *Corky* (1972, Leonard Horn), *Foxtrot* (1975, Arturo Ripstein), *Orca* (1977, Michael Anderson).

○

BASIL RATHBONE (1892–1967) This South African–born ex-Shakespearean actor, with precise, weaponlike diction; piercing, knowing, intimidating eyes; and slim features, including a sharp nose that all snoopers should have, could have played Margaret Hamilton's brother. Instead he established himself as a great screen villain and then went on to play one of the screen's great heroes, Sherlock Holmes. His villainy was on display in costume pictures, where he was a formidable foe of Errol Flynn's Robin Hood, Tyrone Power's Zorro, and other heroes. He was unafraid of anyone. When he brandished a sword, it was like an extension of his sharp-edged body. His sword fight with Flynn's Robin Hood (with director Michael Curtiz's trademark giant shadows covering the wall) is one of the adventure cinema's most exciting confrontations. Though Flynn won on the screen, in reality, Rathbone was the more skilled swordsman of the two. What distinguished Rathbone's ruthless kings and palace advisers is that they weren't evil just because they enjoyed being evil but because they saw their cold-hearted acts as the correct conduct for men in power (who want to stay in power). Rathbone's Holmes grew tiresome as the years went on, simply because he seemed to lose the lust for the hunt—his motives became less personal—but in the beginning, and sporadically thereafter, he was a lot of fun as he solved cryptic mysteries, patronized Watson, was equally aloof and ostentatious, let hatred creep into his eyes as he discussed Moriarty, and

delighted in his own cunning. His Holmes never made great, uncanny deductions when solving crimes—although he cleverly pieced together many minor clues—but Rathbone had such presence, and conveyed that his character had such confidence in a crisis, that viewers forget Holmes never has the chance to show what a great detective he can be.

• **Cult Favorites:** *The Adventures of Robin Hood* (1939, Michael Curtiz and William Keighley), *The Hound of the Baskervilles* (1939, Sidney Lanfield), *The Adventures of Sherlock Holmes* (1939, Alfred L. Werker).

• **Sleepers:** *The Sun Never Sets* (1939, Rowland V. Lee), *Tower of London* (1939, Lee), *The Scarlet Claw* (1944, Roy William Neill).

• **Also Recommended:** *David Copperfield* (1935, George Cukor), *Anna Karenina* (1935, Clarence Brown), *The Last Days of Pompeii* (1935, Ernest B. Schoedsack), *A Tale of Two Cities* (1935, Jack Conway), *Captain Blood* (1935, Curtiz), *If I Were King* (1938, Frank Lloyd), *Son of Frankenstein* (1939, Lee), *The Mark of Zorro* (1940, Rouben Mamoulian), *Above Suspicion* (1943, Richard Thorpe), *The Court Jester* (1956, Norman Panama and Melvin Frank), *The Last Hurrah* (1958, John Ford), *Tales of Terror* (1962, Roger Corman), *The Comedy of Terrors* (1964, Jacques Tourneur), *Queen of Blood/Planet of Blood* (1966, Curtis Harrington).

• **Other Key Films:** *Sherlock Holmes and the Voice of Terror* (1942, John Rawlins), *Sherlock Holmes and the Secret Weapon* (1942, Neill), *Sherlock Holmes in Washington* (1943, Neill), *Sherlock Holmes Faces Death* (1943, Neill), *Sherlock Holmes and the Spider Woman* (1944, Neill), *Pearl of Death* (1944, Neill), *House of Fear* (1945, Neill), *The Woman in Green* (1945, Neill), *Pursuit to Algiers* (1945, Neill), *Terror by*

Night (1946, Neill), *Dressed to Kill* (1946, Neill).

○

ALDO RAY (1926–91) Hoarse, husky, rough-looking ex–Navy frogman in World War II who was convincing as sailors and foot soldiers in fifties war films. His soldiers were brave, reliable, sensitive yet tough, poorly educated (some were rednecks) yet opinionated, and patriotic. Though they were outspoken, they followed orders. His civilian characters acted the way you'd expect his soldiers (and ex-cons) to turn out once they got their releases: men who try their hardest to adjust to the new world and just get by in blue-collar jobs. He was an offbeat lead out of uniform, but did well in minor films, as well as in George Cukor's perceptive comedy-drama *The Marrying Kind,* giving a realistic performance as Judy Holliday's flawed but well-meaning husband. Probably Ray's cult status has more to do with his later appearances in low-grade exploitation films, including *Nigger Lover, Biohazard, Human Experiments,* and, of course, *Bog.* He had the distinction of being the first "name" actor to be in a porno film, *Sweet Savage,* although he remained clothed in the hard-core western. He made much worse films.
• **Cult Favorites:** *The Marrying Kind* (1952, George Cukor), *Sweet Savage* (1979, Ann Perry).
• **Sleeper:** *Nightfall* (1956, Jacques Tourneur).
• **Other Key Films:** *Pat and Mike* (1952, Cukor), *Miss Sadie Thompson* (1953, Curtis Bernhardt), *We're No Angels* (1955, Michael Curtiz), *Battle Cry* (1955, Raoul Walsh), *Three Stripes in the Sun* (1955, Richard Murphy), *Men in War* (1957, Anthony Mann), *God's Little Acre* (1958,

Mann), *The Naked and the Dead* (1958, Walsh), *Riot on Sunset Strip* (1967, Arthur Dreifuss), *The Green Berets* (1968, John Wayne), *Psychic Killer* (1975, Ray Danton), *Haunts* (1977, Herb Freed).

○

RONALD REAGAN (1911–) If he was expected to play world-weary heroes, he didn't shave for a couple of days, narrowed his eyes, didn't open his mouth so much when he talked, and muddled through hard-boiled dialogue. He merely seemed tired. When he had light roles, he shaved and smiled more. That pretty much sums up his range as an actor. Our ex-President was one of our blandest, most wooden leading men on the screen. He had good moments in *King's Row* (especially when he discovers that his legs have been amputated: "Where's the rest of me?!") and *The Hasty Heart,* and was likable in *Knute Rockne—All American,* as dying halfback George Gipp ("Win one for the Gipper!"), and properly detestable as the villain in his last film, *The Killers*—but that's not much for a 27-year career. I did like his liberal(!) lawyer in *Storm Warning,* but maybe because I was grateful for anyone who helps Ginger Rogers against the KKK. As his political stature rose, some of his movies gained attention, particularly among camp movie fans. In the dull *Hellcats of the Navy,* he romances his future wife, Nancy Davis, and, frighteningly, gives orders to fire missiles. In his most famous film, *Bedtime for Bonzo,* his college professor raises a chimpanzee to prove that environment, not heredity, is the reason people become good or bad. Interestingly, Val Burton, one of the scriptwriters responsible for the almost-leftist philosophy that Reagan's character expounds, would soon be blacklisted as a suspected communist. Attempts by Democrats to ridicule Reagan by showing this film at fundraisers backfired, because the picture is surprisingly amusing, and Reagan comes across as reliable, friendly, earnest, and an all-around good sport. If Bonzo is a better performer, it is because he had the comic range to surprise us, while Reagan is predictable—a characteristic that would appeal to voters.

• **Cult Favorites:** *Bedtime for Bonzo* (1951, Frederick de Cordova), *Hellcats of the Navy* (1957, Nathan Juran), *The Killers* (1964, Don Siegel).

• **Sleeper:** *Storm Warning* (1950, Stuart Heisler).

• **Other Key Films:** *Brother Rat* (1938, William Keighley), *Dark Victory* (1939, Edmund Goulding), *Hell's Kitchen* (1939, Lewis Seiler and E. A. Dupont), *Angels Wash Their Faces* (1939, Ray Enright), *Knute Rockne—All American* (1940, Lloyd Bacon), *Santa Fe Trail* (1940, Michael Curtiz), *Kings Row* (1942, Sam Wood), *Juke Girl* (1942, Curtis Bernhardt), *Desperate Journey* (1942, Raoul Walsh), *Stallion Road* (1947, James V. Kern), *Night unto Night* (1949, Siegel), *The Girl from*

Ronald Reagan in a publicity shot with Barbara Stanwyck for Cattle Queen of Montana.

Jones Beach (1949, Peter Godfrey), *The Winning Team* (1952, Seiler), *Tropic Zone* (1953, Lewis R. Foster), *Cattle Queen of Montana* (1954, Allan Dwan), *Tennessee's Partner* (1955, Dwan).

○

OLIVER REED (1938–) Early in his career, this dark-haired, solidly built English actor played young toughs who maybe are out for a good time but are really too angry to have one. His first starring role was in the Hammer horror film *The Curse of the Werewolf,* with good and evil fighting for possession of his soul. Throughout his career, Reed would move back and forth between evil characters and good but flawed men. His mean eyes, tough (though handsome) face, dark scowl, imposing build, and intense manner, the way his voice boomed when he was enraged, and his practice of loudly inhaling before delivering a line all made him an ideal villain. His Bill Sikes in his uncle Carol Reed's *Oliver!,* uncaring father in *Tommy,* and other shrewd brutes are genuinely hateful. He has never been as good playing heroes, but it's fun rooting for him as Athos in Richard Lester's "Three Musketeers" movies. Perhaps Reed does well as this hero because he is as cynical about the world as Reed's villains. Except Athos doesn't try to spread misery. All Reed's characters seem to have permanent migraines. His most intriguing character is his morally corrupt yet politically enlightened priest in Ken Russell's harrowing witchcraft drama, *The Devils.* He's a sinner who becomes a saint by refusing to confess he is a witch, although this means he'll be tortured and burned alive. Reed earlier gave a strong performance in Russell's *Women in Love,* as Gerald, who has a combative relationship with Gudrun (Glenda Jackson) that eventually drives them apart, and has a strong bond with Alan Bates's Birkin, culminating in their famous symbolic nude wrestling scene. Gerald is another of his physical, self-destructive characters.

• **Cult Favorites:** *These Are the Damned/The Damned* (1963, Joseph Losey), *The Assassination Bureau* (1969, Basil Dearden), *Women in Love* (1969, Ken Russell), *The Devils* (1971, Russell), *The Three Musketeers* (1974, Richard Lester), *Tommy* (1975, Russell), *The Brood* (1979, David Cronenberg), *Castaway* (1987, Nicolas Roeg).

• **Other Key Films:** *The Curse of the Werewolf* (1961, Terence Fisher), *Night Creatures* (1962, Peter Graham Scott), *Paranoiac* (1963, Freddie Francis), *The Girl-Getters/The System* (1966, Michael Winner), *The Jokers* (1966, Winner), *I'll Never Forget What's 'is Name* (1967, Winner), *The Trap* (1966, Sidney Hayers), *Oliver!* (1968, Carol Reed), *Hannibal Brooks* (1969, Winner), *The Lady in the Car with Glasses and a Gun* (1970, Anatole Litvak), *The Four Musketeers* (1975, Lester), *Royal Flash* (1975, Lester), *Burnt Offerings* (1976, Dan Curtis), *Ransom/Maniac* (1977, Richard Compton), *Venom* (1982, Piers Haggard), *The Black Arrow* (1984, John Hough).

○

HARRY REEMS Herbert Streicher appeared in off-off-Broadway productions and had bits with the National Shakespeare Company before he realized he could make a good living acting by making porno loops and features. He played numerous zany doctors before Gerard Damiano cast him as another one in *Deep Throat,* gave him $100, and changed his name to Harry

Reems. As the burlesque-style doctor who diagnoses the reason for Linda Lovelace's sexual frustration—her clitoris is in her throat—and helps her achieve ultimate satisfaction, he played a major part in the porno industry's breakthrough film and gained instant fame. He soon appeared in a dramatic role, as Georgina Spelvin's sexual mentor in hell, in Damiano's more erotic *The Devil in Miss Jones,* solidifying his claim as porno's top leading man. He was sought by other porno producers and newspaper and television interviewers, and he also gave lectures. The mustached actor was an adequate performer with a flair for comedy, though he tended to ham it up because he didn't take these projects seriously. He usually starred in light comedies in which he played doctors—Dr. Scrotum in *Intensive Care*—and several women would service him. He was in *Sometimes Sweet Susan,* the first union-made adult film. In 1976, he became the first performer to be prosecuted on a federal level, when the Department of Justice charged him with being part of a "conspiracy" to make and distribute *Deep Throat.* He was convicted in Memphis, Tennessee, but prior to his appeal the case was dismissed. He tried his hand at legitimate R-rated films, and didn't make another X-rated film until *Society Affair* in 1982. He remains an outsider in the porno industry.

• **Cult Favorites:** *Deep Throat* (1972, Gerard Damiano), *The Devil in Miss Jones* (1972, Damiano).

• **Other Key Films:** *It Happened in Hollywood* (1972, Peter Locke), *High Rise* (1972, Danny Stone), *Sometimes Sweet Susan* (1974, Fred Donaldson), *Wet Rainbow/Rainbow* (1974, Duddy Kane), *Butterflies* (1974, Joseph W. Sarno), *Intensive Care* (1974, David Sear), *Bel Ami* (1974, Bert Torn), *Every Inch a Lady* (1975, John and Lem Amero), *Society Affair* (1982, Robert McCallum).

○

STEVE REEVES (1926–) In 1959, about the time George Reeves, television's Superman, committed suicide, unrelated Steve Reeves emerged as a new idol for young boys in America playing another superhero living among mortals on earth. The bearded, handsome, incredibly muscular former "Mr. America" and "Mr. Universe" was the title character in Joseph E. Levine's successful, trend-setting Italian epics, *Hercules* (made in 1957, but released in America two years later) and the less impressive *Hercules Unchained.* He was the best of the early beefcake stars, with more presence than the other American and European bodybuilders and actors (Reg Park, Mark Forest, Kirk Morris, Alan Steel, Brad Harris, and even Gordon Scott) who played mythic musclemen in Italian epics. He was strong and built so well that you could believe his powerful feats; his Hercules is sympathetic and poignant because he yearns to be mortal so he can love and fight like other men. Reeves and delectable Sylva Koscina were an eye-opening couple. Reeves played other mythic heroes in Italian films, but his best post-*Hercules* film was the enjoyable swashbuckler *Morgan the Pirate,* in which he played (without a beard) a real-life, quite human pirate from the not-too-distant past. In his dubbed films, Reeves had a deep voice that suited someone with his physique, but rumors persisted that his real voice was high-pitched. I don't know—I can't remember seeing him on a talk show.

• **Cult Favorites:** *Hercules* (1957, Pietro Francisci), *Morgan the Pirate* (1961, André de Toth).

Steve Reeves as Hercules.

• **Other Key Films:** *Jail Bait* (1954, Edward D. Wood, Jr.), *Hercules Unchained* (1959, Francisci), *The White Warrior* (1959, Riccardo Freda), *The Last Days of Pompeii* (1960, Mario Bonnard), *Goliath and the Barbarians* (1960, Carlo Campogalliani), *Thief of Bagdad* (1961, Arthur Lubin), *The Trojan Horse* (1961, Giorgio Ferroni), *Duel of the Titans* (1961, Sergio Corbucci), *The Slave* (1962, Corbucci), *Sandokan the Great* (1964, Umberto Lenzi).

○

LIZ RENAY (1927–) The blond, buxom show-girl, Hollywood starlet, and girlfriend of gangster Mickey Cohen went to Arizona to play a jailed gangster's moll in the 1959 indie *A Date with Death*. Coincidentally, a couple of years later she went to prison on perjury charges, after refusing to rat on Mafia acquaintances. Released, she returned to movies and was kidnapped by "Clash Flagg," aka Ray Steckler, in Steckler's cheap bit of sensationalism, *The Thrill Killers.* She went on to become a stripper (bringing her daughter into the act), appearing on rare occasion in films. However, an enraptured John Waters recruited her to play Muffy St. Jacques in *Desperate Living.* She fit in comfortably among Waters's oddball cast, playing Mink Stole's lesbian lover—who insists Mink cut off the penis she just got in an operation—and lounging in the nude while cockroaches race across her body. It was just another strange experience in Renay's eventful life.

- **Cult Favorite:** *Desperate Living* (1977, John Waters).
- **Other Key Films:** *A Date with Death* (1959, Harold Daniels), *The Thrill Killers* (1965, Ray Steckler), *Day of the Nightmare* (1965, John Bushelman).
- **Also of Interest:** *Blackenstein* (1973, William A. Levy), *Deep Roots* (1980, Lisa Barr).

○

CANDICE RIALSON (1950–) It could be said that this beautiful young blonde was playing herself in Roger Corman's funny New World self-parody, *Hollywood Boulevard,* as a starlet who gets work in sex-and-violence exploitation films for an independent film company. Rialson was New World's up-and-coming star for a while, making her mark in their silly, nudity-filled nurse-and-teachers comedies. But she never got anywhere, despite her looks, bubbly personality, flair for comedy, and sex appeal. She virtually disappeared, leaving her mark in such weird roles as a young woman with a vagina that sings and talks (griping about bad lovers!) in the ghastly *Chatterbox!* She did get to play Gloria Grahame's daughter in *Mama's Lit-*

tle Girls, but that was a truly sleazy film. If she had a prestige film it was *Winter Kills,* but she had only a bit as one of the young nurses who plays around with John Huston's old rake as they ride in a golf cart.

- **Cult Favorites:** *Hollywood Boulevard* (1976, Joe Dante and Allan Arkush), *Winter Kills* (1979, William Richert).
- **Other Key Films:** *Pets* (1973, Raphael Nussbaum), *Mama's Dirty Girls* (1974, John Hayes), *Candy Stripe Nurses* (1974, Allan Holleb), *Summer School Teachers* (1975, Barbara Peeters), *Chatterbox!* (1976, Tom DeSimone).

○

KANE RICHMOND (1906–73) The former Fred Bowditch was a legitimate contender with Buster Crabbe for the title "King of the Serials." The handsome, square-jawed actor starred in seven serials between 1935 and 1947, playing strong, determined men of action. He was good in a clinch with the likes of serial queen Kay Aldridge in *Haunted Harbor* but his athletic endeavors were accomplished by stand-in David Sharpe. His best serial is, arguably, *Spy Smasher,* in which an American agent (he also played his twin brother) romances the lovely Marguerite Chapman, and uncovers the identity of the Mask, dastardly leader of a Nazi spy ring. Although the death of the twin may have precluded it, it's unfortunate that Spy Smasher wasn't brought back for future serials. Richmond also appeared in features, mostly taking leads in low-budget action pictures. He is best remembered for his three films as the radio hero The Shadow, at Monogram.

- **Cult Favorites:** *The Lost City* (1935 serial, Harry Revier), *Spy Smasher* (1942 serial, William Witney).
- **Other Key Films:** *The Adventures of Rex*

and Rinty (1935 serial, Ford Beebe and Reeves Eason), *Haunted Harbor* (1944 serial, Spencer Bennet and Wallace Grissell), *Brenda Starr, Reporter* (1945 serial, Wallace W. Fox), *Jungle Raiders* (1945 serial, Lesley Selander), *The Shadow Returns* (1946, William Beaudine), *Brick Bradford* (1947 serial, Bennet).

○

MOLLY RINGWALD (1968–) The daughter of blind musician Bob Ringwald, she sang with his Great Pacific Jazz Band before she was 4, and was the cinema's teen princess from 1984 to 1986, adored by female "Ringlets" throughout America. She had a look they liked: orange-red hair; large lips smothered with lipstick; a pretty, pouty face; intelligent, expressive eyes; and the latest teen fashions. They could identify with the precocious 13-year-old in Paul Mazursky's *Tempest* and, better, the confused high-school girls she played so convincingly in writer-producer-director John Hughes's *Sixteen Candles, The Breakfast Club,* and *Pretty in Pink* (which Hughes had Howard Deutch direct). They worry about boys, images, and what to wear to the dance; they think every bad thing is a catastrophe; they assume all adults in the world have conspired against them; they roll their eyes to the sky any time anybody says anything uncool; they are a bit affected and narcissistic but are nice girls; and they finally let their defenses down and open up to boys and fathers (who *do* care and understand after all)—and good things happen to them in return. Young girl movie fans identified with her, and boys wanted to take her to their proms. Surprisingly, she has had a succession of flops in adult roles—her acting hasn't improved with age—but those who grew up with her wait patiently for her breakthrough.

• **Cult Favorites:** *Tempest* (1982, Paul Mazursky), *Sixteen Candles* (1984, John Hughes), *The Breakfast Club* (1985, Hughes), *Pretty in Pink* (1986, Howard Deutch).

• **Also of Interest:** *The Pick-Up Artist* (1987, James Toback), *Betsy's Wedding* (1990, Alan Alda).

○

TEX RITTER (1907–74) Texas-born singing cowboy—elected to both the Cowboy Hall of Fame and the Country and Western Hall of Fame—starred in 58 westerns between 1936 and 1945. Billed as "America's Most Beloved Cowboy," he moved from Grand National to Monogram to Columbia, where he teamed up with Wild Bill Elliott, and rode his horse White Flash to Universal, where his partners were Johnny Mack Brown and comic Fuzzy Knight, and to PRC for a "Texas Rangers" series. He was an amiable, unassuming hero, shyly courting the ladies and killing villains with workmanlike precision. He claimed he killed Charles King in 20 films and that "it usually was behind the same rock." His plots were unremarkable, with Tex trying to clear his name (or Johnny Mack Brown's) or, as a sheriff or government agent, trying to round up rustlers, bank robbers, or land-grabbers. His films had a lot of action and several songs. What distinguished him from other singing cowboys is that, being genuinely interested in western folklore, he sang traditional songs of the West. When he retired from cowboy films, he continued his successful singing career. The most memorable of his ballads was the Oscar-winning theme to *High Noon,* heard throughout that movie. The father of actor John Ritter.

• **Sample Films:** *Song of the Gringo* (1936, John P. McCarthy), *Arizona Days* (1937, John English), *Westbound Stage* (1939, Spencer Bennet), *The Cowboy from Sundown* (1940, Bennet), *King of Dodge City* (1941, Lambert Hillyer), *Raiders of San Joaquin* (1942, Lewis D. Collins), *Deep in the Heart of Texas* (1942, Elmer Clifton), *The Old Chisholm Trail* (1942, Clifton), *Cheyenne Roundup* (1943, Ray Taylor), *Marshall of Gunsmoke* (1944, Vernon Keays), *Oklahoma Raiders* (1944, Collins).

○

THELMA RITTER (1905–69) Brooklyn-born character actress debuted in *Miracle on 34th Street* as the shopper who swears allegiance to Macy's after its new Santa, Edmund Gwenn's Kris Kringle, generously sends her to Gimbel's for an inexpensive toy. She would have been marvelous playing flighty eccentrics, but instead she was wonderful as straight-from-the-hip, down-to-earth "characters" who put in a hard day's work, understand what it takes to survive in a tough world, and know the value of money, friendship, and having a place of importance in other people's lives. They wear inexpensive coats, flowery dresses, and an odd assortment of hats; they are feisty, cynical, opinionated and outspoken, quick with the wisecracks (Ritter was very funny), and ready with common-sense advice. Rather than being interfering, they are good-hearted and caring. She played housekeepers and mother's helpers, Marilyn Monroe's landlady in *The Misfits,* an ex-vaudevillian who has become Bette Davis's aide and live-in companion in *All About Eve,* James Stewart's nurse–physical therapist in *Rear Window,* a poor tie peddler in *Pickup on South Street.* They all have pride and dignity, and with good

reason: they are loyal and willing to put themselves on the line. In *Rear Window,* Ritter does "leg" work for Stewart, who is temporarily wheelchair-bound, taking part in some dangerous sleuthing; in *Pickup on South Street,* she makes herself a target of execution rather than turning in Richard Widmark to the commies. In film after film, men and women (like Davis, Monroe, and Doris Day) are glad she is around. So is the moviegoer, for she is a joy to watch. Nominated for six Supporting Actress Oscars.

• **Cult Favorites:** *Miracle on 34th Street* (1947, George Seaton), *All About Eve* (1950, Joseph L. Mankiewicz), *Pickup on South Street* (1953, Samuel Fuller), *Rear Window* (1954, Alfred Hitchcock), *Pillow Talk* (1959, Michael Gordon), *The Misfits* (1961, John Huston).

• **Other Key Films:** *Call Northside 777* (1948, Henry Hathaway), *A Letter to Three Wives* (1949, Mankiewicz), *Father Was a Fullback* (1949, John M. Stahl), *Perfect Strangers* (1950, Bretaigne Windust), *The Mating Season* (1951, Mitchell Leisen), *As Young As You Feel* (1951, Harmon Jones), *The Model and the Marriage Broker* (1951, George Cukor), *Titanic* (1953, Jean Negulesco), *Lucy Gallant* (1955, Robert Parrish), *Daddy Long Legs* (1955, Negulesco), *The Proud and the Profane* (1956, Seaton), *A Hole in the Head* (1959, Frank Capra), *The Second Time Around* (1961, Vincent Sherman), *Birdman of Alcatraz* (1962, John Frankenheimer), *Move Over, Darling* (1963, Gordon).

○

ADAM ROARKE His costume was a leather jacket and a three-day beard. He was also reasonably handsome and rugged-looking, and could ride a motorcycle and talk tough.

That was enough to qualify him as the star of a number of the better outlaw-biker films, ideal drive-in movies. His bikers could be real bastards, but a few—in *The Savage Seven, The Losers*—had morality that made them choose the right side. You always got the feeling he was only an actor playing a tough guy—although he had been in gangs back in Brooklyn. You also got the feeling that he was holding back on his talents, saving them for more significant roles that never came. At least he got to escape the biker milieu for two artier films, *Play It As It Lays* and *The Stunt Man*, in the latter film as the actor for whom Steve Railsback doubles. There were hints he could play comedy.

• **Cult Favorites:** *El Dorado* (1967, Howard Hawks), *Hell's Angels on Wheels* (1967, Richard Rush), *The Savage Seven* (1968, Rush), *Psych-Out* (1968, Rush), *The Losers* (1970, Jack Starrett), *Dirty Mary Crazy Larry* (1974, John Hough), *The Stunt Man* (1980, Rush).

• **Also of Interest:** *Hell's Belles/Girl in a Mini-Skirt* (1969, Maury Dexter), *Play It As It Lays* (1972, Frank Perry), *The Four Deuces* (1975, William H. Bushnell, Jr.), *Trespasses* (1986, Loren Bivens and Adam Roarke).

○

JASON ROBARDS/ROBARDS, JR. (1922–) Of all great actors, possibly the one most taken for granted. He has given brilliant starring and supporting performances for 20 years, in all kinds of roles: Jamie Tyrone in *Long Day's Journey into Night*, George S. Kaufman in the otherwise mundane *Act One*, a nonconformist who must go back to work if he wants to support nephew Barry Gordon in *A Thousand Clowns* (one of the first pictures identified as a "cult movie"),

Al Capone in *The St. Valentine's Day Massacre*, a comical outlaw in *Once Upon a Time in the West*, an honest westerner in *The Ballad of Cable Hogue*, Ben Bradlee in *All the President's Men*, Dashiell Hammett in *Julia*, Howard Hughes in *Melvin and Howard*, a mild-mannered father who wants his young son's respect in *Something Wicked This Way Comes*, and so on. Typically, his characters are iconoclasts who are wise, unpretentious, and philosophical. They love telling interesting stories, making wise observations about the present, and giving advice about the future. They have had many experiences so they have smart perspectives on all situations. Sensitive men, they understand the people they speak to and can help them deal with many of their problems (as in his scenes with Jane Fonda's Lillian Hellman in *Julia*). Since these characters don't feel sorry for themselves, they see no need to mince words with others. He is usually the calm voice of reason, there for anyone in a jam, whether with sound advice or with deeds. When Robards is on the screen, viewers and characters feel things are under control. The son of actor Jason Robards, he has been a standout stage actor since the mid-fifties. He was married to Lauren Bacall.

• **Cult Favorites:** *A Thousand Clowns* (1965, Fred Coe), *The St. Valentine's Day Massacre* (1967, Roger Corman), *Once Upon a Time in the West* (1969, Sergio Leone), *Isadora/The Loves of Isadora* (1969, Karel Reisz), *The Ballad of Cable Hogue* (1970, Sam Peckinpah), *Johnny Got His Gun* (1971, Dalton Trumbo), *Pat Garrett and Billy the Kid* (1973, Peckinpah), *A Boy and His Dog* (1975, L. Q. Jones), *Melvin and Howard* (1980, Jonathan Demme).

• **Sleeper:** *Something Wicked This Way Comes* (1983, Jack Clayton).

• **Other Key Films:** *Long Day's Journey into Night* (1962, Sidney Lumet), *A Big Hand for the Little Lady* (1966, Fielder Cook), *Any Wednesday* (1966, Robert Ellis Miller), *All the President's Men* (1976, Alan J. Pakula), *Julia* (1977, Fred Zinnemann).

• **Also of Interest:** *Tender Is the Night* (1962, Henry King), *Act One* (1983, Dore Schary), *Divorce American Style* (1967, Bud Yorkin), *The Night They Raided Min-* sky's (1968, William Friedkin), *Comes a Horseman* (1978, Pakula), *Max Dugan Returns* (1983, Herbert Ross), *Bright Lights, Big City* (1988, James Bridges), *Parenthood* (1989, Ron Howard).

○

TANYA ROBERTS (1957–) A gorgeous former model, with long brown hair and light blue

Tanya Roberts is Sheena, *queen of the jungle*.

eyes, and one of the three leads in the final year of TV's "Charlie's Angels," she is one of the few movie stars whose acting has worsened with experience. She was adequate and eye-catching as an uppity teenager in *California Dreaming* and didn't embarrass herself in supporting decorative parts early in her career. But beginning with her slavegirl role in the sword-and-sandal film *Beastmaster*—a juvenile picture except for her topless swim (to satisfy those who saw her *Playboy* pictorial)—she has turned in cardboard performances. Surely she has had difficulty trying to cover up her Bronx accent, which just wasn't appropriate for such roles as Sheena, Queen of the Jungle. I don't agree with most critics that *Sheena* is a lot worse than most Tarzan-style jungle films, but Roberts's performance—though still watchable because the filmmakers exploit her physical attributes—is undeniably wretched. You want to root for her, but you start feeling guilty about talented actresses who can't find work. Since her failure as *Sheena,* she has had trouble getting meaty (but not fleshy) roles.

• **Cult Favorite:** *Fingers* (1978, James Toback).

• **Sleeper:** *California Dreaming* (1979, John Hancock).

• **Key Films:** *Beastmaster* (1982, Don Coscarelli), *Sheena* (1984, John Guillermin), *A View to a Kill* (1985, John Glen).

• **Also of Interest:** *The Yum-Yum Girls* (1976, Barry Rosen), *Tourist Trap* (1979, David Schmoeller), *Hearts and Armour* (1982, Giacomo Battiato), *Forced Entry* (1975/84, Jim Sotos).

○

BILL "BOJANGLES" ROBINSON (1878–1949)
The legendary black tap dancer began hoofing for change on street corners and in saloons before he was 10. He starred in vaudeville, had success on Broadway in *Bluebirds* and *Buddies,* and went to Hollywood in 1930. He had a dancing cameo in *Dixiana* and appeared in an all-black film experiment titled *Harlem Is Heaven* before shooting to stardom in Shirley Temple's *The Little Colonel.* As a white-haired, well-dressed (regal black jacket, striped vest, brass buttons, patent-leather shoes), well-mannered, reliable, satisfied slave-servant on a southern plantation, he played his first "Uncle Tom" role. On the other hand, when he cheerfully danced with his talented young costar up and down the mansion steps in a marvelous routine—Robinson was the originator of the "staircase tap dance"—he was part of the cinema's first interracial dance team. They were a lovely couple, feeding off each other's happiness: she had spunk and he had grace, and together they conveyed the joy of dancing. As Temple later wrote: "Although bubbling with energy, his physical motions were so controlled and fluid, they came out looking relaxed." In *The Littlest Rebel,* Robinson and Temple did several more happy tap routines. His steps seem extensions of his shuffle walk. It's interesting that Temple's soldier father entrusts Robinson, a black man, to be her guardian while he is away at war. On the down side, Robinson's "Uncle Billy" is content to be a slave: so satisfied is he with his lot in life and that of other slaves that he admits he doesn't understand Lincoln's call for emancipation. Robinson would be in two more Temple films, *Rebecca of Sunnybrook Farm* and *Just Around the Corner,* in which the little girl and his hotel doorman sing "I Love to Walk in the Rain" as they dance on a hydraulically operated dance floor. Robinson closed out his movie

Bill "Bojangles" Robinson and Shirley Temple in The Little Colonel.

career as the male lead, Lena Horne's boyfriend, in the classic all-black musical, *Stormy Weather*. His dancing is superb, but Horne seems too classy for his character. In *Swing Time,* Fred Astaire put on blackface to pay tribute to Robinson in the classic number "Bojangles of Harlem"; years later, Jerry Jeff Walker immortalized him in song with the touching ballad "Mr. Bojangles."

• **Cult Favorite:** *Stormy Weather* (1943, Andrew L. Stone).

• **Other Key Films:** *The Little Colonel* (1935, David Butler), *Hooray for Love* (1935, Walter Lang), *In Old Kentucky* (1935, George Marshall), *The Littlest Rebel* (1935, Butler), *Rebecca of Sunnybrook Farm* (1938, Allan Dwan), *Just*

Around the Corner (1938, Irving Cummings).

○

GERMAN ROBLES Slim, slick, noble-looking Mexican actor who gained fame playing villains in horror movies. He was best known for his vampires, the Hungarian Count Lavud/Duval, whom he portrayed in the seminal vampire film *El Vampiro,* and one sequel, and for his Nostradamus, whom he played four times. His vampire was well dressed, had gray strands in his hair that added to his distinguished look, and bared the longest fangs in the vampire business. Not convincing, he looked like he was dressed up for a costume party.

The pictures have some atmosphere but are hampered by low-budget production values and dubbing. The films are not only confusing, but extremely boring. Robles should have been given an energy boost, real blood if necessary.

• **Cult Favorites:** *El Vampiro* (1959, Fernando Mendez), *The Curse of Nostradamus* (1960, Frederico Curiel).

• **Other Key Films:** *The Vampire's Coffin* (1959, Mendez), *The Blood of Nostradamus* (1961, Curiel), *Nostradamus and the Genie of Darkness* (1960, Curiel), *Nostradamus and the Destroyer of Monsters/Monster Demolisher* (1962, Curiel).

○

JEAN ROGERS (1916–) A fetching blonde with a long list of credits, especially in B movies; she's remembered almost exclusively for playing Dale Arden, opposite Buster Crabbe, in the enormously popular serials *Flash Gordon* and *Flash Gordon's Trip to Mars*. Little boys didn't come back episode after episode just to see their hero: Rogers's curly-locked heroine was gorgeous and sexy (her outfit had a bare midriff), and she would throw her arms around Crabbe's neck, pushing her chest against his, or fearfully cower against a wall, breathing so heavily that her ribs would show. Flash treats her like a child, but even the youngest viewers knew differently. Ming the Merciless wasn't the only one who lusted after her. Rogers couldn't act, so her dialogue was kept to a minimum: often she said just one word, like "Stop!" or "Hurry!" or "Flash!" If she was given two words they might be something as easy as "Stop, Flash!" or "Hurry, Flash!" One thing she could do was scream, opening her eyes wide and throwing her hands over her ears. She screamed

a lot, because she was always scared about Flash's safety or her own. Not a heroine for today, as, with Flash around, she never had to save herself.

• **Cult Favorites:** *Flash Gordon* (1936 serial, Frederick Stephani), *Flash Gordon's Trip to Mars* (1938 serial, Ford Beebe and Robert Hill).

• **Also of Interest:** *Tailspin Tommy in the Great Air Mystery* (1934 serial, Ray Taylor), *Ace Drummond* (1936, Beebe and Cliff Smith), *The Adventures of Frank Merriwell* (1936 serial, Smith), *Secret Agent X-9* (1937, Beebe and Smith), *Night Key* (1937, Lloyd Corrigan), *Charlie Chan in Panama* (1940, Norman Foster).

○

ROY ROGERS (1912–) Leonard Slye was an original member of the great country-and-western singing group the Sons of the Pioneers. Once they gained attention on a Los Angeles radio station, they were asked to make appearances in shorts and features, including Gene Autry's *The Old Corral*. Slye became Dick Weston when he embarked on a solo acting career in B westerns. In 1938, his name was changed to Roy Rogers (because Will Rogers was so popular), and he took the lead in *Under Western Stars*. Viewers would respond to this slightly built but handsome young singing cowboy, with brown hair and squinty blue eyes, a friendly face and manner, a pleasant singing voice, funny sidekick George "Gabby" Hayes, and marvelous horse, Trigger. They didn't mind that he couldn't act very well. When Autry went off to war, Republic promoted Rogers as "The King of the Cowboys." The studio even gave him old Autry scripts to remake. Indeed, he replaced Autry as the nation's top cowboy star in 1943 and remained so until 1954. Beginning in the forties, he made over 35 pictures with Dale Evans, many after their marriage. Rogers's early films were his best, ably directed by Joseph Kane and smoothly blending action and songs (the Sons of the Pioneers became regulars). Later films made no attempt to be as authentic to the Old West, had Roy and Dale wear glitzy costumes, added juvenile humor, and minimized action to accommodate extravagant musical interludes. Plots about uncovering the identities of those responsible for local crimes were quite lame. If the films succeeded (and they obviously did with many western fans), it was strictly on the strength of the couple's strong, likable personalities.

• **Some Key Films:** *Under Western Stars* (1938, Joseph Kane), *Dark Command* (1940, Raoul Walsh), *Red River Valley* (1941, Kane), *Heart of the Golden West* (1942, Kane), *King of the Cowboys* (1943, Kane), *Silver Spurs* (1943, Kane), *The Man from Music Mountain* (1943, Kane), *My Pal Trigger* (1946, Frank McDonald), *Helldorado* (1947, William Witney), *Pals of the Golden West* (1951, Witney), *Son of Paleface* (1952, Frank Tashlin).

○

MICHAEL ROOKER (1955–) His name isn't familiar, but you might recognize his face on some sick passerby's T-shirt: liking the brutal, controversial *Henry: Portrait of a Serial*

Michael Rooker in Henry: Portrait of a Serial Killer.

Killer is one thing, but wearing a picture of Henry is another. This solidly built, Alabama-born actor, whose eyes appear gentle but hint that he has a few screws loose, and whose voice is shyly soft, slightly high, a bit jittery, and definitely creepy, was terrifying—and convincing—as the emotionally vacuous murderer in the critically acclaimed shocker. Rooker succeeded because, ironically, at the end of this particular character study, you have no idea what makes Henry, and all those men like Henry, tick. His are merely the actions of a man who thinks society deserves him roaming its streets. By the time the independently made Chicago film was released nationwide, Rooker had already played other hissable villains. He was a vicious racist in *Mississippi Burning,* in which he showed no feelings except when Gene Hackman grabs his testicles and squeezes. And he was the murderer, Ellen Barkin's jealous ex-husband, in *Sea of Love.* Rooker defended his villains to Lawrence Van Gelder: "I don't approach a role by saying I'll be unsavory or unlikable. I think all the roles I've done have been very passionate people who go to absolute extremes to make their points."

• **Cult Favorite:** *Henry: Portrait of a Serial Killer* (1990, John McNaughton).
• **Other Key Films:** *Eight Men Out* (1988, John Sayles), *Mississippi Burning* (1988, Alan Parker), *Sea of Love* (1989, Harold Becker), *Days of Thunder* (1990, Tony Scott).

○

RICHARD ROUNDTREE (1942–) Handsome, broad-shouldered New York actor who made a splash as the title character in the trendsetting blaxploitation film *Shaft.* His hip, black detective lived in a groovy Greenwich Village apartment, wore spiffy clothes, and had sexy black and white women lusting for him. He talked back to white policemen and muscled his way through the bad black community, a loner who refused to knuckle under to anyone. He had some presence, but his performance and his superstud hero lacked the flash and fire of Ron O'Neal in *Superfly.* Roundtree repeated his role in two equally sexy and violent, though better, sequels, and a cleaned-up TV series of the same name, breaking from his character by becoming part of the mainstream. He would take supporting roles in later action films, sometimes playing villains, without causing much stir. When he first came on the screen, you may have wondered where you saw him before. The roles were unpredictable: in *Jocks,* which has some funny moments, he plays a tennis coach.

• **Cult Favorites:** *Shaft* (1971, Gordon Parks), *Eye for an Eye* (1981, Steve Carver), *Q* (1982, Larry Cohen).
• **Other Key Films:** *Shaft's Big Score!* (1972, Parks), *Shaft in Africa* (1973, John Guillermin), *Earthquake* (1974, Mark Robson), *Diamonds* (1975, Menahem Golan), *Man Friday* (1976, Jack Gold).
• **Also of Interest:** *Escape to Athena* (1979, George Pan Cosmatos), *The Big Score* (1983, Fred Williamson), *One Down, Two to Go* (1983, Williamson), *City Heat* (1984, Richard Benjamin), *Game for Vultures* (1986, James Fargo).

○

MICKEY ROURKE (1950–) He has the face and manner of a punk kid grown up, an annoying whisper that passes for a voice, and often looks like he needs a shave or bath—so when he plays characters you aren't supposed to like (the slick sicko who dominates lover Kim Basinger in 9½ *Weeks*) or who are supposed to get on your nerves (boozy writer Charles Bukowski in *Barfly*), he needn't do very much. Rourke's sleaziest characters can make you shudder. Since getting noticed as the arsonist in *Body Heat* and the friend who is in big trouble with bad guys in *Diner*, he has become popular despite being in a succession of unpopular, disappointing films. Audiences admire him for choosing chancy, out-of-the-mainstream projects, and don't blame him when they fail; recognize his talent for creating unusual, if not always likable, characters; are excited by those characters' unpredictability and attraction to danger; and are as charmed by his sweet crunched-lips smile as are those people his characters con. His films have emotional scenes, brutal action sequences, and full-throttle sex (such as the controversial, blood-dripping sex scene with Lisa Bonet in *Angel Heart*). He is particularly popular in France.

• **Cult Favorites:** *Body Heat* (1981, Lawrence Kasdan), *Eureka* (1981, Nicolas Roeg), *Diner* (1982, Barry Levinson), *Rumble Fish* (1983, Francis Coppola), 9½ *Weeks* (1986, Adrian Lyne), *Angel Heart* (1987, Alan Parker).

• **Also of Interest:** *The Pope of Greenwich Village* (1984, Stuart Rosenberg), *Year of the Dragon* (1985, Michael Cimino), *A Prayer for the Dying* (1987, Mike Hodges), *Barfly* (1987, Barbet Schroeder), *Johnny Handsome* (1989, Walter Hill).

Mickey Rourke does his sleazy act in Angel Heart, *seducing young Lisa Bonet.*

CANDIDA ROYALLE A high-school valedictorian who has been one of the porno industry's top leading ladies for more than a decade. With long, dark hair—shortened in recent years—a shapely, if occasionally fleshy, body, a lovely face, a huge (if insincere) smile, and rosy cheeks, she is known for her looks and sexuality rather than her passable talent. Her film roles were varied, but she often played smart, uppity, controlling women, more interested in achieving pleasure than giving it to her husbands and male lovers. If anything, she tried to bring sensuality to her love scenes with other women—note particularly her steam bath sequence with Laurien Dominque in *Hot Rackets*. In recent years, Royalle has become the writer-producer of a successful line of erotic but not raunchy X-rated videos designed for couples.

• **Key Films:** *Hard Soap* (1977, Bob Chinn), *Hot and Saucy Pizza Girls—They Deliver* (1978, Damon Christian), *Hot Rackets* (1979, Sam Norvill), *Sunny* (1980, Warren Evans), *Ball Game* (1980, Ann Perry), *Fascination* (1980, Larry Revene), *Delicious* (1981, Philip Drexler, Jr.), *The Tiffany Minx* (1981, Robert Walters), *Outlaw Ladies* (1981, Henri Pachard), *Blue Magic* (1981, Par Sjostedt).

○

ZELDA RUBINSTEIN Chubby 4'3" actress with an irritating voice was the clever choice to play Tangina, the kooky, boastful house exorciser, in *Poltergeist*. By alerting JoBeth Williams and Craig T. Nelson of everything they have to fear—and obviously getting a kick out of the challenge—she adds humor, hysteria, and eeriness to the proceedings. She helps Williams and Nelson retrieve young daughter Heather O'Rourke from the other world, but she doesn't do as good a job of cleansing the house of evil spirits as she brags about when she thinks the job is done. Rubinstein reappeared in the film's inferior sequels. Of more interest was her creepy role as a mother urging her son (Michael Lerner) to commit ghastly murders in the film-within-a-film sequence of *Anguish*.

• **Cult Favorites:** *Poltergeist* (1982, Tobe Hooper), *Anguish* (1987, Bigas Luna).

• **Also of Interest:** *Poltergeist II* (1986, Brian Gibson).

○

BETSY RUSSELL This very pretty, shapely, sexy, dark-haired actress took a shot at stardom in the mid-eighties, making R-rated films that would get frequent play on cable. She didn't make it, mostly because these films were bad, but I thought she was quite appealing and certainly worthy of more parts than she got. I liked her young characters, who were usually smart, confident, independent, and aggressive, willing to take on imposing males one-on-one, whether driving race cars, as in *Tomboy,* or engaging in gunfire, as in *Avenging Angel*. With the exception of her snooty school girl in *Private School,* none of her characters were flirts or sexual teases—they had moral standards. Yet none were shy about disrobing in front of a male; their nonchalance when stripping (the kind Jennifer Beals exhibited when she reached beneath her sweater and removed her bra while Michael Nouri looked on in *Flashdance*) contributed to Russell's sex appeal. And yes, so did her body. Her best film was the brutal L.A.-set exploitation film *Avenging Angel*. She took over a character created by Donna Wilkes in *Angel,* now an ex–child hooker grown up and back on the streets to protect young streetwalkers and find a killer. The character did a good job, and so did the actress.

- **Key Film:** *Avenging Angel* (1985, Robert Vincent O'Neil).
- **Also of Interest:** *Private School* (1983, Noel Black), *Out of Control* (1984, Allan Holzman), *Tomboy* (1985, Herb Freed), *Cheerleader Camp* (1987, John Quinn).

○

CRAIG RUSSELL (1948–90) Round-faced, young Canadian actor, with a striking talent for female impersonation, was a refreshingly unusual lead in the rewarding comedy-drama *Outrageous!,* playing a different kind of underdog. His Robin Turner was a gay hairdresser who alienated many of his "conservative" gay friends by becoming a professional female impersonator (and being "too" outrageous), revealing prejudice within a minority that itself suffers discrimination. The film is noteworthy for having a gay lead character played by a gay actor and making the important statement that gays aren't necessarily depressed by their homosexuality (the grim theme of *The Boys in the Band*), and for being a commercial film featuring a relationship between a young man and a young woman (Hollis McLaren as a schizophrenic) that is based on friendship rather than romance—together they struggle to retain their crazy brand of individualism in our dehumanized world and to have fun. Rather than playing him as one-dimensional so straight audiences can read him quickly, Robin has great range: he is kind-hearted, angry, witty, philosophical, moody, very sensitive to criticism, strong and even heroic when necessary, extremely sarcastic, and harmlessly bitchy (McLaren thinks Robin has Tallulah Bankhead living inside him). And when he does his witty impersonations of Streisand, Crawford, Channing, Garland, Davis, West, etc., he becomes what he wants to be: dazzling. Russell played Robin in a less successful and controversial sequel ten years later. He died of heart failure related to AIDS in 1990.

- **Cult Favorite:** *Outrageous!* (1977, Richard Benner).
- **Other Key Films:** *Too Outrageous* (1987, Benner).

○

ELIZABETH RUSSELL (1916–) A former model with a slim build, high cheekbones, and haunted eyes, she was a friend of horror-movie producer Val Lewton, who gave her a one-word part in *Cat People.* It was a scene-stealing role, nonetheless, in which she approaches stranger Simone Simon in a restaurant, calls her "sister," and departs, as someone comments that she resembles a cat. Lewton would use Russell four more times, in supporting roles. Most notably, she was in *Curse of the Cat People,* disheartened by an elderly mother who insists she is an imposter, and the bizarre *The Seventh Victim,* as a woman bedridden with consumption. In the gloomy ending of the latter film—a candidate for most depressing ending in any film—she goes off for a night on the town though she knows it will kill her; neighbor Jean Brooks walks past her and, we hear, hangs herself. Russell was also in Lewton's *Youth Runs Wild* and *Bedlam,* dolled up as the wife of sadistic Boris Karloff. Her only lead was in Paramount's *Girl of the Ozarks.*

- **Cult Favorites:** *Cat People* (1942, Jacques Tourneur), *The Seventh Victim*

(1943, Mark Robson), *Curse of the Cat People* (1944, Gunther von Fritsch and Robert Wise), *Bedlam* (1946, Robson).

• **Other Key Films:** *The Corpse Vanishes* (1942, Wallace Fox), *Hitler's Madman* (1943, Douglas Sirk), *Weird Woman* (1944, Reginald LeBorg), *Youth Runs Wild* (1944, Robson).

○

GAIL RUSSELL (1924–61) Lovely, fragile actress with dark hair and blue eyes stepped out of Santa Monica High and into a Paramount contract, unprepared for the pressures of stardom. Her first starring role was in the intelligent ghost story *The Uninvited,* opposite Ray Milland, giving a sympathetic portrayal of a young woman being driven to suicide by an evil spirit while the spirit of her good mother tries to protect her. Russell began drinking to quiet her nerves. Her vulnerability came through to great advantage, and that she withdrew and seemed remote just made her seem beguiling. Viewers also liked the sweetness and gentleness of her characters, though Paramount was disappointed she couldn't also play women with a hard edge to them. Russell was a governess who suspects her employer of murder in *The Unseen,* a disappointing mystery that tried to cash in on *The Uninvited.* She also made an impression in *Night Has a Thousand Eyes* as a woman who listens to Edward G. Robinson's portentous tales and realizes she fits into them. Best of all was her kind, understanding Quaker girl who convinces outlaw John Wayne to put away his gun and become a farmer in the Wayne-produced pacifist western, *Angel and the Badman.* The film was charming, and Wayne and Russell made a sweet couple—when they looked at and spoke to each other, it really seemed like they were in love. Years later, "Chata" Wayne would name Russell as Wayne's corespondent when suing him for divorce. In the mid-fifties, her life touched by scandal, her career on the downslide, and her marriage to Guy Madison on the rocks, Russell was arrested several times for drunk driving and spent time in sanitoriums. She attempted a comeback—Wayne got her the female lead in *Seven Men from Now,* the first Randolph Scott–Budd Boetticher western. She looked older than her years in less innocent roles; in *The Tattered Dress,* she shoots her lover. But in 1961, at 36, she was found dead in her apartment, surrounded by empty liquor bottles and vials of barbiturates.

• **Cult Favorites:** *The Uninvited* (1944, Lewis Allen), *Angel and the Badman* (1947, James Edward Grant), *Seven Men from Now* (1955, Budd Boetticher).

• **Other Key Films:** *The Unseen* (1945, Allen), *Night Has a Thousand Eyes* (1948, John Farrow), *The Tattered Dress* (1957, Jack Arnold).

• **Also of Interest:** *Lady in the Dark* (1944, Mitchell Leisen), *Our Hearts Were Young and Gay* (1944, Allen), *Salty O'Rourke* (1945, Raoul Walsh), *Moonrise* (1948, Frank Borzage), *Wake of the Red Witch* (1948, Edward Ludwig).

○

JANE RUSSELL (1921–) Buxom brunette received tremendous unwanted publicity for her screen debut, in Howard Hughes's infamous western, *The Outlaw,* which was banned for three years because of minor sexual innuendo and major cleavage. As Billy the Kid's love interest—they have a memorable roll in the hay—she was subjected to wearing Hughes's specially

Wearing a special bra designed by Howard Hughes, Jane Russell caused a sensation in The Outlaw, *with Jack Beutel.*

designed bra, and, by means of a pulley system, having her size 38 breasts raised and lowered, according to her character's fluctuating passion. The picture turned out to be far less scandalous than anticipated, but Russell was indeed sexy (though some think she would be more alluring in a bathing suit in *Underwater!*). She would have many more roles as "hot-blooded" females, coming off best with brawny Robert Mitchum as her leading man. But surprisingly, she shined more in comedy roles, most notably opposite Bob Hope in the popular *The Paleface* and *Son of Paleface,* and in *Gentlemen Prefer Blondes,* where she gave a vivacious performance singing, dancing, and exchang-

ing funny lines with Marilyn Monroe, her friend on- and off-camera. She is the funny, sexually aggressive, confident female Jayne Mansfield might have played, if she had Russell's talent.

• **Cult Favorites:** *The Outlaw* (1943, Howard Hughes), *Gentlemen Prefer Blondes* (1953, Howard Hawks), *The Born Losers* (1967, T. C. Frank/Tom Laughlin).

• **Other Key Films:** *The Paleface* (1948, Norman Z. McLeod), *His Kind of Woman* (1951, John Farrow), *Macao* (1952, Josef von Sternberg), *Son of Paleface* (1952, Frank Tashlin), *Underwater!* (1955, John Sturges), *Gentlemen Marry Brunettes* (1955, Richard Sale), *The Revolt of Mamie Stover* (1956, Raoul Walsh).

KURT RUSSELL (1947–) Talented, boyishly handsome actor made a difficult transition from child to teen to adult star, and from an old-style Disney lead to a science-fiction/action hero to a witty, versatile leading man, specializing in physical, playful, funny, amiable, not entirely grown-up men. Today he is established in the mainstream, but from 1979 to 1982, he was exclusively a cult star, thanks to several films with John Carpenter and one with Robert Zemeckis. Breaking away from silly Disney sci-fi comedies, he was the title character in Carpenter's 1979 TV movie, *Elvis*, surprising everyone with his electrifying, interestingly conceived dramatic performance. With an eyepatch and a dry, Clint Eastwood–like voice, he was a troublesome renegade who is forced by our fascistic futuristic government to attempt a daring rescue on a prison island, New York, in Carpenter's ambitious but disappointing *Escape from New York*. He was physical and charismatic enough to carry that film, but like all the other actors he was dwarfed by Carpenter's special effects in *The Thing*. Best of all was his car dealer in Zemeckis's *Used Cars*. His fast-talking, fast-thinking (when desperate), benevolently amoral hustler is truly a funny character. It showed the industry what he could do, if turned loose.

• **Cult Favorites:** *Used Cars* (1980, Robert Zemeckis), *Escape from New York* (1981, John Carpenter), *The Thing* (1982, Carpenter).

• **Other Key Films:** *Silkwood* (1983, Mike Nichols), *Swing Shift* (1984, Jonathan Demme), *The Mean Season* (1985, Phillip Boros), *The Best of Times* (1986, Roger Spottiswoode), *Overboard* (1987, Garry Marshall), *Tequila Sunrise* (1988, Robert Towne), *Backdraft* (1991, Ron Howard).

THERESA RUSSELL (1957–) Michael Crichton's *Physical Evidence* was expected to be Russell's breakthrough as a leading lady (she'd been paired with Debra Winger in *Black Widow*), outside the films of her husband, Nicolas Roeg. The reason it flopped was quite evident: as a straitlaced lawyer, Russell wasn't allowed to be physical. You don't take away Dirty Harry's magnum, and you don't take away Russell's greatest weapon. This shapely, long-haired blonde with mysterious green eyes, a heart-melting and unexpected smile, and catlike features became "the thinking man's sex symbol" (as *Playboy* referred to her) by playing women who are sensual and passionate, who have unbridled sexuality, who are the screen's most seductive predators. Neurotic, often. Repressed, never. One remembers her raising a bare leg to block Art Garfunkel's path at a party in *Bad Timing: A Sensual Obsession*; giving herself to just-parolled Dustin Hoffman in *Straight Time*; giving aging Romeos their last sexual bliss before killing them (after mating with them) in *Black Widow*. She's a super actress but is at ease only when her acting incorporates sex. Everything she does has sexual overtones, even her wonderfully played Marilyn Monroe–like character's doozy of an explanation/demonstration of relativity to an Einstein-like scientist in *Insignificance*. Sex is on the surface of her troubled women, while below there is both sadness and mystery: she lies in *Black Widow*; is an undercover cop who poses as hookers in *Impulse*; has deep, dark secrets in *Black Widow*, *Track 29*, and other films. Her characters are on the sexual prowl because most of them sense they are doomed.

• **Cult Favorites:** *Straight Time* (1978, Ulu

Theresa Russell in The Razor's Edge.

Grosbard), *Eureka* (1981/83, Nicolas Roeg), *Bad Timing: A Sensual Obsession* (1980, Roeg), *Insignificance* (1985, Roeg).

• **Also of Interest:** *The Last Tycoon* (1976, Elia Kazan), *The Razor's Edge* (1984, John Byrum), *Black Widow* (1986, Bob Rafelson), *Impulse* (1990, Sondra Locke), *Whore* (1991, Ken Russell).

○

TINA RUSSELL (1951–78) Probably the best known of the pre–Linda Lovelace porno stars. This slim brunette made more than 100 loops and features with her husband, Jason Russell. None were particularly in-ventive or interesting—they weren't much better than XXX-rated home movies—and though active, Russell lacked the spark of future porno queens. In a typical plot, a group of people spending a weekend to-gether in a cabin have individual sexual encounters and, finally, an orgy. The Rus-sells had an open marriage that encouraged outside sexual relationships (both were bisexual), and they wanted their films to be further expressions of their philosophy. Tina discussed their views in an autobiog-raphy, *Porno Star,* and in Armand Weston and Howard Winters's documentary, *Personals.* The Russells split up, and Tina costarred with such male superstuds as

Harry Reems and John Holmes in *French Schoolgirls* and Marc Stevens in films like *Big Thing, Campus Girls,* and *Dr. Teen Dilemma.* Tragically, Russell died of cancer at an early age.

• **Key Films:** *Miss September (Whatever Happened to Her?)* (1973, Jerry Deney), *Dark Dreams, Sleepyhead.*

• **Sample Titles:** *Whistle Blowers, Bottoms Up* (1974, Gerard Damiano), *Big Thing, Campus Girls, French Postcard Girls, French Schoolgirls, Hardy Girls, Madame Zenobia.*

○

MARGARET RUTHERFORD (1892–) Wonderful, white-haired British comic actress always reminded me of an eccentric piano teacher—so I wasn't surprised to learn that she *was* a piano teacher (and an elocution teacher, which also makes sense) before becoming an actress in the mid-twenties. She first appeared in films in 1936, at age 44, and began cultivating an eccentric screen persona, playing a village busybody, a dotty old lady, a champion of migratory birds, and so on. British critic David Shipman writes: "The fact is that Margaret Rutherford was a rather special actress. She had, it must be admitted, a funny face. Unattractive, no; but funny, yes. She had the demeanor of a startled turkey-cock, the jaws of a bloodhound. The element of *grotesquerie,* allied to a rather unwieldy frame, restricted her for a while to weirdies. When her comic skill was recognized, she played a variety of eccentric English spinsters, intense, gushing and woolly-minded—all of which she embraced with a nonpatronizing warmth." Her breakthrough was in *Blithe Spirit,* reprising her stage role as the wacky, bicycle-riding medium, Madame Arcati.

Arcati is a delightful character, who is thrilled by the appearances of a ghost (the remarried Rex Harrison's first wife) after her séance, and doesn't feel responsible for the mess she caused but can't rectify. Her best scene has her telling off Constance Cummings for not respecting her trade. Rutherford would continue to play oddball spinsters throughout her career, obstinate, opinionated old ladies who loved being at the center of something, anything, even the most catastrophic problems. She portrayed women from all classes, and they were equally daffy: an usherette, a rich aunt, a girls' school headmistress, a racehorse owner, a mermaid's nurse, a Grand Duchess (in *The Mouse on the Moon*), and, of course, a detective. She played her most famous part, the intrepid Miss Marple, Agatha Christie's detective, in four films (plus a cameo). The mysteries weren't particularly interesting, but it was fun watching Rutherford as she personally conveyed the theme that it takes a special brand of loony to *want* to solve murders and mingle with suspects.

• **Cult Favorites:** *I'm All Right, Jack* (1960, John and Roy Boulting), *Chimes at Midnight/Falstaff* (1968, Orson Welles).

• **Key Films:** *Yellow Canary* (1943, Herbert Wilcox), *Blithe Spirit* (1945, David Lean), *Miranda* (1948, Ken Annakin), *Passport to Pimlico* (1949, Henry Cornelius), *The Happiest Days of Your Life* (1950, Frank Launder), *The Importance of Being Earnest* (1952, Henry Asquith), *The Smallest Show on Earth* (1957, Basil Dearden), *On the Double* (1961, Melville Shavelson), *Murder, She Said* (1962, George Pollock), *The V.I.P.s* (1963, Asquith), *Murder at the Gallop* (1963, Pollock), *The Mouse on the Moon* (1963, Richard Lester), *Murder Ahoy* (1964, Pollock), *Murder Most Foul* (1965, Pollock).

BRUNO S. German director Werner Herzog discovered his squat, double-chinned, strange-looking star working as a lavatory attendant. At the age of 3, he'd been abandoned by his prostitute mother, and then spent 23 years in institutions, including mental and corrections facilities. Herzog cast him as the lead in his compelling *The Mystery of Kaspar Hauser,* as a real-life nineteenth-century figure whose life was similar to his own. Shackled and limited to bread and water until he was 17 (by his father?), deprived of human contact, and having no language, his Kaspar Hauser is abandoned in Nuremberg in 1828, where he learns to speak and write and develops a cynical, philosophic view of the world he has entered. He becomes impatient with the priests and professors who try to brainwash him with their unsound championing of faith and logic, respectively, and rebels against those who try to exploit him. He is an outsider, a naturalist, whose presence causes everyone to question their orderly vision of their world, their faith in God, their way of leading their lives. In *Stroszek,* Herzog cast him as an ex-prisoner who finds the outside world more restrictive than jail. He flees from Germany to Wisconsin with his elderly neighbor and a prostitute, and tries to realize the American Dream. In a wild finale, he robs a barbershop at gunpoint and . . . buys a frozen turkey. Fleeing police, he ends up broke, hungry, and alone, spinning on a chairlift. Again human potential has been crushed.

• **Cult Favorites:** *The Mystery of Kaspar Hauser/Every Man for Himself and God Against All* (1974, Werner Herzog), *Stroszek* (1977, Herzog).

SABU (1924–63) There were no teenagers of color in the mainstream American cinema of the late thirties and early forties, so it's significant that this dark-skinned Indian was a star in the British cinema. America's Robert Flaherty found Sabu Dastagar working in the elephant stables of a maharajah in Mysore, India, and cast him in the British production *Elephant Boy,* which Flaherty codirected with Zoltan Korda. Sabu was an instant success as a native boy who knows the whereabouts of a secret elephant burial ground, and Korda would use him again in two Kipling tales—in *Drums,* as a native drummer boy for a British regiment, and in *The Jungle Book,* as a boy who has been raised by wolves. His most famous part was the title role in Britain's greatest fantasy film, the Alexander Korda–produced *The Thief of Bagdad,* more mischievous than usual but again playing a shrewd, spirited, brave, witty, resourceful, and imaginative youngster. The symbol of freedom, he gives up a chance for wealth, power, and, worst of all, an education, and flees on a magic carpet. The film's highlights are his scenes with the giant genie, imposingly played by black American actor Rex Ingram—it was the rare instance when two nonwhite actors were allowed to share the screen in a film that wasn't all-black. In Hollywood, Sabu costarred in a few Jon Hall–Maria Montez escapist Arabian Nights fantasies, adding to the adventure, humor, and color (in more ways than one). As an adult, he'd continue to play in exotic turbaned and bare-chested roles, usually in films set in the jungle and dealing with elephants and wild tigers. But as he got older, his success diminished. His most unusual adult role, a

Sabu in The Thief of Bagdad.

secondary part, was in the erotic master-piece about nuns, *Black Narcissus,* as a native general in the Himalayas who wears the intoxicating Black Narcissus cologne as he courts sensual native girl Jean Simmons. The cheery, talented actor died at 39 from a heart attack.

• **Cult Favorites:** *The Thief of Bagdad* (1940, Ludwig Berger, Tim Whelan, and Michael Powell), *Arabian Nights* (1942, John Rawlins), *Cobra Woman* (1944, Robert Siodmak), *Black Narcissus* (1947, Powell and Emeric Pressburger).

• **Other Key Films:** *Elephant Boy* (1937, Robert Flaherty and Zoltan Korda), *Drums/The Drum* (1938, Z. Korda), *Jungle Book* (1942, Z. Korda), *White Savage* (1943, Arthur Lubin).

• **Also of Interest:** *Tangier* (1946, George Waggner), *The End of the River* (1948, Derek Twist), *Man-Eater of Kumaon* (1948, Byron Haskin), *Song of India* (1949, Albert S. Rogell), *Hello Elephant* (1952, Gianni Franciolini), *Jaguar* (1956, George Blair), *Sabu and the Magic Ring* (1958, Blair), *Rampage* (1963, Phil Karlson), *A Tiger Walks* (1964, Norman Tokar).

○

MARIANNE SÄGEBRECHT Heavy but nimble, sweet-faced German actress gave enchanting performances as the offbeat, romantic leads in Percy Adlon's *Sugarbaby, Bagdad Cafe,* and *Rosalie Goes Shopping,* comedies which either annoyed or captured the fancy of moviegoers. In the first picture, her plump mortician cleverly plots how to snare a handsome, skinny, blond, married subway conductor. When she finally takes him home and nourishes him with sex and food, she makes him happier than any other woman could. Sägebrecht proves that big isn't only beautiful, but sexy as well. In *Bagdad Cafe,* her abandoned woman takes a job in a cafe in the California desert and, as if by magic, drums up business and brings many diverse, squabbling people together in happy harmony. She doesn't need to chase after slim Jack Palance. He watches her dance in the desert and detects a beauty others may have overlooked; you don't get to see Palance propose often in movies, so she must be special. Secure in a relationship with pilot Brad Davis in *Rosalie Goes Shopping,* she can devote her time to shopping schemes.

• **Cult Favorite:** *Bagdad Cafe* (1988, Percy Adlon).

• **Other Key Films:** *Sugarbaby* (1985, Adlon), *Rosalie Goes Shopping* (1990, Adlon).

• **Also of Interest:** *War of the Roses* (1989, Danny DeVito).

○

HAROLD SAKATA (1920–82) Block-of-granite, bull-necked Japanese actor—if he wasn't a wrestler, then he should have been—played the greatest of the countless henchmen in the James Bond films. His Oddjob, in *Goldfinger,* dresses like a gentleman but is an invincible fighting machine, smiling, grunting, flinging his blade-rimmed bowler with deadly accuracy, using judo chops and brute force. Even when he is killed fighting Sean Connery, we realize that the better fighter lost. Sakata had no other good film roles—he was Pig in Al

Adamson's 1978 cheapie clinker, *Black Eliminator*—but I remember him being effectively cast years ago as a furniture-smashing headache-sufferer in a humorous television commercial.

• **Cult Favorite:** *Goldfinger* (1964, Guy Hamilton).

• **Also of Interest:** *The Jaws of Death* (1976, William Grefe).

○

SANTO/SAMSON (1917–84) Santo, the ring name for Cuzman Huerta, was the most popular wrestler in the history of Mexico, becoming a true phenomenon in his native country. His legions of fans never saw his face because he always wore a silver mask. Supposedly, he wore it even when out of the public eye. He was past 40 when he became the first star of Mexico's masked-wrestler movies, appearing in numerous laughably bad low-budget pictures throughout the sixties (and becoming a comic-book hero as well). Santo played Santo—his character was called Samson or Superman in other countries—and on screen, the chunky hero wore his silver mask and a cape, wrestled, drove a two-seat British sports car, and like Batman, hung out in an underground cave. Beginning with vampire women and zombies, he defeated a gallery of unconvincing monsters. On at least one occasion, a masked wrestling opponent turned out to be a monster! In later years, he teamed up with another masked-wrestler idol, Blue Demon.

• **Cult Movies:** *Santo vs. the Vampire Women* (1962, Alfonso Corona Blake), *Santo Against the Zombies* (1962, Benito Alzraki), *Santo in the Wax Museum* (1964, Blake), *Santo Against the Baron Brakola*

(1965, Jose Diaz Morales), *Santo and the Blue Demon vs. Dracula and the Wolf Man* (1967, Miguel M. Delgado), *Santo and Dracula's Treasure* (1968, Rene Cordona), *Santo and the Blue Demon vs. the Monsters* (1969, Gilberto Marinez Solares), *Santo en la Venganza de las Mujeres Vampiras* (1969, Frederico Curiel).

○

SUSAN SARANDON (1946–) Playing Janet ("Dammit!") in *The Rocky Horror Picture Show* guaranteed this pretty, sexy, amusing New York actress eternal cult adulation. Nonetheless, her cult reputation would be enhanced with leads in the kitschy *The Other Side of Midnight*, Andy Warhol's all-time favorite movie; *Pretty Baby*, playing Brooke Shields's prostitute mother; *The Hunger*, featuring her love scene with vampire Catherine Deneuve; and *Atlantic City*, which gave her respectability. However, she didn't really "make it" in Hollywood until a few years later, when she starred in the hits *Compromising Positions*, *The Witches of Eastwick*, and, especially, the bawdy baseball film *Bull Durham*, which established her as the lusty sex symbol for "real men." In a famous scene, she teaches Tim Robbins how to remove a garter belt. In *White Palace*, she again has an affair with a much younger man, James Spader. Throughout her career, she has exhibited a refreshing naturalness, particularly when funny. Audiences recognize that she is an adventurous actress who will accept a role for the challenge, regardless of whether she'll get top billing or top dollar. She has tackled roles few actresses would touch. For *Rocky Horror*, she spent almost the entire film in a half-slip and bra. In *The Hunger*, she sits wretching in front of a toilet and breaks into convulsions, a victim's blood covering her face. In the off-Broadway play *Extremities*, she suffered broken bones, fractures, and black eyes playing a would-be rape victim. Sarandon's women are free-spirited and express a healthy sexuality. Like her prostitute in *Pretty Baby*, Sarandon has an admitted pride in her body and has been willing to tastefully display it. Her first movie scene, in *Joe*, called for her to strip and take a nude bath; several years later, she still was willing to open *Atlantic City* with a graceful scene in which she rubs lemon juice on her breasts. Her characters' sexy dress isn't meant to tease, just to indicate that they are available to the men who attract them. Unfortunately, their choice of men is as bad as Sarandon's choice of films. Sarandon's women are ambitious, but their goals aren't terribly monumental—a little money, a husband, a good job. That's just as well, since they rarely realize their dreams. Until *Bull Durham* and *White Palace*, her women haven't been assertive or self-assured. They can be pushed around or intimidated . . . up to a point. They are women who roll with the punches and are perhaps too understanding when dumped by men—which happens to many of them. They are appealingly quirky and flighty, and though undereducated, have clever wits. If these women can be criticized, it is because they rarely touch us deeply and, unlike the women played by most contemporary actresses, aren't particularly vulnerable. While we like Sarandon very much, we don't really care what happens to most of her characters.

• **Cult Favorites:** *Joe* (1970, John G. Avildsen), *The Rocky Horror Picture Show* (1975, Jim Sharman), *The Other Side of Midnight* (1977, Charles Jarrott), *Pretty*

Baby (1978, Louis Malle), *Atlantic City* (1980, Malle) *The Hunger* (1983, Tony Scott).

• **Other Key Films:** *Lovin' Molly* (1974, Sidney Lumet), *The Great Waldo Pepper* (1975, George Roy Hill), *King of the Gypsies* (1978, Frank Pierson), *Tempest* (1982, Paul Mazursky), *Compromising Positions* (1985, Frank Perry), *The Witches of Eastwick* (1987, George Miller), *Bull Durham* (1988, Ron Shelton), *White Palace* (1990, Luis Mandoki), *Thelma & Louise* (1991, Ridley Scott).

○

TURA SATANA Part Apache, part Japanese, raven-haired ex-stripper not only was an amazing physical specimen but also knew karate, so Russ Meyer cast her in the lead of his raunchy action film *Faster, Pussycat! Kill! Kill!* (Before that she'd appeared uncredited in *Irma La Douce* and *Who's Been Sleeping in My Bed?*) Her lewd, rude, black-garbed villainess Varla, bisexual leader of a busty trio of buxom go-go dancers turned criminals, is out for kicks and money. So she challenges a stranger to a fistfight, beats him up with karate chops, breaks his back, and kills him; kidnaps his girlfriend; plots to rob a handicapped old lecher; kills one of his partners with a well-aimed knife; runs over the old man as he sits in his wheelchair; attempts to run over the old man's retarded son, Vegetable; and beats another man with karate blows—before being run over herself. For her dirty deeds, she qualifies as Meyer's second-best female, behind Erica Gavin's *Vixen*. Satana appeared in only a few more films, *The Astro-Zombies* and *Doll Squad*, as part of a tantalizingly dressed all-female band of CIA assassins. Unfortunately, her fame didn't come until the eighties, when John

Waters championed *Faster, Pussycat* as his favorite film. By that time she had long since retired and become a nurse.

• **Cult Favorite:** *Faster, Pussycat! Kill! Kill!* (1966, Russ Meyer).

• **Other Key Films:** *The Astro-Zombies* (1968, Ted V. Mikels), *Doll Squad* (1973, Mikels).

○

JOHN SAXON (1935–) Handsome, solidly built Brooklyn actor who initially played sensitive yet volatile juveniles and young adults. Although *Cry Tough* got a lot of publicity because of a hot lovemaking scene he did with Linda Cristal for the European market, Saxon didn't have enough magnetism to become a box-office star, and he usually ended up playing in comedies and dramas that top-billed older, established actors. However, Saxon did a commendable job as the lead in the obscure *War Hunt*, Robert Redford's debut film. In the sixties, he took a step in the right direction by starring in low-budget horror/science-fiction films. However, Saxon's second career began in 1973, when he costarred with Bruce Lee in *Enter the Dragon*, showcasing his martial-arts skills. Since then, Saxon has worked regularly, playing leads in violent, action-packed exploitation and horror films. He still doesn't have much charisma, but he is serious even in such atrocities as *The Bees, Cannibals in the Streets,* and *Blood Beach,* is convincing in action scenes, and if his character should be killed, no one really cares.

• **Cult Favorites:** *Queen of Blood* (1966, Curtis Harrington), *Enter the Dragon* (1973, Robert Clouse), *Battle Beyond the Stars* (1980, Jimmy T. Murakami), *Tenebrae* (1982, Dario Argento), *A Nightmare on Elm Street* (1984, Wes Craven), *A*

John Saxon and Jim Kelly, participants in a martial-arts contest in Enter the Dragon.

Nightmare on Elm Street 3: Dream Warriors (1987, Chuck Russell).

• **Sleepers:** *War Hunt* (1962, Denis Sanders), *Night Caller from Outer Space* (1965, John Gilling), *Death of a Gunfighter* (1969, "Allen Smithee" [Robert Totten and Don Siegel]), *Black Christmas/Stranger in the House* (1975, Bob Clark), *Moonshine County Express* (1977, Gus Trikonis).

• **Also of Interest:** *Running Wild* (1955, Abner Biberman), *Rock, Pretty Baby* (1956, Richard Bartlett), *This Unhappy Feeling* (1958, Blake Edwards), *Summer Love* (1958, Charles Haas), *Cry Tough* (1959, Paul Stanley), *The Unforgiven* (1960, John Huston), *Portrait in Black* (1960, Michael Gordon), *The Cardinal* (1963, Otto Preminger), *The Cavern* (1965, Edgar G. Ulmer), *Joe Kidd* (1972, John Sturges), *The Swiss Conspiracy* (1977, Jack Arnold), *The Glove* (1978, Ross Hagen), *The Big Score* (1983, Fred Williamson).

○

MARIA SCHNEIDER (1952–) A sensual French actress, with curly dark hair and a sexy teenager's pout, she caused a sensation opposite Marlon Brando in the controversial *Last Tango in Paris.* She played a soon-to-be-married young woman with a fear of the future and an obsession with anything old (she works in an antique store). She has an affair with Brando's much older stranger, agreeing to any sexual act he demands in their apartment rendezvous. It is one of the few films in which characters communicate through sex. Many justifiably complained that Schneider was nude most of the time, while Brando kept his clothes on. Those who were appalled by the film suggested that the specific nature of the sex, with the man in control and the woman debased through his insulting words and acts, was consistent with the standard sadomasochistic male fantasy relationship found in the crudest pornography. But in fact, he is trying—with her consent—to get this spoiled young woman to reject her bourgeois shackles (which he demands she renounce in the sodomy scene) so that she will be able to freely explore herself as a sexual animal. Schneider next appeared in the African-set *The Passenger,* encouraging politically apathetic stranger Jack Nicholson to commit himself to political action. The picture was interesting but slow, and

Schneider kept her clothes on, providing no fireworks. Stardom immediately vanished. The daughter of actor Daniel Gélin.
- **Cult Favorites:** *Last Tango in Paris* (1973, Bernardo Bertolucci), *The Passenger* (1975, Michelangelo Antonioni).
- **Also of Interest:** *The Love Mates* (1971), *Memoirs of a French Whore* (1974), *The Babysitter* (1975, René Clément), *Violanta* (1978, Daniel Schmid).

○

MAX SCHRECK (1879–1936) German stage and screen character actor who made film history as the vampire in F. W. Murnau's *Nosferatu,* among the greatest of all vampire movies. With his bald head, pale, batlike face, pointed ears, fangs, hungry eyes and lips, long nails on bony hands, and movements that imply he isn't much more than a skeleton beneath his clothes, he was a vampire for the ages—a figure all horror fans know well. Many images are unforgettable: him standing on the deck of the rat-infested ship after draining the

Maria Schneider in The Passenger *with Jack Nicholson.*

blood of the sailors; him leaning over Greta Schroeder's bed to drink her blood although the sun is rising, and then dying by the brightly lit window. Schreck's terrifying look would be copied by Klaus Kinski in Werner Herzog's remake, *Nosferatu, the Vampyre,* and by Reggie Nalder for the TV movie *Salem's Lot.* He was in other films, but few would recognize him as anything other than the hideous vampire.

• **Cult Favorite:** *Nosferatu* (1922, F. W. Murnau).

• **Sample Films:** *The Street* (1923, Karl Grune), *The Grand Duke's Finances* (1923, Murnau), *The Strange Case of Captain Ramper* (1927), *At the Edge of the World* (1927, Grune), *Rasputin: The Holy Devil* (1928), *Ludwig II* (1929), *Der Tunnel* (1933, Curtis Bernhardt).

○

ARNOLD SCHWARZENEGGER (1947–) Austrian-born muscleman had appeared in a couple of films before giving up competitive bodybuilding, and had been impressive as a fiddle-playing bodybuilder in *Stay Hungry.* But after winning his final "Mr. Olympia" title, in the competition seen in the documentary *Pumping Iron,* he turned to acting

Arnold Schwarzenegger is The Terminator.

full-time. It would have been easy to laugh at this hunk with a thick accent and a body that, as Danny DeVito says in *Twins,* looks like it is about "to explode," but he has been a surprisingly competent actor and an exciting screen presence; in recent films, he has even become deliberately funny. Until *Twins* and *Kindergarten Cop,* his starring roles had been exclusively in action pictures, many having mythical or science-fiction themes. His characters invariably embark on dangerous missions. He was convincing as Robert E. Howard's *Conan the Barbarian,* and he and Sandahl Bergman came across as filmdom's best romance-combat duo. Significantly, Schwarzenegger, by no means insecure enough to try to dominate the screen, has consistently left room for such leading ladies as Bergman, Rae Dawn Chong, Maria Conchita Alonso, and Linda Hamilton to turn in strong performances. Having modeled his fighting attitude/style—"serenity in combat"—on Toshiro Mifune in his samurai films, he has come off best when battling formidable villains, like the invincible alien in *Predator,* Vernon Wells's kidnapper in *Commando,* and the various killers unleashed by an egocentric, sadistic host of a brutal game show (inspiringly played by "Family Feud's" Richard Dawson) in *The Running Man.* While he is a killing machine, he shows his human side. However, in his best film, *The Terminator,* he played an *evil* killing machine with no human side (except for a wicked sense of humor). In fact, he *is* a machine, a state-of-the-art cyborg from the year 2029, which has come to the present to kill a woman (Hamilton) before she gives birth to the man who will lead a revolution in the cyborg's time. His terminator kills without emotion—he is big enough to rip anyone apart, yet he shoots people in the head from arm's length. The terminator's famous, witty warning: "I'll be back . . ."

• **Cult Favorites:** *Stay Hungry* (1976, Bob Rafelson), *Pumping Iron* (1977, George Butler), *Conan the Barbarian* (1982, John Milius), *The Terminator* (1984, James Cameron), *Predator* (1987, John McTiernan).

• **Sleeper:** *The Villain* (1979, Hal Needham).

• **Other Key Films:** *Conan the Destroyer* (1984, Richard Fleischer), *Commando* (1985, Mark L. Lester), *Red Sonja* (1985, Fleischer), *Raw Deal* (1986, John Irvin), *Red Heat* (1988, Walter Hill), *Twins* (1988, Ivan Reitman), *Total Recall* (1990, Paul Verhoeven), *Kindergarten Cop* (1990, Ivan Reitman), *Terminator 2: Judgment Day* (1991, Cameron).

○

GORDON SCOTT (1927–) Handsome Gordon Werschkul, a 6'3" Las Vegas lifeguard with 19" biceps, became the eleventh screen Tarzan, starring in the final three Tarzan films produced by Sol Lesser. *Tarzan's Hidden Jungle* (Scott and leading lady Vera Miles would marry), *Tarzan and the Lost Safari,* and *Tarzan's Fight for Life* were unexciting and unimaginative. However, the next two Scott pictures, produced by Jay Weintraub, rank with Johnny Weissmuller's best Tarzan films. *Tarzan's Greatest Adventure* and *Tarzan the Magnificent* were shot in color, mostly on location, had exciting, adult stories, riveting action, and mean villains—Anthony Quayle and Sean Connery, followed by Jock Mahoney and John Carradine. Scott may not have been convincing as the famous ape-man, but he was a fine jungle hero, with charisma, and was believable in fight sequences. His Tarzan wasn't invin-

Gordon Scott and Sara Shane in Tarzan's Greatest Adventure.

cible, relying on smarts as well as athleticism to edge out opponents. Following his Tarzan success, Scott starred in Italian muscleman pictures.

• **Cult Favorite:** *Tarzan's Greatest Adventure* (1959, John Guillerman).

• **Also Recommended:** *Tarzan the Magnificent* (1960, Robert Day).

• **Other Key Films:** *Tarzan's Hidden Jungle* (1955, Harold Schuster), *Tarzan and the Lost Safari* (1957, H. Bruce Humberstone), *Tarzan's Fight for Life* (1958, Humberstone), *Samson and the Seven Miracles of the World* (1961, Riccardo Freda), *Duel of the Titans* (1961, Sergio Corbucci), *Conquest of Mycene* (1963, Giorgio Ferroni), *The Lion of St. Mark* (1963, Luigi Capuano), *Goliath and the Vampires* (1964, Giacomo Gentilomo), *The Tramplers* (1966, Albert Band).

○

HAZEL SCOTT (1920–81) Attractive, gifted young black singer and pianist, a former child prodigy who combined jazz with classical music; she was a sensation as a performer in an integrated club in Greenwich Village before going to Hollywood. She didn't want to be forced into maid or shady-lady roles, so she signed an M-G-M contract that stipulated she wouldn't play characters. Instead she appeared exclusively in specialty numbers, singing and playing the piano. Her highlights include a duet with Lena Horne on "Jericho" in *I Dood It* and her soulful solo of "The Man I Love" in the George Gershwin film biography, *Rhapsody in Blue*. She was extremely conscious of her image, and her hair, makeup, and dress were always immaculate; at the piano, her back was straight, her attitude almost defiantly confident. However, some blacks accused her of exploiting her physical attributes and acting "native" when she rose and belted an upbeat song, while others thought she was too haughty and bourgeois, especially when she performed in nightclub sets in front of all-white audiences—which she refused to do outside of movies. Outspoken politically, she married Harlem Congressman Adam Clayton Powell, Jr., the most formidable black politician of the day. They divorced in 1961, the year she made her final movie, *The Night Affair.*

• **Key Films:** *I Dood It* (1943, Vincente Minnelli), *Something to Shout About* (1943, Gregory Ratoff), *The Heat's On* (1943, Ratoff), *Broadway Rhythm* (1944, Roy Del Ruth), *Rhapsody in Blue* (1945, Irving Rapper).

○

RANDOLPH SCOTT (1898–1987) This tall, blond Virginian, with a handsome, lined face, deep voice, and cultured southern accent, was an icon of the movie western, adored by some genre fans as much as John Wayne. He appeared in 10 Zane Grey adaptations at Paramount between 1933 and 1936, but also starred in such non-westerns as *The Last of the Mohicans;* the H. Rider Haggard adventure *She;* two Fred Astaire–Ginger Rogers musicals; and *My Favorite Wife,* doing a solid comedic turn as Cary Grant's rival for Irene Dunne's affections. But after the war, he appeared exclusively in westerns, many of which he produced with Harry Joe Brown, culminating with an outstanding, offbeat adult series directed by Budd Boetticher. His aging cowboys are playful and funny, but when things get serious, they become ob-

sessed with seeing justice done, righting wrongs, or getting revenge. Some of his cowboys have lost their wives or fiancées (who were murdered, committed suicide, or, as in *Comanche Station,* were kidnapped by Indians). Loners, they must come to terms with their own flaws, obsessions, blindness, and self-hatred for having failed to protect those they loved. Most of these films are set in a West that is becoming increasingly civilized but is no less violent or corrupt. While his lawmen are determined to assure that the transition to civilization is peaceful (in *Abilene Town,* he and the armed townsfolk let a gang of outlaws ride away rather than gunning them down), some of his brooding loners must decide whether to continue their violent ways or become part of the new West. Often, he is friends with or likened to a villain—Richard Boone, Claude Akins, Lee Marvin, and Pernell Roberts in various Boetticher films—but what makes him better than them, and the better candidate for civilization, is his code of honor. In Scott's final film, Sam Peckinpah's glorious *Ride the High Country,* he is the bad guy and Joel McCrea is his opposite, the good man he once rode with. McCrea's code of honor inspires Scott to return to his once virtuous ways and be the rare and desperately needed defender of morality in the new West. At the end, he rides tall. Investing in real estate, Scott became one of the richest men in Hollywood.

• **Cult Favorites:** *She* (1935, Irving Pichel and Lansing C. Holden), *Follow the Fleet* (1936, Mark Sandrich), *Seven Men from Now* (1955, Budd Boetticher), *The Tall T* (1957, Boetticher), *Decision at Sundown* (1957, Boetticher), *Buchanan Rides Alone* (1958, Boetticher), *Ride Lonesome* (1959, Boetticher), *Westbound* (1959, Boetticher),

Comanche Station (1960, Boetticher), *Ride the High Country* (1962, Sam Peckinpah).

• **Sleepers:** *Murders in the Zoo* (1933, A. Edward Sutherland), *Abilene Town* (1946, Edwin L. Marin), *Seventh Cavalry* (1953, Joseph H. Lewis).

• **Also Recommended:** *Roberta* (1936, William A. Seiter), *The Last of the Mohicans* (1936, George B. Seitz), *Go West, Young Man* (1936, Henry Hathaway), *Jesse James* (1939, Henry King), *Frontier Marshal* (1939, Alan Dwan), *Virginia City* (1940, Michael Curtiz), *My Favorite Wife* (1940, Garson Kanin), *When the Daltons Rode* (1940, George Marshall), *Western Union* (1941, Fritz Lang), *Belle Starr* (1941, Irving Cummings), *To the Shores of Tripoli* (1942, H. Bruce Humberstone), *The Spoilers* (1942, Enright), *Return of the*

Bad Men (1948, Enright), *Sugarfoot* (1952, Marin), *The Stranger Wore a Gun* (1953, André de Toth), *Tall Man Riding* (1955, Lesley Selander).

○

STEVEN SEAGAL The emerging star of martial-arts films. A tall, dark-haired actor, with a thin ponytail that hints he is a nonconformist, Seagal has been an impressive, explosive hero in *Above the Law* and *Hard to Kill* (a smash hit with wife Kelly Le Brock), playing maverick cops who are hunted when they try to expose corruption in the "system." Though soft-spoken and not expressive, he has a strong screen presence. Since he, like his characters, studied (all kinds of things) in the Far East and had a

Steven Seagal in combat in Above the Law.

background with American intelligence agencies, he has a built-in mystery that makes him intriguing on the screen—you don't know exactly what's on his mind. But you realize he's intelligent, focused, and unafraid of the odds against him. He's an exciting fighter, but he breaks too many bones and too often puts down his weapons in order to destroy someone in hand-to-hand combat. He's so big and formidable next to those around him that often it looks like he's bullying 98-pound weaklings. His characters in these films do have soft sides (both have been family men) and they are moral. Interestingly, both films have leftist slants (in the second picture, we see George Bush kiss a pig). Without doubt, he's destined to be a major star.

• **Sleeper:** *Above the Law* (1988, Andrew Davis).
• **Other Key Films:** *Hard to Kill* (1990, Bruce Malmuth), *Marked for Death* (1990, Dwight H. Little), *Out for Justice* (1991, John Flynn).

○

JEAN SEBERG (1938–79) Gorgeous blonde from Marshalltown, Iowa, was plucked off the University of Iowa campus by Otto Preminger to star in *Saint Joan,* ending a much-publicized talent hunt. Although she was understandably self-conscious in her debut (and having her long hair shorn couldn't have made her too comfortable), her performance and the film weren't as bad as American critics contended. Preminger brought her back to star as Françoise Sagan's willful heroine in *Bonjour Tristesse.* Her notices for that film were only slightly better, but she caught the eye of French critic Jean-Luc Godard, who wanted her for his first film, *Breathless,* playing opposite Jean-Paul Belmondo as an American living in Paris and supporting herself by hawking newspapers ("New York *Herald-Tribune!*") on the Champs-Élysées. Godard wanted her callow character, who casually turns in her murderer boyfriend to the police so she won't lose her passport, to be a continuation of her girl in *Bonjour Tristesse,* who is indifferent to a death she causes. Seberg's biographer, David Richards, notes Godard saw that Seberg had the "potential for casual destruction behind her innocent features." *Breathless* was a sensation, and both Belmondo and Seberg (again with short hair) excited the young French viewers with their portrayals of characters who act impetuously without regard to consequences. They both became sex symbols and cult figures in France. Seberg would become the first American actress to work regularly and successfully in France. Among her films there were her then-husband Romain Gary's lamentable *Birds in Peru,* in which she played a woman who has sex with every man she encounters but can't achieve sexual satisfaction. It was the first picture to receive an X-rating in America. Her one American triumph was as *Lilith,* an asylum patient Warren Beatty falls in love with, has hopes for because she has moments of lucidity, but can't cure (she has, among other things, nymphomania). In this controversial film, Lilith causes another patient's suicide, has sex with a woman, and shocks a young boy by whispering something wicked into his ear. Seberg's cult reputation has grown considerably (along the lines of Frances Farmer's) since her suicide in 1979, and startling proof has surfaced that the FBI, angered at her support of the Black Panthers, tried to ruin her by planting false accusations in the press that she was carrying the baby of a black lover. She was under great stress, and her baby, who turned out to be white, died at birth. Seberg never recovered from the tragedy.

- **Cult Favorites:** *The Mouse That Roared* (1959, Jack Arnold), *Breathless* (1959, Jean-Luc Godard), *Lilith* (1964, Robert Rossen), *Playtime* (1967, Jacques Tati).
- **Other Key Films:** *Saint Joan* (1957, Otto Preminger), *Bonjour Tristesse* (1958, Preminger), *Let No Man Write My Epitaph* (1960, Philip Leacock), *Five Day Lover/ Time Out for Love* (1961, Philippe de Broca), *In the French Style* (1963, Robert Parrish), *A Fine Madness* (1966, Irvin Kershner), *Birds in Peru* (1968, Romain Gary), *Paint Your Wagon* (1969, Joshua Logan), *Airport* (1970, George Seaton).

○

EDIE SEDGWICK (1943–71) Ill-fated pop culture phenom of 1965, when she was Andy Warhol's constant party-hopping companion and film star, a trend-setting model for *Vogue* (which called the slim, long-legged girl in microskirts and black leotards "a youthquaker"), Bob Dylan's lover (he wrote "Just Like a Woman" about her), and celebrity known to everyone in New York's art, fashion, and literary worlds—as well as those in the decadent drug and orgy scene. She appeared in about a dozen of Warhol's Factory films written by Ronald Tavel and utilizing a stationary camera and minimal sets (the revealing *Poor Little Rich Girl* was filmed in her apartment). Sedgwick is considered the one Warhol Superstar with genuine star quality. She was quite striking, with her bleached white hair, black eyes, Twiggy build, endless legs, and a radiant face that resembled Jean Seberg's. She was also completely comfortable in front of the camera, whether flicking ashes on a youth being tortured in *Vinyl*, repeatedly sneezing in *Kitchen* to cue the other actors that she had forgotten her lines (and was trying to find dialogue sheets while the camera rolled), or wearing a black lace bra and panties in a love scene in *Beauty Part II*. Today, her most famous film is the unfortunate *Ciao! Manhattan*. It was begun in New York in 1967 (two years after she'd left Warhol), abandoned for various reasons, including Sedgwick's drug dependency, and resumed in California three years later. The new story had the spacey Sedgwick, as Susan, talking about her rebellious past; her flashbacks comprise the black-and-white footage taken of Sedgwick back in 1967. Sadly, the pathetic, unhealthy, mixed-up later Sedgwick—so different from the slim (she'd recently had silicone injections), fresh-faced, relatively coherent young girl who was the talk of the modeling world—is not putting on an act. She would die soon after filming ended—and *that* is what you think about while watching the film. You get the impression that Sedgwick was exploited for the sake of bringing a bizarre touch to the project. In essence, she is DOA. She was the subject of *Edie*, the bestseller by Jean Stein and George Plimpton.

- **Cult Favorites:** *Vinyl* (1965, Andy Warhol), *Kitchen* (1965, Warhol), *Beauty Part II* (1965, Warhol), *Poor Little Rich Girl* (1965, Warhol), *Lupe* (1965, Warhol), *Space* (1965, Warhol), *Face* (1965, Warhol), *Restaurant* (1965, Warhol), *Afternoon* (1965, Warhol), *Ciao! Manhattan* (1967/ 72, John Palmer and David Weisman).

○

SEKA Pretty platinum blond porno queen; burst on the scene in the late seventies, playing women who, she said, were much like herself. They were sexually aggressive, uninhibited pleasure-seekers, not the type who would console a lover who goes limp. Proving herself "all woman," she engaged in wild sex with male superstuds like John Holmes and Jamie Gillis—in fact, both have sex with her at the same time in one memorable movie scene. Her theory is that if she can excite her screen lovers by what she is willing to do (which is almost anything), then the men in the audience will become excited. So the most important thing in her sex scenes is how she contributes to her lovers' orgasms. It's no wonder that men are her biggest fans. Publicized for a time as "Porno's Marilyn Monroe"—although there are no similarities—she has heavily promoted her films, her videos, and herself.

• **Some Key Films:** *Blonde Fire* (1979, Bob Chinn), *Heavenly Desire* (1979, Jaacov Jaccovi), *Prisoner of Paradise* (1980, Bob Palmer), *Beyond Shame* (1980, Fred J. Lincoln and Sharon Mitchell), *Inside Seka* (1980, Howard A. Howard), *Aunt Peg* (1980, Arthur Cutter and Wes Brown), *Rockin' with Seka* (1980, Ziggy Zigowitz), *Tara* (1980, Leon Gucci), *Downstairs/Upstairs* (1980, Lisa Barr), *Plato's, the Movie* (1980, Joe Sherman), *"F"* (1980, Svetlana), *Love Goddesses* (1981, Adele Robbins), *Blondes Have More Fun* (1981, John Seeman), *Between the Sheets* (1982, Anthony Spinelli), *Anytime, Anyplace* (1982, Kirdy Stevens).

○

SERENA Lusty, red-haired porno star Serena Blacquelord first gained popularity in the mid-seventies and stayed at the top for many years, helped by her success in the video market. Although she was never a great actress, she was considered a "terrific sensual emoter," who convinced ev-

eryone that she was loving the screen sex. She did many lesbian and straight sex scenes but was best known for strong, kinky sex, often employing vibrators and dildos. In several movies with her ex-boyfriend Jamie Gillis, she took the passive role in S&M sequences.

• **Cult Favorites:** *Dracula Sucks* (1979, Phillip Marshak), *Aunt Peg* (1980, Arthur Cutter and Wes Brown), *Insatiable* (1980, Godfrey Daniels).

• **Other Key Films:** *Honeypie* (1975, Howard Ziehm), *The Maids* (1975, Jack Jackson), *Sweetcakes* (1976, Hans Johnson), *The Ecstasy Girls* (1979, Robert McCallum), *Taxi Girls* (1979, Jaacov Jaccovi), *Heavenly Desire* (1979, Jaccovi), *Small Town Girls* (1979, Tony Janovich), *Screwples* (1979, Clair Dia), *Serena—An Adult Fairy Tale* (1979, Fred J. Lincoln), *Bound* (1979), *For the Love of Pleasure* (1979, Ed Brown), *Sensual Fire* (1979, Troy Benny), *Blonde in Black Silk* (1980, Philip Drexler, Jr.), *Inside Desiree Cousteau* (1980, Leon Gucci), *Every Which Way She Can* (1981, Louie Lewis), *Afternoon Delights* (1981, Warren Evans), *Never So Deep* (1982, Gerard Damiano), *Extremes*.

○

MICHEL SERRAULT This French character actor had been around for years before starring in what would become the most successful foreign film ever to play in the United States: the gay farce *La Cage aux Folles*. He played the effeminate Albin, who, under the stage name Zaza, is the star attraction in a scandalous transvestite nightclub; for 20 years, he has been the lover of Renato (Ugo Tognazzi). Renato tells Albin he loves him because he makes him laugh—but the film forgets to include any time when Albin even makes Renato smile broadly. I sense no warmth or affection between the two. Serrault is a talented actor and does what the director asks of him, but his character comes across as so silly, weak, fussy, irrational, self-pitying, cloying, annoying, and temperamental that it is a wonder Renato puts up with him. However, it's not surprising that he caused straight viewers to laugh. Since 1981, he has made several films for director Christian de Chalonge, playing men who are after other people's money; in some, they kill to get it.

• **Cult Favorites:** *Diabolique* (1955, Henri-Georges Clouzot), *King of Hearts* (1967, Philippe de Broca), *La Cage aux Folles* (1978, Edouard Molinaro), *Get Out Your Handkerchiefs* (1978, Bertrand Blier), *Buffet Froid* (1979, Blier).

• **Other Key Films:** *Le Viager* (1972, Pierre Tcherina), *Les Gaspards* (1973, Tcherina), *La Cage aux Folles II* (1980, Molinaro), *Malevil* (1981, Christian de Chalonge), *Merry Christmas . . . Happy New Year* (1989, Luigi Comenici), *Docteur Petiot* (1989, de Chalonge).

• **Also of Interest:** *Love on a Pillow* (1963, Roger Vadim), *Male Hunt* (1965, Molinaro), *La Cage aux Folles 3: The Wedding* (1985, Georges Lautner).

○

DELPHINE SEYRIG (1932–90) Lebanon-born French stage actress was well cast in her first major film, Alain Resnais's infuriatingly cryptic *Last Year at Marienbad,* where she played the beautiful, nameless Woman whose thoughts may (or may not) be what is visualized in the film. A cerebral actress, she would continue to give intriguing performances as other enigmatic, intelligent, stylish women, though her later characters would be more expressive and more emotional, and exhibit a Dietrich-like sense of irony. In fact, in *Daughters of Darkness,* she partly based her stylish, mysterious vampire, Elizabeth Bathory, on Dietrich. An ardent feminist, Seyrig appeared in several films directed by women; offscreen, she was extremely active in a move to change antiquated rape laws in France.

• **Cult Favorites:** *Last Year at Marienbad* (1961, Alain Resnais), *Stolen Kisses* (1968, François Truffaut), *Daughters of Darkness* (1971, Harry Kumel), *The Discreet Charm of the Bourgeoisie* (1972, Luis Buñuel).

• **Other Key Films:** *Muriel* (1963, Resnais), *La Musica* (1966, Marguerite Duras and Paul Seban), *Accident* (1967, Joseph Losey), *The Milky Way* (1970, Buñuel), *Donkey Skin* (1971, Jacques Demy), *The Day of the Jackal* (1973, Fred Zinnemann), *A Doll's House* (1973, Losey), *The Black Windmill* (1974, Don Siegel), *India Song* (1975, Duras), *Vera Baxter* (1976, Duras), *I Sent a Letter to My Love* (1981, Moshe Mizrahi).

○

FRANK SHANNON (1875–1959) Character actor interrupted an otherwise undistinguished career to play Flash Gordon's traveling companion, Dr. Zarkoff, in the three popular serials. The bewhiskered doctor's main purpose was to relate scientific mumbo jumbo to Buster Crabbe's hero—e.g., he explains how the futuristic devices on the planet Mongo work—and on occasion, to do something scientific. Other than when science was involved, he was not particularly keen. Zarkoff is of special interest to the science-fiction cinema, a genre in which brilliant men are looked on with suspicion and are usually villains, because he is one of the few scientists whose knowledge is to be admired.

• **Cult Favorites:** *Flash Gordon* (1936 serial, Frederick Stephani), *Flash Gordon's Trip to Mars* (1938 serial, Ford Beebe and Robert F. Hill), *Flash Gordon Conquers the Universe* (1940 serial, Beebe and Ray Taylor), *The Return of Frank James* (1940, Fritz Lang).

• **Other Key Film:** *The Phantom* (1943 serial, B. Reeves Eason).

• **Also of Interest:** *The Prisoner of Shark Island* (1936, John Ford), *The Texas Rangers* (1936, King Vidor).

○

DICK SHAWN (1929–87) Handsome, wild comic who appeared to best effect in broad comedies. He was funny in *Wake Me When It's Over,* using military supplies to help build a hotel in the Far East—the kind of thing Phil Silvers was doing on TV—and in another army comedy, *What Did You Do in the War, Daddy?,* as one of a bunch of G.I. misfits trying to manipulate the odd population of an Italian town into surrendering. But Shawn's cult status is due to parts in two even more outrageous films, playing much zanier characters. In *It's a Mad Mad Mad Mad World,* he was obnoxious Ethel Merman's wacked-out, spacey son Sylvester, who beats up Milton Berle and Terry-Thomas when he wrongly concludes they've been abusing his mother. In *The Producers,* he had his best role as middle-aged hippie Lorenzo St.

Dick Shawn in The Producers *with Renee Taylor.*

Dubois, aka LSD, who plays a hippie Hitler in the ghastly musical, *Springtime for Hitler.* The film's high point is LSD's audition, when he sings "Love Power," which begins with sweet lyrics about flowers and concludes with harsh lyrics about the flower being flushed down the toilet, where it goes "in the sewer with the yuck running through 'er" and ends up in the "water that we drink." An anything-goes actor, he played a transvestite in the exploitation film *Angel.*

• **Cult Favorites:** *It's a Mad Mad Mad Mad World* (1963, Stanley Kramer), *The Producers* (1968, Mel Brooks), *Love at First Bite* (1979, Stan Dragoti), *Angel* (1983, Robert Vincent O'Neil).

• **Also of Interest:** *Wake Me When It's Over* (1960, Mervyn LeRoy), *What Did You Do in the War, Daddy?* (1966, Blake Edwards), *The Happy Ending* (1969, Edwards), *The Secret Diary of Sigmund Freud* (1984, Danford B. Greene), *Maid to Order* (1987, Amy Jones).

○

WALLACE SHAWN (1943–) Short, bald, funny-looking, and funny New York playwright-actor who has become a familiar supporting player since Louis Malle cast him as "himself" in *My Dinner with André,* an amusing, if sense-dulling, talkfest which Shawn cowrote with his costar, theater director André Gregory. Shawn has always been funniest in films that allow him to have conversations. Not only does he look like a cartoon character, but his manner of speech is something out of Mel Blanc, with a high voice that sounds like it's escaping from a balloon, and strong emphasis on one random word in each sentence. He seems distrustful, and his questions have an accusatory ring to them.

He usually doesn't care that much about what the other person has to say. In *My Dinner with André,* he struggles to hold up his end of the conversation by thinking up properly stimulating questions and often bluffing his way through his own responses to André's answers. In other pictures, he is even more cynical—complaints dominate his chatter—and far angrier. He might make an ideal Santa's helper or perhaps a hobbit, but he never plays someone who is so pure of heart. While only his smug lawyer in *The Bedroom Window* (a rare noncomedy) and assassin in *The Princess Bride* are hateful, his whiners, weasels, and assorted egocentrics (e.g., his film professor/filmmaker in *The First Time*) aren't particularly likable; the best are annoying, tolerable eccentrics. In a bit in *Manhattan*, he was Diane Keaton's ex-husband, whom she'd described as being "virile" and having "animal magnetism."

• **Cult Favorites:** *My Dinner with André* (1981, Louis Malle), *Strange Invaders* (1983, Michael Laughlin), *The Moderns* (1988, Alan Rudolph).

• **Sleepers:** *Starting Over* (1979, Alan J. Pakula), *The First Time* (1983, Charlie Loventhal), *The Bostonians* (1984, James Ivory), *The Hotel New Hampshire* (1984, Tony Richardson), *Heaven Help Us* (1985, Michael Dinner).

• **Also of Interest:** *Micki & Maude* (1984, Blake Edwards), *Crackers* (1984, Malle), *Prick Up Your Ears* (1987, Stephen Frears), *The Bedroom Window* (1987, Curtis Hanson), *The Princess Bride* (1987, Rob Reiner), *Scenes from the Class Struggle in Beverly Hills* (1989, Paul Bartel).

○

MOIRA SHEARER (1926–) Scottish-born, red-haired Moira King took up ballet at the age

Moira Shearer performs the title ballet in The Red Shoes.

of 6 and was dancing professionally in her mid-teens. At 16, she joined the Sadler's Wells Ballet, where she was discovered by Michael Powell when he was casting the lead in his classic dance tragedy *The Red Shoes,* inspired by Hans Christian Andersen's fairy tale. In this mixture of backstage musical and highbrow art, she was captivating as Vicky Page, who says ballet is her life, yet when she ultimately chooses dance over her marriage, her red shoes cause her to leap to her death (not a particularly enlightened theme). As an actress, Shearer is remarkably composed, and her dancing is marvelous. The lengthy, expressionistic "Red Shoes Ballet" is one of the cinema's most exciting dances. In her white chiffon ballet costume with a blue-trimmed white bodice, a blue ribbon in her flaming red hair, and those "living" red shoes on her feet, she is stunning. Many women regard *The Red Shoes* as their favorite film; Shearer's tremendous talent and breathtaking beauty influenced many of them to take dance lessons as children. Shearer appeared in only a few more films, in which her dancing was usually the highlight. Her strangest role choice was as an acting understudy who becomes a murder victim in Powell's controversial *Peeping Tom.*

• **Cult Favorites:** *The Red Shoes* (1948, Michael Powell and Emeric Pressburger), *Peeping Tom* (1960, Powell).

• **Also of Interest:** *Tales of Hoffman* (1951, Powell and Pressburger), *The Story of Three Loves* (1953, Vincente Minnelli), *The Man Who Loved Redheads* (1955, Harold French), *Black Tights* (1960, Terence Young).

○

JOHNNY SHEFFIELD (1931–) Curly-haired, blond youngster was 7 when he was cast as Boy in *Tarzan Finds a Son!*, the fourth of six "Tarzan" films starring Johnny Weissmuller and Maureen O'Sullivan. He was a cute little kid, but his unfortunate purpose was to make the adult series appeal more to family audiences. He'd swim with Pop, ride a baby elephant, disobey Pop's orders, go where he shouldn't and have to be rescued—in the finale, his parents had to go to New York to get him back. O'Sullivan left the series, but Sheffield stuck around for several years and Boy grew into a strapping teenager and a dull, unnecessary character. His teenage Boy reminds me of James MacArthur in a loincloth. Not too exciting, huh? Having outgrown that part, Sheffield starred in *Bomba, the Jungle Boy*. He'd play Roy Rockwell's juvenile Tarzan 10 more times, still riding elephants, but now rescuing people himself, stopping poachers and treasure hunters, outthinking hostile African tribes, and bringing peace to the jungle. The juvenile, copycat "Bomba" films would be popular on television beginning in the late fifties.
• **Cult Favorite:** *Tarzan's New York Adventure* (1942, Richard Thorpe).
• **Also Recommended:** *Tarzan Finds a Son!* (1939, Thorpe), *Tarzan's Secret Treasure* (1941, Thorpe).
• **Other Key Films:** *Tarzan Triumphs* (1943, William Thiele), *Tarzan's Desert Mystery* (1943, Thiele), *Tarzan and the*

Amazons (1945, Kurt Neumann), *Tarzan and the Leopard Woman* (1946, Neumann), *Tarzan and the Huntress* (1947, Neumann), *Bomba, the Jungle Boy* (1949, Ford Beebe), *Bomba on Panther Island* (1949, Beebe), *The Lost Volcano* (1950, Beebe), *The Hidden City* (1950, Beebe), *The Elephant Stampede* (1951, Beebe), *The Lion Hunters* (1951, Beebe), *The African Treasure* (1952, Beebe), *Bomba and the Jungle Girl* (1952, Beebe), *Safari Drums* (1953, Beebe), *The Golden Idol* (1954, Beebe), *Killer Leopard* (1954, Beebe), *Lord of the Jungle* (1955, Beebe).

○

BARBARA SHELLEY (1933–) British actress couldn't get her career off the ground in Italy, so she returned home and became a leading lady in horror movies, beginning with *Cat Girl,* a Val Lewton–like chiller that was done in by budget restrictions. The best of her early films was the classic *Village of the Damned,* as the mother of one of the evil, brainy children. She worked often for Hammer Studios, and though she wasn't quite as pretty or sexy as the typical Hammer pinup girl, she had more talent, class, and maturity. Throughout her career, she played women who either are possessed by something evil—as in *Cat Girl, The Gorgon,* and, for a brief time, *Five Million Years to Earth*—or are controlled by someone who is evil—as in *Rasputin—the Mad Monk* and *Dracula—Prince of Darkness.* In the latter film, she again is possessed by something evil, a vampire, after being bitten by Christopher Lee.
• **Cult Favorites:** *Village of the Damned* (1960, Wolf Rilla), *Quatermass and the Pit/Five Million Years to Earth* (1967, Roy Ward Baker).
• **Also Recommended:** *The Shadow of the*

Barbara Shelley in Village of the Damned *with George Sanders.*

Cat (1961, John Gilling), *The Gorgon* (1965, Terence Fisher).
• **Other Key Films:** *Cat Girl* (1957, Alfred Shaughnessy), *The Camp on Blood Island* (1958, Val Guest), *Blood of the Vampire* (1958, Henry Cass), *The Secret of Blood Island* (1965, Quentin Lawrence), *Rasputin—the Mad Monk* (1966, Don Sharp), *Ghost Story/Madhouse Mansion* (1974, Stephen Weeks).

○

FU SHENG/ALEXANDER FU SHENG (1954–83)
This martial-arts star made a big impression as one of the spectacular five-man fighting force in *Five Masters of Death*, toplining David Chiang and Ti Lung. Always an impulsive hothead, in *Chinatown Kid* he kills and is killed because he desperately wants a digital watch. In 1978, director Chang Cheh cast him as the star of his "Brave Archer" series, beginning with *Kung Fu Warlord*; he played a Sung Dynasty hero named Kuo Tsing in the bloody films. By the end of the decade, the acrobatic, boyishly handsome (he often wore a ponytail), charismatic actor had become one of Hong Kong's biggest martial-arts stars. He broke his legs doing a stunt, and it seemed his career was over, but he came back. At first it appeared that he was going to do mostly comedic parts, but his last film, *The Eight Diagram Pole Fighter*, required him to go crazy because of deaths in his family. He didn't get to finish that film: at the age of 29, he was killed in a car crash.
• **Cult Favorite:** *Five Masters of Death* (1975, Chang Cheh).
• **Other Key Films:** *The Chinatown Kid* (1977, Cheh), *Kung Fu Warlord* (1978, Cheh), *Kung Fu Warlord II* (1978, Cheh),

Blast of the Iron Palm (1979, Cheh), *Brave Archer and His Mate* (1979, Cheh), *Ten Tigers of Kwantung* (1979, Cheh), *Master of Disaster* (1982, Liu Chia Liang), *Legendary Weapons of Kung Fu* (1982, Liang), *The Eight Diagram Pole Fighter* (1983, Liang).

○

BROOKE SHIELDS (1965–) Beautiful child phenom, a model since the age of 11 months. She was promoted as a pre-

pubescent sex symbol, an image that was reinforced when the 12-year-old played a child prostitute in Louis Malle's controversial *Pretty Baby*. In the film, she appeared nude, played scenes with nude adults, and had an adult lover, Keith Carradine as photographer E. J. Bellocq. She may not have been exploited, but other than when she poses for Bellocq's camera, her nude scenes are embarrassing: she looks downright foolish when interrupted in her bath by the madam and a male customer, and when standing bare-assed in

Brooke Shields and Keith Carradine in Pretty Baby.

front of Bellocq's door, banging on it to be let inside. Yet Shields was surprisingly good, giving her best delivery of lines (outside of *Wanda Nevada*), offering an acceptable southern accent, moving well, and seeming natural in the difficult part. But she'd become more amateurish. Her later films are insufferable, especially the teenage-sex dramas *The Blue Lagoon*, where she's stuck on an island with Christopher Atkins, and *Endless Love*. Maybe the plan was to cover up her new teenager's modesty and acting discomfort by casting her in films (and commercials) with overt sexual themes. Since her virginity was much publicized, the smart, likable, proper teenager (who insisted on body doubles) seemed as miscast as a Marie Osmond.

• **Cult Favorites:** *Alice, Sweet Alice/ Communion/Holy Terror* (1977, Albert Sole), *Pretty Baby* (1978, Louis Malle), *The Blue Lagoon* (1980, Randal Kleiser).

• **Also of Interest:** *King of the Gypsies* (1978, Frank Pierson), *Wanda Nevada* (1979, Peter Fonda), *Endless Love* (1981, Franco Zeffirelli).

○

HENRY SILVA (1928–) A menacing-looking, Brooklyn-born actor, with dark hair, high cheekbones, and a wide, cruel grin, he looks like a cross between an Italian and an Apache, but is actually the rare Puerto Rican to have success in the movies. He has played vicious, often crazy villains, who aren't as cerebral or self-torturing as Jack Palance's classic scoundrels (Silva has been called "the poor man's Palance") but are more energetic and just as threatening. One of his most memorable roles was the title character in *Johnny Cool*, a sadistic, revenge-seeking gangster. Silva

hasn't received top billing otherwise, but he has still made memorable impressions as borderline crazies in the Randolph Scott western *The Tall T*, as Richard Boone's gun-happy henchman, "Chink"; as a foolishly fearless big-game hunter (funny doing self-parody) in the horror-satire *Alligator;* and, scariest of all, as the doped-up assassin in *Sharky's Machine*.

• **Cult Favorites:** *The Tall T* (1957, Budd Boetticher), *The Manchurian Candidate* (1962, John Frankenheimer), *Alligator* (1980, Lewis Teague), *Chained Heat* (1983, Paul Nicolas), *Code of Silence* (1985, Andrew Davis).

• **Sleepers:** *Johnny Cool* (1963, William Asher), *Shoot* (1976, Harvey Hart), *Above the Law* (1988, Davis).

• **Also of Interest:** *A Hatful of Rain* (1957, Fred Zinnemann), *The Law and Jake Wade* (1958, John Sturges), *A Gathering of Eagles* (1963, Delbert Mann), *The Secret Invasion* (1964, Roger Corman), *Love and Bullets* (1979, Stuart Rosenberg), *Buck Rogers in the 25th Century* (1979, Daniel Haller), *Sharky's Machine* (1981, Burt Reynolds), *Thirst* (1988, Robin Hardy).

○

SIMONE SIMON (1911–) Sensual, ethereal, dark-haired beauty starred in films in her native France, America, and England. She achieved major international success in Jean Renoir's adaptation of Emile Zola's *La Bête Humaine,* a precursor of America's film noir. After engineer Jean Gabin witnesses Simone and her husband emerging from a compartment where a man (her lover) was murdered, she seduces him into an affair so he won't squeal, and then convinces him to murder her husband. The way her femme fatale uses sex to control Gabin, to make him act stupidly so he'll fall into a trap, anticipates how Kathleen Turner handles William Hurt in *Body Heat.* Other notable French roles include her chambermaid in *La Ronde* and model in *Le Plaisir,* multiple story films by Max Ophüls that contend that only women can appreciate love on other than a physical level. Simon's major film role in America was the lead, Irena, in *Cat People,* the first of Val Lewton's fascinating "psychological" horror classics. She played a sweet, lonely Serbian-born New York artist who believes that she, like the rest of her cursed tribe, will turn into a large cat (the actress had feline qualities) if she has sex—which makes things dicey when she marries Kent Smith. Like Lewton's other tragic heroines, she doesn't have the willpower to reject her evil side; when she is jealous or physically threatened, she reverts to her cat side, leading to several scary scenes. Simon returned in the excellent sequel, *Curse of the Cat People,* but this unusual picture has nothing to do with cats. Instead it deals with the imagination of Kent Smith's lonely child, and Irena is her kind, supportive imaginary playmate, whose image she conjures up after seeing Irena's picture in her father's belongings. A highlight is Simone singing a French lullaby to the child. In a nonhorror role for producer Lewton, Simone did well as the heroine of *Mademoiselle Fifi,* as a "laundress" who proves more gallant than her richer, condescending fellow passengers on a French coach that is threatened by Prussians.

• **Cult Favorites:** *La Bête Humaine* (1938, Jean Renoir), *Cat People* (1942, Jacques Tourneur), *Curse of the Cat People* (1944, Gunther von Fritsch and Robert Wise), *La Ronde* (1950, Max Ophüls).

• **Other Key Films:** *Lac aux Dames* (1934, Marc Allégret), *Girls' Dormitory* (1936, Irving Cummings), *Seventh Heaven* (1937, Henry King), *Josette* (1938, Allan Dwan), *The Devil and Daniel Webster* (1941, William Dieterle), *Mademoiselle Fifi* (1944, Wise), *Johnny Doesn't Live Here Anymore* (1944, Joe May), *Le Plaisir* (1952, Ophüls).

○

TOD SLAUGHTER (1885–1956) England's "King of the Grand Guignol" made an art of overplaying Victorian villains. The heavyset actor swaggered, rolled his eyes, and broke into an evil grin as he perpetrated cruel acts. His roles included Sweeney Todd, who turns victims into meat pies; Spring-Heeled Jack (Jack the Ripper) in *The Curse of the Wraydons;* a graverobber in *The Greed of William Hart;* Sir Percival Glyde in the adaptation of Wilkie Collins's *The Woman in White, Crimes at the Dark House;* and Tiger, killer of the underworld, in *The Ticket-of-Leave Man.* Slaughter's films haven't played on American television for years, but I remember enjoying his overblown villainy in *Sweeney Todd, the Demon Barber of Fleet Street* and other thirties films. In *A Pictorial History of Horror Movies,* Britisher Denis Gifford explained his appeal: "The blood of the melodrama ran red, yet such was the gusto of Tod Slaughter . . . that his films never offended. Slashing throats or snapping spines, he weltered in his glorious gore, leering and chuckling, winking and nudging his audience to laugh along with him on the road to hell."

• **Cult Favorite:** *Sweeney Todd, the Demon Barber of Fleet Street* (1936, George King).

• **Also of Interest:** *The Murder in the Red Barn/Maria Marten* (1935, King), *It's Never Too Late to Mend* (1937), *The Ticket-of-Leave Man* (1937, King), *Sexton Blake and* the Hooded Terror (1938, King), *The Face at the Window* (1939, King), *Crimes at the Dark House* (1939, King), *The Curse of the Wraydons* (1946, Victor M. Gover), *The Greed of William Hart* (1948, Gilbert Church), *Horror Maniacs* (1948), *A Ghost for Sale* (1952).

○

JACK SMITH (1932–89) A major figure in New York underground movies, beginning in the late fifties. He directed the notorious *Flaming Creatures,* which was banned in New York State, and starred for Ken Jacobs, George Kuchar, Bill Vehr, Ron Rice, Andy Warhol, and others. These were mostly nonnarrative, experimental films in which images, often sexual, were more important than characters or plots. But Smith still stood out, whether as a Fairy Vampire in *Death of P'Town* or as a passionate gypsy dancing lady in *Little Cobra Dance: Saturday Afternoon Blood Sacrifice;* severing his ear for Marie Menken in *Eargogh,* or participating in an orgy scene. The star, who, according to Sheldon Renan, "looks like Punch of Punch and Judy, and also like a thin, tall, hairy Peter Ustinov," was instrumental in developing a nonacting style that would later be prevalent in Andy Warhol movies.
• **Key Films:** *Little Cobra Dance: Saturday Afternoon Blood Sacrifice* (1957, Ken Jacobs), *Star-Spangled Death* (1957, Jacobs), *Little Stabs at Happiness* (1958/61, Jacobs), *The Death of P'Town* (1961, Jacobs), *Blonde Cobra* (1959/62, Jacobs), *The Queen of Sheba Meets the Atom Man* (1963, Ron Rice), *Chumlum* (1964, Rice), *The Lovers of Eternity* (1964, George Kuchar), *Batman* (1964, Andy Warhol), *The Devil Is Dead* (1964, Carl Linder), *Skin* (1965, Linder), *Camp* (1965, Warhol), *Jeremelu* (1965,

Naomi Levine), *Brothel* (1966, Bill Vehr), *The Illiac Passion* (1964/66, Gregory Markopoulos), *The Mysterious Spanish Lady* (Vehr), *Eargogh* (Dov Lederberg), *Dirt* (Piero Heliczer).
• **Also of Interest:** *Silent Night, Bloody Night* (1973, Theodore Gershuny).

○

RAINBEAUX SMITH/CHERYL SMITH This pretty, shapely, fragile, long-haired blonde was one of my favorite supporting players in seventies exploitation films. She first caught my attention playing a 13-year-old in the arty, surreal *Lemora—Lady Vampire.* She looked familiar, like a high-school cheerleader (which she played a couple of times in movies), or someone you saw stoned and lost at a sixties rock concert. Her roles were typically of a sexual nature (requiring nudity) and were usually found in films with a lot of violence, although *Slumber Party '57* (Debra Winger's debut film) is strictly a sex comedy. I remember her most as the frightened, childlike prisoner in *Caged Heat;* she held her own with Barbara Steele, Erica Gavin (who said Smith was "cosmic"), and Roberta Collins. In *Massacre at Central High,* an interesting political allegory masquerading as an exploitation film, she and Lani O'Grady are Mary and Jane, the constantly stoned companions of Robert Carradine's Spoony. They all get blown up. In Cheech and Chong's *Up in Smoke,* all she was asked to do was laugh.
• **Cult Favorites:** *Lemora—Lady Vampire* (1973, Robert Blackburn), *Caged Heat* (1974, Jonathan Demme), *Massacre at Central High* (1976, Renee Daalder), *Up in Smoke* (1978, Lou Adler).
• **Also of Interest:** *Drum* (1976, Steve Carver), *Revenge of the Cheerleaders* (1976,

Rainbeaux Smith in Jonathan Demme's Caged Heat.

Richard Lerner), *Slumber Party '57* (1977, William E. Levey), *The Incredible Melting Man* (1978, William Sachs).

○

WILLIAM SMITH Handsome, muscular actor has been a major figure in low-budget action films since the early seventies. Always playing tough, violent men, he has moved back and forth between hard-living heroes, villains, and antiheroes. Many of his characters are Vietnam veterans. His villains are frightening, but I prefer his heroes, who are dependable, great fighters, and always seem to care. He is most identified with the motorcycle films he made early in his career—my favorite is the exciting *Run, Angel, Run*, in which his attempt to reform, and live on a farm with the woman he loves, is threatened by his old biker buddies. Smith also has made an impression as a sympathetic vampire in *Grave of the Vampire*, the government worker who stifles the *Invasion of the Bee Girls*, Arnold Schwarzenegger's father in *Conan the Barbarian*, and Clint Eastwood's bare-knuckles boxing opponent in the otherwise uninteresting *Any Which Way*

You Can. I got to like Smith in the mid-sixties when he was a strong-as-an-ox Texas Ranger (the partner of Peter Brown and Neville Brand) on TV's "Laredo." Recently, he has sported a bald look.

• **Cult Favorites:** *The Losers* (1970, Jack Starrett), *Invasion of the Bee Girls* (1973, Denis Sanders), *Conan the Barbarian* (1982, John Milius), *Rumble Fish* (1983, Francis Coppola), *Red Dawn* (1984, Milius).

• **Sleepers:** *Run, Angel, Run* (1963, Starrett), *Grave of the Vampire* (1972, John Hayes), *The Last American Hero* (1973, Lamont Johnson), *The Frisco Kid* (1979, Robert Aldrich).

• **Also of Interest:** *Angels Die Hard* (1970, Richard Compton), *C.C. & Company* (1970, Seymour Robbie), *The Thing with Two Heads* (1972, Lee Frost), *Deadly Trackers* (1973, Barry Shear), *The Ultimate Warrior* (1974, Robert Clouse), *Twilight's Last Gleaming* (1977, Aldrich), *Gentle Savage* (1978, Sean McGregor), *Any Which Way You Can* (1980, Buddy Van Horn), *Moon in Scorpio* (1987, Gary Graver), *Hell Comes to Frogtown* (1987, R. J. Kizer and Donald G. Jackson).

○

P. J. SOLES (1956–) In *Carrie,* Pamela Jayne Soles was a mean teenager, the best friend of vicious Nancy Allen; she wears pigtails and a red baseball cap (even to the prom)— and she's the one who laughs when pig's blood pours on Sissy Spacek. And in *Private Benjamin,* with dark hair, she was unfriendly to Goldie Hawn. But usually this pretty, slender, high-spirited blonde comes across as the ideal fun date, someone who will keep the energy level up, provide more

than her share of the humor, take chances, and initiate the romance. Soles, Jamie Lee Curtis, and Nancy Loomis were perfect as chatty, boy-crazy high-school friends in the horror film *Halloween.* Of the three, she was the most impulsive, aggressive, and promiscuous—because she's having wild sex she's oblivious to the intruder in the house—and as a result she is the first victim. She was the solo star in the ready-made cult film *Rock 'n' Roll High School,* again as a teenager, Riff Randall, obsessed with the punk group the Ramones. She carries the movie, bebopping and high-kicking nonstop, drooling over how Joey Ramone "slithers pizza into his mouth," and repeatedly injecting life into the picture when the humor has gone limp. In *Stripes,* she is an MP who should arrest Bill Murray but instead becomes his lover and cohort in his wild escapades. Even as a soldier, she is a great date.

• **Cult Favorites:** *Carrie* (1976, Brian De Palma), *Halloween* (1978, John Carpenter), *Rock 'n' Roll High School* (1979, Allan Arkush).

• **Other Key Film:** *Stripes* (1981, Ivan Reitman).

• **Also of Interest:** *Private Benjamin* (1980, Howard Zieff), *Sweet Dreams* (1985, Karel Reisz), *Saigon Commandos* (1987, Clark Henderson).

○

GALE SONDERGAARD (1899–1985) Black-haired, imperious, impressive character actress won the first Best Supporting Actress Oscar for her first role, a scheming housekeeper in *Anthony Adverse.* She would appear in sympathetic parts, but be better remembered as Hollywood's top villainess of the forties. Cunning, sadistic, and humorless, her wicked women were the brains behind evil plots, but on occasion they had cruel accomplices or lent their services to evil governments. Often she played foreigners. The most famous of her Eurasian "'Dragon Lady" roles was in *The Letter,* in which she blackmails Bette Davis. She also is remembered as "the Spider Woman," having played both the leader of a murderous gang pursued by Basil Rathbone in *Sherlock Holmes and the Spider Woman* and a fiend who carries on diabolical experiments in *The Spider Woman Strikes Back.* Sondergaard and her husband, director Herbert Biberman, one of the "Hollywood Ten," were blacklisted and disappeared from movies for 20 years. Her best role after returning was as Richard Harris's Indian friend-mother figure in *The Return of a Man Called Horse.*

• **Recommended:** *Anthony Adverse* (1936, Mervyn LeRoy), *The Life of Emile Zola* (1937, William Dieterle), *Juarez* (1939, Dieterle), *The Cat and the Canary* (1939, Elliott Nugent), *The Mark of Zorro* (1940, Rouben Mamoulian), *The Letter* (1940, William Wyler), *My Favorite Blonde* (1942, Sidney Lanfield), *Christmas Holiday* (1944, Robert Siodmak), *Anna and the King of Siam* (1946, John Cromwell), *The Time of Their Lives* (1946, Charles T. Barton), *Road to Rio* (1948, Norman Z. McLeod), *The Return of a Man Called Horse* (1976, Irvin Kershner).

• **Also of Interest:** *Maid of Salem* (1937, Frank Lloyd), *A Night to Remember* (1943, Richard Wallace), *Appointment in Berlin* (1943, Alfred E. Green), *The Strange Death of Adolf Hitler* (1943, James Hogan), *The Spider Woman/Sherlock Holmes and the Spider Woman* (1944, Roy William Neill), *The Invisible Man's Revenge* (1944, Ford Beebe), *Gypsy Wildcat* (1944, Neill), *The Climax* (1944, George Waggner), *The Spider Woman Strikes Back* (1946, Arthur Lubin).

○

RENÉE SOUTENDIJK Blond Dutch actress captured everyone's attention with sex-charged performances in two Paul Verhoeven pictures that had international success. In the sexually explicit and complex "youth" film *Spetters,* she is a beautiful, flirtatious short-order cook, with curly hair and tight tops, a sympathetic "bad" girl who makes a play for three male friends, one at a time, when she thinks they can provide her with the money and security she desires. She is a more stylish and wicked temptress in Verhoeven's eerie, erotic, perversely hilarious horror film, *The Fourth Man,* a spider woman who seduces men, marries them, films them, and becomes a widow after their horrible "accidental" deaths. A death-obsessed, bisexual writer (Jeroen Krabbe) is her latest conquest—he worries when he learns what happened to the men in her past. Recently, Soutendijk has attempted to break into American films, as have Verhoeven, Krabbe, and Rutger Hauer (who had a bit in *Spetters*). But she had to be restrained and not particularly glamorous as Ben Kingsley's wife in the acclaimed TV movie *Murderers Among Us: The Simon Wiesenthal Story.*

• **Cult Favorites:** *Spetters* (1980, Paul Verhoeven), *The Fourth Man* (1979/83, Verhoeven).

• **Also of Interest:** *Pastorale '43* (Wim Verstappen), *A Leg to Stand On* (Victorine Habet), *Deadly Sin* (Rene van Hie), *A Woman Like Eve* (Nouchka van Brakel), *Forbidden Bacchanal* (Verstappen), *The Girl with Red Hair* (1981, Ben Verbong).

SISSY SPACEK (1949–) At the prom in *Carrie,* her super-shy outcast finally feels comfortable enough to reveal her true self and, sure enough, her handsome date realizes that this unusual girl is wonderfully special, radiantly beautiful, genuinely sensitive, and far superior to the more popular girls who dance around them—he is visibly thrilled to discover a true gem among the clones. That's how critics and fans came to respond to this pale, freckled, 85-pound strawberry blonde from Texas. They initially figured she was too offbeat to be a successful leading lady, but were swayed by Spacek's one terrific performance after another. Because of her strong accent, she almost always plays someone who either lives in the South or has southern roots, but it's amazing how many different types of females she has played. It's difficult to imagine any two of them being friends (set aside Loretta Lynn, who makes friends with anyone she meets)—in fact, it's unlikely that their paths would ever cross. Among them are dreamers, romantics, kooks (like her topless maid in *Welcome to*

Sissy Spacek and Shelley Duvall are an unforgettable team in Robert Altman's bizarre 3 Women.

L.A.), troubled teenagers; there are practical women, warmhearted women, talented women, independent women, lonely women, mature women, funny women (she has an offbeat sense of humor), sexy women, and, in *3 Women,* a woman without any personality whatsoever (which is why she tries to steal Shelley Duvall's identity). She has played timid, slouch-shouldered teens in *Carrie* and *Coal Miner's Daughter* who pull their sweater sleeves over their hands, but in *Missing,* her courageous political activist rolls her sleeves above her elbows and confronts the authorities. In *Marie,* the once-abused housewife takes off her apron, puts on a suit, and takes on the government. Her teenager in *Badlands,* her most romantic and pathetic character, is without emotion (embodying the vacuous fifties). But her mother who wrongly believes she's a widow in *Raggedy Man,* perhaps her best performance, and her young woman who fears she's a widow in *Missing* are highly emotional, truly caring people who put themselves on the line for those they love. After capturing the cult audience with her troubled teens in *Badlands* and *Carrie,* Spacek broke into the mainstream with a brilliant Oscar-winning performance in *Coal Miner's Daughter,* even doing a fine job singing. But she didn't settle into the Hollywood mold. On the contrary, she continues to take unusual projects (sometimes acting for director husband Jack Fisk) and surprise us with every performance.
• **Cult Favorites:** *Badlands* (1973, Terrence Malick), *Carrie* (1986, Brian De Palma), *Welcome to L.A.* (1977, Alan Rudolph), *3 Women* (1977, Robert Altman), *Raggedy Man* (1981, Jack Fisk).
• **Other Key Films:** *Coal Miner's Daughter* (1980, Michael Apted), *Missing* (1982,

Costa-Gavras), *Marie* (1986, Roger Donaldson).
• **Also of Interest:** *Prime Cut* (1972, Michael Ritchie), *Heart Beat* (1980, John Byrum), *Crimes of the Heart* (1986, Bruce Beresford), *The Long Walk Home* (1990, Richard Pearce).

○

FAY SPAIN (1937–) Beginning in the late fifties, this pretty young actress played tough, slightly amoral sexpots with a variety of hairstyles and colors. They all insisted on having a good time, even if that meant trouble. No one could tell them what to do. In *Dragstrip Girl,* she was, as the promo poster indicated, "Car Crazy! Speed Crazy! And Boy Crazy!" In producer Albert Zugsmith's *The Beat Generation,* she was threatened by rapist Ray Danton, but more often she was a temptress, teasing men she didn't consider good enough for her, testing the others. Her most famous scene is in Anthony Mann's adaptation of Erskine Caldwell's *God's Little Acre,* in which she takes an open-air bath and delights in having Buddy Hackett pour water into her tub without being allowed to look at her. She is the devil's envoy in *The Private Lives of Adam and Eve* and, as an adult and more controlled, the evil queen of Atlantis in the Italian *Hercules and the Captive Women.*
• **Cult Favorites:** *The Private Lives of Adam and Eve* (1959, Albert Zugsmith and Mickey Rooney), *The Godfather Part II* (1974, Francis Ford Coppola).
• **Other Key Films:** *Dragstrip Girl* (1957, Edward L. Cahn), *Teenage Doll* (1958, Roger Corman), *God's Little Acre* (1958, Anthony Mann), *Al Capone* (1959, Richard Wilson), *The Beat Generation* (1959, Charles Haas), *Hercules and the Captive*

Women (1961, Vittorio Cottafavi), *Flight to Fury* (1966, Monte Hellman).

• **Also of Interest:** *The Abductors* (1957, Andrew V. McLaglen), *The Crooked Circle* (1957, Joseph Kane), *Thunder Island* (1963, Jack Leewood), *Welcome to Hard Times* (1967, Burt Kennedy).

○

GEORGINA SPELVIN (1937–) Former ballet and erotic dancer gave what is considered the best performance in a porno film as the star of the critics' favorite porno film, *The Devil in Miss Jones,* which along with *Deep Throat* and *Behind the Green Door* attracted young, mixed middle-class audiences to adult movies. She was in her mid-thirties and wasn't as pretty or well-built as her bimbo competitors, but she was incredibly sensual and probably the only person on the planet who could deliver Miss Jones's raunchy lines with skill and conviction and also skillfully perform the unusual sex the part required. Wishing she had led a lusty life, Justine Jones is a virgin spinster who commits suicide and then finds herself in an unearthly pleasure world where she is educated (by Harry Reems) in various sex acts, comes to love sex, and then learns her punishment is she can't ever be sexually fulfilled—at the end, the frustrated woman can't even bring herself to a climax. Porno meets Sartre. What turned on viewers was not only the strong sex (including a double insertion in which the young men involved apparently didn't realize the camera was on), but Spelvin's lack of inhibitions, the way she emotes during sex, and her obvious sexual experience. As Kenneth Turan and Stephen F. Zito wrote in *Sinema,* "she has a way of making sex seem intellectual as well as animal." Spelvin would continue to be in porno films and amaze everyone with her physical talents, but she was rarely provided with adequate room to act. She was funny in a small, sexy part in the mainstream comedy *Police Academy.*

• **Cult Favorites:** *The Devil in Miss Jones* (1972, Gerard Damiano), *The Private Afternoons of Pamela Mann* (1974, Henry Paris/Radley Metzger), *The Erotic Adventures of Candy* (1978, Gail Palmer).

• **Other Key Films:** *Wall of Frenzy* (1973), *High Priestess of Sexual Witchcraft* (1973), *Wakefield Poole's Scandals* (1973/74, Wakefield Poole), *Inside Georgina Spelvin* (1974, John Christopher), *Wet Rainbow* (1974, Duddy Kane), *3 A.M.* (1976, Robert McCallum), *Desires Within Young Girls* (1977, Ramsey Karnson), *Take-Off* (1978, Armand Weston), *Fantasy* (1979, Damiano), *Tropic of Desire* (1979, Bob Chinn), *Babylon Pink* (1979, Henri Pachard), *Mystique* (1979, Robert Norman), *For Richer, for Poorer* (1980, Damiano), *All the Way* (1980, Chuck Williams), *Exposed* (1980, Jeffrey Fairbanks), *The Devil in Miss Jones II* (1983, Chuck Vincent), *Police Academy* (1984, Hugh Wilson).

○

BUD SPENCER (1929–) Burly Italian Carlo Pedersoli became an unexpected star as the screen partner of Terence Hill in several rambunctious spaghetti westerns. In the "Trinity" films, the barrel-chested, black-bearded Spencer is the half-brother of the blond, slim Hill. They squabble constantly and get on each other's nerves; because of his laziness, Hill bothers Spencer more. Spencer is usually the "straight man," but when the fighting starts, they join forces and the real fun starts. The action is violent, but is geared for comedy. Spencer uses his brute strength, while Hill uses more finesse. (Spencer may remind some of Paul Smith, who played Bluto in the film *Popeye*.) Without varying from their Trinity characters, the duo appeared together in later films, including some set in the present. On his own, Spencer was the genie in the juvenile *Aladdin*.

 • **Cult Favorites:** *Four Flies in Gray Velvet* (1971, Dario Argento), *They Call Me Trinity* (1970, E. B. Clucher), *Trinity Is Still My Name* (1972, Clucher).
 • **Other Key Films:** *Beyond the Law* (1969, Giorgio Stegani), *God Forgives, I Don't* (1969, Giuseppe Colizzi), *Boot Hill* (1969, Colizzi), *Aces High* (1969, Colizzi), *Trinity Sees Red* (1972, Mario Camus), *Massacre at Fort Holman/A Reason to Live . . . a*

Reason to Die (1984, Tonino Valeri), *Aladdin* (1987, Bruno Corbucci).

○

JOE SPINELL (1936–89) Brawny, New York–born Joseph Spagnuolo was a tough guy on- and offscreen. For nine years he was part of The Theatre of the Forgotten, which put on plays for prisoners. Then he won a role in *The Godfather*—the right film for a mean-looking Italian with a New York accent—and thereafter was a sought-after character actor in violent urban pictures. With his strong, untoned build, unattractive mustache, ruddy complexion, double chin, and menacing, slightly crazed

Joe Spinell experiences his worst nightmare in Maniac.

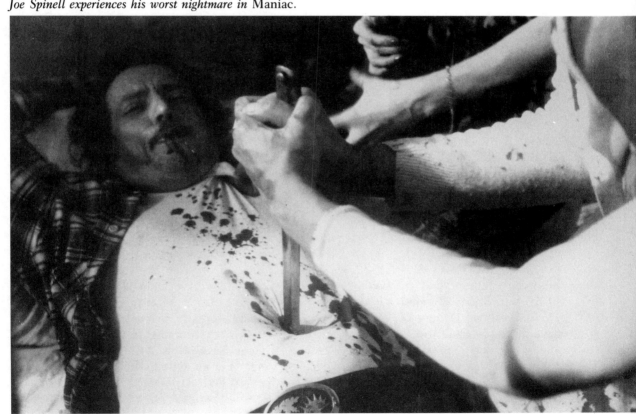

eyes, he was often cast as vicious thugs or seedy gang leaders. In the first two *Godfather* movies, he was a hit man; in *Rocky*, one of several films he made with Sylvester Stallone, he was the loanshark who employs Stallone as a collector. Otherwise, he was usually cast as tough New York types, including cops and Robert De Niro's boss in *Taxi Driver*. His most disgusting role is probably the one for which he is best remembered: his title character in the abominable *Maniac* brutally kills women, scalps them, and attaches their hair to the female mannequins he keeps in his apartment—only Caroline Munro gets away. Not surprisingly, the film was picketed by feminist groups. Undaunted, Spinell always planned on doing sick sequels; he was prevented by his unexpected heart attack. Good directors used him because he always gave good performances, even in *Maniac,* but his choice of projects became increasingly suspect. Mass child murderer John Wayne Gacy wanted Spinell to play him in a movie.

• **Cult Favorites:** *The Godfather* (1972, Francis Ford Coppola), *The Godfather Part II* (1974, Coppola), *Farewell, My Lovely* (1975, Dick Richards), *92 in the Shade* (1975, Thomas McGuane), *Rancho Deluxe* (1975, Frank Perry), *Next Stop, Greenwich Village* (1976, Paul Mazursky), *Stay Hungry* (1976, Bob Rafelson), *Taxi Driver* (1976, Martin Scorsese), *Big Wednesday* (1978, John Milius), *Winter Kills* (1979, William Richert), *The Last Embrace* (1979, Jonathan Demme), *Melvin and Howard* (1980, Demme), *Forbidden Zone* (1980, Richard Elfman), *The Ninth Configuration* (1980, William Peter Blatty), *Maniac* (1980, William Lustig), *Eureka* (1981, Nicolas Roeg).

• **Other Key Films:** *Cops and Robbers* (1973, Aram Avakian), *Rocky* (1976, John V. Avildsen), *Rocky II* (1978, Sylvester Stallone), *Nighthawks* (1981, Bruce Malmuth), *The Big Score* (1983, Fred Williamson), *The Last Horror Show* (1984, David Winters), *Married to the Mob* (1988, Demme).

• **Also of Interest:** *The Seven-Ups* (1973, Philip D'Antonio), *Sorcerer* (1977, William Friedkin), *One Man Jury* (1977, Charles Martin), *Nunzio* (1978, Paul Williams), *Cruisin'* (1980, Friedkin), *Vigilante* (1983, Lustig), *The Last Fight* (1983, Williamson), *Losin' It* (1983, Curtis Hanson), *Deadly Illusion* (1987, Larry Cohen).

○

ANNIE SPRINKLE This busty brunette porno actress–performance artist has gained popularity by showcasing deviant behavior in a cheerful manner, often in XXX-rated comedies. In *Deep Inside Annie Sprinkle,* the "First Lady of Kink" gives happy instructions to the viewers, calling on her friends to help her demonstrate various acts. Although a bit plump, she has terrific screen presence and is truly uninhibited in front of the camera—she can excite you. She has done S&M, as the aggressor, but her specialty is indicated by her name—she even edited a magazine devoted to the subject. She always is upbeat and ready for sex, which is why she is more likable than most porno actresses. She claims sex is her religion and that she studies and attempts sexual practices from all parts of the world. I once heard her say she is working on being sexually primed at all times. Recently she promoted a video in which she demonstrates sex with an ex-female who has become a "male hermaphrodite." She also practices photography!

• **Cult Favorite:** *Deep Inside Annie Sprinkle* (1981, Annie Sprinkle).

• **Some Other Key Films:** *Seduction* (1974, Ralph Ell), *Honeypie* (1975, Howard Ziehm), *Expose Me Lovely* (1976, Armand Weston), *Teenage Deviate* (1976, Ell), *Mash'd* (1979, Emton Smith), *Jack 'n' Jill* (1979, Felix Miguel Arroyo), *For Richer, for Poorer* (1980, Gerard Damiano), *Pandora's Mirror* (1981, Warren Evans), *The Satisfiers of Delta Blue* (1981, Damiano), *Centerfold Fever* (1982, Richard Milner), *Consenting Adults* (1982, Damiano), *The Affairs of Janice, Satan Was a Lady*.

○

LIONEL STANDER (1908–) Former radio and Broadway actor with a gravelly, foghorn voice, a stocky build with perfect posture,

Lionel Stander is Liza Minnelli's agent in New York, New York.

and the face of a clownish tough guy (with prominent cheeks when he grins widely) became one of Hollywood's top supporting actors in the thirties and forties, mostly in comedies, mostly at Columbia. His specialties were cheery, loud henchmen who, though they are uneducated ruffians, worked at being gentlemen by wearing immaculate clothes, being well groomed, and spicing their dumb chatter with witty sarcasm, highfalutin vocabulary, and smart phrases they picked up somewhere. Their meanness is usually tempered by humor. Stander's career came to an abrupt halt in the early fifties when he was blacklisted after refusing to name names for HUAC. Tony Richardson resurrected him in 1965 with a part in *The Loved One.* Then he played one of his old-style henchmen in the absurdist black comedy *Cul-de-Sac,* perhaps his greatest role. In addition to his extensive film work, including westerns in Italy, he spent several years as Max, the chauffeur-butler, on TV's "Hart to Hart."

• **Cult Favorites:** *A Star Is Born* (1937, William Wellman), *Specter of the Rose* (1946, Ben Hecht), *Call Northside 777* (1948, Henry Hathaway), *The Loved One* (1965, Tony Richardson), *Cul-de-Sac* (1966, Roman Polanski), *Once Upon a Time in the West* (1969, Sergio Leone), *New York, New York* (1977, Martin Scorsese).

• **Also Recommended:** *The Scoundrel* (1935, Hecht and Charles MacArthur), *The Milky Way* (1936, Leo McCarey), *Mr. Deeds Goes to Town* (1936, Frank Capra), *The Last Gangster* (1937, Edward Ludwig), *Hangmen Also Die* (1943, Fritz Lang), *Guadalcanal Diary* (1943, Lewis Seiler), *The Kid from Brooklyn* (1946, Norman Z. McLeod), *Unfaithfully Yours* (1948, Preston Sturges), *The Sin of Harold Diddlebock/ Mad Wednesday* (1948/51, Sturges).

• **Also of Interest:** *Hooray for Love* (1935, Walter Lang), *Meet Nero Wolfe* (1936, Herbert Biberman), *Professor Beware* (1938, Elliott Nugent), *A Dandy in Aspic* (1968, Anthony Mann), *The Gang That Couldn't Shoot Straight* (1971, James Goldstone), *Pulp* (1972, Michael Hodges), *The Cassandra Crossing* (1977, George Pan Cosmatos).

○

HARRY DEAN STANTON (1926–) One of our best, most prolific character actors. He usually gives offbeat characterizations in films with hard, sharp edges. He has an authentic, non-Hollywood look: a puzzled, dazed, puppy dog expression; brown hair combed onto a forehead that rises over a sharp nose; a five o'clock shadow at noon; and a friendly smile that makes lines in his face and at the corners of his eyes. At first, you may think him backward—sort of like one of Arthur Hunnicutt's backwoods characters—but when he speaks, you quickly realize his intelligence. He has played a number of religious zealots and other self-righteous individuals. He's the country singer who ruthlessly criticizes Bette Midler in *The Rose,* a guardian angel in *One Magic Christmas,* Molly Ringwald's kind father in *Pretty in Pink,* and a jilted husband who finally gets to know and love his young son in *Paris, Texas,* his one starring role. But he's best as likable sleazes who exist on the fringes, as in *Repo Man,* in which he teaches young Emilio Estevez how to repossess cars; *Cisco Pike,* in which his nice-guy musician, once part of Kris Kristofferson's group, is an ill-fated heroin addict; *Death Watch,* in which he produces a tasteless, popular television series for which he secretly films a woman with a terminal illness; and many other films where he has played con men or police detectives. A singer-musician off-screen.

• **Cult Favorites:** *Ride in the Whirlwind* (1965, Monte Hellman), *Rebel Rousers* (1967, Martin B. Cohen), *Cool Hand Luke* (1967, Stuart Rosenberg), *Cisco Pike* (1972, B. W. L. Norton), *Cockfighter/Born to Kill* (1974, Hellman), *Farewell, My Lovely* (1975, Dick Richards), *92 in the Shade* (1975, Thomas McGuane), *Rancho Deluxe* (1975, Frank Perry), *Straight Time* (1978, Ulu Grosbard), *Alien* (1979, Ridley Scott), *Escape from New York* (1981, John Carpenter), *Repo Man* (1984, Alex Cox), *Paris, Texas* (1984, Wim Wenders), *Red Dawn* (1984, John Milius), *Pretty in Pink* (1986, Howard Deutch), *UFOria* (1980/86, John Blinder), *The Last Temptation of Christ* (1988, Martin Scorsese).

• **Sleepers:** *Where the Lilies Bloom* (1974, William A. Graham), *Wise Blood* (1979, John Huston), *Death Watch* (1980, Bertrand Tavernier).

• **Also of Interest:** *Dillinger* (1973, Milius), *Rafferty and the Gold Dust Twins* (1975, Richards), *The Missouri Breaks* (1976, Arthur Penn), *The Rose* (1979, Mark Rydell), *The Black Marble* (1980, Harold Becker), *One from the Heart* (1982,

Harry Dean Stanton and Adrienne Barbeau talk with Isaac Hayes in John Carpenter's Escape from New York.

Francis Coppola), *Slamdance* (1987, Wayne Wang).

○

CHARLES STARRETT (1903–86) Handsome, Massachusetts-born, ex–Dartmouth football player was Columbia's top B-western star from 1935 to 1952. He had minor success at Paramount as romantic and second leads in other genres before strapping on the holster. He'd make over 130 quickie westerns, more than any other actor. His films were pretty conventional, with fisticuffs, gun fights, riding stunts, and romance (Iris Meredith was his most frequent leading lady). His most famous character was the Durango Kid, whom he'd play 56 times, with Smiley Burnette as his comic sidekick. The athletic actor could be easygoing or tough, depending on the situation; he wasn't shy with women, or the type who minds his own business until pushed too far—he was always ready for action. His best films were made in the early forties, with Joseph H. Lewis or Lambert Hillyer at the helm; Hillyer directed Starrett's personal favorite, *The Medico of Painted Springs,* about a frontier doctor. Later he made tired formula films, unimaginatively directed by Fred Sears.

• **Cult Favorite:** *The Mask of Fu Manchu* (1932, Charles Brabin).

• **Other Key Films:** *Rio Grande* (1938, Spencer G. Bennet), *Blazing Six-Shooters* (1940, Lewis), *Two-Fisted Rangers* (1940, Lewis), *Texas Stagecoach* (1940, Lewis), *The Durango Kid* (1940, Lambert Hillyer), *The Pinto Kid* (1941, Hillyer), *The Medico of Painted Springs* (1941, Hillyer), *The Prairie Stranger* (1941, Hillyer), *Thunder Over the Prairie* (1941, Hillyer), *The Royal Mounted Patrol* (1941, Hillyer).

○

BARBARA STEELE (1938–) The most fascinating actress ever to appear with regularity in horror films, including the spooky, atmospheric classic *Black Sunday* and others made in Italy during the sixties. This British actress is revered by her fans for her talent, emotional range, wit, intelligence, erotic sexuality, and a beauty that is mysterious and unique. Her jet black hair, large green eyes, prominent cheekbones, thick bottom lip, and somewhat knobby chin don't seem synchronized, and as a result her face can be looked on as either evil or sweet, depending on the beholder. So in *Black Sunday*, she was effective playing both the evil vampire-witch and the gentle heroine; in other horror films, she alternated between heroines and wicked women with blood lusts. Video distributor Sinister Cinema pitches its Barbara Steele line by reminding horror fans that she "played witches, ghosts, hideously scarred undead monsters, reincarnates, murderous mistresses, and more. She's been tortured, poisoned, electrocuted, burned at the stake, killed by plague, had acid thrown in her face . . ." One critic of the sixties called her "the only girl in films whose eyebrows can snarl"; *Variety* said she resembled Jackie Kennedy; and another described her as "a blank-eyed manikin with an earthbound figure, and a voice from outer space." Others also took note: Fellini used her in 8½; her one-time husband James Poe wrote a part for her in his script for *They Shoot Horses, Don't They?* (a part Susannah York eventually played); and Jonathan Demme wrote a part for her which she did play in *Caged Heat.* That role, perhaps the strangest in her strange career—a cruel,

The compelling Barbara Steele in Mario Bava's Black Sunday.

repressed, wheelchair-bound women's prison warden who has perverse sexual fantasies—was her first role in six years and her first American film since 1961. More offers from other cult directors would follow. Still, one feels she never received the recognition or major roles she deserved. At least she earned the title "Queen of the Horror Film."

• **Cult Favorites:** *Black Sunday* (1961, Mario Bava), *The Pit and the Pendulum* (1961, Roger Corman), *The Horrible Dr. Hitchcock* (1962, Robert Hampton/ Riccardo Freda), *8½* (1963, Federico Fellini), *The Dance Macabre/Castle of Blood* (1963, Anthony Dawson/Antonio Margheriti), *The Spectre/The Ghost* (1965, Hampton/Freda), *She-Beast/Revenge of the Blood Beast* (1965, Michael Reeves), *Young Torless* (1967, Volker Schlöndorff), *Caged Heat* (1974, Jonathan Demme), *They Came from Within* (1976, David Cronenberg), *Pretty Baby* (1978, Louis Malle), *Piranha* (1978, Joe Dante).

• **Other Key Films:** *The Long Hair of Death* (1964, Dawson/Margheriti), *The Faceless Monster/Nightmare Castle* (1965, Allan Grunewald/Mario Caiano), *The Silent Scream* (1980, Denny Harris).

○

BOB STEELE (1906–88) Robert North Bradbury, Jr.'s father was a movie director, and his twin, Bill, was his partner in a touring comedy stage act. He was briefly a pro boxer before beginning a lengthy career in pictures at the end of the silent era. He'd be effective as bad guys in *Of Mice and*

Men and *The Big Sleep* (he has a memorable death scene), but he made his mark as a hero in B westerns. Steele maintained his popularity despite moving from the silent to the sound film and shifting between studios: FBO, Syndicate Pictures, Tiffany-Stahl, Monogram (where he worked with his father, and also joined Ken Maynard and Hoot Gibson for three "Trail Blazers" films), Supreme Pictures, RKO, PRC (where he starred as Billy the Kid in several 1940–41 films), and Republic (playing Tucson Smith in 20 fast-moving "Three Mesquiteers" films). In later years, he was cast in small parts for nostalgia value (often joining other old-timers) in both A and B westerns. Most western fans prefer his work with producer A. W. Hackel at Supreme and Republic in the mid to late thirties. Those films were loaded with action, though there also was time for romance and comedy (supplied by Si Jenks). While Steele's cowboy was usually easygoing, his films had a serious, recurring theme: the search for his father's murderer. The question was: what will his characters do when they unmask the scoundrels?

• **Cult Favorites:** *The Big Sleep* (1946, Howard Hawks), *Decision at Sundown* (1957, Budd Boetticher), *Rio Bravo* (1959, Hawks).

• **Some Other Key Films:** *With Sitting Bull at the Spirit Lake Massacre* (1926, Robert North Bradbury), *Davy Crockett at the Fall of the Alamo* (1926, Bradbury), *The Mohave Kid* (1927, Bradbury), *The Bandit's Son* (1927, Wallace Fox), *Laughing at Death* (1929, Fox), *The Amazing Vagabond* (1929, Fox), *The Man from Hell's Edges* (1932, Bradbury), *Galloping Romeo* (1933, Bradbury), *Powdersmoke Range* (1935, Fox), *Cavalry* (1936, Bradbury), *The Border Phantom* (1936, S. Roy Luby), *Arizona Gunfighter* (1937, Sam Newfield), *The Colorado Kid* (1937, Newfield), *Of Mice and Men* (1939, Lewis Milestone), *The Carson City Kid* (1940, Joseph Kane), *Billy the Kid in Texas* (1940, Peter Stewart and Newfield), *Billy the Kid Outlawed* (1940, Stewart and Newfield), *Trail Blazers* (1940, George Sherman), *Under Texas Skies* (1940, Sherman), *Lone Star Raiders* (1940, Sherman), *The Great Train Robbery* (1941, Kane), *Billy the Kid's Fighting Pals* (1941, Sherman Scott and Newfield), *Revenge of the Zombies* (1943, Steve Sekely), *Death Valley Rangers* (1943, Robert Tansey), *Westward Bound* (1944, Tansey), *Arizona Whirlwind* (1944, Tansey), *The Lion and the Horse* (1952, Louis King).

• **Also of Interest:** *Killer McCoy* (1947, Roy Rowland), *Cheyenne* (1947, Raoul Walsh), *The Enforcer* (1951, Bretaigne Windust), *The Atomic Submarine* (1959, Spencer G. Bennet), *Hell Bent for Leather* (1960, Sherman), *Bullet for a Badman* (1964, R. G. Springsteen), *The Bounty Killer* (1965, Bennet), *Requiem for a Gunfighter* (1965, Bennet), *Town Tamer* (1965, Lesley Selander), *Rio Lobo* (1970, Hawks).

○

BRINKE STEVENS Eye-catching star of several recent cheapo science-fiction films, some of the direct-to-cable and direct-to-video variety. As an imperiled teen in *Sorority Babes at the Slimeball Bowl-a-Rama*, she even grabbed audience attention away from more famous scream queens Linnea Quigley and Michelle Bauer. Equally suited for heroines and villainesses, this dark-haired brunette has a sensual face but the wicked eyes and thick eyebrows of a soap-opera vixen, and a body that writhes with abandon. She usually wears tantalizing outfits—or less. She spends most of her screen time in chains in the villain's dungeon in *Slave Girls from Beyond Infinity*—and dies with a knife in her back. Stevens scripted *Teenage Exorcist* and hosted the compilation film *Monsters and Maniacs*.

• **Cult Favorite:** *Sorority Babes at the Slime-ball Bowl-a-Rama* (1988, David De-Coteau).

• **Some Other Key Films:** *Slave Girls from Beyond Infinity* (1987, Ken Dixon), *Nightmare Sisters* (1988, DeCoteau), *Bad Girls from Mars, Warlords, Teenage Exorcist.*

○

MARC STEVENS This tall, slim, light-haired porno actor was one of the first male stars in adult films. In the early and mid-seventies, he often costarred with Andrea True and the ill-fated Tina Russell. He also starred in gay films. He wasn't hired for his acting, but for his stud service—he had a remarkably long penis. Often, he turned up just for one sex scene, as in my favorite porno film, *Teenage Cheerleader*. He was extremely prolific in his heyday (which lasted many years), and for a time it was rare that a porno film wouldn't star him and/or Jamie Gillis. He seemed sleazier than Gillis, though Gillis's screen acts were far more perverse. He died from AIDS in 1989.

• **Some Key Films:** *High Rise* (1972, Danny Stone), *Miss September* (*Whatever Happened to Her?*) (1973, Jerry Denny), *Inside Georgina Spelvin* (1974, John Christopher), *Teenage Cheerleader* (1974), *Thrilling and Drilling* (1974, Stan Cory), *A Touch of Genie* (1974, Jason Russell), *Flipchicks* (1975), *All About Gloria Leonard* (1979, Gloria Leonard), *Veronica's Kiss* (1979, Bruce Wilson), *Consenting Adults*

(1982, Gerard Damiano), *Centerfold Fever* (1982, Richard Milner), *Big Thing* (Peter Higgins), *Lady on a Couch, Slip-Up.*

○

STELLA STEVENS (1936–) Even some of the most serious male film critics have wild crushes on this sexy former *Playboy* centerfold from Hot Coffee, Mississippi. Beautiful, curvaceous, with long blond hair and dimples below her sensual lips (she has a slight resemblance to Barbara Eden), she has so much sex appeal that few producers have cared about her talent. She showed a flair for comedy in *Li'l Abner*, playing Appassionata von Climax, and for drama in *Man-Trap*, as the title character, and in John Cassavetes's offbeat *Too Late Blues*, but that wasn't why she was cast. She has played a lot of sexy klutzes and tarts and tough whores with hearts of gold, always catching one's leering eye. But only rarely did her roles tap into her acting skills. She's most likable as the college student whom Jerry Lewis's clumsy professor, Julius Kelp, and his suave, narcissistic alter ego, Buddy Love, court in *The Nutty Professor*. Though her klutzy pose opposite Dean Martin's secret agent Matt Helm in *The Silencers* grates on my nerves, that is one of her most popular characters. Undoubtedly, she was at her best as the western whore whom Jason Robards treats like a lady in *The Ballad of Cable Hogue*, although she was angered that Sam Peckinpah trimmed about a third of her scenes. I love watching her responses to Robards's sincere flattery—not in any other film has a Stevens character received such respect or met a man so capable of saying the right words or so unafraid of expressing his feelings. Their relationship is novel in the western genre, and the most mature relationship Stevens has had on the screen. The movie's highlight is probably her taking an outdoor bath after a night of their lovemaking, and singing "Butterfly Morning"—an unforgettable scene for us Stevens cultists. I think what has made Stevens come across as so sexy is that she has always been uninhibited offscreen as well, posing for the famous *Playboy* shots and wearing revealing clothes in public (she showed up at a horror-movie awards ceremony in a transparent negligee with nothing underneath). She told an interviewer that her inquisitive fans should "buy a copy of the illustrated *Kama-Sutra*—that'll give them a good idea what I do in my private life." Since the mid-seventies, Stevens has directed a documentary, played a couple of exploitation-film villainesses, and appeared in television movies and soaps.

• **Cult Favorites:** *The Nutty Professor* (1963, Jerry Lewis), *The Ballad of Cable Hogue* (1970, Sam Peckinpah), *The Poseidon Adventure* (1972, Ronald Neame), *Cleopatra Jones and the Casino of Gold* (1975, Chuck Bail), *Chained Heat* (1983, Paul Nicolas).

• **Other Key Films:** *Li'l Abner* (1959, Melvin Frank), *Too Late Blues* (1962, John Cassavetes), *Girls! Girls! Girls!* (1962, Norman Taurog), *The Courtship of Eddie's Father* (1963, Vincente Minnelli), *Advance to the Rear* (1964, George Marshall), *The Silencers* (1966, Phil Karlson), *Rage* (1966, Gilberto Gazcon), *The Mad Room* (1969, Bernard Girard), *Slaughter* (1972, Jack Starrett), *Stand Up and Be Counted* (1972, Jackie Cooper).

• **Also of Interest:** *Man-Trap* (1961, Edmund O'Brien), *Synanon* (1965, Richard Quine), *Sol Madrid* (1968, Brian G. Hutton), *Arnold* (1973, Georg Fenady), *Las Vegas Lady* (1976, Noel Nosseck), *Nickel-odeon* (1976, Peter Bogdanovich), *Monster in the Closet* (1986, Bob Dahlin).

○

CATHERINE MARY STEWART (1959–) Pretty Canadian-born ex–soap actress has been the female lead in a number of futuristic science-fiction films, teenage comedies, and low-grade exploitation films, most unworthy of her. This energetic, witty, and feisty actress has shown a lot of range within a limited framework, even singing in a couple of movies. She was sweet as Lance Guest's teenage girlfriend in *The Last Starfighter,* her best-known role, but she really sparkles as a survivor in the highly original apocalyptic comedy *Night of the Comet,* not only handling the romance and action, but also joining Kelli Moroney, as her younger sister, in a delightful shopping sequence set in an empty department store. The two make a fabulous comic duo. Stewart has a lot of talent—I hope that, just once, a talented major filmmaker gives her a shot.

• **Sleeper:** *Night of the Comet* (1984, Thom Eberhardt).

• **Other Key Films:** *The Last Starfighter* (1984, Nick Castle), *Mischief* (1985, Mel Damski), *Dudes* (1987, Penelope Spheeris), *World Gone Wild* (1988, Lee H. Katzin), *Weekend at Bernie's* (1989, Ted Kotcheff).

• **Also of Interest:** *The Apple* (1980, Menahem Golan), *Nighthawks* (1981, Bruce Malmuth), *Night Flyers* (1987, T. C. Blake/Robert Collector), *Scenes from the Goldmine* (1987, Marc Rocco).

○

JAMES STEWART (1908–) This tall, handsome, gangly Pennsylvanian drawls and

James Stewart in The Man from Laramie, *one of several rugged cult westerns he made with director Anthony Mann.*

stutters amiably and talks with his hands when he's excited. He had cult status even before *It's a Wonderful Life* emerged as our favorite Christmas film. He also may be our most popular actor. His image is that of a shy, cheery, awkward boy-next-door, yet his best films are those in which he revealed a darker side. Many of his characters are naive, optimistic Americans who become cynical: his politician in *Mr. Smith Goes to Washington*, George Bailey in *It's a Wonderful Life*, his pacifist in *Destry Rides*

Again, his lawyer in *The Man Who Shot Liberty Valance*. By the time we meet his cowboys in his fascinating, violent Anthony Mann adult westerns, they are already hard-bitten. Many characters have psychological problems: Mr. Smith becomes terribly depressed; George Bailey wants to commit suicide; alcoholic Elwood P. Dowd imagines a giant rabbit friend in *Harvey*; his detective in *Vertigo* becomes, essentially, a necrophiliac (making over shopgirl Kim Novak into his dead lover);

his photographer becomes a Peeping Tom in *Rear Window;* many of his cowboys are obsessed with vengeance. Many characters also suffer physically: he collapses during a wrenching filibuster in *Mr. Smith,* he's shot in his gun hand in *The Man from Laramie,* he has a broken leg in *Rear Window,* and more. His men are, typically, outsiders. Some arrive in a new town and find themselves at odds with an element. Some aren't newcomers, but their idealism or neurosis sets them apart—even in *It's a Wonderful Life,* George becomes a stranger in his own town when his "guardian angel" makes him experience how it would be if he never existed. His outsiders find no one will believe what they are saying, in such films as *Mr. Smith Goes to Washington, Call Northside 777, Harvey, No Highway in the Sky,* and *Rear Window.* But Stewart's characters don't give up the fight. We trust that they will help anyone in trouble—they just have no idea how to help themselves.

• **Cult Favorites:** *Rose Marie* (1936, W. S. Van Dyke), *Born to Dance* (1936, Roy Del Ruth), *Mr. Smith Goes to Washington* (1939, Frank Capra), *Destry Rides Again* (1939, George Marshall), *The Shop Around the Corner* (1940, Ernst Lubitsch), *The Philadelphia Story* (1940, George Cukor), *It's a Wonderful Life* (1946, Capra), *Call Northside 777* (1948, Henry Hathaway), *Rope* (1948, Alfred Hitchcock), *The Stratton Story* (1949, Sam Wood), *Winchester '73* (1950, Anthony Mann), *Harvey* (1950, Henry Koster), *Bend of the River* (1952, Mann), *The Naked Spur* (1953, Mann), *Rear Window* (1954, Hitchcock), *The Far Country* (1955, Mann), *The Man from Laramie* (1955, Mann), *The Man Who Knew Too Much* (1956, Hitchcock), *Vertigo* (1959, Hitchcock), *Bell, Book and Candle* (1958,

Richard Quine), *The Man Who Shot Liberty Valance* (1962, John Ford), *Cheyenne Autumn* (1964, Ford).

• **Sleeper:** *The Shootist* (1976, Don Siegel).

• **Other Key Films:** *You Can't Take It with You* (1938, Capra), *Made for Each Other* (1939, John Cromwell), *The Mortal Storm* (1940, Frank Borzage), *Broken Arrow* (1950, Delmer Daves), *The Jackpot* (1950, Walter Lang), *No Highway in the Sky* (1951, Koster), *The Greatest Show on Earth* (1952, Cecil B. De Mille), *Carbine Williams* (1952, Richard Thorpe), *The Glenn Miller Story* (1954, Mann), *The Spirit of St. Louis* (1957, Billy Wilder), *Night Passage* (1957, James Neilson), *Anatomy of a Murder* (1959, Otto Preminger), *The Flight of the Phoenix* (1966, Robert Aldrich).

○

STING (1951–) Blond, handsome, charismatic British rock singer (born Gordon Sumner)—he was with the enormously popular group Police before going solo—has made the successful transition to film. He debuted in a small, nonspeaking but dynamic part in England's first street film, *Quadrophenia,* as Ace Face, the top Mod who battles police in one era and is a bellboy in the next. He proved he could handle lines in the unusual, often unpleasant film *Brimstone and Treacle,* giving a flesh-crawling performance as a disturbed young man who cons his way into the home of a middle-class couple by claiming to be the ex-boyfriend of their mute, bedridden daughter—and ends up taking sexual advantage of the helpless girl. The most intriguing aspect of the film is that you can never figure out his motives. Since then Sting has had leads in a few films,

Sting (right) *and Phil Daniels in* Quadrophenia.

mostly mainstream failures. He was boring as Baron Frankenstein in *The Bride,* but so was Jennifer Beals as his creation. He did better as a shady jazz-club owner in the odd British film noir, *Stormy Monday*. His characters are best when they have elements of mystery and danger. *Bring On the Night* is a documentary about Sting forming a new, temporary band. He starred briefly in *The Three Penny Opera* on Broadway. A political activist, he has worked closely with Brazilian tribal leaders to protest further razing of the rain forest.

• **Cult Favorites:** *Quadrophenia* (1979, Franc Roddam), *Brimstone and Treacle* (1982, Richard Loncraine), *Dune* (1984, David Lynch), *Stormy Monday* (1988, Mike Figgis).

• **Other Key Films:** *Plenty* (1985, Fred Schepisi), *The Bride* (1985, Roddam), *Bring On the Night* (1985, Michael Apted), *Julia and Julia* (1987, Peter Del Monte).

○

LINDA STIRLING (1921–) When Kay Aldridge left Republic, this tall, lovely former model replaced her as the studio's "Queen of the Serials." Fetchingly garbed in *The Tiger Woman,* playing a white woman who was raised by and is queen of a dark-skinned jungle tribe, but is entitled to an inheritance (the reason greedy villain LeRoy Mason wants to kill her), she immediately won the hearts of male serial fans. She next starred as the masked justice-fighter, "The Whip," in the swashbuckler *Zorro's Black Whip*. But in her subsequent serials,

Serial queen Linda Stirling in *The Tiger Woman.*

she'd leave most of the fighting to the male leads, settling for being a woman in distress. Her various heroines are nearly killed by a rocket blast, a flooding mine tunnel, a water-filling pit, a wine press, a collapsing bridge that plunges into a volcano and over a cliff, and, in *The Crimson Ghost,* a "control collar" that will kill her if removed. Stirling usually was so perfectly made up that it was hard to forget she was a model, but the dimple on her right side softened her appearance and contributed to her likability. While still in her twenties, she retired to get married.

• **Cult Favorite:** *The Tiger Woman* (1944 serial, Spencer G. Bennet and Wallace Grissell).
• **Other Key Films:** *Zorro's Black Whip* (1944 serial, Bennet and Grissell), *Manhunt of Mystery Island* (1945 serial, Bennet, Grissell, and Yakima Canutt), *The Purple Mask Strikes* (1945 serial, Bennet and Fred C. Bannon), *The Crimson Ghost* (1945 serial, William Witney and Bannon), *Jesse James Rides Again* (1947 serial, Bannon and Thomas Carr).
• **Also of Interest:** *The Pretender* (1947, W. Lee Wilder).

DEAN STOCKWELL (1936–) The brother of actor Guy Stockwell, he began as a curly-haired, blond child actor at M-G-M. Quite likable and intuitively talented, he specialized in smart, sensitive boys, including the title character in the allegorical antiwar movie *The Boy with Green Hair,* still one of the finest children's films. Except for making that picture, he hated the entire experience and dropped out of movies when he got older. He returned in the late fifties and tried to change his wholesome image, playing a genius youth who commits murder for the fun of it in *Compulsion,* and the tubercular Edmund Tyrone in *Long Day's Journey into Night.* However, his Paul Morel in the film based on D. H. Lawrence's *Sons and Lovers* could have been one of his sensitive young characters grown up. In the late sixties, he took roles in antiestablishment exploitation films. In the eighties, he entered a new phase, giving terrific, scene-stealing performances in quirky character parts, usually bad men and none stranger than his vile, effeminate criminal who lip-synchs to Roy Orbison's "In Dreams" in *Blue Velvet.* Even in that role, his comical, bemused expression, with lips tightened and eyes twinkling, is evident. Once known for his hard living—he has long been friends with Dennis Hopper—he is now one of the weirdest members of the Hollywood mainstream (even starring on TV's "Quantum

Dean Stockwell in Blue Velvet.

Leap"), although his film choices and portrayals remain offbeat.

- **Cult Favorites:** *The Boy with Green Hair* (1948, Joseph Losey), *Psych-Out* (1968, Richard Rush), *Tracks* (1977, Henry Jaglom), *Dune* (1984, David Lynch), *Paris, Texas* (1984, Wim Wenders), *To Live and Die in L.A.* (1985, William Friedkin), *Blue Velvet* (1986, Lynch).
- **Sleepers:** *Stars in My Crown* (1950, Jacques Tourneur), *Alsino and the Condor* (1982, Miguel Littin).
- **Other Key Films:** *Anchors Aweigh* (1945, George Sidney), *The Green Years* (1946, Victor Saville), *Gentleman's Agreement* (1947, Elia Kazan), *The Secret Garden* (1949, Fred M. Wilcox), *Kim* (1950, Victor Saville), *Compulsion* (1959, Richard Fleischer), *Sons and Lovers* (1960, Jack Cardiff), *Long Day's Journey into Night* (1962, Sidney Lumet), *Rapture* (1965, John Guillermin), *The Loners* (1972, Sutton Roley), *The Werewolf of Washington* (1973, Milton Moses Ginsberg), *Gardens of Stone* (1987, Francis Coppola), *Married to the Mob* (1988, Jonathan Demme), *Tucker: A Man and His Dream* (1988, Coppola).

○

MINK STOLE There have been numerous intentionally annoying characters in John Waters's bizarre comedies, but none is more repellent than Mink Stole's in *Desperate Living.* Just out of the mental institution and back in her middle-class home, Peggy Gravel is on the verge of another breakdown. You'll want to strangle her because she won't stop screaming at the top of her lungs that everyone is trying to kill her. She and her enormous maid (Jean Hill) kill her husband and go on the lam. They are stopped by a cop who lets them go only when they give him their panties and wet soul kisses. In Mortville, she rents space from a lady wrestler (Susan Lowe) and sides with evil queen Carlotta (Edith Massey), because she respects Carlotta's plan to inject everyone with rabies. Stole played other obnoxious women for Waters, including a mental patient who does a topless dance in *Mondo Trasho,* a religious pervert who becomes Divine's lover in *Multiple Maniacs,* Divine's belligerent, illegitimate daughter who becomes a Hare Krishna to annoy her mother in *Female Trouble,* and Connie Marble, who with husband Raymond (David Lochary) competes with Divine for the title of "the filthiest human being in the world."

- **Cult Favorites:** *Mondo Trasho* (1969, John Waters), *Multiple Maniacs* (1970, Waters), *Pink Flamingos* (1972, Waters), *Female Trouble* (1974, Waters), *Desperate Living* (1977, Waters), *Polyester* (1981, Waters), *Hairspray* (1988, Waters), *Cry-Baby* (1990, Waters).

○

SHIRLEY STOLER (1929–) Obese, unfriendly-looking redhead who made her first *big* impression as the ill-tempered, sexually frustrated, 200-pound nurse Martha Beck in *The Honeymoon Killers.* This low-budget gem was a chilling reenactment of the harrowing "Lonely Hearts Club Murders" which made national headlines in the late forties. Slender Tony Lo Bianco was her costar, playing a Spanish gigolo, Ray Fernandez, who is more charming than smart. He became her lover and accomplice in the murders of the lonely, monied women whose ads he answered. These are cold-blooded killers, whose amoral behavior matches their sexual drive. Stoler plays Martha as a cross between Divine, Big

Shirley Stoler is romantically involved with Tony Lo Bianco in The Honeymoon Killers.

Nurse in *One Flew Over the Cuckoo's Nest,* and an angry Godfrey Cambridge. She is strong when dishing out violence (killing one old lady with a hammer, when Ray can't bring himself to do it) but turns to mush when Ray is untrue to her, attempting suicide and finally having the police arrest them both. It's funny watching the harassed Ray constantly trying to keep the jealous Martha, who poses as his sister, from arguing with the women he pursues for their money. Their scenes together are brilliant. In *Seven Beauties,* Stoler was used for effect as the brutal, grotesque-looking German prison camp commandant to whom Italian Giancarlo Giannini must make love in order to stay alive. In *Miami Blues,* she chops off Alec Baldwin's fingers with a meat cleaver. She'd be perfect as a regular on Pee-Wee Herman's kiddie show.

• **Cult Favorites:** *The Honeymoon Killers* (1970, Leonard Kastle), *Seven Beauties* (1976, Lina Wertmuller), *Miami Blues* (1990, George Armitage), *Frankenhooker* (1990, Frank Hennenlotter).

• **Also of Interest:** *The Displaced Person* (1976, Glenn Jordan), *Below the Belt* (1974/80, Robert Fowler).

○

SHARON STONE (1958–) This gorgeous blonde, a former model, had small parts in *Stardust Memories* and *Irreconcilable Differences,* but has had better luck in action-adventure films. Her two movies with Richard Chamberlain, *King Solomon's Mines* and *Allan Quatermain and the Lost City of Gold* (a sequel that was shot while cast and crew were still on location in Africa), were good only for giving Stone practice in women-in-distress roles. She was used to better effect in 1988, in the violent urban melodramas *Above the Law*, as Steven Seagal's wife, and *Action Jackson,* as the blond counterpart to black beauties Pam Grier and Vanity. She was spirited, sexy, and likable—which was unfortunate in the second film, because she is killed by husband Craig T. Nelson. She earned the female villain role, almost killing husband Arnold Schwarzenegger in hand-to-hand combat, in the futuristic action-thriller *Total Recall.* She was the *Playboy* cover girl when that smash hit was released. One can predict a bright career for her.

• **Cult Favorite:** *Stardust Memories* (1980, Woody Allen).

• **Sleepers:** *Irreconcilable Differences* (1984, Charles Shyer), *Above the Law* (1988, Andrew Davis).

• **Other Key Films:** *King Solomon's Mines* (1985, J. Lee Thompson), *Allan Quatermain and the Lost City of Gold* (1987, Gary Nelson), *Cold Steel* (1987, Dorothy Ann Puzo), *Action Jackson* (1988, Craig R. Baxley), *Total Recall* (1990, Paul Verhoeven).

○

JUNE STOREY With the possible exception of Gail Davis, this pretty actress with light-colored hair and a gentle disposition was Gene Autry's most popular leading lady. She was charmed and serenaded by Autry in 10 films in 1939 and 1940, as he was solidifying his position as the number-one cowboy star. As Autry was the most chaste of the cowboy stars, his courtship of Storey was, to say the least, polite. He'd rescue her spunky heroines from the bad guy at the end—proving to many that *he* wasn't the bad guy—and she and her father would thank him for his deed. They'd smile at each other, there'd be a hint of love in their eyes, but that was about it. There was a harder edge to her B melodramas, but she didn't get any of the juicy parts.

• **Key Films:** *Home on the Prairie* (1939, Jack Townley), *Blue Montana Skies* (1939, B. Reeves Eason), *Mountain Rhythm* (1939, Eason), *Colorado Sunset* (1939, George Sherman), *In Old Monterey* (1939, Joseph Kane), *South of the Border* (1939, Sherman), *Rancho Grande* (1940, Frank McDonald), *Gaucho Serenade* (1940, McDonald), *Carolina Moon* (1940, McDonald), *Ride, Tenderfoot, Ride* (1940, McDonald).

• **Also of Interest:** *Girls' Dormitory* (1936, Irving Cummings), *First Love* (1939, Henry Koster), *Dance Hall* (1941, Irving Pichel), *The Strange Woman* (1947, Edgar G. Ulmer), *Killer McCoy* (1948, Roy Rowland), *Cry of the City* (1948, Robert Siodmak), *The Snake Pit* (1948, Anatole Litvak).

○

GLENN STRANGE (1899–1973) Tall Irish–Cherokee Indian had dark hair, thick eyebrows, a square jaw, and a lined face, but his face was disguised in his most famous role: the Frankenstein Monster. He played the part three times and was the best Monster other than Boris Karloff. He projected neither the poignancy nor subtlety that made Karloff's Monster so fascinating, but he looked frightening (Strange was probably Fred Gwynne's model in TV's "The Munsters"), growled as if he meant it, and was a killing machine that couldn't be soothed with a little kindness. In *Abbott and Costello Meet Frankenstein,* the film for which he is most appreciated, he didn't make the Monster a buffoon, but smartly played him as if he didn't know the film was a comedy—perhaps that's why

Glenn Strange in a publicity shot for Abbott and Costello Meet Frankenstein.

Costello looks genuinely frightened when Strange chases him. Strange appeared in other horror films, often as monsters and brutes. A former rodeo performer, he also played in many westerns. He usually was a heavy, but he was Dick Foran's comic sidekick in a number of B westerns.

• **Cult Favorite:** *Abbott and Costello Meet Frankenstein* (1948, Charles Barton).

• **Other Key Films:** *House of Frankenstein* (1944, Erle C. Kenton), *House of Dracula* (1945, Kenton), *Red River* (1948, Howard Hawks), *The Red Badge of Courage* (1952, John Huston).

• **Also of Interest:** *The Mummy's Tomb* (1942, Harold Young), *The Mad Monster* (1942, Sam Newfield), *The Monster Maker* (1944, Newfield), *The Black Raven* (1943, Newfield), *Master Minds* (1949, Jean Yarbrough), *Double Crossbones* (1951, Barton), *Comin' Round the Mountain* (1951, Charles Lamont), *The Lawless Breed* (1952, Raoul Walsh), *The Great Sioux Uprising* (1953, Lloyd Bacon).

○

SUSAN STRASBERG (1938–) She was a beautiful, sexy brunette, and because she was the daughter of Lee and Paula Strasberg, founders of the Actors Studio, much was expected of her. After *The Cobweb* and *Picnic*, as Kim Novak's brainy sister, she was cast as the lead in *Stagestruck*, playing

Susan Strasberg found more success in low-budget exploitation films than she did in major Hollywood productions.

an aspiring actress. It was her own star-making role, but she was a disappointment. She must have felt too much was riding on her shoulders, because later in the sixties, in less important films, she loosened up and came across much better. Her first good performance was in the scary British horror film *Scream of Fear,* as a wheelchair-bound young woman who is suspicious of her father's disappearance. She was sexy as a deaf girl in the best of the drug-hippie movies, *Psych-Out,* searching for her brother in Haight-Ashbury. And she still wasn't all there in *Psycho Sisters.* She may have weakened major films, but the presence of this lovely, intelligent actress in horror films has given them class.

• **Cult Favorites:** *Scream of Fear/Taste of Fear* (1961, Seth Holt), *The Trip* (1967, Roger Corman), *Psych-Out* (1968, Richard Rush), *Psycho Sisters/So Evil, My Sister* (1972, Reginald LeBorg).

• **Other Key Films:** *Picnic* (1955, Joshua Logan), *Stagestruck* (1958, Sidney Lumet), *Hemingway's Adventures of a Young Man* (1962, Martin Ritt), *The Brotherhood* (1968, Ritt).

• **Also of Interest:** *The Cobweb* (1955, Vincente Minnelli), *McGuire, Go Home!* (1966, Ralph Thomas), *Chubasco* (1968, Allen H. Miner), *In Praise of Older Women* (1978, George Kaczender), *The Manitou* (1978, William Girdler), *Bloody Birthday* (1986, Ed Hunt).

○

DOROTHY STRATTEN (1960–80) Beautiful, buxom blonde from Vancouver was *Playboy's* 1979 Playmate of the Year before embarking on a film career. She played the title character, a gorgeous twenty-eighth-century robotic spaceship pilot in the insipid, low-budget science-fiction parody

Dorothy Stratten in Galaxina.

Galaxina. When Galaxina falls in love, she reprograms herself to be humanoid, but the director forgot to tell his neophyte actress to humanize her acting style at this point. Stratten's natural charm and budding talent wouldn't be revealed until boyfriend Peter Bogdanovich's breezy comedy *They All Laughed.* But by the time it was released, Stratten was dead, shot by her estranged husband, Paul Snyder, in one of Hollywood's saddest tragedies. Her story, the story of a vulnerable, insecure innocent who is trapped by a vicious, domineering wolf, would be made into both a feature, *Star 80,* directed by Bob Fosse and starring Mariel Hemingway, and a TV movie with Jamie Lee Curtis; Bogdanovich would also write a book about her.

• **Key Films:** *Galaxina* (1980, William Sachs), *They All Laughed* (1981, Peter Bogdanovich).

○

WOODY STRODE (1914–) This 6'4" UCLA All-American end, along with halfback Kenny Washington, broke the NFL color barrier in 1946 (a year before UCLA's Jackie Robinson played in major league baseball) when they joined the Los Angeles Rams (blacks Marion Motley and Bill Willis simultaneously joined the AAFC's Browns). Strode's time in the NFL and CFL was brief, but in the early fifties he began a lengthy film career as a supporting player in action and adventure films. Tall, bald, and handsome, with a muscular face that has impressive bone structure, a bodybuilder's physique, and eyes that said "You'd better not mess with me," he made up for his stilted acting style with a strong physical presence. He could play a warrior or a king. In fact, in *The Ten Commandments,* he played a tribal king and a slave, though both roles were tiny. Among his most memorable roles are the noble gladiator whom Kirk Douglas battles in the arena but doesn't want to kill in *Spartacus;* John Wayne's companion and housemate in *The Man Who Shot Liberty Valance;* two brothers, one a formidable foe to hero Jock Mahoney, in *Tarzan's Three Challenges;* and an African leader modeled on Patrice Lumumba in *Black Jesus.* His most significant role was the title character in John Ford's *Sergeant Rutledge,* giving a touching and, as always, dignified portrait of a black cavalry officer who is tried for rape and murder. Since the late sixties, Strode has played—with the exception of an amusing, pre-titles cameo in *Once Upon a Time in the West*—in a string of innocuous look-alike and equally bloody westerns (from *The Revengers* to *The Ravagers*) and exploitation films (from *The Bronx Executioner* to *The Violent Executioner*). At least he got leads in some made in Italy.

• **Cult Favorites:** *Bride of the Gorilla* (1951, Curt Siodmak), *The Ten Commandments* (1956, Cecil B. De Mille), *Spartacus* (1960, Stanley Kubrick), *The Man Who Shot Liberty Valance* (1962, John Ford), *Seven Women* (1966, Ford), *Once Upon a Time in the West* (1968, Sergio Leone).

• **Sleepers:** *The Last Voyage* (1960, Andrew L. Stone), *Sergeant Rutledge* (1960, Ford).

• **Other Key Films:** *Pork Chop Hill* (1960, Lewis Milestone), *Two Rode Together* (1961, Ford), *Tarzan's Three Challenges* (1963, Richard Thorpe), *Genghis Khan* (1965, Henry Levin), *The Professionals* (1966, Richard Brooks), *Black Jesus* (1968).

• **Also of Interest:** *City Beneath the Sea* (1953, Budd Boetticher), *The Gambler from Natchez* (1954, Levin), *Tarzan's Fight for Life* (1958, H. Bruce Humberstone), *The Sin of Rachel Code* (1961, Gordon Douglas), *The Gatling Gun* (1972, Robert Gordon), *King of the Spiders* (1977, John "Bud" Cardos), *The Cotton Club* (1984, Francis Coppola).

○

GRADY SUTTON (1908–) Chubby, moon-faced, funny character actor with rolling eyes and a Tennessee accent. He started in films at 16, and for many years he played silly, unathletic collegians, without bothering to ask for billing. He became popular in a series of shorts, "The Boy Friends," directed by George Stevens. He'd have a lengthy career playing dumb assistants, soda jerks and other countermen, snoopy office workers, dumped suitors, and other small roles. He's best remembered for three films with W. C. Fields. In *The Man on the Flying Trapeze*, the kindly Fields despises but puts up with his babied, unemployed, moocher brother-in-law who takes naps after breakfast. In *You Can't Cheat an Honest Man*, shrewd carnival owner Fields gets Sutton's numskull to pay him in order to work at the carnival; Sutton agrees to do anything Fields asks but is too stupid to even attempt anything. Fields complains, "There's too much of the dictator in you." Sutton was Ogg Oggilby, the fiancé of Fields's daughter, Una Merkel, in *The Bank Dick*. He also was in Fields's classic short *The Pharmacist*.

• **Cult Favorites:** *The Freshman* (1925, Sam Taylor and Fred Newmeyer), *The Man on the Flying Trapeze* (1935, Clyde Bruckman), *My Man Godfrey* (1936, Gregory La Cava), *The Bank Dick* (1940, Eddie Cline), *A Star Is Born* (1954, George Cukor), *I Love You, Alice B. Toklas* (1968, Hy Averback).

• **Also of Interest:** *Alice Adams* (1935, George Stevens), *Stage Door* (1937, La Cava), *You Can't Cheat an Honest Man* (1939, George Marshall), *A Lady Takes a Chance* (1943, William A. Seiter), *The Great Moment* (1944, Preston Sturges).

○

CARL "ALFALFA" SWITZER (1926–59) One of the most popular members of "Our Gang," and arguably the most talented, he was with Hal Roach's little rascals from 1935 to 1942. He wasn't adorable like the others, but you could see why Darla thought he was cute: he had freckles, dimples, beady eyes, and dark hair with a pronounced cowlick, which, along with his cracking voice, was his most famous feature. Alfalfa was probably the character with whom young viewers most identified. Plots usually centered around Alfalfa's problems, though best friend Spanky and Buckwheat had equal screen time. A romantic, he spends much time courting Darla or trying to prove himself to her: he writes poetry, acts in plays, serenades her (with an off-key voice) until interrupted by hiccups or the croaking of a runaway frog hidden inside his clothes. Like the others, he panics when in trouble (his eyes widen, his voice becomes high, he screams, and he'll want to run away). But, when forced to fight the bully, Butch, for Darla's honor or hand, he stands his ground, clinches his teeth, tightens a fist, and, after some manhandling, wins because of luck or the help of his friends. Extremely likable on screen, he was, surprisingly, the only rascal Darla Hood actually disliked because he played vicious pranks on her offscreen. Growing up, he had bits in such features as *The Human Comedy*, *Going My Way*, *It's a Wonderful Life* (dancing with Donna Reed), and *A Letter to Three Wives*, but his lack of success led him to drink excessively. In 1959, he was drunk when he went after a friend who claimed Alfalfa owed him $50, and was shot to death.

• **Cult Favorites:** "Our Gang"/"Little Rascals" shorts (1935–42).

○

SHIH SZU (1953–) Next to Angela Mao, this lovely, raven-haired former dancer was the most popular of the female kung fu stars of the Chinese cinema. At 16, she joined the Shaw brothers and, after receiving third billing in *The Crimson Charm* (and dying halfway through the picture), she moved up to star rank. Her costumed women, who have determined eyes, invariably embark on missions of revenge, often with male companions. In Hammer's *Legend of the Seven Golden Vampires,* a British–Hong Kong coproduction, she travels with six brothers, including David Chiang, to battle Dracula. Most of her films are period pieces, but the comic-bookish *Supermen Against the Orient* is set in the present, allowing her to dress and wear her hair much differently. She's deadly as ever, but comes across as perky at times. In all her films, her fight scenes are exciting because of her graceful body movements, physical beauty, and the fact that she's thrashing many men who are twice her size.

• **Cult Favorite:** *Legend of the Seven Golden Vampires/The Seven Brothers Meet Dracula* (1973, Roy Ward Baker).

• **Other Key Films:** *The Crimson Charm* (1969), *Lady Hermit* (1969), *The Young Avenger* (1970), *The Rescue* (1970), *Thunderbolt Fist* (1971), *Supermen Against the Orient* (1973), *The Shadow Boxer* (1974).

○

HIDEKO TAKAMINE (1924–) One of Japan's greatest, most beautiful actresses, best remembered for her 11 films for Keisuke Kinoshita and 17 films, over 25 years, for Mikio Naruse. She began as a child actress—she was referred to as "the Mary Pickford of Japan"—but had her greatest successes after the war. She proved to be a fine comedienne in *Carmen Comes Home,* as a stripper who is treated with disdain when she returns to her rural hometown, until she puts on a benefit for the local school and becomes a heroine. More often she played serious roles: teachers, mothers, lovers, and neurotic or exploited women who fight for self-respect. She played abandoned women who refuse to stay abandoned; girls and young women who struggle with their parents; geishas; and mistresses of irresponsible men, as in Naruse's classic, *Floating Clouds.* Her portrayals in Naruse's films helped him convey his major theme: the ill-treatment of women was the reason postwar Japan was such a miserable country. Her typical character, writes Japanese film historian Audie Block, had "large, vulnerable, somewhat prideful eyes given to flashes of obstinacy and annoyance. She rebels from the start, but with a weariness which suggests she knows she may have to give up eventually."

• **Key Films:** *Composition Class* (1938, Kajiro Yamamoto), *Horse* (1941, Yamamoto), *Carmen Comes Home* (1951, Keisuke Kinoshita), *Carmen's Pure Love* (1952, Kinoshita), *Lightning* (1952, Mikio Naruse), *Wild Geese/The Mistress* (1953, Shiro Toyoda), *The Garden of Women* (1954, Kinoshita), *Twenty-Four Eyes* (1954, Kinoshita), *Where Chimneys Are Seen* (1954, Heinosuke Gosho), *Floating Clouds* (1955, Naruse), *Flowing* (1956, Naruse), *Untamed Woman* (1957, Naruse), *The Times of Joy and Sorrow* (1957, Kinoshita), *Candle in the Wind* (1957, Kinoshita), *The River Fuefuki* (1960, Kinoshita), *When a Woman Ascends the Stairs* (1960, Naruse), *The Bitter Spirit/Immortal Love* (1961, Kinoshita), *A Wanderer's Notebook/Her Lonely Love* (1962, Naruse), *Yearning* (1964, Naruse).

○

LYLE TALBOT (1902–87) Handsome, slick-haired actor never played leads in A films, but had a long career starting in the thirties, often playing gangsters and shady nightclub owners. However, Talbot is a cult figure because as a washed-up actor in the fifties he appeared in several campy films, not just "Jungle Jim," "Bomba," and bad Jon Hall movies, but worse: Edward D. Wood awful-movie classics. In *Glen or Glenda?*, he's the concerned policeman who questions a doctor about men who dress as women. In *Plan 9 from Outer Space,* he's General Roberts—no great shakes.

• **Cult Favorites:** *Atom Man vs. Superman* (1950 serial, Spencer Bennet), *Glen or Glenda?/I Changed My Sex* (1953, Edward D. Wood, Jr.), *High School Confidential* (1958, Jack Arnold), *Plan 9 from Outer Space* (1959, Wood).

• **Also of Interest:** *Three on a Match* (1932, Mervyn LeRoy), *The Thirteenth Ghost* (1932, Albert Ray), *20,000 Years in Sing Sing* (1933, Michael Curtiz), *The Life of Jimmy Dolan* (1933, Archie Mayo), *Return of the Terror* (1934, Howard Bretherton), *Oil for the Lamps of China* (1935, LeRoy), *Go West, Young Man* (1936, Henry Hathaway), *Batman and Robin* (1949 serial, Bennet), *Champagne for Caesar* (1950, Richard Whorf), *Gold Raiders* (1951, Edward Bernds), *Hurricane Island* (1951, Lew Landers), *Fury of the Congo* (1951, William Berke), *African Treasure* (1952, Ford Beebe), *Tobor the Great* (1954, Lee Sholem), *Jail Bait* (1955, Wood).

○

GLORIA TALBOTT (1931–) Slim brunette with sharp features and smart, sexy eyes wasn't glamorous enough, I suppose, to star in mainstream A films, though she was appealing in minor daughter roles in both *We're No Angels* and *All That Heaven Allows*. But she was a terrific, offbeat heroine in low-budget exploitation pictures. Somehow the talent came through in troubled-youth movies; B westerns like

Gloria Talbott worries about her choice of husband in I Married a Monster from Outer Space.

The Oklahoman, in which she was an Indian maid; and even such horrors as *The Cyclops* (what radiation did to her poor husband!) and Edgar G. Ulmer's dismal *Daughter of Dr. Jekyll,* where she is unhappy because she thinks she is under a curse to commit murders. She was good again in the enjoyably silly *The Leech Woman,* confronting Coleen Gray. However, her best performance was as the young bride who discovers that *I Married a Monster from Outer Space.* As a sympathetic, intelligent woman in this much-underrated paranoia film, Talbott is super, properly projecting both strength and vulnerability. In other films, too, she was believable as women who are scared about what is happening to them but still stand their ground.

• **Cult Favorites:** *All That Heaven Allows*

(1955, Douglas Sirk), *Daughter of Dr. Jekyll* (1957, Edgar G. Ulmer), *I Married a Monster from Outer Space* (1958, Gene Fowler, Jr.).

• **Other Key Films:** *We're No Angels* (1955, Michael Curtiz), *The Young Guns* (1956, Albert Band), *The Oklahoman* (1957, Francis D. Lyon), *The Cyclops* (1957, Bert I. Gordon), *Taming Sutton's Daughter* (1957, Lesley Selander), *Alias Jesse James* (1959, Norman Z. McLeod), *Girls Town* (1959, Charles Haas), *The Leech Woman* (1960, Edward Dein), *Talion* (1966, Michael Moore).

○

RUSS TAMBLYN (1934–) Curly-haired, boyish-looking former child performer (as Rusty Tamblyn) broke into the big time with some unusually athletic dancing in Stanley Don-en's spirited musical *Seven Brides for Seven Brothers,* as the youngest of the all-male clan. He also displayed his distinct dancing style—which seemed to mix acrobatics, tumbling, and Dick Button's leaping-spinning, quite revolutionary ice-skating style—as the title character in George Pal's children's film, *tom thumb,* and as a gang leader in *West Side Story.* In *The Wonderful World of the Brothers Grimm,* he was partner to Yvette Mimieux's "Dancing Princess." Tamblyn also appeared in dramatic roles, usually as troubled youths and young cowboys who are cocky and don't seem to care much about anything, including the negative way people perceive them. He received a Best Supporting Actor Oscar nomination for *Peyton Place,* but his most memorable nonmusical role was in Albert Zugsmith's zany production *High School Confidential,* in which he played a brash, obnoxious de-

Russ Tamblyn's narc flirts to get the goods on dopers in High School Confidential.

linquent who turns out to be a narc. His energetic undercover cop has time to flirt with three sexy blondes: his teacher; a pretty teenage addict; and his seductive married aunt, lustily played by Mamie Van Doren. To keep his career going after musicals died out, the talented actor was forced to make a western in Spain and a science-fiction/horror film in Japan, and even put himself in the untalented hands of American exploitation filmmaker Al Adamson, for whom he played psycho bikers and worse.

• **Cult Favorites:** *The Boy with Green Hair* (1948, Joseph Losey), *tom thumb* (1958, George Pal), *High School Confidential* (1958, Jack Arnold), *The Haunting* (1963, Robert Wise).

• **Also Recommended:** *Take the High Ground* (1953, Richard Brooks), *Seven Brides for Seven Brothers* (1954, Stanley Donen), *Peyton Place* (1957, Mark Robson), *West Side Story* (1961, Wise and Jerome Robbins), *The Wonderful World of the Brothers Grimm* (1962, Henry Levin and Pal).

• **Also of Interest:** *The Kid from Cleveland* (1949, Herbert Kline), *Father of the Bride* (1950, Vincente Minnelli), *Hit the Deck* (1955, Roy Rowland), *The Fastest Gun Alive* (1956, Russell Rouse), *The Young Guns* (1956, Albert Band), *Follow the Boys* (1963, Richard Thorpe), *The Long Ships* (1964, Jack Cardiff), *War of the Gargantuas* (1967, Inoshiro Honda), *Satan's Sadists* (1969, Al Adamson), *The Female Bunch* (1969, Adamson), *Dracula vs. Frankenstein* (1971, Adamson).

○

ZOË TAMERLIS (1964–) An intriguing actress with an otherworldly resemblance to Bianca Jagger, Simone Simon, and Nastassia Kinski, she was just 17 when she gave a fascinating performance as the title character in *Ms. 45,* by far the best exploitation film about women avenging their rapes. Her mute garment shop seamstress is related to Catherine Deneuve's beauty parlor worker in *Repulsion,* except that after killing and chopping up one male in her apartment, she goes into the streets to methodically, savagely, and silently avenge the abuse she has received from *all* men. Her mute Thana comes to represent all women who don't speak out against the daily outrages they are subjected to from boyfriends, male bosses, male strangers. She kills a rapist with an iron, the symbol of the stereotypical unliberated woman, signifying that woman's passivity is not insurmountable, and then takes his gun (obviously a phallic symbol). She will use the male weapon to destroy men. The young Tamerlis gave a surprisingly composed and intelligent performance, and when dressed in a nun's habit with heavy makeup, high boots, and a .45 stuck in her garter, she had astounding sex appeal. Tamerlis went blond, did nudity, and played two women in Larry Cohen's bloody and silly *Special Effects,* but she was better in her debut, where she invested herself in her character. She has played in other low-budget films, here and in Italy, as Zoë Tamerlaine Lund (in *Exquisite Corpses*) and Tamara Tamerind.

• **Cult Favorite:** *Ms. 45/Angel of Vengeance* (1981, Abel Ferrara).

• **Other Key Film:** *Special Effects* (1984, Larry Cohen).

○

AKIM TAMIROFF (1899–1972) Russian emigré who became one of Hollywood's finest scene-stealing character actors, a lively, funny presence even in dramatic films. He had a thick Russian accent and played an assortment of foreigners, even Spaniards and Asians. Some of his quirky characters in foreign-set films, like Pablo in *For Whom the Bell Tolls*, are virtuous and on the "right side," but others are shiftless, untrustworthy, unsavory, even ruthless, as is his Mexican crime boss, Uncle Joe Grandi, in *Touch of Evil*. Many of his immigrants are mobsters or, as in *The Great McGinty*, crooked political bosses. However, even his worst scoundrels are hard to dislike because Tamiroff supplied them with his loud, flustered, humorous delivery and accent (he would have been a great stand-up comic); his hurt expression when his character isn't trusted and his teddy-bear body add to the effect. He convinces us that even his authority figures are underdogs who have little chance of staying on top.

• **Cult Favorites:** *Naughty Marietta* (1935, W. S. Van Dyke), *The Miracle of Morgan's Creek* (1944, Preston Sturges), *Touch of Evil* (1958, Orson Welles), *The Trial* (1963, Welles), *Alphaville* (1965, Jean-Luc Godard), *After the Fox* (1966, Vittorio de Sica).

• **Other Key Films:** *Anthony Adverse* (1936, Anthony Asquith), *The General Died at Dawn* (1936, Lewis Milestone), *The Great Gambini* (1937, Charles Vidor), *Spawn of the North* (1938, Henry Hathaway), *Dangerous to Know* (1938, Robert Florey), *King of Chinatown* (1939, Nick Grinde), *The Magnificent Fraud* (1939, Florey), *Disputed Passage* (1939, Frank Borzage), *The Way of All Flesh* (1940, Louis King), *The Great McGinty* (1940, Sturges), *Tortilla Flat* (1942, Victor Fleming), *Five Graves to Cairo* (1943, Billy Wilder), *For Whom the Bell Tolls* (1943, Sam Wood), *Mr. Arkadin/Confidential Report* (1955,

Welles), *Anastasia* (1956, Anatole Litvak), *Romanoff and Juliet* (1961, Peter Ustinov), *Topkapi* (1965, Jules Dassin).

○

KINUYO TANAKA (1910–77) A major figure in the Japanese cinema, she was an actress when just 14, and became her country's first female director, beginning in 1953 with *Love Letter* and *The Moon Doesn't Rise*. She starred in 1931 in Japan's first successful talkie, *The Neighbor's Wife and Mine*, by the influential Heinosuke Gosho, and in the ambitious *The Loyal Forty-Seven Ronin*, and soon was the most popular actress in Japan. Into the early fifties, she played in many contemporary dramas, usually as smart, resilient, and loyal (to a fault) lower-middle-class women (lovers, wives, mothers), in a changing and, in the postwar years, distressed society. The West knows her best for period films she made in the fifties with Kenji Mizoguchi, a director sympathetic to women. In the mystical *Ugetsu*, she is killed after her potter husband abandons her to have an affair with a beautiful witch ghost—then as a ghost herself, she welcomes and comforts him upon his return home, before she vanishes. In *The Life of Oharu*, she gives a lovely performance as a seventeenth-century woman whose entire life, which ends with her being a hungry, aged street whore, is characterized by ill-treatment by men. Oharu is often pointed to by feminists as the screen character that best epitomizes the victimization of women throughout history. Interestingly, Tanaka broke away from Mizoguchi when he tried to prevent her from directing.

• **Cult Favorites:** *The Life of Oharu* (1952, Kenji Mizoguchi), *Ugetsu* (1953, Mizoguchi).

• **Some Other Key Films:** *The Neighbor's Wife and Mine* (1931, Heinosuke Gosho), *The Loyal Forty-Seven Ronin* (1932, Teinosuke Kinugasa), *Army* (1944, Keisuke Kinoshita), *Mother* (1952, Mikio Naruse), *Where the Chimneys Are Seen/Three Chimneys* (1954, Gosho), *Sansho the Bailiff* (1954, Mizoguchi), *Flowing* (1956, Naruse).

○

SHARON TATE (1943–69) She'll always be remembered first as a tragic murder victim of Charles Manson and his cult followers, and secondly as the wife of Roman Polanski, who has often directed macabre, bloody films (as was invariably pointed out in her obituaries). Forgotten is that this gorgeous redhead was an actress with some promise. She had a pinup's beauty and was pushed as a sex symbol, posing for risqué photo layouts, taking a bubble bath in her husband's *The Fearless Vampire Killers*, and playing a bust-exercising porno actress in *The Valley of the Dolls*—she got (and deserved) her worst reviews for what was also her most serious role, in the trashy Jacqueline Susann adaptation. But she was affectionately silly in the Tony Curtis–Claudia Cardinale comedy, *Don't Make Waves;* Dean Martin's fourth Matt Helm spy-comedy, *The Wrecking Crew;* and *The Fearless Vampire Killers.* I think she had

Sharon Tate in Roman Polanski's The Fearless Vampire Killers.

the most potential for light comedy, but I suspect that Polanski would have cast her in a black comedy, probably something like the role played by Catherine Deneuve (whose beauty was similar) in his *Repulsion.*

• **Cult Favorite:** *The Fearless Vampire Killers/Dance of the Vampires* (1967, Roman Polanski).

• **Other Key Films:** *Valley of the Dolls* (1967, Mark Robson), *The Wrecking Crew* (1969, Phil Karlson).

• **Also of Interest:** *Don't Make Waves* (1967, Alexander Mackendrick), *Eye of the Devil* (1967, J. Lee Thompson).

○

JACQUES TATI (1908–82) A tall, gangly former rugby pro and pantomime star in cabarets and music halls, he wrote, directed, and starred in only five pictures, but they were more than enough to make him France's most famous movie comic. Beginning with *Jour de Fête,* in which his small-town mailman tries to speed up service, and in the four films in which he played the polite, silent, storklike gentleman Mr. Hulot, he satirized a world that is modernizing too quickly, where fads, gimmicks and gadgets, and impersonal machinery and architecture are replacing warmth, taste, and patience. He conceived brilliant sight gags, using props, strange characters, and sound effects. Hulot is an observer of the strange world, sort of like comic-strip character Mr. Mum, except that he decides to interact with the props he finds in each seemingly tranquil but actually hostile environment. He invariably destroys the entire set—as would a Jerry Lewis character (Lewis also reacted comically to sound effects and music) or Peter Sellers's Inspector Clouseau. What's

Jacques Tati as Monsieur Hulot.

most childlike and appealing about this well-meaning, high-stepping character in hat and raincoat (and carrying an umbrella) is that each time he does something wrong, he runs away and hides. Of the Hulot films, only the first, *Mr. Hulot's Holiday,* is consistently funny and doesn't drag toward the end, but there are treasures to be found in all of them. Hulot is one of the cinema's greatest, most cleverly conceived comic characters.

• **Cult Favorites:** *Mr. Hulot's Holiday* (1953, Jacques Tati), *Mon Oncle* (1958, Tati), *Playtime* (1967, Tati).

• **Other Key Films:** *Jour de Fête* (1949, Tati), *Traffic* (1972, Tati).

○

SHIRLEY TEMPLE (1928–) The most popular and, arguably, the most talented of child stars, this cute, blond, doll-like curly top skillfully sang, danced, acted, strutted, pouted, and flirted her way into America's collective heart. Her sentimental films were, for the most part, well made, and Temple usually avoided being cloying or ingratiating despite playing little girls who seemed ready-made for annoyance. Her optimistic, spunky, and loving 6- to 12-year-olds soften the hearts of numerous old people, including irascible grandfathers Lionel Barrymore in *The Little Colonel*, C. Aubrey Smith in *Wee Willie Winkie*, and Jean Hersholt in *Heidi*; book-maker Adolphe Menjou in *Little Miss Marker*; even Abraham Lincoln in *The Littlest Rebel* and Queen Victoria in *The Little Princess*, Temple's best film. She brings opponents together: separated couples, soldiers from different armies, and—by tap dancing in delightful routines with Bill "Bojangles" Robinson—people from different races. Temple's wise little charmers teach everyone the recipe for happiness, which is, simply, be nice, be civil, and be warm to *everybody*. All Temple had to do was sit in characters' laps and speak from the heart to win their instant

Shirley Temple first grabbed attention in the "Baby Burlesks" series.

love. She did it so often with elderly characters that Graham Greene accused 20th Century-Fox of trying to appeal to the prurient interests of dirty old men. Richard Harmetz suggests that Temple's appeal to children was not that she was so sweet or innocent, but that her youngster always manipulates, bosses around, and dominates adults. When she herself grew up and her characters no longer had such power, her popularity dissipated.

• **Key Films:** *Stand Up and Cheer* (1934, Hamilton MacFadden), *Little Miss Marker* (1934, Alexander Hall), *The Little Colonel* (1935, David Butler), *The Littlest Rebel* (1935, Butler), *Poor Little Rich Girl* (1936, Irving Cummings), *Dimples* (1936, William A. Seiter), *Wee Willie Winkie* (1937, John Ford), *Heidi* (1937, Allan Dwan), *Rebecca of Sunnybrook Farm* (1938, Dwan), *The Little Princess* (1939, Walter Lang), *Fort Apache* (1948, Ford).

• **Also of Interest:** "Baby Burlesks" shorts (1932–34, Charles Lamont), *Baby Take a Bow* (1934, Harry Lachman), *Bright Eyes* (1934, Butler), *Our Little Girl* (1935, John Robertson), *Curly Top* (1935, Cummings), *Captain January* (1936, Butler), *Stowaway* (1936, Seiter), *Little Miss Broadway* (1938, Cummings), *Just Around the Corner* (1938, Cummings), *Susannah of the Mounties* (1939, Seiter), *The Blue Bird* (1940, Lang), *Kathleen* (1941, Harold S. Bucquet), *Since You Went Away* (1944, John Cromwell), *The Bachelor and the Bobby-Soxer* (1947, Irving Reis).

○

MAX TERHUNE (1891–1973) Ex-vaudevillian who was one of the most popular comic sidekicks in B westerns, often using the

Max Terhune (upper left) *and Ray "Crash" Corrigan backed John Wayne in several "Three Mesquiteers" movies.*

nicknames "Lullaby" and "Alibi." He broke in at Republic as part of the original and best "Three Mesquiteers," a Zane Grey trio that foiled outlaws in the old and current West. His partners were Bob Livingston and Ray "Crash" Corrigan, who were both handier with a gun, better riders, fancier dressers (Terhune usually wore multicolored, mismatched outfits), and in better physical shape—even if they didn't have such cheery smiles. Livingston would be replaced by John Wayne and eventually Corrigan and Terhune moved on, too, joining Dennis Moore for the passable but far less exciting "Range Busters" series. In time, Terhune provided comedy relief in Ken Maynard's last western, *Harmony Trail,* and some quickies with an overweight Johnny Mack Brown at Monogram.

• **Some Key Films:** *Ride, Ranger, Ride* (1936, Joseph Kane), *Riders of the Whistling Skull* (1937, Mack Wright), *Santa Fe Stampede* (1938, George Sherman), *Call the Mesquiteers* (1938), *Pals of the Saddle* (1938, Sherman), *Overland Stage Raiders* (1938, Sherman), *The Night Riders* (1939, Sherman), *Harmony Trail* (1947, Robert Emmett/Tansey), *Along the Oregon Trail* (1947), *Gunning for Justice* (1949).

○

TERRY-THOMAS (1911–90) Born Thomas Terry Hoar-Stevens, this successful English comic with a thick mustache and large front teeth separated by a wide gap (displayed with every pompous grimace, whine, or remark) gave hilarious performances as "silly ass" Britishers. His loud, condescending, upper-crust authority figures (schoolmasters, officers, ex-majors) usually end up in ridiculous, humiliating predicaments, providing Thomas the op-

portunity for great physical comedy. He had success in England in madcap comedies (often for the Boulting brothers) with Peter Sellers, Ian Carmichael, and Alistair Sim before taking roles in America and throughout Europe. He played villains in *tom thumb,* along with Peter Sellers, and in *Those Magnificent Men in Their Flying Machines,* but even his nonvillains were fun to root against. I particularly like his savagely conceited bore in the sidesplitting *School for Scoundrels,* who loses all pride and dignity once timid rival Ian Carmichael learns the art of one-upmanship. The best part of *It's a Mad Mad Mad Mad World* is an argument that escalates into a bumbling, down-and-dirty Laurel and Hardy–type fight between Thomas's smug Britisher, Algernon Hawthorne, and Milton Berle's British-insulting American, J. Russell Finch. Thomas played essentially only one screen character—but he was a pip!

• **Cult Favorites:** *tom thumb* (1958, George Pal), *I'm All Right, Jack* (1960, Roy Boulting), *It's a Mad Mad Mad Mad World* (1963, Stanley Kramer), *The Abominable Dr. Phibes* (1971, Robert Fuest).

• **Sleepers:** *The Green Man* (1957, Robert Day), *School for Scoundrels* (1960, Robert Hamer).

• **Other Key Films:** *Private's Progress* (1956, John Boulting), *Brothers in Law* (1957, R. Boulting), *Lucky Jim* (1957, J. Boulting), *Your Past Is Showing/The Naked Truth* (1957, Mario Zampi), *Blue Murder at St. Trinian's* (1958, Frank Launder), *Too Many Crooks* (1958, Zampi), *Man in the Cocked Hat* (1959, Jeffrey Dell and R. Boulting), *Make Mine Mink* (1960, Robert Asher), *Bachelor Flat* (1961, Frank Tashlin), *The Wonderful World of the Brothers Grimm* (1962, Henry Levin and Pal), *Mouse on the Moon* (1963, Richard Lester), *Those Magnificent Men in Their Flying*

Ernest Thesiger has Boris Karloff's Monster doing his bidding, forcing Colin Clive to manufacture a mate in Bride of Frankenstein.

Machines (1965, Ken Annakin), *How to Murder Your Wife* (1965, Richard Quine), *La Grande Vadrouille/Don't Look Now . . . We're Being Shot At!* (1966, Gérard Oury), *Arabella* (1969, Adriano Barocco), *Dr. Phibes Rises Again* (1972, Fuest), *The Last Remake of Beau Geste* (1977, Marty Feldman).

○

ERNEST THESIGER (1879–1967) Brittle British character actor is best remembered for his delicious performances as wide-eyed mad hatters in thirties horror and fantasy films. He was already over fifty when he made his first sound picture, James Whale's *The Old Dark House,* a spooky film in which he pro-

vides much sardonic humor. He and Eva Moore (as his sister) play the Femms, strange hosts to several uncomfortable travelers who are stranded in their house for the night. He is *some* host, miserly telling his dinner guests, "Have a potato," treating everyone with absolute condescension, and making them feel frightened about something in the attic. The arguments between this prissy, sarcastic, cowardly atheist and Moore's partially deaf, unfriendly religious fanatic are brilliantly written and played—they both make viewers laugh and feel nervous. Boris Karloff was Thesiger's servant in this film, and in *The Ghoul,* Thesiger returned the favor. The two again were reunited in Whale's classic *Bride of Frankenstein,* in which Thesiger's eccentric scoundrel, Dr. Septimus Praetorius, creates a mate for Karloff's Monster, forcing Colin Clive's doctor to help him. Praetorius, a birdlike figure who looks like he goes to Harpo Marx's hair stylist, is one of the horror cinema's greatest, most bizarre creations—effeminate, witty, philosophical, sophisticated, brilliant . . . and criminally insane. Whale loved filming angular faces at odd angles, and his close-ups of Thesiger, particularly during the creation scene, are quite thrilling. While Thesiger would have many fine moments in his long career, playing mostly unlikable characters, he wouldn't find roles to equal his diabolical oddballs in *The Old Dark House* and *Bride of Frankenstein*.

• **Cult Favorites:** *Bride of Frankenstein* (1935, James Whale), *A Christmas Carol* (1951, Brian Desmond Hurst), *The Man in the White Suit* (1952, Alexander Mackendrick), *The Horse's Mouth* (1959, Ronald Neame), *The Roman Spring of Mrs. Stone* (1961, José Quintero).

• **Sleepers:** *The Old Dark House* (1932, Whale), *The Man Who Could Work Miracles* (1937, Lothar Mendes), *Quartet* (1949, Ken Annakin).

• **Also of Interest:** *The Ghoul* (1934, T. Hayes Hunter), *My Heart Is Calling* (1935, Carmine Gallone), *Henry V* (1946, Laurence Olivier), *Caesar and Cleopatra* (1946, Gabriel Pascal), *Last Holiday* (1950, Henry Cass), *The Winslow Boy* (1950, Anthony Asquith), *The Battle of the Sexes* (1960, Charles Crichton), *Sons and Lovers* (1960, Jack Cardiff).

○

DYANNE THORNE She had the embarrassing distinction of playing the title character, a haughty, sadistic torture camp comman-

dant, in *Ilsa: She Wolf of the SS*, a cult film for the sick set that has a plot suitable for S&M porno books. In the worst of all women-in-prison films, the not particularly attractive, though extremely buxom, SS officer conducts heinous experiments to prove—get this—that women can take more punishment than men. Also: each night she makes love to a different male prisoner and, after he fails to satisfy her, castrates and kills him. The prisoners take over at the end and give Ilsa several doses of her own medicine. But she was healthy enough for an equally detestable sequel, *Ilsa, Harem Keeper of the Oil Sheiks*. She had a new job but wasn't any nicer. She ends up in a pit of excrement. If anything can be said in defense of the two pictures, it's that, contrary to their notorious reputations, the brutality looks staged rather than authentic, and the audience is not

Dyanne Thorne in Ilsa, Harem Keeper of the Oil Sheiks.

manipulated into rooting for Ilsa and thrilling to her torture sessions. Still, the films are vile, and Thorne makes no better an impression than Ilsa. I assume she was no more endearing as *Wanda, the Wicked Warden*.

• **Cult Favorites:** *Ilsa: She Wolf of the SS* (1974, Don Edmonds), *Ilsa, Harem Keeper of the Oil Sheiks* (1976, Edmonds).

• **Other Key Films:** *The Erotic Adventures of Pinocchio* (1971, Corey Allen), *Wanda, the Wicked Warden/Greta the Torturer* (1979, Jesus Franco).

• **Also of Interest:** *The Swinging Barmaids* (1975, Gus Trikonis), *Ilsa, Tigress of Siberia.*

○

THE THREE STOOGES Moe Howard (1905–75), Curly Howard (1911–52), and Larry Fine (1911–74) were the most famous incarnation of film's most popular, stupid, and destructive slapstick team, but at various times Curly's spot was filled by Shemp Howard (1901–55), Joe Besser (1907–88), and "Curly Joe" De Rita (1909–). In fact, the genesis of the trio was a duo: Moe and

The best Three Stooges trio (left to right): *Curly, Larry, and Moe.*

older brother Shemp did a black-face act in vaudeville, and in 1923 they became comedian Ted Healy's background "Stooges." Five years later, Larry became the third stooge. After success in vaudeville and Broadway revues, "Ted Healy and His Stooges" made a film, *Soup to Nuts,* with Moe, Shemp, and Larry in support as "The Racketeers." When Healy returned to Hollywood three years later, Shemp dropped out of the group and was replaced by his younger brother, Curly. Curly's nitwit, who was always at odds with Moe, would be the most likable and sympathetic of all the Stooges. Moe would beat him for being stupid; Larry would serve as a buffer and be slapped in the process. After providing wild background support to Healy in a few features at M-G-M, including Joan Crawford's *Dancing Lady,* and two-reelers at Columbia, The Three Stooges went off on their own to make the first of their mind-boggling 191 shorts for Columbia. In 1946, when Curly suffered a debilitating stroke (he would die six years later), Shemp returned—he'd play the only Stooge who could outsmart Moe. When Shemp died in 1955, veteran comic Joe Besser ("Stinky" on TV's "The Abbott and Costello Show") replaced him. His kidlike character would be the only Stooge to hit Moe back, though it would be a self-defense reflex. Besser left in 1958, when the shorts were discontinued, and the group almost disbanded. However, the shorts were sold to television, and young children were introduced to the group. Immediately, The Three Stooges were back in demand. With ex–burlesque comic "Curly Joe" De Rita as Besser's replacement (as a child, I thought he was Curly, only aged and fatter), they began making features. Their career wouldn't end until 1970, when Larry had a stroke. There has been renewed interest in The Three Stooges over the last five years or so. There have been numerous books about them; "The Curly Shuffle" was a pop music hit, and the song and accompanying Stooges video clip plays on giant screens at ballparks. Their return to fame coincides with the increased popularity of pro wrestling, campy movies, and other lowbrow entertainment. While the Stooges weren't without talent—which is enough to surprise many who had always avoided them—their repetitious, violent acts (with Moe, whom I never could stand, poking Curly's eyes, smacking his nose, and clubbing his head) grow tiresome, like watching the same silly circus clowns night after night. If you're in the right mood and patient enough to get into the wild rhythm of this infantile trio, you might enjoy bits of their best films, those Curly shorts when the boys' plumbers, cooks, firemen, painters, and so on infiltrate staid high society. Those weird haircuts, the pie fights, Curly's squealing, grunting, and running in place, the destruction (but not the abuse Curly takes from Moe), and the dumbness of it all can be funny. Still, The Three Stooges are the group we point to in order to show just how good other comedy teams are.

• **Cult Favorites:** 191 shorts (1934–58, most directed by either Del Lord or Jules White).

• **Key Features:** *Have Rocket, Will Travel* (1959, David Lowell Rich), *The Outlaws Is Coming* (1965, Norman Maurer).

○

LAWRENCE TIERNEY (1919–) Strong, rugged leading man of the forties and fifties began as a supporting player in two films for Val Lewton's unit at RKO, *The Ghost Ship* and *Youth Runs Wild.* He stayed in low-budget films, playing tough, weapon-carrying characters, including cops, convicts, ex-cons, crooks, and gangsters. His heroes usually tried to prove themselves innocent of crimes. His bad guys didn't bother to prove themselves innocent of anything. He worked best for little-known director Max Nosseck, giving a particularly effective mean turn as *Dillinger*. He gave his other top-rate performance as a killer lusting after sister-in-law Claire Trevor in *Born to Kill*, a hard-edged film noir directed by Robert Wise, another Val Lewton alumnus. Tierney dropped out of acting for many years. He would make the news after being stabbed in a bar (he was a tough guy offscreen as well), and after being discovered working as a hansom cab driver in New York. Bald and burly, and still looking mean, he returned to Hollywood, playing a semiregular station cop on TV's "Hill Street Blues," and showing up in an occasional low-budget film, acting unpleasant.

• **Cult Favorites:** *Dillinger* (1945, Max Nosseck), *Born to Kill* (1947, Robert Wise), *Andy Warhol's Bad* (1971, Jed Johnson).

• **Also of Interest:** *The Ghost Ship* (1943, Mark Robson), *Youth Runs Wild* (1944, Robson), *Back to Bataan* (1945, Edward Dmytryk), *Step by Step* (1946, Phil Rosen), *San Quentin* (1946, Gordon Douglas), *The Devil Thumbs a Ride* (1947, Felix Feist), *The Hoodlum* (1951, Nosseck), *Female Jungle/The Hangover* (1956, Bruno VeSota), *Midnight* (1980, John Russo).

○

KENNETH TOBEY (1919–) Red-haired actor has taken mostly character parts in his long film career, but he was the best leading man of fifties science-fiction films, playing as-sured, stalwart military men who success-fully supervise the destruction of the monsters in *The Thing, The Beast from 20,000 Fathoms,* and *It Came from Beneath the Sea,* three of the better films of the genre. His most memorable part is un-doubtedly Air Force Captain Pat Hendry in Howard Hawks's production of *The Thing.* Like other Hawks action heroes, he is a strong, brave leader who can outthink any enemy, but is easily outmaneuvered by a beguiling, quick-witted female (Margaret Sheridan). He's an assuring figure because he is confident in himself and his men; is relaxed and maintains his humor in a crisis; works alongside his men to solve problems; and isn't afraid to give decisive orders or to listen to any expert suggestions from his men—which is why his men work so well under his command and are able to show that they, America's finest, are prepared to turn back *any* invasion. Outside of science-fiction films, Tobey had numerous roles, often as other military men, particularly fliers (he was a flier offscreen). Unfortu-nately, he wasn't given the significant parts he could have easily handled. A pro, Tobey has always taken what has been offered, even bits and cameos he gets from filmmak-ers who affectionately remember his fine contributions to the science-fiction genre, his Jim Bowie in *Davy Crockett, King of the Wild Frontier,* and his fifties TV series, "The Whirlybirds."

• **Cult Favorites:** *The Thing* (1950, Chris-tian Nyby and, uncredited, Howard Hawks), *Angel Face* (1953, Otto Prem-inger), *Davy Crockett, King of the Wild Frontier* (1955, Norman Foster), *The Wings of Eagles* (1957, John Ford), *Billy Jack* (1971, Tom Laughlin), *Walking Tall* (1973, Phil Karlson), *Dirty Mary Crazy Larry* (1974, John Hough), *Airplane!* (1980, Jim Abrahams, David Zucker, and

Jerry Zucker), *The Howling* (1981, Joe Dante), *Strange Invaders* (1983, Michael Laughlin).

• **Sleepers:** *Homebodies* (1974, Larry Yust), *Baby Blue Marine* (1976, John Hancock).

• **Other Key Films:** *I Was a Male War Bride* (1949, Hawks), *The Beast from 20,000 Fathoms* (1953, Eugene Lourie), *It Came from Beneath the Sea* (1955, Robert Gordon), *The Search for Bridey Murphy* (1956, Noel Langley), *The Vampire* (1957, Paul Landres).

○

THELMA TODD (1905–35) After winning a "Miss Massachusetts" beauty contest, this vivacious, curly-haired blonde was recruited by Hollywood, where she worked for both Paramount (in features) and Hal Roach (in shorts). She was pretty enough to be a dramatic lead, but since she was the rare looker with natural comedy talents, she supported a number of the cinema's top comics, including Harry Langdon, Laurel and Hardy, Charlie Chase, Wheeler and Woolsey, Joe E. Brown, Buster Keaton, and the Marx Brothers. She was particularly effective as a vamp. She and Groucho casually flirt and trade quips in *Monkey Business* (there's a funny bit where he hides in her closet) and in *Animal Crackers,* where he holds her "college widow" tightly ("If I held you any closer, I'd be in back of you")—in the absurd finale, Groucho, Chico, and Harpo *all* marry her. Hal Roach rewarded her with a series of her own, teaming her with ZaSu Pitts in 17 lively comedy shorts. The flip, wisecracking Todd and Pitts were meant to be like a female Laurel and Hardy, but while their characters' camaraderie is strong and they always get into

Thelma Todd.

trouble, they aren't nearly as stupid or childish as their male counterparts. Pitts left the series and was replaced by Patsy Kelly without the quality of the shorts diminishing. Todd was at the height of her popularity when she was found slumped in her car in her garage, dead of carbon-monoxide poisoning. According to some reports, her clothes were disheveled and covered with blood, so her death remains one of Hollywood's most intriguing unsolved mysteries. Recently, it was conjectured that director Roland West closed the garage door, not aware of Todd's presence.

• **Key Films:** 17 Hal Roach shorts with ZaSu Pitts (1931–33), 21 Hal Roach shorts with Patsy Kelly (1933–35).

• **Also Recommended:** *Nevada* (1927, John Waters), *Seven Footsteps to Satan* (1929, Benjamin Christenson), shorts with Harry Langdon, Laurel and Hardy, and Charlie Chase (late 1920s–early 1930s), *The Maltese Falcon* (1931, Roy Del Ruth), *Monkey Business* (1931, Norman Z. McLeod), *Horse Feathers* (1932, McLeod), *Speak Easily* (1932, Edward Sedgwick), *Call Her Savage* (1932, John Francis Dillon), *Sitting Pretty* (1933, Harry Joe Brown), *Counsellor-at-Law* (1933, William Wyler), *The Bohemian Girl* (1936, James Horne).

○

UGO TOGNAZZI (1922–90) Debonair Italian romantic lead who had a successful run in the early to mid-sixties in farces about marital infidelity in a country without divorce. He usually played successful, respected gentlemen who fancy themselves great lovers. But the romance has gone out of their married lives, and they either are cuckolds or are stepping out on their wives. When their wives cheat on them, they probably deserve it; when they cheat on their wives—whom they underestimate—they will likely learn a terrible, humbling lesson about their wives, all women (particularly Italian women), and marriage. In 1978, Tognazzi got a large dose of international fame by teaming with France's Michel Serrault in the wildly popular gay comedy, *La Cage aux Folles,* which spawned two sequels. His Renato, the less ostentatious of the two aging male lovers, is funny and romantic—though more so, unfortunately, with his ex-wife than with Serrault's Albin—but he is also remote, tired, and inconsiderate. He tolerates Albin's flamboyant eccentricities like a man who accepts his wife's "childishness" because she is female. Tognazzi seems scared of his own character and makes no connection with Serrault's.

• **Cult Favorites:** *La Cage aux Folles* (1978, Edouard Molinaro), *Barbarella* (1968, Roger Vadim), *La Grande Bouffe* (1973, Marco Ferreri).
• **Other Key Films:** *The Conjugal Bed* (1963, Ferreri), *The Ape Woman* (1964, Ferreri), *Crazy Desire* (1964, Luciano Salce), *The Fascist* (1965, Salce), *Hours of Love* (1965, Salce), *High Infidelity* (1965, Salce), *The Magnificent Cuckold* (1966, Antonio Pietrangela), *La Cage aux Folles II* (1981, Molinaro), *Joke of Destiny* (1984, Lina Wertmuller).

○

SIDNEY TOLER (1874–1947) This stocky, Missouri-born actor had numerous character roles in the thirties and forties: he was in jungle pictures, a western, a Maria Montez–Jon Hall exotic island tale, and a Laurel and Hardy comedy; he played Daniel Webster, he tracked down Marlene Dietrich. Yet he is remembered almost solely for taking over the role of Charlie Chan after Warner Oland died. He went on to play Earl Derr Bigger's sly, methodical, cocky detective 21 times at 20th Century-Fox and Monogram, until his own death. His films at 20th were much better written and produced—*Charlie Chan at Treasure Island* is considered the best—with intriguing mysteries and characters, and a good mix of comedy and excitement. Toler was both a lively and a formidable presence. In the later films, he seemed increasingly slow and bored. Because of poor writing, his detective didn't seem especially astute (for example, he'd question suspects who had been situated in *front* of a victim, even though he saw that the victim was shot from behind), and his poorly written "words of wisdom" were silly rather than clever. At times, he would bully suspects; at other times, he'd put innocent people in jeopardy by asking questions (even a little boy is killed in one movie). He only seemed perky when he was responding to the comic antics of his Number Two Son (Victor Sen Young) and chauffeur Birmingham Brown (Mantan Moreland).

• **Cult Favorites:** *Blonde Venus* (1932, Josef von Sternberg), *Charlie Chan at Treasure Island* (1939, Norman Foster).

• **Other Key Films:** *Charlie Chan in Honolulu* (1938, H. Bruce Humberstone), *Charlie Chan in Rio* (1941, Harry Lachman), *Charlie Chan in City of Darkness* (1939, Herbert I. Leeds), *Charlie Chan in Panama* (1940, Foster), *Charlie Chan's Murder Cruise* (1940, Eugene Forde), *Charlie Chan at the Wax Museum* (1940, Lynn Shores), *Murder Over New York* (1940, Lachman), *Dead Men Tell* (1941, Lachman), *Castle in the Desert* (1942, Lachman).

• **Also of Interest:** *The Gorgeous Hussy* (1936, Clarence Brown), *Our Relations* (1936, Lachman), *If I Were King* (1938, Frank Lloyd), *King of Chinatown* (1939, Nick Grinde), *A Night to Remember* (1943, Richard Wallace), *White Savage* (1943, Arthur Lubin), 10 "Charlie Chan" films at Monogram (1944–47).

○

ANGEL TOMPKINS Tall, sensuous, blue-eyed blonde broke into films in the early seventies, after modeling in Chicago, and seemed to have a bright future. She won a Golden Globe nomination for Best New Actress after her first film, *I Love My Wife,* in which she tantalizes Elliott Gould. She did an adequate job, adding a hard edge to her sexy women in a number of action films, and was featured in a *Playboy* pictorial. She was particularly impressive and likable in the amusing caper movie *Little Cigars,* as a tough ex-moll who heads a gang of midgets and runs off with her little lover, Billy Curtis. Tompkins dropped out of films for years, reemerging in the eighties, in a small part in the witty horror film *Alligator,* written by John Sayles. She then took the kinky female villain role in the exploitive women's prison picture *The Naked Cage,* featuring a torrid lesbian love scene. Other than being shot to death by Carrie Snodgrass in the Charles Bronson thriller *Murphy's Law,* this once promising actress hasn't been seen much since. Perhaps she should have gone after Claudia Jennings or even Tiffany Bolling roles.

• **Cult Favorite:** *Alligator* (1980, Lewis Teague).

• **Other Key Films:** *I Love My Wife* (1970, Mel Stuart), *Prime Cut* (1972, Michael Ritchie), *The Don Is Dead* (1973, Richard Fleischer), *Little Cigars* (1973, Chris Christenberry), *The Teacher* (1974, Hikmet Avedis), *The Bees* (1978, Alfredo Zacharias), *One Man Jury* (1978, Charles Martin), *The Naked Cage* (1982, Paul Nicholas), *Murphy's Law* (1986, J. Lee Thompson).

○

RIP TORN (1931–) This much respected Texas-born stage actor, who was married to Geraldine Page, could have been in a lot more films throughout his career, but he consistently took parts only in films that he considered artistic and/or politically correct. He did occasionally lower his standards in the seventies and eighties and appeared as villains in such exploitation films as *Slaughter, The Beastmaster,* and *A*

Stranger Is Watching. He is a forceful performer who likes to play eccentrics, powerful rich men, and volatile, on-the-edge characters. Like a scene-stealer on stage who doesn't have many lines, he'll give his minor parts extra stature by wearing a large hat, using a strong accent or unusual delivery, or signaling madness with his eyes. I think he overdoes it in his broad comical-villain roles, as in *Nadine,* but he can be quite effective developing true-life characters: his borderline crazy psychiatrist (who secretly videotapes all his sessions) in the semiexperimental *Coming Apart,* Henry Miller in *Tropic of Cancer,* the proud backwoodsman in *Cross Creek,* the alcoholic country music star in *Payday,* Judas in *King of Kings.* An intelligent, interesting actor who hasn't really found the roles to match his talents.

• **Cult Favorites:** *You're a Big Boy Now* (1967, Francis Ford Coppola), *Beach Red* (1967, Cornel Wilde), *Beyond the Law* (1968, Norman Mailer), *Coming Apart* (1969, Milton Moses Ginsberg), *Tropic of Cancer* (1970, Joseph Strick), *Maidstone* (1971, Mailer), *Payday* (1973, Daryl Duke), *The Man Who Fell to Earth* (1976, Nicolas Roeg), *The Private Files of J. Edgar Hoover* (1977, Larry Cohen).

• **Other Key Films:** *Time Limit* (1957, Karl Malden), *Pork Chop Hill* (1959, Lewis Milestone), *King of Kings* (1961, Nicholas Ray), *Sweet Bird of Youth* (1962, Richard Brooks), *The Cincinnati Kid* (1965, Norman Jewison), *Birch Interval* (1977, Delbert Mann), *Coma* (1978, Michael Crichton), *Heartland* (1979, Richard Pearce), *A Stranger Is Watching* (1982, Sean S. Cunningham), *Cross Creek* (1983, Martin Ritt), *Flashpoint* (1984, William Tannen), *Defending Your Life* (1991, Albert Brooks).

ANDREA TRUE A top porno star of the mid-seventies, this beautiful, high-energy performer usually played married women whose domestic sex lives leave much to be desired. Often they are seduced by an experienced, unfeeling male (often played by Jamie Gillis) who makes them do his sexual bidding and causes them to become addicted to sex. True always performed at full throttle, as if she were auditioning for the role of a lifetime. She was probably one of the few porno actresses who expected to become a legitimate star from being in XXX-rated movies. When that didn't work, she formed a singing group, the Andrea True Connection, and had a popular disco song, "More, More, More," that made use of her porno acting experience.

• **Key Film:** *The Seduction of Lynn Carter* (1975, Wes Brown).

• **Also of Interest:** *Pleasure Cruise* (Don Lang), *Seduction* (1974, Ralph Ell), *Hardy Girls* (Allen Ruskin), *Both Ways* (1975, Jerry Douglas), *Every Inch a Lady* (1975, John and Lem Amero), *Mash'd* (1979, Emton Smith).

LORENZO TUCKER (1907–86) This handsome black actor was a dancer and minstrel show performer before he was discovered by Oscar Micheaux, the famous black director and distributor of all-black, non-Hollywood "race" films. Micheaux cast him in several romantic melodramas over the years, promoting his suave star as "the black John Gilbert" and, later, "the black Valentino." Tucker also appeared in "race" pictures for other black filmmakers, often in minor parts. Seeing Tucker today in clips (he was often interviewed for "race" movie documentaries) and an occasional film that plays on the black television network, it's not readily apparent why he rather than one of the other black actors (some of whom were taller, livelier, and equally good-looking) was a matinee idol. Also, since most of these pictures were poorly written, statically directed, and hampered by low-budget production values (see the frequently telecast *Reet, Petite, and Gone*), it's hard to tell if he had any special talent.

• **Sample Films:** *Wages of Sin* (1927, Oscar Micheaux), *When Men Betray* (1928), *Easy Street* (1930), *Daughter of the Congo* (1931, Micheaux), *The Black King* (1932), *Veiled Aristocrats* (1932), *Harlem After Midnight* (1934), *Temptation* (1936, Micheaux), *Straight to Heaven* (1939), *One Round Jones* (1947), *Underworld* (1947, Micheaux), *Boy, What a Girl* (1947), *Sepia Cinderella* (1947), *Reet, Petite, and Gone* (1947).

○

SONNY TUFTS (1911–70) This 6′4″ blond singer-actor was pitched as a sex symbol when he joined Paramount in 1943, stripping off his shirt to reveal a powerful chest in his debut film, the World War II drama *So Proudly We Hail*. He and Paulette Goddard would be reunited in *I Love a Soldier;* he often played soldiers opposite Veronica Lake, Olivia de Havilland, and Betty Hutton in innocuous comedies. Everyone (not just Johnny Carson) likes to joke about how bad Sonny Tufts was, but in truth he was no worse than a mediocre actor in bad films. In fact, he was perfectly acceptable in *So Proudly We Hail*; as the second male lead in *The Virginian*, turning against hero Joel McCrea; and in RKO's *Easy Living*, as a football player. But you can't deny that he was bland—imagine combining the worst of Forrest Tucker and Van Johnson. Tufts does deserve his camp reputation because of embarrassing offscreen activities (arrests for being drunk; a suit by a dancer for disfiguring her leg with his teeth; etc.) as well as the atrocious roles he took beginning in the mid-fifties, in films with tell-all titles like *Cat Women of the Moon, Serpent Island, The Parson and the Outlaw,* and *Cotton-pickin' Chickenpickers.* Of the group, only *Cat Women of the Moon,* a bona fide camp classic with Marie Windsor, is enjoyably bad. In the excruciating *Serpent Island,* he again strips off his shirt, only this time his chest is the ugliest in movie history, with lines and deep crevices that remind one of the canals on the moon. Interestingly, in *Town Tamer,* Tufts was joined by other veteran actors with drinking problems. He died of pneumonia.

• **Cult Favorites:** *Cat Women of the Moon* (1954, Arthur Hilton), *The Seven Year Itch* (1955, Billy Wilder).

• **Also of Interest:** *So Proudly We Hail* (1943, Mark Sandrich), *Government Girl* (1944, Dudley Nichols), *I Love a Soldier* (1944, Sandrich), *Here Come the Waves* (1944, Sandrich), *Bring On the Girls* (1945, Sidney Lanfield), *The Virginian* (1946, Stuart Gilmore), *Easy Living* (1949, Jacques Tourneur), *The Crooked Way* (1949, Robert Florey), *The Parson and the Outlaw* (1957, Oliver Drake), *Town Tamer* (1965, Lesley Selander).

○

LANA TURNER (1920–) In their book *Dames,* Ian and Elisabeth Cameron correctly ob-

Right to left: *Lana Turner, Hedy Lamarr, and Judy Garland in M-G-M's* Ziegfeld Girl.

served, "Lana Turner deserves a prize for her great achievement: staying at the top the longest without any discernible talent." The beautiful blonde, a one-time "Sweater Girl," was a Hollywood High student when, the tall tale goes, she was discovered sipping a soda (and supposedly wearing a tight sweater) at the counter in Schwab's. She had a movie career that didn't merely survive on glitz and glamour alone, but thrived. It's not surprising that she comes off particularly well, despite stilted performances, as actresses in *The Bad and the Beautiful* and *Imitation of Life*—after all, the producers wisely cast an actress who, like her characters, was

entirely artifice. Turner was sexy in her first film, *They Won't Forget,* as a promiscuous teenager (the first of her sexy hometown girls) who is slain on the way to a rendezvous; in the best of her many melodramas, *The Postman Always Rings Twice,* she seduces John Garfield into disposing of her husband. M-G-M would have been wise to let her other characters be openly sexual, but while it promoted her as the "Sweater Girl" and made her a top pinup, her characters (even including, to a large degree, her platinum, dressed-in-white femme fatale in *Postman*) are icy and untouchable. It was fitting that she would be selected to play the appropriately named

Lady de Winter in *The Three Musketeers.* In *A Life of Her Own,* she forgoes men to pursue a career, a course she would take years later in Universal's *Imitation of Life,* where she tells fiancé John Gavin of her decision as the cold snow falls behind her. It's too bad that Turner didn't get to play some cheap tramps, as Beverly Michaels and Cleo Moore did in Hugo Haas's sleazy films—anything to dirty her image. Turner could have stood it. In fact, her career got a boost from a scandal: after her troubled teenage daughter, Cheryl Crane, stabbed to death Turner's gangster boyfriend, Johnny Stompanato (she testified she was protecting Turner), Turner capitalized on the publicity by playing a mother with a troubled daughter in both *Imitation of Life,* where lonely Sandra Dee falls for her mother's boyfriend, and *Portrait in Black,* where Turner's boyfriend is accidentally killed while menacing Dee. Thus began Turner's successful comeback, where she'd play more women whose isolation is less a sign of independence than of selfishness. I find almost all of Turner's dramas enjoyable, but even Turner cultists should be wary of her comedies—as the Camerons write, "Turner does not give the impression . . . of possessing any sense of humor at all."

• **Cult Favorites:** *The Postman Always Rings Twice* (1946, Tay Garnett), *Imitation of Life* (1959, Douglas Sirk).

• **Also Recommended:** *They Won't Forget* (1937, Mervyn LeRoy), *Ziegfeld Girl* (1941, Robert Z. Leonard), *Dr. Jekyll and Mr. Hyde* (1942, Victor Fleming), *Johnny Eager* (1942, LeRoy), *The Three Musketeers* (1948, George Sidney), *A Life of Her Own* (1950, George Cukor), *The Bad and the Beautiful* (1952, Vincente Minnelli), *Diane* (1957, David Miller), *Peyton Place* (1958, Mark Robson), *Portrait in Black* (1961, Michael Gordon), *Madame X* (1966, David Lowell Rich).

○

TOM TYLER (1903–54) Handsome action hero began his career in the mid-twenties making solid, innovative low-budget westerns for Joseph Kennedy's FBO pictures. In the early thirties he switched back and forth between B westerns and serials, and ended the decade with small parts in *Stagecoach* and *Gone With the Wind.* In the forties, other than two starring roles in serials, costarring with Bob Steele and Rufe Davis in some efficient, enjoyable "Three Mesquiteers" B westerns, and playing the monster in the lousy *The Mummy's Hand,* he took minor roles in such films as *Brother Orchid, The Westerner, Talk of the Town, Blood on the Moon, I Shot Jesse James,* and *She Wore a Yellow Ribbon.* Tyler's cult status is due to his popularity as a dashing, athletic serial star; he played two cowboys, a mountie, a pilot, a hunter, and two colorful, uniformed comic-strip superheroes, the Phantom and Captain Marvel. *The Adventures of Captain Marvel* is considered Republic's finest serial and Tyler the studio's most exciting hero (thanks to the stunt work of Don Sharpe). When the word "Shazam" is spoken, Billy Batson (young Frank Coghlan, Jr.) turns into Captain Marvel (Tyler), and the villainous Scorpion is in deep trouble.

• **Cult Favorite:** *The Adventures of Captain Marvel* (1941 serial, William Witney and John English).

• **Other Key Films:** *The Phantom of the West* (1931 serial, Ross Lederman), *Battling with Buffalo Bill* (1931 serial, Ray Taylor), *Clancy of the Mounted* (1933 se-

Susan Tyrrell is the wicked Queen Doris and Herve Villechaize is King Fausto in Forbidden Zone.

rial, Taylor), *Jungle Mystery* (1932 serial, Taylor), *The Phantom of the Air* (1933, Taylor), *The Mummy's Hand* (1940, Christy Cabanne), *The Phantom* (1943 serial, B. Reeves Eason and Witney).

○

SUSAN TYRRELL (1941–) This out-of-the-mainstream character actress, a Warhol graduate and one-time roommate of transvestite Candy Darling, has given some funny deadpan performances as pathetic lowlifes and assorted grotesques. Her loud women pout, complain, blubber, swear, sneer, drink too much, are on makeup over-load, dress tastelessly, and have ugly hairstyles—yet even those who are repulsive sluts consider themselves sexy. I figured, if only she couldn't act, she'd be perfect for John Waters films. But he cast her anyway, in *Cry-Baby,* and she fit in snugly. She worked well with Stacy Keach, playing his has-been boxer's boozy girlfriend in *Fat City,* and, in what may be her best role, the greedy, masochistic, and quite loathsome cheap whore whom his psycho cop tries to murder in *The Killer Inside Me.* Other memorable oddball parts include Carroll Baker's annoying, dumpy daughter-in-law in *Andy Warhol's Bad,* the friendly butch landlady in *Angel,* a sexually repressed, overprotective murderous aunt in *Night Warning,* and the female leader (Herve Villechaize is the male ruler) of the Sixth Dimension in *Forbidden Zone.* She took a small part, as Kris Kristofferson's Tom Thumb–size wife, in the dreadful *Big Top Pee-Wee.*

• **Cult Favorites:** *Andy Warhol's Bad* (1971, Jed Johnson), *Forbidden Zone* (1980, Richard Elfman), *Angel* (1984, Robert Vincent O'Neil), *Flesh + Blood* (1985, Paul Verhoeven), *Tapeheads* (1988, Bill Fishman), *Cry-Baby* (1990, John Waters).

• **Sleepers:** *Fat City* (1972, John Huston), *Fast-Walking* (1982, James B. Harris).

• **Other Key Films:** *The Killer Inside Me* (1976, Burt Kennedy), *Tales of Ordinary Madness* (1983, Marco Ferrari), *Avenging Angel* (1985, O'Neil).

• **Also of Interest:** *The Steagle* (1971, Paul Sylbert), *Another Man, Another Chance* (1977, Claude Lelouch), *Loose Shoes/ Coming Attractions* (1980, Ira Miller), *Liar's Moon* (1981, David Fisher), *Night Warning* (1982, William Asher).

○

RUDOLPH VALENTINO (1895–1926) The Italian-born Rodolfo Guglielmi di Valentina d'Antonguolla was a waiter, taxi

Rudolph Valentino with Alice Terry in The Sheik.

dancer, and gigolo before finding success in the movies. He started out playing oily Latin villains, but scriptwriter June Mathis saw his potential for romantic leads and wrote starring vehicles for him—*The Four Horsemen of the Apocalypse, The Conquering Power, Camille, Blood and Sand,* and *The Young Rajah.* Those roles, along with his most famous film, *The Sheik,* established him permanently as the screen's greatest lover. Today we are disappointed by his slight acting talent and even his lovemaking technique, but women of the day were thrilled by this gloriously handsome, graceful Latin lover, with his bulging eyes and sensuous glances (caused by nearsightedness), rippling muscles and bare chest (he stripped in most films), and his forceful, unrestrained passion when taking women in his arms—often against their wills. To the bored, fantasizing women of the world, this exotic figure, in turbans, tuxedos, and foreign uniforms, represented escape—partly of a sexual nature. They wanted him to dance the tango with them, as he did with Beatrice Dominguez in *The Four Horsemen of the Apocalypse,* a classic sequence that anticipated Fred Astaire's sexual seduction dances with Ginger Rogers by ten years. And they wanted him to make love to them as he did with Nazimova, Alice Terry, Vilma Banky, Bebe Daniels, Nita Naldi, and particularly Agnes Ayres, whom he abducted in *The Sheik* and then charmed and excited into giving herself to him completely. He was, wrote critic Alexander Walker, "the seducer who could be trusted to act like a gentleman." Valentino's screen character became more effeminate and his box-office power plunged when Natasha Rambova guided her passive husband's career, but when United Artists executives stipulated she no longer inter-

fere, he regained his masculinity and full popularity with *The Eagle* and *Son of the Sheik,* his last two films. After his sudden death from a perforated ulcer, thousands of heartbroken women paraded past his body at a New York funeral home—newsreels of this event are shown as often as clips from his films—and a death cult would take hold, even greater than the later ones for James Dean, Marilyn Monroe, and Elvis Presley.

- **Cult Favorites:** *The Four Horsemen of the Apocalypse* (1921, Rex Ingram), *The Sheik* (1921, George Melford).
- **Other Key Films:** *The Conquering Power* (1921, Ingram), *Blood and Sand* (1922, Fred Niblo), *The Young Rajah* (1922, Philip Rosen), *Monsieur Beaucaire* (1924, Sidney Olcott), *The Eagle* (1925, Clarence Brown), *Son of the Sheik* (1926, George Fitzmaurice).
- **Also of Interest:** *Eyes of Youth* (1919, Albert Parker), *Stolen Moments* (1920, James Vincent), *Unchartered Seas* (1921, Wesley Ruggles), *Moran of the Lady Letty* (1922, Melford), *Beyond the Rocks* (1922, Sam Wood), *A Sainted Devil* (1924, Joseph Henabery), *Cobra* (1925, Henabery).

○

VAMPIRA (1921–) The niece of the legendary "Flying Finn," Olympic long-distance running champion Paavo Nurmi, Maila Nurmi was discovered by Howard Hawks, who thought she looked like Lauren Bacall. The film he planned for her never came off, but as Vampira, she became a cult figure in Los Angeles in the fifties as a horror-movie hostess on television (anticipating Elvira by 30 years); as a local eccentric; and as a companion of James Dean. Using Charles Addams's Morticia as her model, she was primed for Halloween the whole year through, with her long black hair (it was originally blond), arched eyebrows, and long nails; she dressed in black, with a belt pulled tightly around her 17″ waist. She looked like a cross between a starving beatnik and a witch. She claimed she was blacklisted and couldn't get legit movie roles, so she accepted Edward D. Wood's $200 for one day's work on *Plan 9 from Outer Space*. She insisted that she be given no dialogue, so all her dead, possessed woman does is walk trancelike through a misty graveyard. She probably gives the best performance in the film—the others, who recite Wood's lines, make fools of themselves. Vampira was given bit parts, adding to the zany ambiance, in three drive-in films by exploitation producer Albert Zugsmith; she also played a hag in *The Magic Sword*. Thanks to *Plan 9*—she has spoken at recent screenings—her fame endures.

• **Cult Favorites:** *Plan 9 from Outer Space* (1959, Edward D. Wood, Jr.), *Sex Kittens Go to College* (1960, Albert Zugsmith).

• **Also of Interest:** *The Big Operator* (1959, Charles Haas), *The Beat Generation* (1959, Haas), *The Magic Sword* (1962, Bert I. Gordon).

○

LEE VAN CLEEF (1925–89) Narrow-eyed, dry-voiced, cruel-looking actor was the police sharpshooter who guns down *The Beast from 20,000 Fathoms* on the Coney Island roller coaster. It would be one of the few times until late in his career, when he got lead roles, that he would be on the right side of the law. He often played sadistic hired killers in melodramas and outlaws in westerns, underlings of the major villains. He was memorable as one of the homosexual killers in *The Big Combo*, but some forget he was also one of the bad guys who threaten Gary Cooper in *High Noon* and James Stewart in *The Man Who Shot Liberty Valance*, backing up Lee Marvin. In the mid-sixties, he put on some weight, grew a thick mustache, developed a sneer, lowered his voice, dressed in black, and became an international star as Clint Eastwood's wiser, confident but tough accomplice (the "good") in *For a Few Dollars More*—he lit a match on Klaus Kinski's hump—and his vicious, evil foe (the "bad") in *The Good, the Bad, and the Ugly*, his most famous role. He was an imposing figure—he said his "feral nose" was his key to success—with surprising presence for someone who had been ignored for so many years. His mean, creviced face was worthy of director Sergio Leone's wide-screen close-ups, especially during the final gun battles. He would star in other bloody, less impressive Italian westerns, usually playing experienced but weary gunfighters and bounty hunters who want money or revenge, or to clear their names. He was usually kinder but not gentler than the villains.

• **Cult Favorites:** *Kansas City Confidential* (1952, Phil Karlson), *The Big Combo* (1955, Joseph H. Lewis), *The Conqueror* (1956, Dick Powell), *China Gate* (1957, Samuel Fuller), *The Tin Star* (1957, Anthony Mann), *Ride Lonesome* (1959, Budd Boetticher), *The Man Who Shot Liberty Valance* (1962, John Ford), *For a Few Dollars More* (1965, Sergio Leone), *The Good, the Bad, and the Ugly* (1966, Leone), *The Stranger and the Gunfighter* (1976, Anthony Dawson/Antonio Margheriti), *The Octagon* (1980, Eric Karson), *Escape from New York* (1981, John Carpenter).

• **Other Key Films:** *The Big Gundown* (1968, Sergio Sollima), *Sabata* (1970, Frank Kramer/Gianfranco Parolini), *Bar-*

Lee Van Cleef and Clint Eastwood in For a Few Dollars More.

quero (1970, Gordon Douglas), *Captain Apache* (1971, Alexander Singer), *Bad Man's River* (1972, Gene Martin/Eugenio Martin), *Return of Sabata* (1972, Kramer), *Take a Hard Ride* (1975, Dawson), *The Hard Way* (1979, Michael Dryhurst), *Code Name: Wild Geese* (1984, Dawson).

• **Also of Interest:** *High Noon* (1952, Fred Zinnemann), *The Beast from 20,000 Fathoms* (1953, Eugene Lourie), *Vice Squad* (1953, Arnold Laven), *A Man Alone* (1955, Ray Milland), *Pardners* (1956, Norman Taurog), *Gunfight at the O.K. Corral* (1957, John Sturges), *The Lonely Man* (1957, Henry Levin).

○

JEAN-CLAUDE VAN DAMME (1961–) High-voltage action star from Brussels, with one of the longest names ever on a marquee. The "Muscles from Brussels" played Russian villains in *No Retreat, No Surrender* and *Black Eagle* (opposite Sho Kosugi), and was the mutating alien who battles Arnold Schwarzenegger to a standstill in *Predator,* before making it big as the hero of such violent films as *Bloodsport,* as real-life American Frank Dux (the first westerner to win the secretive Kumite karate competition in Hong Kong), and the futuristic *Cyborg,* as Gibson Rickenbacker. He also starred in *Kickboxer,* again in a martial-arts tournament, and *Death Warrant,* as an undercover cop who takes on a psycho-slasher in prison. *Death Warrant* used the promo slogan "Wham! Bam! Van Damme!" He can't act a lick and his speech is often unintelligible, but his films don't require thespian skills. He's handsome, muscular, graceful (he studied ballet), and impressive in combat, whether engaging in karate or kickboxing—and that's been enough for him to win a strong following (although I've never met a Van Damme fan).

• **Cult Favorites:** *Predator* (1987, John McTiernan), *Bloodsport* (1987, Newt Arnold), *Cyborg* (1989, Albert Pyun), *Kickboxer* (1989, Mark DiSalle and David Worth).

• **Also of Interest:** *No Retreat, No Surrender* (1986, Corey Yuen), *Black Eagle* (1988, Eric Carson), *Death Warrant* (1990, Deran Sarafian), *Lionheart* (1991, Sheldon Lettich).

MAMIE VAN DOREN (1931–) In the fifties, the decade of buxom platinum blondes, push-up bras, tight sweaters, and hip-hugging skirts, she was Universal Studios' dime-store Marilyn Monroe. She was a vivacious sexpot who had many well-publicized affairs, wore outfits in public that guaranteed photographs of her would be in the morning papers, was the first singing actress—she claims—to have a rock-'n'-roll connection (though it's hard to find anyone who bought her records), and was a familiar face on television and in the movies. She was billed for *Untamed*

Jean-Claude Van Damme (right) *gets revenge in* Kickboxer.

Youth as "the girl built like a platinum powerhouse"; her movies were mostly of the drive-in variety—silly sex comedies (in *Sex Kittens Go to College,* she takes over a college science department!), sleazy pot-boilers, and "hip" films about troubled young women. Her fans waited for her character to sing (because she'd also do some semiobscene gyrating!), attempt a seduction, or be placed in a compromising position while wearing a top several sizes too small. Her acting was of secondary concern, which was just as well because she wasn't particularly talented, although she had enough range to be bubbly or sensuous—she was always sexually provocative. She had presence, immense sex appeal, and was a lot of fun. Among her most memorable roles was as narc Russ Tamblyn's nymphomaniac aunt in *High School Confidential,* one of many films she made for producer Albert Zugsmith. She walks around in erotic outfits, rolls on her nephew's bed as if she were a cat in heat, bites into his apple with thoughts of Eden in her naughty head, drinks herself into a stupor, gets slapped around in classic cheap-dame style, and tells a prim teacher, "Don't tell me you never rode in a hot rod or had a late-night date in the balcony." Van Doren returned to the spotlight with a recent autobiography, *Playing the Field,* in which she recalls her sexual interludes with such figures as Rock Hudson and Bo Belinsky. Obviously all types of men were attracted to her.

• **Cult Favorites:** *Untamed Youth* (1957, Howard W. Koch), *High School Confidential* (1958, Jack Arnold), *Sex Kittens Go to College* (1960, Albert Zugsmith), *The Private Lives of Adam and Eve* (1960, Zugsmith and Mickey Rooney), *College Confidential* (1960, Zugsmith), *Voyage to the Planet of Prehistoric Women* (1966/68,

Mamie Van Doren in Albert Zugsmith's production, Girls Town.

Derek Thomas/Peter Bogdanovich).

• **Other Key Films:** *The All American* (1953, Jesse Hibbs), *Yankee Pasha* (1954, Joseph Pevney), *Ain't Misbehavin'* (1955, Edward Buzzell), *The Second Greatest Sex* (1955, George Marshall), *Running Wild* (1955, Abner Biberman), *Star in the Dust* (1956, Charles Haas), *The Girl in Black Stockings* (1957, Koch), *Teacher's Pet* (1958, George Seaton), *Born Reckless* (1958, Koch), *Guns, Girls, and Gangsters* (1959, Edward L. Cahn), *The Beat Generation* (1959, Haas), *The Big Operator* (1959, Haas), *Girls Town* (1959, Haas), *Vice Raid* (1959, Cahn), *The Navy vs. the Night Monsters* (1966, Michael Hoey), *Las Vegas Hillbillys* (1966, Arthur C. Pierce).

○

VANITY (1963–) Gorgeous Canadian-born black actress-singer, once romantically and musically linked to rock superstar Prince (she had a hit record, "Nasty Girl"), has played leads and supporting roles in a number of seamy, violent melodramas. Her women are extremely sexy, funny, and gritty; understanding the ways of the world, they expect no free favors from any man. They are ideal companions to suave Billy Dee Williams in *Deadly Illusion* and tough Carl Weathers in *Action Jackson*. With beauty, talent, and a natural style that is most appealing, Vanity could be what Pam Grier was in the seventies—but, when one considers today's scripts, it is unlikely she'll get the chance. Her real name is Denise Matthews, but it's probable (though I can't tell positively) that early in her career she was the "D. D. Winters" who starred in the lurid *Tanya's Island,* fought over by a jealous man and an ape.
- **Cult Favorite:** *The Last Dragon/Berry Gordy's The Last Dragon* (1985, Michael Schultz).
- **Other Key Film:** *Action Jackson* (1988, Craig R. Baxley).
- **Also of Interest:** *52 Pick-Up* (1986, John Frankenheimer), *Never Too Young* (1986, Gil Bettman), *Deadly Illusion* (1987, William Tannen and Larry Cohen).

○

EDWARD VAN SLOAN (1882–1964) Thirties character actor had the distinction of being in Universal's three horror classics: *Dracula, Frankenstein,* and *The Mummy*. Graywhite haired, serious, pensive, and intelligent-looking, he played doctors, scientists, and lots of professors: Professor Hawley, Professor Carlisle, Professor Bostwick, etc. His most famous professor was Van Helsing, the indefatigable pursuer of Bela Lugosi in *Dracula,* then, several years later, Gloria Holden in the superior sequel, *Dracula's Daughter*. Van Helsing and Count Dracula's battle of wills in *Dracula* is quite memorable. But for some reason I can never remember what Van Sloan looks like—I expect someone who looks like a thin Edmund Gwenn and an impostor appears. Yet I am always impressed that he can convince sane people of the existence of vampires. His classic words to skeptics: "The superstition of yesterday can become the scientific reality of today."
- **Cult Favorites:** *The Mummy* (1932, James Whale), *The Scarlet Empress* (1934, Josef von Sternberg), *Dracula's Daughter* (1936, Lambert Hillyer).
- **Other Key Films:** *Dracula* (1931, Tod Browning), *Frankenstein* (1931, Whale), *Deluge* (1933, Felix E. Feist), *The Last Days of Pompeii* (1934, Merian C. Cooper and Ernest B. Schoedsack).
- **Also Recommended:** *Behind the Mask* (1932, John Francis Dillon), *The Death Kiss* (1933, Edward L. Marin), *Death Takes a Holiday* (1934, Mitchell Leisen), *Murder on Campus* (1934, Richard Thorpe), *The Black Room* (1935, Roy William Neill), *The Crime of Dr. Crespi* (1935, John Auer), *A Shot in the Dark* (1935, Charles Lamont), *The Phantom Creeps* (1939 serial, Ford Beebe and Saul A. Goodkind), *Before I Hang* (1940, Nick Grinde).
- **Also of Interest:** *Forgotten Commandments* (1932, Louis Gasnier and William Schoor), *The Story of Louis Pasteur* (1936, William Dieterle), *Penitentiary* (1938, John Brahm), *The Song of Berna-*

dette (1943, Henry King), *The Mask of Dijon* (1946, Lew Landers).

○

MONIQUE VAN VOOREN (1933–) Blond, glamorous Belgian nightclub performer (with a large gay following) was a Hollywood starlet in the fifties. She had bit and supporting parts in several innocuous comedies, but she was the female lead in *Tarzan and the She-Devil,* as an evil temptress who enslaves an African tribe, kidnaps Jane, and captures and tortures Lex Barker's Lord of the Jungle—too bad for her that he escapes. Van Vooren resurfaced in American films in 1967, playing Jon Voight's lover, Plethora, in the obscure *Fearless Frank.* In the mid-seventies (when she was in her early forties), she appeared with Mary Woronov and Lynn Lowry in *Sugar Cookies,* which contains nudity, lesbian sex, and murder, and as a decadent baroness in *Andy Warhol's Frankenstein,* in which she interrupts the bloodshed for a funny sex scene with Joe Dallesandro, during which there is some loud armpit slurping. She always seemed the type of woman—an overly glamorous, ostentatious performer who is famous for no real reason—who would interest Warhol.

• **Cult Favorites:** *The Gospel According to St. Matthew* (1966, Pier Paolo Pasolini), *Andy Warhol's Frankenstein* (1974, Paul Morrissey).

• **Other Key Films:** *Tarzan and the She-Devil* (1953, Kurt Neumann), *Fearless Frank* (1967, Philip Kaufman), *Sugar Cookies* (1975, Theodore Gershuny).

• **Also of Interest:** *Ten Thousand Bedrooms* (1957, Richard Thorpe), *Happy Anniversary* (1959, David Miller).

○

CONRAD VEIDT (1893–1943) Slender, striking, agile—he moved like a dancer as the somnambulist in *The Cabinet of Dr. Caligari*—refined German actor, a former student of Max Reinhardt. He had an unusual (and successful) career, playing, at various junctures, tormented men who become instruments of evil, in German fantasy-horror films; historical figures including Richard III, Cesare Borgia, Ivan the Terrible (in *Waxworks*), Lord Nelson, Chopin, and Louis XI; romantic leads—he was most dashing opposite Vivien Leigh in *Dark Journey;* and despicable scoundrels. What's unusual is that even in the later part of his career, when he played only villains, he remained a romantic idol, a symbol of European sophistication—he even did promotional ads ("If Conrad Veidt offered you a cigarette, it would be a De Rozke—of course!"). That the public was never able to pigeonhole him as a villain is understandable. His face was at once handsome and cruel (he had a wrinkled forehead, receding hairline, and, at times, a monocle), with eyes that seemed haunted by past horrors—many of which his characters perpetrated themselves. And from the beginning, there was a strong duality in his screen characters, as they came to represent the struggle between good and evil. In *The Hands of Orlac,* he is a good man onto whose arms are grafted the hands of a murderer; in *The Man Who Laughs,* he is given a monster's disfigured face—the model of Batman's Joker—and breaks horror conventions by remaining good; Cesare, in *Caligari,* is controlled by a madman. On the other hand, in *The Student of Prague,* he sells his soul and is tortured by his mirror reflection. In *The*

Conrad Veidt is aroused by Werner Krauss in The Cabinet of Dr. Caligari.

Head of Janus, he played Jekyll and Hyde (though different names are used); and he played twins, one good and one bad, in *The Two Brothers* and, years later, in *Nazi Agent.* He portrayed spies with divided loyalties, and Germans who just happened to have been born on the wrong side. As cruel as is his Hitler-like wizard in *The Thief of Bagdad,* we sympathize with him because his love for the princess (June Duprez) is pure. Among the only villains for whom we can feel only hatred are his Lucifer in *Satanas,* the despicable aristocrat who tries to force Joan Crawford to kill a child in *A Woman's Face,* and the Nazis he played in American films. He is best remembered for *Casablanca*—his Nazi officer pulls a gun on Bogart, although Bogie already has one pointed at him; like many of Veidt's Nazi villains, he is killed because of stupidity based on conceit.

• **Cult Favorites:** *The Cabinet of Dr. Caligari* (1919, Robert Wiene), *Dark Journey* (1937, Victor Saville), *The Thief of Bagdad* (1940, Ludwig Berger, Tim Whelan, and Michael Powell), *Casablanca* (1943, Michael Curtiz).

• **Other Key Films:** *The Hands of Janus* (1919, F. W. Murnau), *Waxworks* (1924, Paul Leni), *The Hands of Orlac* (1925, Wiene), *The Student of Prague* (1926, Henrik Galeen), *The Beloved Rogue* (1927, Alan Crosland), *The Man Who Laughs* (1927, Leni), *F.P.I. Does Not Answer* (1932, Karl Hartl).

• **Also Recommended:** *The Spy in Black*

(1939, Powell and Emeric Pressburger), *Contraband* (1940, Powell and Pressburger), *Escape* (1940, Mervyn LeRoy), *A Woman's Face* (1941, George Cukor).

• **Also of Interest:** Numerous German films (1917–32), *I Was a Spy* (1933, Victor Saville), *All Through the Night* (1941, Vincent Sherman), *Nazi Agent* (1942, Jules Dassin), *Above Suspicion* (1943, Richard Thorpe).

○

JOHN VERNON (1935–) This deep-voiced, ruddy-faced, handsome but cold-looking Canadian actor has been a strong villain in crime dramas, westerns, horror films, and comedies since the late sixties. His cads are typically intelligent, smug, humorless, cruel, and in positions of power—political figures, gangster chiefs, movie directors, prison wardens, heads of schools (as in *National Lampoon's Animal House*). Too sure of themselves, they are either foiled (by the frat pranksters, by Jim Varney's Ernest) or killed. He has particularly nifty deaths at the hands of Lee Marvin in *Point Blank* and Clint Eastwood in *The Outlaw Josey Wales*. On occasion, Linda Blair has gotten the best of him.

• **Cult Favorites:** *Point Blank* (1967, John Boorman), *Dirty Harry* (1971, Don Siegel), *The Outlaw Josey Wales* (1976, Clint Eastwood), *National Lampoon's Animal House* (1978, John Landis), *Chained Heat* (1983, Paul Nicholas), *Ernest Goes to Camp* (1987, John R. Cherry III).

• **Other Key Films:** *Topaz* (1969, Alfred Hitchcock), *Charley Varrick* (1973, Siegel), *The Black Windmill* (1974, Siegel), *Curtains* (1983, Jonathan Stryker/Richard Ciupka), *Nightstick* (1987, Joseph L. Scanlon), *I'm Gonna Git You Sucka* (1988, Keenen Ivory Wayans).

• **Also of Interest:** *One More Train to Rob* (1971, Andrew V. McLaglen), *W/I Want Her Dead* (1974, Richard Quine), *Brannigan* (1975, Douglas Hickox), *The Uncanny* (1977, Denis Heroux), *Jungle Warriors* (1984, Ernst R. von Theumer), *Killer Klowns from Outer Space* (1988, Stephen Chlodo).

○

BRUNO VESOTA (1922–76) In one of the most unnerving scenes in fifties science-fiction/horror films, VeSota's weakling bartender uses a rifle to force his cheating wife, Yvette Vickers, and her lover, Michael Emmett, into the swamp . . . which wouldn't be so bad if they weren't in a movie called *Attack of the Giant Leeches*. AIP's resident fat man—he looked like a squashed and sweaty William Conrad—would play unpleasant characters in numerous low-budget science-fiction, horror, western, and hot-rod/motorcycle films in the fifties and sixties. Many were directed by Roger Corman; among VeSota's own directorial efforts were *The Female Jungle, The Brain Eaters,* and *Invasion of the Star Creatures.* His bad-tempered, untrusting troublemakers and cowards usually had unfortunate ends: they were stabbed or axed, or, in *Leeches,* even hung themselves.

• **Cult Favorites:** *The Wild One* (1953, Laslo Benedek), *Bait* (1954, Hugo Haas), *Attack of the Giant Leeches* (1959, Bernard Kowalski), *Night Tide* (1961, Curtis Harrington), *Hell's Angels on Wheels* (1967, Richard Rush).

• **Also of Interest:** *The Fast and the Furious* (1954, John Ireland and Edwards Sampson), *Apache Woman* (1955, Roger Corman), *Oklahoma Woman* (1955, Corman), *Dementia* (1955, John Parker), *The Un-*

dead (1956, Corman), *Gunslinger* (1956, Corman), *Rock All Night* (1957, Corman), *Teenage Doll* (1957, Corman), *War of the Satellites* (1957, Corman), *Hot Car Girl* (1958, Kowalski), *The Wasp Woman* (1959, Corman), *Code of Silence* (1960, Mel Welles), *The Haunted Palace* (1963, Corman), *A Man Called Dagger* (1967, Rush), *Single Room Unfurnished* (1968, Matteo Ottaviano).

○

VICTORIA VETRI (1944–) California blonde of Italian descent, with a cute face and a curvy body, appeared on television and in her first movies as Angela Dorian. In *Rosemary's Baby,* she was Mia Farrow's dark-haired Italian neighbor, who falls out a window to her death. After that film, director Roman Polanski convinced her to use her real name, Victoria Vetri. Hoping to boost her career, she was one of the first actresses to pose for *Playboy,* and became "Playmate of the Year." This "exposure" resulted in her being offered the lead in Hammer Studios' *When Dinosaurs Ruled the Earth,* as a Rock Tribe princess. Nude publicity shots (by *Playboy* photographers) and stills and posters of her in a warrior pose while wearing a tiger-skin bikini made her a pinup favorite at the time. She was amusing as part of an ensemble in *Group Marriage,* and alluring (nude when rescued by William Smith) as the second female lead, behind Anitra Ford, in *Invasion of the Bee Girls,* written by Nicholas Meyer. But she never approached stardom. Her attempt to be a rock music singing star also failed.

• **Cult Favorites:** *Rosemary's Baby* (1968, Roman Polanski), *Invasion of the Bee Girls/Graveyard Tramps* (1973, Denis Sanders).

• **Other Key Films:** *When Dinosaurs Ruled the Earth* (1970, Val Guest), *Group Marriage* (1972, Stephanie Rothman).

• **Also of Interest:** *Chuka* (1967, Gordon Douglas).

○

YVETTE VICKERS (1936–) Curvaceous, super-sexy blonde (a *Playboy* Playmate in 1959), first discovered by Billy Wilder, who gave her the unbilled bit part of a giggly girl who won't get off the phone at a party in *Sunset Boulevard.* James Cagney then gave her a major part in *Short Cut to Hell,* a remake of *This Gun for Hire.* She had bits and minor roles throughout the fifties, playing juvenile delinquents or tarts, before she played tramps in two low-budget science-fiction films that forever made her a major sex symbol of the genre. In *Attack of the 50 Ft. Woman,* she was so sexy she almost stole the film from another cult figure, Allison Hayes, although Hayes had a much "bigger" part. Vickers played Honey Parker, scheming mistress of Hayes's husband, who plots with him to institutionalize and then kill his wife—but Hayes gets mighty big and goes on the offensive. Vickers was even more provocative in *Attack of the Giant Leeches,* slithering around in a Japanese robe, rubbing skin lotion on her legs, acting rudely toward her meek husband (Bruno VeSota), having a hot date with the town lech, begging her husband (who has discovered her infidelity) not to force them into the swamp (where she knows something is lurking). Although ravaged and dying, she even looked fetching hanging in the leeches' cave, waiting for them to climb on her and drain more blood from her body. This was the high point of her career. She would have a small but eye-catching part in *Hud,* but do little else of significance.

• **Cult Favorites:** *Sunset Boulevard* (1950, Billy Wilder), *Attack of the 50 Ft. Woman* (1958, Nathan Hertz), *Beach Party* (1963, William Asher), *What's the Matter with Helen?* (1971, Curtis Harrington).

• **Sleeper:** *Attack of the Giant Leeches/The Giant Leeches* (1959, Bernard Kowalski).

• **Also Recommended:** *Short Cut to Hell* (1957, James Cagney), *Reform School Girl* (1957, Edward Bernds), *Hud* (1963, Martin Ritt).

• **Also of Interest:** *Sad Sack* (1957, George Marshall), *Juvenile Jungle* (1958, William Witney), *The Saga of Hemp Brown* (1958, Richard Carlson), *I, Mobster* (1958, Roger Corman), *Pressure Point* (1962, Hubert Cornfield), *Vigilante Force* (1976, George Armitage).

○

KATHERINE VICTOR (1928–) Born Katena Ktenavea, this statuesque, raven-haired model, nightclub torch singer, pianist, and theater and live-television actress began making films in the early fifties as Katherine Vea, playing bits in *The Eddy Duchin Story, Sabrina,* and the Grade-Z horror film *Lost Women.* Unfortunately, the last title was an indication of the sorry direction her career would take. Victor would be the female star of untalented producer-director Jerry Warren, exhibiting class and sex appeal in otherwise ghastly horror and science-fiction films. As the late actor Barry Brown, Victor's greatest fan, recalled, she typically played a "half-smiling villain, beautiful, elegant, and supremely menacing." Her imperious, mysterious, ruthless, and sexy villainesses included Dr. Sheila Myra, who uses nerve gas to turn young water skiers into *Teenage Zombies,* and a high priestess of devil worshippers in *Creature of the Walking Dead.* Away from Warren, in Phil Tucker's *The Cape Canaveral Monsters,* another low-budget disaster, she was the mean Maida, a cohort of alien invaders. With such credits (*The Wild World of Batwoman* was never even released), it's little wonder she stopped making movies to work on the production side for various television animation companies.

• **Key Films:** *Teenage Zombies* (1957/60, Jerry Warren), *The Cape Canaveral Monsters* (1959, Phil Tucker), *Curse of the Stone Hand* (1965, Warren), *House of the Black Death* (1965, Warren), *Creature of the Walking Dead* (1966, Warren), *The Wild World of Batwoman/She Was a Hippie Vampire* (1966, Warren).

• **Also of Interest:** *Lost Women/Mesa of Lost Women* (1952, Herbert Tevos and Ron Diamond), *Justine* (1963, George Cukor).

○

JAN-MICHAEL VINCENT (1944–) Blond, boyish-looking action hero of the seventies and early eighties, with jeans, a genial smile, and modest talent. He occasionally played rebels—in the acclaimed TV movie *Tribes* (shown theatrically abroad as *The Soldier Who Declared Peace*), his long-haired recruit refuses to buckle under to a stern drillmaster. More often he was someone who just wanted to be left alone; when his privacy was infringed upon, he became a reluctant hero, fighting the bad guys with fists, baseball bats, and guns. Other than *Tribes,* his most interesting roles were in *Buster and Billie,* as the only boy to see the worth in a plump, "easy" local girl (Joan Goodfellow); *Big Wednesday,* as an over-aged surfer who still searches for the perfect wave; and *Baby Blue Marine,* as a marine reject during World War II who steals a uniform and is treated like a hero in a small town he passes through. Unfortunately, the roles required sensitivity, and that has never been Vincent's strong suit.

• **Cult Favorites:** *White Line Fever* (1975, Jonathan Kaplan), *Big Wednesday* (1978, John Milius).

• **Sleepers:** *The Soldier Who Declared Peace* (1970, Joseph Sargent), *Buster and Billie* (1974, Daniel Petrie), *Bite the Bullet* (1975, Richard Brooks), *Baby Blue Marine* (1976, John Hancock).

• **Other Key Films:** *Going Home* (1971, Herbert B. Leonard), *The Mechanic* (1972, Michael Winner), *The World's Greatest Athlete* (1973, Robert Scheerer), *Vigilante Force* (1976, George Armitage), *Damnation Alley* (1977, Jack Smight), *Hooper* (1978, Hal Needham), *Defiance* (1980, John Flynn), *Hard Country* (1981, David Greene), *Last Plane Out* (1983, David Nelson), *Born in East L.A.* (1987, Cheech Marin).

○

VIVA Actress-journalist-personality, with frizzy hair, a slim build, sunken cheeks, and sharp features—she always reminded me of a loopy Vanessa Redgrave. But she was from New York, a nonactress with natural talent who became one of the last of Andy Warhol's Superstars. In *Blue Movie/Fuck* she broke new ground with Louis Waldon, when Warhol showed the sexual act in its entirety for the first time in his work. In addition to being sexually uninhibited on screen, Viva was amusing, interesting, and real when she delivered her often improvised lines, as the two characters discuss Vietnam, his unhappy marriage, social issues, and so on. She was weird enough to grab attention in only a few minutes of screen time, which is why she got comic cameos in some mainstream films set in New York, L.A., and San Francisco. In *Play It Again, Sam*, Woody Allen realizes how bad his luck with women is when her nymphomaniac rebukes his advances. High and spacey in *Cisco Pike*, she doesn't reject dealer Kris Kristofferson (or probably anybody else). It's too bad she didn't get more parts—she was funny and bizarre. She is the author of *Superstar* and *The Baby*.

• **Cult Favorites:** *Lonesome Cowboys* (1967, Andy Warhol), *Blue Movie/Fuck/Louis and Viva* (1969, Warhol), *Play It Again, Sam* (1972, Herbert Ross), *Cisco Pike* (1972, B. W. L. Norton), *Ciao! Manhattan* (1967/73, John Palmer and David Weisman), *Forbidden Zone* (1980, Richard Elfman).

• **Also of Interest:** ★★★★ (1968, Warhol), *Midnight Cowboy* (1969, John Schlesinger).

○

ERICH VON STROHEIM (1885–1957) As an actor, the Vienna-born Erich Oswald Stroheim quickly gained a reputation as "The Man You Love to Hate," and that never changed throughout his long career. In the films he directed and (after he was no longer given assignments because of his directorial extravagances) the films of others, he was thoroughly dislikable, playing Prussian career officers, mad doctors, and, in *The Lost Squadron*, an autocratic, anything-for-his-art director that was the height of self-parody (after he causes a stuntman's death, other stuntmen murder him!). His aristocratic Europeans are relics of a bygone era of pageantry, order, and chivalrous codes—but, with exceptions like his gentlemanly German officer in

Grand Illusion, they are also perverse, cultured but barbaric. Ruthless, rigid men, they wear uniforms and monocles and smoke cigarettes in holders; they speak only with sarcasm or conceit. They love giving orders. They are imposing but, ultimately, pathetic men, without friends and detested by the women they desire, whose downfalls come because they are too arrogant to believe anyone would challenge someone of their power and brilliance. They accept defeat with the stoicism of a captain going down with his ship. Von Stroheim always seemed unhappy on the screen, as if he felt his very appearance reminded viewers of his fall from being a towering director to an actor—a mere mortal. Perhaps, in his eyes, Max von Mayerling in *Sunset Boulevard,* a once-great director who now is servant to his greatest actress and former wife (Gloria Swanson), represented how low he himself had sunk in the film world.

• **Cult Favorites:** *The Wedding March* (1928, Erich von Stroheim), *Grand Illusion* (1937, Jean Renoir), *Sunset Boulevard* (1950, Billy Wilder).

• **Other Key Films:** *Blind Husbands* (1919, von Stroheim), *Foolish Wives* (1922, von Stroheim), *The Great Gabbo* (1929, James Cruze), *Five Graves to Cairo* (1943, Wilder), *The North Star* (1943, Lewis Milestone), *The Lady and the Monster* (1944, George Sherman).

• **Also Recommended:** *Hearts of the World* (1918, D. W. Griffith), *Three Faces East* (1930, Roy Del Ruth), *The Lost Squadron* (1932, George Archainbaud), *Les Pirates de Rail* (1938, Christian-Jaque), *La Danse de Mort* (1947, Marcel Cravenne).

• **Also of Interest:** *As You Desire Me* (1932, George Fitzmaurice), *The Crime of Dr. Crespi* (1935, John Auer), *Mademoiselle Docteur* (1937, Edmund Gréville), *I Was* *an Adventuress* (1940, Gregory Ratoff), *So Ends Our Night* (1941, John Cromwell), *Storm Over Lisbon* (1944, Sherman), *The Great Flamarion* (1945, Anthony Mann), *The Mask of Dijon* (1946, Lew Landers).

○

MAX VON SYDOW (1929–) This tall, gaunt, blond, deep-voiced Swedish actor was memorable in many Ingmar Bergman classics, a strong leading man opposite Bergman's formidable actresses, Ingrid Thulin, Harriet Andersson, Bibi Andersson, and Liv Ullmann. He played philosophic, troubled, confused men who struggle to cope with guilt, dwindling faith, marital instability, and a number of moral issues. His brave knight in *The Seventh Seal* quests for the meaning of life; other characters, particularly his musicians and painters, withdraw into near isolation—not particularly brave, they are unwilling to commit themselves emotionally or politically. It is often their angry women who force them to make difficult choices. His passivity again is a key element in the heralded *Pelle the Conqueror,* in which his character's young son must be the one to take action and test the waters. Von Sydow's face exudes gentleness, confidence, patience, and a sense of peace, which doesn't explain why he has been asked to play killers in a couple of his English-speaking films, but is likely the reason he was chosen to play both the title role in *The Exorcist* and Christ in *The Greatest Story Ever Told.* In the funny Bergman spoof, *The Dove,* he was parodied by a high-stepping, bowlegged blond actor.

• **Cult Favorites:** *The Seventh Seal* (1957, Ingmar Bergman), *Wild Strawberries* (1957, Bergman), *The Virgin Spring* (1959, Bergman), *Hour of the Wolf* (1968, Bergman), *The Exorcist* (1973, William Friedkin), *Steppenwolf* (1974, Fred Haines), *The Exorcist II: The Heretic* (1978, John Boorman), *Dune* (1984, David Lynch), *Hannah and Her Sisters* (1986, Woody Allen).

• **Sleepers:** *Death Watch* (1980, Bertrand Tavernier), *Wolf at the Door* (1987, Henning Carlsen), *Pelle the Conqueror* (1988, Billie August).

• **Other Key Films:** *The Magician/The Face* (1958, Bergman), *Through a Glass Darkly* (1961, Bergman), *Winter Light* (1962, Bergman), *The Greatest Story Ever Told* (1965, George Stevens), *The Shame* (1967, Bergman), *The Passion of Anna/A Passion* (1969, Bergman), *The Emigrants* (1971, Jan Troell), *The New Land* (1973, Troell), *Three Days of the Condor* (1975, Sidney Pollack), *Flight of the Eagle* (1982, Troell), *Never Say Never Again* (1983, Irvin Kershner).

• **Also of Interest:** *The Night Visitor* (1970, Laslo Benedek), *Foxtrot* (1975, Arturo Ripstein), *Voyage of the Damned* (1976, Stuart Rosenberg), *Duet for One* (1987, Andrei Konchalovsky).

○

TOMISABURO WAKAYAMA He looked like a grumpy, dumpy, double-chinned building super, but this Japanese actor played one of the deadliest fighters in screen history, Itto Ogami, in the bloody but fascinating "Sword of Vengeance" films. Derived from a comic book, *Kozure Ogami/Lone Wolf and Cub,* and directed by his brother, Kenji Misumi, the series is about a disgraced, scowling, seventeenth-century ex-samurai who travels through Japan as an assassin for hire. His companion is his small, big-eyed boy (Masahiro Tomikana), whom he rolls in a baby carriage equipped with

weapons. He is the most honorable of men, yet is willing to use the boy as a decoy, even killing a bad guy who tries to save the youngster from drowning (he was just pretending). The expressionless boy is always present during the tremendous carnage. Some of the bloody fight scenes are incredible. A clever, vicious fighter, Ogami kills one swordsman by leaping over him and pushing his sword directly into his skull . . . and he wasn't even in a worse mood than usual. For American distribution, the first two "Baby Cart" pictures were joined together and re-edited, scored, and dubbed as 1980's *Shogun Assassin.* The third film came to America in 1974 as *Lightning Swords of Death,* which concludes with Ogami shooting, blowing up, and slicing-and-dicing an entire army. He isn't even impressed with himself.

• **Key Films:** *The Sword of Vengeance* (1972, Kenji Misumi), *Baby Cart at the River Styx* (1972, Misumi), *Baby Cart to Hades* (1973, Misumi), *Baby Cart in Peril* (1972, Misumi), *Baby Cart in the Land of the Demons* (1973, Misumi).

○

ANTON WALBROOK (1900–1967) He came from a family of clowns, but this handsome, mustached Austrian projected refined, European elegance in German, French, English, and American pictures. He exhibited grace, charm, and a wry wit as a "master of ceremonies" in French director Max Ophüls's film adaptation of Arthur Schnitzler's play *La Ronde,* introducing several tales of love and infidelity. In Ophüls's *Lola Montès,* he played the small but integral part of the King of Bavaria, risking his kingdom for the love of the title character (Martine Carole), her final hope for love and happiness. In the previous decade, Walbrook also made indelible impressions in the films of English directors Michael Powell and Emeric Pressburger. His most familiar role was the ballet impresario Boris Lermontov in *The Red Shoes*. He acts like a villain, is photographed like a villain, yet his seemingly selfish desire to force Moira Shearer's ballerina Vicky Page to give up her husband and concentrate on dancing actually keeps her doing what she *must* do to be happy—and it's what she wants, too.

• **Cult Favorites:** *The Life and Death of Colonel Blimp* (1943, Michael Powell and Emeric Pressburger), *The Red Shoes* (1948, Powell and Pressburger), *La Ronde* (1950, Max Ophüls), *Lola Montès/The Sins of Lola Montez* (1955, Ophüls).

• **Other Key Films:** *Cinq Gentilshommes Maudits* (1931, Julien Duvivier), *The Soldier and the Lady/Michael Strogoff* (1937, Richard Eichberg), *Victoria the Great* (1937, Herbert Wilcox), *Gaslight/Angel Street* (1940, Thorold Dickinson), *49th Parallel/The Invaders* (1941, Powell and Pressburger), *The Queen of Spades* (1948, Dickinson), *L'Affaire Maurizius* (1954, Duvivier), *Saint Joan* (1957, Otto Preminger), *I Accuse* (1957, Jose Ferrer).

○

CHRISTOPHER WALKEN (1943–) Queens-born film and stage actor, tall, slim, and muscular, with brown-blond hair and a face that is pretty-boy handsome but looks a bit dazed, even crazed. He usually plays men who walk a fine line between sanity and lunacy, or reality and illusion, or good and evil. Several of his characters fall in the wrong direction. He has played frightening men who are insane and/or mean, and dangerous to others and/or themselves. His Russian roulette–playing soldier in

The Deer Hunter and several other characters are suicidal—even his supporting character (Diane Keaton's brother) in *Annie Hall* desires to be in a head-on car crash (which is why poor Woody Allen doesn't have such a comfortable ride with him). Few of his characters fear death; most are capable of killing. Even his good guys don't know when to stop. Walken has never reached the superstardom predicted for him after his Best Supporting Actor Oscar–winning performance in *The Deer Hunter*. But his strong characterizations in *The Dead Zone*, in which he gives a sensitive portrayal of a man who can foresee the horrible future in the best of the Stephen King adaptations; the grim *Pennies from Heaven*, in which he does a dazzling tap routine; and, as Sean Penn's vile father, in *At Close Range*, show that the early plaudits were justified.

• **Cult Favorites:** *Next Stop, Greenwich Village* (1976, Paul Mazursky), *Annie Hall* (1977, Woody Allen), *Roseland* (1977, James Ivory), *The Last Embrace* (1979, Jonathan Demme), *Pennies from Heaven* (1981, Herbert Ross), *Brainstorm* (1983, Douglas Trumbull), *The Dead Zone* (1983, David Cronenberg), *The Comfort of Strangers* (1991, Paul Schrader).

• **Other Key Films:** *The Deer Hunter* (1978, Michael Cimino), *The Dogs of War* (1980, John Irvin), *Heaven's Gate* (1980, Cimino), *A View to a Kill* (1985, John Glen), *At Close Range* (1986, James Foley), *Biloxi Blues* (1988, Mike Nichols), *The Milagro Beanfield War* (1988, Robert Redford).

• **Also of Interest:** *The Anderson Tapes* (1971, Sidney Lumet), *The Happiness Cage/The Mind Snatchers* (1972, Bernard Girard), *Communion* (1989, Philippe Mora), *King of New York* (1990, Abel Ferrara).

○

DEE WALLACE/DEE WALLACE STONE (1949–)
Talented, wholesomely pretty, blue-eyed blonde has played the female lead in a number of popular fantasy and horror films. In *E.T. The Extra-Terrestrial, Cujo,* and *Critters,* she played protective mothers in frightening situations. In *The Howling,* her television newscaster (her best role) has no kids to protect; she herself is the one facing the most danger. Her women are warm and loving but usually have troubles picking men. In *E.T.,* she's divorced; in *Cujo,* she's having an unsatisfying affair; in *The Howling,* her husband fools around and becomes a werewolf. She sighs a lot—life has worn her out. One of our most emotional actresses, she also cries and screams often, sometimes at the same time. She's always on edge, exhibiting controlled hysteria; when there is danger, she goes berserk, although she is resourceful enough and loves her kids enough to overcome most crises. It isn't easy for her to get over shocks—for instance, in *The Howling,* she must get therapy after a werewolf encounter. Because of family obligations and a "Lassie" TV series with husband Christopher Stone, she has cut down on movies in the last few years. A former teacher and dancer, she got her big break playing a prostitute on TV's "Lou Grant"; she subsequently won a part in the film *'10'.*
• **Cult Favorites:** *The Hills Have Eyes* (1977, Wes Craven), *The Howling* (1981, Joe Dante), *Critters* (1986, Stephen Herek).
• **Other Key Films:** *'10'* (1979, Blake Edwards), *E.T. The Extra-Terrestrial* (1982, Steven Spielberg), *Cujo* (1983, Lewis Teague).
• **Also of Interest:** *Secret Admirer* (1985,

David Greenwalt), *Shadow Play* (1986, Susan Shadburne), *Miracle Down Under* (1987, George Miller).

○

M. EMMET WALSH (1935–) Superb, much-in-demand, middle-aged character actor. Heavyset, he comes across as either formidable or the type of fat guy everyone picks on in grade school. His manipulative, slippery, annoyed delivery makes it apparent that he isn't to be trusted. He was Michael Keaton's protective A.A. sponsor in *Clean and Sober,* but more often he plays characters who are extremely unlikable: cowards, mean authority figures, and bullies (Dustin Hoffman's parole officer in *Straight Time,* Harrison Ford's policeman boss in *Blade Runner*), and, preferably, vicious

M. Emmet Walsh is a vicious private eye in Blood Simple.

killers, as in *Blood Simple* and *The Mighty Quinn*. In a part written specifically for him, he had a chance to strut his stuff in *Blood Simple*, playing a slimy Texas private eye who is hired by a bar owner to kill his wife and her lover. He proceeds with his assignment with frightening arrogance, joy, and brutality. Such Walsh characters are the type of amoral, wormy individuals who seize power where law and order don't exist.

• **Cult Favorites:** *Slap Shot* (1977, George Roy Hill), *Straight Time* (1978, Ulu Grosbard), *Blade Runner* (1982, Ridley Scott), *Missing in Action* (1984, Joseph Zito), *Blood Simple* (1985, Joel Coen).

• **Also of Interest:** *The Gambler* (1974, Karel Reisz), *Ordinary People* (1980, Robert Redford), *Cannery Row* (1982, David S. Ward), *Silkwood* (1983, Mike Nichols), *The Best of Times* (1986, Roger Spottiswoode), *Back to School* (1986, Alan Metter), *Critters* (1986, Stephen Herek), *Wildcats* (1986, Michael Ritchie), *Clean and Sober* (1986, Glenn Gordon Caron), *Sunset* (1988, Blake Edwards), *The Mighty Quinn* (1989, Carl Schenkel).

○

DAVID WARNER (1941–) After a small part in *Tom Jones*, this lanky, blond British stage actor caused a stir as the star of *Morgan!* Like other major cult films of the era, it didn't just feature a nonconformist lead character but dealt with nonconformity per se. Morgan is a London artist, and lapsed communist, who is obsessed with getting back Leonie (Vanessa Redgrave). She divorced him because he is hopelessly childish and withdraws from reality, often fantasizing he is a gorilla. Because the film is directed as a comedy, we laugh at Morgan's hazardous pranks involving

knives, explosives, and a kidnapping, and wrongly cheer his devil-may-care behavior. However, Leonie is wise to turn him away although she loves him—for he is truly insane, a serious danger to her and himself. Warner would play other strange but sympathetic characters, most notably his rakish, self-ordained minister in the elegiac western *The Ballad of Cable Hogue*, but with his coltish looks, intense eyes, gruff voice, and strident manner, he would gravitate toward shrewd, sadistic villains, from Nazis to Jack the Ripper in *Time After Time* to Evil in *Time Bandits*.

• **Cult Favorites:** *Morgan!* (1966, Karel Reisz), *The Ballad of Cable Hogue* (1970, Sam Peckinpah), *Straw Dogs* (1971, Peckinpah), *The Omen* (1976, Richard Donner), *Time After Time* (1979, Nicholas Meyer), *Tron* (1982, Steven Lisberger).

• **Sleepers:** *The Sea Gull* (1968, Sidney Lumet), *The Thirty-Nine Steps* (1978, Dan Sharp), *The Company of Wolves* (1985, Neil Jordan).

• **Other Key Films:** *Tom Jones* (1963, Tony Richardson), *The Bofors Gun* (1968, Jack Gold), *The Fixer* (1968, John Frankenheimer), *From Beyond the Grave* (1973, Kevin Connor), *A Doll's House* (1973, Joseph Losey), *The Old Curiosity Shop/Mr. Quilp* (1975, Michael Tuchner), *Providence* (1977, Alain Resnais), *Cross of Iron* (1977, Peckinpah), *The Man with Two Brains* (1983, Carl Reiner).

○

FREDI WASHINGTON (1903–) Perhaps the only actress who couldn't have a movie career because she was too beautiful. She was a black actress decades before blacks would be considered for romantic leads; with her looks and sophistication, no one would be-

Fredi Washington breaking mother Louise Beavers's heart in Imitation of Life.

lieve her as a maid, the only kind of part available at the time—not that she would have taken such parts. She was a former dancer and Broadway star who moved from musicals to the drama *Black Boy,* opposite Paul Robeson. Light-skinned, with green eyes and straight hair, she played an unhappy, haunted black girl who wanted to pass the color line—the type of character she would be known for. In real life, Washington refused to pass as white to further her career. She broke into movies opposite Duke Ellington in the musical short *Black and Tan,* as a fatally ill dancer. In 1933, she played a racially mixed island girl in *Drums in the Night,* and Paul Robeson's sluttish, hot-tempered Harlem girlfriend in *The Emperor Jones*—she wore dark makeup so au-

diences would know she was black. Her major film role came in 1934: the tragic mulatto, Peola, in *Imitation of Life,* a tormented young woman whose determination to pass for white breaks her mother Louise Beavers's heart. Her scenes with Beavers are quite emotional and poignant. She was also in the melodrama-farce *One Mile from Heaven* (billed behind Claire Trevor) as a black raising a white orphan child. Again, her role at least called attention to the position of blacks, specifically light-skinned blacks, in America.

• **Key Films:** *Black and Tan* (1929 short, Dudley Murphy), *The Emperor Jones* (1933, Murphy), *Imitation of Life* (1934, John M. Stahl), *One Mile from Heaven* (1937, Allan Dwan).

JOHN WAYNE (1907–79) An actor of mythic proportions, symbolizing American spirit, grit, and conservative values, he was the preeminent figure of the western and also dominated war films, two-fisted action pictures, and even a few comedies in his 50-year movie career. The 6'4" former Marion Michael Morrison, discovered while playing football at USC, played brave, formidable men who can handle themselves in gunfights, fistfights, or battles. Ideal leaders (as in *Fort Apache, She Wore a Yellow Ribbon, Sands of Iwo Jima*), they understand the opponent, know the logistics of the land, think clearly under pressure, care about the welfare of their men, and won't tolerate cowardice or selfish interests, but understand that mistakes are part of the maturing process. Professionals, they expect everyone to do a good job. They are determined to get impossible tasks done, such as tracking down kidnapped Natalie Wood in Wayne's greatest film, *The Searchers,* driving a cattle herd west in *Red River,* or leading unseasoned soldiers to victory in battle. They *always* speak the truth, are tough but tender and sentimental, are loyal friends or father figures, and are polite and

John Wayne with Ricky Nelson in Rio Bravo.

considerate toward women. One admires Wayne's relationships with Claire Trevor in *Stagecoach,* Gail Russell in *The Angel and the Badman,* Maureen O'Hara in *The Quiet Man* and other pictures, Patricia Neal in *In Harm's Way,* Angie Dickinson in *Rio Bravo,* and Lauren Bacall in *The Shootist,* among many others, because they are mature, sensitive, open, and mutually respectful, with each person holding equal power. Wayne recognizes that women are unique individuals and doesn't want to change or tame them. Exceptionally handsome, he was an excellent romantic lead. Wayne was a fine, much underrated actor, and his characters varied more than critics contended. He could be funny, boisterous, clownish (as in *True Grit*), dignified (his dying gunfighter in *The Shootist*), quiet and innocent (*The Long Voyage Home*). He was heroic, but he could be mean and pigheaded (as in *Red River*), even wrongheaded (his racist Ethan Edwards in *The Searchers*). Some of his characters are extremely complex. Some even die. But like Wayne when he died, they continue to exist in our mythology.

• **Cult Favorites:** *Angel and the Badman* (1947, James Edward Grant), *Three Godfathers* (1948, John Ford), *The Quiet Man* (1952, Ford), *The Conqueror* (1955, Dick Powell), *The Searchers* (1956, Ford), *Jet Pilot* (1957, Josef von Sternberg), *Rio Bravo* (1959, Howard Hawks), *The Man Who Shot Liberty Valance* (1962, Ford), *The Longest Day* (1963, Ken Annakin, Andrew Marton, and Bernhard Wicki), *Donovan's Reef* (1963, Ford), *El Dorado* (1967, Hawks).

• **Sleepers:** *The Long Voyage Home* (1940, Ford), *They Were Expendable* (1945, Ford), *The Shootist* (1976, Don Siegel).

• **Other Key Films:** *The Big Trail* (1930, Raoul Walsh), *The Three Musketeers* (1933 serial, Colbert Clark), *Stagecoach* (1939, Ford), *Dark Command* (1940, Walsh), *Pittsburgh* (1942, Lewis Seiler), *Back to Bataan* (1945, Edward Dmytryk), *Fort Apache* (1948, Ford), *Red River* (1948, Hawks), *She Wore a Yellow Ribbon* (1949, Ford), *Sands of Iwo Jima* (1949, Allan Dwan), *Flying Leathernecks* (1951, Nicholas Ray), *Hondo* (1953, John Farrow), *The Wings of Eagles* (1957, Ford), *The Alamo* (1960, John Wayne), *North to Alaska* (1960, Henry Hathaway), *Hatari!* (1962, Hawks), *McClintock!* (1963, Andrew V. McLaglen), *In Harm's Way* (1965, Otto Preminger), *The War Wagon* (1967, Burt Kennedy), *True Grit* (1969, Hathaway), *Rio Lobo* (1970, Hawks), *The Cowboys* (1972, Mark Rydell).

○

JOHNNY WEISSMULLER (1904–84) The greatest swimmer of all time—he broke 67 world free-style records and won five Olympic gold medals—went on to be the best movie Tarzan, a surprising sex symbol of the thirties, and a hero to young boys, generation after generation. One of my favorite screen moments is in *Tarzan's New York Adventure,* when to escape the police of the "concrete jungle," he dives off the Brooklyn Bridge; when friends try to console Maureen O'Sullivan's Jane, they find that she isn't worried about her husband's safety—like us boys, Jane knew that Weissmuller's Tarzan could survive such a leap and far worse. He was such an invulnerable hero that Weissmuller's death in 1984 was as disconcerting as that of George Reeves, television's Superman. Weissmuller's Tarzan was, at 6'3", barechested, and in a loincloth, very physical. In the course of a day, he flew through the jungle on vines, swam, fought victorious life-and-death battles with lions, crocodiles, and rampaging rhinos, rode elephants to the rescue into pygmy-cannibal villages, and still had enough energy to make love to Jane. Since he was brought up in the jungle, he got away with what other movie heroes weren't allowed—it was obvious that he was *sexually,* not just romantically, attracted to O'Sullivan's sexy Jane, and we knew what went on between the two when the camera left them alone at night, whether in a cave (in *Tarzan, the Ape Man*) or in their elaborate tree house (in *Tarzan's New York Adventure*). In the six best Weissmuller Tarzan films, he is her protector, her teacher about the jungle, her father figure after her father dies, her playmate, friend, and lover. Like her, he is strong, considerate, faithful, and extremely stubborn. And she gives much to him. Their lone conflict arises from the clash between his primitive instincts and her woman's intuition. A great couple, they respect and love each other—he is forgiving, she never has to be because he never makes mistakes. Weissmuller's acting was always criticized, but he was better than the schooled O'Sullivan during silent passages. She said he could have been a *great* silent actor, because his gestures were so natural and his face and eyes were so sensitive and sincere. He does have a silent passage in *Tarzan Escapes* that is very moving, when he falls limp on the ground and cries, thinking Jane has deserted him. O'Sullivan deserted the series and Weissmuller went on to play opposite several other Janes, the best being Brenda Joyce. When he started to look old and flabby in his loincloth next to Johnny Sheffield's Boy, he moved on to his other familiar (and clothed) character, Jungle Jim, in movies and then television.

• **Cult Favorites:** *Tarzan, the Ape Man*

Johnny Weissmuller as Tarzan.

(1932, W. S. Van Dyke), *Tarzan and His Mate* (1934, Cedric Gibbons and, uncredited, Jack Conway).

• **Other Key Films:** *Tarzan Escapes* (1936, Richard Thorpe), *Tarzan Finds a Son!* (1939, Thorpe), *Tarzan's Secret Treasure* (1941, Thorpe), *Tarzan's New York Adventure* (1942, Thorpe), *Jungle Jim* (1948, William Berke).

• **Other Key Films:** *Tarzan Triumphs* (1943, William Thiele), *Tarzan's Desert Mystery* (1943, Thiele), *Tarzan and the Amazons* (1945, Kurt Neumann), *Tarzan and the Leopard Woman* (1946, Neumann), *Tarzan and the Huntress* (1947, Neumann), *Tarzan and the Mermaids* (1948, Robert Florey).

○

RAQUEL WELCH (1940–) The international sex goddess of the sixties and early seventies. Beautiful, shapely, long-haired brunette was a movie superstar before she'd really starred in any movies, due to her shrewd, personally conducted publicity campaign, which included a whirlwind tour of Europe; she wound up on the covers of hundreds of magazines and became a pinup queen. As a teenager, I didn't even like her, but I had a poster of blond Raquel in her revealing two-piece cavewoman outfit from *One Million Years B.C.* She was amusingly bad in Hammer Studios' prehistoric nonsense, tolerable as one of the shrunken scientists in *Fantastic Voyage* (where she is attacked by antibodies, appropriately enough!), and well cast as Lust, tempting Dudley Moore, in *Bedazzled*—but otherwise her perfor-

mances in the sixties were even worse than her films. You listened to her too-strong voice, looked into her empty eyes, and realized she was incapable of showing any feeling for the women she played. In her defense, her prostitutes and other busty babes weren't real people. What made her especially intolerable is that she played the role of star to the hilt, giving less than humble interviews and feuding with actor Jim Brown (despite their interracial, nude sex scene) on *100 Rifles,* actress Mae West on the unwatchable *Myra Breckinridge* (she was so bad that one almost wanted her to switch back to being the pre-op Rex Reed character), and, later, director James Ivory on *The Wild Party,* among others. She got such a bad

Raquel Welch fights off John Richardson in One Million Years B.C.

reputation as an actress that no one noticed when she created her first real character, an unhappy roller-derby queen, and gave a sensitive, perceptive performance (even doing her own difficult stunts!) in *Kansas City Bomber*. Then she further improved her image by doing some funny slapstick and allowing herself to be the butt of jokes in *The Three Musketeers* and *The Four Musketeers*. She got her best reviews and seemed to want to play other challenging parts, but her do-or-die follow-up, *The Wild Party*, died at the box office, and her career stalled.

• **Cult Favorites:** *Fantastic Voyage* (1966, Richard Fleischer), *One Million Years B.C.* (1966, Don Chaffey), *Bedazzled* (1967, Stanley Donen), *The Magic Christian* (1970, Joseph McGrath), *The Three Musketeers* (1974, Richard Lester).

• **Sleeper:** *Kansas City Bomber* (1972, Jerrold Freedman).

• **Other Key Films:** *Fathom* (1967, Leslie H. Martinson), *Bandolero* (1968, Andrew V. McLaglen), *Lady in Cement* (1968, Gordon Douglas), *100 Rifles* (1969, Tom Gries), *Myra Breckinridge* (1970, Michael Sarne), *Hannie Calder* (1971, Burt Kennedy), *The Four Musketeers* (1975, Lester), *The Wild Party* (1975, James Ivory).

• **Also of Interest:** *A House Is Not a Home* (1964, Russell Rouse), *Flare Up* (1969, James Neilson), *Fuzz* (1972, Richard A. Colla), *Bluebeard* (1972, Edward Dmytryk), *The Last of Sheila* (1973, Herbert Ross), *Mother, Jugs and Speed* (1976, Peter Yates), *The Prince and the Pauper* (1977, Fleischer).

○

TUESDAY WELD (1943–) An original talent, with beauty, wit, and exciting sex appeal. This energetic, long-haired blonde has a slim, shapely, squeezable body; a baby-doll face with large, animated eyes, sensuous lips, and a broad smile that reveals dimples and large, slightly spaced, pearly white teeth; and a distinct, seductive, I-want-something, self-pitying delivery. She has never gotten the roles she deserves (reportedly, she rejected *Lolita* and, pregnant, couldn't do *Bonnie and Clyde*), but has been the crush of millions of males since the fifties. In dramas like *The Cincinnati Kid,* where she is touching and vulnerable, she usually has a rough go of it, but in comedies, where Weld thrives, her emotional sex kittens usually succeed quite easily. In her debut, *Rock, Rock, Rock!,* Weld was barely a teenager but already scheming to get enough money to buy a strapless gown and go to the prom with Tommy. In her much-remembered role as teenager Thalia Menninger on the TV series "The Many Loves of Dobie Gillis," she loves Dobie, but won't be his until he (a high school student) can figure out how to make enough money to support her (and her family) for the rest of his life. Thalia is the prototypical Weld role. In their search for expensive clothes, money, position in society, and freedom, her many young women use their bodies to manipulate weak men into giving them what they desire. In the absurd, often tasteless *Lord Love a Duck,* she puts both her principal and her father(!) under her spell by fondling herself and almost swooning in her lemon-meringue, papaya-surprise, and periwinkle-pussycat cashmere sweaters. Male viewers understood why Dobie Gillis, Anthony Perkins in the dark comedy *Pretty Poison* (in which Weld's unforgettable teenage "Bad Seed" coldly shoots her interfering mother), and all those other men try to satisfy her greedy, egocentric young women. Weld just gets so excited

Tuesday Weld (right) *with Ruth Gordon and Roddy McDowell in* Lord Love a Duck.

talking about getting what she wants, as if she were a youngster anticipating Christmas—her eyes light up, she laughs, squeals, rubs her body against the men— that the young men don't want to let her down (especially since the physical rewards will be great). In her early films, Weld's women try to destroy men; later they become self-destructive (her gangster's moll in *Once Upon a Time in America* is a masochist). They are confused, troubled, and resigned to a life that is not full of happiness—it is as if the young Weld has come down to earth.

• **Cult Favorites:** *Sex Kittens Go to College* (1960, Albert Zugsmith), *Lord Love a Duck* (1966, George Axelrod), *Pretty Poison* (1968, Noel Black), *A Safe Place* (1971, Henry Jaglom), *Who'll Stop the Rain?* (1978, Karel Reisz), *Thief* (1981, Michael Mann), *Once Upon a Time in America* (1984, Sergio Leone).

• **Sleepers:** *Wild in the Country* (1961, Philip Dunne), *Soldier in the Rain* (1963, Ralph Nelson).

• **Other Key Films:** *Rock, Rock, Rock!* (1956, Will Price), *Rally 'Round the Flag, Boys!* (1958, Leo McCarey), *The Private Lives of Adam and Eve* (1961, Zugsmith and Mickey Rooney), *Bachelor Flat* (1962, Frank Tashlin), *The Cincinnati Kid* (1965, Norman Jewison), *I Walk the Line* (1970, John Frankenheimer), *Play It As It Lays* (1972, Frank Perry), *Looking for Mr. Goodbar* (1977, Richard Brooks), *Serial* (1980, Bill Persky), *Author! Author!* (1982, Arthur Hiller), *Heartbreak Hotel* (1988, Chris Columbus).

PETER WELLER (1947–) He was well cast as Diane Keaton's lover in *Shoot the Moon*, an almost likable presence until he viciously beats up her husband, Albert Finney, and as Teri Garr's instantly unsympathetic boyfriend in *Firstborn*. However, he has generally played heroic parts and given less compelling performances in science-fiction, horror, and action films. He is cool and handsome but stone-faced and humorless, and with his slight build, has little physical presence. In those roles that call for dynamism, like the title character in *The Adventures of Buckaroo Bonzai*, he fails to deliver; in that film Bonzai himself is less captivating than any of his buckaroos. It's no compliment to say that he's better cast as emotionless characters, such as his half-human *RoboCop*. In that surprise hit, he has physical presence because of his gigantic machine garb. No one is upset when he is transformed after his body is destroyed, because he wasn't much different beforehand.

• **Cult Favorites:** *Shoot the Moon* (1982, Alan Parker), *The Adventures of Buckaroo*

Peter Weller is RoboCop.

Bonzai Across the Eighth Dimension (1984, W. D. Richter), *RoboCop* (1987, Paul Verhoeven).

• **Also of Interest:** *Just Tell Me What You Want* (1980, Sidney Lumet), *Of Unknown Origin* (1983, George Pan Cosmatos), *Firstborn* (1984, Michael Apted), *Shakedown* (1988, James Glickenhaus), *Leviathan* (1989, Cosmatos), *RoboCop II* (1990, Irvin Kershner).

○

JENNIFER WELLES Blond, slightly overweight porno star from the mid- to late seventies, who gave way to more vivacious and younger actresses. Her acting was limited and her tiresome star vehicles had limp, convoluted plots. Many people who say that porno films bore them after fifteen minutes must have seen those starring Jennifer Welles. Still, she had many fans—maybe because she promoted herself as a star.

• **Key Film:** *Inside Jennifer Welles* (1977, Howard A. Howard).

• **Some Other Films:** *Honeypie* (1974, Howard Ziehm), *Little Orphan Sammy* (1975, Arlo Schiffin), *Expose Me Lovely* (1976, Armond Weston), *Sweetcakes* (1976, Hans Johnson), *The Little Blue Box* (1978, Schiffin), *Temptations, Thunderbuns.*

○

MEL WELLES Since the mid-fifties, character actor (and later director—e.g., of Sarah Bay in *Lady Frankenstein*) of bargain-basement comedies (Abbott and Costello, the Bowery Boys), teen-music, horror, and science-fiction films. He has appeared in a number of films written by Charles B. Griffith, most of them for producer-director

Roger Corman. His characters have typically been unlikable. He was Blackbeard in Huntz Hall's dream in *Hold That Hypnotist,* and a repulsive, lecherous innkeeper in Michael Reeves's first film, *She-Beast,* starring Barbara Steele. His most memorable performance was in the Corman-Griffith witty black comedy, *The Little Shop of Horrors.* He was hilarious, perhaps parodying a Yiddish-theater actor, as a greedy skid-row florist, Gravis Mushnick, whose store does great business when his young employee (Jonathan Haze) nurtures a gigantic, blood-drinking alien plant. He has done voice-overs on countless projects.

• **Cult Favorites:** *The Little Shop of Horrors* (1960, Roger Corman), *The She-Beast* (1974, Michael Reeves).

• **Sleeper:** *Dr. Heckyl and Mr. Hype* (1980, Charles B. Griffith).

• **Also of Interest:** *Abbott and Costello Meet the Mummy* (1955, Charles Lamont), *The Undead* (1956, Corman), *Hold That Hypnotist* (1957, Austin Jewell), *Rock All Night* (1957, Corman), *Attack of the Crab Monsters* (1957, Corman).

○

ORSON WELLES (1915–88) His achievements as a director are so staggering that his acting talent has always been underestimated. Even before he put on an obscene amount of weight, he was an imposing figure—dominating *The Third Man* although he had little screen time—with a deep, powerful, clear, mesmerizing voice that made movie-goers *listen* for a change (which is why he was asked to narrate many films). He had magician's eyes, sometimes sparkling, sometimes spooky, and rarely focused them directly at other characters, leaving them unable to tell when he was deceiving them. He was a moral director who played amoral villains. His Charles Foster Kane, Nazi killer in *The Stranger*, Harry Lime in *The Third Man*, *Macbeth*, *Mr. Arkadin*, and police detective Hank Quinlan in *Touch of Evil* all have greatness in them, but they take short cuts to power and sell their souls; to maintain their lofty, lonely positions, they must continue to be corrupt, brutal, unsentimental, arrogant, even criminal. Their idealism has given way to ruthlessness. These men have betrayed those who loved them, and many of the films ultimately are about whether those they have betrayed will now betray them or remain loyal. Those who do turn against Welles's characters won't regret their decisions, but always will suffer guilt. In *Chimes at Midnight*, featuring Welles's greatest performance, the tables are turned, and his fat, cowardly, bawdy, undignified but goodhearted Falstaff, who has always loved and cared for Prince Hal (Keith Baxter), is discarded by the young man once he becomes king. Falstaff dies of a broken heart. Friendship was sacred to Welles, which is why Hal's act is so despicable. And I believe Welles regarded it as personal, for Falstaff is surely the character closest to the real Welles. Falstaff is a victim (much like Charles Foster Kane, after everyone deserts him), and I believe Hal was meant to represent one of the young talents Welles nurtured along, only to watch them move to the top of show biz and pretend they never knew him.

• **Cult Favorites:** *Citizen Kane* (1941, Orson Welles), *The Lady from Shanghai* (1948, Welles), *The Third Man* (1949, Carol Reed), *Touch of Evil* (1958, Welles), *The Trial* (1963, Welles), *Chimes at Midnight/Falstaff* (1966, Welles), *Casino Royale* (1967, John Huston, Ken Hughes, Robert Parrish, Joe McGrath, and Val Guest), *Start the Revolution Without Me* (1969, Bud Yorkin), *Catch 22* (1970, Mike Nichols), *Butterfly* (1981, Matt Cimber).

• **Other Key Films:** *Journey into Fear* (1942, Norman Foster and, uncredited, Welles), *Jane Eyre* (1944, Robert Stevenson), *The Stranger* (1946, Welles), *Prince of Foxes* (1948, Henry King), *Black Magic* (1949, Gregory Ratoff and, uncredited, Welles), *Othello* (1952, Welles), *Mr. Arkadin/Confidential Report* (1955, Welles), *Moby Dick* (1956, Huston), *Man in the Shadow* (1957, Jack Arnold), *The Long Hot Summer* (1957, Martin Ritt), *The Roots of Heaven* (1958, Welles), *Compulsion* (1959, Richard Fleischer), *Crack in the Mirror* (1960, Fleischer), *A Man for All Seasons* (1966, Fred Zinnemann), *The Kremlin Letter* (1969, Huston), *The Immortal Story* (1969, Welles), *A Safe Place* (1971, Henry Jaglom), *F for Fake* (1975, Welles and François Reichenbach), *Voyage of the Damned* (1976, Stuart Rosenberg).

○

OSKAR WERNER (1922–84) Blond, boyish-looking, Austrian-born leading man starred in films of several countries, beginning in the late forties. In the mid-fifties, he had a small part in Max Ophüls's final film, *Lola Montès*, playing a student who has a fling with the heroine and recognizes, with admiration, that she "represents love and liberty." He would continue to play romantic men who perceive poetic, noble, or life-affirming qualities in beautiful women. They are intelligent men but need women to stimulate their senses and reveal the treasures of life (for instance, Julie Christie introduces him to books in *Fahrenheit 451*). They give women the physical love and warmth they need, then are willing to allow them their need for

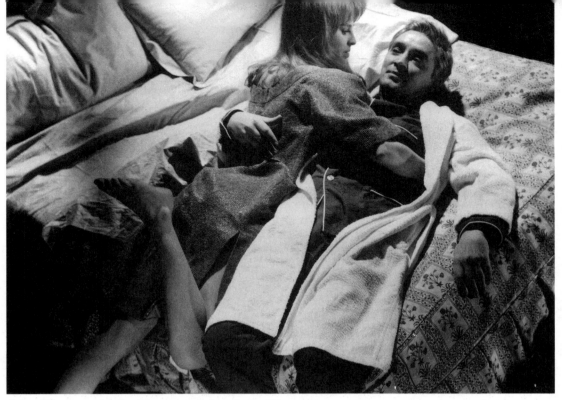

Oskar Werner and Julie Christie in Fahrenheit 451.

freedom without taking it as a personal slight. In *Jules and Jim,* the picture that made Werner familiar to moviegoers worldwide, his Jules tolerates his wife, Catherine (Jeanne Moreau), periodically leaving him to have affairs, including one with his best friend, Jim (Henri Serre). He doesn't want to tie her down because he loves that she is a free spirit. A romantic held down by practicality (he's a scientist), he feeds off her reckless, liberated lifestyle, which ends in suicide, content to be pawn to her queen. Women all over the world were enchanted by Werner's intellect, handsome face, sensitivity, talent, and distinguished accent, and he decided to take a crack at being a Hollywood-style romantic lead in the early sixties. A disappointed Truffaut says Werner's acting was no longer natural when they made

Fahrenheit 451. After a few more English-speaking films, he returned to the stage. There had been rumors of fights with directors and of heavy drinking. *Voyage of the Damned* was a one-shot attempt at a movie comeback. He and Truffaut died only a day apart.

• **Cult Favorites:** *Lola Montès/The Sins of Lola Montez* (1955, Max Ophüls), *Jules and Jim* (1962, François Truffaut), *Fahrenheit 451* (1966, Truffaut).

• **Other Key Films:** *Eroica (The Beethoven Story)* (1949, Walter Kolm-Veltée), *Decision Before Dawn* (1951, Anatole Litvak), *The Last Ten Days* (1955, G. W. Pabst), *Ship of Fools* (1965, Stanley Kramer), *Voyage of the Damned* (1976, Stuart Rosenberg).

• **Also of Interest:** *Angel with the Trumpet* (1949, Anthony Bushell), *The Spy Who*

Came in from the Cold (1965, Martin Ritt), *Interlude* (1968, Kevin Billington), *The Shoes of the Fisherman* (1968, Michael Anderson).

○

MAE WEST (1893–1980) After scandalizing Broadway by writing, producing, directing, and starring in such plays as *Sex* (for which she was jailed for 10 days on obscenity charges), *Diamond Lil,* and *The Pleasure Man,* this outrageous, bosomy blond performer strutted her way into the cinema and, as she moved into her forties, entertained and shocked a nation. Beginning with *Night After Night,* in which she excited George Raft, and then in her first starring vehicles, *She Done Him Wrong* (an adaptation of *Diamond Lil*) and *I'm No Angel* (her best film), playing opposite newcomer Cary Grant in both, she showcased her self-assured and uninhibited pre–Legion of Decency brand of sexuality. She let fly with witty double entendres, usually related to her own sexual prowess, and displayed a brazen sex-is-fun, sex-is-exciting, sex-is-necessary attitude that only Jean Harlow openly shared. At times she looks so overweight and ridiculous in

Mae West and W. C. Fields in My Little Chickadee.

her films, strapped into her tight garments and swathed in feathers, furs, and diamonds, that today it's hard to believe she was a leading lady and sex symbol. But a second later, she is mysteriously seductive as she bats her dark lashes over her blue eyes, raises her eyebrows, slightly opens her sensual mouth, grins knowingly, swings out a hip, and in her familiar husky, purring Brooklyn accent says something women are supposedly too shy to say. Her sex appeal was definitely the result of her attitude and her willingness to be outrageous. While she certainly made a contribution as a living endorsement for the enjoyment of sex, equally important was that she was one of the few actresses in film history (Katharine Hepburn and Ruth Gordon were others) who championed nonconformity in their films (she played *herself*), a domain usually reserved for rebel actors. Her characters know that society disapproves of them, but they never change to suit the stuffed shirts who refuse to recognize that these women aren't harming anyone with their sexual exploits (West *never* steals another woman's man) and, in fact, are making a lot of men happy. *My Little Chickadee* was a disappointment, but it was inspiring to team West with W. C. Fields because both always played flamboyant, conceited, and boastful nonconformists. Both had a way with words (and much-mimicked deliveries); a unique way of looking at a cockeyed world run by bluenoses; and, to maintain their independence, were resigned to endure public scorn and punishment for breaking society's rules. When West laughs at herself, she is recognizing the irony that she, a tiny, solitary blonde without protection or power, only benevolent sexual allure, is taken so seriously by society that it actually considers her a

threat. But the prigs were correct: West forever changed attitudes toward sex, for both participants and aghast onlookers.

• **Cult Favorites:** *She Done Him Wrong* (1933, Lowell Sherman), *I'm No Angel* (1933, Wesley Ruggles), *My Little Chickadee* (1940, Edward Sutherland), *Sextette* (1978, Ken Hughes).

• **Other Key Films:** *Belle of the Nineties* (1934, Leo McCarey), *Goin' to Town* (1935, Alexander Hall), *Klondike Annie* (1936, Raoul Walsh), *Every Day's a Holiday* (1938, Sutherland).

• **Also of Interest:** *Night After Night* (1932, Archie Mayo), *The Heat's On* (1943, Gregory Ratoff), *Myra Breckinridge* (1970, Michael Sarne).

○

PEARL WHITE (1889–1938) The most famous of all serial heroines and, for a few of her 10 years of stardom (1913–1923), the most popular of all silent movie actresses, including Mary Pickford. She was a bareback rider in a circus before she signed her first film contract, and then knocked about for a few years before she was cast in what would become the most well-known serial of them all, *The Perils of Pauline*. White told everyone in the movie business that she was 24, but after her death her father claimed she was actually born in 1897 and was just 16 when she made the star-making serial. Pauline is a pretty young woman who wants to spend a year pursuing her writing ambition and adventure before agreeing to marry handsome Crane Wilbur. Villain Paul Panzer realizes that for him to inherit the fortune left by Pauline's stepfather, he must kill her, preferably before she marries and produces another heir. In chapter after chapter (*not* all of them cliffhangers), the fair-haired heroine finds herself in great danger, mostly initiated by Panzer. White thus established the formula that would prevail in her later serials: the pacing would be slow and deliberate and the emphasis would be less on action than on the enormity of the dangers that were created for her. The excitement would come from watching White, who did almost all of her own stunts, save herself—or be saved by Wilbur or other heroes—from sure death. Her characters were quite appealing, not only because of White's natural beauty (she had fabulous eyes) but because her characters were calm in the face of danger, not only willing to take chances but able to survive all obstacles. Off-camera, White also took part in daredevil publicity stunts. In 1923, she retired and moved permanently to Paris, suffering from a spinal injury that occurred either during her stint in the circus or while she was making her first serial, and from failing eyesight due to years under movie lights.

• **Cult Favorite:** *The Perils of Pauline* (1914 serial, Donald MacKenzie).

• **Other Key Films:** *The Exploits of Elaine* (1914 serial), *The New Exploits of Elaine* (1915 serial), *The Iron Claw* (1916 serial), *Pearl of the Army* (1916 serial), *The Fatal Ring* (1917 serial), *The Black Secret* (1919 serial), *The Lightning Rider* (1919 serial), *Plunder* (1923 serial).

○

GENE WILDER (1935–) He has an appropriate name—there are few wilder comic actors. With curly, out-of-control hair, expressive eyes, and the odd but affable face of a court jester, he has played an assortment of eccentrics and other strange men, almost all with loony streaks. They do outrageous things: in *The Producers,* his timid accountant (who has "crazy spells") and a fellow Jew, Zero Mostel, produce a musical (which they hope will fail) glorifying Hitler; his sadistic nobleman in *Start the Revolution Without Me* carries an obviously dead falcon on his arm; his sweet nonconformist in *Quackser Fortune Has a Cousin in the Bronx* makes a living following horses around Dublin and collecting manure for fertilizer; his respectable character in *Everything You've Always Wanted to Know About Sex (But Were Afraid to Ask)* falls madly in love with a sheep; his mad scientist in *Young Frankenstein* creates a monster; his Polish rabbi, perhaps his best performance, in *The Frisco Kid* travels across the Wild West. Good or bad (or good but seemingly bad in his most chancy role, a confectioner in *Willy Wonka and the Chocolate Factory*), his characters dance to their own drummers. But they are funniest when Wilder can play off other funny actors or actresses. Certainly, he and Richard Pryor have worked well together in *Silver Streak, Stir Crazy,* and *See No Evil, Hear No Evil,* because they take turns as straight men, and each allows the other to exhibit his own brand of lunacy (plus these black and white screen partners obviously like each other). Wilder has also been funny playing off Zero Mostel, Teri Garr, Cleavon Little, Peter Boyle, Harrison Ford, and many others—he just needs somebody with a sense of humor. He is quite funny talking quietly, enunciating every word in a patronizing manner, and trying to stay levelheaded when someone has just done or said something he considers stupid. Eventually he explodes and has very loud and animated tantrums, which are quite amusing. But this isn't to say he is predictable. You are never exactly sure how he will respond to something, so it's more comforting when he goes berserk

Gene Wilder in Willy Wonka and the Chocolate Factory.

than when he keeps everything inside and continues to speak softly, clearly, and without emotion, which is what he does until the end of *Willy Wonka and the Chocolate Factory.* Some of Wilder's work bordered on genius early in his career; since then, mostly in films he wrote and directed, his work has been erratic. He dropped temporarily out of films to be with his wife, Gilda Radner, who was dying of cancer.

• **Cult Favorites:** *Bonnie and Clyde* (1967, Arthur Penn), *The Producers* (1968, Mel Brooks), *Start the Revolution Without Me* (1970, Bud Yorkin), *Quackser Fortune Has a Cousin in the Bronx* (1970, Waris Hussein), *Willy Wonka and the Chocolate Factory* (1971, Mel Stuart), *Everything You've Always Wanted to Know About Sex (But Were Afraid to Ask)* (1972, Woody Allen), *Blazing Saddles* (1974, Brooks), *Young Frankenstein* (1974, Brooks).

• **Sleeper:** *The Frisco Kid* (1979, Robert Aldrich).

• **Other Key Films:** *The Adventures of Sherlock Holmes' Smarter Brother* (1975, Gene Wilder), *Silver Streak* (1976, Arthur Hiller), *The World's Greatest Lover* (1977, Wilder), *Stir Crazy* (1980, Sidney Poitier), *The Woman in Red* (1984, Wilder), *See No Evil, Hear No Evil* (1989, Hiller).

○

DAWN WILDSMITH The sexy wife of Z-budget director Fred Olen Ray. She rarely has a major role in his awful action, science-fiction, and horror films, which, considering their quality, may be a nice gesture on Ray's part. So if you want to see what a bad—but forgivably so—actress Wild-smith is, you may have to track down the absurd beach film *Surf Nazis Must Die,* a video hit which Ray didn't direct. A favorite of bad horror movie fans—although I think her name is more familiar than her face.

• **Cult Favorite:** *Surf Nazis Must Die* (1987, Peter George).

• **Other Sample Films:** *The Phantom Empire* (1987, Fred Olen Ray), *Beverly Hills Vamp* (1988, Ray), *It's Alive III: Island of the Alive* (1988, Larry Cohen), *Star Slammer* (1988, Ray), *Terminal Force.*

○

JUNE WILKINSON (1941–) British-born blond starlet of the late fifties and sixties and, according to a 1967 magazine, "one of three contenders in Hollywood's sex symbol sweepstakes, along with Raquel Welch and Ursula Andress." She lost. Wilkinson got a lot of press because of her 43-22-37 figure, and posed nude for a lot of girlie magazines; she had financially, if not critically, successful tours with *Pajama Tops* and *Any Wednesday,* but got nowhere in her movie career. The public already had Jayne Mansfield, and even she was passé at this time. The best Wilkinson could do was go bosom-to-bosom with Mamie Van Doren in a couple of silly sex comedies, including the much-publicized *The Private Lives of Adam and Eve,* with Mickey Rooney.

• **Cult Favorite:** *The Private Lives of Adam and Eve* (1959, Albert Zugsmith and Mickey Rooney).

• **Also of Interest:** *Career Girl* (1959, Harold David), *Twist All Night* (1961, William Hole, Jr.), *The Playgirls and the Bellboy* (1958/62, Fritz Umgelter and Francis Ford Coppola), *The Candidate/ Playmates for the Candidate* (1964, Robert

Angus), *Sno-Line* (1984, Douglas F. O'Neons).

○

BILLY DEE WILLIAMS (1937–) That this gifted, intelligent, suave, mustached actor, so handsome and masculine that he has been billed as the "black Clark Gable," hasn't been offered significant film roles is living proof of the industry's unwillingness to produce films featuring black romantic leads, and its refusal to consider blacks for leads in scripts that are not specifically designated for blacks. After work in the theater and on television, Williams shot into the limelight with a sensitive portrayal of the Chicago Bears' star running back Gale Sayers in the award-winning made-for-TV movie *Brian's Song,* with James Caan matching him as Sayers's best friend, dying teammate Brian Piccolo. He then played opposite Diana Ross in her two features, *Lady Sings the Blues* and *Mahogany,* establishing himself, as Donald Bogle asserts, as "the screen's first authentic black romantic leading man, a real lover." Adored by females of all races and admired by men, Williams's men are cool, confident, and calm; rather than being aggressive in their pursuit of women, they are polite, gently seductive, even gallant, like modern-day Sir Walter Raleighs. They have tempers but are capable of keeping them under control, and though they won't back down in an argument with women even if they will lose, they are caring and supportive; they are smart and sophisticated, men of taste and good breeding. Writes Bogle: "Some might prefer minimizing Williams's importance in American films. But in the world of pop images, his was a new one, filling a void that had in the past rendered black men asexual or incapable of romance. His was a mature black male, perhaps dreamy and idealized but a clear mark in an evolutionary line of heroic black male images." Other than a funny, often joyous, insightful performance as a black baseball star in *The Bingo Long Traveling All-Stars and Motor Kings,* and an engaging performance as Sylvester Stallone's detective partner in *Nighthawks,* Williams hasn't had many worthwhile parts. George Lucas should be commended for giving him the chance to get some deserved fame by casting him as Lando Calrissian in the second and third "Star Wars" films, but his character was pretty much wasted. Ironically, Williams has recently been seen to best effect as a virile, suave ladies' man in a series of liquor commercials—playing himself.

• **Cult Favorite:** *The Bingo Long Traveling All-Stars and Motor Kings* (1976, John Badham).

• **Other Key Films:** *Lady Sings the Blues* (1972, Sidney J. Furie), *The Hit!* (1973, Furie), *Mahogany* (1975, Berry Gordy), *The Empire Strikes Back* (1980, Irvin Kershner), *Nighthawks* (1981, Bruce Malmuth).

• **Also of Interest:** *The Last Angry Man* (1959, Daniel Mann), *The Out-of-Towners* (1970, Arthur Hiller), *Marvin and Tige* (1982, Eric Weston), *Return of the Jedi* (1983, Richard Marquand), *Fear City* (1984, Abel Ferrara), *Deadly Illusion* (1987, William Tannen and Larry Cohen).

○

CINDY WILLIAMS (1947–) Before her movie career was sidelined for several years while she found fame on television's successful "Laverne and Shirley," this cute, dimpled, bouncy, dark-haired actress played sexy, innocent-faced teenagers and young women in a number of offbeat, low-budget projects. She was sweet, romantic, and quite wonderful, much like the few girls we remember with fondness from high school, in *American Graffiti,* worried that boyfriend Ron Howard will graduate and forget her. It was this movie role (and especially her dance with Howard to the Platters' "Smoke Gets in Your Eyes") for which she'll always be remembered. Then she turned around and surprised us—and eavesdropper Gene Hackman (who assumes she's the one in trouble)—as a young woman planning a murder in *The Conversation.* She refused to do nudity in *The First Nudie Musical,* but was her usual adorable, spunky, funny, wisecracking, *naughty*-girl-next-door self, singing and saying dirty lines while smiling. Back for an occasional film since her television series ended, she still seeks zany projects.

• **Cult Favorites:** *Drive, He Said* (1971, Jack Nicholson), *American Graffiti* (1973, George Lucas), *The Conversation* (1974, Francis Ford Coppola), *The First Nudie Musical* (1976, Mark Haggard and Bruce Kimmel), *UFOria* (1980/86, John Binder).

• **Also of Interest:** *Gas-s-s-s* (1970, Roger Corman), *Travels with My Aunt* (1972, George Cukor), *Mr. Ricco* (1975, Paul Bogart), *More American Graffiti* (1979, B. W. L. Norton).

○

EDY WILLIAMS Publicity-chasing sexpot who shows up each year at Cannes to strip for photographers. Big-breasted and shapely, she married Russ Meyer, who then put her in *Beyond the Valley of the Dolls* as porno star Ashley St. Ives, a sexual vulture who likes to make love anywhere but a bed. He promised to cast her as other aggressive sluts and to make her a star. He did neither. They divorced. Her career has gone nowhere, possibly because she has, in her search for fame, become a semi-joke.

• **Cult Favorites:** *The Naked Kiss* (1964, Samuel Fuller), *Beyond the Valley of the Dolls* (1970, Russ Meyer).

• **Also of Interest:** *The Pad and How to Use It* (1966, Brian Hutton), *Good Times* (1967, William Friedkin), *The Secret Life of an American Wife* (1968, George Axelrod), *The Seven Minutes* (1971, Meyer), *Hellhole* (1985, Pierre de Moro).

○

ESTHER WILLIAMS (1923–) The cleanest act in Hollywood. A former freestyle swimming champion (one forgets she was a world-record holder at 100 and 220 meters) and performer in Billy Rose's Aquacade, she became an enormous star at M-G-M in the forties and fifties in poolside musical comedies and romances. "Hollywood's Mermaid" couldn't sing (she was dubbed) and, though she tried, couldn't really dance or act, but she could swim and looked fetching in a bathing suit, so the studio came up with projects that emphasized her strong points. She played swimmers, bathing-suit designers, actress-swimmers, women who lived near water and invariably took swims. And not ordinary plunges, but spectacular, often Busby Berkeley–choreographed extravaganzas, with underwater cameras, an orchestra playing, elaborate waterworks, and maybe a hundred lovelies sharing the pool, all smiling and swimming in synch, parting to let the "Queen of the Surf" swim directly toward the camera. I liked her best as a baseball club owner opposite Gene Kelly in *Take Me Out to the Ball Game,* in which she swam only once, but her legions preferred her around the pool.

(In the 1987 Yugoslavian nostalgia piece *Hey Babu Riba,* friends from the fifties reflect back to when they were obsessed with Williams in *Bathing Beauty*.) Williams definitely had appeal: she was pretty, cheerful, likable, and healthy. But she had that water-proofed, painted-on grin of today's synchronized swimmers; not surprisingly, today, Williams is that stupid event's most famous spokesperson.

• **Key Films:** *Bathing Beauty* (1944, George Sidney), *Thrill of a Romance* (1945, Richard Thorpe), *Easy to Wed* (1946, Edward Buzzell), *Fiesta* (1947, Thorpe), *This Time for Keeps* (1947, Thorpe), *On an Island with You* (1948, Thorpe), *Take Me Out to the Ball Game* (1949, Busby Berkeley), *Neptune's Daughter* (1949, Buzzell), *Duchess of Idaho* (1950, Robert Z. Leonard), *Pagan Love Song* (1950, Robert Alton), *Skirts Ahoy!* (1952, Sidney Lanfield), *Million Dollar Mermaid* (1952, Mervyn LeRoy), *Dangerous When Wet* (1953, Charles Walters), *Easy to Love* (1953, Walters), *Jupiter's Darling* (1955, George Sidney).

• **Also of Interest:** *Andy Hardy's Double Life* (1942, George B. Seitz), *A Guy Named Joe* (1943, Victor Fleming), *Ziegfeld Follies* (1946, Vincente Minnelli), *The Hoodlum Saint* (1946, Norman Taurog), *The Unguarded Moment* (1956, Harry Keller), *Raw Wind of Eden* (1958, Richard Wilson), *The Big Show* (1960, James B. Clark).

○

FRED WILLIAMSON (1938–) "The Hammer" was a defensive back in the NFL and AFL before becoming an actor, debuting in Robert Altman's *M*A*S*H,* which concludes with a football game. After another supporting role in Otto Preminger's *Tell Me That You Love Me, Junie Moon,* he left the mainstream cinema, toughened his screen persona, and became a star of the black exploitation cinema. On occasion he played villains, like his ruthless gangster in *Black Caesar* and its sequel, *Hell Up in Harlem,* but more often he was the "buck" hero: a boxer, a loner who battles the mafia, or, in "Nigger Charley" westerns, a former slave. Handsome and brawny, at 6'2" and 210 pounds, he was a solid action star—smooth, hip, violent, virile, and humorous, not averse to self-parody. He was, according to Donald Bogle, "a sleazily likable rogue." Comparing Williamson favorably to his occasional screen partner, Jim Brown, Bogle contended that he "learned to communicate thought on screen; his physical feats seemed to grow out of the workings of his mind." Williamson may have been underrated, as Bogle suggests, but his seventies films—with few exceptions, like *Three Tough Guys, Black Eye,* and *Three the Hard Way*—were pretty intolerable and, even in terms of the genre, not that important. Even though most of his later films have been rubbish, he has maintained a career the hard way, sometimes going to Italy, starring in (writing, directing, and producing in some cases) westerns and black exploitation films long after such films had gone out of style.

• **Key Films:** *The Legend of Nigger Charley* (1972, Martin Goldman), *Hammer* (1972, Bruce Clark), *Black Caesar* (1973, Larry Cohen), *The Soul of Nigger Charley* (1973, Larry G. Spangler), *That Man Bolt* (1973, Henry Levin and David Lowell Rich), *Hell Up in Harlem* (1973, Cohen), *Black Eye* (1974, Jack Arnold), *Three the Hard Way* (1974, Gordon Parks, Jr.), *Take a Hard Ride* (1975, Anthony M. Dawson), *Adios Amigo* (1975, Fred Williamson), *Meet Johnny Barrows* (1976, Williamson), *Vigi-*

lante (1982, William Lustig), *The Last Fight* (1983, Williamson), *The Big Score* (1983, Williamson), *One Down, Two to Go* (1983, Williamson), *The Messenger* (1987, Williamson).

○

MARLENE WILLOUGHBY Very slim, black-haired, half-Polish, half-Italian exotic dancer and porno star. She played Fidel Castro in an off-Broadway production of *Che,* the role Jack Palance had in the movie. She began making hard-core sex films in the seventies, eventually appearing in over 200, from the erotic to the raunchy to the kinky. She was best in humorous sex films, but since her tongue was in her cheek even in dramatic films, she probably didn't take her movie career too seriously. She wasn't strong enough to carry a picture by herself, and usually was just one of several female stars in vignette films. Nonetheless, she is well known; for a time a columnist for one of the New York dailies repeatedly inserted news items about Willoughby and referred to her as "The Queen of Porno Films." Smart and funny, she has long been an advocate for sexual freedom.

• **Key Films:** *Marlene's World* (1977, Mister Mustard), *Fiona on Fire* (1978, Warren Evans), *Damiano's People* (1979, Gerard Damiano), *The Pink Ladies* (1980, Richard Mahler), *Sunny* (1980, Evans), *Outlaw Ladies* (1981, Henri Pachard), *The Tiffany Minx* (1981, Robert Walters), *Foxtrot* (1982, Cecil Howard).

• **Some Other Titles:** *The Fur Trap* (1973), *Inside Jennifer Welles* (1977, Howard A. Howard), *Angels in Distress* (Joseph Scarpelli), *The Trouble with Young Stuff, Venture into the Bizarre, Mistress Electra*

(1983), *Backdoor Girls* (1983), *Nasty Girls* (1983).

○

DOOLEY WILSON (1894–1953) A former minstrel show, vaudeville, and nightclub performer, he was a singing drummer, not a pianist, but he'll always be remembered at the keyboard as Sam, Bogart's friend and piano player, in *Casablanca*. No true movie fan will forget his rendition of the poignant "As Time Goes By" upon Bogart's request, as the tough guy's sentimentality returns. In Murray Burnett and Joan Alison's un-produced play, *Everybody Goes to Rick's*, Sam is just a performer, a wild African who is weirdly dressed and decked out in native jewelry. Wilson's Sam isn't native to Africa (he'd been with Bogart in Paris), wears a suit, and is quiet and dignified. Wilson would continue to play polite, smart, soft-spoken men throughout his career, but his choice of roles was limited and, other than the all-black musical *Stormy Weather*, he never appeared in another film—or role—of consequence.

• **Cult Favorites:** *Casablanca* (1942, Michael Curtiz), *Stormy Weather* (1943, Andrew L. Stone).

Dooley Wilson plays for Humphrey Bogart and Ingrid Bergman in Casablanca.

Marie Windsor was usually in classier B movies than Cat Women of the Moon.

• **Also of Interest:** *My Favorite Blonde* (1942, Sidney Lanfield), *Cairo* (1942, W. S. Van Dyke), *Higher and Higher* (1944, Tim Whelan), *Come to the Stable* (1949, Henry Koster), *Passage West* (1951, Lewis R. Foster).

○

MARIE WINDSOR (1922–) Attractive, tough, dark-haired former "Miss Utah" was one of many over the years to be called the "Queen of the Bs." Beginning in the late forties, she was a lead and supporting player in many low-budget melodramas, action films, and westerns; she was *Dakota Lil*, a pirate in *Hurricane Island*, a victim of *The Sniper*, and one of the *Swamp Women*, *Island Women*, *Outlaw Women*, and *Cat Women of the Moon* (opposite Sonny Tufts). She occasionally played women who were likable, if not pure, but she was much better as vulgar, heartless schemers,

as underhanded as the bitches played by Barbara Stanwyck. Her most memorable role was as Elisha Cook's greedy, cheating, manipulative wife, a peroxide blonde, in *The Killing*. Watch how she seduces Cook in order to get him to be part of a robbery, and you'll see early evidence that director Stanley Kubrick equates sexuality with perversity and evil.

• **Cult Favorites:** *Force of Evil* (1948, Abraham Polonsky), *Cat Women of the Moon* (1954, Arthur Hilton), *The Killing* (1956, Stanley Kubrick), *The Story of Mankind* (1957, Irwin Allen), *Paradise Alley* (1961, Hugo Haas).

• **Sleepers:** *The Little Big Horn* (1951, Charles Marquis Warren), *The Sniper* (1952, Edward Dmytryk), *The Narrow Margin* (1952, Richard Fleischer), *Freaky Friday* (1977, Gary Nelson).

• **Other Key Films:** *Outpost in Morocco* (1949, Robert Florey), *Dakota Lil* (1950, Lesley Selander), *Hurricane Island* (1951,

Lew Landers), *The Tall Texan* (1953, Elmo Williams), *The Bounty Hunter* (1954, André de Toth), *Swamp Women* (1955, Roger Corman), *Abbott and Costello Meet the Mummy* (1955, Charles Lamont), *The Day Mars Invaded the Earth* (1962, Maury Dexter).

○

SHELLEY WINTERS (1922–) Today she remains in the spotlight as a tactlessly outspoken—and thus entertaining—guest on talk shows. She often pitches her best-selling tell-all-and-even-more autobiographies, detailing her love affairs with an infinite number of movie idols. Most took place many, many pounds ago, in the late forties and fifties, when she was a svelte, pretty leading lady (or second female lead), and one of the most temperamental actresses of her day. She usually played women at the low end of the social spectrum: waitresses, saloon and dance-hall girls, factory workers, Hollywood extras. Most were luckless losers, pathetic women who give of themselves too easily and wind up ditched or dead. She is killed in *A Double Life* (by psychotic lover Ronald Colman), and in *Take One False Step, A Place in the Sun* (in a classic scene with husband Montgomery Clift on a lake), *The Night of the Hunter* (by husband Robert Mitchum—another classic murder followed by a haunting shot of her corpse in a lake), and *The Big Knife*. Even when she

Shelley Winters (right) *stops being friendly toward Debbie Reynolds in* What's the Matter with Helen?

began playing character parts, her luck with men didn't improve (as we see with her women who chase young men in *Alfie* and *The Chapman Report*), and their lives usually ended in misfortune (she is taken to concentration camps in *The Diary of Anne Frank* and *Wild in the Streets;* she dies in a car crash in *Lolita;* in *Bloody Mama,* as Ma Barker, she goes down fighting). Her character parts included bawdy, loud-mouthed wives; meddlesome, nagging, overly maternal mothers; madams—and a former swimming champion who can hold her breath a long, long time(!) in *The Poseidon Adventure.* Many were dizzy dames who talk so much that words spoken to them never cut through the confusion to reach their brains. In a few horror movies, Winters got to strike back and be mean, making up for her victimization in her early films. Winters is always a lot of fun to watch but has never been a camp star (even though some of her movies are campy). She can be forgiven her excesses because she has always been an excellent actress.

• **Cult Favorites:** *Winchester '73* (1950, Anthony Mann), *A Place in the Sun* (1951, George Stevens), *The Night of the Hunter* (1955, Charles Laughton), *Lolita* (1962, Stanley Kubrick), *Wild in the Streets* (1968, Barry Shear), *Bloody Mama* (1970, Roger Corman), *The Poseidon Adventure* (1972, Ronald Neame), *Next Stop, Greenwich Village* (1976, Paul Mazursky), *The Tenant* (1976, Roman Polanski).

• **Sleepers:** *Cry of the City* (1948, Robert Siodmak), *The Great Gatsby* (1949, Elliott Nugent), *I Am a Camera* (1955, Henry Cornelius), *Enter Laughing* (1967, Carl Reiner), *Blume in Love* (1973, Mazursky).

• **Other Key Films:** *A Double Life* (1947, George Cukor), *Take One False Step* (1949, Charles Erskine), *He Ran All the Way* (1951, John Berry), *Phone Call from a Stranger* (1952, Jean Negulesco), *Mambo* (1954, Robert Rossen), *Executive Suite* (1954, Robert Wise), *The Big Knife* (1955, Robert Aldrich), *Odds Against Tomorrow* (1959, Wise), *The Young Savages* (1961, John Frankenheimer), *The Chapman Report* (1962, Cukor), *The Balcony* (1963, Joseph Strick), *A Patch of Blue* (1965, Guy Green), *Alfie* (1966, Lewis Gilbert), *The Scalphunters* (1968, Sidney J. Pollack), *What's the Matter with Helen?* (1971, Curtis Harrington), *Who Slew Auntie Roo?* (1971, Harrington).

○

ANNA MAY WONG (1907–61) The only Chinese actress to play substantial roles in Hollywood films and to become a sex symbol in America. Wong Liu Tsong ("Frosted Yellow Willow") was born in Los Angeles. She began appearing in movies in the early twenties and made an exciting impression at 16 as an exotic slave girl in Douglas Fairbanks's popular *The Thief of Bagdad.* By the end of the decade and into the thirties, having starred in melodramas with Chinese themes in America, Great Britain, and Germany, she was an international celebrity, the movie symbol of the mysterious East, one of the world's great beauties. Dressed in exotic and often daring Chinese costumes, she was tall and slim, with black hair and bangs that fell to her arched eyebrows, and a complexion that, according to a writer of the day, "rose blushing through old ivory." When she appeared in 1932 with Marlene Dietrich in Josef von Sternberg's deliriously enjoyable *Shanghai Express,* she more than held her own in terms of beauty. The two actresses' characters were quite similar—resigned to the fact that they are looked

Anna May Wong and Warner Oland in Shanghai Express.

down upon by "moral" men, and not trying to change anyone's unfair opinion of them, they secretly make noble sacrifices for the welfare of those that condemn them. Wong killed villain Warner Oland in that film, but had played Oland's daughter when he was the evil Dr. Fu Manchu in *Daughter of the Dragon.* Today, we remember that Wong almost always played sinister women during the thirties and early forties, but it should be noted that she had top billing in a number of now-hard-to-see B melodramas, playing brave, sympathetic heroines. She was the only leading lady who never kissed on screen; she did kiss John Longden before the cameras for the British film *The Road to Dishonor,* but that scene was deleted. After making a comeback in 1960 with roles in *The Savage Innocents* and *Portrait in Black,* she died of a heart attack at age 54.

• **Cult Favorites:** *The Thief of Bagdad* (1924, Raoul Walsh), *Shanghai Express* (1932, Josef von Sternberg), *The Savage Innocents* (1960, Nicholas Ray).

• **Other Key Films:** *Forty Winks* (1925), *Mr. Wu* (1927, William Nigh), *Old San Francisco* (1927), *The Chinese Parrot* (1928), *Piccadilly* (1929, E. A. Dupont), *Daughter of the Dragon* (1931, Lloyd Corrigan), *A Study in Scarlet* (1933, Edward L. Marin), *Chu Chin Chow* (1934, Walter

Forde), *Limehouse Blues* (1934, Alexander Hall), *Java Head* (1934, Walter Ruben), *Daughter of Shanghai* (1937, Robert Florey), *Dangerous to Know* (1938, Florey), *King of Chinatown* (1939, Nick Grinde), *Island of Lost Men* (1939, Kurt Neumann), *Lady from Chunking* (1942, Nigh), *Bombs Over Burma* (1942, Joseph H. Lewis), *Impact* (1948, Arthur Lubin).

○

NATALIE WOOD (1938–1981) I don't think anyone, not even Marilyn Monroe, touched as many hearts as this beautiful actress whom so many Americans watched grow up and felt they knew. No one claimed she was a great actress—though she *was* great in *Splendor in the Grass,* and perfect in *Rebel Without a Cause* and other films—but few actresses made you root so much for them or care so much about the well-being of their characters. Her girls and women have guts but are brittle. Often they are out of their element—in relationships, in occupations (like the burlesque stage of *Gypsy* and the movie world of *Inside Daisy Clover*)—and frighteningly alone. More than once, they are kidnapped and kept in hostile environments. Typically, they love unattainable men—drifters, older men, men with money, the gay Robert Redford character in *Inside Daisy Clover.* Her Puerto Rican Maria loves Polish Tony in *West Side Story;* her Mexican-American loves WASPy Tab Hunter in *The Burning Hills;* and Frank Sinatra and Tony Curtis vie for her affections, unaware she is half-black, in *Kings Go Forth.* In her noncomedies, only James Dean in *Rebel Without a Cause* and, to a lesser extent, Steve McQueen in *Love with the Proper Stranger* seem ideal for her. Her characters are unhappy through no fault of their own—in *Miracle on 34th Street,* her mother has divorced and, though loving, has projected her cynicism onto her young daughter; in *Rebel Without a Cause,* her father thinks his teenage daughter is too old to get his affection; in *The Searchers,* she is kidnapped as a girl and becomes squaw to a brutal Indian; in *Splendor in the Grass,* boyfriend Warren Beatty leaves her when she refuses to sleep with him unless they marry; in *Gypsy,* she grows up in the background while her talented sister enjoys fame and her mother's attention; in *West Side Story,* boyfriend Tony is killed by her brother's gang; in *Inside Daisy Clover,* she is manipulated, bruised and battered, and made a prisoner of her stardom. Her characters all have a profound sense of loss: of their childhoods, fathers, mothers, innocence, boyfriends, husbands, freedom, identities, dreams (in *Marjorie Morningstar,* she becomes a housewife rather than a star), and, in *Splendor in the Grass* and *Inside Daisy Clover,* their sanity. It's such a relief when Santa gets her the home she dreams about in *Miracle on 34th Street,* when James Dean loves her in *Rebel Without a Cause,* and when John Wayne lifts her into his arms and brings her home in *The Searchers.* I just wish someone was there for her during her emotional breakdown (what a raw, remarkable performance!) in *Splendor in the Grass.* She was my favorite actress and, like many, I get chills when, in that picture, she almost drowns.

• **Cult Favorites:** *Miracle on 34th Street* (1947, George Seaton), *The Silver Chalice* (1954, Victor Saville), *Rebel Without a Cause* (1955, Nicholas Ray), *The Searchers* (1956, John Ford), *Splendor in the Grass* (1961, Elia Kazan), *Inside Daisy Clover* (1966, Robert Mulligan), *Brainstorm* (1983, Douglas Trumbull).

• **Other Key Films:** *Marjorie Morningstar* (1958, Irving Rapper), *Kings Go Forth* (1958, Delmer Daves), *West Side Story* (1961, Robert Wise and Jerome Robbins), *Gypsy* (1962, Mervyn LeRoy), *Love with the Proper Stranger* (1963, Mulligan), *Sex and the Single Girl* (1964, Richard Quine), *The Great Race* (1965, Blake Edwards), *This Property Is Condemned* (1966, Sidney Pollack), *Bob and Carol and Ted and Alice* (1969, Paul Mazursky).

○

THOMAS WOOD/WILLIAM KERWIN/ROONEY KERWIN Under various names, he appeared in numerous "nudies" and "gore" films directed by Herschell Gordon Lewis and produced by David Friedman. As Thomas Wood, he starred in Lewis's two most famous gore films, *Blood Feast* and *Two Thousand Maniacs*. His last name describes his acting style for Lewis, but he came off like an Oscar winner in comparison to his leading lady, ex-*Playboy* Bunny Connie Mason. In *Blood Feast*, he is the officer in charge of a murder investigation involving a maniac who hacks off and pulls out body parts of his female victims. When Wood tries to seduce Mason (as Suzette) in his convertible, only to have her get the shivers because of the maniac on the loose, he jokes, "You may be safer with the killer than you are with me!" Talk about tasteless. My favorite moment has the boyfriend of one of the victims ranting and raving, shouting indecipherable inanities, while Wood stands inches away calmly taking notes with his pencil and pad; it's like a sports interviewer standing still yet somehow staying next to a skier who's on his way down the slope. Wood is able to track down killer Fuad Ramses, who meets his death in a garbage truck. Wood's success rate remains at 100 percent when he and Mason are the only northerners to escape a southern town containing *Two Thousand Maniacs*. Also shot in Florida on a low budget, the film is a variation of *Brigadoon*, with the vengeful townspeople being the ghosts of people wiped out by a northern regiment in the Civil War. The film's so unnerving because of the gruesome murders and tortures that I'm relieved *anyone* escapes the town—even Wood and Mason.

• **Cult Favorites:** *Blood Feast* (1963, Herschell Gordon Lewis), *Two Thousand Maniacs* (1964, Lewis), *The Playgirl Killer/ Decoy for Terror* (1965, Erick Santamaria), *A Taste of Blood* (1967, Lewis).

• **Also of Interest:** *The Living Venus* (1960, Lewis), *The Adventures of Lucky Pierre* (1961, Lewis).

○

HOLLY WOODLAWN Talented female impersonator gave a hilarious performance in *Trash*, Andy Warhol and Paul Morrissey's tribute to squalor and decadence, Lower East Side style. She played junkie Joe Dallesandro's female live-in lover, Holly, a nympho who picks up teenage boys for sex because Joe can't get it up, masturbates in frustration with a beer bottle (one of the weirdest scenes in film history, considering she is played by a male), collects furniture from trash piles, and orders Joe to shape up so they can qualify for welfare and become respectable. Her scene with the welfare worker, in which she wears a pillow under her sweater to make him believe she's pregnant, is a superb comedy sequence, brilliantly conceived and played. It's too bad Woodlawn didn't appear in films outside of Warhol's, because s/he was a genuine talent (even poignant at times), capable of dominating the screen.

Holly Woodlawn in Trash.

Woodlawn would, however, team with Divine in the off-Broadway play *Women Behind Bars,* definitely a candidate for movie cultdom—if only it had been filmed.

• **Cult Favorite:** *Trash* (1970, Paul Morrissey).

• **Other Key Film:** *Women in Revolt/Sex* (1971, Andy Warhol and Morrissey).

○

BAMBI WOODS This pretty, energetic blonde was rejected when she tried out for the Dallas Cowboy Cheerleaders, but she achieved more fame than any of the women who made it. She played Debbie in the porno film with the most familiar title other than *Deep Throat,* the notorious box-office hit *Debbie Does Dallas.* It is a terrible film, in which Woods and her friends on a high-school cheerleading squad take part-time jobs so they can travel to Dallas and try out as professional cheerleaders. They end up having sex with all their male employers, and it's clear that the male director's lone interest was to show young girls giving men pleasure. All the females, including Debbie, are obnoxious, and all the actresses are dreadful—with Woods the worst of all. She would return for the sequel. I wouldn't.

• **Cult Favorite:** *Debbie Does Dallas* (1978, Jim Clark).

• **Also of Interest:** *Debbie Does Dallas II* (1983, Clark).

○

JAMES WOODS (1947–) An offbeat, intense, yet funny and riveting leading man whose popularity increases with every performance. He's entertaining, even in bad films. Slim but intimidating, with a lean, lined, pockmarked face and potent eyes that don't seem to fit, he made his first impression as a chilling, remorseless cop-killer in *The Onion Field*. He was so suited for villainy—playing intelligent, fearless men whose crazy, brutal streaks make them frightening to cross—that it was surprising when he started playing characters on our side. Not that they weren't also menacing—as is his cult deprogrammer in *Split Image*. Even some of his semiheroes are, for the most part, jerks, but his real-life writer, Richard Boyle, in the compelling political drama *Salvador* (a brilliant, live-wire performance that won him an Oscar nomination) and low-grade lawyer in *True Believer* turn out to be, much to their own surprise, jerks with consciences. His bad guys often have sympathetic traces, his good guys nasty ones—and he plays them in similar fashion. The actor is typically hyper, on edge, as if his character is on speed or hasn't slept because he secretly bet all his company's money on a 100-to-1 long shot. His sleazy, trying-to-be-slick characters smoke (in *Cat's Eye*, he can't quit smoking although his family will suffer), drink, and talk incessantly. Their rhythmic patter is all B.S., the self-serving hustling and bluffing of a used-car salesman or William Morris agent. After listening to his con and looking into those weird eyes, only a few fools on screen think he is reliable and trustworthy. Others are frightened away.

• **Cult Favorites:** *The Way We Were* (1973, Sidney Pollack), *Night Moves* (1975, Arthur Penn), *Videodrome* (1983, David Cronenberg), *Once Upon a Time in America* (1984, Sergio Leone), *Salvador* (1986, Oliver Stone).

• **Sleepers:** *The Onion Field* (1979, Harold Becker), *Eyewitness* (1981, Peter Yates), *Fast-Walking* (1982, James B. Harris), *Joshua Then and Now* (1985, Ted Kotcheff).

• **Other Key Films:** *Split Image* (1982, Kotcheff), *Against All Odds* (1984, Taylor Hackford), *Cop* (1987, Harris), *True Believer* (1989, Joseph Ruben).

• **Also of Interest:** *Cat's Eye* (1985, Lewis Teague), *Best Seller* (1987, John Flynn), *The Boost* (1988, Becker), *The Hard Way* (1991, John Badham).

○

HANK WORDEN (1901–) Thin, wide-eyed character actor who has played minor, oddball parts since the late forties. He appeared most often in westerns, usually as characters whose minds have weakened after years in the uncivilized West. Before he had really aged, he already looked old and worn out. He appeared in numerous John Wayne films, mostly westerns, including several directed by John Ford. Both Wayne and Ford liked his wit, and his familiar, rhythmic delivery in which he left out the pronoun, politely addressed whomever he was speaking to, and repeated the sentence. He was creepily demented as one of the sadistic outlaws who seize a wagon train in Ford's *Wagonmaster* (without Wayne), but usually Ford cast him as sympathetic, humorous characters. His best role was "Mose" in *The Searchers*, who, after escaping from Indians by "pretending" he was crazy, just wants to sit by a fire in his rocking chair. In the mid-seventies, I'd sometimes spot Worden at screenings, and get him to tell me anecdotes about Ford, Wayne, and that old rocking chair. A nice memory. In 1990, Worden turned up on David Lynch's TV series "Twin Peaks."

• **Cult Favorites:** *Angel and the Badman* (1947, James Edward Grant), *Three Godfathers* (1949, John Ford), *The Quiet Man* (1952, Ford), *The Searchers* (1956, Ford), *Forty Guns* (1957, Samuel Fuller),

Big Wednesday (1978, John Milius), *UFOria* (1980/86, John Binder).

• **Sleepers:** *Wagonmaster* (1950, Ford), *The Big Sky* (1952, Howard Hawks), *Sergeant Rutledge* (1960, Ford), *Hammett* (1983, Wim Wenders).

• **Also of Interest:** *Fort Apache* (1948, Ford), *Yellow Sky* (1948, William Wellman), *When Willie Comes Marching Home* (1950, Ford), *The Indian Fighter* (1955, André de Toth), *The Horse Soldiers* (1959, Ford), *McClintock!* (1963, Andrew V. McLaglen).

○

MARY WORONOV (1946–) This tall, attractive, long-haired brunette has played leads and supporting roles in low-budget horror, science-fiction, and action films, soft-core sex films, and, best of all, the black comedy *Eating Raoul.* A few of her women have been lesbians; many are physically imposing (including her race-car driver Calamity Jane in *Death Race 2000*); all are sexually aggressive. The films themselves are usually R-rated, with Woronov providing some of the sex scenes. She is drawn toward offbeat roles, but none has been stranger than her prudish Mrs. Bland in *Eating Raoul,* who, in order to steal money so she and her husband (director Paul Bartel) can buy a restaurant, poses as a dominatrix to attract perverts to their house so they can kill and rob them. She is extremely funny (she and Bartel make a

Mary Woronov with director and costar Paul Bartel in Eating Raoul.

great team) and sexy—the scene in which she is seduced by Raoul (Robert Beltran) is genuinely erotic. Originally from New York's underground cinema.

• **Cult Favorites:** *Seizure* (1974, Oliver Stone), *Death Race 2000* (1975, Paul Bartel), *Hollywood Boulevard* (1976, Joe Dante and Allan Arkush), *Jackson County Jail* (1976, Michael Miller), *Rock 'n' Roll High School* (1979, Arkush), *Eating Raoul* (1982, Bartel).

• **Sleeper:** *Night of the Comet* (1984, Thom Eberhardt).

• **Other Key Films:** *Silent Night, Bloody Night* (1973, Theodore Gershuny), *Sugar Cookies* (1975, Gershuny).

• **Also of Interest:** *Angel of H.E.A.T.* (1982, Myrl A. Schriebman), *Get Crazy* (1983, Arkush), *Movie House Massacre* (1984, Alice Raley), *Hellhole* (1985, Pierre de Moro), *Nomads* (1986, John McTiernan), *Scenes from the Class Struggle in Beverly Hills* (1989, Bartel).

○

JACK WRANGLER One of the most famous porno stars, regarded as the renegade-beat figure of adult films because of an eventful life in and out of the business, all detailed in his autobiography. He wasn't in a lot of major adult films, but he got a reputation for his good looks and masculinity, love-making skills, and acting ability. Among his screen lovers were porn queens Leslie Bovee, Candida Royalle, and, most memorably in *Jack 'n' Jill*, Samantha Fox. He played Lucifer in the comedic *Devil in Miss Jones II*.

• **Key Films:** *Misbehavin'* (1978, Chuck Vincent), *Jack 'n' Jill* (1979, Mark Ubell), *Games Women Play* (1980, Vincent), *Blue Magic* (1981, Par Sjostedt), *Dirty Looks*

(1982, Vincent), *Devil in Miss Jones II* (1983, Henri Pachard).

○

FAY WRAY (1907–) Her fame as Ann Darrow in *King Kong* and as other screaming heroines in the thirties has eclipsed her romantic leading-lady status during the twenties, which culminated with her moving performance as Mitzi in Erich von Stroheim's monumental *The Wedding March*. In fact, she was at her best in sound films during long silent passages (especially in *King Kong*), when both subtle and exaggerated acting were called for: the *gorgeous* eyes of her imperiled heroines grow wide in terror yet look for escape, their breasts rise and fall, their lips fight to open, their hands rise to their faces, and finally they scream and scream. Of course, in sound films, her screams could be heard, and they were heard often in most of her films. Light-haired, with a pretty, innocent face, but a willingness to wear sexy, ripped outfits in *King Kong* and be naked and strapped to a table in *The Mystery of the Wax Museum,* she remains one of the most fetching horror-movie stars. It's little wonder that several men were attracted to her in each film. In *King Kong,* it seems only one man, Bruce Cabot's Jack Driscoll, covets her. But Robert Armstrong's woman-hating Carl Denham also falls for her. The giant gorilla that chases her and takes her up the most phallic building in the world (he who can distinguish Ann from other women only by her smell) actually represents the sexually repressed Denham's uncontrollable desire for Ann. The "Girl in the Hairy Paw" retired in

Fay Wray with Bruce Cabot in King Kong.

1942; she returned in the fifties, and played a lot of mothers.
• **Cult Favorites:** *The Wedding March* (1928, Erich von Stroheim), *The Mystery of the Wax Museum* (1933, Michael Curtiz), *King Kong* (1933, Merian C. Cooper and Ernest B. Schoedsack).
• **Other Key Films:** *Four Feathers* (1929, Lothar Mendes), *Thunderbolt* (1929, Josef von Sternberg), *The Conquering Horde* (1931, Edward Sloman), *Doctor X* (1932, Curtiz), *The Most Dangerous Game* (1932, Schoedsack and Irving Pichel), *Viva Villa!* (1934, Jack Conway), *The Clairvoyant/ The Evil Mind* (1935, Maurice Elvy).
• **Also of Interest:** *Legion of the Condemned* (1928, William A. Wellman), *Dirigible* (1931, Frank Capra), *Shanghai Madness* (1933, John G. Blystone), *Madame Spy* (1934, Karl Freund), *Murder in Greenwich Village* (1937, Albert S. Rogell), *Adam Had Four Sons* (1941, Gregory Ratoff), *Hell on Frisco Bay* (1955, Frank Tuttle).

○

TERESA WRIGHT (1918–) A surprising number of people have told me that this talented, attractive brunette is their all-time favorite actress. She had something special as she played scrubbed-faced but strong-willed young women in the forties, women who represented the typical middle-American daughter-girlfriend-wife (family women) of the period, and in *Mrs. Miniver,* as Greer Garson's daughter-in-law, the typical young English woman. These women are symbols of crushed but uncorrupted innocence, women of great drive and resolve, who are smart, reliable and devoted, strong and solid, willing—even impatient—to learn and to solve problems (or a mystery, in *Shadow of a Doubt*), thoughtful, and understanding, offering a steady hand to troubled men like the dying Lou Gehrig in *Pride of the Yankees,* or returning vets Dana Andrews in *The Best Years of Our Lives* and handicapped Marlon Brando in *The Men.* These women were the reason our men went to war, and the reason they will be able to readjust to society.
• **Cult Favorites:** *Pride of the Yankees* (1942, Sam Wood), *Shadow of a Doubt* (1943, Alfred Hitchcock), *The Best Years of Our Lives* (1946, William Wyler), *Roseland* (1977, James Ivory).
• **Also Recommended:** *The Little Foxes* (1941, Wyler), *Mrs. Miniver* (1942, Wyler), *Pursued* (1947, Raoul Walsh), *The Men* (1950, Fred Zinnemann), *The Steel Trap* (1952, Andrew L. Stone), *The Actress* (1953, George Cukor).
• **Also of Interest:** *Casanova Brown* (1944, Wood), *Enchantment* (1948, Irving Reis), *Count the Hours* (1953, Don Siegel), *Track of the Cat* (1954, William A. Wellman),

The Search for Bridey Murphy (1956, Noel Langley), *The Happy Ending* (1969, Richard Brooks), *Somewhere in Time* (1980, Jeannot Szwarc).

○

SEAN YOUNG (1959–) Tall, slim, dark-haired beauty (she resembles Kay Kendall) usually plays sexy party-girl types with vivacious personalities. Her wild back-of-the-limo sex scene with Kevin Costner in *No Way Out* will keep that picture among video rental favorites for many years. However, she gave her most captivating performance in a subdued role in the melancholy science-fiction film *Blade Runner,* as a young woman who is heartbroken to discover that she is an android, and that all her memories are false. Although dressed conservatively, she is as provocative as she has ever been in movies. Her tearful love scene with Harrison Ford is just as stirring as the heated one with Costner. Amazingly, she didn't get along with either actor. In fact, Young has the reputation of being extremely difficult to work with. She and Charlie Sheen warred on *Wall Street;* after having an affair with her while filming *The Boost,* James Woods brought a lawsuit (later dismissed) against her for $2 million for harassing him and his fiancée. *Wall Street* director Oliver Stone fired her before she completed her role; *Dick Tracy* star-director Warren Beatty fired her after a week of shooting. She has talent and she has a strong personality—so her future should be very interesting.
• **Cult Favorites:** *Blade Runner* (1982, Ridley Scott), *Dune* (1984, David Lynch).
• **Other Key Films:** *No Way Out* (1987, Roger Donaldson), *Wall Street* (1987, Oliver Stone).

• **Also of Interest:** *Stripes* (1981, Ivan Reitman), *Young Doctors in Love* (1982, Garry Marshall), *The Boost* (1988, Harold Becker), *Cousins* (1989, Joel Schumacher), *A Kiss Before Dying* (1991, James Dearden).

○

SEN YOUNG/VICTOR SEN YOUNG (1915–80) From 1938 to 1948, this Chinese-American actor played Charlie Chan's Number Two Son, Jimmy, in the films in which Sidney Toler portrayed the famous detective. He was good-natured, polite, well-dressed, and respectful of his brilliant, idiosyncratic "Pop," whom he always tried to impress with foolhardy sleuthing. During the war, Hollywood portrayed few Asians in a good light, and Young had few other opportunities to play likable, trustworthy characters—mostly he played spies and other nefarious figures that either were Japanese or were presented to audiences as Japanese-like. Playing a friendly character again, he was the Cartwrights' houseboy, Hop Sing, on the TV western series "Bonanza."
• **Key Films:** *Charlie Chan in Honolulu* (1938, H. Bruce Humberstone), *Charlie Chan in Reno* (1939, Norman Foster), *Charlie Chan at Treasure Island* (1939, Foster), *The Letter* (1940, William Wyler), *Charlie Chan in Panama* (1940, Foster), *Charlie Chan at the Wax Museum* (1940, Lynn Shores), *Charlie Chan's Murder Cruise* (1940, Eugene Forde), *Charlie Chan in Rio* (1941, Harry Lachman), *Across the Pacific* (1942, John Huston), *Night Plane from Chunking* (1943, Ralph Murphy), *The Flower Drum Song* (1961, Henry Koster), *Men in War* (1957, Anthony Mann).

WANG YU/JIMMY WANG YU Hero of the Chinese martial-arts cinema, beginning with the Shaw Brothers studio in 1963; an independent actor-writer-director in the seventies. He is best known as Silver Roc, the original "One-Armed Swordsman," a part later played by David Chiang (as Lei Li), but he also is remembered as "The One-Armed Boxer." He played intense, tortured loners who are usually out to clear their names or avenge dastardly acts, like the loss of a wife or, of course, a limb. His films were full of action and long battle sequences, usually involving swordplay and the severing of heads and limbs. A Yu trademark was his killing several enemies with one motion. Many of the villains were Japanese. The pictures had a pain motif—first Yu suffered, then his enemies did. His best film was *Zatoichi and the One-Armed Swordsman*, in which his Chinese hero teamed with Shintaro Katsu's blind samurai hero of Japanese martial-arts films.

• **Cult Favorites:** *The One-Armed Swordsman* (1968, Chang Cheh), *Zatoichi and the One-Armed Swordsman* (1970, Kimiyoshi Yasudi), *The Chinese Boxer* (1970, Wang Yu).

• **Also of Interest:** *The Return of the One-Armed Swordsman* (1969, Cheh), *Golden Swallow* (1970, Cheh), *A Man Called Tiger* (1972, Cheh), *The Tattooed Dragon* (1972, Cheh), *Beach of the War Gods* (1973, Yu), *Wang Yu's Seven Magnificent Fights* (1973, Lo Wei), *The Man from Hong Kong* (1974, Brian Trenchard Smith), *Killer Meteor* (1977, Wei).

O

PIA ZADORA (1954–) She was a little girl when she appeared as an alien in the ridiculous *Santa Claus Conquers the Martians,* and when she made her movie comeback seventeen years later, she still looked like a little girl. However, she tried to pass herself off as a sexy leading lady in two trashy films, playing, with tongue in cheek (though critics didn't seem to notice), a sluttish sex kitten who seduces the man who may be her father in *Butterfly* (from the James Cain novel) and a screenwriter determined to climb to the top no matter what she must do or endure in *The Lonely Lady* (from the Harold Robbins potboiler). Pia also did an enormous amount of publicity and posed nude in various men's magazines. She somehow won a Golden Globe for Best New Actress, but critics and the mass audience—who figured she was a star only because her multimillionaire husband, Meshulam Riklis, was putting his money behind her—despised her films and didn't take her seriously as an actress or a sex symbol. However, she had her fans. Director John Waters wrote: "She's shorter than Elizabeth Taylor, cuter than Alvin the Chipmunk, richer than Cher, more publicized than Zsa Zsa, and has a better hairdo than Farrah. She may be a national joke to some, but I think Pia Zadora will get the last laugh. . . . I'd kill to have her in one of my own films." Pia got the last laugh by becoming an acclaimed singer. This paved the way for another return to movies . . . in Waters's *Hairspray.*

• **Cult Favorites:** *Butterfly* (1981, Matt Cimber), *Hairspray* (1988, John Waters).

• **Other Key Films:** *Santa Claus Conquers the Martians* (1964, Nicholas Webster),

Fakeout (1982, Cimber), *The Lonely Lady* (1983, Peter Sasdy).

○

NICK ZEDD The major figure of the New York underground's "Cinema of Transgression," the "depraved," taboo-breaking 8mm satirical-experimental cinema that features punk types in hard-core sex and S&M sequences. He has made influential shorts as director and actor, at times playing females. Slim and good-looking, he was the one-time boyfriend of Lydia Lunch, the top female star of this controversial cinema. Among the films he directed are *They Eat Scum* (1985) and *Geek Maggot Bingo* (1983).

• **Some Key Films (As Actor):** *Thrust in Me* (1984, Nick Zedd and Richard Kern), *Submit to Me* (1985, Kern), *Me Minus You* (1985, Zedd and Jessica Jason), *No Such Thing As Gravity* (1990, Alyce Wittenstein).

○

GEORGE ZUCCO (1886–1960) Middle-aged, balding British stage actor played some of Hollywood's most venomous villains in the thirties and forties. His scoundrels were always unredeemable. If you couldn't get Lionel Atwill, you'd go after George Zucco . . . and vice versa. They even costarred in *Fog Island*. Like Atwill, he played the sinister Moriarty in Basil Rathbone's Sherlock Holmes series, and starred as mad scientists in B horror films that were far beneath his talents. And like Atwill, he is admired by horror fans for playing even his silliest roles to the hilt, without ever mocking his material. Always inventing new serums, his scientists could turn human beings into monsters with the best of them.

• **Cult Favorite:** *Adventures of Sherlock Holmes* (1939, Alfred L. Werker).
• **Other Key Films:** *The Man Who Could Work Miracles* (1937, Lothar Mendes), *The Mummy's Hand* (1940, Christy Cabanne), *The Monster and the Girl* (1941, Stuart Heisler), *Dr. Renault's Secret* (1942, Harry Lachman), *Sherlock Holmes in Washington* (1943, Roy William Neill), *The Mad Ghoul* (1943, James Hogan), *House of Frankenstein* (1944, Erle C. Kenton), *The Mummy's Ghost* (1944, Reginald LeBorg), *The Flying Serpent* (1946, Sherman Scott/Sam Newfield), *Tarzan and the Mermaids* (1948, Robert Florey).
• **Also of Interest:** *The Cat and the Canary* (1939, Elliott Nugent), *The Hunchback of Notre Dame* (1939, William Dieterle), *The Mummy's Tomb* (1942, Harold Young), *The Mad Monster* (1942, Newfield), *Dead Men Walk* (1943, Newfield), *The Black Raven* (1943, Newfield), *Return of the Ape Man* (1944, Philip Rosen), *Fog Island* (1945, Terry Morse), *The Pirate* (1947, Vincente Minnelli), *Madame Bovary* (1949, Minnelli).

George Zucco points a gun at David Bruce in The Mad Ghoul.

INDEX OF CULT FAVORITES